Fundamentals of Financial M

Fundamentals of Financial Management

D. CHANDRA BOSE

Reader
Research and Postgraduate Department of Commerce
Sree Narayana College
(University of Kerala)
Kollam

PHI Learning Private Limited

New Delhi-110001
2009

Rs. 350.00

FUNDAMENTALS OF FINANCIAL MANAGEMENT
D. Chandra Bose

ISBN-978-81-203-2984-3

The export rights of this book are vested solely with the publisher.

Third Printing · · · · · · **May, 2009**

Published by Asoke K. Ghosh, PHI Learning Private Limited, M-97, Connaught Circus, New Delhi-110001 and Printed by Rajkamal Electric Press, Plot No. 2, Phase IV, HSIDC, Kundli-131028, Sonepat, Haryana.

To

my beloved wife G.R. Ajita

and

daughters Divya and Daya
(Kuttamangalam, Valathungal, Kollam, Kerala)

Contents

Contents

Preface

I have great pleasure in bringing out this book entitled "Fundamentals of Financial Management" keeping in mind both the students of management science and practising managers. The objective of the book is to assist and enable the readers in developing an understanding of the theory and art of financial management and to integrate the knowledge with practice in evaluating the firm's investment, financing and dividend decisions. The various theories have been critically evaluated and compared with practical situations assessing their contribution in the field of finance.

The entire text has been divided into twenty-four chapters and is a sincere attempt to provide the means of improving basic skills in the field of financial management. Moreover, each financial function is identified and discussed in the most concise, lucid and illustrative manner with a conscientious effort to present the subject-matter in a way that is easily comprehensible to students. Suggestions from teachers and students are solicited so as to enable me to further improve this work in the near future.

D. CHANDRA BOSE

1

Financial Functions of Management

Business Finance may be said to deal with acquisition of funds, use of funds and distribution of Profits by a business organisation.

— CHARLES W. GERSTENBERG

CONTENTS

- Introduction
- Meaning of financial management
- Significance of financial management
- Objectives of financial management
- Profit maximisation vs. wealth maximisation
- Decision-making in financial management
- Functions of financial manager
- Financial management and other areas of management
- Indian financial system
- Time value of money
- Review questions

INTRODUCTION

Finance is an important function in any business as money is required to support its various activities. It has given birth to "Financial Management" as a separate subject. As a separate subject, financial management is of recent origin and has not acquired a body of knowledge of its own. It draws heavily on "Economics" for its theoretical concepts. In the early half of the last century, the job of financial management was largely confined to the acquisition of funds. But as business firms continued to expand their markets and they became larger and more diversified, greater control of financial operation became highly important. Thus now the scope of financial

1

management is very wide and it should not be considered to be merely restricted for raising of capital. It also covers other aspects of financing such as assessing the needs of capital, raising sufficient amount of funds, cost of financing, budgeting, maintaining liquidity, lending and borrowing policies, dividend policy and so on.

MEANING OF FINANCIAL MANAGEMENT

Finance is considered as the life-blood of any business. It is defined as *the provision of money at the time it is needed*. All the plans of a businessman would remain mere dreams unless adequate money is available to convert them into reality.

Financial management is very important to every type of organisation. It refers to that part of managerial activity concerned with the procurement and utilisation of funds for business purposes. In the words of Howard and Upton:

> Financial management involves the application of general management principles to financial operations.

Thus financial management is concerned with:

(a) estimation of the fixed and working capital requirements,

(b) formulation of capital structure,

(c) procurement of fixed and working capital, and

(d) management of earnings.

SIGNIFICANCE OF FINANCIAL MANAGEMENT

Financial management occupies a significant place because it has an impact on all the activities of a firm. Its primary responsibility is to discharge the finance function successfully. No one can think of any business activity in isolation from its financial implications. The management may accept or reject a business proposition on the basis of its financial variabilities. In other words, the live executives who are directly involved in the decision-making process should give supreme importance for financial consideration.

The finance function centres round the management of funds raising and using them effectively. But the dimensions of financial management are much broader than mere procurement of funds. Planning is one of the primary activities of the financial manager. It helps him to obtain funds and the best time in relation to their cost of the conditions under which they can be obtained. However, Financial Management should not be taken as a profit extracting device. It implies a more comprehensive concept than the simple objective of profit-making. Its broader mission should be to protect the interest of the different sections of the community undisturbed and protected through maximising the value of the firm.

The concepts of financial management are applicable to an organisation, irrespective of its size, nature of ownership and control. They can be applied to any activity of an organisation which has financial implications. In the words of Raymond Chambers:

> The term financial management may be applied to any kind of undertaking or organisation regardless of its aims or constitution.

The term Corporate Financial Management is often used to emphasise the financial management of companies or corporations. Thus, it consists of the decisions relating to: (a) investment—concerned with capital budgeting and current assets management (b) financing—concerned with determining the best financing mix, and (c) dividend—concerned with the solution to the decision of dividend policy.

OBJECTIVES OF FINANCIAL MANAGEMENT

Financial management is concerned with the efficient use of capital funds. It evaluates how funds are used and procured. In all cases, financial management involves sound judgement, combined with a logical approach to decision-making. Different alternatives having different implications are available to a business enterprise in the process of decision-making. These alternatives have to be evaluated on the basis of some analytical framework and commercial strategies of an enterprise.

There can be many financial objectives. Two of them are notable because of wide support for them. These are:

(i) Profit Maximisation, and

(ii) Wealth Maximisation

If profit maximisation is the maximising the rupee income of the business, wealth maximisation refers to the maximisation of the market price per share of the company. Although profit maximisation is traditionally considered as the main objective of the firm, it has been strongly attacked for not having logical managerial justifications. But the wealth maximisation is regarded as operationally and managerially the better objective because it: (a) considers the time value of money, (b) takes into account, the risk or uncertainty of future earnings, and (c) considers the effects of dividend policy on the market price of the shares.

In short, the objectives of financial management are such that they should be beneficial to owners, management, employees and customers. These objectives can be accomplished only by maximising the value of the firm through the following ways:

1. **Increase in Profits:** A firm can maximise its value through increasing its revenue. The revenue can be enhanced by way of stepping up the volume of sales or any other activities. In theory, when a firm is in equilibrium, its profits are said to be maximum. At this stage, the average cost is minimum and the marginal cost and marginal revenue are equal. An increase of sales beyond this limit will not necessarily result in a rise in profits unless markets are increased for increased supply of goods and overhead costs are controlled.

2. **Reduction in Cost:** A firm should work by all means to reduce the cost of capital and to launch economy drive in its operations.

3. **Sources of Funds:** A firm can raise funds in various ways or sources. The risks involved in all these sources are to be assessed beforehand. While the issue of equity shares increases the ownership funds of the corporation, the issue of debentures and preference shares enhances the fixed and recurring obligations of it.

4. **Minimise Risks:** "No pain, no gain"—is a common adage. Before embarking on any particular course of action, a firm will have to calculate different types of risks which it

confronts. The firm will have to consider the interest of equity shareholders as the central focus of financial policies, while keeping the goal of maximising the value of the firm.

5. **Long-run Value:** The objective of financial management must be to maximise the long-run value of the firm. This objective should be followed for the permanent progress and sound reputation of the firm. Thus a firm may profitably follow the principle "more haste, less speed".

PROFIT MAXIMISATION vs WEALTH MAXIMISATION

Should the goals of financial decision-making be profit maximisation or wealth maximisation? There are certain objections against profit maximisation as the goal of the firm. They are as follows:

(a) It does not specify the time of expected returns.

(b) It does not take into consideration, the uncertainty of future earnings.

(c) It does not consider the effect of dividend policy on the market price of shares.

(d) It does not consider the interest of consumers, workers and the society.

(e) It does not differentiate between the short-term and long-term profits.

Prof. Solomon of Stanford University has handled this issue logically. He argues that it is useful to differentiate between Profits and Profitability. Maximisation of profit in the sense of maximising the wealth, accruing to shareholders is clearly an unreal motive. On the contrary, profitability maximisation in the sense of using resources to yield economic values higher than the joint values of inputs required is a useful objective. The object of profitability accomplished in terms of greater outputs than input values, involves a different set of considerations. He has also made clear that wealth maximisation also maximises the accomplishment of other operating objectives such as maximising the sales or size, growth or market share, or maximising the chances of company's survival and improving the investors' and managers' peace of mind.

DECISION-MAKING IN FINANCIAL MANAGEMENT

The financial management decisions can be broadly classified into:

(a) investment decisions,

(b) financing decisions, and

(c) dividend decisions.

These three components of the finance function interact among themselves through the medium of capital with a view to attaining the objective of wealth maximisation. Figure 1.1 shows the components of the finance function and the inter-relationship among them.

Investment decisions are concerned with the decisions about the investment of funds. Funds are to be invested in fixed assets and current assets. Investment of funds in fixed assets has long-term implications as funds are blocked for a long duration. But immediate returns can be expected from investment in current assets, such as cash, receivables and inventories. The purpose behind

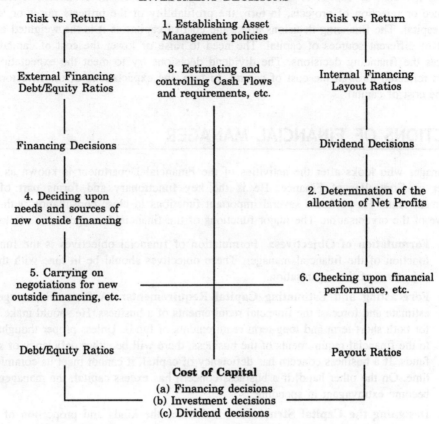

FIGURE 1.1 Components of finance function and their interaction.

the investment decisions is to find out the projects which are acceptable through discounted cash flow (DCF) techniques using the cost of capital as the cut-off criterion and also to choose the projects with high net present values (NPV) or internal rate of return (IRR) if the resources are limited. The investment decisions are also subject to risk versus return analysis as future cash flows are subject to uncertainty.

Financing decisions are concerned with the financing of business activities. They are intimately bound with the investment decisions. The financing decisions are helpful in planning for a balanced capital structure. Risk, return and control are the crucial factors relevant in formulating the financing decisions. Various analytical techniques like EPS/EBIT computations, leverage calculations and interest and dividend coverage estimates are used in the process of making the financing decisions.

Dividend decisions are concerned with the disposal of profits. Dividend is generally paid as some percentage of earnings on the paid-up capital. The internal profitability versus the external profitability (Walter's Approach) analysis helps in developing the pay out ratio. The part of the profits which is not paid out as dividend constitutes the source of internal financing.

The cost of capital is the nucleus in the financial decision-making. It has a two-way effect on the investment, financing and dividend decisions. It influences and in turn is influenced by them. As the cost of capital is the cut-off criterion in investment decisions, it leads to the acceptance or rejection of projects. In turn, the profitability of the projects raises or lowers the cost of capital. The financing decisions affect the cost of capital as it is the weighted average of the cost of different sources of capital. The need to raise or lower the cost of capital, in turn, influences the financing decisions. The dividend decisions try to meet the expectations of the investors reflected through the cost of capital. In turn, the expectations of the investors raise or lower the cost of capital.

FUNCTIONS OF FINANCIAL MANAGER

The manager who looks after the activities of the Financial Department is known as Financial Manager or Controller of Finance. He is the key functionary and forms part of the top management team. He performs several important functions in close consultation with the chief executive of the organisation. The major functions of the financial manager are as follows:

1. **Formulation of Objectives:** Formulation of financial objectives is the fundamental function of the financial manager. These objectives should be in tune with the overall objectives of the organisation.

2. **Forecasting and Estimating Capital Requirements:** A financial manager has to estimate and forecast the financial requirements of a business. He should make estimates for both short-term and long-term requirements of funds. Unless proper thought is given to the financial requirements of the business, there will be either deficiency or surplus of funds. If a business concern has deficiency of capital, it cannot meet its commitments in time. On the other hand, if a business concern has excess capital, the management may become extravagant in spending.

3. **Designing the Capital Structure:** It denotes the kinds and proportion of different securities. Thus the capital structure of a company is said to be the composition of equity and preference capital and debt capital. After estimating the financial requirements, the financial manager will have to design the kind and proportion of various sources of funds. This should be based on the analysis of cost of capital, consideration of factors such as risk, return and control conditions in money and capital market.

4. **Determining the Suitable Source of Finance:** The decision to tap various sources of finance depend upon the capital structure designed. On the basis of it, the finance manager has to determine the sources from which the funds are to be raised. The management can raise finance from various sources such as shares, debentures, financial institutions, commercial banks and so on. The financial manager should analyse the pros and cons of all these sources before making a final decision.

5. **Procurement of Funds:** After estimating the capital requirements and deciding about the sources of finance, the financial manager has to take necessary steps to procure the funds.

6. **Investment of Funds:** The funds procured should be prudently invested in various projects. The technique of capital budgeting may be helpful in selecting a project. While taking investment decisions, the financial manager has to keep in mind the principles of profitability, liquidity and safety. The principle of profitability should not be the only

criterion of investment because, if the funds are blocked in unsafe projects, the solvency of the company will be in danger.

7. **Dispersal of Profits:** The financial manager has to decide how much is to be retained for internal use and how much is to be declared as dividend out of profits of the company. A large number of factors like the trend of earnings of the company, the trend of market price of its shares, the requirement of funds for self-financing, the future prospects, the cash flow position and so on, should influence these decisions. Thus, this is an important area of financial management.

8. **Maintaining the Proper Liquidity:** Every organisation is required to keep some liquidity for meeting its day-to-day needs. Availability of cash is necessary to maintain its liquidity. Cash is needed to pay off creditors, purchase stock of materials, pay labour and to meet day-to-day expenses. The finance manager has to decide the need for liquid assets and then arrange them in such a way that there is no scarcity of funds.

9. **Maintaining Relation with Outside Agencies:** The financial manager should establish and maintain cordial business relations with outside agencies like financial institutions, stock exchanges, tax authorities and so on.

FINANCIAL MANAGEMENT AND OTHER AREAS OF MANAGEMENT

Since every business activity is in need of money, financial management has a close relationship with all other areas of management such as marketing, personnel management, production management, asset management, cost accounting and financial accounting. The following are the relationships between financial management and other areas of management.

Financial Management and Marketing

Marketing management is the most important operative function of management. It deals with planning and controlling the entire marketing activities of a concern and comprises the formulation of marketing objectives, policies, programmes and strategies. The purpose behind marketing management is to enhance the sales volume, to develop new markets, and to reach new customers. However, the philosophy and approach to the pricing policy are critical elements in the company's marketing effort, image and sales level. Since the determination of approximate price of the company's product is very important both to the marketing and financial managers, there should be a joint decision. While the financial manager can supply the vital information regarding costs, changes in costs at different levels of production and the profit margin required to carry on the business, the marketing manager provides information as to how different prices will affect the demand for the firm's product in the market and the firm's competitive position. Thus, the role of financial manager for the formulation of the pricing policies of the firm cannot be undermined.

Financial Management and Personnel Management

The personnel management has gained a unique status in the modern industrial concerns. The personnel manager organises the personnel department which is generally assigned the operative functions of employment, compensation, training, etc. These functions are performed in consultation with the heads of other departments. However, all these require finances and thereby the decision relating to these aspects can be taken by the personnel department, only after consulting with the finance department.

In short, it is needless to point out that the financial management is closely linked with all other areas of management. Further, the firm's attitude towards other areas of management largely depends on its financial position. Usually, a firm having a comfortable financial position may give flexibility to the other management functions such as personnel, production and marketing. On the other hand, a firm which faces a financial crisis will have to devise its personnel, marketing and production strategies keeping the overall financial position in view. Thus the function of personnel department of a firm mainly banks upon the attitude of the finance department.

Financial Management and Production Management

Production is the conversion of raw materials into finished products which is also called manufacturing of goods. The production department will have to ensure that production is carried on in the best manner at the lowest cost. However, production is indirectly related to the key day-to-day decisions made by the financial manager. For instance, changes in the production process may necessitate capital expenditures, which the firm's financial manager should evaluate and then finance. Thus, financial management and production management are related.

Financial Management and Assets Management

Assets, both fixed and current, are resources necessary for the business of the firm. But the acquisition of assets and their maintenance and utilisation require finances. Thus, the financial manager is concerned with both the acquisition and utilisation of the firm's assets. The finance manager together with other officials of the firm, will have to take decisions regarding the current and future utilisation of firm's assets and their proper mix so as to accomplish the firm's goals in the best possible manner.

Financial Management and Cost Accounting

Cost accounting is the steering wheel which keeps the organisation on a steady path of prosperity. Most large firms have a separate cost accounting department to monitor expenditures in their operational areas. It helps the management in carrying out its functions by providing cost information. The finance manager is concerned with the proper utilisation of funds and thereby he is rightly concerned with the operational costs of the firm. Moreover, as the financial manager of the firm will have to make suitable recommendations to keep the cost under control, the information supplied by cost accounting department is very pertinent to him.

Financial Management and Financial Accounting

Financial accounting is that part of accounting which is employed to communicate the financial information of a business unit. Thus, it aims at ascertaining the profitability and providing information about the financial position of the concern. However, financial accounting is distinct from financial management although both play roles complementary to each other. If financial accounting is concerned with the recording, reporting, and measuring of business transactions, the financial management is concerned with the task of ensuring that the funds are procured at optimum cost and involve minimum financial risk. The information supplied by financial accounting is used by the financial manager to take decisions so as to help the concern in accomplishing its goals.

INDIAN FINANCIAL SYSTEM

The Indian financial system is divided into two sectors such as organised sector and informal sector. While the organised sector comprising all the institutions, markets and instruments come under the effective purview of the Reserve Bank of India and the government, the informal sector is beyond the purview of the regulatory and government authorities. But these two sectors are differentiated on the basis of the categories of customers, interest rate structures, credit conditions and business practices. However, the organised sector dominates the Indian financial system.

The financial system facilitates the transformation of savings into investment and consumption. In other words, it provides the means by which savings surplus units in the economy can transfer savings to those who require these savings for investment and consumption purposes. Although an understanding of the financial system is beneficial to all citizens, it is particularly relevant for financial managers who participate actively in raising and investing resources. Thus this discussion is limited to the following five sections which comprise the Indian financial system.

   (i) Financial assets
   (ii) Financial intermediaries
   (iii) Financial markets
   (iv) Financial rates of return
   (v) Financial development measures

(i) Financial Assets

Financial assets consist of money, debt and stock. Money is issued by the Reserve Bank of India and the Ministry of Finance, Government of India (as paper currency and coins) and by commercial banks (as demand deposits). While the debt is issued by a variety of organisations comprising the government and its agencies, the stock (equity and preference) is issued by business organisations. From the point of view of finance managers, the debt and stock are more significant.

A firm can raise debt capital by way of term loans from financial institutions, working capital advances from commercial banks, and issue of debentures. In this connection, it is noted that debt capital involves a fixed interest and principal repayment burden. However, a firm can issue two types of stocks. They are: equity and preference. While equity stock represents ownership capital, preference stock represents a hybrid form of financing in that it possesses some features of equity and some characteristics of debt.

(ii) Financial Intermediaries

In the organised sector, financial intermediation is conducted by a number of institutions. These institutions are functioning under the overall control of RBI. The following are the various kinds of financial intermediaries.

(a) **Reserve Bank of India:** Reserve Bank of India (RBI) is at the apex of the Indian financial system. Apart from traditional functions, RBI performs several functions aimed at developing the Indian financial system. They are:

  (i) integrating the unorganised financial sector with the organised financial sector;

  (ii) encouraging the extension of the commercial banking system in the rural areas;

  (iii) influencing the allocation of credit;

  (iv) supporting innovation in co-operative banks, and

  (v) promoting the development of new institutions.

(b) **Commercial Banks:** After RBI, commercial banks are the most unique institutions in the financial system. One of the major functions of commercial banks is to provide working capital advance to an industry. The State Bank of India, the largest commercial bank in India, was established in 1955 when the Imperial Bank was nationalised and merged with some banks of the princely states.

(c) **Term-lending Financial Institutions:** A number of financial institutions have been established to meet the term-finance needs of industry. They consist of three all-India term lending institutions such as Industrial Development Bank of India, Industrial Finance Corporation of India and Industrial Credit and Investment Corporation of India, and State Financial Corporations and State Industrial Development Corporations.

(d) **Agricultural Financing Institutions:** The agricultural financing system prevailing in India is very complex. The all-India level institutions engaged in this field are National Bank of Agriculture and Rural Development (NABARD) and the National Co-operative Development Corporation (NCDC). These institutions channelise their assistance through an elaborate network of regional, state level and field level institutions.

(e) **Insurance Companies:** The Life Insurance Corporation of India and the General Insurance Corporation of India are the two insurance companies in India. While the Life Insurance Corporation of India provides life insurance, the General Insurance Corporation of India engages in the business of property insurance. Both of them have massive resources for investment.

(f) **Other Public Sector Financial Institutions:** Unit Trust of India, Post Office Savings Bank and Industrial Reconstruction Bank of India are the unique public sector financial institutions which mobilise public savings and channelise them into corporate sector.

(g) **Non-banking Private Financial Institutions:** Non-banking private financial institutions such as hire-purchase companies, leasing companies, investment companies and finance corporations in the private sector are the other institutions functioning in the Indian financial system.

(iii) *Financial Markets*

Financial markets exist wherever financial transactions take place. A financial transaction is said to have taken place when a financial asset is created or transferred. For instance, issue of equity shares by a company, deposit of money in a bank and so on.

Money market and capital market are the two classes of financial markets. While money market deals in short-term debt, the capital market deals in long-term debt and stock. Capital market can be divided into two parts, the first covering the market for corporate securities and the second covering the market for gilt-edged securities. Securities issued by the central government, state governments, semi-government authorities autonomous institutions and public sector enterprises are referred to as gilt-edged securities.

(iv) *Financial Rates of Return*

Both as the principal borrower and an important lender, the government fixes the level and structure of interest rates in the organised sector.

(v) *Financial Development Measures*

The Indian financial system is judged by various indicators of financial development such as finance ratio, financial inter-relations ratio, new issue ratio and intermediation ratio.

$$\text{Finance Ratio} = \frac{\text{Total Financial Claims}}{\text{National Income}}$$

$$\text{Financial Inter-relations Ratio} = \frac{\text{Total Financial Claims}}{\text{Net Physical Capital Formation}}$$

$$\text{New Issue Ratio} = \frac{\text{Primary Issues (Claims created by non-financial sectors)}}{\text{Net Physical Capital Formations}}$$

$$\text{Intermediation Ratio} = \frac{\text{Issues of Financial Institutions}}{\text{Total Financial Issues in the Economy}}$$

TIME VALUE OF MONEY

The time value of money is a common denominator for discussing financial transactions and financial opportunities. However, the time value of money is fundamental in many areas of finance to determine trade-off between risk and return. Thus time value of money or time preference for money is one of the central ideas in finance. Money has a time value on account of the following reasons:

(i) An investor can invest a rupee received today for a greater value to be received tomorrow or after a certain period.

(ii) Generally, individuals prefer current consumption.

(iii) The money received today should have greater purchasing power than the same to be received in future during boom or inflation.

Needless to say, the concept of time value of money is based on the principle that a sum of money received today is worth more than the same amount received after some days. In other words, money to be received in future is less valuable than what it is today. For instance, in case a person is given an alternative either to receive Rs. 20,000 now, or after one year, he will prefer Rs. 20,000 at present. This may happen on account of any one of the following facts:

(a) He may invest this money and earn some interest on it.

(b) He may need money for current consumption.

(c) He is in a position to buy more goods with this money than what he is going to get for the same amount after one year.

When individuals and organisations face the situations involving cash receipts and disbursements over several periods of time, the time value of money becomes of paramount consideration in decision-making. This can be amplified with the help of following examples.

EXAMPLE 1

P gives a loan of Rs. 5000 to Q for one year. The market rate of interest is 8% p.a. Thus at the end of the year, P will get Rs. 5,400 for the initial loan of Rs. 5,000 given by him to Q. In other words, the amount of Rs. 5,000 today at 8% interest is equivalent to Rs. 5,400 to be received after a year.

EXAMPLE 2

A project requires an initial investment of Rs. 25,000. It is expected to provide a return of Rs. 4,000 per annum for eight years at the end of each year. Thus the project involves a cash outflow of Rs. 25,000 in the 'zero' year (i.e., initially) and cash inflows of Rs. 4,000 per year for eight years. A decision regarding the acceptance or rejection of the project can be arrived at only if the present value of cash inflows received annually for eight years is computed and compared with the initial investment of Rs. 25,000. However, the project can be accepted only when the present value of the cash inflows at the desired rate of return is at least equal to initial investment of Rs. 25,000.

In the light of the above discussion, it is clear that there is a preference of having money at present to a future point of time. This indicates that

(i) an individual will have to pay in future more for a rupee received today, and

(ii) an individual may accept less for a rupee to be received in future. These statements relate to two different concepts. They are as follows:

(a) Compound Value Concept

(b) Present Value Concept

(a) Compound Value Concept

Under this concept, the interest earned on the initial principal becomes a part of the principal at the end of the compounding period. For instance, Rs. 1,000 is invested at 8% compound interest for two years, the return for the first year will be Rs. 80 and for the second year, interest will be received on Rs. 1080 (i.e., Rs. 1,000 + 80). Thus the total amount due at the end of second year will become Rs. 1166.40 (i.e., Rs. 1,000 + 80 + 86.40).

(b) Present Value or Discounting Concept

Present value is the exact opposite or mirror image of the future value. While present value shows what the value is today (at present) of future sums of money, future value shows how much a sum can become at a future date. This process of decreasing future income payments to their present value is known as discounting. The value today of the sum to be received in the future is known as its present value.

For instance, "deposit Rs. 100 and take back Rs. 110 after one year", stated in another way means that Rs. 100 is the present value of Rs. 110 to be received a year later.

— REVIEW QUESTIONS —

1. What is Financial Management? Explain the significance of Financial Management.
2. Discuss the objectives of Financial Management.
3. Distinguish between wealth maximisation and profit maximisation. Explain briefly the various types of financial management decisions.
4. State in brief, the principal functions of a Finance Manager.
5. Discuss the relationship of financial management with other areas of management.
6. Discuss the principal components of Indian financial system.
7. Write notes on:
   (a) Time value of money
   (b) Gilt-edged securities
   (c) Financial intermediaries.

2
Financial Planning

*Whilst making profit is the mark of corporation success
money is the energizer which makes it possible.*

— G.D. BONDS

CONTENTS

- Introduction
- Steps in financial planning
- Characteristics of a good financial plan
- Fixed capital
- Working capital
- Tax implications and financial planning
- Review questions

INTRODUCTION

Planning is one of the most important functions of the financial manager. Like a doctor who wishes to know the condition of his patient before prescribing a remedy, a financial manager should first know his organisation's immediate position in order to formulate plans. This is because of the fact that the plans should fit the financial capabilities of the company. *Financial Planning*, therefore, is a part of the overall planning of any business. It refers to the application of planning for finance function. In other words, *Financial Planning is the process of determining the objectives, policies, procedures and programmes to deal with the financial activities of an organisation.* In short, financial planning is essentially concerned with the economical procurement and profitable use of funds. In this connection, G.D. Bonds points out that

> Whilst making profit is the mark of corporation success, money is the energizer which makes it possible.

An organisation, whether it is big or small, requires some sort of financial planning. It helps management to avoid waste by providing policies and procedures, which enable a closer co-ordination between various functions of the organisation. It helps the organisation in preparing for the future. Thus an organisation without sound financial planning is susceptible to shortage of funds, misapplication of funds and inefficient financial management.

In short, the significance of financial planning to a business concern arises because of the following benefits:

1. It ensures adequate capital from various sources for the smooth functioning of an organisation.

2. It ensures stability of business operations by reducing uncertainty about the availability of capital.

3. It ensures liquidity throughout the year by achieving a balance between the inflow and outflow of funds.

4. It helps to minimise cost of financing through the judicious application of scarce financial resources.

5. It facilitates financial control.

STEPS IN FINANCIAL PLANNING

Financial planning involves the following four steps:

1. **Establishing Objectives:** The first step in financial planning is the formulation of financial objectives in tune with business objectives. Even though the extent to which capital is employed varies from firm to firm, the objective is similar in all firms. The financial planners should formulate both short- and long-run objectives in order to be successful in the changing economic conditions. The use of capital in the correct proportion is the long-run objective of any firm.

2. **Estimating the Amount of Capital Required:** The basic aim of financial planning is the determination of capital requirements. Thus, the financial planners should estimate the amounts of both fixed and working capital required for various needs of the business.

3. **Determining the Capital Structure:** It refers to the proportion of different kinds of securities raised by a firm as long-term finance. Thus the financial planners should determine the types of securities to be issued and the relative proportion of each type of security.

4. **Formulating Financial Policies:** Financial policies are the guides to all actions. They deal with procuring, administering and disbursing the funds of business firms. Financial policies of a business firm may be brought into the following broad categories:

   (a) Policies governing the amount of capital required.

   (b) Policies which determine the control by the parties who furnish the capital.

(c) Policies which act as a guide in the use of debt or equity capital.

(d) Policies which guide management in the selection of sources of funds.

(e) Policies which govern credit and collection activities.

CHARACTERISTICS OF A GOOD FINANCIAL PLAN

A sound financial plan should possess the following characteristics:

1. **Simplicity:** A good financial plan should be free from complexity. In other words, a financial plan should be drafted in terms of the purpose for which the enterprise is organised.

2. **Flexibility:** A good financial plan of a firm should be in a position to finance expansion programmes without much difficulty. As the environment or organisational structure of a firm may change from time to time, it is desirable to have a more flexible and versatile plan than a routine stereotyped one.

3. **Intensive Use:** A good financial plan should be such that it will provide for an optimum use of capital. Capital should not remain idle, nor should there be any paucity of capital. If this is not done, the profitability will suffer.

4. **Foresight:** A financial plan should be based on the vision and experience of the management. There should be systematic prediction of various contingencies. In this connection, Henry Hoagland observes:

> No business management can assume that it will always have smooth sailing.

5. **Cost:** The cost of raising funds is an important consideration in the formulation of a financial plan. The selection of various sources should be such that the cost burden should be minimum. An excessive burden of fixed charges on the earnings of the firm might inflate its cost of capital.

6. **Objectivity:** The figures and reports to be used for a financial plan should be free from partiality, prejudice and personal bias. Thus a lapse from objectivity is not desirable.

7. **Liquidity:** A good financial plan should be based on the principle of liquidity which means the ability to produce cash on demand. This is made possible only when there is adequate net working capital. The degree of liquidity to be maintained depends on the size of the organisation, its age, its credit standing and nature of its business.

8. **Profitability:** A good financial plan should also be based on the principle of profitability. It means, the ability to enhance the profit-earning capacity of the concern. Thus a financial plan should maintain the required proportion between the fixed charges, the obligations and the liabilities in such a manner that the profitability of the organisation is not adversely affected.

Forecasting or Estimating Financial Requirements

Financial forecasting is a systematic projection of the expected action of finance through financial statements. It is a kind of plan which will be formulated at a future date for a specified period. There are three methods of forecasting financial requirements. They are as follows:

1. **Traditional Method:** Under this method, a firm's needs in terms of the number of days for which its sales are tied up in an individual balance sheet item are taken into account. It is a tie in between forecasting sales and forecasting financial requirements.

2. **Engineering Analysis:** It is a combination of technical know-how and judgement.

3. **Operation Analysis:** It relies mainly on judgement and on an understanding of the different kinds of operations in which a firm is engaged.

Factors Considered for Estimating Financial Requirements

1. **Cost of Financing:** Cost of financing such as advertisement expenses, brokerage on securities, commission on underwriting, etc., are expenses incurred for raising finance from the public. It should be the minimum.

2. **Repayment Date:** The time for which finance is required should be taken into account while estimating financial requirements of a concern. This helps for determining the repayment date.

3. **Liquidity:** Liquidity means ability to produce cash on demand. Due regard should be given to it as poor liquidity may lead to insolvency.

4. **Interest Payment:** Interest payment should be the minimum as heavy interest charges are embarrassing.

5. **Claim on Assets:** The borrowings of the concern may result in a charge on its assets. This may restrict their use and jeopardise the manoeuverability of the concern.

6. **Control:** The capital structure of a concern should be such as to ensure that control does not pass into the hands of outsiders. If too many people are allowed to control the concern, the operations and performance may go out of control.

7. **Risk:** The financial manager is more concerned about the financial risk which is created by a high debt-equity ratio than about any other risk. Thus it is better not to launch risky projects when equity finance is not available to the desired extent.

8. **Seasonality:** The financial requirements of a concern are highly influenced by seasonality which cannot be easily predicted. The events like strikes, product failures, changes in the supply prices, changes in technology or consumer tastes significantly affect financial requirements.

9. **Cost of Promotion:** Expenses incurred before the incorporation of a company are called promotion expenses. These include expenses on preliminary investigation, accounting, marketing and legal advice, etc.

10. **Cost of Fixed Assets:** The amount invested in fixed assets like land and buildings, plant and machinery, furniture, etc., is called fixed capital. The need of fixed capital should be based on estimates supplied by the production and engineering departments.

11. **Cost of Current Assets:** The requirements of current assets such as cash, stock of goods, book debts, etc., should be assessed on the basis of estimated sales and production schedules or projections.

12. **Cost of Establishing the Business:** It consists of operating losses which have to be sustained during the initial or gestation period of a company. The fixed capital requirement of a concern is a matter of promotional expenses, cost of establishing the business, cost of financing and cost of fixed assets. Of these, the cost of promotion and cost of establishing the business are relevant for new companies. On the other hand, working capital requirements is a matter of cost of current assets. Thus the capital requirements of a concern may be studied under the heads: fixed capital and working capital.

FIXED CAPITAL

Fixed capital is represented by fixed assets like plant and machinery, land and building, furniture, etc. Capital investment in such assets is more or less of a permanent nature. It does not mean, however, that fixed assets remain fixed for all the time to come. The amount of investment over fixed assets may diminish from time to time due to depreciation and sales.

The amount of fixed capital investment of a concern depends on the following factors:

1. **Nature of Business:** The fixed capital requirements of a manufacturing concern in general is much higher than that of a trading concern.

2. **Scale of Operation:** A small-scale concern requires less fixed capital than a large-scale concern. For example, public utility concerns like railways and water supply undertakings require a large investment in fixed assets.

3. **Type of Manufacturing Process:** Processing industries require a much larger amount of fixed capital than what is required in service and assembly industries.

4. **Mode of Acquiring Fixed Assets:** Fixed assets can be acquired either on ready cash or on instalment basis. The fixed capital requirement of cash purchase is much higher than that of instalment purchase.

WORKING CAPITAL

Working capital is the amount of capital which is required for the day-to-day working of a business. In simple language, working capital refers to that part of capital which is available and used for carrying out routine business operations of financing current assets such as cash, marketable securities, debtors and inventories. Working capital is also known as *Circulating Capital* because of the fact that it keeps on revolving or circulating from cash to current assets and back. Figure 2.1 shows the operating cycle of working capital.

Concepts of Working Capital

There are two concepts of working capital. They are:

1. Gross working capital and
2. Net working capital

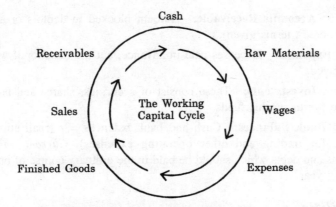

FIGURE 2.1 Operating Cycle of Working Capital.

1. Gross Working Capital

Gross Working Capital is the funds invested in total current assets. Current assets are those which in the ordinary course of business can be converted into cash within a short span of time. The concept of gross working capital is a going-concern concept which is helpful in providing the right amount of working capital at the right time. Thus the concern can realise the greatest return on its investment.

2. Net Working Capital

Net Working Capital refers to the difference between current assets and current liabilities (CA – CL). It is a broader and perhaps more useful concept, as working capital management is concerned with the problems that crop-up in managing the inter-relationship between current assets and current liabilities. It is also a useful concept for determining the ability of the concern to meet future needs.

Net working capital may be *positive or negative*. When the current assets exceed the current liabilities, the working capital is positive. On the other hand, when the current liabilities are more than the current assets, it is known as negative working capital.

Components of Working Capital

Net working capital is the difference between current assets and current liabilities. Current assets are either the assets which are used in the selling activities or the assets which are expected to be converted into cash within one accounting year. Both these meanings of current assets are considered together for the purpose of working capital management.

Current Assets

The major elements of current assets are:

1. **Stock or Inventories:** Investment blocked in inventories of raw materials, work-in-progress and finished goods = f (production) = f (sales).

2. **Debtors or Accounts Receivable:** Amount blocked in debtors or account receivable = f (sales, credit terms given).

3. **Pre-paid Expenses:** Expenses paid in advance, but the benefits of which have not yet been received.

4. **Short-term Investments:** These consist of securities, shares and bonds purchased to invest short-term surplus funds.

5. **Cash and Bank Balances:** Cash and bank balances = f (realisation of book debts, payments for trading and other operating expenses). *Current liabilities* are those obligations and debts which should be paid in the ordinary course of business within one accounting year.

Current Liabilities

The major elements of current liabilities:

1. **Accounts Payable or Trade Creditors:** These are the purchase of materials on credit from the sellers.

2. **Overdraft:** It is a temporary financial accommodation granted to an existing current account. Under this arrangement, the bank allows his customer to overdraw his account. Bank overdraft is considered as a current liability as there is no legal obligation on the part of the banks to continue it for long-term.

3. **Bank Loan:** This is the sum which is given by banks for a fixed time. Under loan scheme, the entire money is disbursed at one time. All loans which are given for short-term are a part of current liabilities.

4. **Cash Credits:** A cash credit is an arrangement whereby a borrower is allowed to withdraw up to a certain limit against securities. In the case of cash credit, a new account is opened in the name of the borrower known as *cash credit account* to which the amount sanctioned is credited. The borrower is entitled to withdraw the amount up to the cash limits as and when he requires money. Interest is charged on the amount actually drawn by the borrower.

   As overdraft and cash credit are similar in basic nature, these are grouped together for the purpose of the management of working capital.

5. **Accrued Expenses:** Expenses incurred but not paid are known as accrued expenses. Outstanding salaries and wages, outstanding rent, outstanding rates and taxes, outstanding interest, creditors for rent, rates and wages are examples of accrued expenses. These are short-term liabilities.

6. **Proposed Dividends:** Usually dividend is declared at the time of Annual General Meeting of a company. Till the period the declared dividend is not paid, the same is known as proposed dividend and treated as current liability.

7. **Tax-payment Due:** Any tax which is due for payment within a period of twelve months is a current liability.

8. **Short-term Loans:** Borrowing from banking and non-banking institutions for a short span of time is a current liability.

Permanent and Variable Working Capital

Permanent Working Capital

Permanent or regular working capital is the minimum amount which is required to ensure the effective utilisation of current assets. It represents the 'hard core' of working capital. The amount of permanent working capital increases with the increase in fixed assets over a long period. The increase in fixed assets leads to increase in sales turnover which in turn leads to increase in permanent working capital.

Figure 2.2 shows this relationship.

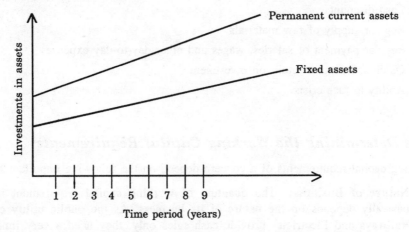

FIGURE 2.2 Relationship between Permanent Current Assets and Fixed Assets.

Variable Working Capital

Variable or temporary working capital is the amount of working capital which is required to meet the seasonal demands and some special exigencies. These seasonal demands are subject to fluctuations and are generally cyclical in nature. Figure 2.3 shows fluctuating current assets or variable working capital.

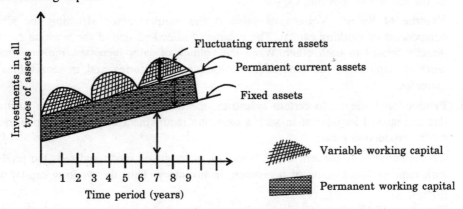

FIGURE 2.3 Variable Working Capital.

Significance of Working Capital

Working capital is very important for the successful conduct of any business. Just as circulation of blood is essential in the human body for maintaining life, working capital is essential for the smooth running of a business. Moreover, the significance of working capital in a firm arises on account of the following reasons:

(a) Solvency of business

(b) Goodwill of the firm

(c) Easy loans

(d) Cash discount

(e) Regular supply of raw materials

(f) Regular payment of salaries, wages and other day-to-day expenses

(g) Quick and regular return on investment

(h) Ability to face crisis

(i) High morale

Factors Determining the Working Capital Requirements

The working capital requirements of a concern depend on the following important factors:

1. **Nature of Business:** The quantum of working capital requirement in a concern basically depends on the nature of its business. As the public utility concerns like Railways and Electricity provide cash sales only, they need a very limited working capital. On the other hand, trading and financial concerns require very less investment in fixed assets but have to invest huge amount in current assets.

2. **Size of Business:** The working capital requirements of a concern are directly influenced by the size of its business. The greater the size of the business unit, the larger will be the amount of working capital.

3. **Manufacturing Process:** The level of working capital depends upon the time required to manufacture goods. The longer the processing period of manufacture, the larger will be the amount of working capital.

4. **Volume of Sales:** Volume of sales is the unique factor affecting the size and components of working capital. The volume of sales and size of the working capital are directly related to each other. When the volume of sales increases, the investment of working capital (in the cost of operations, in inventories and in receivables) also increases.

5. **Production Policy:** In certain industries, the demand is subject to wide fluctuations due to seasonal variations. In such a case, the requirement of working capital depends on the production policy.

6. **Credit Policy:** A concern which buys raw materials on credit and sells the product on cash requires less amount of investment in inventory. Thus the working capital will be low.

7. **Turnover of Working Capital:** Turnover means the speed with which the working

capital is converted into cash by the sale of goods. The speedier the turnover, the smaller will be the amount of working capital required.

8. **Seasonal Variation:** Since in certain industrial concerns, raw materials are not available throughout the year, they have to buy these materials during the season to ensure uninterrupted flow of production. In such cases a large amount of working capital is required.

9. **Business Cycle:** Usually, business expands during the periods of prosperity and declines during the periods of depression. Thus, more working capital is required during the periods of prosperity and less during the periods of depression.

10. **Production Cycle or Operating Cycle:** It is the time required to convert raw materials into finished goods. The longer the operating cycle, the larger will be the amount of working capital requirements.

11. **Earning Capacity and Dividend Policy:** The earning capacity and dividend policy of a concern also influences the requirements of its working capital. Firms which have high earning capacity may generate cash profits from operations and contribute to their working capital. A firm that maintains a steady high rate of cash dividend irrespective of its generation of profits requires a large sum as working capital.

12. **Price Level Changes:** The price level changes also influence the working capital requirements of a concern. Usually, a firm will have to maintain larger amount of working capital during rising prices as more funds are required to maintain the same current assets.

Adequacy of Working Capital

Working capital is an investment in current assets. Like other investments, it costs money. Thus, the working capital position of a concern should be neither excess nor inadequate. In other words, every concern should have adequate working capital to run its operations. The adequacy of working capital arises on account of the following reasons:

1. It helps the company to pay all the current obligations in time.
2. It helps to enjoy the advantage of cash discounts.
3. It helps the company to extend favourable credit terms to customers.
4. It helps the company to withstand the period of depression.
5. It enables the company to operate its business efficiently as there is no delay in obtaining materials.
6. It protects the company from the unfavourable effects of shrinkage in the values of current assets.
7. It helps the company to a larger extent to maintain its credit.

Excess or Inadequate Working Capital

Redundant working capital means idle funds which earn no profit for the business. On the other hand, inadequate working capital means shortage of working capital. A concern which has inadequate working capital cannot pay its short-term liabilities in time. Thus both redundant and shortage of working capital positions are bad for any business. However, out of the two, it is the shortage of working capital which is more dangerous from the point of view of the firm.

Dangers of Redundant Working Capital

A concern which has excess working capital should face the following problems:

1. overtrading,
2. improper rate of return on investment,
3. big inventories,
4. imbalance between liquidity and profitability,
5. fall in value of shares,
6. speculative transactions, and
7. overall inefficiency in the organisation.

Dangers of Inadequate Working Capital

A concern which has inadequate working capital cannot:

1. pay its short-term liabilities in time,
2. exploit favourable market conditions and undertake profitable projects,
3. buy its requirements in bulk,
4. pay day-to-day expenses of its operations,
5. utilise the fixed assets efficiently due to non-availability of liquid funds, and
6. enjoy the advantage of cash discount facilities.

TAX IMPLICATIONS AND FINANCIAL PLANNING

Since the income of all firms is subject to tax at the rates determined by the Finance Act passed every year by the Parliament, the taxation provisions have a vital effect on the Financial Planning of a firm. They are as follows:

(i) Decisions on Capital Structure

The tax implications play a vital role while determining the Debt-Equity mix of the firm. A firm can raise funds either through shares or loans including debentures. But it is pointed out that the interest paid on loan is deductible as an expense for tax purpose while the dividend paid on share capital is not deductible as an expense. Thus raising money through loan is cheaper than that of through shares.

(ii) Decisions on Capital Budgeting

A firm should also consider tax implications while taking capital budgeting decisions. For instance, a company should consider the following amounts in order to determine the amount of investment required in a capital investment project.

(a) The amount of tax, the company can save on account of writing off the loss on the sale of the old assets.

(b) The amount of tax the company is required to pay on any profit made on the disposal of old assets.

(c) The amount of tax, the company can save by virtue of investment allowance or other benefits on acquisition of new plant and machinery, ship or aircraft etc.

(d) The amount of tax saved by the company as a result of depreciation on the assets being allowed as a business expenditure for the purpose of tax.

(iii) Decisions on Dividend

The company should consider the tax implications as and when it takes dividend decision. Although the company should pay income tax when it earns income, the dividends are taxed as and when they are paid to individual shareholders. In this connection, it is needless to mention that the shareholders need not pay income tax unless dividends are received. Thus, the companies whose shareholders are in the high tax brackets, should retain the earnings rather than distributing them by way of dividends. But at any rate, in case dividends are to be paid, it is advisable to pay such dividends by way of shares. This is because of the fact that dividends in the form of shares (i.e., bonus shares) are subject to lower rate of tax.

(iv) Method of Depreciation

The company should also consider the tax implications while determining the method of depreciation. This is because the rate of depreciation in the case of written down value method is generally three times that of the rate of depreciation in the case of straight line method. Thus if a company desires to have huge funds during the initial periods of the project by making savings through taxation, it is advisable to charge depreciation as per the written down value method.

— REVIEW QUESTIONS —

1. What is meant by Financial Planning? Explain the various steps involved in Financial Planning?

2. Discuss the characteristics of a good financial plan.

3. What is financial planning? Discuss the factors to be considered while estimating financial requirements?

4. What is fixed capital? Discuss the factors to be considered for determining the fixed capital investment of a concern.

5. What is working capital? Discuss the factors which determine the working capital requirements of a company.

6. Write notes on:

   (a) Concepts of Working Capital

   (b) Components of Working Capital

   (c) Adequacy of Working Capital

   (d) Tax Implications and Financial Planning

   (e) Permanent and Temporary Working Capital.

3

Financial Forecasting

Financial forecasting is a systematic projection of the expected action of finance through financial statements.

INTRODUCTION

Forecast is a prediction of what is going to happen as a result of a given set of circumstances. When estimates of future conditions are made on a systematic basis, the process is referred to as 'forecasting' and the figure or statement obtained is called the forecast. In other words forecasting is peeping into the future, i.e., ascertaining the probabilities about the future. It consists of deciding, beforehand, the quantitative estimates of the firm's performance in terms of sales, production, costs and expected profits. Thus financial forecasting implies the technique of determining in advance, the requirement and utilisation of funds for a future period. It means, a systematic projection of the expected action of finance through financial statements. In short, it is a sort of working plan formulated for a particular period by arranging future activities.

Uses of Financial Forecasting

Following are the merits of financial forecasting:

(i) It helps to anticipate financial needs and effects on new policies and reduce emergency decisions.

(ii) Financial forecasting works as a control device in a firm as it provides a standard of financial performance for the future.

(iii) It is an aid in explaining the requirements of funds for the firm together with the funds of the suppliers.

(iv) It is used to pre-test the financial feasibility of various programmes.

(v) It helps to explain the proper requirements of funds and their optimum utilisation.

(vi) It assists the firm for the successful financial planning by providing significant information.

TOOLS OR ELEMENTS OF FINANCIAL FORECASTING

Financial forecasting of a business firm involves the preparation of: (a) pro forma financial statements, and (b) cash budget.

(a) Pro forma Financial Statements

Financial statements which are meant to display the effects of future circumstances are described as proforma statements. There are no rigid set of rules for constructing pro forma statements. Thus the formats of these projected financial statements vary in accordance with the ingenuity of the financial executives. There are two types of pro forma financial statements. They are: (i) projected income statement and (ii) projected balance sheet.

(i) Projected Income Statement

This statement is a projection of income for a period of time in future. In other words, projected income statement is a statement which furnishes a fair and reasonable estimate of expected revenue, cost, profits, taxes, dividends and other financial items. This statement is built around the estimate of the expected sales for the forecast period. The sales may be estimated on the basis of the detailed analysis of competitive firms, market research and professional economic surveys. Production cost can be estimated on the basis of the formulated production schedule. But this can be accurately predicted through the detailed analysis of purchases, productive wages and overhead costs. Having made the forecast of sales and production cost, the finance manager should estimate the administrative and selling expenses. As both of them are usually budgeted beforehand, their estimates are seldom correct. The estimates should also be made for other incomes and expenses along with interest for computing net income before taxes. For calculating net income after taxes, income-taxes at the prescribed rate should also be deducted. Finally, dividend payments should be predetermined at the appropriate level. Such payments are required to be deducted from the estimated net income/profit after tax.

A typical form of projected income statement with imaginary figures is given below:

Projected Income Statement
for the year ended 31st December 2002

	Rs.	Rs.
Revenues/Sales		16,00,000
Expenses		
Cost of Goods Sold:		
Raw Materials	4,00,000	
Direct Wages	6,00,000	
Factory Overheads	1,00,000	11,00,000
Gross Profit		5,00,000
Administrative Expenses	80,000	
Interest	20,000	
Selling and Distribution Expenses	60,000	
Depreciation	40,000	2,00,000
Operating profits/Net Income Before Tax		3,00,000
Less: Taxes 50%		1,50,000
Profit after Tax/Net Income		1,50,000
Add: Retained Earnings b/d		50,000
		2,00,000
Less: Dividend		1,00,000
Retained Earnings c/d		1,00,000

Although pro forma income statement may serve as a satisfactory estimate of profits for the projected period, it does not serve as a device to control expenses.

(ii) Projected Balance Sheet

The projected balance sheet is essentially a forecast of expected funds flows. Its construction is based on the information available in the projected income statement together with supporting schedules and budgets. However, the following four steps are involved in its preparation.

(a) Calculation of the net investment in each of the assets of the company to carry out operations at the planned level on the target date.

(b) Calculation of the net worth of the company after adjusting the projected income of the company from the period of forecasting.

(c) Listing of the liabilities that can be relied upon without negotiation.

(d) Comparison of the projected assets with total sources of funds, i.e., liabilities and net worth.

Interpretation of Projected Balance Sheet Items

(a) **Fixed Assets:** As outlays of plant and machinery are generally planned beforehand, the amount of fixed assets can be estimated without much difficulty. However, adjustments are to be made for additions and sales of old assets along with the amount of depreciation. Other assets such as pre-paid expenses, patents, goodwill, etc., will remain as they are unless it is specially mentioned.

(b) Current Assets:

(i) *Cash:* Usually a minimum amount of cash is to be maintained in hand for meeting various needs of the firm. It can also be a balancing or 'plug' figure to equalise assets and liabilities. This is particularly the case when borrowings from banks are taken as fixed.

(ii) *Sundry Debtors (Accounts Receivable):* Sales budget can be used to forecast the magnitude of debtors. However, it depends on the number of days credit allowed to customers. It can be computed with the help of a formula:

$$\text{Sundry Debtors} = \frac{\text{Credit Sales}}{\text{Average Debtors}}$$

or

$$= \frac{\text{Debtors}}{\text{Credit Sales}} \times 365$$

(iii) *Inventories:* The inventory level in relation to production programme is a unique item in the projected balance sheet. Its estimate is made on the basis of turnover ratio or through careful estimates of purchase, production, and selling schedules. It is computed as under:

$$\text{Stock Turnover Ratio} = \frac{\text{Cost of Goods Sold}}{\text{Average Inventories}}$$

or

$$= \frac{\text{Sales}}{\text{Average Inventories}}$$

(c) Liabilities:

1. *Shareholder's Fund/Net Worth:* It consists of the amount of share capital and reserves and surplus (fixed assets plus current assets minus current and long-term liabilities). Moreover, shareholders' funds should be computed by taking into consideration, the items such as fresh issue of shares, redemption of preference shares and retained earnings from profit as well. The profit figures are taken from the projected income statement. In case there is allocation of profit to reserve it can be incorporated in the respective reserves.

2. *Creditors:* They can be estimated by analysing schedules of purchases, payments for the period or by ascertaining the ratio of accounts payable with purchases or cost of goods sold. Creditors can be computed as under:

$$\text{Creditors} = \frac{\text{Credit Purchases}}{\text{Average Creditors}}$$

or

$$= \frac{\text{Creditors}}{\text{Credit Purchase}} \times 365$$

3. *Outstanding Liabilities:* Outstanding or accrued liabilities can be analysed by examining the pattern of wage payments, tax payments and interest obligations. Past and future data relating to these items should also be considered for this purpose.

4. *Provision for Tax and Dividends:* The projected balance sheet should be prepared only after providing proper provision for taxes and dividends. However, these items also depend on past and future data, the rate of tax and dividend, etc.

Having estimated all the components of the projected balance sheet, the financial analyst should combine and present them in a Balance Sheet. Further, all the Balance Sheet items can be estimated by projecting financial ratios for the future.

ILLUSTRATION 3.1

The Balance Sheet of Z Co. Ltd. on 31-3-2001 is as follows:

	Rs.		Rs.
Capital	20,00,000	Fixed Assets	10,00,000
Creditors (Trade)	2,80,000	Stock	5,00,000
Profit and Loss A/c	1,20,000	Debtors	2,00,000
		Cash and Bank	7,00,000
	24,00,000		24,00,000

The purchases and sales are estimated for the year ended 31-3-2002 as under:

	Upto 28-2-2002 Rs.	March 2002 Rs.
Purchases	28,20,000	2,20,000
Sales	38,40,000	4,00,000

The management decided to invest Rs. 2,00,000 in purchase of fixed assets which are depreciated at 10% on cost. The time-lag for payment to trade creditors for purchases and receipts from sales is one month. The business earns a gross profit of 25% on turnover. The sundry expenses are 10% of the turnover. The amount of depreciation is not included in these expenses. Draft a Projected Balance Sheet including the Projected Income Statement for the period 31-3-2002 assuming that creditors are all trade creditors for purchases and debtors for sales and there is no other item of current assets and liabilities apart from Stock and Cash and Bank Balances.

Solution

Projected Income Statement
for the period ending 31st March 2002

	Rs.	Rs.
Sales (Rs. 38,40,000 + Rs. 4,00,000)		42,40,000
Less: Cost of goods sold:		
Opening Stock	5,00,000	
Add: Purchases		
(Rs. 28,20,000 + Rs. 2,20,000)	30,40,000	
	35,40,000	
Less: Closing Stock (bal: fig.)	3,60,000	
Gross Profit (25% on Sales)		31,80,000
		10,60,000
Less: Sundry Expenses		
(10% on Sales)	4,24,000	
Depreciation: 10% on	1,20,000	5,44,000
Rs. 12,00,000		
(Rs. 10,00,000 + Rs. 2,00,000)		
Retained Earnings		5,16,000

Projected Balance Sheet
as at 31st March 2002

Liabilities	Rs.	Rs.	Assets	Rs.	Rs.
Capital		20,00,000	Fixed Assets	10,00,000	
Profit & Loss A/c			Additions	2,00,000	
Balance	1,20,000			12,00,000	
Add: Profit for			Less Depreciation		
the year	5,16,000		@10%	1,20,000	
		6,36,000			10,80,000
Sundry Creditors		2,20,000	Closing Stock		3,60,000
(Only for March			Sundry Debtors		4,00,000
purchases)			(Only for March's		
			Sales)		
			*Cash and Bank		10,16,000
		28,56,000			28,56,000

*Cash and Bank Balances	Rs.	Rs.
Opening Balance	7,00,000	
Receipts from Debtors	40,40,000	47,40,000
(Rs. 2,00,000 + Rs. 38,40,000)		
Less: Payments:		
Sundry Creditors		
(Rs. 2,80,000 + Rs. 28,20,000)	31,00,000	
Fixed Assets	2,00,000	
Expenses	4,24,000	
		37,24,000
Closing Balance		10,16,000

Cash Budget

Cash budget is one of the most important tools in the budgetary kit of the financial executive. It is prepared to estimate the expected cash receipts and payments during a specific period in future. Thus cash budget is a forecast of how much cash will be required during a particular period in future. However, the estimates are made on a day-to-day, week-to-week or month-to-month basis depending upon the requirement of cash.

The following are the main objectives of preparing cash budget.

(i) To ensure the availability of adequate amount of cash for the purpose of various capital and revenue expenditures.

(ii) To arrange cash in advance in the case of expected shortage of funds.

(iii) To employ surplus amount of cash, if any, in any profitable investment outside the business.

In short, cash budget provides information about the sources of expected cash that will be required for the business as and when necessary. But at the same time, in case the synchronisation of cash between receipts and payments is found impossible, the firm cannot earn expected profit shown in the Budgeted Profit and Loss Account. Thus the performance of all other functional budgets becomes useless.

Benefits of Preparing Cash Budget

The various advantages which can be derived from the cash budget are as follows:

(i) **Cash Requirements:** The cash budget provides a clear picture about the quantum of cash requirement at a particular moment of time. This helps the firm to make necessary arrangements for various purposes.

(ii) **Additional Cash Requirements:** The cash budget also informs the firm the quantum of additional cash requirement during the peak period. It also suggests the way in which such funds are to be mobilised.

(iii) **Deficit or Surplus:** The result of cash budget is either surplus or deficit cash. Thus, surplus cash, if any, can be invested properly.

(iv) **Cash Discount:** A firm can derive the benefit of cash discount by making payments before the date as the surplus amount of cash can be known by the preparation of cash budget.

Methods of Preparing Cash Budget

A cash budget is prepared in any one of the following ways: (a) Receipts and payments method, (b) The adjusted profit and loss method, (c) The balance sheet method.

For short-term forecasting, the receipt and payment method is very useful as the inflow and outflow of cash can be estimated by a proper analysis under this method. However, the adjusted profit and loss method and the balance sheet method are useful for long-term forecasting.

(a) Receipts and Payments Method

Under this method, all the anticipated cash receipts and payments which are expected during the budget period are considered. In other words, the estimates of sales, purchases, production, etc., form the basis for cash budget. It considers only cash receipts, regardless of their nature and period. Similarly, it recognises payments irrespective of the particular point of time at which the liability for expenditure arises. Moreover, the nature of cash payment is also irrelevant. But it is needless to point out that the accrued expenses and incomes are not to be considered at all in this budget.

Under this method, the budget is divided into two parts. They are receipts and payments. The receipts part of the budget is constructed in accordance with the sales budget, as the chief sources of funds are from sales. But the payments part of the budget is constructed as per other functional budgets.

The cash budget prepared under this method provides the following information:

(i) Information as to the quantum of sales to be made and also about the time-lag in the case of credit sales.

(ii) Information about the raw materials to be bought. This is furnished from purchase budget.

(iii) Information about the total amount of wages to be paid and the lag in payment of wages.

(iv) Information about the amount to be paid for various overheads and the lag in payment of overheads.

(v) Information about the cost to be considered for acquiring fixed assets. This is required for preparing capital expenditure budget.

All other information relating to receipts such as issue of shares, overdrafts, etc., and payments such as dividend, taxation, repayment of loans, etc., are also available from cash budget.

ILLUSTRATION 3.2

From the information given below, prepare a monthly Cash Budget for the four months ending 31st March.

Expected Sales:

	Rs.
December	1,00,000
January	1,20,000
February	90,000
March	1,60,000

Expected purchases:

December	64,000
January	1,20,000
February	1,40,000
March	90,000

Other relevant information:

(a) Wages to be paid to workers Rs. 12,000 each month.
(b) Dividend from investments amounting to Rs. 2,000 are expected on 31st March.
(c) Income-tax to be paid (in advance) in March Rs. 4000.
(d) Preference share dividend of Rs. 10,000 is to be paid on 28th February. Balance at Bank on 1st December is expected to be Rs. 12,000.

Solution

Cash Budget
Period: 4 months ending 31st March

Details				
Receipts	December Rs.	January Rs.	February Rs.	March Rs.
Balance b/d	12,000	36,000	24,000	
Sales	1,00,000	1,20,000	90,000	1,60,000
Dividend	—			2,000
Deficit c/d	—	—	48,000	—
	1,12,000	1,56,000	1,62,000	1,62,000
Payments:				
Deficit b/d				48,000
Creditors	64,000	1,20,000	1,40,000	90,000
Wages	12,000	12,000	12,000	12,000
Pref: Dividend	—		10,000	—
Income-Tax	—	—	—	4,000
Balance c/d	36,000	24,000	—	8,000
	1,12,000	1,56,000	1,62,000	1,62,000

N.B. Deficit implies overdraft

(b) Adjusted Profit and Loss Method

Adjusted profit and loss method is practically useful for long-term forecasting which attempts to indicate the effect of proposed long-range plans such as acquisitions, new product development and long-range charges on the company's balance sheet three, five or even ten years in the future. This method is based on the assumption that profit is equivalent to cash and both cash and non-cash transactions are considered. Under this method, it is started by taking the balance from budgeted profit and loss account (that is why it is called Adjusted Profit and Loss Method) and then various non-cash charges (e.g., depreciation) are added back with it and non-cash credits are deducted from it. Thereafter, the changes of assets and liabilities are to be added or deducted, as the case may be, which ultimately affect cash.

Under adjusted profit and loss account method, cash budget often resembles the projected source and application of funds statement. The adjusted profit implies the estimated cash available. Thus under this method, available cash can be estimated only by preparing budgeted profit and loss account for the budget period and budgeted balance sheet both for the current as well as previous periods.

However, the Adjusted Profit and Loss Method differs from Receipts and Payments Method in the sense that the former takes non-cash transaction into consideration and at the same time considers profit equivalent to cash.

ILLUSTRATION 3.3

Following is the Balance Sheet of X Ltd. as on 31st December 2001.

Balance Sheet
As on 31st December 2001

Liabilities	Rs.		Assets		Rs.
Share Capital	10,000		Goodwill at Cost		60,000
Equity Shares of			Fixed Assets:		
Rs. 10 each, fully paid		1,00,000	Land and Building		40,000
Reserve and Surplus:			Plant and Machinery	1,00,000	
General Reserve		40,000	Less Depreciation	10,000	90,000
Capital Reserve		60,000	Furniture and Fixtures		30,000
Profit and Loss Account		80,000	Current Assets:		
Future Taxation		30,000	Stock	1,00,000	
Current Liabilities:			Debtors	80,000	
Creditors	80,000		Cash and Bank	40,000	2,20,000
Taxation	40,000				
Proposed					
Dividend	10,000	1,30,000			
		4,40,000			4,40,000

Details for the next twelve months ending on 31st December 2002 are:

	Rs.
Wages (Direct)	2,40,000
Wages (Indirect)	1,20,000
Salaries (Office)	1,00,000
Payments to Creditors	6,00,000
Receipts from Debtors	10,00,000
Cash Sales	4,00,000
Purchase of Land and Building	50,000
Interim Dividend	15,000
Debtors' Balance (Closing)	70,000
Creditors' Balance (Closing)	50,000

Depreciation is to be charged @10% on Plant and Machinery (on Straight-Line Method)

Stock is expected to be valued at Rs. 1,40,000 at the end of the year.

Future Taxation to be reserved for the following year amounted to Rs. 40,000.

Transfer Rs. 40,000 for General Reserve

Prepare a Cash Flow Statement under Adjusted Profit and Loss Method assuming that last year's tax and dividend are to be paid. Prepare also the Forecast Balance Sheet.

Solution

Cash Flow Statement

	Rs.		Rs.
Opening Balance of Cash	40,000	Outflow of Cash:	
Add: Inflows of Cash:		Interim Dividend	15,000
Net Profit	3,90,000	Taxation	40,000
Depreciation on plant and Machinery	10,000	Proposed Dividend	10,000
Decrease in Debtors	10,000	Purchase of Land & Building	50,000
		Decrease in Creditors	30,000
		Increase in Stock	40,000
			1,85,000
		Closing Balance of Cash	2,65,000
	4,50,000		4,50,000

Forecast Balance Sheet
as at 31st December 2002

Liabilities	Rs.	Assets	Rs.
Share Capital	1,00,000	Goodwill at cost	60,000
Reserves & Surplus:		Fixed Assets:	
General Reserve	80,000	Land & Building:	40,000

Continued

Liabilities		Rs.	Assets		Rs.	
Capital Reserve		60,000	Addition		50,000	90,000
Profit and Loss Account		3,75,000	Plant and Machinery		1,00,000	
Future Taxation		40,000	Less: Depreciation		20,000	
Current Liabilities:						80,000
Sundry Creditors	50,000		Furniture and Fixtures			30,000
Taxation	30,000		Current Assets:			
		80,000	Stock		1,40,000	
			Debtors		70,000	
			Cash		2,65,000	
						4,75,000
		7,35,000				7,35,000

Working Notes:

Debtors Account

	Rs.		Rs.
To Balance b/d	80,000	By Cash	10,00,000
To Sales (Credit)	9,90,000	By Balance c/d	70,000
	10,70,000		10,70,000

Creditors Account

	Rs.		Rs.
To Cash	6,00,000	By Balance b/d	80,000
To Balance c/d	50,000	By Purchases (Credit)	5,70,000
	6,50,000		6,50,000

Profit and Loss Account (Adjusted)
for the year ended 31st Dec. 2002

		Rs.			Rs.
To Opening Stock		1,00,000	By Sales		
To Purchases (Credit)		5,70,000	By Cash	4,00,000	
By Wages			By Credit	9,90,000	13,90,000
Direct:	2,40,000				
Indirect:	1,20,000		By Closing		1,40,000
		3,60,000	By Stock		
By Gross					
Profit c/d		5,00,000			
		15,30,000			15,30,000

Continued

	Rs.		Rs.
To Salaries	1,00,000	By Gross profit b/d	5,00,000
To Depreciation on			
Plant & Machinery	10,000		
To Net Profit c/d	3,90,000		
	5,00,000		5,00,000
To General Reserve	40,000	By Net Profit b/d	3,90,000
To Provision of Taxation	40,000	By Balance b/d	80,000
To Interim Dividend	15,000		
To Balance c/d	3,75,000		
	4,70,000		4,70,000

(c) Balance Sheet Method

In this method, a budgeted balance sheet is prepared by recording all expected assets and expected liabilities except cash. In case the liabilities side is more than the assets side, the difference will be cash balance. On the contrary, if the assets side is higher than the liabilities side, the balance will represent bank overdraft.

Balance sheet method is highly useful for long-term forecasting.

ILLUSTRATION 3.4

The following are the particulars of Z Ltd.:

	Rs.
Share Capital	8,00,000
General Reserve (against Rs. 6,00,000 invested in Fixed Assets)	1,00,000
Stock	1,00,000
Debtors	1,00,000
Creditors (Trade and Others)	80,000

Additional information:

Stock level is proposed to be increased by	100%
Additions to be for Machinery amounted to (as per Capital Budget)	80,000
Advance Income-Tax payment is estimated at	1,00,000
Estimated profit after charging Depreciation	
Rs. 60,000 and 50% of profit for Taxation amounted to	1,60,000

6% Dividend to be paid, also make a provision for proposed dividend @ 10%

Sales Budget shows Rs. 24,00,000 sales and debtors are estimated to be outstanding for 3 months

Creditors (Trade and others) are likely to be doubled

Make an estimate of cash position as at the end of the budget period

Solution

Budgeted Balance Sheet
as at ....

Liabilities	Rs.		Assets	Rs.	
Share Capital		8,00,000	Fixed Assets:		
Reserve & Surplus:			Balance	6,00,000	
Generally Reserve		1,00,000	Additions	80,000	
				6,80,000	
Profit and Loss A/c	1,60,000		Less:		
Less` Dividend	48,000		Depreciation	60,000	
	1,12,000				6,20,000
Less: Proposed Dividend	80,000				
		32,000	Current Asset:		
Current Liabilities:			Stock	2,00,000	
Proposed Dividend		80,000	Debtors	6,00,000	
Provision for Taxation		1,60,000	Advance		
Creditors (Trade & others)		1,60,000	Income-Tax	1,00,000	
Bank Overdraft (bal. fig)		1,88,000			9,00,000
		15,20,000			15,20,000

Financial Forecasting—Other Methods

The elements of financial forecasting have been discussed so far with the help of projected financial statements (i.e., projected income statement and projected balance sheet) and cash budget. Here some other methods of financial forecasting are also to be discussed. They are: (i) Percentage of sales method, (ii) Simple regression method, and (iii) Multiple regression method.

(i) Percentage of Sales Method

Percentage of sales method is the simplest forecasting technique and is suitable for short-term forecasting. This method is commonly used in estimating financial requirements of the firm based on forecast of sales. Under this method, each component of Balance Sheet item is expressed in terms of percentage of sales. Financial data can now be developed for projected sales at different levels.

(ii) Simple Regression Method

Simple regression or scatter diagram method is used to estimate the financial forecasting in a more logical way. This method provides estimates of values of the dependent variables from values of independent variables. Under this method, on the basis of past relationship between sales and different items, a regression line or line of best fit can be drawn. It is needless to mention that the said line may either be linear or curved. However, this method requires linking sales with one item at a time. Thus, data about different items can be projected with the change in the sales level.

(iii) Multiple Regression Method

Multiple regression analysis is a further application and extension of the simple regression method for multiple variables. While under simple regression method, the sale is considered to be a function of one variable, under multiple regression method the sale is considered to be a function of several variables. Thus multiple regression method is a better technique for calculating the amount of different items.

— REVIEW QUESTIONS —

1. What is financial forecasting? Describe the elements of financial forecasting.
2. What is a cash budget? Discuss the various methods of cash budget.
3. Write notes on:
   (a) Scatter Diagram
   (b) Percentage of Sales Method
   (c) Projected Income Statement
   (d) Projected Balance Sheet
4. Define financial forecasting. What are the utilities of financial forecasting?
5. The Balance Sheet of ABC Ltd. as at 31st December is as follows.

Balance Sheet
As at 31st December 2000

Liabilities		Rs.	Assets		Rs.
Share Capital			Goodwill at cost		30,000
5000 Equity shares of Rs. 10			Fixed Assets:		
each fully paid		50,000	Land and Building		20,000
Reserves and Surplus:			Plant and Machinery	50,000	
General Reserve		20,000	Less: Depreciation	5,000	
Capital Reserve		30,000			45,000
Profit and Less Account		40,000	Furniture and		
Future Taxation		15,000	Fixtures		15,000
Current Liabilities:			Current Assets:		
Creditors	40,000		Stock	50,000	
Taxation	20,000		Debtors	40,000	
Proposed			Cash and Bank	20,000	
Dividend	5,000				1,10,000
		65,000			
		2,20,000			2,20,000

Information for the next twelve months ending on 31st December 2001 is

	Rs.
Wages (Direct)	1,20,000
Wages (Indirect)	60,000
Salaries (Office)	50,000
Payments to Creditors	3,00,000
Receipts from Debtors	5,00,000
Cash Sales	2,00,000
Purchase of Land and Building	25,000
Interim Dividend	7,500
Debtors Balance (Closing)	35,000
Creditors Balance (Closing)	25,000

Depreciation is to be charged @10% on Plant and Machinery (on Straight-Line Method).

Stock is expected to be valued at Rs. 70,000 at the end of the year.

Future Taxation to be reserved for the following year amounted to Rs. 20,000.

Transfer Rs. 20,000 for General Reserve

You are required to prepare a Cash Flow Statement under Adjusted Profit and Loss Method assuming that last year's tax and dividend are to be paid. Prepare also the Forecast Balance Sheet.

(Ans.: Closing balance of cash Rs. 1,32,500 Forecast Balance Sheet total Rs. 3,67,500)

6. From the following information, prepare a monthly Cash Budget for the four months ending 31st December.

Expected Sales:	Rs.
September	50,000
October	60,000
November	45,000
December	80,000

Expected purchase:	
September	32,000
October	60,000
November	70,000
December	45,000

Other relevant information is:

(a) Wages to be paid to workers Rs. 6,000 each month.

(b) Dividend from investments amounting to Rs. 1,000 are expected on 31st December.

(c) Income-tax to be paid (in advance) in December Rs. 2,000.

(d) Preference share dividend of Rs. 5,000 are to be paid on 30th November. Balance at Bank on 1st September is expected to be Rs. 6,000.

(Ans.: Balance c/d, September Rs. 18,000, October Rs. 12,000, December Rs. 4,000, Deficit c/d November Rs. 24,000)

7. The following is the operation budget of your company phased by quarters for a calender year. From this and the additional information given, prepare a Cash Flow Forecast by quarters.

Figures in Rs. lakhs

	1st Qr	2nd Qr	3rd Qr	4th Qr
Sales:				
Credit	13.50	12.60	8.20	13.20
Cash	0.50	0.60	0.40	0.80
	14.00	13.20	8.60	14.00
Material Consumed	9.40	8.80	5.60	9.20
Operation Expenses (variable)	0.60	0.60	0.50	0.60
Fixed Expenses (includes Rs. 80,000 per quarter as depreciation)	1.30	1.30	1.30	1.30
	11.30	10.70	7.40	11.10
Operating Profit	2.70	2.50	1.20	2.90
End-of-the-quarter Balances:				
Debtors	7.70	7.70	6.50	7.70
Stock—Raw Materials	6.50	5.00	6.50	6.50
Stock—Finished Goods	3.45	3.75	5.35	3.75
Creditors	2.50	2.50	2.50	2.50
Operating Balance at the beginning of 1st Qr				
Debtors		7.00		
Stock-Raw Materials		6.00		
Finished Goods		3.75		
Creditors		2.40		
Bank Borrowings (Overdraft)		4.70		
Additional plant on order		4.50	(to be paid in Sept.)	
Anticipated loan for new plant		3.00	(available in Sept.)	
Sales of old car		0.08	(in August)	
Loan instalment due last quarter		1.50		
Advance tax payable each quarter		0.08		

(I.C.W.A. Final)

(**Ans.:** Balance c/d 2nd Qr. Rs. 0.90 lakhs, 3rd Qr. Rs. 0.38 lakhs, 4th Qr. Rs. 0.58 lakhs, Deficit c/d 1st Qr. Rs. 3.10 lakhs)

4

Capitalisation and Capital Structure

Capitalisation refers to the total amount in securities issued by a company.

CONTENTS
● Capitalisation
● Theories of capitalisation
● Capital structure
● Classification of capital structure
● Case study
● Review questions

CAPITALISATION

The term capitalisation is derived from the word capital. '*Capital*' in the business aspect means the actual wealth or assets of a concern. But in the accounting aspect 'capital' means the net worth of a business, i.e., *Assets-Liabilities*. Thus, the term capitalisation refers to the total amount in securities issued by a company. It consists of share capital, reserves, debenture capital and long-term borrowings of the company. It is a quantitative aspect of financial planning.

The terms capitalisation and share capital are used only in the case of a joint-stock company. But the term share capital is used for the paid-up value of shares of a company. It consists of both equity and preference share capital as given below:

Share Capital = Equity Shares + Preference Shares

Capitalisation = Share Capital + Debenture Capital + Long-term Borrowings
+ Free Reserves.

THEORIES OF CAPITALISATION

The following are the two recognised bases for capitalising new companies.

(i) Cost Theory

The cost theory suggests that the value of a company is the aggregate of the value of fixed assets, working capital, the cost of establishing business and expenses of promotion. While fixed assets include plant, machinery, patents, etc., working capital consists of the capital which is regularly required for the continuous operation of the business. Such a method of computation of capitalisation of a concern helps the promoters to determine the amount of capital to be raised. In spite of this advantage, the cost theory of capitalisation is subject to an objection that it is based on a figure (i.e., cost of establishing and starting business) which will not vary with variation in the earning capacity of the company. Thus the true value of a concern is judged from its earning capacity rather than from the capital invested in it. For instance, the earnings and the earning capacity of the concern will naturally come down when some assets become obsolete and some other assets remain idle. But such a decrease will not come below the value of investment made in the company's business.

(ii) Earnings Theory

The earnings theory suggests that the true value (capitalisation) of a company depends on its earnings and earning capacity. Thus the value or capitalisation of a company is equal to the capitalised value of its estimated earnings. With this end in view, the financial manager of a new company should prepare an estimated profit and loss account. For the first few years of its life, he has to forecast sales and determine the probable cost with the help of his experience. The earnings so estimated may be compared with the actual earnings of similar concerns in the industry so as to make necessary adjustments in it. Then the promoters will have to study the rate of earning of other concerns of the same industry similarly situated. The rate is then applied to the estimated earnings of the company for determining the capitalisation. For instance, a company may estimate its average profit in the first few years at Rs. 1,00,000. It is assumed that other companies of the same type are earning a return of 20 per cent on their capital. Then the capitalisation of the company is [(1,00,000 × 100)/20].

In this connection, it is noted that the earning theory has the advantage of capitalising a company at an amount which is directly related to its earning capacity. Thus a company is worth what it can earn. But the new companies will find it difficult and even risky to depend merely on estimates of their earnings as the generally expected return in an industry. Thus in the case of new companies, the cost theory provides a better basis for capitalisation than the earning theory.

However, in established companies, the capitalisation can be determined on the basis of either cost theory or earning theory. In case, cost is adopted as the basis, the true worth of the company cannot be determined with the help of capitalisation. Although the assets of such a company stand at their original values, its earnings may have reduced substantially. In such a situation, it will be risky to presume that the capitalisation of the company is high. Thus in established companies, earnings provide a better basis of capitalisation than cost.

Actual and Proper Capitalisation

The aggregate value of the shares, debentures and non-divisible retained earnings of the company is called the actual capitalisation of the company. The actual capitalisation in accordance with the balance sheet of AB Co. Ltd. given below is Rs. 20,00,000.

AB Co. Ltd.
Balance Sheet as on 31st December 2002

Liabilities	Amount Rs.	Assets	Amount Rs.
Paid-up Capital			
1,00,000 Equity Shares of Rs. 10 each	10,00,000	Sundry Assets	20,00,000
50,000, 7% Preference Shares of Rs. 10 each	5,00,000		
5,000 Debentures of Rs. 100 each	5,00,000		
	20,00,000		20,00,000

But the proper capitalisaton of a company can be determined by capitalising the average annual profits at the normal rate of return earned by comparable companies in the same line of business. In case a company gets an annual return of Rs. 2,00,000 and the normal rate of return in the industry is 10 per cent, the proper or normal capitalisation is:

$$\frac{2,00,000}{10} \times 100 = Rs. \, 20,00,000$$

Whether the company is properly capitalised, over-capitalised or under capitalised can be known through a comparison between the actual and proper capitalisation.

Over-Capitalisation

The situation of over-capitalisation arises when a company raises more capital than is justified by its expected earnings. A company is said to be over-capitalised "when its profits are not large enough to yield a fair return on the amount of shares and debentures that have been issued". This situation can be explained with the help of an illustration.

Suppose a company earns a profit of Rs. 4 lakhs. With the expected earnings of 20 per cent, the capitalisation of the company should be Rs. 20 lakhs. But if a company issues shares and debentures to the extent of Rs. 25 lakhs, the rate of earnings will be only 16 per cent. As the rate of interest on debenture is fixed, the equity shareholders will get only a lower dividend in the future.

Watered Capital

Water is said to be present in the capital when a part of the capital of a company is not represented by assets. In other words, the capital of the company is said to have been "watered" whenever its stock is issued to persons in excess of the benefits received from them. This generally occurs when assets are acquired by a company at high price. But the shares issued against such assets are in fact issued against water. This can be explained by taking into account a specific instance of a newly formed company.

Balance Sheet

	Rs.		Rs.
Share Capital	5,00,000	Machinery	2,00,000
		Buildings	2,50,000
		Other assets	50,000
	5,00,000		5,00,000

In the above case, the worth of machinery and buildings is in fact only Rs. 1,50,000 and Rs. 2,00,000 respectively. Thus there is water in each case to the extent of Rs. 50,000. In case the value of other assets is in their book value, the total amount of water comes to Rs. 1,00,000.

Both "watered capital" and "over-capitalisation" are not synonymous terms. Stock may be watered and yet it may not result in over-capitalisation as the earnings are up to the general expectation. Further, although water enters the capital usually in the initial period—at the time of promotion, over-capitalisation can be found out only after the company has worked for some time.

Effects of Over-Capitalisation

The situation of over-capitalisation has evil consequences both to the shareholders and company.

The shareholders of an over-capitalised company are losers in all transactions as a result of the following reasons:

1. The value of shares diminishes because of lower profitability.
2. The shareholders get lower rate of dividend because of reduced earnings of the company.
3. The return on investment is uncertain and irregular.
4. The shareholders will have to suffer on account of speculation which is encouraged in the shares of over-capitalised company.
5. Even in the case of reorganisation, the shareholders are the worst sufferers.

From the point of view of the company, the situation of over-capitalisation has the following evil consequences:

1. The reputation of the company diminishes as a result of low profitability.
2. The company is not in a position to raise fresh capital from the market.
3. The financial status of the company may be adversely affected due to inadequate provision for depreciation, replacement, etc.

4. The shares of the company may not be easily sold.

5. The management of the over-capitalised company may be forced to follow unfair practices on account of reduced earnings.

Under-Capitalisation

Under-capitalisation is a state when the capital of the company is less in proportion to its total requirements. It is just the reverse of over-capitalisation. A company is said to be under-capitalised "when it is earning exceptionally high profits as compared to other companies".

Suppose, the capitalisation of a company is Rs. 10,00,000 and the average rate of return of the industry is 10 per cent. But if the company is earning 15 per cent on the capital investment, it is a case of under-capitalisation.

Under-capitalisation is associated with an effective utilisation of investments, a high rate of dividend and enhanced price of shares. Sometimes an under-capitalised company, on the face of it, may have an insufficient capital but it may have large secret reserves.

Effects of Under-Capitalisation

The situation of under-capitalisation has the following effects on shareholders:

1. The rate of earning per share is high because of the high earning of the company.

2. The market value of shares increases.

3. Regular dividend can be expected.

4. The reputation of the company increases.

From the point of view of the company, the situation of under-capitalisation has the following consequences:

1. The goodwill of the company increases because of high profitability.

2. The high dividend rates give an opportunity to workers to demand higher wages.

3. The consumers feel that they are being exploited by the company.

4. The high rate of earnings attracts competition in the market.

5. It attracts Government control and high taxation.

Comparison of Over-Capitalisation and Under-Capitalisation

Over-Capitalisation	Under-Capitalisation
1. It is the situation of high total capital as compared with the existing earnings.	1. It is the situation of low total capital as compared with the existing earnings.
2. It is the situation of idle capital.	2. It is the situation of efficient use of capital.
3. In an over-capitalised company, the rate of earnings per share is very low.	3. In an under-capitalised company, the rate of earnings per share is very high.
4. It is the case of irregular dividend.	4. It is the case of regular dividend.
5. The market value of shares of an over-capitalised company is very low.	5. The market value of shares of an under-capitalised company is very high.
6. The reputation of an over-capitalised company goes down.	6. The reputation of an under-capitalised company goes up.
7. The management of an over-capitalised company may follow unfair practices to pay high dividend.	7. The management of an under-capitalised company may create secret reserves and avoid tax on higher income.

CAPITAL STRUCTURE

The term capital structure involves decisions related to the kinds of securities to be issued and the relative proportion of each kind of security. The capital structure of a company is made up of debt and equity securities. In the words of Gerstenberg:

> Capital structure or financial structure is the types of securities to be issued and proportionate amounts that make up the capitalisation.

Thus capital structure refers to the proportion of different kinds of securities raised by a company as long-term finance. Long-term funds can be raised either by the issue of (a) Shares or (b) Debentures or long-term loans and borrowings. However, there is a difference between two types of long-term finance. When the company raises funds by the issue of equity shares, it requires to pay dividend only if there is sufficient profit. But if the company raises funds by issuing debentures, it has to pay a fixed rate of interest irrespective of the profit or loss. Thus the question of capital gearing arises as to which fund a fixed rate of interest or dividend is paid.

Capital Gearing

Capital gearing is the relationship between the ownership capital and creditorship capital. In other words, it stands for the ratio between the various kinds of securities to the total capitalisation. The gearing may be either high or low. A company is said to be highly geared when the ownership capital is less than the creditorship capital. On the other hand, a company is said to be low geared when the ownership capital is greater than creditorship capital.

A company should prefer low gear during its initial stage of development. But after gaining momentum, it can change the gear from low to high. This is the principle adopted in the case of operating an automobile. This can be explained with the help of an illustration.

Let two companies, each having issued the total securities worth rupees forty lakhs, have equity shares worth rupees ten lakhs and rupees thirty lakhs respectively. The first company is highly geared as the ratio between ownership capital and creditorship capital is 1:3. But in the case of the second company, this ratio is 3:1, so it is lowly geared.

Factors Affecting Capital Structure

While planning the capital structure, the following significant factors are to be considered carefully:

1. **Trading on Equity or Financial Leverage:** A company is said to be trading on equity when it uses owned and borrowed capital for the conduct of its business. The term equity denotes the ownership of the company. Thus trading on equity means taking the advantage of equity share capital to borrowed funds on a reasonable basis.

Trading on equity is based on the assumption that if the rate of interest on creditorship capital is less than the general rate of the company's earnings, the equity shareholders will get a benefit in the form of additional profit. This can be amplified with the help of an illustration:

Suppose, a company has an equity capital of 2,000 shares of Rs. 100 each fully paid and earns an average profit of Rs. 60,000. Now the company wishes to make an expansion and needs another Rs. 2,00,000. The options with the company are either to issue new shares or to raise loans at 10 per cent per annum.

Assuming that the company would earn the same rate of profits, it is advisable to raise loans. Thus the earnings per share will increase. The company shall pay only Rs. 20,000 as interest and the profit expected shall be Rs. 1,40,000 (before payment of interest). After the payment of interest, the profit left for equity shareholders shall be Rs. 1,20,000. It is 50 per cent return on the equity capital against 30 per cent return otherwise.

However, leverage can operate adversely when the rate of interest on long-term loan is greater than the expected rate of profits of the company.

2. **Control:** The control of a company is vested in the hands of a board of directors elected by the equity shareholders. Equity shareholders have a full-fledged voting right. But debentureholders have no voting right and the preference shareholders possess only limited voting right. If the equity shareholders wish to retain control over the company, they should not permit to issue further equity shares to the public. In such a case, debt financing is recommended.

3. **Cost of Financing:** The capital structure should provide for the minimum cost of capital. Usually, debt is a cheaper source of finance when compared to preference and equity capital. Preference capital is also cheaper than equity capital because of the less risk involved and a fixed rate of dividend payable to the preference shareholders.

4. **Flexibility of Financial Structure:** The capital structure of a company should be adjustable in accordance with the needs of the changing conditions. Redeemable preference shares and convertible debentures may be preferred on account of flexibility.

5. **Period of Financing:** When the company requires funds for permanent investment, it should prefer equity share capital. Otherwise, it may issue redeemable preference shares and debentures.

6. **Statutory Requirements:** A company should also fulfil the requirements of the statute when its capital structure is framed. For example, the banking companies are permitted to issue only equity shares as per the Banking Companies Regulation Act.

7. **Capital Market Conditions:** The conditions prevailing in the capital market influence the determination of securities to be issued. The market conditions are either depression or boom. During depression, debentures and preference shares which carry a fixed rate of return may be marketed more easily as people do not like to take risks. But during boom, people are ready to take risk and invest in equity shares.

Features of Capital Structure

The following are the salient features of sound capital structure.

Return: The capital structure of a company is said to be sound, if it generates maximum returns to the shareholders without incurring additional costs to them.

Flexibility: The capital structure of the company should be flexible. It implies the capability of the company to adapt its capital structure in accordance with the changing situations.

Risk: Usually, excessive risk threatens the solvency of the company. Thus the debt of the company should be such that it should not add significant risk.

Capacity: A company should frame its capital structure within its debt capacity which depends on its ability to generate future cash flows. This helps the company to have enough cash to pay creditors fixed charges and principal sum.

Control: A company's capital structure should be sound and effective if it involves only minimum risk of loss of control of the company. Needless to point out here, the owners of closely-held companies are particularly concerned about dilution of control.

CLASSIFICATION OF CAPITAL STRUCTURE

The capital structure can be classified according to:

    (i)   sources

    (ii) ownership

    (iii) cost

    (iv) nature and type

(i) According to Sources

The sources of capital are broadly divided into:

    (a) internal, and (b) external

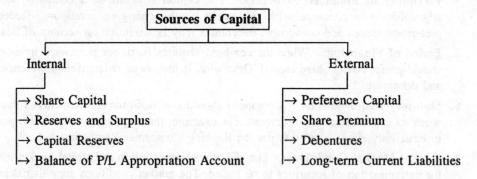

(ii) According to Ownership

According to ownership, capital is brought into:

    (a) owned capital, and (b) borrowed capital

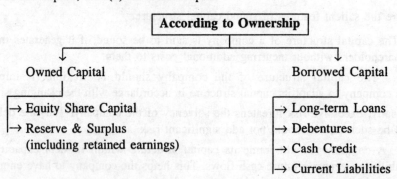

(iii) According to Cost

According to cost, capital structure is brought into: (a) fixed cost capital and (b) variable cost capital:

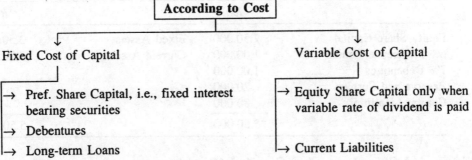

According to Cost

Fixed Cost of Capital

→ Pref. Share Capital, i.e., fixed interest bearing securities
→ Debentures
→ Long-term Loans

Variable Cost of Capital

→ Equity Share Capital only when variable rate of dividend is paid
→ Current Liabilities

(iv) According to Nature or Type

According to the nature and type of the firm, the capital structure may be (a) simple and (b) complex.

(a) Simple

The capital structure of a firm is said to be simple when it is composed of equity capital only or with retained earnings.

EXAMPLE 1

Balance Sheet as at ....

	Rs.		Rs.
Equity Share Capital	2,00,000	Fixed Assets	1,50,000
		Current Assets	50,000
	2,00,000		2,00,000

(b) Complex

The capital structure of a firm is said to be complex when it is composed of equity share capital, preference share capital, retained earnings, debentures, long-term loans and current liabilities, etc.

EXAMPLE 2

Balance Sheet as at ....

	Rs.		Rs.
Equity Share Capital	2,50,000	Fixed Assets	3,50,000
6% Preference Capital	1,00,000	Current Assets	2,00,000
7% Debentures	1,00,000		
Reserve and Surplus	20,000		
Current Liabilities	80,000		
	5,50,000		5,50,000

Financial Structure and Capital Structure

In a broader sense, there will be no difference between financial structure and capital structure. In narrow sense, the financial structure comprises all long-term and short-term liabilities, while the capital structure includes only long-term liabilities.

CASE STUDY

Capital Structure Analysis of United Electrical Industries Limited (UEI)

United Electrical Industries Limited (UEI) was incorporated in 1950. It commenced its activities with the assembling of single phase house service meters. At present, the main products of the company consist of electricity meters, motor starters, plastic film capacitors and street light contractors. It has a total sales of Rs. 1006.84 lakh, total assets of Rs. 1693.02 lakh and loss of Rs. 322.16 lakh in 2003-04. The capital structure of the company is given in Table 4.1.

TABLE 4.1   Capital Structure of UEI as on 31st March, 2004

Source of capital	Books Value (Rs. In lakh)	Proportion/Mix
Equity Capital	399.03	0.45
Reserve & Surplus	166.66	0.18
Long-term Loans	331.28	0.37
Total Capital	896.97	1.00

Source: Review of Public Enterprises in Kerala.

Table 4.2 shows the capital structure ratios of UEI in 2004.

TABLE 4.2   Capital Structure Ratios of UEI in 2004

Capital Gearing	1.71:1
Debt-Equity	0.83:1
Total Investment to Long-term Liability	2.21:1
Fixed Assets to Funded Debt	0.17:1
Reserve to Equity Capital	0.42:1

Source: Review of Public Enterprises in Kerala

While analysing the capital structure with the help of gearing ratio, it is found that UEI is a low geared one. The company has kept its gearing (i.e., 1.71:1) in such a way that it is able to maintain a steady rate of dividend. Moreover, a low debt-equity ratio (i.e., 0.83:1) of the company is considered as favourable from the long-term creditors point of view because a high proportion of owners funds provide a larger margin of safety for them.

When the total investment of UEI is compared with long-term liability, it is found that the proportion of long-term liability is not high. While measuring the relationship between fixed assets and funded debt of the company, it is found that the company's investment in fixed assets is not satisfactory.

The ratio of reserves to equity capital establishes relationship between reserves and equity share capital of the UEI. This ratio indicates how much of profits are generally retained by the company for future growth. As far as UEI is concerned, this ratio is 0.42:1 which is not at all satisfactory.

— REVIEW QUESTIONS —

1. What is meant by capitalisation? Explain the consequences of over-capitalisation and under-capitalisation.

2. What do you understand by the term 'capital structure'? Explain the factors to be taken into account for determining the capital structure of a company.

3. Write notes on:
   (a) Capital Gearing
   (b) Trading on Equity
   (c) Under-Capitalisation
   (d) Watered Capital.

4. Distinguish between over-capitalisation and under-capitalisation.

5. What is capitalisation? Explain briefly the Cost and Earning Theory of capitalisation.

6. Define capital structure. What are the salient features of a good capital structure of a firm?

5
Capital Structure Planning

Planning capital structure implies selecting a desired debt-equity mix.

CAPITAL STRUCTURE PLANNING

While capital structure refers to the mix of long-term sources of funds, capital structure planning implies selecting a desired debt-equity mix. Some companies do not plan their capital structure, but it develops as a result of the financial decision taken by the financial manager without any formal planning. Although such companies may prosper in the short-run, they may face a lot of hurdles in raising funds for various needs and also fail to economise the use of their funds in the long-run. As a result, it is being increasingly realised that all companies should plan their capital structure to maximise the use of funds. Now, it is required to find how the financial manager may determine an appropriate capital structure for his particular firm in real world situations. For this purpose, various methods with their applications are to be examined. However, the identification of the exact percentage of debt-equity mix is a too tough task. Once the desired level is identified, the same is continued so long as it becomes necessary to change/amend it.

APPROACHES OF CAPITAL STRUCTURE PLANNING

A company should plan its capital structure immediately on its incorporation and all its subsequent financing decisions should be made for accomplishing the same. Thus capital structure

54

decision is a continuous process and has to be made as and when a firm requires additional finances.

There are three most common approaches to determine a firm's capital structure. They are:

(a) EBIT-EPS Analysis

(b) Cost of Capital

(c) Cash Flow Analysis

Apart from these approaches governing the capital structure decisions, the following factors should also be considered in practice.

(d) Control

(e) Timing and Flexibility

(f) Nature and Size of the Firm, and

(g) Industry Standard.

(a) EBIT-EPS Analysis

With a view to examining the effect of leverage, the relationship between EBIT (Earnings Before Interest and Tax) and EPS (Earnings Per Share) should be analysed. However, it is in need of a comparative study of various alternative methods of financing under various alternative assumptions relating to Earning Before Interest and Taxes. The effects of leverage on the shareholders' return and risk will be discussed in detail in Chapter 8, Leverages. But some of its significant aspects shall be emphasised here. Financial leverage or trading on equity arises when fixed assets are financed from debt and preference share capital. In case the assets financed the use of debt yield a return more than the cost of debt, the earning per share also goes up without an enhancement in the owners' investment. The same is also applicable in the case of preference share capital. But the debt has some edges over the preference shares on account of the following: (i) interest on debt capital is an allowable deduction under Income Tax rule while computing profit, (ii) the cost of debt is usually less than that of the preference share. However, when the capital structure of a firm is planned, the effects of leverage and EPS are to be duly considered. The firms with high level of EBIT can make profitable use of the high degree of leverage to enhance return on the shareholders equity. It is already pointed out here that the effect of leverage can be examined in case the relationship between the EBIT and EPS are analysed. This principle can be amplified in the light of the following.

ILLUSTRATION 5.1

Z Ltd. has a capital structure comprising equity capital only. It has 1,00,000 equity shares of Rs. 10 each. Now the company wants to raise a fund of Rs. 2,50,000 for its various investment purposes after considering the following three alternative methods of financing:

(i) Issuing 25,000 equity shares of Rs. 10 each.

(ii) Borrowing a debt of Rs. 2,50,000 at 10% interest; and

(iii) Issuing 2,500 10% preference shares of Rs. 100 each.

Show the effect of EPS under various methods of financing if EBIT (after additional investment) are Rs. 3,20,000 and rate of taxation is @50%.

Solution

Computation of the effect of EPS under various alternative methods of financing

	Equity Financing Rs.	Debt Financing Rs.	Preference Share Financing Rs.
EBIT (after additional investment)	3,20,000	3,20,000	3,20,000
Less: Interest on Debt financing @10% on Rs. 2,50,000	—	25,000	—
Earnings After Interest Before Tax	3,20,000	2,95,000	3,20,000
Less: Income Tax @50%	1,60,000	1,47,500	1,60,000
	1,60,000	1,47,500	1,60,000
Less: Preference Dividend @10%	—	—	25,000
Earnings for Equity Shareholders	1,60,000	1,47,500	1,35,000
No. of Equity Shares	1,25,000	1,00,000	1,00,000
EPS = $\dfrac{\text{Earnings for Equity Shares}}{\text{No. of Equity Shares}}$	1.28	1.48	1.35

In the light of the above table it is clear that EPS is maximum when the company uses debt-financing even if the rate of preference dividend and the rate of debt-financing are the same. This occurs as preference dividend is not a tax deductible item, while the interest on debt is a tax deductible item.

It is seen that EPS will go up with a high degree of leverage with the corresponding increase in EBIT. But in case the company fails to get a rate of return on its assets more than the rate of debt financing or preference share financing, it will have to experience a reverse effect on EPS. This is shown in the following illustration.

Suppose in the above illustrations the EBIT is Rs. 80,000 in lieu of Rs. 32,000, the EPS under various methods of financing is as given below:

Computation of the effect of EPS under various alternative methods of financing

	Equity Financing Rs.	Debt Financing Rs.	Preference Share Financing Rs.
EBIT	80,000	80,000	80,000
Less: Interest on Debt Financing @10% on Rs. 2,50,000	—	25,000	—
Earnings After Interest Before Tax	80,000	55,000	80,000
Less: Income-Tax @50%	40,000	27,500	40,000
Earnings After Tax	40,000	27,500	40,000
Less: Preference Dividend @10%	—	—	25,000
Earnings for Equity Shareholders	40,000	27,500	15,000
No. of Equity Shares	1,25,000	1,00,000	1,00,000
EPS = $\dfrac{\text{Earnings for Equity Shares}}{\text{No. of Equity Shares}}$	0.32	0.28	0.15

It is clear from the above table that in case the rate of debt financing is greater than the rate of earning before tax, the EPS will decrease with the corresponding degree of leverage which directly affects the EPS.

The EBIT-EPS analysis is a very potent tool in the hands of the financial manager to get an insight into the company's capital structure management. He has to find the possible fluctuations in EBIT and analyse their effect in various financial plans. In case the chance of earning a rate of return on the company's assets lower than the cost of debt is insignificant, a large amount of debt can be used by the company to enhance the earnings per share. This may have a favourable impact on the market value of each equity share. In the reverse case, however, i.e., when EBIT is less or cost of debt capital is higher than the rate of earnings, a company should not go for debt financing. Thus it is concluded that if there is a higher level of EBIT and less chance of downward fluctuations, a company can effectively use debt in the capital structure.

(b) Cost of Capital

The minimum rate of return expected by the suppliers of finance is called the cost capital. This return depends on the degree of risk assumed by the investors. Usually, the debtholders assume less risk than shareholders as the rate of interest is fixed and the company is legally bound to pay interest whether it makes profit or not. Moreover, debt capital should be returned within a specified period, but shareholders will have to share the residue only when the company is wound up. Thus it is concluded that debt is a cheaper source of finance than equity. Although this is the general case without considering the tax, the tax deductibility of interest charges further decreases the cost of debt. The preference share capital is also cheaper than equity capital, but not as cheap as debt. Thus a firm would always like to employ debt as a source of finance, if it considers cost of capital (component or specific) as a criterion for financing decision (ignoring risk).

The cost of equity capital comprises the cost of both fresh issue of shares and retained earnings. However, the cost of debt is cheaper than that of both these sources of equity funds. But in between retained earnings and cost of equity, the former is cheaper as the personal taxes are paid by the shareholders on their dividend income. Moreover, retained earning is a tax-free source and it also does not require any floatation cost. Thus a company prefers retained earnings to new issues. If the internal finance is found insufficient, a company goes for external finance. It starts with debt, then possibly hybrid securities such as convertible debentures, then perhaps equity as a last resort. Myers has called it the Pecking Order Theory since there is no well-defined debt equity target and there are two kinds of equity, internal and external, one at the top of the pecking order and one at the bottom.

As the specific cost of capital criterion ignores risk and the effect on equity value and cost, the impact of financing decision on the overall cost of capital should be considered. In case a company continuously takes debt-financing to minimise the overall cost of capital, the debt after attaining a certain limit, will become costly and risky. Moreover, when the degree of leverage increases, the creditors demand a high rate of interest for increased risk and do not provide any more loan to the company. Further, excessive debt makes the shareholder's position very risky. Thus the combination of debt and equity should be in such a manner that the market value per share enhances and minimises the average cost of capital of a company. In real world situation, there is generally a range of debt-equity ratio within which the cost of capital is minimum or the value is maximum.

From the above analysis, it is clear that the excessive debt will decrease the share price and hence decline the overall return to shareholders in spite of the increase in EPS. Thus the effect of debt-equity ratio should be appraised on the basis of value, rather than EPS.

(c) Cash Flow Analysis

A company is said to be prudently financed if it is able to service its fixed charges under any reasonably predicable adverse conditions. The fixed charges of a company comprise payment of interest, preference dividends and principal. Thus cash flow analysis is very significant to know the ability of the company to meet its various commitments including the service fixed charges. When the company employs a large amount of debt or preference capital with short-term maturity, the amount of fixed charges will be high. However, a company which expects a larger and stable cash inflow in the future can employ a large amount of debt in its capital structure. But it is quite risky to employ a large amount of debt by those companies whose cash inflows are unstable and unpredictable. Thus, before taking any additional debt capital, analysis of expected future cash flows should carefully be considered as the fixed interest charges are paid out of cash.

The cash flow analysis can be carried out by preparing pro forma cash flow statements to show the company's financial conditions. The expected cash flows can be brought into three groups. They are:

   (i) operating cash flows—relating to the operations of the company.

   (ii) non-operating cash flows—comprising capital expenditure and working capital changes, and

   (iii) financial flows—consisting of interest, dividends, lease rentals, repayment of debts, etc.

A company should carry out the analysis of all these three groups of cash flows to get a clear picture of its ability to service debt obligations even under adverse conditions. This can be done by examining the effect of alternative debt policies on the company's cash flow ability. The company should then choose the proper amount of debt in the capital structure.

The liquidity and solvency position of a company through cash flow analysis can also be judged with the help of the following measures.

(i) Ratio of Fixed Charges to Net Cash Inflows

This ratio measures the relationship between fixed financial charges and the net cash inflow of a company. In other words, this ratio reveals that the number of times the fixed financial charges are covered by the net cash flows of a company. The higher the ratio, the larger amount of debt can be used by the company.

(ii) Cash Budget

The other measure is the preparation of cash budget. It is prepared to find out the possible deviation between the expected cash flows and the actual cash flow of the company. The information so obtained from such budget is helpful to know the ability of the company to pay its fixed charge obligation through the application of budget.

Moreover, the various advantages arising from the analysis of cash flow are highly helpful in preparing the debt-equity mix in the total capital structure of a company. They are as follows:

   (i) It highlights on the solvency and liquidity position of a company at the time of adverse condition.

(ii) It considers the financial trouble in a dynamic context over a number of years.

(iii) It takes into account the various changes made in Balance Sheet and other cash flow which are not exhibited in P/L A/c.

(d) Control

Since the equity shareholders are the owners of the company, they can exercise control over its affairs. Thus debentureholders and preference shareholders, have no say in the management of a company till their interest is not affected legally. If the primary objective of the company is to control efficiently, more weight should be given to debt capital for additional requirement of capital while designing capital structure. In such a case, the management does not have to make any sacrifice regarding the control of the company. In case the company borrows higher than its repayment capacity, they (lenders and creditors) may seize the asset of the company against their claims. In this case the management loses all control over the affairs of the company. In order to avoid such a situation, the management should sacrifice a part of its control by issuing additional equity shares. Thus in view of control, issuing equity shares may be considered as a better source of financing in the hands of the company. Moreover, it is also pointed out that if the company can maintain its profitability and liquidity position and the existing management prefers to keep control in its own hands, it may encourage borrowings rather than issuing fresh equity shares. In such a situation if the company issues fresh equity shares, there is the possibility of losing control over the affairs of the company. Thus after considering the company's overall profitability, it should select a suitable debt-equity mix.

(e) Timing and Flexibility

Having determined an appropriate capital structure, a company should face the problem relating to timing of security issues. Thus a company has to face the question of what should be the timing of issuing such securities for maintaining the strict proportion of debt and equity. Simultaneously, the decision should also be made about which one is to be issued at first, i.e., whether debt at first and equity at last or vice-versa. In case the existing rate of interest on debt is high and there is a chance to decrease the rate of such interest in near future, the equity shares should be issued now and the debt issues should be postponed. On the other hand, if the market for company's equity shares are dull and there is the possibility of improving the same in near future, the debt issues should be made now and the equity issues should be postponed.

In case a company chooses these alternatives, it is required to sacrifice a certain amount of flexibility which is one of the most serious considerations in setting up the capital structure. Flexibility means the ability of the company to adapt its capital structure in accordance with the changing conditions. In other words, the financial plan of the company should be flexible enough to change the composition of the capital structure as warranted by the company's operating strategy and needs. However, flexibility depends on loan convents, option to early retirement of loans and the excess resources at the command of the company.

Although flexibility is the most desirable, it can be accomplished at a cost. A company which tries to obtain loans on easy terms will have to pay interest at a higher rate. Further, a company which wants to get the right of refunding may have to compensate lenders by paying a higher interest. Thus a company should compare the costs and benefits for achieving the desired degree of flexibility and balance them properly.

(f) Nature and Size of the Firm

While designing the appropriate capital structure, the nature and size of a firm have a unique role. For instance, although a small firm has good credit status, it cannot easily raise funds from long-term sources. If the same is available, it should be at a comparatively high rate of interest with inconvenient repayment terms. Thus such a firm cannot function normally and is forced to make its capital structure very inflexible. That is why a small firm has to depend on its own source of finance for long-term funds such as equity shares, retained earnings/ploughing back of profits, etc. Further, the cost of issuing such shares is higher than that of a big firm. However, a small firm has a distinct edge over the big one. That is, if there are dissident shareholders in a small firm, they can be controlled and organised easily as its shares are not scattered widely throughout the country. But the same is highly impossible in the case of a big firm as its shares are widely scattered throughout the country. That is why, a small firm prefers to restrict the business and use its retained earnings as a source of long-term finance. But a big firm can raise long-term funds such as debentures, preference shares on easy terms and comparatively at low cost, and thereby it has got more flexibility while framing its capital structure. In short, what should be the appropriate capital structure of a firm, depends on its size and nature.

(g) Industry Standard

While designing the capital structure of a firm and the industrial position, the capital structure of other similar risk-class firms should also be evaluated. This is because of the fact that in case a firm follows a capital structure other than that of the similar firm in the same industry, it may not be accepted by the investors. Thus while designing the capital structure of a firm, certain common factors such as general state of economy, nature, type and size of the firm, etc., are to be considered. Moreover, the nature and size of the firm may have direct impact on the capital structure composition. For instance, a firm which has to make a heavy investment in fixed assets and has a high operating leverage will naturally prefer less financial risk and design the capital structure in a manner other than the public utility concerns (e.g., electricity) where day-to-day transactions are done primarily on cash basis. Besides, a firm having stable sales and better prospects for development may use more debt capital in its capital structure than those firms having unstable sales and no prospects for growth.

Optimum Capital Structure

A firm is said to be in optimum capital structure when the market value per equity share is the maximum. Thus optimum capital structure may be defined as that relationship of debt and equity which maximises the value of a firm's share in the stock exchange. If the borrowing results in increase in market value of the firm's equity shares, it can be said that the borrowing has moved the firm towards its optimum capital structure and vice-versa. Thus the object of optimum capital structure is to select a debt-equity mix having maximum value of the firm.

In the words of Ezra Solomon, "Optimum leverage can be defined as that mix of debt and equity which will maximise the market value of a company, i.e., the aggregate value of the claims and ownership interests represented on the credit side of the balance sheet. Further, the advantages of having an optimum financial structure, if such an optimum does exist, is two-fold, it maximises the company's cost of capital which in turn increases its liability to find new wealth creating investment opportunities. Also, by increasing the firm's opportunity to engage in future wealth-creating investment, it increases the economy's rate of investment and growth."

Considerations

A finance manager can attain his object of optimum capital structure up to a certain extent with the help of the following considerations:

(i) The finance manager should choose a source of finance having a fixed cost for enhancing the return on equity shareholders in case the ROI is more than the fixed cost of funds. Thus he can take the advantage of favourable financial leverage.

(ii) A high corporate tax provides some form of leverage with respect to the capital structure management. The high cost of equity financing can, therefore, be avoided by using debt which in effect provides a form of income tax leverage to the equity shareholders. Thus the finance manager should take the advantage of the leverage offered by the corporate taxes.

(iii) The price of the equity shares should come down in case the equity shareholders perceive an excessive amount of debt in the capital structure of a firm. The finance manager must not therefore, issue debentures, whether risky or not if it is likely to depress the market price of equity shares. Thus he can avoid a perceived high risk capital structure.

CASE STUDY

Capital Structure Analysis of Larsen & Toubro (L&T) Limited

L&T was established in the year 1938. It is a large engineering company with varied and diversified activities. Its main activities comprise dairy equipment, cement and cement equipment, steel, paper, nuclear power and space exploration, hydraulic excavators, switch gears, electronic controls, valves, welding alloys, computer peripherals, test and measuring equipment, etc.

The company has five divisions. They are (i) Engineering and constructions, (ii) Electrical and Electronics, (iii) Machinery and Industrial products, (iv) IT and Technology Services, and (v) Finance and HR.

The authorised and paid-up capital of the company as on 31st March 2005 is Rs. 325 crores and Rs. 25.98 crores respectively. It has a gross sales of Rs. 13,269 crores, net assets of Rs. 51,323 crore and net profit of Rs. 1,286 crores during 2004–05.

Table 5.1 provides L&T's debt-equity ratio, interest coverage and interest as a percentage of sales for the period from 1995–96 to 2004–05. L&T's debt-equity ratio shows a fluctuating pattern during the past ten years. After remaining at a low level from 1995–96 to 1998–99, it has significantly increased to a very high level of 1.05 in 1999–2000. The company has maintained this increasing trend up to 2001–02 when it increased to a level of 1.07. The ratio again decreased to 92%, 49% and 56% respectively in 2002–03, 2003–04 and 2004–05 (see Figure 5.1).

TABLE 5.1 L&T's Capital Structure and Other Financial Data

Year (1)	D/E Ratio (Times) (2)	Int. Cover (Times) (3)	Int./Sales (%) (4)
1995–1996	0.41	6.52	1.84
1996–1997	0.65	5.12	2.17
1997–1998	0.84	7.52	1.31
1998–1999	0.92	3.74	2.21
1999–2000	1.05	2.12	4.48
2000–2001	1.09	1.94	4.62
2001–2002	1.07	2.27	3.87
2002–2003	0.92	3.89	1.80
2003–2004	0.49	21.79	0.38
2004–2005	0.56	24.82	0.41
Average	0.80	7.98	2.31

Source: Annual Report of L&T.

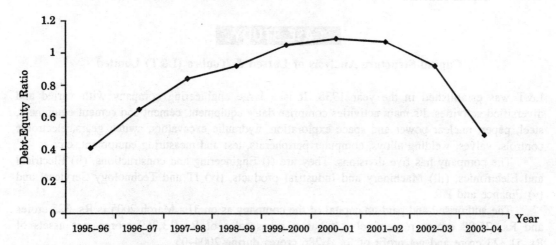

FIGURE 5.1 L&T's Debt-Equity Ratio from 1995-96 to 2004-05.

L&T's interest coverage ratio has been showing wide fluctuation and it has been at a healthy level during the past two years (Figure 5.2). Its interest coverage ratio has never been less than 1.75 times in the past ten years. Hence, L&T has been maintaining a good debt-servicing ability and has also been employing debt to take advantage of interest tax shield.

Interest, as a percentage of sales, was quite high in the beginning of the year 2000 but it has come down to less than one per cent of sales in the past two years.

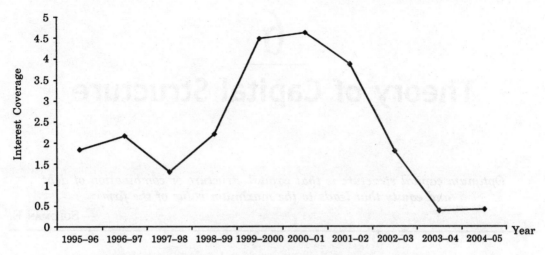

FIGURE 5.2 L&T's Interest Coverage from 1995-96 to 2004-05.

— REVIEW QUESTIONS —

1. Define the term capital structure. Name the items that are included in capital structure.
2. "The total value of a firm remains unchanged regardless of variations in its financing". Explain.
3. Explain briefly the factors that affect the planning of capital structure of a firm.
4. What do you mean by the optimal capital structure of a firm? How do you ascertain the optimal capital structure?

6
Theory of Capital Structure

Optimum capital structure is that capital structure or combination of debt and equity that leads to the maximum value of the firm.

— SOLOMAN E.

CONTENTS

- Introduction
- Theories of capital structure
- Review questions

INTRODUCTION

The capital structure of a firm is represented by long-term funds which can be raised either by issue of (a) shares or (b) debentures or long-term loans and borrowings. In case a firm raises funds by the issue of equity shares, it is required to pay dividends only if there is enough profit. On the contrary, if a firm raises funds through debentures or long-term borrowings, it is required to pay a fixed rate of interest irrespective of the profit or loss. Then the key question with which it is concerned is whether a firm can affect its total valuation (debt plus equity) and its cost of capital by changing its financing mix. If so, what should be the proportion of equity and debt in the capital structure of a firm. The answer of this question should be based on an understanding of the relationship between financial leverage (debt-equity mix) and firm's valuation. This relationship can better be understood with the help of the following assumptions.

(i) The firm employs only two types of capital-debt and equity.

(ii) The firm's total assets are presented and they do not change.

(iii) The firm has no retained earnings as 100% of its earning is paid as dividend to the shareholders.

(iv)   The firm should enjoy a perpetual life.

(v)   The firm's operative earnings (EBIT) are not expected to grow or decline over time.

(vi)   The firm's business risk remains constant and is independent of capital structure and financial risks.

(vii)   The total financing of the firm remains constant.

(viii)   The investors should bear the same subjective probability distribution relating to future operating income.

(ix)   There is no income tax, corporate or personal. Later, this assumption was removed.

There are several theories which are used to explain the relationship between capital structure, cost of capital, and value of the firm. They are as follows:

THEORIES OF CAPITAL STRUCTURE

1. Net Income (NI) Approach
2. Net Operating Income (NOI) Approach
3. Traditional Approach
4. Modigliani-Miller Approach

With a view to explaining the theories of capital structure, the following systems should also be used apart from the above assumptions.

S = Total Market Value of the Equity

T = Total Market Value of the Debt

V = Total Market Value of the Firm (i.e., $S + T$)

I = Total Interest Payable on Debt Capital

NOI/EBIT = Net Operating Incomes Available to the Equity Shareholders.

(a) Cost of Equity $(K_e) = \dfrac{\text{EBIT} - I}{S}$

or, it can be given as under

$$K_e = \frac{\text{DPS}}{\text{MPS}} + g = \frac{\text{EPS}}{P} + 0 = \frac{\text{EPS}}{P}$$

where,

DPS = Dividend per Share

MPS = Market Price per Share

EPS = Earning per Share

g = Rate of Growth

Thus, Value of Equity = $S = \dfrac{\text{EBIT} - I}{K_e}$

(b) Cost of Debt $(K_d) = \dfrac{I}{T}$

Thus, Value of Debt $= T = \dfrac{I}{K_d}$

To compute the total value of the firm, the Equity (S) and Debt (T) are summed up as under

$$V = S + T = \dfrac{I}{K_d} + \dfrac{\text{EBIT} - I}{K_e}$$

To compute the weighted average cost of capital

$$K_w = W_d K_d + W_e K_e = \left(\dfrac{T}{V}\right) K_d + \left(\dfrac{S}{V}\right) K_e$$

where,

W_d = Proportion of Debt to Total Value
W_e = Proportion of Equity to Total Value

1. Net Income (NI) Approach

This approach is suggested by David Durand. According to him, the total value of the firm may be enhanced by lowering its cost of capital. Thus the value of the firm depends on its capital structure decision. When cost of capital is the lowest, the value of the firm is the highest. At this point, the market price per share is maximum and the firm is said to have optimum ·capital structure. The same is possible continuously by lowering its cost of capital by the use of debt capital. A high debt content in the capital structure (i.e., high financial leverage) will lead to the reduction of the overall cost of the capital and consequently enhance the value of the firm. Similarly, the value of the firm will get reduced if the amount of debt is reduced by issuing additional equity shares. The same is possible only when:

(i)   There are no corporate taxes.

(ii) Cost of debt (K_d) is less than cost of equity (K_e)

(iii) The debt content does not change the risk perception of the investors.

According to this approach, the value of the firm can be computed by using the following formula.

$$V = S + T$$

where,

V = Value of the Firm
S = Market Value of the Equity
T = Market Value of the Debt

The market value of equity can be computed as under:

$$S = \dfrac{\text{EBIT} - I}{K_e} \quad \text{or} \quad \dfrac{\text{EBT}}{K_e}$$

where,

S = Market Value of Equity
EBIT = Earnings Before Interest and Tax
I = Interest Payable on Debt Capital
K_e = Equity Capitalisation Rate
EBT = Earnings Before Tax

The net income approach is graphically presented in Figure 6.1. The degree of leverage is plotted on the abscissa and K_e, K_d and K_w are plotted on the ordinate.

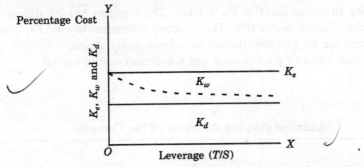

FIGURE 6.1 Behaviour of K_w, K_d and K_e under the Net Income Approach.

In the light of the graph, it is clear that as T/S enhances, K_w decreases because the proportion of debt (i.e., the cheaper source of finance) enhances in the capital structure.

ILLUSTRATION 6.1

A Ltd. is expecting on annual EBIT of Rs. 2 lakhs. The company has 8% debentures of Rs. 5 lakhs. The cost of equity or capitalisation rate is 10%. Compute the total value of the company and overall cost of capital.

Solution

Statement showing the value of the Company

	Rs.
Earning Before Interest and tax (EBIT)	2,00,000
Less: Interest at 8% on Rs. 5 lakhs	40,000
Earnings available to Equity Sharehoders (EBT)	1,60,000
Equity Capitalisation Rate (K_e)	10%
Market Value of Equity (S)	
$\dfrac{EBT}{K_e} = \dfrac{1,60,000}{10} \times 100$	16,00,000
Market Value of Debt (T)	5,00,000
Total Value of the Company ($S + T$)	21,00,000

Overall Cost of Capital:

$$K_e = \frac{EBIT}{V} = \frac{2,00,000}{21,00,000} \times 100 = 9.52\%$$

The effect of change in debt-equity mix in the capital structure of a company can be examined with the help of the following illustration.

Increase in Value

According to Net Income Approach, if the amount of equity is reduced debentures are issued to the equity shareholders, the value of the company will get enhanced.

ILLUSTRATION 6.2

'A' Ltd. is expecting an annual EBIT of Rs. 2 lakhs. The company has 8% debentures of Rs. 5 lakhs. The equity capitalisation rate is 10%. The company determines to raise Rs. 2 lakhs by issue of 8% debentures and use the proceeds thereof to redeem equity shares.

Compute the total value of the company and the overall cost of capital.

Solution

Statement showing the value of the Company

	Rs.
Earnings Before Interest and Tax (EBIT)	2,00,000
Less: Interest at 8% Debentures of Rs. 7,00,000	56,000
Earnings available to Equity Shareholders (EBT)	1,44,000
Equity Capitalisation Rate (K_e)	10%
Market Value of Equity (S):	
$\dfrac{EBT}{K_e} = \dfrac{1,44,000}{10} \times 100$	14,40,000
Market Value of Debt (T)	7,00,000
Total Value of Company ($S + T$)	21,40,000
Overall Cost of Capital	
$K_e = \dfrac{EBIT}{V} = \dfrac{2,00,000}{21,40,000} \times 100$	= 9.35%

In the light of the above statement, it is clear that raising of additional debt has enhanced the total value of the company and curtailed the overall cost of capital.

Decrease in Value

According to Net Income (NI) approach, if the amount of debt is curtailed by issuing additional equity shares, the value of the company will get reduced.

ILLUSTRATION 6.3

'A' Ltd is expecting an annual EBIT of Rs. 2 lakhs. The company has 8% debentures of Rs. 5

lakhs. The equity capitalisation rate is 10%. The company desires to redeem debentures of Rs. 2 lakhs by issuing additional equity shares of Rs. 2 lakhs.

Compute the value of the company and the overall cost of capital.

Solution

Statement showing the value of the Company

	Rs.
Earnings Before Interest and Tax (EBIT)	2,00,000
Less: Interest at 8% on Debentures of Rs. 3,00,000	24,000
Earnings available to Equity Shareholders (EBT)	1,76,000
Equity Capitalisation Rate (K_e)	10%
Market Value of Equity Shares (S):	
$\dfrac{EBT}{K_e} = \dfrac{1,76,000}{10} \times 100$	17,60,000
Market Value of the Debt (T)	3,00,000
Total Value of the Company ($S + T$)	20,60,000
Overall Cost of Capital:	
$K_e = \dfrac{EBIT}{V} = \dfrac{2,00,000}{20,60,000} \times 100 = 9.71\%$	

In the light of the above statement, it is clear that the reduction in debt has curtailed the overall value of the company and enhanced the overall cost of capital.

2. Net Operating Income (NOI) Approach

The net operating income approach is advocated by David Durand. According to him the value of a firm depends on its net operating income and business risk. Thus the change in the degree of leverage employed by a firm cannot change its net operating income and business risks. But it merely brings variation in distribution of income and risk between debt and equity without affecting the total income and risk which influence the market value of the firm. Thus, under this approach any capital structure will be optimum. Theoretically there will be optimum capital structure when there is 100% debt content. This is because with every increase in debt, 'content K' decreases and the value of the firm increases.

The net operating income approach is based on certain assumptions which are as follows:

(i) The overall cost of capital (K_w) remains constant for all degrees of leverage (i.e., debt-equity mix).

(ii) The net operating income is capitalised at an overall capitalisation rate to find out the total market value of the firm. Thus the split between debt and equity is irrelevant.

(iii) There are no corporate taxes.

(iv) The use of low cost debt enhances the risk of equity shareholders, this in turn, enhances the equity capitalisation rate. Thus the benefit of debt is nullified by the increase in the equity capitalisation rate.

According to the NOI hypothesis, the value of a firm is determined with the help of the following equation.

$$V = \frac{EBIT}{K_w}$$

where,

V = Value of the Firm
EBIT = Earnings Before Interest and Tax
K_w = Overall Cost of Capital

The value of equity (S) which is a residual value, can be ascertained by the following equation:

$$S = V - T$$

where,

S = Value of Equity
V = Value of Firm
T = Value of Debt

The NOI approach can be explained with the help of Figure 6.2.

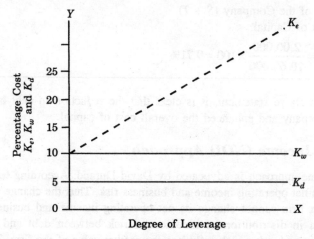

FIGURE 6.2 Behaviour of K_e, K_w and K_d as per Net Operating Income Approach.

Figure 6.2 shows that the division between debt and equity is not relevant. An increase in the use of debt funds which are 'apparently cheaper' is offset by an increase in the equity capitalisation rate. This occurs because the equity investors seek more compensation as they are exposed to higher risk arising from increase in the degree of leverage.

ILLUSTRATION 6.4

AB Ltd. has an EBIT of Rs. 2 lakhs. The company has 8% debentures of Rs. 5 lakhs. Presuming the overall capitalisation rate as 10%, compute the total value of the company and equity capitalisation rate.

Solution

Statement showing the value of the company

	Rs.
Earning Before Interest and Tax (EBIT)	2,00,000
Overall Capitalisation Rate (K_w)	10%
Market Value of the Company (V)	
$\dfrac{2,00,000}{10} \times 100$	20,00,000
Total Value of Debt (T)	5,00,000
Market Value of Equity (S)	15,00,000

$S = (V - T)$

Equity Capitalisation Rate (K_e)

$$K_e = \frac{\text{EBIT}-I}{S} \times 100 = \frac{2,00,000 - 40,000}{15,00,000} \times 100$$

$$= \frac{1,60,000}{15,00,000} \times 100 = 10.67\%$$

The validity of NOI approach can be checked by ascertaining the overall cost of capital.

$$K_w = K_d \left(\frac{T}{V}\right) + K_e \left(\frac{S}{V}\right)$$

where,

K_w = Overall Cost of Capital
K_d = Cost of Debt
T = Total Debt
V = Total Value of the Company
K_e = Cost of Equity Capital
S = Market Value of Equity

$$K_w = 8\% \left(\frac{5,00,000}{20,00,000}\right) + 10.67\% \left(\frac{15,00,000}{20,00,000}\right)$$

$$= 8\% \left(\frac{1}{4}\right) + 10.67\% \left(\frac{15}{20}\right) = 2\% + 8\%$$

$$= 10\%$$

Increase in Debt

If the company increases the debt content for decreasing its equity content, the total value of the company would remain unchanged. But the capitalisation rate will increase.

ILLUSTRATION 6.5

AB Ltd. has an EBIT of Rs. 2 lakhs. Its cost of debt is 8% and the outstanding debt amounts to

Rs. 5 lakhs. The overall capitalisation rate is 10%. The company determines to raise a sum of Rs. 2 lakhs through debt at 8% and use the proceeds to pay off the equity shareholders. Compute the total value of the company and also the equity capitalisation rate.

Solution

Statement showing the value of the company

	Rs.
Earnings Before Interest and Tax (EBIT)	2,00,000
Overall Capitalisation Rate (k)	10%
Market Value of the Company (V)	
$\dfrac{2,00,000}{10} \times 100$	20,00,000
Total Value of Debt (T)	7,00,000
Market Value of Equity (S)	13,00,000
$S = V - T$	
Equity Capitalisation Rate	

$$K_e = \frac{\text{EBIT} - I}{S} \times 100 = \frac{2,00,000 - 56,000}{13,00,000} \times 100$$

$$= \frac{1,44,000}{13,00,000} \times 100 = 11.08\%$$

The overall cost of capital under NOI approach can be checked as under:

$$K_w = K_d \left(\frac{T}{V}\right) + K_e \left(\frac{S}{V}\right) = 8\% \frac{7,00,000}{20,00,000} + 11.08\% \frac{13,00,000}{20,00,000}$$

$$= 2.80\% + 7.20\% = 10\%$$

3. Traditional Approach

According to this approach, the cost of capital is dependent on the capital structure and there is an optimal capital structure which minimises the cost of capital. The real marginal cost of debt and equity is the same at the optimum capital structure. But the real marginal cost of debt is lower than the real marginal cost of equity before the optimal point. On the contrary, beyond the optimal point, the real marginal cost of debt is greater than the real marginal cost of equity.

Figure 6.3 illustrates the traditional approach graphically.

In the above graph, the average cost curve is U-shaped. It implies that at this stage, the cost of capital is minimum which is expressed by the letter 'A'. If a perpendicular is drawn to the X-axis, the same will indicate the optimum capital structure for the firm.

The main propositions of this approach are as under:

(i) The cost of debt capital, K_d, remains more or less constant up to a certain degree of leverage and thereafter rises.

(ii) The cost of equity capital, K_e remains constant more or less or rise gradually up to a certain degree of leverage and thereafter increases rapidly.

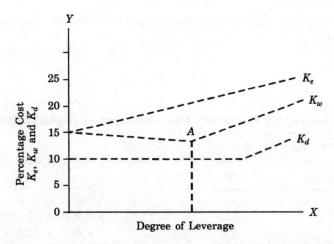

FIGURE 6.3 Behaviour of K_e, K_w and K_d under the traditional approach.

(iii) The average cost of capital, K_w, reduces up to a certain point, and remains more or less unchanged for moderate increase in leverage and thereafter rises after attaining a certain point.

The traditional approach or intermediate approach is a midway between the net income approach and the net operative income approach. Thus it partly contains the characteristics of both the approaches. They are as follows:

(i) The traditional approach is similar to NI approach to the extent that it accepts that the capital structure of a firm affects the cost of capital and its valuation. But it does not subscribe to the NI approach that the value of the firm will necessarily enhance with all levels of leverage.

(ii) It subscribes to the NOI approach that after attaining a certain level of leverage, the overall cost of capital enhances resulting in decline in the total value of the firm. But it varies from NOI approach in the sense that the overall cost of capital will not remain constant for all levels of leverage.

ILLUSTRATION 6.6

In considering the most desirable capital structure for a company, the following estimates of the cost of debt and equity capital (after tax) has been at various levels of debt equity mix:

Debt as percentage of total Capital employed	Cost of Debt (%)	Cost of Equity (%)
0	5.0	12.0
10	5.0	12.0
20	5.0	12.5
30	5.5	13.0
40	6.0	14.0
50	6.5	16.0
60	7.0	20.0

You are required to determine the optimal debt-equity mix for the company by calculating composite cost of capital.

(C.A. Final, May 1978)

Statement showing the Company's Composite Cost of Capital (After tax)

Cost of Capital (After Tax) Debt as percentage of total Capital employed	Cost of Debt %	Cost of Equity %	Composite Cost of Capital	
0	5.0	12.0	5 × 0 + 12 × 1	= 12.00
10	5.0	12.0	5 × 0.10 + 12 × 0.90	= 11.30
20	5.0	12.5	5 × 0.20 + 12.5 × 0.80	= 11.00
30	5.5	13.0	5.5 × 0.30 + 13 × 0.70	= 10.75
40	6.0	14.0	6 × 0.40 + 14 × 0.60	= 10.80
50	6.5	16.0	6.5 × 0.50 + 16 × 0.50	= 11.25
60	7.0	20.0	7 × 0.60 + 20 × 0.40	= 12.20

In the light of the above calculations, it is clear that the optimal debt-equity mix is 30% debt and 70% equity, where the composite cost of capital is the least.

4. Modigliani-Miller Approach (MM)

According to Modigliani-Miller, the total market value of the firm and the cost of capital are independent of the capital structure. They mention that the weighted average cost of capital does not make any change with a proportionate change in debt-equity mix in the total capital structure of the firm (Figure 6.4).

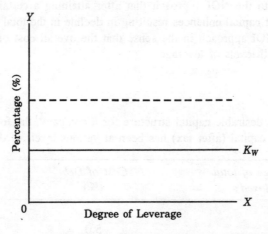

FIGURE 6.4 Weighted Average Cost of Capital does not make any change (MM hypothesis)

MM approach is similar to the Net Operating Income (NOI) approach. But there are some basic variations between the two. The NOI approach is purely conceptual and does not provide operational justification for irrelevance of the capital structure in the valuation of the firm. However, Modigliani and Miller have restated and amplified the NOI position in terms of three basic propositions.

Propositions

The following are the basic propositions of the MM approach.

(i) The cost of capital and the total market value of the firm are independent of its capital structure. The cost of capital is equal to the capitalisation rate of equity stream of operating earnings for its class. But the total market value of the firm is determined by capitalising the expected NOI by the rate appropriate for the risk class.

(ii) The expected cost of equity (K_e) is equal to the appropriate capitalisation rate of a pure equity stream with a premium for financial risk. The difference between the pure-equity capitalisation rate (K_e) and cost on debt (K_d) is equal to a premium for financial risk. In a nutshell, increased K_e is offset exactly by the use of cheaper debt.

(iii) The cut-off rate for investment is always independent of the way in which an investment is financed.

Assumptions

The following are the various assumptions underlying MM analysis:

(i) Existence of perfect capital market.
This means that (a) capital markets are perfect, (b) information is freely available, (c) transactions are costless and (d) securities are indefinitely divisible.

(ii) Homogeneous Expectation
All the investors should have the same expectation of a firm's net operating income (EBIT).

(iii) Homogeneous risk class.
Firms can be classified into equivalent risk classes on the basis of their business risk.

(iv) The dividend payout ratio is 100%.
It means that there are no retained earnings.

(v) Taxes do not exist. No taxes
There are no corporate taxes. But, later on, this assumption has been removed.

Proof of MM Argument—The Arbitrage Mechanism

MM have suggested an arbitrage mechanism to prove their argument. Arbitrage is an act of buying an asset or security in one market having lower price and selling it in another market at a higher price. The result of such an action is that the market price of the securities of the two firms cannot remain different for long period in different markets (firms are similar in all respects except their capital structures). Thus equilibrium in value of securities can be restored with the help of arbitrage process. This is because in case the market value of the two firms (firms are similar in all respects except their capital structures) are not similar, investors of the overvalued firm should dispose their shares, borrow additional funds on personal account and invest in the undervalued firm with a view to getting the same return on less investment. When the investor uses debt for the purpose of arbitrage, it is termed as 'personal leverage' or 'home made'. This can be amplified in the light of the following illustration.

ILLUSTRATION 6.7

Two firms X and Y are identical in all respects except that the firm 'X' has 8% of Rs. 1,00,000 debentures. Both the firms have the same earnings before interest and tax amounting to Rs. 20,000. The equity capitalisation rate of firm 'X' is 15% and that of firm 'Y' is 12%.

Compute the total market value of each of the firm and explain with an example the working of the arbitrage process.

Solution

Statement showing the total value of the firms

Particulars	Firm X Rs.	Firm Y Rs.
Earnings Before Interest and Tax EBIT	20,000	20,000
Less: Interest	8,000	—
Earnings available for Equity Shareholders	12,000	20,000
Equity Capitalisation Rate (K_e)	15%	12%
Total Market Value of Equity (S)		
Firm 'X' $\dfrac{12,000}{15} \times 100$	80,000	
Firm 'Y' $\dfrac{20,000}{12} \times 100$		1,66,667
Total Market Value of the Debt (T)	1,00,000	—
Total Value of the Firm (V)	1,80,000	1,66,667
Overall Cost of Capital (K_w) EBIT/V		
Firm 'X' $\dfrac{20,000}{1,80,000} \times 100$	11.11%	—
Firm 'Y' $\dfrac{20,000}{1,66,667} \times 100$		12%
Debt Equity Ratio (T/S)		
Firm 'X' $\dfrac{1,00,000}{1,80,000}$	0.56	

From the above table, it is clear that the market value of the firm 'X' (having debt content in its capital structure) is greater than that of the firm 'Y' (having no debt content in its capital structure). M-M state that this situation cannot remain for long period by virtue of the operation of arbitrage process. The investors in firm 'Y' can earn a higher return on their investment with a lower financial risk. Thus the investors in firm 'X' will commence selling their shares and commence buying-shares in firm 'Y'. However, these processes will continue so long as the price of the firm's 'X' shares decrease and the price of the firms's 'Y' shares enhance so as to bring the total value of the two firms identical. This is made clear with the help of the following example.

Suppose an investor 'A' holds 20% of the outstanding shares of firm 'X'. This means his holding amounts to Rs. 16,000 (i.e., 20% of Rs. 80,000) and his share in the earning which belongs to equity shareholders amounts to Rs. 2,400 (i.e., 20% of Rs. 12,000).

Mr. 'A' will sell his holdings in firm 'X' and invest money in firm 'Y'. Firm 'Y' has no debt in its capital structure and thereby, Mr. 'A's financial risk in firm 'Y' would be less than that of firm 'X'. With a view to having the same degree of financial risk in firm 'Y', Mr. 'A' will borrow additional funds equivalent to his proportionate share in firm 'X's debt on his personal account, i.e., Rs. 20,000 (20% of Rs. 1,00,000) at 8% interest. The effect of such a borrowing is that he will substitute personal leverage for the corporate leverage. The proportionate holding of Mr 'A' in firm 'Y' now amounts to Rs. 33,333, i.e., 20% of Rs. 1,66,667. Thus the present position of Mr 'A' is as follows:

				Rs.
(A)	Mr. 'A's position in firm 'X' with 20% Equity Holding			
	(i) Investment Outlay Rs. 80,000			
	(ii) Dividend income 20% of Rs. 12,000			2,400
(B)	Mr. 'A's position in firm 'Y' with 20% Equity Holding			
	(i) Investment Outlay Own funds Rs. 15,833 + borrowed funds Rs. 17,500			33,333
	(ii) Dividend Income: Total income 20% of Rs. 20,000		4,000	
	Less: Interest payable on Borrowed Funds 8% on Rs. 17,500		1,400	2,600
(C)	Mr. 'A's position in firm Y, if he invests the total available funds			
	(i) Total investment outlay (own funds Rs. 16,000 + borrowed funds Rs. 17,333)			33,333
	(ii) Total Income $\left(\dfrac{20,000}{1,66,667}\times 33,500\right)=$		4,020	
	Less: Interest Payable on Borrowed Funds		1,400	2,620

In the light of the above analysis it is clear that Mr. 'A' can have greater income if he shifts his investments from firm 'X' to firm 'Y'. The same process will be followed by other investors as well. By virtue of this fact, there shall be an enhancing demand for firm Y's securities. This in turn, will lead to an enhance in the market price of its shares. Simultaneously, the share price of firm 'X' will come down. This process remains so long as it is able to bring down the investment outlays and get the same return. However, shifting from firm 'X' to firm 'Y' beyond this point is not beneficial. This is known as the point of equilibrium. At this point, the overall cost of capital and the total value of both these firms should be the same.

Thus, Modigliani and Miller point out that, the total value of a levered firm (i.e., a firm having debt content in its capital structure) cannot be greater than that of the unlevered firm. The opposite is also true.

Criticisms of the MM Hypothesis

The arbitrage process of MM hypothesis fails to bring the desired equilibrium in the capital markets by virtue of the following facts:

(i) **Different Rates of Interest for the Individuals and Firms:** Modigliani and Miller assume that the firms and individuals can borrow and lend at the same rate of interest cannot hold good in reality. This is due to the firms' greater credit standing than that of individuals on account of firms' large holding of fixed assets.

(ii) **Personal Leverage is not the Perfect Substitute for Corporate Leverage:** The hypothesis that personal leverage is the substitute for 'corporate leverage' is not true as there is unlimited liability in the case of individuals, and firms may have a limited liability. Thus both the firms and individuals have different stand in capital market.

(iii) **Institutional Restrictions:** The choice of the switching over from levered to unlevered firm and vice-versa is available to all investors, particularly, institutional investors such as LIC, UTI, commercial banks, etc. Thus in reality arbitrage process is retarded by institutional restrictions.

(iv) **Existence of Transaction Cost:** Usually transaction costs in the form of brokerage or commission etc., are involved in buying and selling of securities. Thus the investors are required to invest a higher amount in the shares of levered/unlevered firms than their present investment to earn the same return.

(v) **Incorporation of Corporate Taxes:** Owing to corporate taxes, the cost of borrowing funds to the firm is lower than the contractual rate of interest. Thus, the total return to the shareholders of a levered firm is more than that of an unlevered firm. On account of this fact, the total market value of a levered firm tends to exceed that of the unlevered firm.

M-M Hypothesis with Corporate Taxes

According to Modigliani and Miller, the value of a firm and its cost of capital will remain constant with leverage (i.e., debt content in the capital structure). This assumption does not hold good when there are corporate taxes. When taxes are levied on income, debt financing is more beneficial as interest paid on debt is a tax-deductible item. However, dividend paid on equity shareholders and retained earnings are not tax deductible items. Thus in case debt capital is used in the total capital structure, the total income available to the equity shareholders and/or debtholders will be higher. In other words, the market value of a levered firm should be higher than that of an unlevered firm. The value of the levered firm should exceed that of the unlevered firm by an amount equal to debt multiplied by the rate of tax. This can be put in the form of the following formula.

$$V_1 = V_n + tD$$

where,

V_1 = Value of the Levered Firm
V_n = Value of the Unlevered Firm
t = Rate of Corporate Tax
D = Amount of Debt

The market value of an unlevered firm is equal to the market value of its shares. This can be explained in the form of an equation which is as under:

$$V_n = S$$

where,

V_n = Market Value of Unlevered Firm

S = Market Value of Equity

$$S = \frac{\text{Profits available for Equity Shareholders}}{\text{Equity Capitalisation Rate}}$$

The value of V_n can also be ascertained with the help of the following equation:

$$V_n = \frac{\text{EBT}(1 - t)}{K_e}$$

where,

EBT = Earnings Before Tax

t = Tax Rate

K_e = Equity Capitalisation Rate

ILLUSTRATION 6.8

Two firms X and Y are identical in all respects except the degree of leverage. Firm 'X' has 6% debt of Rs. 2,00,000. But firm 'Y' has no debt. Both the firms are earning an EBT of Rs. 1,00,000 each. The corporate tax is 60% and equity capitalisation rate is 10%.

Calculate the market value of the two firms.

Solution

The market value of the firm 'Y' (unlevered)

$$V_n = \frac{\text{EBT}(1 - t)}{K_e} = \frac{1,00,000(1 - 0.6)}{10\%} = \frac{1,00,000 \times 0.4}{10\%} = \text{Rs. } 4,00,000$$

Thus, the value of firm 'Y' (unlevered) is Rs. 4,00,000.

The market value of the firm 'X' (levered)

$V_1 = V_n + tD$

$\quad = 4,00,000 + 0.6 \times 2,00,000$

$\quad = 5,20,000$

Thus, the value of Firm 'X' (levered) is Rs. 5,20,000.

ILLUSTRATION 6.9

Firms P and Q are in the same risk class, and are identical in every respect except that firm P uses debt while firm Q does not. The levered firm has Rs. 10,00,000 debentures, carrying 8% rate of interest. Both the firms earn 16% before interest and taxes on their total assets of

Rs. 20,00,000. Assume perfect capital markets, rational investors and so on. Capitalisation rate is @12% and corporate tax is @50%.

(i) Calculate the value of firms P and Q using the net income (NI) approach.

(ii) Calculate the value of each firm using the net operating income (NOI) approach.

(iii) Using the NOI approach, compute the overall cost of capital (K_w) for firms P and Q.

Which of the firms P and Q have optimum capital structure as per NOI approach

Solution

(i)

	Levered Firm P Rs.	Unlevered Firm Q Rs.
EBIT (16% of Rs. 20,00,000)	3,20,000	3,20,000
Less: Interest	80,000	—
Taxable Income	2,40,000	3,20,000
Less: Taxes	1,20,000	1,60,000
Earnings for Equity Holders	1,20,000	1,60,000
Equity-Capitalisation Rate (K_e)	0.12	0.12
Market Value of Equity (S)	10,00,000	13,33,333
Market Value of Debt (T)	10,00,000	—
Total Value of the Firm (V)	20,00,000	13,33,333

(ii) The value of an unlevered firm under the NOI approach when taxes are considered, can be computed by the following formula suggested by MM.

$$\text{Value of Unlevered Firm } (V_n) = \frac{\text{EBT}(1-t)}{K_e}$$

Value of Levered Firm (V_1) $= V_n + Dt$

Accordingly, value of unlevered firm 'Q' can be ascertained as under:

$$V_n = \frac{3,20,000(1-0.5)}{0.12} = \frac{3,20,000 \times 0.5}{0.12} = \text{Rs. } 13,33,333$$

Value of levered firm 'P' can be computed as under:

$V_1 = 13,33,333 + 10,00,000(0.5)$

$\quad = 13,33,333 + 5,00,000$

$\quad = \text{Rs. } 18,33,333$

(iii) To determine the overall cost of capital, cost of debt (K_d) and cost of equity (K_e) are required.

Firm 'P'

$K_d = 8\% \ (1 - 0.5) = 4\%$

$$K_e = \frac{\text{Income available to Equity Holders}}{\text{Market Value of Equity}} = \frac{\text{NI}}{S}$$

Rs.

EBIT	3,20,000
Less: Interest	80,000
Taxable Income	2,40,000
Less: Taxes at 50%	1,20,000
NI available to Equity Holders	1,20,000
Market value of firm (V) as determined in part (ii)	18,33,333
Market Value of Debentures (T)	10,00,000
Market Value of Equity (S) = $V - T$	8,33,333

$$K_e = \frac{1,20,000}{8,33,333} = 14.40\%$$

$$K_w = 4\%\left(\frac{10,00,000}{18,33,333}\right) + 14.40\%\left(\frac{8,33,333}{18,33,333}\right)$$

$$= 2\% + 7\% = 9\%$$

K_w for firm P = 9%

K_w for firm Q (as given in the problem) is = 12%

According to NOI approach where there are no corporate taxes every capital structure is optimum. However, in those cases where there are corporate taxes, capital structure will be optimum as per NOI approach where there is maximum possible debt content in the capital structure. By virtue of this fact none of the firms P and Q has optimum capital structure.

ILLUSTRATION 6.10

Firms A and B are identical in every respect, except that A is unlevered and B is levered. Firm B has 10% debentures of Rs. 25 lakhs outstanding. Assume (i) that all the M-M assumptions are fulfilled, (ii) that the tax rate is 50%, (iii) the EBIT is Rs. 8,00,000 and that equity capitalisation rate for firm B is 12%.

(a) What would be the value of each firm as per M-M's approach.

(b) Suppose V_n = Rs. 30,00,000 and V_1 = Rs. 40,00,000. According to M-M, do they represent equilibrium values? If not, explain the process by which equilibrium will be resorted.

No calculations are required.

Solution

(a) $V_n = \dfrac{\text{EBT}(1-t)}{K_e}$

$$= \frac{8,00,000(1-0.5)}{0.12}$$

$$= \frac{8,00,000 \times 0.5}{0.12} = \text{Rs. } 33,33,333$$

$$V_1 = V_n + Dt$$
$$= 33,33,333 + 25,00,000 \ (0.5)$$
$$= 33,33,333 + 12,50,000$$
$$= Rs. \ 45,83,333$$

(b) Firm 'A' is undervalued. But the firm 'B' is overvalued. Thus the investors can be better-off by investing in the undervalued firm since they require only lower investment outlay to earn the same income as they earn in the overvalued firm. Hence, they will sell their holding of the overvalued firm 'B' and buy shares of the undervalued firm 'A'. As a result, the prices of shares of firm 'B' decline and those of firm 'A' increase. This process remains so long as equilibrium in the values of the firms are restored.

ILLUSTRATION 6.11

The values for two firms X and Y in accordance with the traditional theory are given below:

	X Rs.	Y Rs.
Expected Operating Income $(\bar{x})$	50,000	50,000
Total Cost of Debt $(K_d \times D = R)$	0	10,000
Net Income $(\bar{x} - R)$	50,000	40,000
Cost of Equity (K_e)	0.10	0.11
Market Value of Shares (S)	5,00,000	3,60,000
Market Value of Debt (D)	0	2,00,000
Total Value of the Firm $(V = S + D)$	5,00,000	5,60,000
Average Cost of Capital (K_0)	0.10	0.09
Debt-Equity Ratio	0	0.556

Compute the values for firms X and Y as per the M-M theories. Assume that (i) corporate income-tax does not exist, and (ii) the equilibrium value of K_0 is 12.50.

(Delhi, M.Com, 1979)

Solution

Computation of the value for the firms under M-M hypothesis

	Firm X Rs.	Firm Y Rs.
EBIT $(\bar{x})$ (Expected Operating Income)	50,000	50,000
Less: Cost of Debt	—	10,000
Net Earnings for Equity Shareholders	50,000	40,000
Equilibrium Value of Cost of Capital (K_0)	0.125	0.125
Total value of the firm $\left(\dfrac{EBIT/\bar{x}}{K_0} \right)$	4,00,000	4,00,000
Market Value of Debt	—	2,00,000
∴ Market Value of Equity	4,00,000	2,00,000
∴ Cost of Equity $\left(\dfrac{Earnings \ for \ Equity}{Market \ Value \ of \ Shares} \right)$	12.5%	20%

ILLUSTRATION 6.12

From the following particulars presented by firm X and firm Y:

(i) Calculate the value of firms 'X' and 'Y' using Net Income (NI) Approach.

(ii) Calculate the value of firms 'X' and 'Y' using Net Operating Income (NOI) approach.

Firm 'X' and Firm 'Y' are identical in all respects except their capital structure. That is Firm 'X' uses debt whereas Firm 'Y' does not. The levered firm had Rs. 5,00,000 long-term loans, carrying 8% interest.

Both the firms earn on their total assets of Rs. 8,00,000 at 16% (before interest and taxes) Rate of tax is 50%

Capitalisation Rate @15% (Assume there are perfect capital market, rational investors and so on).

Solution

(i) **According to NI Approach**

	Firm X Levered Rs.	Firm Y Unlevered Rs.
EBIT (@16% on Rs. 8,00,000)	1,28,000	1,28,000
Less: Interest on Long-term Loans @8%	40,000	—
	88,000	1,28,000
Less: Taxes @50%	44,000	64,000
Earnings for Equity Shareholders	44,000	64,000
Equity Capitalisation Rate (K_e)	0.15	0.15
Market Value of Equity (S)	2,93,333	4,26,667
Market Value of Debt (T)	5,00,000	—
Total value of the firm	7,93,333	4,26,667

(ii) **According to NOI Approach**

The value of the firms, in the case of tax consideration, suggested by M-M is ascertained with the help of the following:

Value of Unlevered Firm

$$V_n = \frac{EBT(1-t)}{K_e}$$

Value of levered firm

$$V_1 = V_n + tD$$

Thus, value of unlevered firm 'Y' will be:

$$V_n = \frac{1,28,000(1-0.5)}{0.15}$$

$$= \frac{1,28,000 \times 0.5}{0.15}$$

$$= \text{Rs. } 4,26,667$$

Similarly, value of levered firm 'X' will be:

$V_1 = 4,26,667 + 0.5 \times 5,00,000$

$\quad = Rs.\ 6,76,667$

– REVIEW QUESTIONS –

1. What do you understand by capital structure of a firm? Explain the Net Operating Income theory of capital structure planning.

2. Explain 'Arbitrage Process' under Modigliani and Miller approach.

3. Critically examine the Net Income and Net Operating Income approaches to capital structure. What is the traditional view on this question?

4. What is 'Optimum Capital Structure'? Explain simple capital structure and complex capital structure.

5. Z Ltd. is expecting on annual EBIT of Rs. 1 lakh. The company has Rs. 4.00 lakhs in 10% debentures. The cost of equity capital or capitalisation rate is 12.5%. Calculate the total value of the firm. Also state the overall cost of capital.

    (**Ans:** Total value of the firm Rs. 8,80,000 Overall cost of capital 11.36%)

6. Two firms P and Q are identical in all respects except that the firm 'P' has 10% Rs. 50,000 debentures. Both the firms have the same earnings before interest and tax amounting to Rs. 10,000. The equity capitalisation rate of firm 'P' is 16% while that of firm Q is 12.5%.

    Compute the total market value of each of the firm.

    (**Ans:** P: Rs. 81,250; Q: Rs. 80,000)

7. A Ltd. wants to determine the optimal capital structure. From the particulars presented below, ascertain the optimal capital structure.

Condition	Equity Rs.	Debt Rs.	Cost of debt after tax (%)	K_e (%)
1	50,000	2,00,000	9	10
2	1,25,000	1,25,000	6	11
3	20,000	50,000	5	14

    (**Ans:** The optimal capital structure will be in the condition '2' where cost of capital is minimum, i.e., the debt-equity mix is 50%-50%)

8. 'Z' Ltd presents the following particulars:

    EBIT (i.e., Net Operating Income) is Rs. 30,000

    The equity capitalisation ratio (i.e., cost of equity) is 15% (K_e)

    Cost of debt is 10% (K_d)

    Total capital amounted to Rs. 2,00,000

    Compute cost of capital and the value of the firm for each of the following alternative leverage after applying the NI approach.

    Leverage (Debt to total capital) 0%, 20%, 50%, 70% and 100%

    (**Ans:** Total value of the firm: 0%–2,00,000, 20%–2,13,333, 50%–2,33,333, 70%–2,46,667, 100–2,66,667. Cost of capital: 0%–30%, 20%–28%, 50%–25%, 70%–23%, 100–20%)

7

Cost of Capital

Cost of capital is the rate of return the firm requires from investment
in order to increase the value of the firm in the market place.

— HAMPTON, JOHN J.

The concept of cost of capital has acquired wide significance at present as it helps to devise an optimal capital structure and it can serve as a discount rate for selecting the capital expenditure projects. However, it is probably one of the most difficult and controversial topics in financial management. There are different opinions among financial experts about its method of computation and measurement. But in view of the crucial operational significance, the discussions that follow are with the general framework of the computation of cost of capital.

MEANING AND CONCEPT OF COST OF CAPITAL

The term cost of capital refers to the minimum rate of return which a firm must earn on its investment. In economic sense, it is the cost of raising funds required to finance the proposed project—the borrowing rate of the firm. Thus under economic terms, the cost of capital may be defined as the weighted average cost of each type of capital. According to Hampton, John. J,

Cost of capital is the rate of return the firm requires from investment in order to increase the value of the firm in the market place.

There are three basic aspects about the concept of cost.

(i) It is not a Cost as Such

The cost of capital of a firm is the rate of return which it requires on the projects. That is why, it is a 'hurdle' rate. Usually such a rate is ascertained on the basis of actual cost of various components of capital. For instance, equity capital has a cost followed by preference share capital and so on.

(ii) It is the Minimum Rate of Return

A firm's cost of capital represents the minimum rate of return which is required to maintain at least the market value of equity shares.

(iii) It Consists of Three Components

A firm's cost of capital includes three components:

(a) **Return at Zero Risk Level:** It relates to the expected rate of return when a project involves no financial or business risks.

(b) **Business Risk Premium:** Generally, business risk premium is determined by the capital budgeting decisions for investment proposals. Business risk relates to the variability in operating profit (earning before interest and taxes) by virtue of changes in sales. If a firm selects a project which has more than the normal risk, the suppliers of the funds for the project will naturally expect a higher rate of return than the normal rate. Thus the cost of capital increases.

(c) **Financial Risk Premium:** Financial risk relates to the pattern of capital structure (i.e., debt-equity mix) of the firm. In general, a firm which has higher debt content in its capital structure should have more risk than a firm which has comparatively low debt content. This is because the former should have a greater operating profit with a view to covering the periodic interest payment and repayment of principal at the time of maturity than the latter. In other words, the chances of cash insolvency are higher in the case of such firms. Thus the suppliers of funds will expect a higher rate of return from such firms as compensation for high risk.

The above three components of cost of capital may be written in the form of the following equation:

$$K = r_0 + b + f$$

where,

K = Cost of Capital

r_0 = Return at Zero Risk Level

b = Business Risk Premium

f = Financial Risk Premium

SIGNIFICANCE OF COST OF CAPITAL

The determination of the firm's cost of capital is very significant from the standpoint of both capital budgeting and capital structure planning decisions.

(i) **Capital Budgeting Decisions:** The concept of cost of capital can serve as a discount rate for selecting the capital expenditure projects. The capital budgeting decision after all is the matching of the costs of the use of funds with the returns of the employment of funds. Thus the financial manager can arrive at the break-even point in the capital structure—the point at which the rate of return of a given project equals the cost of procuring funds for that project.

(ii) **Capital Structure Decisions:** The concept of cost of capital is an important consideration in capital structure decisions. It helps to devise an optimal capital structure with an ideal debt-equity mix based on minimum costs.

CLASSIFICATION OF COST OF CAPITAL

Cost of capital can be brought as under:

1. Explicit Cost and Implicit Cost
2. Future Cost and Historical Cost
3. Specific Cost and Combined Cost
4. Average Cost and Marginal Cost

1. Explicit Cost and Implicit Cost

The explicit cost of any source of finance may be defined as the discount rate that equates the present value of the cash inflows (that are incremental to the taking of the financing opportunity) with the present value of its expected cash outflows. When a firm raises funds from different sources, it involves only a cash inflow at the beginning by the amount raised which is followed by a series of cash outflows in the form of interest payments, repayment of principal or repayment of dividends. In other words, the explicit cost is the internal rate of return the firm pays for financing. For instance, if a firm issues 2,000, 10% debentures of Rs. 100 each, redeemable after the 20 years at par, there will be an inflow of cash to the extent of Rs. 2,00,000 (2,000 × Rs. 100) at the beginning, but the annual cash outflow will be Rs. 20,000 (Rs. 2,00,000 × 10/100) in the form of interest and there also will be an outflow of Rs. 2,00,000 at the end of 20th year when the debentures will be redeemed. Thus explicit cost is that rate of internal return which equates Rs. 2 lakhs, the initial cash inflow with Rs. 20,000 payable every year for 20 years and Rs. 2 lakhs at the end of 20 years. However, it is noted that if a firm takes any non-interest bearing loan, there will be no explicit cost as there is no outflow of cash by way of interest payment although the principal should be repaid.

The explicit cost of capital may be computed by using the following equation:

$$I_0 = \frac{C_1}{(1+K)^1} + \frac{C_2}{(1+K)^2} + \dots + \frac{C_n}{(1+K)^n}$$

where,

I_0 = Net amounts of funds received by the firm at time zero.

C = Outflow in the period concerned

n = Period for which the funds are provided

K = Explicit Cost of Capital

The implicit cost may be defined as the rate of return associated with the best investment opportunity for the firm and its shareholders that will be forgone if the projects presently under consideration by the firm were accepted. When the earnings are retained by a firm, the implicit cost is the income which the shareholders could have earned if such earnings would have been distributed and invested by them. In short, the explicit cost arises when the capital is raised and which is also the IRR of the financial opportunity. On the other hand, implicit cost of capital arises whenever funds are used. Thus funds raised from any source have implicit costs once they are invested.

2. Future Cost and Historical Cost

If future cost is the expected cost of funds for financing a project, historical cost is the cost which has already been incurred for financing a particular project. In financial decision-making process, the relevant cost is future cost. But however, historical cost is useful while projecting future cost and providing an evaluation of past performance in comparison with standard or predetermined cost.

3. Specific Cost and Combined Cost

The cost of each component of capital, i.e., equity shares, preference shares, debentures, loan, etc., is called the specific cost of capital. The firm should consider the specific cost, while determining the average cost of capital. This is particularly useful where the profitability of a project is judged on the basis of the specific source of funds taken for financing the said projects. For instance, if a firm's estimated cost of equity capital is 10%, a project which is financed out of equity shareholders' funds would be accepted only when it provides a rate of return of at least 10%.

When specific costs are combined to find out the overall cost of capital, it is called the combined cost or composite cost. In other words, the combined or composite cost of capital is inclusive of all costs of capital from all sources (i.e., equity shares, preference shares, debentures and other loans). This concept of capital is used as a basis for accepting or rejecting the proposal in capital investment decisions although various proposals are financed through various sources.

4. Average Cost and Marginal Cost

Average cost of capital is the weighted average of the cost of each component of funds invested by the concern. But the weights are in proportion of the shares of each component of capital in the total investment. However, the computation of average cost involves certain problems. They are as follows:

(i) It needs measurement of costs of each specific source of capital.

(ii) It needs the assignment of proper weights to each component of capital.

(iii) It raises a question whether the average cost is affected by changes in the composition of the capital.

Marginal cost of capital is the cost of additional amount of capital which is raised by a firm for current and/or fixed capital investment. When a firm procures additional capital from one particular source only in a given proportion, then the marginal cost is known as specific or explicit cost of capital. The marginal cost of capital is the most significant factor to be considered in the case of capital budgeting and financing decisions.

ILLUSTRATION 7.1

A company presents the following information relating to the cost of capital:

Sources	Amount Rs.	After-tax Cost of Capital
Equity	1,00,000	8%
Debt	1,00,000	3%

The company wants to raise funds for Rs. 50,000 for an investment proposal. It also determines to raise the same from a bank at a cost of 10%. Calculate the marginal cost of capital and compare the same with the average cost of capital before and after additional financing assuming that the corporate rate of tax is 50%.

Solution

It is clear from this problem that the marginal cost for raising an additional capital of Rs. 50,000 is 10% before tax and 5% after tax (i.e., 10 – 50% of 10%). The same is also called the explicit or specific cost of financing Rs. 50,000 as there is only one source, i.e., bank. But the marginal cost differs from the average cost which is computed as follows:

Before additional financing

	Proportion	Cost After-tax	Weighted Average Cost (%)
Equity	0.5	8	4.0
Debt*	0.5	3	1.5
	1.0		5.5

After financing Rs. 50,000:

	*Proportion	Specific Cost After-tax	Weighted Average Cost (%)
Equity	0.4	8	3.2
Debt:			
Old	0.4	3	1.2
New	0.2	5	1.0
	1.0		5.4

* Proportion:
 Equity   1,00,000
 Debt
    Old   1,00,000
    New   50,000
∴ Ratio:
 Equity: Debt(New): Debt(Old) = 1,00,000 : 1,00,000 : 50,000
                           2   :   2   :   1
        or   4   :   4   :   2

Here, the weighted average cost comes down from 5.5% to 5.4%. The cost of new debt is greater than that of old debt and the cost of new debt is less than that of equity capital. Thus average cost of capital comes down as there is an increase in the proportion of debt capital to total capital invested.

When a company raises additional capital, it should use various sources of financing proportionately for maintaining the optimum capital structure. In case, the capital is raised from various sources at a given proportion, it requires a calculation of average cost of capital for knowing the cost of the total additional amount raised. Hence, in this case, marginal cost of capital may also be called the weighted average cost for the same. If there is no change in specific cost, there will be no difference between the two. Find the following example.

ILLUSTRATION 7.2

In Illustration 7.1, if the company raises the additional amount of Rs. 50,000 from equity and debt at the existing specific cost, there will be no difference between the weighted average cost and the marginal cost of capital since both of them are one and the same which is as follows:

Sources	Amount Rs.	Proportion	Specific Cost After-tax (%)	Marginal Cost (%)
Equity	25,000	0.5	8	4.0
Debt	25,000	0.5	3	1.5
		1.0		5.5

Thus, the cost of raising Rs. 50,000 is only 5.5% which is the marginal cost.

In case the specific cost changes, there will be a difference between the marginal cost of capital and the average cost of capital of a company although additional capital is raised at a given proportion. Find the following example.

ILLUSTRATION 7.3

In case it is assumed that cost of debt is 10% (before tax) and the rate of tax is 50% and the company prefers to procure Rs. 50,000 proportionately, calculate the marginal cost of capital and the average cost of capital.

Solution

(a) Marginal Cost of Capital

Sources	Amount Rs.	Proportion	Cost After-tax (%)	Marginal Cost of Capital (%)
Equity	25,000	0.5	8	4.0
Debt	25,000	0.5	5	2.5
		1.0		6.5

(b) Average Cost of Capital

Sources	Amount Rs.	Proportion	Cost After-tax (%)	Weighted Average Cost (%)
Equity	1,25,000	0.5	8	4.0
Debt				
Old	1,00,000	0.4	3	1.2
New	25,000	0.1	5	0.5
		1.0		5.7

Here, the overall cost of capital goes up since there is an increase in the cost of new debt capital. The same actually varies from the marginal cost of 6.5% for procuring additional capital of Rs. 50,000 to 5.7%.

Controversy Regarding Cost of Capital

In spite of the practical utility and importance of cost of capital, it is the most disputed topic in financial management. In this regard, there are mainly two approaches. They are as follows:

1. Traditional Approach

Under this approach, the cost of capital of a firm relates to its capital structure. In other words, the cost of capital of the firm is the weighted average cost of debt and the cost of equity. For instance, in case a company has 10% debentures (issued and payable at par) the cost of funds raised from this source comes to only 5% (assuming 50% tax rate). But other sources such as equity shares and preference shares also involve cost. However, the raising of funds by way of debentures is cheaper. This is mainly due to the following facts:

(i) Usually, interest rate is less than dividend rates.

(ii) Interest is allowed as an expense while taxable profit of the company is computed. But dividend is not allowed as an expense.

The main argument in favour of this approach is that the weighted average cost of capital will go up with every increase in the debt content in the total capital employed. However, the debt content in the total capital employed must be maintained at a proper level as the cost of debt is a fixed burden. Moreover, when the debt content goes up beyond a certain level, the investors consider the company too risky and their expectations from equity shares will go up.

2. Modigliani and Miller Approach

Under this approach, the total cost of capital of a company is constant and independent of its capital structure. In other words, a change in the debt-equity ratio does not affect the total cost of capital. For instance, the company has at present even debt-equity ratio. It has been paying dividend at the rate of 15% on equity shares. If the debt-equity ratio changes to say 55% and 45%, the consequences are as follows:

(i) The overall cost of capital will decrease as the debt is cheaper.

(ii) The expectation of the equity shareholders from present dividend of 15%, will go up as they consider the company too risky.

On account of the above reasons, the overall cost of the company will not be affected by change in the debt-equity ratio. Thus, Modigliani and Miller argue that within the same risk class, mere change of debt-equity ratio does not affect the cost of capital. Their observations in their article "Cost of Capital, Corporation Finance and Theory of Investment" are:

(i) The total market value of the firm and its cost of capital are independent of its capital structure. The total market value of the firm can be calculated by capitalising the expected stream of operating earnings at a discount rate considered appropriate for its risk class.

(ii) The cut-off rate for investment purposes is completely independent of the way in which investment is financed.

Assumptions

The Modigliani-Miller approach is based on the following assumptions:

(i) **Perfect Capital Market:** Trading of securities takes place in perfect capital market. This indicates that:

(a) Investors have full-fledged freedom to buy and sell securities.

(b) As investors are completely knowledgeable and rational persons, they can know at once all information and changes.

(c) The buying and selling of securities does not involve costs such as broker's commission, transfer fees, etc.

(d) The investors can borrow against securities on the same basis as the firms can do so.

(ii) **Homogeneous Risk Classes:** In case the firms expected earnings have identical risk features, they should be considered to belong to a homogeneous class.

(iii) **Same Expectations:** All investors have the same expectations of the net operating income (EBIT) of firm which is used for its evaluation. There is 100 per cent dividend pay out, i.e., all the net earnings of the firm are distributed to the shareholders.

(iv) **No Corporate Taxes:** At the formulation stage of hypothesis, Modigliani and Miller assume that there are no corporate taxes. However, they have removed this assumption later on.

In short, despite the correctness of the basic reasoning of Modigliani and Miller, the traditional approach is more realistic because of the following:

(i) The companies are subject to income-tax. Thus by virtue of tax effect, the cost of debt is less than that of equity capital.

(ii) The assumption of perfect market in Modigliani and Miller hypothesis is seldom true.

By virtue of the foregoing discussion, the Modigliani and Miller approach is subject to vehement criticism. According to Mr. Ezra Soloman, "The thesis that the company's cost of capital is independent of its financial structure is not valid. As far as leverage effect alone is concerned (and ignoring all other considerations that might affect the choice between debt and equity) there does exist a clearly definable optimum position—namely, the point at which the marginal cost of more debt is equal to or greater than a company's average cost of capital". But Mr. E.W. Walker very aptly remarks that "the criticisms lodged against Modigliani and Miller's thesis are valid thus limiting its use in actual situations. Nevertheless, the proportions as well as their criticisms should be carefully studied, since they will serve as an aid to understanding capital structure theory".

COMPUTATION OF COST OF CAPITAL

Computation of the cost of capital involves: (i) computation of specific costs (i.e., computation of cost of each specific source of finance) and (ii) computation of composite cost (i.e., weighted average cost).

Computation of Specific Costs

It is the computation of the cost of each specific source of finance such as debt, preference capital and equity capital.

Cost of Debt

It is the rate of return which is expected by lenders. This is actually the interest rate specified at the time of issue.

Debt may be issued at par, at premium or discount. It may be perpetual or redeemable. The following are the techniques of computation of cost in each case.

(i) **Debt Issued at Par:** The cost of debt issued at par is the explicit interest rate adjusted further for the tax liability. It is computed in accordance with the following formula:

$$K_d = (1 - T)R$$

where

K_d = Cost of Debt
T = Marginal Tax Rate
R = Interest Rate

ILLUSTRATION 7.4

A company has issued 7% debentures and the tax rate is 50%, the after tax cost of debt is 3.5%. It is calculated as follows:

$K_d = (1 - T)R = (1 - 0.5)7 = 0.5 \times 7$
     = 3.5%

As the interest is treated as an expense while calculating firm's income for tax purposes, the tax is deducted out of interest payable. However, the tax adjusted interest rate is used only if the EBIT (Earnings/Profits Before Interest and Tax) is equal to or exceeds the interest. But in case EBIT is negative, the cost of debt should be computed before adjusting the interest rate of tax. For instance, in the above case, the cost of debt (before adjusting the rate of tax) is 7% only.

(ii) **Debt Issued at Premium or Discount:** When the debentures are issued at a premium (more than the face value) or at a discount (less than the face value) the cost of debt should be computed on the basis of net proceeds realised on account of issue of such debentures. Such cost may further be adjusted in view of the tax rate applicable to the company. The formula for ascertaining the cost of debt in such cases is as under:

$$K_d = \frac{C}{P}(1-T)$$

where

K_d = Cost of Debt
C = Annual Interest
P = Net Proceeds
T = Tax Rate

ILLUSTRATION 7.5

A company issues 10% debentures for Rs. 1,00,000. Rate of tax is 50%. Calculate the cost of debt (before and after tax) if the debentures are issued at (i) par; (ii) 10% discount and (iii) 10% premium.

Solution

Cost of debt is:

$$K_d = \frac{C}{P}(1-T)$$

where

K_d = Cost of Debt
C = Annual Interest
P = Net Proceeds
T = Tax

(i) Issued at par

$$K_d = \frac{10,000}{1,00,000}(1-0.50)$$

$$= \frac{1}{10} \times 0.50 = 0.50 \text{ or } 5\%$$

(ii) Issued at discount

$$K_d = \frac{10,000}{90,000}(1-0.50)$$

$$= \frac{1}{9} \times 0.50 = 0.056 \text{ or } 5.6\%$$

(iii) Issued at premium

$$K_d = \frac{10,000}{1,10,000}(1-0.50)$$

$$= \frac{1}{11} \times 0.50 = 0.045 \text{ or } 4.5\%$$

(iii) Cost of Redeemable Debt: When debentures are redeemed after the expiry of a fixed period, the cost of debt before tax can be computed with the help of the following formula:

$$K_d \text{ (before tax)} = \frac{C + \dfrac{(D - P)}{n}}{\dfrac{(D + P)}{2}}$$

where,

C = Annual Interest
D = Par Value of Debentures
n = Number of Years to Maturity
P = Net Proceeds

ILLUSTRATION 7.6

A company issues 10% debentures for Rs. 1,00,000 and realises Rs. 95,000 after allowing 5% commission to brokers. The debentures are due for maturity at the end of the 10th year. Compute the effective cost of debt before tax.

Solution

$$K_d \text{ (before tax)} = \frac{C + \dfrac{(D - P)}{n}}{\dfrac{(D + P)}{2}}$$

where,

C = Rs. 10,000 (10% of Rs. 1,00,000)
P = Rs. 95,000
D = Rs. 1,00,000
n = 10

$$K_d = \frac{10,000 + \left(\dfrac{1,00,000 - 95,000}{10}\right)}{\dfrac{1,00,000 + 95,000}{2}}$$

$$= \frac{10,000 + 500}{97,500} = 10.77\%$$

In the above illustration, if the tax rate is 50%, the cost of debt after tax can be computed as under:

$$K_d \text{ (after tax)} = K_d \text{ (before tax)} \times (1 - T) = 10.77 \times (1 - 0.50)$$
$$= 10.77 \times 0.50 = 5.39\%$$

It should be pointed out that while computing the real cost of debt, the contractual interest rate as well as certain other imputed costs of raising funds from debts should be considered.

When financing of funds from the debt goes up, the expectation of the equity shareholders on their capital also goes up because of increase in the risk factor. Moreover, with increase in the amount of borrowed funds, the interest rate is also likely to rise. Hence the imputed cost of raising funds through debt financing comprises the increase in the expectation of the equity shareholders from their capital employed in the business.

Cost of Preference Share Capital

The calculation of the cost of preference capital creates some conceptual problems. It is argued that as the preference dividend is not legally binding on the part of the company, it does not constitute cost. However, this argument is not correct. This is because, although it is not legally binding on the part of the company to pay preference dividend, it is generally paid as and when the company earns enough profits. The failure to pay preference dividend is a matter of serious concern on the part of the equity shareholders. They may even lose control of the company as the preference shareholders will enjoy the right to take part in the general meeting with equity shareholders under certain conditions if the company fails to pay preference dividend. Moreover, the accumulation of arrears of preference dividend may adversely affect the right to equity shareholders. By virtue of these reasons, the cost of preference capital should also be calculated at par with the cost of debentures. The method of its calculation is given below:

$$K_P = \frac{D_P}{P}$$

where,

K_P = Cost of Preference Shares
D_P = Fixed Preference Dividend
P = Net Proceeds of Preference Shares

ILLUSTRATION 7.7

A company raises preference share capital of Rs. 1,00,000 by issuing 10% preference shares of Rs. 100 each. Compute the cost of preference capital when they are issued at (i) 10% premium, and (ii) at 10% discount.

Solution

(i) When preference shares are issued at a premium of 10%

$$K_P = \frac{D_P}{P}$$

where,

K_P = Rs. 10,000 (@10% on Rs. 1,00,000)
P = Rs. 1,10,000 (Rs. 1,00,000 + Rs. 10,000)

i.e., = $\frac{10,000}{1,10,000}$ = 9.09%

(ii) When preference shares are issued at a discount of ·10%

$$K_P = \frac{D_P}{P}$$

$$= \frac{10,000}{90,000(1,00,000 - 10,000)} = 11.11\%$$

Cost of Redeemable Preference Shares

The cost of redeemable preference shares is the discount rate which equates the net proceeds of sale of preference shares with the present value of future dividend and repayment of principal. Such cost can be computed as per the same formula for computing the cost of redeemable debentures (discussed in the preceding pages). But the cost of preference share capital is not adjusted for taxes as it is not a charge against profit but an appropriation of profit. Thus the cost of preference capital is substantially higher than that of debt.

ILLUSTRATION 7.8

A company issues 10% redeemable preference shares for Rs. 1,00,000, redeemable at the end of the 10th year from the year of their issue. The underwriting cost is 5%. Calculate the effective cost of preference share capital.

$$K_P = \frac{C + \dfrac{(D - P)}{n}}{\dfrac{(D + P)}{2}}$$

where,

C = Annual Dividend
D = Par Value of Preference Shares
n = Number of Years to Maturity
P = Net Proceeds

$$= \frac{10,000 + \left(\dfrac{1,00,000 - 95,000}{10}\right)}{\dfrac{1,00,000 + 95,000}{2}} = \frac{10,000 + 5,000}{97,500}$$

$$= 10.77\%$$

Cost of Equity Capital

The calculation of the cost of equity capital is a tedious task. As observed in the case of preference shares, it is argued that the equity capital does not involve any cost because the company is not legally bound to pay dividend to the equity shareholders. This is not true as the equity shareholders invest money in shares with the expectation of getting dividend· from the company. Moreover, the company also does not issue equity shares without the motive of paying them dividend. Thus the market value of equity shares highly depends on the return expected by the sharehoders.

Cost of equity capital may be defined as the minimum rate of return that a firm must earn on the equity-financed portion of an investment project in order to leave unchanged the market price of its stock.*

For instance, in case the required rate of return (RRR) is 13% and cost of debt is 10% and the company has the policy to finance with 70% equity and 30% debt, the required rate of return on the project could be computed as under:

$$13\% \times 0.70 = \quad 9.1\%$$
$$10\% \times 0.30 = \quad \underline{3.0\%}$$
$$\underline{12.1\%}$$

It indicates that in case the company accepts a project involving an investment of Rs. 50,000 and giving an annual return of Rs. 6,050, the project would provide a return which is just enough to keep the market value of the company's equity shares unchanged. The rate of return on equity financed portion can be ascertained as under.

	Rs.
Total Return	6,050
Less Interest on Debentures: $\dfrac{15,000 \times 10}{100}$	1,500
Amount available for Equity Shareholders	4,550
Rate of Return on Equity = $\dfrac{4,550 \times 100}{35,000}$ = 13%	

Hence, the expected rate of return is 13% which just equals the required rate of return on investment. In case the project earns less than Rs. 6,050 a year, it would provide a return less than required by the investors. Thus the market value of the company's share would come down. Conceptually, this rate of return may be considered as the cost of equity capital.

The equity capital may be brought into two categories for the purpose of computing the cost of capital. They are:

(i) New Issue or External Equity

(ii) Retained Earnings.

New Issues

To find out the cost of external equity, different authorities have different approaches and explanations. Some of these approaches are as follows:

1. Dividend Price (D/P) Approach

According to this approach, the cost of equity capital is computed against a required rate of return in terms of future dividends. Thus cost of capital is defined as "the discount rate that equates the present value of all expected future dividends per share with the net proceeds of the sale (or the current market price) of a share". In other words, the cost of equity capital will be that rate of expected dividends which will maintain the present market price of equity shares.

*Van Horne, J.I., op. cit., p. 198.

This approach provides due importance to dividends. But it ignores one basic aspect that retained earning has also an impact on the market price of equity shares. Thus this does not seem to be very logical.

The cost of equity in this approach is computed according to the following formula.

$$K_e = \frac{D}{P}$$

where,

K_e = Cost of Equity Share Capital
D = Dividend/Earnings per Share
P = Net Proceeds per Share/Current Market Price per Share.

ILLUSTRATION 7.9

A company offers equity shares of Rs. 10 each for public subscription at a premium of 5%. The company pays 2% of the issue price as underwriting commission. The rate of dividend expected by equity shareholders is 30%.

You are required to compute the cost of equity capital. Will your cost of capital be different if it is calculated on the basis of present market value of equity share which is only Rs. 13.

Solution

The cost of capital is computed as under:

$$K_e = \frac{D}{P}$$

where,

K_e = Cost of Equity Share Capital
D = Dividend/Earnings per Share
P = Net Proceeds per Share

$$K_e = \frac{3}{10.29^*} = 0.29 \text{ or } 29\%$$

In the case of existing equity shares, it is appropriate to compute cost of equity shares on the basis of market price. It can be computed as under:

$$K_e = \frac{D}{MP}$$

where,

K_e = Cost of Equity Share Capital
D = Dividend per Share
MP = Market Price per Share

$$K_e = \frac{3}{13} = 0.2307 \text{ or } 23.07\%$$

---

*Rs. 10.50 – Rs. 0.21.

2. Dividend Price Plus Growth [(D/P) + g] Approach

In this approach, the cost of equity capital is calculated on the basis of the expected dividend rate plus the rate of growth in dividend. But the rate of growth is ascertained on the basis of the amount of dividends paid by the company for the last few years.

Under this method, the cost of capital can be computed by using the following formula,

$$K_e = \frac{D}{P} + g$$

where,

K_e = Cost of Equity Share Capital
D = Dividend per Share
P = Net Proceeds per Share
g = Growth Rate in Dividend

In the case of existing equity shares, the cost of equity capital can also be computed by the same formula, instead of P (Net proceeds of shares), MP (Market Price) should be used.

ILLUSTRATION 7.10

The current market price of an equity share of the company is Rs. 70. The current dividend per share is Rs. 5. Dividends are expected to grow at 7%. Calculate the cost of equity capital.

Solution

$$K_e = \frac{D}{P} + g = \frac{5}{70} + 0.07 = 0.07 + 0.07$$

$$= 0.14 \text{ or } 14\%$$

ILLUSTRATION 7.11

From the following particulars of XY company, calculate the cost of equity capital.

(i) Current Market price of a share is Rs. 160

(ii) The underwriting cost per share on new share is 3%.

(iii) The following are the dividends paid on the outstanding shares for the last five years.

Year	Dividend per Share
1997	10.50
1998	11.00
1999	11.50
2000	12.50
2001	13.40

(iv) The company has a fixed dividend payout ratio.

(v) The expected dividend on the new shares at the end of the first year is Rs. 14.10 per share.

Solution

With a view to computing the cost of funds raised by equity share capital, the growth rate of dividends should be estimated. During the five years, the dividends have increased from Rs. 10.50 to Rs. 13.40 presenting as compound factor of 1.276 (i.e., 13.40/10.50). After applying the "compound sum of one rupee table" a sum of Rs. 1 would accumulate to Rs. 1.276 in five years at 5% interest.* This means that the growth rate of dividends is 5%. Thus the cost of equity can be computed as under:

$$K_e = \frac{D}{P} + g$$

$$= \frac{14.10}{155.2(160 - 4.8)} + 5\%$$

$$= 9.08\% + 5\% = 14.08\%$$

Although the "dividend price growth approach" is helpful in satisfactorily determining the expectation of the investors, the quantification of the expectation of growth of dividends is a tough task. Generally, it is presumed that the growth in dividends is equal to the growth rate in earnings per share.

3. Earning Price (E/P) Approach

Under this approach, it is the earning per share which determines the market price of the shares. This is based on the assumption that the shareholders capitalise a stream of future earnings for evaluating their shareholdings. Thus the cost of capital relates to that earning percentage which can keep the market price of the equity shares constant. This approach, therefore, recognises both dividend and retained earnings. But the advocates of this approach differ on the applicability of both earnings and market price figures. Some prefer to use the current earning rate and current market price. While others recommend average rate of earning (based on the earnings of past few years) and the average market price of equity shares (based on market price for the last few years).

The formula used for computing cost of capital under this approach is as follows:

$$K_e = \frac{E}{P}$$

where,

K_e = Cost of Equity Capital
E = Earning per Share
P = Net Proceeds of an Equity Share

It is noted that in the case of existing equity shares, it is better to apply market price (MP) in lieu of net proceeds (P).

ILLUSTRATION 7.12

The capital employed by a company comprises two lakhs equity shares of Rs. 100 each. Its

---

*Refer to Appendix 3 at the end of the book.

current earnings are Rs. 20 lakhs per annum. The company wants to raise additional funds of Rs. 30 lakhs by issuing new shares. The floatation costs are expected to be 10% of the face value of the shares. What will be the cost of equity capital if it is assumed that earnings of the company are stable?

Solution

$$K_e = \frac{E}{P}$$

where,

E = Earning per Share = $\dfrac{20,00,000}{2,00,000}$

   = Rs. 10 per Share

P = Net Proceeds of Share = Face Value – Floatation Cost

   = 100 – 10 = Rs. 90

K_e = $\dfrac{10}{90}$ = 11.1%

4. Realised Yield Approach

Under this approach, the cost of equity capital should be ascertained on the basis of return actually realised by the investors on their investment (i.e., on equity shares). Thus in this approach, the past records in a given period regarding dividends and the actual capital appreciation in the value of the equity shares held by the shareholders should be taken to calculate the cost of equity capital. This approach provides fairly good results in those companies where the dividends are stable and the growth rate is almost constant.

ILLUSTRATION 7.13

Mr. 'A' purchased 5 shares at a cost of Rs. 250 on 1st January 1997. He held them for 5 years and sold them in January, 2002 for Rs. 312. The dividends which he received for the last five years are as follows:

Year	Dividends
1997	14
1998	15
1999	15
2000	15
2001	16

Compute the cost of equity capital.

Solution

Before computing the cost of capital, it is necessary to calculate the internal rate of return. This rate of return can be calculated with the help of "Trial and Error Method" (See Chapter 19, Capital Budgeting). The rate comes to 10% which is shown as under:

Year	Dividends Rs.	Sale Proceeds Rs.	Discount Factors at 10%	Present Value Rs.
1997	14	—	0.909	12.72
1998	15	—	0.826	12.39
1999	15	—	0.751	11.26
2000	15	—	0.683	10.24
2001	16	—	0.621	9.93
2002	—	312	0.621	193.75
				250.29

The purchase price of the 5 shares on 1st January 1997 was Rs. 250. The present value of cash inflows (as on 1st January 2002) amounts to Rs. 250.29. Thus at 10%, the present value of the cash inflows over a period of 5 years is equal to the cash outflow in the year 1997. The cost of equity capital can, therefore, be considered as 10%.

Cost of Retained Earnings

Equity capital usually comprises two components. The first is the amount of funds available in the form of net income that may be used to pay dividend or may be retained in the business to purchase assets. The second source of equity capital is the amount of funds raised by a new issue. This section deals with the cost associated with using retained earnings as a source of financing.

Generally, the companies do not distribute the whole of the profits earned by them by way of dividend among their shareholders. A part of such profits is retained by them for future expansion of the business. Some people view that such retained earnings are cost free. But this view is not true as the amount retained by company would have given some earning to the shareholders if it had been distributed among them by way of dividend. Hence, the cost of retained earnings are the earnings foregone by the shareholders. In other words, the opportunity cost of retained earnings may be taken as the cost of retained earnings. It is equal to the income what a shareholder could have earned otherwise by investing the same in alternative investment. For instance, if the shareholders had invested the said funds in an alternative channel they could have earned a return of 15%. This return of 15% is actually foregone by them as the company does not distribute the entire profits to them. In this case, the cost of retained earnings may be taken at 15%.

The above analysis can also be explained in the following way.

Suppose the company does not retain the profit and passes on to the shareholders and the same is invested by them in purchasing shares of the same company. Now, the shareholders' expectation about the return on such new equity shares would be taken as the opportunity cost of retained earnings. In other words, if earnings were distributed as dividend and at the same time an offer for the right shares was made, the shareholders would have subscribed the right issues on the expectation of certain return. Such an expected return can be considered as the cost of retained earnings of the company.

Moreover, the shareholders have to pay tax on the dividends received, incur brokerage cost for making investment, etc. Hence, the funds available with the shareholders are less than what they would have been with the company, had they been retained by it. By virtue of it, the cost of retained earnings to the company is always less than the cost of new equity shares issued by the company. Thus the following adjustments are required for determining the cost of retained earnings.

    (i) Income Tax Adjustment: Usually, the dividends receivable by the shareholders are subject to income tax. Thus the dividends actually received by them are the amount of net dividend (i.e., gross dividends less income tax).

    (ii) Brockerage Cost Adjustment: Usually, the shareholders cannot utilise the whole amount of dividend received from the company for the purpose of investment as they have to incur some expenses by way of brokerage, commission, etc., for purchasing new shares against the dividend.

    The cost of retained earnings after making proper adjustments (i.e., income tax and brokerage cost) can be computed by using the following formula:

$$K_r = K_e(1 - T)(1 - C)$$

where,

    K_r = Cost of Retained Earnings
    K_e = Cost of Equity Capital
    T = Marginal Tax Rate applicable to the Shareholders
    C = Commission and Brokerage costs, etc., in terms of percentage

ILLUSTRATION 7.14

A company is earning a profit of Rs. 60,000 per annum. The shareholders' required rate of return is 10%. It is expected that retained earnings, if distributed among the shareholders, can be invested by them in securities of similar type carrying return of 10% per annum. Shareholders also have to incur by way of brokerage and commission @3%. Rate of tax is 40%.

    Calculate the cost of retained earnings.

Solution

For computing the cost of retained earnings to the company, it is required to ascertain the net amount available to the shareholders for investment and the likely return earned by them. This is calculated as under.

	Rs.
Dividends Payable to the Shareholders	60,000
Less: Income Tax @40%	24,000
After Tax Dividends	36,000
Less: Brokerage Cost @3%	1,080
Net Amount Available for Investment.	34,920
Earnings on Investment: 10% of Rs. 34,920	

i.e., $\dfrac{34,920 \times 10}{100}$ = Rs. 3,492

If the company had not distributed the earnings among its shareholders, it could have made the whole of Rs. 60,000 for investment as no expenses such as income tax and brokerage cost, as above, would have been payable. Had the company earned a return of 5.82% (calculated as under), it could have paid a sum of Rs. 3,492 to the shareholders.

$$\frac{3,492 \times 100}{60,000} = 5.82\%$$

The rate of return expected by the shareholders from the company on their retained earnings comes to 5.82%. Hence it may be taken as the cost of the retained earnings.

The cost of retained earnings after making adjustment for income tax and brokerage cost payable by the shareholders, can also be calculated with the help of the following formula.

$$K_r = K_e(1 - T)(1 - C)$$

i.e., $\qquad 10(1 - 0.40)(1 - 0.03) = 5.82\%$

Composite or Weighted Average Cost of Capital

The term cost of capital is used to denote the overall composite cost of capital or weighted average of the cost of each specific type of funds i.e., weighted average cost. In other words, the composite or weighted average cost of capital is the combined specific costs used to find out the overall cost of capital. The computation of weighted average cost of capital involves the following steps:

  (i)   Calculate the cost of each specific source of funds.

  (ii) Assign proper weights to specific costs.

  (iii) Multiply the cost of each source by the appropriate weight.

  (iv) Divide the total weighted cost by the total weights to get the overall cost of capital.

Assignment of Weights

This involves the determination of the proportion of each source of funds in the total capital structure of the company. For this purpose, the following three possible weights may be used.

  (i)   Book Value Weights   —   used for actual or historical weights.

  (ii) Market Value Weights   —   used for current weights.

  (iii) Marginal Value Weights —   used for proposed future financing.

(i) Book Value Weights

Under this method, the relative proportions of various sources to the existing capital structure are used to assign weights. The advantages of these weights are as follows:

  (i)   Book values are easily available from the published annual report of a company.

  (ii) All companies set their targets of capital structure in terms of book values rather than market value.

  (iii) The analysis of capital structure on the basis of debt-equity ratio also depends on book value.

ILLUSTRATION 7.15

The cost of capital (after tax) of a company of the specific sources is as follows:

Cost of Debt	4.00%
Cost of Preference Shares	11.5%
Cost of Equity Capital	15.50%
Cost of Retained Earnings	14.50% (assuming external yield criterion)

Capital Structure are:

Sources	Amount Rs.
Debt	3,00,000
Preference Share Capital	4,00,000
Equity Share Capital	6,00,000
Retained Earnings	2,00,000
	15,00,000

Calculate the weighted average cost of capital using 'Book Value Weights'.

Solution

**Computation of Weighted Average
Cost of Capital Under Book Value Weights**

Sources (a)	Amount (b)	Proportion (c)		After Tax Cost (d)	Weighted Cost (e) = (c) × (d)
Debt	3,00,000	0.200	(20%)	0.0400	0.0080
Preference Share Capital	4,00,000	0.267	(26.7%)	0.1150	0.0307
Equity Share Capital	6,00,000	0.400	(40%)	0.1550	0.0620
Retained Earnings	2,00,000	0.133	(13.3%)	0.1450	0.0193
	15,00,000	1.000	(100%)		0.1200

∴ Weighted average cost of capital: 12%

Alternative approach

An alternative method is to calculate the total cost of capital and then divide the figure by the total capital which actually avoids fractional calculations as computed above.

Computation of Weighted Average Cost of Capital

Sources (a)	Amount (b)	Cost (c)	Total cost (d) = (b) × (c)
Debt	3,00,000	4.00%	12,000
Preference Capital	4,00,000	11.50%	46,000
Equity Share Capital	6,00,000	15.50%	93,000
Retained Earnings	2,00,000	14.50%	29,000
	15,00,000		1,80,000

$$\text{Weighted Average Cost of Capital} = \frac{1,80,000}{15,00,000} = 12\%$$

(ii) Market Value Weights

Theoretically, the use of market value weights for computing the cost of capital is more appealing due to the following facts:

(a) The market values of the securities are approximate to the actual amount to be obtained from the sale of such securities.

(b) The cost of each specific source of finance is computed in accordance with the prevailing market price.

However, there are some practical difficulties for using market value weights. They are as follows:

(a) Frequent fluctuation in the market value of securities is a common phenomenon.

(b) Market values of securities are not readily available like book values. But book values are available from the published records of the company.

(c) The book value and not the market value is the base for analysing the capital structure of the company in terms of debt-equity ratio.

In spite of the operational difficulties of market value weights (particularly the market value of retained earnings) in comparison with book value weights, the former are theoretically consistent and sound. Thus market value weights may be used as better indicators of the company's cost of capital.

According to Gitman*, as retained earnings are treated as equity capital for computing cost of specific sources of funds, the market value of equity shares may be considered as the combined market value of both equity shares and retained earnings. Individual market value (equity shares and retained earnings) may also be found out by allocating each of the percentage share of the total market value equal to their respective percentage share of the total values.

ILLUSTRATION 7.16

From the information mentioned in the Illustration 7.15, compute the weighted average cost of capital taking into account that the market value of various sources of funds are as follows:

---

*Gitman, L.J., *Principles of Managerial Finance*, Harper & Row, 1976, p. 353.

Sources	Market Value Rs.
Debt	2,50,000
Preference Shares	4,50,000
Equity and Retained Earnings	10,00,000

Solution

A sum of Rs. 10,00,000 may be allocated between equity share capital and retained earnings as follows:

Sources (a)	Book Value Rs. (b)	Percentage (%) (c)	Market Value Rs. (d)
Equity Shares	6,00,000	$\dfrac{6,00,000}{8,00,000} \times 100 = 75\%$	$10,00,000 \times 75\% = 7,50,000$
Retained Earnings	2,00,000	$\dfrac{2,00,000}{8,00,000} \times 100 = 25\%$	$1,00,000 \times 25\% = 2,50,000$

Thus after computing the market value, weighed average cost of capital is ascertained as follows.

Computation of Weighted Average Cost of Capital
(Market Value Weights)

Sources (a)	Market Value Rs. (b)	Cost Rs. (c)	Total Cost Rs. (d) b × c
Debt	2,50,000	4.00%	10,000
Preference Share	4,50,000	11.50%	51,750
Equity Share Capital	7,50,000	15.50%	1,16,250
Retained Earnings	2,50,000	14.50%	36,250
	17,00,000		2,14,250

Weighted Average Cost of Capital $= \dfrac{2,14,250}{17,00,000} = 12.60\%$

(iii) Marginal Value Weights

Under this method, weights are assigned to each source of funds in proportions of financing inputs the firm intends to employ. This method is based on a logic that the firm is with the new or incremental capital and not with capital raised in the past.

Usually, a firm should provide utmost care to long-term implications while framing its financing strategy. However, under marginal weighing the firm does not consider the long-term implications of its current financing. For instance, a firm may accept a project giving an after-tax return of 9% as it intends to raise the funds required by issue of debentures having an after-tax cost of 8%. In the coming year, if the firm intends to raise funds by issue of equity shares having a cost of 12%, it will have to reject a project which gives a return of only 11%. Thus, marginal weighting method does not consider the fact that to-day's financing affects tomorrow's cost. Moreover, in case only a single source is being employed in lieu of a number of sources, the application of marginal weights for calculating weighted average cost will be of no use.

ILLUSTRATION 7.17

The cost of capital (after tax) of a firm of the specific sources is as follows:

Cost of Debt	4.00%
Cost of Preference Shares	11.50%
Cost of Equity Capital	15.50%
Cost or Retained Earnings	14.50% (assuming external yield criterion)

Capital Structures are:

Sources	Amount Rs.
Debt	3,00,000
Preference Share Capital	4,00,000
Equity Share Capital	6,00,000
Cost of Retained Earning	2,00,000
	15,00,000

The firm desires to raise Rs. 6,00,000 for extending its plant capacity. It also estimates that Rs. 2,00,000 may be utilised from retained earnings and Rs. 4,00,000 may be raised as follows.

	Rs.
Long-term Debt	1,50,000
Preference Shares	2,50,000

Calculate the weighted average cost of capital after applying marginal weight.

Solution

Weighted Average Cost of Capital
(Marginal Weights)

Sources (a)	Amount (b)	Proportion (c)		Cost (d)	Total Cost (e) = (c) × (d)
Debt	1,50,000	0.25	25.00%	4.00%	1.00
Preference Share	2,50,000	0.42	41.67%	11.50%	4.83
Retained Earnings	2,00,000	0.33	33.33%	14.50%	4.79
	6,00,000	1.00	(100%)		10.62%

Weighted average Cost of capital 10.62%

This weighted average cost under marginal weight is substantially lower than that of under the book value and market value weights. This is simply on account of the use of large scale preference capital. Moreover, the above computed average cost of capital would have even been lower than the present one if 'debt' had been used at a large amount as its interest rate is very low.

ILLUSTRATION 7.18

Your company's share is quoted in the market at Rs. 20 currently. The company pays a dividend of Rs. 1 per share and the investor expects a growth rate of 5% per year.

Compute:

(a) the company's cost of equity capital;

(b) if the anticipated growth rate is 6% p.a., calculate the indicated market price per share;

(c) if the company's cost of capital is 8% and the anticipated growth rate is 5% p.a., calculate the indicated market price if the dividend of Rs. 1 per share is to be maintained.

(ICWA Final, June 1980)

Solution

The relationship among cost of capital, dividend, price and expected growth rate is given by the formula:

(a) Cost of Equity Capital

$$= \frac{\text{Dividend Per Share}}{\text{Current Market Price}} \times 100 + \text{Growth Rate (\%)}$$

$$= \frac{\text{Rs. 1}}{20} \times 100 + 5\% = 5\% + 5\%$$

$$= 10\%$$

(b) Market price

$$= \frac{\text{Dividend Per Share}}{\text{Cost of Equity Capital} - \text{Growth Rate (\%)}}$$

$$= \frac{\text{Rs. 1}}{10\% - 6\%} = \frac{\text{Rs. 1}}{4\%} = \text{Rs. 25}$$

(c) Market price

$$= \frac{\text{Rs. 1}}{8\% - 5\%} = \frac{\text{Rs. 1}}{3\%} = \text{Rs. 33.33}$$

ILLUSTRATION 7.19

The particulars about the existing capital structure of AB Ltd. are given:

	Amount Rs.	Before-tax Cost (%)
Equity Share Capital	8,00,000	12%
Preference Share Capital	1,00,000	7%
Long-term Debt	6,00,000	8%

The company wants to undertake an expansion project costing Rs. 5,00,000 which can be taken from a bank at 10%. The minimum acceptable rate of return from the new project is based on the company's cost of capital. What is the minimum acceptable rate of return to the company in the case of the proposed expansion projects? You may assume a 50% tax rate.

Solution

The minimum acceptable rate of return of an expansion project should be based on the cost of capital of the company. In this case, the weighted average cost is to be computed which is given below:

Weighted Average Cost (after tax)

Sources	Amount Rs.	Capital Structure Proportion (Weights)	Weighted Average Cost		
			Before-tax cost (%)	Before-tax (%)	After-tax (%)
Equity Share Capital	8,00,000	0.40	12	4.80	4.80
Preference Share Capital	1,00,000	0.05	7	0.35	0.35
Long-term Debt Existing	6,00,000	0.30	8	2.40	1.20
New	5,00,000	0.25	10	2.50	1.25
	20,00,000	1.00		10.05	7.60

∴ The minimum acceptable rate of return from the new project would be 7.6%.

ILLUSTRATION 7.20

The capital structure of a Limited company is as follows:

	Rs.
Equity Share Capital (1,00,000 Shares)	20,00,000
5% Preference Shares	5,00,000
6% Debentures	15,00,000
	40,00,000

The market price of the company's equity share is Rs. 20. It is expected that the company will pay a current dividend of Rs. 3 per share which will grow at 8 per cent for ever. The tax rate may be presumed at 50 per cent. Calculate the following:

(a) A weighted average cost of capital based on existing capital structure.

(b) The new weighted average cost of capital in case the company raises an additional Rs. 10,00,000 debt by issuing 8 per cent debentures. This would result in increasing the expected dividend to Rs. 4 and leave the growth rate unchanged but the price will fall to Rs. 15 per share.

(c) The cost of capital if in (b) above, growth rate increases to 10 per cent.

Solution

(a) Statement Showing Weighted Average Cost of Capital

	Amount Rs.	After-tax Cost	Weights	Weighted Cost
Equity Share Capital*	20,00,000	0.23	0.500	0.1150
Preference Share Capital	5,00,000	0.05	0.125	0.0063
Debentures	15,00,000	0.03	0.375	0.0113
Weighted Average Cost of Capital (K_e)			13.26% or	0.1326

*The Cost of Equity Shares is:

$$K_e = \frac{D}{P} + g = \frac{3}{20} + 0.08 = 0.15 + 0.08 = 0.23 \text{ or } 23\%$$

(b) Statement Showing Weighted Average Cost of Capital

	Amount Rs.	After-tax Cost	Weights	Weighted Cost
Equity Share Capital*	20,00,000	0.35	0.40	0.140
5% Preference Share Capital	5,00,000	0.05	0.10	0.005
6% Debentures	15,00,000	0.03	0.30	0.009
8% Debentures	10,00,000	0.04	0.20	0.008
Weighted Average Cost of Capital (K_e)				0.162
				or 16.20 %

*Cost of Equity Shares is:

$$K_e = \frac{D}{P} + g = \frac{Rs.\,4}{Rs.\,15} + 0.08 = 0.27 + 0.08 = 0.35 \text{ or } 35\%$$

(c) Statement Showing Weighted Average Cost of Capital

	Amount Rs.	After-tax Cost	Weights	Weighted Cost
Equity Share Capital*	20,00,000	0.37	0.40	0.148
5% Preference Share Capital	5,00,000	0.05	0.10	0.005
6% Debentures	15,00,000	0.03	0.30	0.009
8% Debentures	10,00,000	0.04	0.20	0.008
Weighted Average Cost of Capital (K_e)				0.170
				or 17%

*Cost of Equity Shares is:

$$K_e = \frac{D}{P} + g = \frac{Rs.\,4}{Rs.\,15} + 0.10 = 0.27 + 0.10 = 0.37 \text{ or } 37\%$$

ILLUSTRATION 7.21

The following information is available from the Balance Sheet of 'Z' Ltd.

	Rs.
Equity Share Capital	
30,000 Shares of Rs. 10 each	3,00,000
Reserves and Surplus	2,00,000
10% Debentures	2,00,000

The rate of tax of the company is 50%. Current level of equity dividend is 15%. Compute the Weighted Average Cost of Capital using the above figure.

Solution

Statement Showing the Weighted Average Cost of Capital

Sources	Amount Rs.	Capital Structure Proportion (Weight)	Before-tax Cost (%)	After-tax Cost (%)	Weighted Average Cost (after-tax) (%)
Equity (including Reserves & Surplus)	5,00,000	0.71	8.99%	8.99%	6.38
Debentures	2,00,000	0.29	10%	5%	1.48
	7,00,000	1.00			7.86%

∴ Weighted Average Cost of Capital is 7.86%.

$$\text{Value per share} = \frac{\text{Rs. } 5,00,000}{30,000} = \text{Rs. } 16.67$$

$$\text{Cost of Equity} = \frac{15}{\text{Rs. } 16.67} \times 100 = 8.99\%$$

(Since rate of dividend is 15%)

CASE STUDY

Cost of Capital Analysis of Larsen & Toubro Limited (L&T)

The capital structure of L&T has been analysed in Chapter 5. In this section, the cost of capital L&T shall be analysed.

The capital structure of L&T for the year 2004–05 is shown in Table 7.1.

The average market price of L&T's one share was Rs. 900. The market value of the company's equity is obtained by multiplying the number of the outstanding shares (13 crore) by the average share price. However, the market value of debt is assumed to be equal to the book value.

TABLE 7.1 L&T's Capital Structure in 2004–05

Sources of Capital	Book value (BV) Rs. crore	BV Weights Proportion	Market Value Rs. crore	MV Weights Proportion
Short-term debt	1660.90	0.31	1660.90	0.13
Long-term debt	293.10	0.06	293.10	0.02
Total debt	1954.00	0.37	1954.00	0.15
Net worth	3369.00	0.63	11700.00	0.85
Total Capital	5,323.00	1.00	13,654.00	1.00

Source: Annual Return

Estimation of L&T's Cost of Equity

The formula for ascertaining the cost of equity is:

$$K_e = \frac{D}{P} + g$$

where,

K_e = Cost of equity share capital
D = Dividend per share
P = Net proceeds per share
g = Expected growth in dividends.

L&T's dividend yield in 2004–05 is 3.5%. The dividend yield of the company has varied between 1.5 per cent to 3.5 per cent with an average yield of 2.2 per cent. It is assumed that the current dividend yield of 3.5 per cent is a fair approximation of L&T's expected yield.

Estimation of Growth Rate

Growth may be approximated by ascertaining the product of retention ratio and return on equity (ROE).

$$g = \text{Retention ratio} \times \text{ROE}$$

L&T's payout ratio has fluctuated over years. However, on an average, it has distributed about 45 per cent of its net profit and retained 55 per cent in the past decade. In the most recent period, 2004–05 about 59 per cent of its profit. The ROE of L&T in 2004–05 is 30.6 per cent and ten year average is 17.9 per cent. Assuming that the current retention ratio of 59 per cent and ROE of 30.6 per cent will continue in the future, then the dividend of L&T is expected to grow at 18.1 per cent per year.

$$g = \text{Retention ratio} \times \text{ROE}$$
$$= 0.59 \times 0.306 = 0.181 \text{ or } 18.1\%$$

Thus K_e or cost of equity of L&T is current dividend yield + growth rate i.e., 3.5% + 18.1% = 21.6%.

Table 7.2 shows data on L&T's EPS, DPS, payout, average price, dividend yield, earnings yield, price to book value per share and ROE during 1995–96 to 2004–05.

TABLE 7.2 L&T's Financial Data from 1995–96 to 2004–05

Year	EPS (Rs.)	DPS (Rs.)	Average Share Price (Rs.)	Book Value Per Share	Dividend Payout Ratio (%)	Dividend yield (%)	Earnings yield (%)	ROE (%)
1995–1996	16.88	6.00	262.00	112.67	0.355	0.023	0.065	0.150
1996–1997	16.55	6.00	260.00	122.04	0.363	0.023	0.064	0.136
1997–1998	21.39	6.50	280.00	134.99	0.304	0.023	0.076	0.158
1998–1999	18.94	6.50	300.50	146.48	0.343	0.022	0.063	0.129
1999–2000	13.74	6.50	290.00	152.13	0.473	0.023	0.047	0.090
2000–2001	25.34	6.50	450.00	157.31	0.257	0.015	0.056	0.161
2001–2002	27.90	7.00	480.00	130.25	0.251	0.015	0.058	0.214
2002–2003	34.83	8.50	500.00	139.15	0.244	0.017	0.700	0.250
2003–2004	42.82	18.00	700.50	216.74	0.420	0.026	0.061	0.198
2004–2005	77.62	31.00	900.00	253.91	0.399	0.035	0.086	0.306
Average	29.60	10.25	442.30	156.57	0.341	0.022	0.065	0.179

Source: L&T's Annual Return

L&T's Cost of Debt

L&T's debt consists of both short-term and long-term debt. It has also current liabilities such as creditors. Should it be included in the calculation of the weighted cost of capital? There is no unanimity on this issue. So current liabilities have been ignored from the computation of L&T's cost of capital.

L&T's debt comprise 85 per cent short-term and 15 per cent long-term debt. In India, bank borrowings and other short-term debts cost about 12 per cent and long-term debt about 10 per cent. It is assumed that L&T will incur these costs in obtaining debt in the future. Moreover, if it is assumed that L&T's short-term debt will continue to be 85 per cent and long-term debt 15 per cent and that corporate tax rate will be 35 per cent, then the after tax weighted marginal cost of its debt will be:

Weighted cost of debt
$$= 0.12(1 - 0.35) \times 0.85 + 0.10(1 - 0.35) \times 0.15$$
$$= 0.0663 + 0.0098$$
$$= 0.761 \text{ or approximately } 7.6\%$$

L&T's Weighted Average Cost of Capital

L&T's cost of equity and debt has already been estimated. The weighted average cost of capital of L&T can be ascertained, if its target capital structure is known. The target capital structure may be expressed in terms of book value or market value. Further, if it is assumed that L&T will maintain its current capital structure in the future, then its weighted average cost of capital will be as follows.

Source of Capital	Cost of Capital	Weight		Weighted Cost	
		BV	MV	BV	MV
Equity	0.216	0.63	0.85	0.136	0.184
Debt	0.076	0.37	0.15	0.028	0.011
Total				0.164	0.195

L&T's weighted average cost of capital is approximately 16 per cent if book value weights are considered and 19 per cent if market value weights are taken. Since the market value of L&T's equity is greater than the book value, the market value weighted average cost of capital is more than the book value weighted average cost of capital.

– REVIEW QUESTIONS –

1. What is cost of capital? What is meant by "explicit cost" and real cost of capital?

   (M.Com., Calcutta, 1979)

2. What do you understand by cost of capital? How is it ascertained?

   (M.Com., Calicut, 1982)

3. (a) What is the relevance of cost of capital in corporate investment and financing decisions?

   (b) Examine the problems in the determination of composite cost of capital.

   (C.A. Final, June 1985)

4. Discuss briefly the different approaches to the computation of the cost of equity capital.

   (C.A. Final, Nov. 1989)

5. Explain how the cost of retained earnings is determined where such retained earnings are proposed to be distributed as bonus shares or right shares to the existing shareholders.

   (C.S. Final, Dec. 1989)

6. (i) Explain the rationale of using weighted cost of capital.

   (ii) Why is it that the 'debt' is the cheapest source of finance for a profit making company?

7. What is meant by cost of capital for a firm? How is it calculated with different types of sources of capital funds?

8. Write short notes on:

   (a) Cost of Capital

   (b) Marginal Cost of Capital

   (c) Modigliani-Miller approach.

9. What are the components of cost of capital? How is the cost of new equity issue determined?

10. The following particulars about the existing structure of 'X' Company Limited are given below:

	Amount Rs.	Before-tax Cost (%)
Equity Share Capital	4,00,000	12%
Preference Share Capital	50,000	7%
Long-term Debt	3,00,000	8%

The company wants to undertake an expansion project costing Rs. 2,50,000 which can be taken from a financial institution at 10%. The minimum acceptable rate of return from the new project is based on the company's cost of capital. What is the minimum acceptable rate of return to the company in the case of the proposed expansion projects? You may assume a 50% tax rate.

(Ans: 7.6%)

11. From the following capital structure of a company, calculate the overall cost of capital, using (a) book value weights and (b) market Value Weights.

Source	Book Value	Market Value
Equity Capital (Rs. 10 Shares)	45,000	90,000
Retained Earnings	15,000	
Preference Share Capital	10,000	10,000
Debentures	30,000	30,000

The after-tax cost of different sources of finance is as follows:

Equity share capital: 14%; Retained earnings: 13%; Preference share capital: 10%; Debentures: 5%.

(Ans: (a) 10.75%, (b) 11.61%)

12. Gopal Industries Ltd. has assets of Rs. 1,60,000 which have been financed with Rs. 52,000 of debt and Rs. 90,000 of equity and a general reserve of Rs. 18,000. The firm's total profits after interest and taxes for the year ended 31st March, 1988 were Rs. 13,500. It pays 8% interest on borrowed funds and is in the 50% tax bracket. It has 900 equity shares of Rs. 100 each selling at a market price of Rs. 120 per share. What is the weighted average cost of capital?

(M.Com, Delhi, 1978)

(Ans: 9.74% approximate.)

13. X purchased 5 shares in a company at a cost of Rs. 240 on January 1, 1996. He held them for 5 years and finally sold them in January, 2001 for Rs. 300. The amount in each of these 5 years was as follows:

1996	Rs.	14
1997	Rs.	14
1998	Rs.	14.50
1999	Rs.	14.50
2000	Rs.	145.50

Calculate the cost of equity capital according to realised yield approach.

(Ans: 10%)

14. From the following details of AB Limited, compute the cost of equity capital under the dividend price plus growth approach.

(i) Each share is of Rs. 150 each.

(ii) The undertaking cost per share amount to 2%.

(iii) The following are the dividends paid by the company for the last five years:

Year	Dividend per Share
1997	10.50
1998	11.00
1999	12.50
2000	12.75
2001	13.40

(iv) The company has a fixed dividend pay out ratio.

(v) The expected dividend on the new shares amounts to Rs. 14.10 per share.

(**Ans:** 15.6%)

15. A firm issues debentures of Rs. 1,00,000 and realises Rs. 98,000 after allowing 2% commission to brokers. The debentures carry on interest rate of 10%. The debentures are due for maturity at the end of the 10th year. Compute the effective cost of debt before tax.

(**Ans:** 0.103 or 10.3%)

16. A company raised preference share capital of Rs. 1,00,000 by issue of 10% preference shares of Rs. 10 each. Compute the cost of preference capital when they are issued (i) 10% premium and (ii) at 10% discount.

(**Ans:** (i) 9.09% (ii) 11.11%)

17. Your company's share is quoted in the market at Rs. 20 currently. The company pays a dividend of Rs. 1 per share and the investor expects a growth rate of 5% per year. Calculate:

(a) the company's cost of equity capital.

(b) if the anticipated growth rate is 6% p.a, calculate the indicated market price per share.

(c) if the company's cost of capital is 8% and the anticipated growth rate is 5% p.a, compute the indicated market price if the dividend of Rs. 1 per share is to be maintained.

(**Ans:** (a) 10%, (b) Rs. 25, (c) Rs. 33.33)

18. The following information is available from the Balance Sheet of XY Limited company.

Equity Share Capital	Rs.
20,000 Shares of Rs. 10 each	2,00,000
Reserves & Surplus	1,30,000
8% Debentures	1,70,000

The rate of tax of the company is 50%. Current level of equity dividend is 12%. Compute the weighted Average Cost of Capital using the above figure.

(I.C.W.A. – Final New)

(**Ans:** Weighted Average Cost of Capital: 6.16%
Value per share: Rs. 16.5
Cost of Equity: 7.27%)

8

Leverages

*Leverage is "the employment of an asset or funds for
which the firm pay a fixed cost of fixed return".*

— JAMES HORNE

CONTENTS

- Meaning of leverage
- Types of leverages
- Case study
- Review questions

Since, the financing or capital structure decision affects the debt-equity mix of the firm, leverage is of vital significance for the management. In this chapter, the discussion is earmarked to know the impact of debt-equity mix on the shareholders' earnings and risk. However, the concept of leverage assists in analysing this aspect.

MEANING OF LEVERAGE

Lever means a bar resting on a pivot which is used to raise a heavier object. When a lever is used properly, a force applied at one point is transformed, or magnified, into another larger force or motion at some other point. In short, the function of lever is to raise a heavy object with a minimum force. The same principle is also applied in business. Thus in a business context, leverage refers to the use of fixed costs in an attempt to increase (or lever up) profitability. According to James Horne, leverage is "the employment of assets or funds for which the firm pays a fixed cost or fixed return".

However, the quantum of fixed costs or returns have considerable impact over the amount of profits available for the shareholders as these are required to be paid or incurred irrespective of the volume of output or sales. When the volume of sales varies, leverage helps in quantifying such influence. Thus there is a relative change in profits on account of a change in sales. Usually, a leverage happens in varying degrees. A high degree of leverage indicates that there will be a large change in profits on account of a relatively small change in sales and vice-versa. Thus, the greater the leverage, the greater are the profits and vice-versa. But a greater leverage obviously implies larger outside borrowings and thereby riskier if the business activity of the firm suddenly takes a dip. On the other hand, a low leverage does not necessarily indicate prudent financial management as the firm might be incurring an opportunity cost for not having borrowed funds at a fixed cost to earn higher profits.

TYPES OF LEVERAGES

There are three types of leverages. They are (i) Operating leverage, (ii) Financial leverage, and (iii) Composite leverage.

1. Operating Leverage

Operating leverage refers to the use of fixed costs in the operation of a firm. If a firm's ratio of fixed costs to total cost is nil, it should not have operating leverage. The operating leverage may be defined as the tendency of the operating profit to vary disproportionately with sales. Thus operating leverage appears from the existence of fixed operating expenses. In other words, operating leverage is the firm's ability to use fixed operating costs to magnify the effect of change in sales on its earnings before interest and tax (EBIT). Usually, the operating expenses of a firm comprise: (i) fixed cost—which remains fixed irrespective of the volume of output (ii) variable cost—which varies directly with volume of sales, and (iii) semi-variable cost—which is partly fixed and partly variable.

A firm's operating leverage is a function of three factors, i.e., (i) the amount of fixed costs, (ii) the contribution margin and (iii) the volume of sales. Thus operating leverage is:

$$\frac{\text{Contribution}}{\text{Operating Profit}} \quad \text{or} \quad \frac{C}{OP}$$

Operating profit here means "Earnings Before Interest and Tax" (EBIT).

Operating leverage is either favourable or adverse. It is said to be favourable, if the contribution is more than the fixed cost. In the opposite case, the operating leverage is termed as adverse.

Degree of Operating Leverage

It is defined as the percentage change in the profits resulting from a percentage change in the sales. In other words, the degree of operating leverage

$$= \frac{\text{Percentage Change in Profits}}{\text{Percentage Change in Sales}}$$

A firm should have a high degree of operating leverage in case it employs a large amount of fixed cost and a small amount of variable cost. On the other hand, a firm is said to have a low degree of operating leverage if it incurs a large amount of variable cost and a small amount of fixed cost. A firm's small change in sales should have a large impact on its operating income if it has a high degree of operating leverage. In other words, the operating profits (EBIT) of such a firm will go up at a faster rate than the increase in sales. Similarly, the operating profits of such a firm will suffer a heavy loss in comparison with the reduction in its sales.

Usually, a firm does not like to operate under conditions of a high degree of operating leverage. This is mainly due to the fact that a small reduction in sales leads to an excessive damage to the firm's efforts to attain profitability.

The effect of operating leverage can be amplified in the light of the following illustrations:

ILLUSTRATION 8.1

The installed capacity of a manufacturing concern is 1200 units. Actual capacity used is 800 units. Selling price per unit is Rs. 10. Variable cost is Rs. 7 per unit. Compute the operating leverage in the following situations:

1. When fixed cost is Rs. 300
2. When fixed cost is Rs. 800
3. When fixed cost is Rs. 1200

Solution

Statement showing Operating Leverage.

		Situation 1	Situation 2	Situation 3
(i)	Sales	8,000	8,000	8,000
(ii)	Variable Cost	5,600	5,600	5,600
(iii)	Contribution (i) – (ii)	2,400	2,400	2,400
(iv)	Fixed Cost	300	800	1,200
(v)	Operating Profit (iii) – (iv)	2,100	1,600	1,200
(vi)	Operating Leverage C/(OP)	$\frac{2,400}{2,100}$ = 1.14	$\frac{2,400}{1,600}$ = 1.50	$\frac{2,400}{1,200}$ = 2.00

In the light of the above illustration, it is clear that the degree of operating leverage increases with every increase in the share of fixed cost in the total cost structure of the concern. It shows, in the illustration in situation '3' that in case amount of sales changes by one, the profit will change by 2 times. This can be examined by taking situation '3' when sales increase to Rs. 16,000, the profit in such an event will be as under:

	Rs.
Sales	16,000
Variable Cost	11,200
Contribution	4,800
Fixed Cost	1,200
Profit	3,600

The sales have, therefore, enhanced from Rs. 8,000 to Rs. 16,000, i.e., a 100% increase. The operating profit has enhanced from Rs. 1,200 to Rs. 3,600 i.e., by Rs. 2,400 (giving an increase of 200%). The operating leverage is '2' in the case of situation '3'. This implies that if amount of sales changes by one, the profit will be change by 2 times. This has been verified by the above illustration where a 100% increase in sales has resulted in 200 per cent increase in profits. Thus the degree of operating leverage is as under:

$$\frac{\text{Percentage change in Operating Income}}{\text{Percentage change in Sales}} = \frac{200}{100} = 2$$

However, in fact, the operating leverage exists only when the quotient in the above equation is more than one.

ILLUSTRATION 8.2

	Companies		
	X	**Y**	**Z**
Fixed Costs	Rs. 1,00,000	Rs. 3,00,000	Rs. 4,75,000
Variable Costs per Unit	Rs. 6	Rs. 5	Rs. 4
Selling Price	Rs. 10	Rs. 10	Rs. 10

Compute:

(a) BEP (Break-Even Points) to all the companies.

(b) Profit earned by the companies if each of them sells 1,50,000 units.

(c) What will be the effect of profit in case:

  (i) sales increase by 30%

  (ii) sales decrease by 30%

Solution

(a) BEP for each company

$$\text{BEP} = \frac{\text{Fixed Costs}}{\text{Contribution (Sales} - \text{Variable Costs)}}$$

For Company 'X' = $\dfrac{1,00,000}{10-6} = \dfrac{1,00,000}{4}$ = 25,000 units.

For Company 'Y' = $\dfrac{3,00,000}{10-5} = \dfrac{3,00,000}{5}$ = 60,000 units.

For Company 'Z' = $\dfrac{4,75,000}{10-4} = \dfrac{4,75,000}{6}$ = 79,167 units.

(b) Computation of profit if the companies sell 1,50,000 units.

		Companies	
	X	Y	Z
Units sold	1,50,000	1,50,000	1,50,000
Contributions	(Rs. 10 – 6)	(Rs. 10 – 5)	(Rs. 10 – 4)
(S – V)	= Rs. 4	= Rs. 5	= Rs. 6
Total Sales (Units × per unit)	15,00,000	15,00,000	15,00,000
Less: Variable Cost	9,00,000	7,50,000	6,00,000
Contribution	6,00,000	7,50,000	9,00,000
Less: Fixed Costs	1,00,000	3,00,000	4,75,000
Profit	5,00,000	4,50,000	4,25,000

(c) Effect of profit when sales increase by 30%

	X	Y	Z
Units Sold 1,50,000 + 30%	1,95,000	1,95,000	1,95,000
	Rs.	Rs.	Rs.
Contribution	4	5	6
Total Sales	19,50,000	19,50,000	19,50,000
Less: Variable Cost	11,70,000	9,75,000	7,80,000
Contribution	7,80,000	9,75,000	11,70,000
Less: Fixed Cost	1,00,000	3,00,000	4,75,000
Profit	6,80,000	6,75,000	6,95,000
Increase in Profit	1,80,000	2,25,000	2,70,000
Percentage increase in Sales	30%	30%	30%
Percentage increase in Profit	$\dfrac{1,80,000 \times 100}{5,00,000}$	$\dfrac{2,25,000 \times 100}{4,50,000}$	$\dfrac{2,70,000 \times 100}{4,25,000}$
	= 36%	= 50%	= 63.53%

(ii) Effect of profit when sales decrease by 30%

	X	Y	Z
Units Sold (1,50,000 – 30%)	1,05,000	1,05,000	1,05,000
	Rs.	Rs.	Rs.
Contribution	4	5	6
Total Sales	10,50,000	10,50,000	10,50,000
Less: Variable Cost	6,30,000	5,25,000	4,20,000
Contribution	4,20,000	5,25,000	6,30,000
Less: Fixed Cost	1,00,000	3,00,000	4,75,000
Profit	3,20,000	2,25,000	1,55,000
Decrease in Profit	3,60,000	4,50,000	5,40,000
Percentage decrease in Sales	30%	30%	30%
Percentage decrease in Profit	$\dfrac{3,60,000 \times 100}{5,00,000}$	$\dfrac{4,50,000 \times 100}{4,50,000}$	$\dfrac{5,40,000 \times 100}{4,25,000}$
	= 72%	= 100%	= 127.06%

2. *Financial Leverage*

Financial leverage is the use of fixed financing costs by the firm. The British expression of financial leverage is gearing. Thus the use of fixed interest/dividend bearing securities such as debt and preference capital along with the owner's equity in the total capital structure of the company is described as financial leverage. The leveraage is said to be high when the fixed interest/dividend bearing securities are more than the equity capital in the capital structure of the company.

In such a case, the interest payment and dividends could drastically decrease the pool available to the ordinary shareholders and their earnings per share falls. This is shown in Figure 8.1.

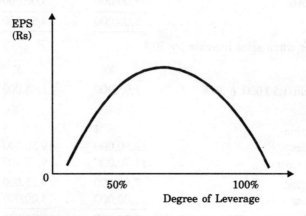

FIGURE 8.1 The relationship between EPS and Leverage.

In the opposite case, the leverage is said to be small.

Trading on Equity and Financial Leverage

Sometimes, financial leverage is also known as trading on equity. But the term trading on equity is used for the term financial leverage only when the financial leverage is favourable. The leverage is said to be favourable so long as the company earns more on assets purchased with the funds than the fixed costs of their use. But negative or unfavourable leverage occurs when the firm does not earn as much as the funds cost.

The company resorts to trading on equity for providing the equity shareholders, a higher rate of return than the general rate of earning on its capital employed. For instance, in case a company borrows a sum of Rs. 1 lakh at 10% interest per annum, and earns a return of 15%, the balance of Rs. 5,000 per annum after payment of interest belongs to the shareholders. Thus the company can pay a higher rate of return than its general rate of earning to the shareholders. But if the company can earn a return of only 8% on Rs. 1 lakh employed by it, the loss of equity shareholders' is Rs. 2,000 per annum. Thus it is clear that although financial leverage creates additional risk to equity shareholders, it has at the same time the potentiality to enhancing their return. That is why the financial leverage is sometimes called a double-edged sword.

Computation

The following are the various methods of computing financial leverage.

(i) When capital structure comprises equity share and debt:

In such a situation, the formula used for calculating financial leverage is:

$$\frac{OP}{PBT}$$

where

OP = Operating profit or earnings before interest and tax (EBIT)

PBT = Profit before tax but after interest

ILLUSTRATION 8.3

A firm has a choice of the following three financial plans. Compute the financial leverage in each situation and interpret it.

	A Rs.	B Rs.	C Rs.
Equity Capital	4,000	2,000	6,000
Debt	4,000	6,000	2,000
Operating Profit (EBIT)	800	800	800

Interest @10% on debt in all situations.

Solution

The computation of financial leverage in all these three situations is as follows:

	A Rs.	B Rs.	C Rs.
Operating Profit (OP)	800	800	800
Interest (10% on Debt)	400	600	200
Profit Before Tax (PBT)	400	200	600
Financial Leverage $\left(\dfrac{OP}{PBT}\right)$	$\dfrac{800}{400}=2$	$\dfrac{800}{200}=4$	$\dfrac{800}{600}=1.33$

Financial leverage indicates the change that will take place in the taxable income on account of change in the operating income. For instance, considering the situation 'A' as the basis, in case the operating profit reduces to Rs. 400, its effect on taxable income is as follows:

Operating Profit (OP or EBIT)	Rs.	400
Less: Interest		400
Profit Before Tax (PBT)		Nil

Financial leverage in situation 'A' is '2'. It indicates that every 1% change in operating profit results in 2% change in the taxable profit. In the above situation operating profit has reduced from Rs. 800 to Rs. 400 (i.e., 50% reduce). As a result the taxable profit has reduced from Rs. 400 to zero. (i.e., 100% reduce).

Degree of Financial Leverage

The degree of financial leverage is the percentage change in taxable profit as a result of percentage change in operating profit. It is the ability of the firm to utilize fixed financial charges in order to magnify the effect of changes in EBIT on EPS of the company.

This may be computed with the help of the following equation. However, financial leverage exists only when the quotient is more than one.

$$\text{Degree of Financial Leverage (DFL)} = \frac{\text{Percentage change in Taxable Income}}{\text{Percentage change in the Operating Income}}$$

For instance, in the above case, the degree of financial leverage is '2'. This is computed as under:

$$\frac{100}{50} = 2$$

(ii) Where the capital structure consists of preference shares and equity shares.

The formula for ascertaining financial leverage can also be used in a financial plan having preference shares. In such a case, the amount of preference dividends should be grossed up (as per the tax rate applicable to the company) and then deducted from the earnings before interest and tax.

ILLUSTRATION 8.4

A firm's capital structure comprises the following securities.

10% Preference Share Capital	Rs. 2,00,000
Equity Share Capital (Rs. 10 shares)	Rs. 2,00,000

The operating profit of the firm is Rs. 80,000. The firm is in 50% tax bracket.
Compute the financial leverage of the firm.
What would be the new financial leverage in case the operating profit enhances to Rs. 1,00,000 and interpret your results.

Solution

Calculation of the Present Financial Leverage

Operating Profit (OP or EBIT)	80,000
Less: Preference Dividend (after grossing up)	40,000
PBT	Rs. 40,000

$$\text{Present Financial Leverage} = \frac{\text{OP}}{\text{PBT}}$$

$$= \frac{80,000}{40,000} = 2$$

Calculation of New Financial Leverage

New Operating Profit	1,00,000
Less: Preference Dividend (after grossing up)	40,000
PBT	Rs. 60,000

$$\text{Financial Leverage} = \frac{\text{OP}}{\text{PBT}}$$

$$= \frac{1,00,000}{60,000} = 1.67$$

The firm's existing financial leverage is '2'. It implies that 1% change in operating profit (OP or EBIT) will lead to 2% change in taxable profit (PBT) in the same direction. For instance, in the present case, operating profit has enhanced by 25% (i.e., from Rs. 80,000 to Rs. 1,00,000). This has resulted in 50% increase in the taxable profit (i.e., from Rs. 40,000 to Rs. 60,000).

(iii) Where the capital structure comprises of equity shares, preference shares and debt.

The financial leverage of a firm in such a case is computed after deducting both interest and preference dividend from operating profit on a before tax basis.

ILLUSTRATION 8.5

A firm's capital structure comprises the following securities:

	Rs.
Equity Share Capital (Rs. 10 shares)	2,00,000
10% Preference Share Capital	2,00,000
9% Debentures	2,50,000

The present EBIT is Rs. 1,00,000. Assuming that the firm is in 50% tax bracket, compute the financial leverage.

Solution

		Rs.
Operating Profit		1,00,000
Less: Interest on Debentures	22,500	
Preference Dividend (pre-tax basis)	40,000	62,500
Profit Before-Tax		37,500

$$\text{Financial Leverage} = \frac{\text{OP}}{\text{PBT}}$$

$$= \frac{1,00,000}{37,500} = 2.67$$

Alternative Definition of Financial Leverage

According to Gitman, financial leverage is "the ability of a firm to use fixed financial charges to magnify the effects of change in EBIT on the firm's earning per share". Thus financial leverage is the relationship between EBIT and EPS. In this sense, a firm should frame its capital structure with a view to maximising the earnings per share (EPS).

As per the above meaning, the degree of financial leverage can be computed by using the following equation:

$$\text{Degree of financial leverage} = \frac{\text{Percentage change in EPS}}{\text{Percentage change in EBIT}}$$

However, financial leverage exists only if the quotient exceeds one, in the equation.

Alternative Approach:

$$\text{Degree of Financial Leverage (DFL)} = \frac{\text{EBIT}}{\text{EBIT} - \text{I}}$$

where,

I = Fixed Interest Charges.

$$\therefore \text{DFL} = \frac{\text{EBIT}}{\text{EBT}}$$

There will be no financial leverage as per the above equation if the quotient does not exceed one.

The above DFL equation can better be understood in the light of the following illustration:

ILLUSTRATION 8.6

Capital Structure

	Rs.
10,000 Equity Share of Rs. 10 each	1,00,000
10% 500, Debenture of Rs. 100 each	50,000
EBIT	40,000
Compute DFL	

Solution

$$\text{DFL} = \frac{\text{EBIT}}{\text{EBIT} - \text{I}} = \frac{40,000}{40,000 - 5,000}$$

$$= \frac{40,000}{35,000} = 1.14$$

ILLUSTRATION 8.7

The capital structure of a firm is as under:

	Rs.
20,000 Equity Shares of Rs. 10 each	2,00,000
4,000 10% Preference Shares of Rs. 100 each	4,00,000
4,000 10% Debentures of Rs. 100 each	4,00,000

Compute the EPS for each of the following levels of EBIT:

(i) 1,50,000 (ii) 1,20,000 and (iii) 2,00,000

The firm is in 50% tax bracket.
Compute also the financial leverage taking EBIT level under (i) base

Solution

Calculation of Earning per Share

	(i) Rs.	(ii) Rs.	(iii) Rs.
EBIT	1,50,000	1,20,000	2,00,000
Less: Interest on Debentures	40,000	40,000	40,000
PBT	1,10,000	80,000	1,60,000
Less: Income Tax	55,000	40,000	80,000
PAT	55,000	40,000	80,000
Less: Preference Dividend	40,000	40,000	40,000
Earnings available for Equity Shareholders (EAS)	15,000	—	40,000
Earning Per Share (EPS)	0.75	Nil	2

The above table shows that:

(a) In case (ii) the EBIT has reduced by 20% (i.e., from Rs. 1,50,000 to Rs. 1,20,000) while the earning per share has reduced by 100% (from Rs. 0.75 per share to nil).

(b) In case (iii) the EBIT has enhanced by 33.33% (from Rs. 1,50,000 to Rs. 2,00,000) as compared to case (i) while the earning per share has enhanced by 166.67% from Rs. 0.75 to Rs. 2).

Thus the DFL (degree of financial leverage) can be calculated as under:

$$\frac{\text{Percentage change in EPS}}{\text{Percentage change in EBIT}}$$

Financial Leverage in between (i) and (ii) $= \dfrac{100}{20} = 5$

Financial Leverage in between (i) and (iii) $= \dfrac{166.67}{33.33} = 5$

The same result can be obtained by using the equation OP/PBT as under:

Calculation of Financial Leverage

		(i) Rs.	(ii) Rs.	(iii) Rs.
OP		1,50,000	1,20,000	2,00,000
Less: Interest	40,000			
Preference Dividend (grossed up)	80,000			
		1,20,000	1,20,000	1,20,000
PBT		30,000	—	80,000

$$\text{Financial Leverage} = \frac{\text{OP}}{\text{PBT}}$$

$$= \frac{1,50,000}{30,000} = 5$$

This implies that with every 1% change in operating profit (OP), the profit before tax (PBT) will change (in the same direction) by 5%. For instance in case (ii) OP has reduced by 20%. This has resulted in reduction of PBT by 100% (i.e., 20 × 5). In case (iii) OP has enhanced by 33.33%. This has resulted in increase of PBT by 166.67 (i.e., 33.33 × 5).

3. Composite/Combined or Total Leverage

Operating leverage explains the degree of operating risk as it measures the relationship between quantity produced and sold and EBIT. But financial leverage explains the degree of financial risk as it measures the relationship between EPS and EBIT. Thus both these leverages are closely related to the firm's capacity to meet its fixed costs (both, operating and financial). If both these leverages are combined, a composite leverage should be obtained. Composite leverage, therefore, expresses the relationship between quantity produced and sold and EPS. In other words, the effect of combining financial and operating leverages is a two-step magnification of any change in sales into a larger relative change in earnings per share. This can be computed as under:

$$\text{Composite leverage} = \text{Operating leverage} \times \text{Financial leverage} = \frac{C}{\text{OP}} \times \frac{\text{OP}}{\text{PBT}} = \frac{C}{\text{PBT}}$$

where,

      C = Contribution (i.e. sales − variable cost)

   OP = Operating Profit or Earning Before Interest and Tax

PBT = Profit Before Tax but after Interest

The calculation of composite leverage can be explained in the light of the following illustration.

ILLUSTRATION 8.8

A firm's sale is Rs. 2 lakhs. The variable cost is 30% of the sales. The fixed operating cost is Rs. 50,000. The amount of interest on long-term debt is Rs. 15,000.

Compute the composite leverage and illustrate its effects in case sales increase by 10%.

Solution

Statement Showing Calculation of Composite Leverage

		Rs.
Sales		2,00,000
Less:	Variable Costs (30% of Sales)	60,000
	Contribution (C)	1,40,000
Less:	Fixed Operating Cost	50,000
	Earning Before Interest and Tax (EBIT)	
	or Operating Profit (OP)	90,000
Less:	Interest	15,000
	Taxable Income (PBT)	75,000

$$\text{Composite Leverage} = \frac{C}{\text{PBT}} = \frac{1,40,000}{75,000} = 1.87$$

The composite leverage of 1.87 implies that with every change of 1% sales, the taxable income changes by 1.87%.

This can be verified by the following calculations when the sales increase by 10%.

		Rs.
Sales		2,20,000
Less:	Variable Costs	66,000
	Contribution (C)	1,54,000
Less:	Fixed Operating Costs	50,000
	Earning Before Interest and Tax (EBIT) or Operating Profit (OP)	1,04,000
Less:	Interest	15,000
	Taxable Income (PBT)	89,000

The above calculation shows that on account of increase in sales by 10%, the profit before tax has increased by 18.67%. This can be verified as under:

$$\text{Increase in Percentage Profit} = \frac{\text{Increase in Profit}}{\text{Base Profit}} \times 100$$

$$= \frac{14,000}{75,000} \times 100 = 18.67\%.$$

Importance of Operating and Financial Leverage

A firm uses the operating and financial leverages to measure its earning per share and market price of equity shares. However, the financial leverage is considered to be superior to the operating leverage as it focuses the attention on the market price of the shares. Generally, the management always tries to enhance the market price of the shares by enhancing the net worth of the firm. With this end in view, the management resorts to trading on equity because when there is a rise in EBIT there is a corresponding rise in the price of the equity shares. In this connection, it is to be noted that in no case can a firm go beyond a certain point in raising the debt content in the total capital structure. However, in case a firm utilises a larger proportion of debt finance, the marginal cost of the debt rises as the subsequent lenders would like to get higher rate of interest. Moreover, a firm's widely fluctuating income and its inability to offer enough security will also stand in the way of further utilisation of debt finance.

In the light of the above discussion, it is clear that a firm should have a balance of both operating and financial leverages. However, a right combination of these leverages is a big challenge before the management. While an improper combination of both operating and financial leverages may prove to be a curse, a right combination is a blessing for the growth of a firm.

A firm's high degree of operating leverage together with a high degree of financial leverage makes its position very risky as it is employing excessive assets and using a huge amount of debt capital. The fixed costs towards using assets and fixed interest charges bring a high risk to the firm. Usually, the presence of a high degree of operating leverage leads to a greater fluctuations in the earnings of the firm and the existence of a high degree of financial leverage brings a wider fluctuation in the earnings to the shareholders. Moreover, a high degree of operating leverage leads to a more than proportionate variation in operating profits even a minor variation in sale and a high degree of financial leverage results in a more than proportionate change in EPS even a small change in EBIT. Thus, in short, a firm should face the problem of inadequate liquidity or insolvency in one or the other year if its operating and financial leverage is high. However, it does not imply that a firm should opt for low degree of both these leverages. Although such lower leverage is a sign of the firm's cautious policy, it will be losing many profit-earning opportunities. Thus a firm should bring all its efforts for combining the operating and financial leverages in such a way that suits the risk-bearing capacity of the firm.

In the light of the above observations, it is stated that a firm with high operating leverage should have a low financial leverage. On the contrary, a firm with low operating leverage should have a high financial leverage if it has sufficient financial opportunities for the use of debt finance. However, a firm's high financial leverage with low operating leverage is considered to be an ideal situation to maximise its profits with minimum risk.

ILLUSTRATION 8.9

Calculate the degree of operating leverage, degree of financial leverage and the degree of combined leverage for the following firms and interpret the result.

	P	Q	R
Ouput (units)	3,00,000	75,000	5,00,000
Fixed Cost (Rs.)	3,50,000	7,00,000	75,000
Unit Variable Cost (Rs.)	1.00	7.50	0.10
Interest Expenses (Rs.)	25,000	40,000	Nil
Unit Selling Price (Rs.)	3.00	25.00	0.50

(C.A. Final)

Solution

Statement showing the computation of leverage (DOL, DFL and DCL)

		P Rs.	Q Rs.	R Rs.
	Sales	9,00,000	18,75,000	2,50,000
Less:	Variable Cost	3,00,000	5,62,500	50,000
	Contribution	6,00,000	13,12,500	2,00,000
Less:	Fixed Costs	3,50,000	7,00,000	75,000
	Earning Before Interest and Tax (EBIT) or Operating Profit (OP)	2,50,000	6,12,500	1,25,000
Less:	Interest Expenses	25,000	40,000	—
	PBT	2,25,000	5,72,000	1,25,000

1. Degree of Operating Leverage

$$= \frac{C}{OP} \qquad \frac{6,00,000}{2,50,000} = 2.40 \qquad \frac{13,12,500}{6,12,500} = 2.14 \qquad \frac{2,00,000}{1,25,000} = 1.00$$

2. Degree of Financial Leverage

$$\frac{OP}{PBT} \qquad \frac{2,50,000}{2,25,000} = 1.11 \qquad \frac{6,12,500}{5,72,500} = 1.07 \qquad \frac{1,25,000}{1,25,000} = 1.00$$

3. Degree of Combined Leverage

$$\frac{C}{PBT} \qquad \frac{6,00,000}{2,25,000} = 2.67 \qquad \frac{13,12,500}{5,72,500} = 2.29 \qquad \frac{2,00,000}{1,25,000} = 1.60$$

Interpretation and Comments

In the above statements, DOL reveals that in case there is a change in sales by 1%, there is a corresponding change in OP by 2.4%, 2.14% and 1.6% in the case of the firms P, Q and R respectively. On the contrary, the DFL shows that in case OP changes by 1% there will be a corresponding change in EPS by 1.11%, 1.07% and 1% in the case of the firms P, Q and R. Similarly, DCL shows that in case sales change by 1%, there will be a corresponding change in EBT by 2.67, 2.29 and 1.60 in the case of the firms P, Q and R respectively. It is also seen from the above statement that firm 'P' has all the three highest leverage followed by Q and R. However, the DFL is less than DOL in all the cases. Composite or combined leverage measures the total risk of the firm. Hence, if the two leverages are high, no doubt, it is a very risky one.

In case a firm enjoys low financial leverage and high operating leverage, the same partly adjust the high operating leverage which has been found in the present problem. Usually, a low operating leverage presents lower fixed cost and greater variable cost. A high financial leverage implies that the firm enhances its ROE after applying debt-financing in its capital structure. Thus it is concluded that a firm should always have a high financial leverage corresponding to a low operating leverage. If this is considered, it is pointed out that none of the three firms has faithfully followed the norms.

ILLUSTRATION 8.10

ABC Ltd. has sales of Rs. 10,00,000 variable cost Rs. 7,00,000 and fixed costs of Rs. 2,00,000 and a debt of Rs. 5,00,000 at 10% rate of interest. (a) Compute the operating, financial and combined leverages. (b) If the company likes to double its Earnings Before Interest and Tax (EBIT), how much of a rise in sales would be needed on a percentage basis.

(C.A. Final, 1979)

Solution

Computation of Operating, Financial and Combined Leverages

$$\text{Operating Leverage} = \frac{\text{Contribution}}{\text{Operating Profit}} = \frac{3,00,000}{1,00,000} = 3$$

$$\text{Financial Leverage} = \frac{\text{Operating Profit}}{\text{Profit Before Tax}} = \frac{1,00,000}{50,000} = 2$$

Combined Leverage = Operating Leverage × Financial Leverage = 3 × 2 = 6

Profit at present:

	Rs.
Sales	10,00,000
Variable Cost	7,00,000
Contribution	3,00,000
Fixed Costs	2,00,000
Operating Profit (EBIT)	1,00,000
Interest (10% on Rs. 5,00,000)	50,000
Profit Before Tax	50,000

Comments

Operating leverage is '3' times. This implies that in case sales increase by 100%, operating profit will increase by 300% (i.e., 3 times the increase in sales). Thus if the company wants to double its earnings before interest and tax (i.e., 100% rise), then a 33.33 per cent rise in sales will be required. This is confirmed by the following calculation:

	Rs.
Sales after 33.33% rise	13,33,333
Variable Cost	9,33,333
Contribution	4,00,000
Fixed Cost	2,00,000
Operating Profit	2,00,000

ILLUSTRATION 8.11

A firm has estimated that for a new product its break even point is 3,000 units, in case the item is sold for Rs. 15 per unit. It has been currently identified by the cost accounting department that the variable cost is Rs. 10 per unit.

Compute the degree of operating leverage for sales volume of 3,500 units, and 4,000 units. What do you infer from the degree of operating leverage at the sales volumes of 3,000 units and 4,000 units and their difference, if any?

Solution

Operating Leverage of a Firm

	Per unit	3,500 units	4,000 units
Sales	Rs. 15	52,500	60,000
Variable Costs	10	35,000	40,000
Contribution	5	17,500	20,000
Fixed Costs (3000 × Rs. 5 per unit)		15,000	15,000
Operating Profit		2,500	5,000
Operating Leverage:			
$\dfrac{\text{Contribution}}{\text{Operating Profit}}$		$\dfrac{17,500}{2,500} = 7$	$\dfrac{20,000}{5,000} = 4$

Inference

The operating leverages at the sales volumes of 3,500 units and 4,000 units are 7 times and 4 times, respectively. It implies that at the sales volume of 3,500 units, the change in operating profit should be 7 times the change in sales volume. A 14.29% enhance in sales volume has resulted in a 100% enhance in operating profits. But at the sales volume of 4,000 units, the degree of operating leverage is only 4 times. This indicates that at this level, the rise in operating profit is only 4 times the rise in sales volume.

However, a very high degree of operating leverage is not desirable since a small fall in sales volume will result in a large fall in operating profit.

ILLUSTRATION 8.12

The following data relate to ABC Ltd:

		Rs.
	Sales	4,00,000
Less:	Variable Expenses (30%)	1,20,000
	Contribution	2,80,000
	Fixed Operating Expenses	1,30,000
	EBIT	1,50,000
Less:	Interest	50,000
	Taxable Income	1,00,000

1. Using the concept of leverage, by what percentage will taxable income enhance in case sales enhance by 10 per cent.

2. Using the concept of operating leverage by what percentage will EBIT increase in case there is a 15% increase in sale?

3. Using the concept of financial leverage, by what percentage will taxable income increase in case EBIT enhances by 10%?

Solution

1. Degree of composite leverage in sales level of Rs. 4,00,000

$$\frac{\text{Contribution}}{\text{Taxable Income}} = \frac{2,80,000}{1,00,000} = 2.80$$

In case sales increase by 10%, taxable income will increase by 2.80 × 10 = 28.

$$\frac{28,000}{1,00,000} \times 100 = 28\%$$

Working Notes

		Rs.
	Sales	4,40,000
Less:	Variable Expenses (30%)	1,32,000
	Contribution	3,08,000
Less:	Fixed Expense	1,30,000
	EBIT	1,78,000
Less:	Interest	50,000
	Taxable Income	1,28,000

Enhance in Taxable Income of Rs. 28,000 i.e., 28% over of Rs. 1,00,000.

2. Degree of operating leverage on sales level of Rs. 4,00,000:

$$\frac{\text{Contribution}}{\text{Operating Income}} = \frac{2,80,000}{1,50,000} = 1.87$$

In case sales enhance by 15% EBIT will enhance by 1.87 × 15 = 28%

Working Notes

		Rs.
	Sales	4,60,000
Less:	Variable Expenses (30%)	1,38,000
	Contribution	3,22,000
Less:	Fixed Expenses	1,30,000
	EBIT	1,92,000

Increase is Rs. 1,92,000 – 1,50,000 or $\dfrac{42,000 \times 100}{1,50,000} = 28\%$.

3. Degree of financial leverage in case EBIT enhances by 10%

$$\frac{\text{EBIT}}{\text{Taxable Income}} = \frac{1,50,000}{1,00,000} = 1.50$$

In case EBIT enhances by 10%, taxable income will enhance by 1.50 × 10 = 15%.

Working Notes

		Rs.
EBIT		1,50,000
Add: 10%		15,000
		1,65,000
Less: Interest		50,000
Taxable income		1,15,000

Increase is Rs. 1,15,000 − 1,00,000 or $\dfrac{15,000}{1,00,000} \times 100 = 15\%$.

ILLUSTRATION 8.13

AB company has to make a choice between debt issue for its expansion programme. Its current position is as follows:

		Rs.
Debts 5%		40,000
Equity Capital Rs. 10 per Share		1,00,000
Surpluses		60,000
Total Capitalisation		2,00,000
Sales		6,00,000
Less: Total Costs		5,00,000
Income Before Interest and Tax		1,00,000
Less: Interest		2,000
		98,000
Income Tax 50%		49,000
Income After Tax		49,000

The expansion programme is estimated to cost Rs. 1,00,000. In case this is financed through debt, the rate of new debt will be 6% and the price earning ratio will be '6' times. If the expansion programme is financed through equity shares, the new shares can be sold netting Rs. 20 per share, and the price earning ratio will be '7' times. The expansion will generate additional sales of Rs. 2,00,000 with a return of 10% on sales before interest and taxes.

If the company is to follow a policy of maximising the market value of its shares, which form of financing should it choose?

Solution

Determination of Market Value of shares under different Financial Plans

	Financial plans	
	6% Debt Issue	*Equity Issue*
	Rs.	*Rs.*
OP or EBIT (present 1,00,000 + 10% of Rs. 2,00,000)	1,20,000	1,20,000
Less: Interest	8,000	2,000
PBT	1,12,000	1,18,000
Less: Income Tax (50%)	56,000	59,000
PAT	56,000	59,000
Earning Per Share (EPS)	$\dfrac{56,000}{10,000} = 5.60$	$\dfrac{59,000}{15,000} = 3.93$
Price Earning Ratio (PER)	Rs. '6' times	'7' times
Market Value of Share (EPS × PER)	5.60 × 6 = 33.60	3.93 × 7 = 27.51

In the light of the above analysis it is clear that the market value of the company's share is higher if it chooses the debt finance. Thus the company should raise additional funds of Rs. 1,00,000 through debt.

CASE STUDY

Leverage Analysis of Transformers and Electricals Kerala Limited (TELK)

TELK was incorporated in 1963 as a government undertaking. The main products of the company consist of transformers, gas circuit breakers and oil integrated paper condenser bushing. The company registered impressive performance during 2003–04. The sales of the company went up by 13% to Rs. 9332.95 lakh as against Rs. 8290.60 lakh during the previous year and it could register a net profit of Rs. 651.88 lakh as compared to Rs. 130.46 lakh during 2002–03. Table 8.1 shows the leverages of TELK for the years 2002-03 and 2003–04.

Table 8.1 Leverages of TELK

Leverages	*2002–03*	*2003–04*
Operating Leverage	5.07	3.16
Financial Leverage	6.11	2.06
Combined Leverage	30.94	6.48

Source: Review of Public Enterprises in Kerala.

As the operating and financial leverages of TELK during 2002–03 are more than that of 2003–04, the company has a higher degree of operating and financial risk during 2002–03. Similarly, the overall risk of TELK during 2002–03 is much higher than that of 2003–04 as the company has higher degree of combined leverage during 2002–03.

— REVIEW QUESTIONS —

1. What is leverage? Explain its significance.

2. What are the different types of leverages? Explain their importance.

3. "Operating leverage is determined by firm's cost structure and financial leverage by the mix of debt-equity funds used to finance the firm's fixed assets. These two leverages combined provide a risk profile of the firm". Discuss.

4. Define operating leverage and financial leverage. Which combination of operating and financial leverages constitutes (i) risky situation, and (ii) ideal situation.

5. The capital structure of 'Z' Ltd. is as under:

   20,000 equity shares of Rs. 10 each fully paid 10%, 1600 Debentures of Rs. 100 each.

   EBIT Rs. 1,00,000

   Tax Rate @50%

   Compute EPS   (**Ans:** Rs. 2.10)

6. Capital structure of AB Ltd. under various financial plans is as follows:

	Plan I 1:1	Plan II 1:3	Plan III 1:4
Equity Share Capital	1,00,000	50,000	40,000
8% Debentures	1,00,000	1,50,000	1,60,000
	2,00,000	2,00,000	2,00,000

   EBIT Rs. 2,00,000

   Tax Rate @50%

   Calculate EPS if the various plans are implemented.

   (**Ans:** Plan I-9.6, Plan II-18.8, Plan III-23.4)

7. An analytical statement of Y Ltd. is as follows:

	Rs.
Sales	9,60,000
Variable Cost	5,60,000
Revenue Before Fixed Cost	4,00,000
Fixed Cost	2,40,000
	1,60,000
Interest	60,000
Earning Before Tax	1,00,000
Tax	50,000
Net Income	50,000

   Compute the degree of (i) Operating Leverage (ii) Financial Leverage, and (iii) The composite Leverage from the above data.

   (**Ans:** (i) 2.50, (ii) 1.60, (iii) 4.00)

8. XYZ company has an EBIT of Rs. 1,60,000. Its capital structure comprises the following securities:

	Rs.
10% Debentures	5,00,000
12% Preference Shares	1,00,000
Equity Shares for Rs. 100 each	4,00,000

The company is in the 55% tax bracket. You are required to ascertain.

(i) the company's EPS

(ii) the percentage change in EPS associated with 30% increase and 30% decrease in EBIT.

(iii) the degree of financial leverage.

(**Ans.:** (i) Rs. 9.375, (ii) 57.6%, (iii) 1.45)

9. The capital structure of the Gopal Ltd. comprises an ordinary share capital of Rs. 10,00,000 (shares of Rs. 100 par value) and Rs. 10,00,000 of 10% debentures. Sales increased by 20% from 1,00,000 units to 1,20,000 units, the selling price is Rs. 10 per unit, variable cost amounts to Rs. 6 per unit and fixed expenses amount to Rs. 2,00,000. The income tax rate is assumed to be 50 per cent.

Compute the following:

(i) Percentage increase in earnings per share.

(ii) Degree of financial leverage at 1,00,000 units and 1,20,000 units.

(iii) Degree of operating leverage at 1,00,000 units and 1,20,000 units.

(**Ans.:** (i) 80%; (ii) 2, 1.71; (iii) 2, 1.55)

10. A firm has sales of Rs. 10,00,000 variable cost of Rs. 7,00,000 and fixed costs of Rs. 2,00,000 and debt of Rs. 5,00,000 at 10% rate of interest. What are the operating, financial and combined leverages? If the firm wants to double its Earnings Before Interest and Tax (EBIT), how much of a rise in sales would be needed on a percentage basis.

(C.A. Final, 1979)

(**Ans.:** Operating leverage = 3; Financial leverage = 2;
Combined leverage = 6; Required rise in sales = 33.33%)

11. A firm has a choice of the following three financial plans. Compute the financial leverage in each case and interpret it.

	P Rs.	Q Rs.	R Rs.
Equity Capital	2,000	100	3,000
Debt	2,000	3,000	1,000
Operating Profit (EBIT)	400	400	400

Interest @10% on Debt in all cases.

(**Ans.:** P = 2; Q = 4; R = 1.33)

12. A firm has sales of Rs. 1 lakh. The variable costs are 40% of the sales while the fixed operating costs amount to Rs. 30,000. The amount of interest on long-term debt is Rs. 10,000.

Calculate the composite leverage and illustrate its effect in case sales increase by 5%.

(**Ans.:** Composite leverage-3)

9

Management of Working Capital

*Working capital is the amount of funds necessary
to cover the cost of operating the enterprise.*

— SHUBIN

CONTENTS

- Dimensions of working capital management
- Forecasting/determining working capital requirements
- Financing of working capital
- Banking norms for financing working capital
- Case study
- Review questions

Meaning

Working capital refers to the excess of current assets over current liabilities. The management of working capital is, therefore, concerned with the problems that arise in administering of both current assets and current liabilities. In other words, working capital management involves deciding upon the amount and composition of current assets and how to finance these assets.

DIMENSIONS OF WORKING CAPITAL MANAGEMENT

The basic objective of working capital management is to maintain a satisfactory level of working capital, i.e., it is neither inadequate nor redundant. This is so because both the excess as well as shortage of working capital positions are bad for any concern. Thus the working capital management policies of a firm have a great impact on its profitability, liquidity, and structural health of the organisation. In this sense, working capital management is concerned with:

(a) the formulation of policies relating to profitability, risk and liquidity,

(b) the decisions about the composition and levels of current assets and,

(c) the decisions about the composition and level of current liabilities.

(a) Profitability, Risk and Liquidity Policies

These policies are formulated in the context of the objectives of the concern. Usually, a concern has diverse objectives such as (i) to produce quality goods (ii) to provide job opportunities (iii) to allocate resources in an efficient manner, (iv) to protect the environment or conserve energy, (v) to substitute import or to promote export, etc.: (vi) to maximise/optimise profits, to maximise shareholders'/owners' wealth and to maximise the market value of the concern.

Although the relative importance of these objectives differs from concern to concern, the objective of profitability receives great attention in management decisions. As far as the working capital management is concerned, the objectives of financial management are profitability (return) and liquidity (risk-liquidity). The profitability object is concerned with maximisation of share-holders' wealth which can be accomplished by efficient use of resources. On the other hand, the liquidity object can be attained by ensuring the capability of the concern to meet current financial obligations.

There is a definite inverse relationship between the aforesaid dual objectives of profitability and liquidity. In other words, the objective of maximisation of profit is contrary to the objective of maximisation of liquidity. Thus the general approaches to risk, liquidity and return policies are:

(i) larger investment in current assets with less dependence on short-term borrowings, increases liquidity and decreases profitability, and

(ii) less investment in current assets with greater dependence on short-term borrowings increases the profitability and decreases liquidity.

A conservative management prefers to minimise the risk by maintaining a higher level of current assets while liberal management assumes greater risk by reducing current assets. However, the risk, liquidity and return policies of the management should be to establish a suitable trade-off between profitability and risk. Risk here refers to the inability of a concern to meet its obligations as and when these become due for payment.

(b) The Level and the Composition of Current Assets

The level and the composition of current assets is concerned with planning the total investment in current assets. Thus the amount of working capital invested in each component should be adequately justified by a concern's equity position. Every rupee invested in the current assets should contribute to the net worth of the concern. In the words of Weston and Brigham,

> current assets holding should be expanded to the point where marginal returns due to increase in these assets would just equal the cost of capital required to finance such increases.

However, this guideline is of limited help for specific working capital decisions on account of restricted availability of short-term borrowings from banks.

The ratios such as: (a) current assets as percentage of total assets and (b) current assets as percentage of total sales are mainly used to measure the level of current assets. The higher the percentage of current assets in total assets, the greater will be the liquidity, other things remaining the same. Similarly, the lower the percentage of current assets to sales, the higher will be the profitability on investments, other things remaining the same.

There are several factors, including management policy decisions which affect in determining the structure of current assets. For instance, in case the management of a concern adopts the policy to use low demand season for building inventories to carry the business of peak demand season, there will be greater average investment in inventory. Moreover, the finance manager of a concern may take the help of relevant industrial averages for determining the appropriate mix of different current assets. However, the structure of current assets of industry as a whole can be determined with the help of the following averages:

1. Daily cash flows $= \dfrac{\text{Net Profits} + \text{Depreciation}}{\text{Number of Trading Days per Year}}$

2. Stock turnover $= \dfrac{\text{Cost of Sales for a Year}}{\text{Stock}}$

3. Receivables as % of finished stock and sales

4. Inventory to current assets

5. Cash to current assets

6. Receivables to current assets

(c) The Level and Composition of Current Liabilities

The level and composition of current liabilities is concerned with planning the sources of finance for working capital. While the level of current liabilities means the total funds to be raised from different sources of current liabilities, the composition of current liabilities refers to the relative proportion of funds from different sources of current liabilities in the total current liabilities.

The level of current liabilities affects the risk, the cost of financing and net earnings. It measures the risk and liquidity when it relates to the level of current assets (Current ratio = CA/CL). While the cost of financing affects average cost of capital, the size of the earnings before taxes (NEBT) is related to the cost of short-term funds. In the words of *Van Horne*, the appropriate level of current liabilities for a firm is the result of fundamental decisions concerning the firm's liquidity and the maturity composition for its debt.

The composition of current liabilities affects risk, cost of financing and profitability. The maturity pattern of various current obligations is an important factor in risk assumptions and risk assessments. Thus a concern should make every effort to relate maturities of payment to its flow of internally generated funds. Generally, the shorter the maturity schedule of current liabilities in relation to expected cash inflows, the greater will be the inability to meet its obligations in time.

The various sources of raising working capital have different cost of capital. Thus the management of composition of current liabilities considers differences in cost of various short-term sources of funds such a borrowings from banks and trade creditors. However, there is a linkage between bank credit and some of the current assets of the firm. The level of current liabilities is affected by this linkage when banks give advances against goods and determine the margin. Moreover, there is also linkage between trade credit financing and pattern of inventory stock. For instance, the optimal order quantity for inventory management is a function of cost of trade credit financing.

To sum up, the management of working capital would be treated as a cardinal part of overall corporate management, with interdependence of the above principles. In the words of Louis Brand,

> We need to know when to look for working capital funds, how to use them and how to measure, plan and control them.

In short, the financial manager of a concern has to carry out the following fundamental functions for accomplishing the various objectives of working capital management:

1. Forecasting/Estimating the working capital requirements
2. Financing of working capital needs
3. An analysis and control of working capital

FORECASTING/DETERMINING WORKING CAPITAL REQUIREMENTS

The estimation of working capital requirements is not an easy task. Before starting this exercise, a large number of factors are to be considered. The study of operating cycle is one among them. It is the circular flow of cash to suppliers, to inventory, to accounts receivables and then to cash.

The concept of operating cycle has the following two important aspects:

(a) the number of stages of conversion of cash, and

(b) the length of time required to complete each stage. Both these aspects help in determining working capital requirements of a concern.

Operating cycle is a continuous process. However, the number of stages in an operating cycle of a concern depends on the nature of its business. Thus the operating cycle in a manufacturing concern involves the following stages (Figure 9.1):

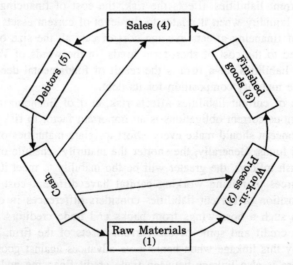

FIGURE 9.1 Operating Cycle of a Manufacturing Concern.

1. Purchase of raw materials and warehousing.
2. Work-in-process (manufacturing activities).
3. Warehousing of finished goods before sale.
4. Sales activities (if all sales are on cash basis, then conversion of sales will be in cash).
5. Debtors (if sales are on credit basis, then time will be taken in collecting receivables).

The number of stages of operating cycle involved in a trading concern are as follows (Figure 9.2):

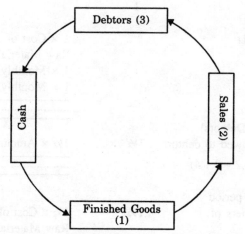

FIGURE 9.2 Operating Cycle of a Trading Concern.

1. Purchase of finished goods.
2. Sales (on cash basis).
3. Debtors (sales on credit basis).

Generally, the larger the number of stages of an operating cycle, the longer is its duration. Moreover, the longer the duration of an operating cycle, the larger will be the amount of working capital requirements. Thus the estimate of working capital requirements of a concern involves the following three major steps:

1. Determining the average length of time for each stage of operating cycle.
2. Determining the size of funds blocked at each stage.
3. Determining the source of financing.

By analysing the operating cycle, the working capital requirements of a manufacturing concern can be determined in the following manner:

	Operating Cycle	Period (Months)	Working Capital Requirements
Stage 1	Raw materials (Storage period)	1	1 × Cost of monthly consumption of Raw Materials
Stage 2	Work-in-process (manufacturing time)	2	

Continued

	Operating Cycle	Period (Months)	Working Capital Requirements
	(a) Raw Material		2 × Cost of monthly consumption of Raw Materials
	+		
	(b) Labour		2 × Monthly Wages
	+		
	(c) Overheads		2 × Monthly Expenses
	Total		....
Stage 3	Finished Goods (storage period)	1	
	(a) Raw Materials		1 × Cost of monthly consumption of Raw Materials
	(b) Labour		1 × Monthly Wages
	(c) Overheads		1 × Monthly Expenses
	Total		....
Stage 4	Sales on Credit (Debtors)		
	Credit period allowed to debtors	1½	1½ × Amount of monthly credit sales
	Total (Stages 1 + 2 + 3 + 4)		....
Less:			
(i)	Creditors (Credit period allowed by suppliers of Raw Materials)	1½	1½ × Cost of monthly consumption of Raw Materials
(ii)	Outstanding Expenses		
	– Wages	2	2 × Monthly Wages
	– Salaries	1½	1½ × Monthly Salary
	Estimated Working Capital Requirements		....

Pro forma of Working Capital Requirements of a Manufacturing Concern

Statement of Working Capital Requirements

Amount Rs.

Current Assets:

  (i) Stock of Raw Material (For .... month's consumption)   ....

  (ii) Work-in-process (For .... months)

      (a) Raw Materials   ....

      (b) Direct Labour   ....

      (c) Overheads   ....

  (iii) Stock of Finished Goods (For .... month's sales)

      (a) Raw Materials   ....

      (b) Labour   ....

      (c) Overheads   ....

Continued

	Amount Rs.

(iv) Sundry Debtors or Receivables (For .... month's sales)	
(a) Raw Materials	....
(b) Labour	....
(c) Overheads	....
(v) Payment in Advance (if any)	....
(vi) Balance of Cash Required to meet day-to-day expenses	....
(vii) Any other (if any)	....
Less Current Liabilities:	
(i) Creditors (For .... month's purchase of raw materials)	....
(ii) Lag in payment of expenses	
(Outstanding expenses .... months)	....
(iii) Others if any	....
Working Capital (CA – CL)	....
Add: Provision/Margin for contingencies	....
Net Working Capital Required	....

Notes:

1. While estimating working capital requirements, the profits should be ignored. This is on account of the following reasons:

   (a) Profits may or may not be used as working capital.

   (b) If profits are used for working capital, it has to be reduced by the amount of income-tax, drawings, dividend paid, etc.

2. Calculation of work-in-process depends upon its degree of completion as regards material, labour and overheads. If nothing is stated in the question, then 100% cost of material, labour and overheads are to be taken. In such a case, the average period of work-in-process should be calculated as equivalent period of completed units.

   But in such a case, some authors have assumed 100% consumption of raw material and 50% (half an average) in the case of labour and overheads.

3. The stocks of finished goods and debtors should be calculated at cost price unless otherwise mentioned.

Pro forma of Working Capital Requirements of a Trading Concern

Statement of Working Capital Requirements

	Amount Rs.

Current Assets:	
(i) Cash	....
(ii) Debtors or Receivables (For month's sales)	....
(iii) Stocks for .... month's sales	....
(iv) Advance payments, if any	....
(v) Others	....

Continued

Amount Rs.

Less Current Liabilities:

(i) Creditors (For .... Month's purchase) ....

(ii) Lag in payment of expenses ....
(Outstanding expenses, if any) ──────

....

Working Capital (CA – CL)
Add: Provision/Margin for Contingencies ....
Net Working Capital Required ──────
....

Notes:

1. While ascertaining the working capital requirements, the profit should be ignored as it may or may not be used as working capital.

2. The stock and debtors should be calculated at cost unless otherwise mentioned.

ILLUSTRATION 9.1

Prepare an estimate of working capital requirements from the following information of a trading concern:

(a) Projected Annual Sales	1,00,000 units
(b) Selling Price	Rs. 10 per unit
(c) Percentage of Net Profit on Sales	25%
(d) Average Credit period allowed to Customers	10 weeks
(e) Average Credit period allowed by Suppliers	5 weeks
(f) Average Stock Holding in terms of Sales Requirements	10 weeks
(g) Allow 10% for Contingencies	

Solution

Statement of Working Capital Requirements

	Rs.
Current Assets:	
Debtors (10 Weeks) (At Cost)	1,44,231
Stock (10 Weeks)	1,44,231
Less Current Liabilities:	2,88,462
Creditors (5 Weeks)	72,115
Net Working Capital	2,16,347
Add 10% for Contingencies	21,635
Working Capital Required	2,37,982

Working Notes:

(i) **Cost of Sales:**

Sales	$= 1,00,000 \times 10$	
	$= $ Rs. 10,00,000	
Profit	$= 25\%$ of Rs. 10,00,000	
	$= $ Rs. 2,50,000	
Cost of Sales	$= 10,00,000 - 2,50,000$	
	$= $ Rs. 7,50,000	

(ii) **Stock:**

Average stock holding is 10 weeks
i.e.,

$$\frac{7,50,000 \times 10}{52}$$

$= $ Rs. 1,44,231 (Approximately)

(iii) **Debtors:**

(At Cost)
Average credit period allowed to customers is 10 weeks.
i.e.,

$$\frac{7,50,000 \times 10}{52}$$

$= $ Rs. 1,44,231 (Approximately)

(iv) **Creditors:**

Average credit period allowed by suppliers is 5 weeks
i.e.,

$$\frac{7,50,000 \times 5}{52}$$

$= $ Rs. 72,115 (Approximately)

(v) As it is a trading concern, cost of sales are assumed to be the purchases.

(vi) Profits have been ignored as funds provided by profits may or may not be used as working capital.

ILLUSTRATION 9.2

XY Ltd. are engaged in a large-scale consumer retailing. From the following information, you are required to estimate their working capital requirement:

Projected Annual Sales	–	Rs. 70 lakhs
Percentage of Net Profit on Cost of Sales	–	25%
Average Credit Period allowed to Debtors	–	8 weeks
Average Credit Period allowed by Creditors	–	3 weeks
Average Stock Carrying	–	6 weeks
(in terms of sales requirements)		

Add 10% of computed figure to allow for contingencies.

Solution

Statement of Working Capital Requirements

	Rs.
Current Assets:	
Stock	6,46,152
Debtors	10,76,920
	17,23,072
Less Current Liabilities:	
Creditors	3,23,076
Working Capital	13,99,996
Add: 10% for contingencies	1,40,000
Total Working Capital Requirement	15,39,996

Working Notes:

(i) Projected Cost per Week:

Projected Annual Sales Rs. 70,00,000

Projected Sales per Week $\dfrac{70,00,000}{52}$

= Rs. 1,34,615 (Approximately)

Less Net Profit @25% on Cost or 20% on sales

Rs. $\left(1,34,615 \times \dfrac{20}{100}\right)$	26,923
Project Cost per Week	1,07,692

(ii) Stock:

6 weeks in terms of Sales requirements i.e., $1,07,692 \times 6$ =	6,46,152

(iii) Debtors:

8 weeks Credit allowed to Debtors i.e., $1,07,692 \times 8 = 8,61,536$ Add Profit @25% on Cost = 2,15,384 =	10,76,920

(iv) Creditors:

3 weeks Credit allowed by Creditors i.e., $1,07,692 \times 3$ =	3,23,076

ILLUSTRATION 9.3

Mr. 'A' wishes to commence a new trading business and gives the following information:

(i) The total estimated sales in a year will be Rs. 15,00,000.

(ii) His expenses are estimated at a fixed expense of Rs. 3,000 per month plus a variable expense equal to 6% of his turnover.

(iii) He expects to fix a sale price for each product which will be 20% in excess of his cost of purchase.

(iv) He expects to turnover his stock five times in a year.

(v) The sales and purchases will be evenly spread throughout the year. All sales will be for cash, but he expects one month's credit for his purchases.

Calculate his average working capital requirements.

Solution

Statement of Working Capital Requirements

	Rs.
Current Assets:	
Stock	2,50,000
Cash	10,500
	2,60,500
Less Current Liabilities:	
Sundry Creditors	1,04,167
Average Working Capital Required	1,56,333

Working Notes:

(i) **Stock:**

Sales	15,00,000
Less Gross Profit	2,50,000
	12,50,000

Stock = $\dfrac{1}{5}$ of 12,50,000 = Rs. 2,50,000

(ii) **Sundry Creditors:**

$\dfrac{1}{12}$ of 12,50,000 = Rs. 1,04,167 (Approximately)

(iii) **Cash:**

It is assumed that Mr. 'A' will have a minimum cash balance to at least cover his expenses for a month which are:

	Rs.
Fixed Expenses	3,000
Variable Expenses	7,500
(6% of one month's Turnover of Rs. 1,25,000)	
	10,500

So, cash = Rs. 10,500

ILLUSTRATION 9.4

From the following particulars, prepare a statement showing working capital needed to finance a level of activity 12,000 units of output per annum.

Analysis of Selling Price per unit	Rs.
Raw Materials	5
Labour	3
Overheads	2
	10
Profit	2
Selling Price	12

Additional Information:

(i) Raw Materials are to remain in store on an average 1 month.
(ii) Materials are in process, on an average 2 months.
(iii) Finished Goods are in stock on an average 3 months.
(iv) Credit allowed to Debtors is 4 months.
(v) Credit allowed by suppliers is 2 months.

It may be assumed that production and overheads accrue evenly throughout the year.

Solution

Statement of Working Capital Requirements

		Rs.
Current Assets:		
Stock of Raw Materials: (1 month)		
Raw Materials	Rs. 5000 × 1 = 5,000	5,000
Work-in-progress: (2 months)		
Raw Materials	Rs. 5,000 × 2 = 10,000	
Labour	Rs. 3,000 × 2 = 6,000	
Overheads	Rs. 2,000 × 2 = 4,000	
		20,000
Stock of Finished Goods: (3 months)		
Raw Materials	Rs. 5,000 × 3 = 15,000	
Labour	Rs. 3,000 × 3 = 9,000	
Overheads	Rs. 2,000 × 3 = 6,000	
		30,000
Debtors: (4 months)		
Raw Materials	Rs. 5,000 × 4 = 20,000	
Labour	Rs. 3,000 × 4 = 12,000	
Overheads	Rs. 2,000 × 4 = 8,000	
		40,000

Continued

	Rs.

Profit: Credit to Debtors

($\frac{1}{5}$ of cost or $\frac{1}{6}$ of sales)   8,000

	48,000

Less: Current Liabilities: 1,03,000

Creditors: (2 months)

Raw Materials   Rs. 5,000 × 2 = 10,000   10,000

Requirements of Working Capital   93,000

Working Notes:

Sales for the Year   12,000 × Rs. 12 =   1,44,000

Sales per Month $\frac{1,44,000}{12}$ =   12,000

Amounts to be blocked in Materials, Labour and Overheads per month are

                                = Rs. 5,000

Materials   Rs. $12,000 \times \frac{5}{12}$ = Rs. 5,000

Labour   Rs. $12,000 \times \frac{3}{12}$ = Rs. 3,000

Overheads   Rs. $12,000 \times \frac{2}{12}$ = Rs. 2,000

Alternatively:

Annual Production   12,000 units

Monthly Production 12,000 ÷ 12 = 1,000 units

Average Cost of Production per Month

Raw Materials   1,000 × Rs. 5 = Rs. 5,000

Labour   1,000 × Rs. 3 = Rs. 3,000

Overheads   1,000 × Rs. 2 = Rs. 2,000

Profit element in Debtors is included.

ILLUSTRATION 9.5

From the following information, you are required to estimate the net working capital.

	Cost per unit (Rs.)
Raw Materials	300
Direct Labour	100
Overheads (excluding Depreciation)	200
Total Cost	600

Additional Information:

Selling Price	Rs. 800 per unit
Output	50,000 units per annum
Raw Materials in Stock	average 4 weeks

Work-in-process:

(assume 50% completion stage with full material consumption)	average 2 weeks
Finished Goods in Stock	average 5 weeks
Credit allowed to Debtors	average 5 weeks
Credit allowed to Creditors	average 10 weeks
Cash at Bank is expected to be	Rs. 60,000

Assume that production is sustained at an even pace during the 52 weeks of the year. All sales are on credit basis.

Solution

Statement Showing Networking Working Capital Requirements

		Rs.

Current Assets:

Stock of Raw Material (4 weeks)

$$50,000 \times 300 \times \frac{4}{52} \qquad 11,53,846$$

Stock of Work-in-progress (2 weeks)

$$\text{Raw Material } 50,000 \times 300 \times \frac{2}{52} = 5,76,923$$

Direct Labour (50% completion)

$$50,000 \times 100 \times \frac{2}{52} \times \frac{50}{100} = 96,154$$

Overhead (50% completion)

$$50,000 \times 200 \times \frac{2}{52} \times \frac{50}{100} = 1,92,308 \qquad 8,65,385$$

Stock of finished goods (5 weeks)

$$50,000 \times 600 \times \frac{5}{52} \qquad 28,84,615$$

Amount blocked in Debtors at cost (5 weeks)

$$50,000 \times 600 \times \frac{5}{52} \qquad 28,84,615$$

Cash at Bank	60,000
Total Current Assets	78,48,461

Less: Current Liabilities:

Creditors for Raw Materials (10 weeks)

$$50,000 \times 300 \times \frac{10}{52} \qquad 28,84,615$$

Net Working Capital Required	49,63,846

Working Notes:

(i) Profit has been ignored and debtors have been taken at cost. The profit has been ignored because this may or may not be used as a source of working capital.

(ii) It has been assumed that raw material is introduced at the beginning of the process.

ILLUSTRATION 9.6

'Z'& Co. are desirous to purchase a business and have consulted you, and one point in which you are asked to advise them is the average amount of working capital which will be required for the first year of running the business.

You are given the following estimates and are instructed to add 10% to your computed figure to allow for contingencies.

		Figures for the year Rs.
(i)	Average amount locked-up for:	
	Stock of Finished Product	5,000
	Stock of Stores, Materials, etc.	8,000
(ii)	Average Credit given:	
	Inland Sales 6 weeks credit	3,12,000
	Export Sales 1½ weeks credit	78,000
(iii)	Lag in Payment of Wages and other outgoings:	
	Wages 1½ weeks	2,60,000
	Stock, Materials, etc., 1½ months	48,000
	Rent, Royalties, etc. 6 months	10,000
	Clerical Staff ½ month	62,400
	Manager ½ month	4,800
	Miscellaneous Expenses 1½ months	48,000
(iv)	Payment in Advance:	
	Payment of (paid quarterly in advance)	8,000
	Undrawn Profit on the Average throughout the year	11,000

Set up your calculations for the average amount of Working Capital.

(C.A. Final)

Solution

Statement of Working Capital Requirements

		Rs.
Current Assets:		
Stock:		
Finished Products	5,000	
Stores, Materials, etc.	8,000	13,000

Continued

Debtors:

Inland Sales (6 weeks credit)

$$\frac{3,12,000}{52} \times 6 = 36,000$$

Export Sales (1½ weeks credit)

$$\frac{78,000}{52} \times 1\frac{1}{2} = 2,250 \qquad\qquad 38,250$$

Advance Payment of tax:

(paid quarterly)

$$\frac{8,000}{4} \qquad\qquad \underline{2,000}$$

Total Current Assets Investment   53,250

Less: Current Liabilities
Lag in payments:

Wages

$$\frac{2,60,000}{52} \times 1\frac{1}{2} = 7,500$$

Stores and Materials

$$\frac{48,000}{12} \times 1\frac{1}{2} = 6,000$$

Rent, Royalties, etc.

$$\frac{10,000}{12} \times 6 = 5,000$$

Clerical Staff

$$\frac{62,400}{12} \times \frac{1}{2} = 2,600$$

Manager

$$\frac{4,800}{12} \times \frac{1}{2} = 200$$

Miscellaneous expenses

$$\frac{48,000}{12} \times 1\frac{1}{2} = 6,000 \qquad 27,300$$

Net Working Capital   25,950
Add 10% for Contingencies   2,595
Average Working Capital required   28,545

Note:

Undrawn profit has been ignored on the assumption that the same may not be used as working capital.

ILLUSTRATION 9.7

A pro forma cost sheet of a company provides the following particulars:

Material	40%
Direct Labour	20%
Overheads	20%

The following further particulars are available:

(a) It is proposed to maintain a level of activity of 2,00,000 units.
(b) Selling price is Rs. 12 per unit.
(c) Raw materials are expected to remain in stores for an average period of one month.
(d) Materials will be in process, on averages half a month.
(e) Finished goods are required to be in stock for an average period of one month.
(f) Credit allowed to debtors is two months.
(g) Credit allowed by suppliers is one month.

You may assume that sales and production follow a consistent pattern.

You are required to prepare a statement of working capital requirements, a forecast Profit and Loss Account and Balance Sheet of the company assuming that:

	Rs.
Share Capital	15,00,000
8% Debentures	2,00,000
Fixed Assets	13,00,000

Solution

Statement of Working Capital Requirements

	Rs.

Current Assets:

Stock of Raw Materials (1 month)

$$\frac{24,00,000 \times 40}{100 \times 12}$$ 80,000

Work-in-Process (½ month)

Materials $\quad \dfrac{24,00,000 \times 40}{100 \times 12} \times \dfrac{1}{2} = 40,000$

Labour $\quad \dfrac{24,00,000 \times 20}{100 \times 12} \times \dfrac{1}{2} = 20,000$

Overheads $\quad \dfrac{24,00,000 \times 20}{100 \times 12} \times \dfrac{1}{2} = \underline{20,000}$

80,000

Stock of Finished Goods (1 month)

Materials $\quad \dfrac{24,00,000 \times 40}{100 \times 12} = 80,000$

Labour $\quad \dfrac{24,00,000 \times 20}{100 \times 12} = 40,000$

Overheads $\quad \dfrac{24,00,000 \times 20}{100 \times 12} = \underline{40,000}$

1,60,000

Debtors at Cost (2 months)

Materials $\dfrac{24,00,000 \times 40 \times 2}{100 \times 12} = 1,60,000$

Labour $\dfrac{24,00,000 \times 20 \times 2}{100 \times 12} = 80,000$

Overheads $\dfrac{24,00,000 \times 20 \times 2}{100 \times 12} = 80,000$ 3,20,000

                                               6,40,000

Less: Current Liabilities

Creditors 1 month for raw materials

                     $\dfrac{24,00,000 \times 40 \times 1}{100 \times 12}$ 80,000

Net Working Capital Required   5,60,000

Notes:

Sales = 2,00,000 × 12 = Rs. 24,00,000

Forecast Profit and Loss Account
For the year ended ....

	Rs.		Rs.
To Materials	9,60,000	By Cost of goods sold	19,20,000
To Wages	4,80,000		
To Overheads	4,80,000		
	19,20,000		19,20,000
To Cost of goods sold	19,20,000	By Sales	24,00,000
To Gross Profit c/d	4,80,000		
	24,00,000		24,00,000
To Interest on Debentures	16,000	By Gross Profit b/d	4,80,000
To Net Profit	4,64,000		
	4,80,000		4,80,000

Forecast Balance Sheet
As at..........

Liabilities	Rs.	Assets	Rs.
Share Capital	15,00,000	Fixed Assets	13,00,000
8% Debentures	2,00,000	Stock:	
Net Profit	4,64,000	Raw Materials	80,000
Creditors	80,000	Work-in-Process	80,000
		Finished Goods	1,60,000
		Debtors	3,20,000
		Cash/Bank Balance	
		(balancing figure)	—
	22,44,000		22,44,000

Working Notes:

(a) Profits have been ignored while preparing working capital requirements for the following reasons:

    (i) Profits may or may not be used for working capital.

    (ii) Even if profits have to be used for working capital, they may have to be reduced by the amount of income tax, dividend, etc.

(b) Interest on debentures has been assumed to have been paid.

ILLUSTRATION 9.8

A newly formed company has applied for a short-term loan to a commercial bank for financing its working capital requirements. You are asked by the bank to prepare an estimate for the requirements of the working capital for that company. Add 10% to your estimated figure to cover unforeseen contingencies. The information about the projected Profit and Loss Account of the company is under:

		Amount Rs.
Sales		21,00,000
Cost of Goods Sold		15,30,000
Gross Profit		5,70,000
Administrative Expenses	1,40,000	
Selling Expenses	1,30,000	
		2,70,000
Profit Before Tax		3,00,000
Provision for Tax		1,00,000
Cost of Goods Sold has been derived as follows:		
Materials used	8,40,000	
Wages and Manufacturing		
Expenses	6,25,000	
Depreciation	2,35,000	
		17,00,000
Less: Stock of finished goods		
(10% products not yet sold)		1,70,000
		15,30,000

The figures given above relate only to the goods that have been finished and not to work-in-progress. Goods equal to 15% of the year's production (in terms of physical units) are in progress on an average requiring full materials but only 40% of the other expenses. The company believes in keeping two months consumption of material in stock.

All expenses are paid one month in arrear, suppliers of materials extend 1½ months credit; sales are 20% cash; rests are at two months credit; 70% of the income-tax has to be paid in advance in quarterly instalments. You can make such other assumptions as you deem necessary for estimating working capital requirements.

(Delhi, M.Com)

Solution

Statement of Working Capital Requirements

		Rs.

Current Assets:

1. Stock of Raw Materials (2 months)

$$8,40,000 \times \frac{2}{12}$$

1,40,000

2. Work-in-process:

Raw Materials $\qquad 8,40,000 \times \frac{15}{100} = 1,26,000$

Wages and Manufacturing Expenses $\qquad$ 6,25,000
Administrative Expenses $\qquad$ 1,40,000

$$7,65,000 \times \frac{40}{100} \quad 3,06,000$$

4,32,000

3. Stock of Finished Goods:

Stock $\qquad$ 1,70,000

Less Depreciation

$$10\% \left(\text{i.e., } 2,35,000 \times \frac{10}{100} \right) \qquad 23,500$$

1,46,500

4. Debtors (2 months):

Cost of Goods Sold – Depreciation
$(15,30,000 - 2,11,500) = \qquad$ 13,18,500
(Dep. $2,35,000 - 23,500$)
Administrative Expenses $\qquad$ 1,40,000
Selling Expenses $\qquad$ 1,30,000

Total $\qquad$ 15,88,500
Less Cash Sales 20% $\qquad$ 3,17,700

$$12,70,800 \times \frac{2}{12}$$

2,11,800

5. **Cash (say)** $\qquad$ 50,700

Total $\qquad$ 9,81,000

Less Current Liabilities :

1. Creditors (1½ months)

$$\frac{8,40,000}{12} \times 1\frac{1}{2}$$

1,05,000

2. Lag in payment of expenses (1 month)

(a) Wages and Manufacturing Expenses

$$6,25,000 \times \frac{1}{12} = 52,083$$

Continued

(b) Administrative Expenses

$$1,40,000 \times \frac{1}{12} = 11,667$$

(c) Selling expenses

$1,30,000 \times \frac{1}{12} = 10,883$		74,583	1,79,583
Net Working Capital			8,01,417
Add 10% for Contingencies			80,142
Estimated Working Capital Required			8,81,559

Working Notes:

1. Depreciation is excluded from the computation of cost of goods sold as it is a non-cash item.
2. Element of profit is excluded here.
3. Assume that cash is required for Rs. 50,700 in order to meet the day-to-day expenses.

ILLUSTRATION 9.9

A pro forma cost sheet of a manufacturing company provides the following particulars:

	Amount per Unit Rs.
Elements of Cost:	
Raw Material	8
Direct Labour	3
Overheads (exclusive of depreciation)	6
	17

The following further particulars are available:

Selling Price	Rs. 20 per unit
Level of Activity	1,04,000 units output per annum (52 weeks)
Raw Material in Stock	On an average 4 weeks
Processing Time	On an average 2 weeks
Finished Goods in Store	On an average 4 weeks
Credit Period:	
(a) Customers	On an average 8 weeks
(b) Suppliers of Materials	On an average 4 weeks
Lag in payment:	
(a) Wages	On an average 1½ weeks
(b) Overhead Expenses	On an average 2 weeks

75% of the output is sold on credit basis. Cash on hand and at bank is expected to be Rs. 5,000.

You are required to prepare a statement in columnar form showing the working capital requirements (a) in total, and (b) as regards each constituent part of the same to finance a level of activity of 1,04,000 units of production per annum. You may assume that all wages and overheads accrue evenly and are completely introduced for half the processing time, i.e., 1 week.

Solution

Statement of Working Capital Requirements

(A) Current Assets Particulars	Period (Weeks)	Total Rs.	Raw Materials Rs	Work-in Process Rs.	Finished Goods Rs.	Debtors Rs.	Cash and Bank Rs.
1. Raw Materials:							
(a) In Stock	4		64,000				
(b) In Work-in-process	2			32,000			
(c) In Finished Goods	4				64,000		
(d) Credit to Debtors	8					96,000	
	18	2,56,000					
2. Direct Labour:							
(a) In Work-in-Process (½ of 2)	1			6,000			
(b) In Finished Goods	4				24,000		
(c) Credit to Debtors	8					36,000	
	13	66,000					
3. Overheads:							
(a) In Work-in-Process (½ of 2)	1			12,000			
(b) In Finished Goods	4				48,000		
(c) Credit to Debtors	8					72,000	
	13	1,32,000					
4. Cash and Bank		5,000					5,000
(A) Total Current Assets		4,59,000	64,000	50,000	1,36,000	2,04,000	5,000

(B) Current Liabilities Particulars	Periods (Weeks) Rs.	Total Rs.	Creditors For Raw Materials Rs.	For Wages Rs.	For Overhead Rs.
5. Credit by Suppliers	4	64,000	64,000		
6. Lag in payment wages	1½	9,000		9,000	
7. Lag in payment of overheads	2	24,000			24,000
(B) Total Current Liabilities		97,000	64,000	9,000	24,000

Working Capital Requirements = (A − B)
i.e., 4,59,000 − 97,000 = Rs. 3,62,000

Working Notes:

1. **Weekly Output** $= \dfrac{1,04,000}{52}$ = 2,000 units

2. **Raw Materials**

   (a) In Stock $= 2,000 \times 4 \times 8$ = Rs. 64,000

   (b) In Work-in-process $= 2,000 \times 2 \times 8$ = Rs. 32,000

   (c) In Finished Goods $= 2,000 \times 4 \times 8$ = Rs. 64,000

   (d) In Credit to Debtors $= 2,000 \times \dfrac{75}{100} \times 8 \times 8$ = Rs. 96,000

3. **Direct Labour:**

   (a) In Work-in-Process $= 2,000 \times 1 \times 3$ = Rs. 6,000

   (b) In Finished Goods $= 2,000 \times 3 \times 4$ = Rs. 24,000

   (c) In Credit to Debtors $= 2,000 \times \dfrac{75}{100} \times 3 \times 8$ = Rs. 36,000

4. **Overheads:**

   (a) In Work-in-process $= 2,000 \times 1 \times 6$ = Rs. 12,000

   (b) In Finished Goods $= 2,000 \times 4 \times 6$ = Rs. 48,000

   (c) In Credit to Debtors $= 2,000 \times \dfrac{75}{100} \times 8 \times 6$ = Rs. 72,000

Working Capital Requirements Under Extra Shift Working

In extra shift working (double shift or triple shift), as there is no further investment in fixed assets, it does not affect the requirements of fixed capital. However, extra shift working shall have the following effects on working capital:

1. It requires increased volume of stock. But the same may not be in proportion to the increase in production as the minimum level of stocks may not increase in the same proportion.

2. Fixed overheads cost per unit will decrease as the fixed overheads remain the same.

3. Variable overheads will increase proportionately. But there may be some savings in purchase cost of materials on account of large orders.

4. Because of higher wages, there may be a change in the amount of work-in-process.

5. There may be an increase of the overall requirements of working capital in extra shift working.

FINANCING OF WORKING CAPITAL

The working capital financing policy of a firm is mainly concerned with the determination of a suitable mix between the long-term sources and short-term sources of finance. Usually this mix is guided by:

(a) the trade off between risk and profitability and

(b) the costs of alternative combinations of short-term and long-term sources.

Moreover, on the basis of risk, profitability and cost, a firm should have different working capital financing policies. But an ideal policy should be such which is least costly, least risky and most profitable. However, as the ideal policy cannot be practised in real market situations, the task of management is to strike a happy balance among these three variables, viz., risks, profitability and cost. For this purpose, the following guidelines are available:

(a) The firm can use only long-term finance. It is the most costly in terms of interest rates and the most conservative policy in terms of certainty of availability of funds.

(b) The firm can use only short-term finance. It is the least costly in the short-run, the most profitable and most risky of availabile of funds.

A choice of suitable financing strategy between these two extremes is influenced by the following factors:

(i) **The Approval of Creditors and the Capital Market:** This approval is reflected in the actual ratios of the two sources in financial statements of firms in industry, in general.

(ii) **The Condition of Money and Capital Markets:** When the market in long-term sources of finance is in depressed condition, there is no choice, but to raise funds from short-term sources.

(iii) **The composition of Current Assets:** In case a firm has quickly convertible non-cash current assets, it may rely more upon short-term sources than upon long-term sources. Retailers of food articles, transport undertakings, hotels, etc., are examples of such firms.

(iv) **Recent Use of Sources:** In case a firm has incurred heavy capital expenditure financed by long-term sources in the recent past, then such a firm has no other choice than to finance increases in current assets by short-term borrowings and vice-versa.

(v) **Management Attitude Towards Risk Associated with a Source of Finance:** The attitude of management on raising funds from long-term and/or short-term sources are important while taking decisions on financing working capital requirements. This attitude is formed by taking into account, cash inflows and outflows (cash budget), funds from business operations (profit and loss account), financial position (balance sheet), conditions in the capital market, banking situations, fiscal and monetary policies.

Advantages of Long-term Sources of Working Capital

(i) **Less Risk:** In the case of long-term sources of finance, the firm will have sufficient time to plan for repayment. Thus the risk that the firm may not have funds to repay loans on maturity date is less.

(ii) **High Stability:** In the case of long-term sources of finance, a firm can have enough funds for comparatively longer period to finance accumulation of inventories or sale on credit (receivables) during off-season. Thus the use of long-term sources of finance increases the degree of stability in operations.

(iii) **High Liquidity:** The use of long-term sources of finance increases the firm's liquidity as the firm has less worry about the repayment of them in the short-run.

Advantages of Short-term Sources of Working Capital

1. **Low Costs:** In the case of short-term sources of finance, interest is paid only for short periods for which funds are used. The overall impact of this is reduction in costs.

2. **Close Relations with Banks:** In the case of short-term sources of finance, the financial manager of a firm has to frequently deal with bank officials. Thus he can establish a close relation with bank officials which can be used beneficially in larger dealings later on.

Approaches to Working Capital Financing Policy

There are three basic approaches for determining appropriate working capital financing policy. Figure 9.3 shows these approaches.

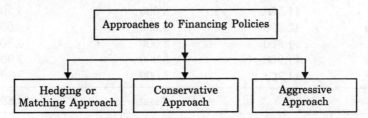

FIGURE 9.3 Approaches of Working Capital Financing Policy.

1. The Hedging or Matching Approach

The term hedging involves simultaneous activities which are opposite to each other and counter balance the effect of each other. With reference to financing policies, the term hedging refers to a process of matching maturities of debt with the maturities of financial needs. Here, the effort is to match the life of assets with the term sources of funds. Thus this approach is also known as "matching approach". For example, if a machine having an expected life of 20 years is to be purchased, long-term loans for 20 years should be borrowed to finance this purchase. Similarly, inventory purchased is expected to be sold in 90 days, then short-term loan for 90 days should be raised.

In the words of *J.C. Van Horne,*

> with the hedging approach, short-term or seasonal variations in current assets
> would be financed with short-term debt, the permanent component of current
> assets would be financed with long-term debt or equity.

This approach classifies the requirements of total working capital into the following two categories:

(a) Funds requirements for seasonally needed current assets (or Variable Working Capital)

(b) Funds requirements for regularly needed current assets (or Permanent Working Capital).

The hedging approach suggests that the variable or seasonal working capital requirements should be financed with short-term funds while the permanent working capital requirements should be financed with funds from long-term sources.

The following example explains the hedging approach:

Estimated Total Investment in Current Assets of AB Company for the year 2002

Month	Investment in Current Assets (Rs.)	Permanent or Fixed Investments (Rs.)	Temporary or Seasonal Investments (Rs.)
January	10,500	8,000	2,500
February	10,000	8,000	2,000
March	9,900	8,000	1,900
April	9,000	8,000	1,000
May	8,500	8,000	500
June	8,000	8,000	—
July	11,000	8,000	3,000
August	11,500	8,000	3,500
September	12,000	8,000	4,000
October	11,800	8,000	3,800
November	11,900	8,000	3,900
December	11,700	8,000	3,700
	Total		**29,800**

In accordance with the hedging approach, the permanent portion of current assets required (Rs. 8,000) should be financed with long-term sources and temporary or seasonal requirements in different months (Rs. 2,500; Rs. 3,000; Rs. 3,700 and so on) should be financed from short-term sources.

2. The Conservative Approach

Under this approach, as far as possible, investments in current assets should be financed by funds from long-term sources and the short-term sources should be used only for emergency requirements. As per this approach, the entire estimated requirements of Rs. 12,000 in the month of September (in the above example) should be financed from long-term sources. The short-term funds should be used only to meet emergencies.

The unique features of this approach are:

(i) Liquidity is relatively greater

(ii) Risk is minimised

(iii) Cost of financing is relatively more.

3. The Aggressive Approach

This approach states that a major part of the total current assets requirements should be financed from short-term sources and even a part of fixed assets requirements be financed from short-term sources. In other words, in the aggressive approach, the trend is towards the use of the short-term sources of financing. Thus, the greater the ratio of short-term funds to total investments in assets, the more aggressive approach in financing is.

The aggressive approach makes finance-mix more risky, less costly and more profitable.

Comparison of Hedging Conservative and Aggressive Approaches

The three approaches of working capital financing can be compared on the basis of cost, profitability and risk considerations. A comparative study of these approaches is given below:

Comparative Study of Financing Approaches

Financing Approaches	Cost	Profitability	Risk
Hedging	Moderate	Moderate	Moderate
Conservative	High	Low	Low
Aggressive	Low	High	High

The following illustrates the above comparison.

ILLUSTRATION 9.10

The following is the summary of balance sheets of XYZ company under the three approaches:

	Policy		
	Hedging	Conservative	Aggressive
Liabilities:			
Current Liabilities	20,000	10,000	30,000
Long-term Loans	20,000	30,000	10,000
Equity	60,000	60,000	60,000
Total	1,00,000	1,00,000	1,00,000
Assets:			
Current Assets:			
(a) Permanent Requirements	25,000	25,000	25,000
(b) Seasonal Requirements	20,000	20,000	20,000
Fixed Assets	55,000	55,000	55,000
Total	1,00,000	1,00,000	1,00,000

Additional Information:

(i) The company earns, on an average 8% on investments in current assets and 20% on investments in fixed assets.

(ii) Average cost of current liabilities is 7% and average cost of long-term funds is 14%.

Compute the costs and returns under the three approaches, and comment on the policies.

Solution

1. Comparison of Costs under the three Approaches

	Hedging	Conservative	Aggressive
Cost of Current Liabilities	7% on 20,000 = 1,400	7% on 10,000 = 700	7% on 30,000 = 2,100
Cost of Long-term Funds	14% on 80,000 = 11,200	14% on 90,000 = 12,600	14% on 70,000 = 9,800
Total Cost	12,600	13,300	11,900

2. Computation of Returns under the three Approaches

	Hedging	Conservative	Aggressive
Returns on Current Assets	8% on 45,000 = 3,600	8% on 45,000 = 3,600	8% on 45,000 = 3,600
Return on Fixed Assets	20% on 55,000 = 11,000	20% on 55,000 = 11,000	20% on 55,000 = 11,000
Total	14,600	14,600	14,600
Less: Cost of Financing	(12,600) *mins.*	(13,300)	(11,900)
Net Return	2,000	1,300	2,700

3. Measurement of Risk of Technical Insolvency under the three Approaches

	Hedging	Conservative	Aggressive
(a) Net Working Capital (CA – CL)	45,000 – 20,000 = 25,000	45,000 – 10,000 = 35,000	45,000 – 30,000 = 15,000
(b) Current Ratio (CA:CL)	$\dfrac{45,000}{20,000}$ = 2.22:1	$\dfrac{45,000}{10,000}$ = 4.5:1	$\dfrac{45,000}{30,000}$ = 1.5:1

Comments:

(i) Cost of financing is the greatest (Rs. 13,300) in conservative approach, and lowest (Rs. 11,900) in aggressive approach (the total fund being the same i.e., Rs. 1,00,000).

(ii) Return on investment (net) is lowest in conservative approach at Rs. 1,300 and highest in aggressive approach at Rs. 2,700.

(iii) Risk is measured by the amount of net working capital. The larger the net working capital, the lesser the risk is. The net working capital is comparatively larger in conservative approach and hence the degree of risk is low. The net working capital is comparatively lower in aggressive approach and hence, the degree of risk is high.

Risk is also measured by the degree of liquidity. However, liquidity can be measured with the help of current ratio. The higher the current ratio, the greater the liquidity, and lessor the risk.

In conservative approach, current ratio is the highest at 4.5:1, and in aggressive approach, this ratio is lowest at 1.5:1. Hence, there is low risk in conservative approach and high risk in aggressive approach.

The following conclusions can be derived from the above analysis:

(i) Hedging approach has moderate costs, risk and return. Its purpose is trade-off between profitability and risk.

(ii) In conservative approach, cost is high, risk is low and return is low.

(iii) In aggressive approach, cost is low, risk is high and return is high.

Sources of Working Capital

The working capital requirements of a concern are brought into two categories. They are: (a) permanent or fixed capital requirements and (b) temporary or variable working capital requirements.

The fixed proportion of working capital should be generally financed from the long-term sources while the temporary or variable working capital requirements of a concern may be met from the short-term sources.

The various long-term sources for financing of working capital requirements are as follows:

(a) Equity Capital (including retained earnings/surplus)

(b) Debentures and Preference Shares

(c) Long-term Loans

The following are the various short-term sources for financing of working capital requirements:

(i) Trade Credit (Sundry creditors, Bills payable)

(ii) Bank Overdraft

(iii) Current Provisions (such as Provision for Taxation)

(iv) Short-term loans from sources other than banks (such as loans from directors, partners, employees, wages and salaries outstanding, income received but not earned or advance payment from customers).

In India, the major portion of working capital finance is provided by commercial banks and trade creditors. But in the case of public enterprises, in spite of Government's directives that they have to meet cent per cent of their working capital needs by the cash credit arrangements with the banks (exclusively with SBI and its subsidiaries), a major portion of their working capital requirements is met by internal sources (including depreciation reserves) and diversion of capital funds. Of late, there has been emphasis on using long-term sources to finance working capital requirements (Tandon Committee Report). Now-a-days, companies are issuing debentures (both convertible and non-convertible) to meet their working capital needs. Moreover, in order to make non-convertible debentures a prominent source for working capital finance, the minimum period of redemption of debentures has been reduced from '12' years to '7' years and the ceiling rate of interest has been raised to 15%.

BANKING NORMS FOR FINANCING WORKING CAPITAL

The availability of bank credit to industry is at present a subject matter of regulation and control. This is required to ensure equitable distribution to various sectors of the Indian economy. The reports submitted by the following four committees are very pertinent in this respect.

    (i)   Dehejia Committee Report, 1969.

    (ii) Tandon Committee Report, 1975.

    (iii) Chore Committee Report, 1980.

    (iv) Marathe Committee Report, 1984.

Dehejia Committee

A committee under the chairmanship of Shri V.T. Dehejia was constituted in 1968 by the National Credit Council to determine the extent to which credit needs of the industry and trade are likely to be inflated and how such trends could be checked. However, the committee made the following recommendations to bring about improvement in the lendig system.

    (i) Credit applications received by the bankers should be evaluated with reference to the present and projected total financial position submitted by borrowers, (ii) The total cash credit requirement of the borrower should be segregated into 'hard core' component and 'short-term' component. While the hard core component represents the minimum level of raw materials, finished goods and stores which the industry is required to maintain a given level of production, the short-term component represents the requirements of funds for temporary purposes such as short-term increase in inventories, tax, dividends and bonus payments, and (iii) The dealings of a customer should be confined to one bank only for avoiding the possibility of double or multiple financing. However, the adoption of consortium arrangement has been recommended in the case of large borrowers.

Tandon Committee

As a result of the failure of implementing Dehejia Committee recommendations, another committee was appointed by the Reserve Bank of India (RBI) in July 1974, under the chairmanship of Shri P.L. Tandon for the urgent necessity of reviewing the existing credit system. The committee submitted its report on 9th August, 1975. It is a landmark in the history of financing of working capital by commercial banks in India and is based on the following three principles.

    (i) The borrower should observe a proper financial discipline. This is required to be ensured by the banker through a realistic appraisal of operational plans submitted by the borrower well in advance, (ii) The banker should supplement the borrower's resources to carry on acceptable level of current assets, and (iii) The loan is used only for the purpose for which it is made. Hence the bank should know the end-use of bank credit.

    The unique features of the Tandon Committee's recommendation relate to the fixation of norms and style of credit for bank lending to industry.

Fixation Norms

The norms for bank lending can be categorized into (i) inventory and receivables norms, and (ii) lending norms.

Inventory and Receivables Norms: The committee has suggested norms for 15 major industries pertaining to the following items for their maximum level of holding.

(a) Raw materials including stores and other items used in the process of manutacfure, (b) Stocks in process, (c) Finished goods, and (d) Receivables and bills discounted and purchased.

The norms have been worked out in accordance with the time element. Thus raw materials are expressed as so many month's cost of production, finished goods and receivables as so many month's cost of sales and sales, respectively.

In this connection, it is noted that in case a borrower has managed with a less investment in the above items as compared to norms in the past, he should continue to do so.

Lending Norms: The committee has suggested three methods of working out the maximum amount that a unit may expect from the bank. The extent of bank finance is more in the first method, less in the second method and least in the third method.

First Method: As per this method, the borrower should continue a minimum of 25 per cent of the working capital gap (i.e., the total of current assets less current liabilities other than bank borrowings). This can be amplified with the help of following example.

EXAMPLE 1

	(Rs.)
Total Current Assets required by the Borrower as per norms	40,000
Current Liabilities	10,000
As per the first method, the amount of Maximum Permissible Bank Borrowings can be computed as under:	
Working capital gap	
(Rs. 40,000 – Rs. 10,000)	30,000
Less: 25% from Long-term Sources	7,500
Maximum permissible Bank Finance (MPBF)	22,500

Second Method: As per this method, the borrower is required to provide the minimum of 25% of the total current assets that will give a current ratio of 1.33:1.

EXAMPLE 2

On the basis of the data in Example 1, the maximum permissible bank borrowings under second method can be computed as under:

	(Rs.)
Current Assets as per norms	40,000
Less: 25% to be provided from Long-term Funds	10,000
	30,000
Less: Current Liabilities other than Bank Finance	10,000
Maximum Permissible Bank Finance (MPBF)	20,000

Third Method: Under this method, the borrower's contribution from long-term funds should be to the extent of the entire core current assets and a minimum of 25% of the balance of the current assets. The term core current asset relates to the absolute minimum level of investment in all current assets which is required in all times to carry out minimum level of business activities.

EXAMPLE 3

In the light of the information given in Example 1, the amount of maximum permissible bank finance can be arrived at as given below, if the current assets are Rs. 4000.

	(Rs.)
Current Assets as per norms	40,000
Less: Core Current Assets	4,000
	36,000
Less: 25% to be provided from Long-term Funds	9,000
	27,000
Less: Current Labilities	10,000
Maximum Permissible Bank Finance (MPBF)	17,000

Thus it is found that under the third method, current ratio has further enhanced.

Style of Credit

In view of serious limitations of cash credit system of the bank, the committee has recommended a change in the style of credit. So far the borrower is sanctioned a limit and is entitled to withdraw money from his cash credit account to the extent of the limit in accordance with his requirements. Thus the banker is not in a position to foresee a demand for credit. This hampers credit planning and results in loss to the banker on account of uncertainties regarding the withdrawal of funds by the borrower.

In view of the above limitations of the cash credit system, the committee recommended for the segregation of annual credit limit into loan component and demand cash credit component. While the loan component comprises the minimum level of borrowings throughout the year, the demand cash credit component takes care of the fluctuating credit requirements of the borrower. Usually, the interest rate of the demand cash credit component is slightly higher than that of loan component.

The committee further recommended that the proposed system of lending and style of credit should be extended to all borrowers having credit limits in excess of Rs. 10 lakh from the banking system. Moreover, the information system should be introduced to commence with in respect of borrowers within limits of Rs. 1 crore and above from the entire banking system.

Chore Committee

Owing to the slow implementation of the recommendation of the Tandon Committee, another committee was appointed by the RBI in March 1979 under the chairmanship of Shri K.B. Chore, Chief Officer, Department of Banking Operations and Development, RBI.

The following are the important recommendations of the committee.

(i) The existing system of three types of lending, namely, cash credits, loans, and bills should continue, (ii) There is no bifurcation of cash credit accounts. This is because for seasonal industries, the difference is too high and for non-seasonal industries the difference is too low, (iii) The banks have been asked to fix separate credit limits for peak level and non-peak level credit requirements, (iv) All borrowers (except sick units) with working capital requirements of Rs. 10 lakh and above should be placed under second method of lending recommended by Tandon Committee, (v) The flow of information from borrower to banks should be simplified, and (vi) A portion of raw-material financing should be taken up by banks through drawee bills.

The measures suggested above should be made compulsory for all borrowers having aggregate working capital limits of Rs. 50 lakh and above from the banking system. However, steps should also be taken by banks to enforce the same discipline in stages on borrowers who are enjoying credit limits of less than Rs. 50 lakh from the banking system.

Marathe Committee

Reserve Bank of India, in 1982, appointed a committee under the chairmanship of Marathe to suggest measures for providing meaningful directions to the credit management function of the RBI. The following are the two major recommendations which have been accepted by the RBI with some modification:

(i) The third method of lending as suggested by the Tandon Committee has been declared to be impractical. Thus, in future, the banks should continue to provide credit for working capital to trade and industry as per the second method of lending, (ii) The introduction of the concept of Fast Track' has been suggested. The concept of 'Fast Track' implies that subject to fulfillment of some conditions, banks can release, without prior approval of the RBI, 50 per cent (75 per cent in the case of predominantly export-oriented manufacturing units) of the additional credit required by the borrowers falling within the ambit of the credit authorisation scheme. Thus the credit disbursement is on a faster rate and, hence, it has been properly termed as the 'Fast Track' Scheme.

In order to place on the 'Fast Track', the concerned borrower should comply with the following five requirements.

(i) Reasonableness of estimates in regard to sales chargeable current assets, current liabilities and net working capital, (ii) Classification of current assets and current liabilities in conformity with the guidelines issued by RBI, (iii) Maintenance of minimum current ratio of 1.33:1 (except under exempted categories), (iv) Prompt submission of operating statements, and (v) Submission of annual accounts and review of accounts.

Analysis of Working Capital or Measuring Working Capital

Working Capital is the lifeblood of a business. The success of a business, therefore, depends on its adequacy. The outside parties such as trade creditors, banks and financial institutions, debentureholders, shareholders, etc., and the management of the firm are highly interested in knowing the overall working capital position of a concern through an analysis. Thus the basic aim of working capital analysis is to evaluate solvency, liquidity and the cost of financing a concern.

The analysis of working capital can be conducted through the following methods:

1. Ratio Analysis
2. Funds Flow Analysis
3. Working Capital Budgeting

1. *Ratio Analysis*

Ratio analysis is the most popular technique of working capital analysis. It can be used for measuring short-term liquidity or the working capital position of a concern. Some commonly used ratios for this purpose are as follows:

   (i)   Current Ratio
   (ii)   Acid Test Ratio
   (iii)   Absolute Liquid Ratio
   (iv)   Inventory Turnover Ratio
   (v)   Receivables Turnover Ratio
   (vi)   Payables Turnover Ratio
   (vii)   Working Capital Turnover Ratio
   (viii)   Working Capital Leverage
   (ix)   Ratio of Current Liabilities to Tangible Net Worth.
        Refer Chapter 15, Ratio Analysis.

2. *Funds Flow Analysis*

It is a technique designated to study the sources from which additional funds are derived and the uses to which these funds are being put. It is an effective management tool to study changes in working capital between the two points of time, along with events causing such changes.

The funds flow analysis consists of: (a) preparing schedule of changes in working capital and (b) statement of sources and application of funds.

This technique of measuring working capital will be explained in detail in Chapter 16, Funds Flow Analysis.

3. *Working Capital Budget*

A budget is a financial and/or quantitative expression of business plans and policies to be pursued in the future period of time. Working capital budget is a part of total budgeting process of a business. It is prepared by estimating future long-term and short-term working capital needs and sources to finance them. At the end of the period, actual performance shall be compared with the budgeted figure to find out the variations, if any, so that corrective actions may be taken in the future. However, the successful implementation of working capital budget involves the preparation of separate budgets for various elements of costs such as inventories, receivables and so on.

One of the fundamental objectives of working capital budget is to ensure the availability of funds and their effective utilisation.

CASE STUDY

Working Capital Management in Kerala Electrical and Allied Engineering Company Ltd. (KEL)

KEL was incorporated on 05 June 1964 with the main objective of carrying on the business of electrical, mechanical and structural engineering equipment and fittings. The main products of the company consist of transformers, HRC fuses, relays/contractors/starters, 18W and 25W alternators, electrical accessories and brushless alternators. The authorized and paid-up capital of the company is Rs. 4000.00 lakh and Rs. 3953.53 lakh respectively as on 31st March 2004.

Table 9.1 provides the working capital position of KEL from 1995–96 to 2003–04.

TABLE 9.1   Working Capital of KEL from 1995–96 to 2003–04

Year	Rs. in lakh
1995–1996	67.63
1996–1997	991.38
1997–1998	1585.69
1998–1999	1444.41
1999–2000	691.15
2000–2001	2072.36
2001–2002	392.37
2002–2003	1290.70
2003–2004	1237.81

Source: Review of Public Enterprises in Kerala.

Table 9.1 shows how Kerala Electrical and Allied Engineering has managed its working capital from 1995–96 to 2003–04. Its level of working capital was very low in 1995–96 and 2001–02, moderate in 1996–97 and 1999–2000, high in 2002–03 and 2003–04 and very high in 1997–98, 1998–99 and 2000–01. Its level of working capital was in the highest level in 2000–01. However, this was brought down during 2001–02, 2002–03 and 2003–04, but not to a satisfactory level.

While the major constituent of current assets of the company comprise raw materials, components, stores and spares, work-in-progress, finished goods, cash on hand or in bank deposits, short-term investments, advances paid and receivables, the current liabilities are made up of borrowings from banks, payables to creditors and suppliers and advances received against sales and statutory dues.

Inventories constitute more than 45 per cent of the current assets in all the years under review except during 2000–01 and 2003–04. The average current ratio is 1.38:1. Stores and spares as percentage of current assets comes to 1.38. But the short-term bank borrowings as a percentage of inventories come averaging around 65.

Table 9.2 shows current assets, current liabilities, current ratio, inventory, inventory as a percentage of current assets, stores and spares as a percentage of current assets and short-term bank borrowings as a percentage of inventories of KEL from 1995–96 to 2003–04.

TABLE 9.2 Current Assets, Current Liabilities and Other Working Capital Data of KEL

Year	Current assets (Rs., lakh)	Current liabilities (Rs., lakh)	Current ratio	Inventory (Rs., lakh)	Inventory as a percentage of current assets	Stores & spares as a percentage of current assets	Short-term borrowing as a percentage of inventories
1995–1996	4396.60	4328.97	1.02:1	2192.73	49.88	1.49	68.07
1996–1997	4813.01	3821.63	1.26:1	2505.46	52.06	1.17	58.34
1997–1998	5387.55	3801.86	1.42:1	2618.24	48.60	1.18	51.91
1998–1999	4482.48	3038.07	1.48:1	2111.90	47.12	1.47	71.52
1999–2000	4290.73	3599.58	1.20:1	2259.73	52.67	1.38	67.10
2000–2001	4060.19	1987.83	1.05:1	1791.31	44.12	1.33	58.43
2001–2002	3224.01	2831.64	1.14:1	1458.01	45.23	1.30	92.91
2002–2003	4122.34	2831.64	1.46:1	2303.13	55.87	1.97	59.43
2003–2004	4294.77	3056.96	1.40:1	1644.32	38.29	1.15	60.64

Source: Review of Public Enterprises in Kerala.

Table 9.2 shows that the efficiency of working capital management in KEL is far from satisfactory. The gross current assets of the undertaking form regular input into the business. They are converted into output which on being sold, brings in money to the organisation. The liquid portion of the gross figure is utilised for meeting the day-to-day business commitments.

The table also reveals that inventory constitutes between 45 and 50 per cent of current assets. The average current ratio is 1.49:1. Thus it can be inferred that as the quick ratio increases, the credibility of the concern also increases. This is because the trade creditors feel more secure about the amounts they have extended.

– REVIEW QUESTIONS –

1. What is meant by working capital management? What are the determinants of working capital needs of an enterprise?
2. How are net working capital, liquidity, technical insolvency and risk related?
3. Explain the various approaches to determine an appropriate financing mix of working capital?
4. Discuss the new trends in financing working capital.
5. What do you understand by working capital? Discuss in detail the various methods of working capital analysis?
6. Write notes on:
   (a) Working Capital Forecasting
   (b) Operating Cycle
   (c) Hedging Approach
   (d) Working Capital Analysis
7. Do you agree? Why?
   (a) High levels of working capital decrease risk and decrease return.
   (b) High levels of working capital decrease risk and increase return.

8. Gopal and Co. are engaged in large scale retail business. From the following information, you are required to forecast their working capital requirements.

Projected Annual Sales	Rs. 130 lakhs
Percentage of Net Profit on cost of Sales	25%
Average Credit Period allowed to Debtors	8 weeks
Average Credit Period allowed by Creditors	4 weeks
Average Stock Carrying (in terms of Sales requirements)	8 weeks

Add 10% to computed figures to allow for Contingencies.

(Ans: Rs. 2,640 lakhs)

9. AB Co. are desirous to purchase a business and have consulted you, and one point on which you are asked to advice them is the average amount of working capital which will be required in the first year of working.

You are given the following estimates and are instructed to add 10% to your computed figure to allow for contingencies.

Figures for the year
Rs.

(i) Average amount blocked up for Stocks:
- Stocks of Finished Product 5,000
- Stocks of Store, Materials, etc. 8,000

(ii) Average credit given:
- Inland Sales 6 weeks Credit 3,12,000
- Export Sales 1½ weeks Credit 78,000

(iii) Lag in payment of wages and other outgoings:

– Wages	1½ weeks	2,60,000
– Stocks, Materials etc.	1½ month	48,000
– Rent, Royalties, etc.	6 months	10,000
– Clerical Staff	½ month	62,400
– Manager	½ month	48,000

(iv) Payment in advance:

Sundry Expenses (paid quarterly in advance)	8,000
Undrawn profits on the average throughout the year	11,000

Set-up your calculations for the average amount of working capital required.

(C.A. Final, May, 1969)

(Hint: Assume 12 months or 52 weeks in a year for calculations; Total current assets (all figures in rupees): 53,250;

Finished stock = 5,000, stores and materials = 8,000 Debtors (inland sales) = 36,000, Debtors export = 2,250; Advance payments = 2,000.

Total Current Liabilities (all figures in rupees): 29,100.

Wages = 7,500, Stocks and materials = 6,000 Clerical staff salary = 2,600, Salary to manager = 2,000, Other outstanding expenses = 6,000.

Net Working Capital = Rs. 24,150 Add 10% contingency, then Net Working Capital = Rs. 26,565.

Undrawn profits may be ignored as these profits may be used for long-term investments (purchase of fixed assets, etc.). Further, the amount of undrawn profits is to be adjusted for tax payments, dividends or drawings, and then only it can be taken as a source of working capital. Information for such adjustments is not available, and therefore, it may be ignored.

10. On 1st January of the year, the Managing Director of 'X' Ltd wanted to know the amount of working capital that will be required during the year.

From the following information, prepare the forecast of working capital requirements.

Production in the last year was 60,000 units. The same will be the production of this year.

Estimated ratios of different costs to selling prices are:

– Raw Materials   60%
– Direct Wages   10%
– Overheads   20%

Raw materials will remain in store, on an average for 2 months, before issued for production.

Each unit will be in production process for '1' month with the raw materials being fed into pipeline immediately. The labour and overhead costs will occur evenly during the period.

Finished goods will stay in the warehouse, awaiting despatch to customers, for approximately '3' months.

Credit allowed by creditors is '2' months from the date of delivery of raw materials.

Credit allowed to debtors is '3' months from the date of despatch.

There are regular production and sales cycles.

Wages are paid on 1st day of a month. The company keeps normally Rs. 20,000 as cash in hand.

Selling price is Rs. 5 per unit.

(**Ans:** Working Capital Requirements = Rs. 1,78,750)

11. 'XYZ' Ltd. earns gross profit of 20% on its sales. Depreciation is allowed as on expenses for computing cost of production.

The following information is available in the financial statements of the company:

	Rs.
– Credit Sales	17,00,000
– Raw Materials	4,00,000
– Direct Wages	3,20,000
– Manufacturing Overheads Outstanding at the end of the year	30,000
– Administrative Expenses	1,10,000
– Promotional Expenses	50,000
– Income Tax, payable in 4 equal instalments	1,40,000

Other Informations:

(i) Credit period allowed to customers = 2 months
(ii) Purchase of raw materials on '1' month credit

(iii) Wages for a month are paid in the next month.

(iv) Cash manufacturing and administrative expenses are paid one month in arrear.

(v) Promotional expenses are paid quarterly and in advance.

(vi) One instalment of income-tax payable is outstanding.

(vii) The inventory policy of the company requires that one month's stock of all the items of raw materials and finished products should be maintained.

(viii) The company wishes to maintain a cash balance of Rs. 80,000 and wants to have a 25% safety margin for its working capital requirements.

Ignoring investments in work-in-progress, estimate the working capital requirements of the company. Consider cash costs only.

(**Ans.:** Net Working Capital = Rs. 2,88,324

Add 20% safety margin = 2,88,324 + 20% of 2,88,324;

= 2,88,324 + 57,665 = Rs. 3,45,989)

12. Shri Ganesh wishes to start a trading business and furnishes the following particulars:

(i) Estimated Annual Sales – Rs. 10,80,000.

(ii) Estimated Fixed Expenses – Rs. 2,100 p.m. of which depreciation amounted to Rs. 500 and estimated variable expenses chargeable to P/L Account equal to 5% of sales.

(iii) Expected Profit on purchases – 20%

(iv) Expected Stock – turnover 5 times

(v) The sales and purchases will occur evenly throughout the year.

(vi) All purchases will be made on one month's credit.

(vii) Customers will be allowed to two month's credit.

(viii) 25% of sales will be made against cash.

You are required to calculate:

(a) His estimated profit for the year.

(b) His average working capital requirements.

(**Ans.:** (a) Rs. 1,00,800 (b) Rs. 2,46,100)

13. From the following information prepare a statement showing the working capital requirements:

Budgeted Sales   Rs. 26,00,000 per annum

Analysis of one rupee of Sales	Rs.
Raw Materials	0.30
Direct Labour	0.40
Overheads	0.20
Total Cost	0.90
Profit	0.10
Sales	1.00

It is estimated that:

(1) Raw materials are carried in stock for 3 weeks and finished goods for 2 weeks.

(2) Factory processing will take 3 weeks.

(3) Suppliers will give 5 weeks credit.

(4) Customers will require 8 weeks credit.

(**Ans.:** Rs. 55,000)

10

Management of Inventories

Inventory management is planning and devising procedures to maintain an optimum level of raw materials, work-in-progress, finished goods, consumables and stores.

CONTENTS

- Introduction
- Techniques of inventory management
- Case study
- Review questions

INTRODUCTION

Industrialisation is an important means of modernization. The increased pace of industrialization in India, in its wake, highlighted a number of managerial problems. Among them, the problem of inventory management is significant. The need for efficient management of available resources in any business organization requires no emphasis and an industrial undertaking which is expected to be run efficiently on business principles is no exception. In several industrial undertakings run by the government cost of input contributes to nearly 60 per cent of the total cost. All the efforts of the government to increase the price of the finished products remain ineffective on account of the acute competition in the business. Left with no choice, the industrial undertakings are forced to manage their available resources more efficiently.

The role of capital is crucial in the context of industrial development. It is all the more true in the case of capital scarce countries like India. The capital raised by a firm is invested in fixed assets and current assets for carrying on its activities. The portion invested in current assets is called the working capital and the inventory constitutes the largest proportion of it. Thus inventories call for efficient management. Good inventory management is good financial management also. One must agree with the observation that "when you need money, look at your inventories before you look to your bankers."

Efficient use of capital in an undertaking helps to provide maximum customer service and earn profit in the process. These objectives can be achieved with the given amount of capital either by maximizing the output or by maximizing the margin of profit or by a combination of both. It would mean that the management must try to make this capital work as fast as possible, which is often difficult to materialize. It is also impossible to raise the margin of profit extensively due to competition in business. Thus capital turnover and productivity of capital often become totally ineffective.

Several modern techniques have been developed and employed by managers as a solution to this problem. Among these, inventory management is the most effective. It enables a manager to increase productivity of capital by reducing material costs, preventing blocking up of large working capital for long periods and improving capital turnover.

The concept of inventory mangement has been one of the many analytical aspects of management. It involves optimization of resources available for holding stock of various materials. Lack of inventory can lead to stock-outs, causing stoppage of production and a very high inventory will result in increased cost due to cost of carrying inventory. Thus optimization of inventory should ensure that inventories are neither too low nor too high.

Inventories like finished products, work-in-progress, components, raw materials, stores, spares, etc., account for 80 per cent or more of the working capital in some of the industries. It would appear that any effort for rationalization of inventories will bring about an appreciable saving. But a scientific system of control can reduce investment in inventories considerably, sometimes as much as 50 per cent or more.

Historical Aspect

In the past, an individual's wealth was usually assessed by the size of his blocks, granaries and warehouses. But with the advent of modern industrialisation, wealth has become more identified with money. There has been a strong tendency towards holding the means to purchase goods and services rather than goods themselves. Inventories are now often referred to as the graveyard of business as surplus stocks have been the principal cause of business failures.

Modern managers have made a complete change in the outlook of inventory holdings on account of:

1. increasing size of the business establishments,
2. wide variety and complexity of modern requirements and
3. urgency of modern requirements.

In USA, there are many professional societies concerned with inventory management. The biggest of these is the National Association of Purchasing Management, which has roughly twice the membership of the American Production and Inventory Control Society is the second ranking organization. While each of these groups is concerned with the broad problems of materials management, it is significant that each focuses its major emphasis on a segment of the materials management process—purchasing in one case and production and inventory control in the other.

In contrast to the situation in the United States, inventory management is firmly established in Japan, where the Material Management Society is the major organisation of this type. Similarly, the Institute of Purchasing and Supply, which is identified as the British equivalent of the National Association of Purchasing Management has been set up to provide greater emphasis on materials management activities other than purchasing.

Inventories in India, whether in the private sector or in the public sector, are much higher than those in the United States and Western Europe mainly on account of the different procurement procedures followed. But even with regard to the nationally available materials the supply position is difficult and the means of transport are inadequate.

Inventory management has been attracting the attention of managers in India for a long time. But with the credit squeeze measures announced by the Government of India and the consideration of the Tandon Committee for inventories, top management is deeply involved in developing suitable norms for inventory control. Tandon Committee appointed by the RBI dealt with prescribing inventory norms towards industries for the smooth running with no stockout.

Meaning and Function

Inventories are resources of any kind having an economic value. It consists of raw materials, work-in-progress, finished goods, consumables and stores. Thus inventory control is planning and devising procedures to maintain an optimal level of these resources.

Inventory functions as a bank and decouples successive stages of operation. Materials, manufacturing and marketing departments are the three operating sub-systems. Finance and personnel control are the non-operating sub-systems. The material sub-system procures the input, the manufacturing sub-system converts it and the marketing sub-system sells the output. The other sub-systems like finance and personnel, serve the needs of the above three operating sub-systems.

Need for Inventory

Primarily, inventory is held for transaction purposes. Today's inventory is tomorrow's consumption. A business cannot maintain a given volume of sales without maintaining sufficient inventory to satisfy its customers. In the field of production, an enterprise cannot ensure uninterrupted production unless it maintains adequate inventory of raw materials.

Inventory is also held as a precaution or as a contingency for increase in lead time or consumption rate. Sometimes, there is speculative element in the reasons for holding inventory. It largely takes into account the expectation of changes in price/cost over a period of time. Finally, inventories are held to decouple the materials department from the consuming department.

Scope and Importance

The industry in various sectors has grown considerably and consequently the working capital blocked up in inventories has also gone up. With rapid modernisation of management, various effective tools and techniques have been evolved for efficient management of inventories. Many firms have taken advantage of these new developments and restructured their inventory management department in tune with the modern trend and have obtained the benefits of cost reduction. Some firms are in the process of getting their personnel trained while many others have not yet initiated to tone up their inventory divisions and get their personnel trained. As a result, the inventories in various forms still remain high in these firms and a major opportunity for cost reduction is being lost.

Private sector undertakings in India are making some savings in inventories by effecting both internal and external economies, as otherwise their very existence itself will be threatened. The internal economies in the public sector are not so effective as those of the private sector on account of social responsibilities and obligations. Most public sector undertakings in India were making heavy losses until a few years back and even now the return on their investment is nowhere comparable to that of the private sector.

There are possibilities to reduce the cost of purchased materials by competitive bidding, value analysis, etc., while savings in the cost of holding inventories can arise out of economic ordering, reducing deterioration and obsolescence in storage, etc., and thereby reducing the working capital blocked up.

Inventory Problem

An analysis of sales of the industrial undertakings during 2000-01 gives the following information:

Direct Material	–	60%
Labour	–	15%
Overheads and Profit	–	25%
Total	–	100%

The above data show that direct materials and indirect materials forming part of the overhead cost, constituting inventories account for a large percentage of the total cost. Inventories, therefore, offer the most important and fruitful area of cost reduction and increased profits.

Inventory problem is one of balancing various costs so that the total cost should be minimized. These costs are:

(a) Cost of ordering

(b) Cost of holding or carrying inventory

(c) Under stocking cost, and

(d) Overstocking cost.

The cost of ordering opposes the cost of carrying while the under-stocking cost opposes overstocking cost. If these costs operate in the same direction, instead of behaving in opposition, there will be no inventory problem. The cost of ordering and the cost of carrying enable us to optimize on the number of orders and the quantity of inventory to be ordered. The understocking and overstocking costs, help an industrial unit to determine the service level that has to be maintained by the inventory.

Cost of Ordering: An organization can attain its need for materials only after fulfilling certain activities. These activities consume executive and non-executive time, stationery and communication charges, thus giving rise to the ordering cost. The cost of an imported order is much greater than that of a cash purchase from the market. This is on account of the variation in the level of activities for different ranges of items.

The ordering cost consists of the costs due to:

(i) Stationery, typing and despatching of orders and reminders.

(ii) Advertisements, tender forms, tender opening formalities, etc.

(iii) Follow-up for expediting. These will be the costs associated with travel, telephone, telegrams and postal bills.

(iv) Costs incurred by the goods received by inspection and handling.

(v) Rent and depreciation on the space and equipment utilized by the concerned purchasing personnel.

(vi) Salaries and all statutory payments to the purchasing personnel.

(vii) Cost of source developments; and

(viii) Cost of entertaining suppliers.

Thus the average ordering cost is:

$$\frac{\text{Total costs incurred on all these heads during a year}}{\text{Number of orders in that year}}$$

In addition to the ordering cost, the set-up cost should also be taken into account while scheduling production in the industrial undertakings. It consists of idle time, cost of labour and tooling involved in the change of product from one to the other.

One of the major components of ordering costs in these undertakings is salaries. This can be controlled if the number of men in purchasing is kept as low as possible. Hence, any jump in the total salary paid should not be allowed unless there is a corresponding increase in the number of orders. The use of overtime can be considered cheaper when there is a marginal increase in the number of orders.

Cost of Holding or Carrying Inventory: One of the motivating factors to control inventory arises on account of its carrying cost. It comes around 30 per cent of the total inventory cost in most of the industrial undertakings, i.e., if the annual average inventory is valued at Rs. 100, then it will cost the concern Rs. 30 to carry it.

Inventory carrying cost is usually expressed as a percentage of the average investment in inventory. Capital cost, cost of storage and handling and deterioration and obsolescence cost are its main components.

Capital costs are mainly represented by interest charges. The storage costs vary widely in accordance with the type of materials stored, type of storage facilities used and other factors. It consists of rent for storage facilities, salaries of personnel and related storage expenses. The total cost on account of deterioration, wastage, obsolescence, etc., may well lie between 10 to 20 per cent of the average value of inventory in most of the industrial undertakings.

Understocking Cost: It is the penalty incurred to the concern on account of the inability to meet the demand in time. The quantum of penalty depends on the nature of the demand. In the cases where the demand is from a customer of the retail establishment, the shortage condition may result in a cost relatively small compared with the item cost. If, on the contrary, the demand arises in a manufacturing activity, the penalty cost for shortage may be extremely high relative to the cost of the item. This is because the entire manufacturing activity would necessarily have to wait for the item which is short.

Overstocking Cost: The overstocking cost arises on account of the opportunity lost when investment in inventories is postponed for a longer period than necessary. In the case of items which will ultimately be used, this cost can be equated with the carrying cost. For items which cannot be used after a certain period, this cost will be the difference between the cost of the item and its salvage value.

As far as an organization is concerned, the situation of both overstocking and understocking is not at all happy. Both shortages and surpluses are required to balance one against the other as they are costly. Arriving at the happy medium between too much and too little is the essence of inventory management.

Lead Time Influences on Inventories

There is a direct relationship between lead time and inventories. During lead time, there will be no delivery of materials and the consuming departments will have to be served from the inventories held. Both lead time and consumption rate can increase without notice and the inventories will have to be geared up for this contingency. Inventories have to be stocked to take care of normal consumption during both average lead time and abnormal lead time. Therefore, as lead time increases, the inventories will have to increase correspondingly.

The influence of various types of lead time on inventory decisions are:

(a) administrative lead time

(b) manufacturing lead time

(c) transporting lead time, and

(d) inspection lead time.

Administrative lead time arises on account of the activities like identification of needs and follow-up orders. In the identification stage the planning section has to compute the requirements of various materials over a time horizon. The actual computing time may be only around half an hour, but the planning department may take two to three weeks to raise an indent. This increase will be due to the waiting time for discussions, meetings, approvals and signatures, especially so in the case of new materials.

An average time required in the industrial undertakings to convert an indent into an order is about two and a half months for new items. First of all locate the source and then negotiate the terms and conditions of supply. Once the negotiations are complete, the order can be placed. For imported items formalities such as DGTD clearance, FE clearance, import license and raising a letter of credit should also be undertaken, thus, leading to an increase in the lead time.

The manufacturing lead time depends entirely on the supplier. Once the order is placed, the purchaser has to wait till the supplier delivers the goods.

The transporting lead time depends on the mode of transport. The time consuming formalities such as insurance, sales tax forms and retiring of documents are involved in it. Customs formalities will add to the lead time requirements for imported items as the trans-shipment is to be made at the port itself.

Inspection lead time arises on account of the non-availability of the standard to compare the quality of the received item. In the case of special equipment, the indenter may himself depute the inspection personnel, which naturally increases the lead time. A pertinent factor which has to be taken note of is that, if an item is rejected during inspection, the lead time will be increased by the time taken to supply the replacement.

Of the various components of lead time, the procurement or manufacturing lead time is the toughest nut to crack. This should be taken care of while negotiating the order and supply details. The administrative and inspection lead time are under the control of the purchaser. The transportation lead time can be reduced by a cost tradeoff but not below the threshold.

TECHNIQUES OF INVENTORY MANAGEMENT

The basic problem of inventory management is to strike a balance between the operating efficiency and the cost of investment and other associated costs with large inventories, with the objective of keeping the basic conflicts at the minimum while optimizing the inventory holding. The decisions as to which item to make and when to keep inventories in balance requires application of a wide range of techniques from simple graphical methods to more sophisticated and complex quantitative techniques. Many of these techniques employ concepts and tools of mathematics and statistics and make use of various control theories from engineering and other fields. They are primarily aimed at helping to make better decisions and getting people employed and follow a wiser policy.

Various techniques applied for inventory management are as follows:

1. Selective Inventory Control
2. Setting of Various Stock Levels
3. Systems of Inventory Control
4. Economic Ordering Quantity or E.O.Q. Formula
5. Re-order Point and Safety Stock
6. Application of Computers for Inventory
7. Just-in-Time Inventory Management
8. Inventory Ratio
9. Aging Schedule of Inventory
10. Inventory Audit.

1. Selective Inventory Control

Effective inventory management requires understanding and knowledge of the nature of inventories and, to gain this understanding, some analysis and classification of inventory are required. They are:

(a) ABC Analysis

(b) HML Analysis

(c) XYZ Analysis

(d) VED Analysis

(e) FSN Analysis

(f) SDE Analysis

(g) GOLF Analysis

(h) SOS Analysis

Classification of Inventories

Sl. No.	Title	Basic	Main use
1.	ABC (Always Better Control)	Value of conception	To control raw material, components and work-in-progress inventories in the normal course of business
2.	HML (High, Medium, Low)	Unit price of the material	Mainly to control purchases
3.	XYZ	Value of the items in storage	To review the inventories and their uses at scheduled intervals
4.	VED (Vital, Essential, Desirable)	Criticality of the component	To determine the stocking levels of spare parts
5.	FSN (Fast moving, Slow moving, Non-moving)	Consumption pattern of of the component	To control obsolescence
6	SDE (Scarce, Difficult, Easy to obtain)	Problems faced in procurement	Lead time analysis and purchasing strategies
7.	GOLF (Government Ordinary, Local, Foreign Sources)	Source of the material	Procurement strategies
8.	SOS (Seasonal, Off-Seasonal)	Nature of supplies	Procurement/holding strategies for seasonal items like agricultural products.

Source: Sandilya, M.S. and Gopalakirshanan, P., *Inventory Management: Text and Cases* (Delhi: Macmillian India Limited, 1981), p. 51.

The motive behind the above analyses and classifications is to tackle important aspects more vigorously. Moreover, an equally critical analyses of all items will be very expensive and will have a diffused effect regardless of priorities.

ABC Analysis

The method follows the general principles of Pareto (Wilfredo Pareto, Italy, 1896). With some practices, the limits of 'A', 'B', and 'C' can be easily determined by a Pareto Analysis; namely, 'A' items do not exceed more than 70 per cent of the investment, 'B' items account for only a moderate share, and 'C' items for less than 10 per cent of total investment.

The ABC Analysis is a rational approach for determining the degree of control that should be exercised on each item in inventories. Obviously, 'A' class items should be subjected to strict management control under either continuous review or periodic review with short review cycles. 'C' class items require little attention and can be relegated down the line for periodic review say, just once a year. Control over 'B' class items should be somewhere in-between.

The Method of ABC classification for managing inventories has been adopted in most of the medium, and large-scale industrial units. Inventories of these undertakings are classified into various categories on the basis of their importance namely their value and frequency of replenishment during a period. One category called group 'A' items, consists of only a small percentage of the total items handled but has a combined value that constitutes a major or large portion of a total stock holding of the concern. The second category consisting of group 'B' items is relatively less important. The third category consisting of 'C' items is of least importance i.e., the group consists of a very large number of items, the value of which is not very high.

ABC Analysis of a Firm

For the purpose of ABC classification of inventories and the method of control to be adopted for each category of items, the firm first of all lists out all the items of inventory. The value is obtained by multiplying the average annual consumption of an item during a period by its unit cost. The items in the list are then rearranged in the descending order of their values irrespective of their quantities. Thus 200 kg. of an item valued at Rs. 2,00,000 should be ranked earlier than 20,000 kg. of another item, the value of which is Rs. 18,000. A running total of all the values is then taken. It is found that a large percentage of the total value is covered by the first few items in the list. They are grouped in the 'A' category, the next few items which have the next least value under 'B' group and the last value items are grouped under 'C' category. So, by controlling the 'A' group items only, a better inventory control is possible. Table 10.1 shows the classification of inventories and its annual consumption value of an electrical industry.

An analysis of the annul consumption of an electrical industry shows that 80 per cent of the total annual consumption value accounts for 10 per cent of the total number of items under category 'A'. Similarly, five per cent of the total annual consumption value accounts for more than 70 per cent of the total number of items under category 'C' and 15 per cent of the total annual consumption value accounts for nearly 20 per cent of the total number of items under category 'B'. Table 5.3 shows the above characteristics.

TABLE 10.1 Classification of Inventory and its Annual Consumption Value of an Electrical Industry

Sl. No.	Name of item	Annual Consumption Value
	A Group	
1.	Magnet	74,00,000
2.	41 S.N.G.	55,00,000
3.	Lamination	41,00,000
4.	Brass Terminals	22,00,000
5.	Magnet Yoke	10,00,000
	B Group	
1.	Copper strips	73,000
2.	M.S. Screws H1	72,000
3.	Sealing Lead	71,000
4.	Press-Phan Sheet	70,000
5.	Charcoal	68,000
	C Group	
1.	Grinding Wheel	14,000
2.	Leather Glouse	14,000
3.	Screw Drivers	13,000
4.	Insulation Tape	12,000
5.	Acid	11,000

Table 10.2 is depicted graphically in Figure 10.1.

TABLE 10.2 ABC Analysis of United Electrical Industries Limited, Kerala

Class	Number of Items (% of total)	Value of Items (% of total)
A	10	80
B	20	15
C	70	5

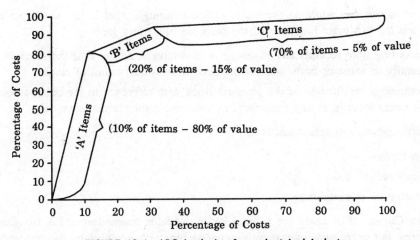

FIGURE 10.1 ABC Analysis of an electrical industry.

2. Setting of Various Stock Levels

The various stock levels fixed for effective management of inventories are maximum level, minimum level, ordering or reordering level and danger level. These levels serve as indices for initiating action on time so that the quantity of each item of material, i.e., the inventory holding is controlled.

Stock levels are not fixed on a permanent basis but are liable to revision in accordance with the changes in the factors determining the levels.

The formulae used for fixing various levels are:

Maximum Level   = Re-Order Level − Expected minimum   + Re-order quantity
                                  consumption in units
                                  during minimum
                                  weeks to obtain delivery

Minimum Level   = Re-Order Level − (Average usage per period ×
                                  Average time to obtain delivery)

Re-Order Level   = Maximum Re-order Period × Maximum Usage

$$\text{Average Stock Level} = \frac{\text{Maximum Level} + \text{Minimum Level}}{2}$$

Danger level is fixed usually below the minimum level. When the stock reaches this level, very urgent action for purchase is indicated. This presupposes that the minimum level contains a cushion to cover such contingencies.

3. Systems of Inventory Control

The main systems of inventory control are:

(a) Perpetual Inventory (Automatic Inventory) system

(b) Double Bin System

(a) Perpetual Inventory System

The control of inventories while in storage is effected through what is known as the perpetual inventory. Thus the two main functions of the perpetual inventory are:

(i) Recording store receipts and issues so as to determine at any time the stock in hand, in quantity or value or both, without the need for physical count of stock.

(ii) Continuous verification of the physical stock with reference to the balance recorded in the stores records, at any frequency, as convenient for the management.

Perpetual inventory system consists of:

(i) Bin cards

(ii) Stores ledger, and

(iii) Continuous stock taking

(i) **Bin Cards:** Bin cards are printed cards used for accounting stock of materials in stores. For every item of materials, separate bin cards are kept by the concerns.

Details regarding the material such as name of material, part number, date of receipt and issue, reference number, name of supplier, quantity received and issued, value of material, rate, balance quantity, etc., are recorded in the bin cards. The bin cards are kept in the bin serially according to part number of the component. At the end of the financial year, the balance quantity in the bin cards is taken as closing stock, and it is valued at rates in the bin cards.

Bin Card Valuation: Stock in certain industrial units are valued under the weighted average system. In this system, the average rate of the item is arrived at by taking into account the value of previous stock. The quantity of the previous stock is added to the receipt. The total value of the previous stock and new receipt is divided by the total quantity. The resultant figure is the weighted average rate of that item, i.e.,

$$\text{Weighted average} = \frac{\text{Value of stock in hand} + \text{Value of the materials received/purchased}}{\text{Quantity of material in hand} + \text{Quantity of material received/purchased}}$$

(ii) **Stores Ledger:** Like bin cards, stores ledger is maintained to record all receipts and issues in respect of materials with the difference that along with the quantities, the values are entered in the receipt, issue and balance columns. Additional information as noted in the bin cards regarding quantity on order and quantity reserved, together with their values may also be recorded in the stores ledger.

(iii) **Continuous Stock Taking:** The perpetual inventory system is not complete without a systematic procedure for physical verification of stores. The bin cards and stores ledger record the balances but their correctness can be verified by means of physical verification only.

There is a proper procedure for the physical verification of stocks in most of the industrial units in India. The excess/shortage found in the verification is reported to higher authorities for action and to avoid differences in stock.

Physical Verification Report: It is necessary to record the result of stock verification in a separate record or report. These reports are maintained date-wise so that when arranged together, they give a chronological list of the items verified. The quantity actually found on stock verification is noted in the proper column by the stock verifier who also enters the verification report, the balance on date as shown in the bin card. The report is then sent to the stores ledger clerk who enters the balance as recorded in the stores ledger. Thus for each item of store in the stock verification report, there are three sets of entries for the quantity.

Value Analysis: Value analysis is a recently developed technique in industrial undertakings to obtain optimum benefit from materials. This implies the minimizing of the value of materials consumed which, in turn, enables reduction of the inventory to be carried out.

Value analysis investigation is usually carried out every year for 'A' and 'B' items in order to:

(i) Minimize its consumption

(ii) Substitute it with cheaper materials in all or some of the application for which it is presently used.

(b) Double Bin System

Double Bin system is a recently developed technique in certain industries in respect of low consumption value items, i.e., items belonging to class 'C' in ABC analysis. This system separates the stock of each item into two bins, one to store the quantity equal to minimum quantity and the other to store the remaining quantity. The staff has instructions not to use the quantity in the smaller portion as long as there is stock in the other portion. As soon as it becomes necessary to use the quantity marked as minimum, it is a signal to place new orders. When the fresh order is received, the minimum quantity is segregated.

Double bin system is ideal for items for which demand and lead time are fairly regular and established. It also avoids the necessity of taking physical inventories as in the case of perpetual inventory system. Since the storekeeper knows automatically when to initiate replenishment action, this being the time when he is forced to dip his hand into the minimum stock bin.

In the fixed order quantity or double bin system, there is built-in safety in that the replenishment interval between two successive orders varies and hence adequate arrangements are required to take care of variations in the rate of demand. If the usage rate rises, the re-order level is reached earlier than expected so that the replenishment interval is shortened. On the other hand, if the rate of usage goes down the replenishment interval is lightened. In either case, safety stock has to provide protection against variation in demand in lead time only.

This is explained with the following illustration relating to an item of low consumption value on which replenishments are obtained.

Let

Expected monthly usage of the item	= 200	units
Provision of safety stock at 2 months supply	= 400	units
Lead time for procurement of the item	= 3	months
Order quantity at 6 months supply	= 1200	units
Actual monthly usage in a period of 6 months	= 300	units

Here, order level is 1000 units comprising 400 units of safety stock and 600 units of expected usage during the lead time of three months. As a result of rise in usage rate, the position would be as shown in Figure 10.2. The re-order level will be reached after two months in lieu of

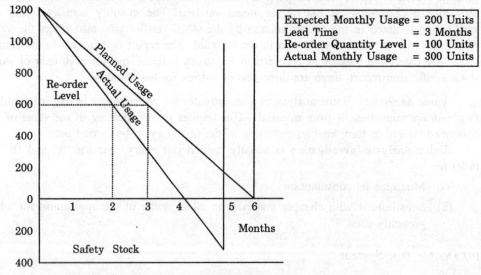

FIGURE 10.2 Double Bin System.

the expected three months. A fresh order will then be placed for 1200 units. The shipment will arrive after another three months, i.e., at the end of the fifth month. By that time 5 × 300 = 1500 units will have been consumed. In other words, all of the 1,200 units of working inventory and 300 units of safety stock will be consumed by the time the new shipment arrives. The amount of safety stock at the time of receiving fresh supplies will be 100 units. The safety stock will be largely eaten up but there will be no stockout.

4. Economic Ordering Quantity or EOQ Formula

In the fixed order quantity system the re-order quantity is the economic order quantity that is fixed in such a manner that would minimize the total variable cost of managing the inventory. The various components of this cost are as follows:

(a) Procurement cost (this includes administrative and provisioning costs)

(b) Storage cost (this includes carrying, handling, etc.)

(c) Stock out cost (this may be laid down by management according to its policy)

The appropriate term economic order quantity appears to be "economic lot size" meaning thereby the quantity that should be accepted per occasion so as to make the inventory procurement cost equal to the inventory carrying cost.

A company is said to be on a point of minimum cost when its ordering cost is just equal to the carrying cost. In other words, a company should neither store excess quantity of material nor should it frequently place too many orders for the same material. When unit price is same regardless of the quantity purchased, the following formula is used. Then it is found that the order quantity varies in proportion to the square root of the demand. There are indices given on scientific basis to order quantity, keeping in view the position cost of inventories, viz., the set up costs, ordering costs and carrying costs. This is known as Economic Order Quantity (EOQ) or Square Root Formula, developed by R.H. Wilson around the thirties and may be modified according to necessity.

$$\text{EOQ or } D = \sqrt{\frac{2Q(a)}{c}}$$

Where,

Q = Annual Requirement in units
a = Unit cost of placing an order
c = Annual Carrying Cost
D = Optimum lot Quantity or Batch Size.

This can be verified with reference to the assumptions in Table 10.3:

Cost of each article is one rupee. Annual demand is 40,000 units. Cost of carrying inventory is 20 per cent. Cost per order is Rs. 10. Using the formula

$$D = \sqrt{\frac{2Q(a)}{c}} = \sqrt{\frac{2 \times 10 \times 40,000}{1 \times 0.20}}$$

$$= \sqrt{40,00,000} \quad D = 2,000 \text{ units}$$

Here, the economic order quantity is 2,000 units. When EOQ is 2,000 units, the number of orders to be placed in a year is 20 and the total cost is Rs. 400 (both total ordering cost and inventory carrying cost are the same, i.e., Rs. 200 + Rs. 200) (Table 10.3).

TABLE 10.3 Tabular Presentation of Economic Order Quantity of 200 Units

Number of Orders Placed	Order Quantity	Average Stock Holding	Inventory Carrying Cost (Rs.)	Ordering Cost (Rs.)	Total Cost (Rs.)
1	40,000	20,000	4,000	10	4,010
2	20,000	10,000	2,000	20	2,020
3	13,333	6,667	1,333	30	1,363
4	10,000	5,000	1,000	40	1040
5	8,000	4,000	800	50	850
10	4,000	2,000	400	100	500
15	2,667	1,334	267	150	417
20	2,000	1,000	200	200	400
25	1,600	800	160	250	410
30	1,333	667	133	300	433

The graphical presentation of the behaviour of ordering and carrying costs is shown in Figure 10.3

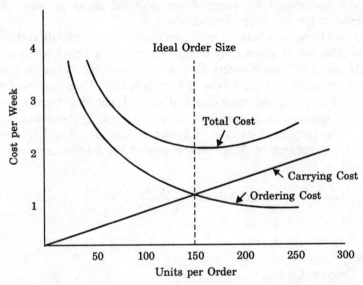

FIGURE 10.3 Behaviour of Ordering and Carrying Costs.

5. Re-order Point and Safety Stock

The computation of re-order point in the industrial units is expressed in terms of number of units per day, multiplied by the lead time in days with adjustments to provide safety stock, thus the formula followed is:

Re-order point = Average daily usage × Lead time in days + Safety stock

Safety stock refers to extra inventory held as a protection against the possibility of a stockout. Stockouts are not only costly but also highly embarrassing to the concern. Thus the safety stock is to be provided to avoid stockout situation that may arise due to unforeseen increase in the rate of consumption during lead time and also increase in the lead time itself.

The problem of safety stock usually does not occur with regard to certain items which are readily available from local sources and those for which substitutes are available. Therefore, the level of safety stock of an item would depend upon whether its shortage would promptly be met, and if not what the stockout cost would be.

The quantity of safety to be carried depends upon how much of safety is to be secured or stockouts incurred. Instances are not rare in the industrial units where at each level of decision making, an ad hoc safety of 10 per cent is added. Such an approach will automatically result in undue overstocking. A larger inventory of safety stock means higher inventory carrying cost. While fixing safety stock in these industrial units, the following factors are considered:

(a) Analysis of lead time in terms of fluctuations.

(b) Usage behaviour-study of fluctuation in rate of consumption.

(c) Importance of the item in the manufacturing programme.

(d) Frequency of the suppliers not honouring commitments on delivery.

(e) Stockout cost.

Safety stock level can also be determined through statistical formula, although there is a good deal of controversy regarding its outright application. There are two commonly employed probability approaches to inventory control in which demand varies. They are:

(a) Fixed Quantity – Variable Cycle System, and

(b) Fixed Cycle – Variable Quantity System.

Fixed quantity-variable cycle system considers buying a fixed lot size at varying intervals. The fixed quantity may be determined by the use of the EOQ formula. This approach is most often used for medium and low value items, where lesser control is allowable.

Fixed cycle-variable quantity system is followed for controlling of high value, critical and rapidly depreciable inventory items where close control is a must. Under this system, it is necessary to vary the lot size as demand changes, while keeping the interval for placing orders constant.

Figure 10.4 demonstrates how inventory should fluctuate when forecasts of lead time and

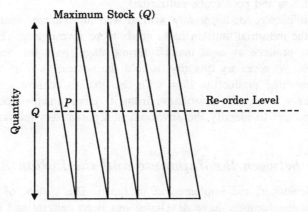

FIGURE 10.4 Fluctuation of Inventory.

usage are accurate. When stock level reaches the order point 'P', the quantity to be ordered is 'Q'. It arrives exactly when stock reaches 'zero' balance. The maximum stock, therefore, is 'Q' and the minimum stock is 'zero'. In such ideal conditions, there would be no fear of shortages and no need for safety stocks. A fixed amount would be re-ordered at fixed intervals.

6. Application of Computers for Inventory

The scope of application of computers in areas like inventory management is really immense. But not many undertakings in India have applied the computer for inventory management and other decision making purposes. The bulk of the applications are in the areas of mundane pay-roll accounting and billing where the computer has been turned into an efficient clerk and printing machine.

Regular inventory management operations can be easily computerized. With the basic issues and receipts document, the materials ledger can be kept up-to-date. The inventory planning, material budgeting and inventory valuation can be efficiently computerized. Applications such as bill of materials, ABC, XYZ and FSN analysis can be done periodically. Similarly, the minimum, maximum and safety stock levels can be fixed with the help of computers. Moreover, if the manual or mechanized system has been properly designed, the implementation of a computerized system will not pose any problem.

The changeover from a mechanized to a computerized system depends on the volume of the work involved. On an average, about 1% to 2% of the turnover can be spent on data processing. If a computer facility can undertake to perform the required job at this cost, the changeover would be advisable. In addition to the job performed by the mechanized process, the computer's access to memory can store data.

The computerized system for managing inventories have not so far been fully introduced in most industrial units in India.

7. Just-in-Time (JIT) Inventory Management

Many successful Japanese companies use a radically different manufacturing philosophy popularly and descriptively termed "just-in-time". It is not just a battery of technique but a grand manufacturing philosophy. The purpose behind the technique is to eliminate waste—not only the conventional form of waste such as scrap, rework and equipment downtime, but also excess lead time, over production and poor space utilization.

JIT as a philosophy has apparently worked well in Japanese manufacturing context but its applicability in the industrial units in India needs to be investigated. The basic principle of this philosophy is to produce at each manufacturing stage, only the necessary products at the necessary time in the necessary quantity to hold the successive manufacturing stages together. It provides a smoother production flow with the goal to achieve a single unit lot size. An organization cannot adopt JIT in isolation from its environment—both internal and external. Hence, it is important to identify the environmental parameters relevant to the success of JIT programme.

Comparison between the Japanese and the Indian Situations

JIT has been developed and implemented in Japan. The system of production and quality management that the Japanese have developed has deep cultural and national roots. Hence, a comparison of Japanese and Indian industries will help examine the applicability of JIT in the

Indian environment and also identify the possible problem areas and steps to be taken to tackle those problems. Table 10.4 shows the comparison of attributes in Japanese and Indian industries.

TABLE 10.4 Comparison of Attributes in Japanese and Indian Industries

Sl. No.	Category	Japanese Industry	Indian Industry
1.	People	a. Japanese workers co-operation, dedication, harmony and group thinking decision process	a. Indian workers have low moral and poor commitment.
		Takes pride in his company high level of motivation	Usually does not identify himself with the company, comparative lack of motivation
		High literacy	Low literacy
		Multi-functional workers	Specialised workers
		b. Enterprise Union (Japan is a homogeneous society)	b. Multifarious union (India is a heterogeneous society
2.	Plants	High-level of automation: CAD/CAM robotics used	Very less automation: CAD/CAM robotics are largely absent
		Group Technology present	Group Technology is absent
		Autonomous Machining, 100% inspection used	These techniques are absent
		Lighted displays to high-light trouble spots are used	Such things are rarely used
		Companies have their own tool makers to build machines	Machines brought from outside usually on the basis of what is available
		Orderliness, cleanliness and arrangement practiced	Comparatively untidy and disorganized
3.	Quality Control	Quality at the source, defect prevention	Statical sampling after lot has been produced, defect detection
		Workers and Foremen have primary responsibility for quality	Quality is the responsibility of Quality Control Department
		100% quality present	Low quality
4.	Production Management	Kanban (Pull System)	MRP (Push System)
		Preventive maintenance	Mostly breakdown maintenance is followed
		Production line slows down for quality problem speeds up when quality is right	Production lines run at fixed rate; quality problems are sent offline
5.	Product and its Value	Customer-oriented product and provides real value	Indigenous R & D lacking. Products customer-oriented but not to the extent desired by a common man.
		Belief in long-term gains, low profit margin	Strive for short-term gains and high profit margins

Source: Prem Vrat, Saurabh Mittal and Kavi Tyagi, "Implementation of JIT in Indian Environment: A Delphi Study", Productivity, Vol. 34, No. 2, July–Sept., 1993, p. 255.

The various problems indentified and imperative to be tackled in most of the industrial units in India for the implementation of JIT are:

(a) Reduction of set-up times

(b) Kanban system

(c) Delivery (from vendor) of exact quantity on exact time

(d) Preventive maintenance, and

(e) Group technology.

All these problems can be tackled only with a very seriously planned effort. Worker motivation and literacy need to be enhanced. These are important for reducing set-up time and introducing Kanban systems. Moreover, the involvement and commitment of top management are needed to bring a drastic change in the working environment and change of attitude in people. These changes are difficult, but possible.

As there are wide differences in the operating environments of Japanese and Indian industries, the work environments in the industrial units in India are to be improved before the implementation of JIT. It requires almost 10 to 20 years.

8. *Inventory Ratio*

Manufacturing firms generally have four kinds of inventories: (i) stores and spares, (ii) raw materials, (iii) work-in-process, and (iv) finished goods. Thus ratios useful to inventory management are:

(i) Inventory Turnover Ratio (ITR)

(ii) Stores and Spares Inventory Holding Period

(iii) Conversion Period of Work-in-process

(iv) Inventory as Percentage of Current Assets

(v) Inventory to Total Assets

(vi) Inventory in terms of Months Cost of Production

(vii) Number of Days Stock in Hand Ratio

(viii) Return Per Rupee Invested Ratio

(i) Inventory Turnover Ratio

This ratio is an important parameter used to evaluate the performance of the inventory function.

$$ITR = \frac{\text{Cost of sales during the period}}{\text{Average stock held during the period}}$$

Here, average stock indicates yearly average (average of opening and closing inventory), where, the numerator of the ratio, i.e., cost of sales means sales minus gross profit. Since inventories are valued in terms of their costs, cost of sales rather than sales have been used in computing turnover ratio.

The inventory turnover shows how quickly the inventory is turning into receivables/cash through sales. This ratio indicates the number of times the stock is turned over on the average and must be replaced during a given period. The liquidity of a firm's inventories is reflected in the number of times the firm's average inventory is turned over during the year.

Inventory turnover has a direct relationship with profit-earning capacity of a firm. Generally, the higher the rate of inventory turnover, the larger the amount of profit, the smaller the amount of working capital tied up in inventory, and the more current the stock of merchandise. Each turnover adds to the volume of profits. While a low inventory turnover implies more excessive inventory levels than warranted by production and sales activities, or a slow-moving or obsolete inventory. A high level of sluggish inventory amounts to unnecessary tie-up of funds, impairment of profits and increased cost. If the obsolete inventories have to be "written off, this will adversely affect the working capital and liquidity position of the firm". Thus a higher turnover is better than a lower turnover.

Weston and Brigham (1975) has suggested that inventory should be in between 12 to 20 per cent of sales value. As such, inventory turnover should be within the range of 5.0 to 8.3 times. While Mohsin (1970) opined that the same should be 9 times. It is, therefore, expected that the inventory turnover in a firm should be in between 5 and 9 times.

Against the above background, the inventory turnover of firms in India is an average of 1.0 times only. This situation suggests that inventory consists of the most slow moving components of current assets. Thus, most of the firms in India keep excessive stock of inventory. Excessive stocks are usually unproductive and represent an investment with a low or zero rate of return.

Table 10.5 gives an insight into the Average Inventory Turnover Ratio of Japanese, American and Indian selected industries to analyse the potential available for cost reduction to Indian industries in inventories.

TABLE 10.5 Inventory Turnover Ratio of Japanese, U.S. and Indian Automobile Industries

Year	Japan	U.S.	Indian
1950	3	3	1
1960	8	10.5	2
1975	21	10.5	3.7
1985	38	12.0	4.2
1990	44	20.3	7.5
1992	45.5	21.0	7.5

Source: Consolidated from the data given in Chartered Financial Analyst (Hyderabad) ASCI Journal of Management and Management Accountant (1993), Calcutta.

A low inventory turnover ratio by Indian companies implies more excessive inventory levels than warranted by production and sales activities or slow-moving inventories. A high level of sluggish inventories amounts to unnecessary tie-up of funds which in turn results in more costs and finally, less profitability. An inventory turnover ratio of 45.5 by Japanese companies is commendable by any standard. It means that Japanese industries are carrying on an average inventory for 8 days at any point of time while the Indian industries for 48 days. American industries have also been able to reduce investments in inventories to a large extent.

Of course, the inventory turnover ratio alone should not serve as the sole determinant of the liquidity of a firm's inventories. More in-depth analysis, involving a thorough item by item check on the existing inventories, is necessary to fully assess inventory liquidity.

(ii) Stores and Spares Inventory holding Period

Stores and spares is a term which commonly covers all kinds of supplies necessary to keep production equipment operating to turn out production to the desired quantity and quality at the desired time. The lack of spares is often one of the most serious bottlenecks in uninterrupted production.

Stores and spares is composed of a large number of items, some of them are most important and require longer periods of time to procure, while most of them are less important and require shorter periods of time to procure. Indiscriminate stocking of each and every item of stores and spares is not wise because a huge amount of funds may unnecessarily be locked up in this component of stores and spares. Thus a firm should keep each and every component of stores and spares to a reasonable level.

Stores and spares is the most slow moving among the four components of inventory. A close watch on the movement of this component of inventory and its effective control can pay rich dividends to a firm. In most of the firms, stores and spares occupy on an average, about two-thirds of the total inventory. Such huge amount of investment in stores and spares inventory should affect both liquidity and profitability of firms.

$$\text{Stores and Spares Inventory Turnover} = \frac{\text{Annual Consumption of Stores and Spares}}{\text{Stores and Spares Inventory}}$$

$$\text{Stores Spares Holding Period} = \frac{365}{\text{Turnover of Stores and Spares}}$$

The suggested norm for the stores and spares inventory holding period should be in between 3 months and 6 months. But in most of the firms, the stores and spares holding period is above the suggested norms. Thus the inference that can be drawn is that there is an over investment in stores and spares on account of its very poor shape management. Long lead time, procedural delays in their procurement and uncertainty about their availability, particularly of imported items are the main reasons which compel the firms to have more stock of stores and spares. Moreover, heavy initial purchase at the time of purchasing new machineries and subsequent purchase without proper assessment of the requirement are also responsible for such huge investment in stores and spares.

(iii) Conversion Period of Work-in-process

Work-in process inventories represent products that need more work before they become finished products for sale. They are semi-manufactured products. The longer the production cycles, the greater the volume of work-in process and vice-versa. It is calculated by dividing W.I.P. inventory by cost of production and multiplied by 365.

The suggested norm is that the work-in-process conversion period should be less than 15 days. But this period is abnormally high in most of the firms. This situation is the result of weak inventory management and hence should affect the profitability of the firms.

(iv) Inventory as Percentage of Current Assets

The share of inventory in the total current assets indicates how much liquidity of a firm is locked up in inventory. Inventory is generally, less liquid than other current assets. As such, inventory is the most non-liquid current asset.

$$\text{Inventory as a percentage of current asset} = \frac{\text{Total Inventory} \times 100}{\text{Total Current Assets}}$$

The quality and liquidity of current assets are largely dependent on the composition of current assets. The lower percentage of inventory to the current assets, the greater the liquidity of current assets and vice-versa. Thus a low ratio is better than a high ratio.

In most of the firms in India, on an average inventory occupies about fifty per cent of the total current assets. Such a high ratio reveals that the quality and liquidity of current assets is very low in various firms.

(v) Inventory to Total Assets

Inventory is an important element in the asset structure of an industrial undertaking. As such, its share in the asset structure and the proportion of funds invested in inventory for operational activities of the undertaking should be examined.

$$\text{Inventory to total assets} = \frac{\text{Total Inventory} \times 100}{\text{Total Asset}}$$

Weston and Brigham (1978) suggested that the ratio of inventory to total assets should be concentrated in the 16 to 30 per cent range. As against this norm, the average ratio in India is 54.4 per cent. Thus, inventory alone occupies more than half of the total assets in most of the firms.

(vi) Inventory in Terms of Months Cost of Production

The main yard stick used to measure the adequacy of inventory is the month's value of its usage. To serve the purpose, aggregate inventory is to be converted into month's value of production, stores and spares to their month's consumption and work-in-process in terms of month's cost of production.

Investment in inventory in terms of month's value of production is ascertained as follows:

$$\frac{\text{Value of Inventory}}{\text{Cost of Production Excluding Depreciation}} \times 12$$

Depreciation is excluded from the cost of production as depreciation does not involve cash outflows.

The Tariff Commission of India has suggested that inventory in public sector enterprises should not exceed 4 to 6 months value of production. Against this background, it is found that most of the firms maintain a large quantity of inventory and thus a considerable overstocking exists therein. Overstocking is due to huge investment in stores and spares. The management of most of the firms fears that it may not get spares in time for repairing of machineries which is likely to disturb production schedule. All these are the main reasons for heavy accumulation of inventories.

(vii) Number of Days Stock in Hand Ratio

Number of Days Stock in Hand Ratio is: $\dfrac{\text{Stock} \times 365}{\text{Cost of Sales}}$

This ratio measures the efficiency in selling the goods. Smaller the number of days stock in hand, higher the efficiency in inventory management.

(viii) Return per Rupee Invested Ratio

Return per rupee invested ratio is given by

$$\frac{\text{Annual Gross Margin}}{\text{Inventory}}$$

This ratio shows efficiency in management of inventory in terms of profitability. Higher the ratio, better the management.

(9) Aging Schedule of Inventory

Classification of the inventories in accordance with the age also assists in identifying inventories which are moving slowly into production or sales. This requires identifying the date of purchase/manufacture of each item of the inventory and classifying them as given in Table 10.6.

TABLE 10.6   Aging Schedule of Inventory as on 31, Dec. 2000*

Age Classification (days)	Date of Purchase/Manufacture	Amount (Rs.)	% of Total
0–20	Dec. 11	10,000	20
21–40	Dec. 7	5,000	10
41–60	Nov. 21	3,000	6
61–80	Nov. 5	25,000	50
81 and above	Oct. 20	7,000	14
	Total	50,000	100

*All figures are imaginary.

In the light of the above table, it is clear that 50% of the inventory is of the age group of 61-80 days, while 14% is older than 80 days. Thus unless steps are taken to clear the inventories, it is possible that more than 50% inventory may suffer deterioration in its value or may even become obsolete.

(10) Inventory Audit

The industrial units in India, particularly, face the problem of inventory build-up and consequent locking up of capital. This calls for an inventory audit. The main aspects of this audit may comprise:

(a) The testing and the appraisal of the policy to be pursued by the industrial unit regarding inventory forecasting, planning and control.

(b) Appraisal of inventory valuation method.

(c) Testing and appraisal of the inventory forecasting and planning models.

(d) Testing and appraisal of control aspects.

(e) Testing the maintenance aspects of inventory as well as inventory records.

Like internal audit, the inventory audit should also be made a routine feature of the industrial units and has to be done with qualified hands within the organization as by an outside inventory audit team.

During inventory audit, certain items should be audited with due care to effect economy in the organization. They are:

(a) raw materials

(b) work-in-progress

(c) finished goods

(d) stores and spare parts

(e) loose tools and others, and

(f) by-products and scrap.

Inventory audit of an industrial unit is to be chalked out with the following programmes (Figure 10.5).

(a) Auditing the process of manufacture

(b) Audit of raw materials

(c) Audit of stores and spares

(d) Auditors observations and conclusions.

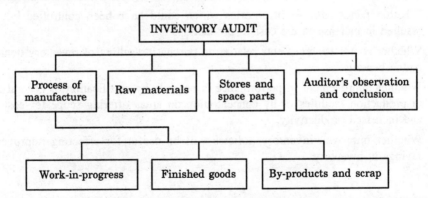

FIGURE 10.5 Inventory Audit Programme.

Source: Ramachandran K.B., "Need for Inventory Audit in Public Sector Enterprises", *Management Accountant*, Vol. 24, No. 8, Aug. 1989: p. 494.

(a) Auditing the Process of Manufacture

The cost auditor should be aware of the technical aspects of the process of manufacture of the main products and by-products and scraps of the industrial unit under audit. He should account the cost aspects involved in the process of manufacture and try to evaluate the possibility of affecting economy of the costs involved in the process of manufacture.

(b) Audit of Raw Materials

The cost auditor should ascertain whether the industrial unit follows standard purchase procedure for purchasing of raw materials. The cost of major raw materials consumed both in terms of quantity and value should be technically evaluated with similar firms in the industry. This will bring to light, the ways and means of utilizing scarce resources in a fruitful manner. The quantity and value of imported and indigenous raw materials used in the manufacturing process and/or production purposes may be reviewed and the usage of main raw materials should be evaluated.

The non-moving materials from one to five years should be seriously viewed and a report covering all the above aspects is to be prepared.

(c) Audit of Stores and Spares

The procurement and utilization of stores and spare parts should be carefully gone through for effective savings. The movement of stores and spare parts at different intervals should be audited. It should be ascertained whether scientific method of procuring is followed. The non-moving items for more than two years and the action taken by top management to avoid such redundant investments should be audited. The type of stores and spare parts for want of which production is affected often should also be audited and reported.

(d) Auditors Observations and Conclusions

The cost auditor should observe the following with respect to the inventory audit:

(i) Whether the firm's funds have been used in a negligent or inefficient manner.

(ii) Whether factors due to inventories which could have been controlled but not done resulted in increase in the cost of production.

(iii) Whether contracts/agreements relating to purchasing/selling of inventory items had any undue benefits.

(iv) Whether improvement in performance is possible by rectification of general imbalance in production facilities or by concentration on areas offering scope for cost reduction and increased productivity.

(v) Whether improved inventory policies will be useful for effecting improvement and savings in inventory.

Conclusion

Most industrial units in India have adopted certain efficient techniques like ABC analysis, perpetual inventory, etc., for controlling their inventories. But with the advent of Electronic Data Processing, better selective inventory control measures are available for the better control of inventory at a reduced amount of investment. The just-in-time inventory control technique can be implemented only after improving the work environment. The control measures such as EOQ and fixing of material stock levels are not strictly adhered to by the industrial units. So, it results in high inventory cost.

CASE STUDY

Inventory Management of Kerala Electrical and Allied Engineering Company Limited (KEL)

Inventories in the Kerala Electrical and Allied Engineering Company Limited (KEL) consist of raw material and components, work-in-progress, finished goods and stores and spares. Table 10.7 shows the raw material and components, work-in-progress, finished goods inventories and stores and spares in KEL from 1995–96 to 2003–04.

TABLE 10.7   KEL's Raw Material, Work-in-progress and Other Inventory Data

(Rs. in lakhs)

Year	Raw materials and components	Work-in-progress	Finished goods	Stores and spares	Value of Inventories	Percentage change in value of inventories
1995–1996	840.30	667.47	619.31	65.65	2192.73	100
1996–1997	720.50	732.28	996.34	56.34	2505.46	14.26
1997–1998	824.93	1164.35	565.45	63.51	2618.24	4.50
1998–1999	658.56	756.60	631.02	65.72	2111.90	−19.34
1999–2000	634.22	605.60	960.77	59.14	2259.73	6.99
2000–2001	502.80	465.13	769.40	53.98	1791.31	−20.73
2001–2002	391.88	425.28	598.96	41.89	1458.01	−18.61
2002–2003	506.89	676.27	1038.79	81.18	2303.13	57.96
2003–2004	394.66	828.50	371.52	49.64	1644.32	−28.60

Source: Review of Public Enterprises in Kerala.

Table 10.7 provides a broad spectrum showing how Kerala Electrical and Allied Engineering has managed its inventory from 1995–96 to 2003–04. Inventory constitutes more than 45 per cent of the current assets in all the years under review except during 2000–01 and 2003–04. The average worth of inventory held comes to Rs. 2098.31 lakh.

The inventory stock in the form of raw materials and components in KEL showed a downward trend from 1995–96 to 2003–04. The average stock of raw materials held during the period under review was Rs. 607.19 lakh. It is also found that there was a considerable increase in consumption of raw materials and components during 2001–02 and 2003–04. This steep increase in consumption can be counted as a good indicator of production.

The work-in-progress inventory in KEL was very high in 1997–98 and then showed a decreasing trend. This trend is also a good indicator of production. The finished goods inventory in KEL showed an upward trend during the period under review except during 1997–98, 2001–02 and 2003–04. This is a sign of wide fluctuation of finished goods stock on account of the inconsistent level of capacity utilization. The stores and spares inventory of the company showed a downward trend except during 1999–2000 and 2002–03.

Figures 10.6 and 10.7 show the time series analysis of value of inventories and percentage change in value of inventories in KEL from 1995–96 to 2003–04.

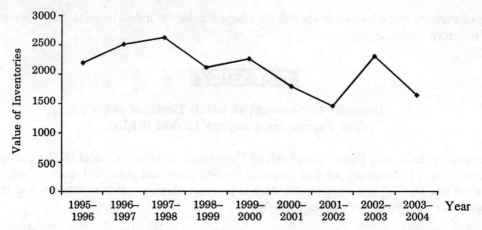

FIGURE 10.6 Time Series Analysis of value of inventories in KEL from 1995-96 to 2003-04.

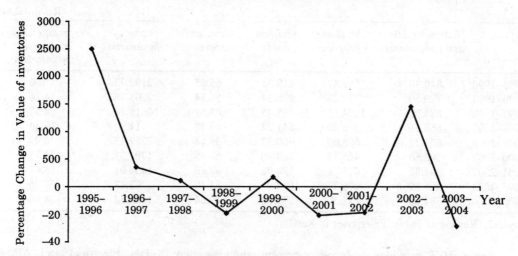

FIGURE 10.7 Time Series Analysis of percentage change in value of inventories in KEL from 1995-96 to 2003-04.

Table 10.2 shows "Inventory Ratios" of KEL from 1996–97 to 2003–04.

TABLE 10.8   Inventory Ratios of KEL

Year	Inventory turnover ratio	Stores and spares inventory holding period (in number of days)	Conversion period of work-in-progress (in number of days)	Inventory as a percentage of current assets	Inventory to total assets (in percentage)	Inventory in terms of months cost of production (in lakhs)	Number of days stock in hand ratio	Return per rupee invested ratio
1996–1997	2.46	376.28	20.15	30.33	22.03	2.65	138.14	2.07
1997–1998	2.63	280.76	58.57	42.47	30.73	2.61	137.14	1.81
1998–1999	2.23	456.25	34.64	31.11	23.90	3.16	170.63	1.49
1999–2000	2.65	350.95	19.78	29.88	24.80	2.53	137.31	1.94
2000–2001	2.76	344.33	20.75	30.68	25.61	2.53	129.26	1.57
2001–2002	1.93	372.44	25.26	37.57	30.75	3.41	191.80	1.30
2002–2003	2.15	357.84	27.55	31.00	26.17	3.04	162.91	1.60
2003–2004	2.64	424.41	25.43	27.76	23.59	2.64	130.48	1.72

Source: Review of Public Enterprises in Kerala.

Table 10.8 reveals that the inventory turnover ratio of the company increased by 0.18 during 2003–04 (i.e., 2.64) from that of 1996–97 (i.e., 2.46). It implies a more efficient use of inventory and reduction in working capital needs. The stores and spares holding period of the company over the period under review comes averaging around 370 days as against suggested norms between 90 days and 180 days. Thus the inference that can be drawn is that there is an over investment of stores and spares on account of poor inventory management. Long lead time, procedural delays in their procurement and uncertainty about their availability, particularly imported items are the main reasons which compel the firms to have more stock of stores and spares.

The conversion period of work-in-progress of the company comes averaging around 29 days as against the suggested norm of less than 15 days. This period is abnormally high in KEL. This situation is the result of weak inventory management and hence is liable to affect the profitability of the firm.

Inventory as a percentage of current assets of the company comes averaging around 25 as against the suggested norm in the 16 to 30 per cent range. Thus inventories share in the asset structure and the proportion of funds invested in inventory for operational activities of the undertaking are considered as satisfactory.

Inventory in terms of months cost of production of the company comes averaging around Rs. 2.82 lakh. Against this background, it is found that the company maintains a large quantity of inventory and thus a considerable overstocking exists therein. Overstocking is due to huge investment in stores and spares. The management of the company fears that it may not get spares in time for repairing machineries. Such a situation is likely to disturb production schedule.

The number of days inventory stock in hand of the company comes averaging around 150. This ratio showed a diminishing trend year by year in the industry except during 1998–99, 2001–02 and 2002–03. This is an indication of increasing efficiency in selling the goods and inventory management.

The return per rupee invested in inventory of the company comes averaging 1.69, i.e., positive. This ratio showed a wide fluctuation year by year from 1996–97 (i.e., 2.07) to 2003–04 (i.e., 1.72). This is an indication of fluctuating efficiency in management of inventories in terms of profitability.

The table also reveals that in KEL, materials (both direct and indirect materials) constituting part of the inventories account for a large percentage of the total cost. Thus the company cannot simply forget the area of materials and think of surviving in the market. At the same time, it is a tough job to direct the control on material at every point. Special attention should, therefore, be paid to point out the important areas where the possibility of loss is more.

— REVIEW QUESTIONS —

1. "Efficient inventory management is reflected in the liquidity and profitability of the firm". Explain.

2. Define inventory management. Explain briefly costs and benefits of inventory.

3. The major objective of inventory management is "to minimise cash outlays for inventories". Explain how this is achieved.

4. Explain briefly the various techniques of inventory management.

5. Write notes on:
   (a) ABC Analysis
   (b) Double Bin System
   (c) Just-in-time Inventory
   (d) Inventory Audit
   (e) Safety Stock
   (f) Inventory Ratio

11

Receivables Management

Receivables are asset accounts representing amounts owed to the firm as a result of sale of goods/services in the ordinary course of business.

— HAMPTON, JOHN J.

CONTENTS

- Introduction
- Receivables-meaning and purpose
- Receivables management—meaning
- Review questions

INTRODUCTION

When a firm sells its products or services on credit, payments are postponed to future dates and thereby receivables/debtors are created. However, no receivables are created when a firm conducts cash sales as payments are received immediately. A firm conducts credit sales to protect its sales from the competitors and to attract the potential customers to buy its products at favourable terms. Usually, the credit sales are made on open account which means that no formal acknowledgements of debt obligations are received from the buyers. This facilitates business transactions and reduces the paperwork required in connection with credit sales.

Receivables or accounts receivable constitute a substantial portion of the total current assets of several firms after inventories. They form about one-third of current assets in India. Since a very substantial amount is tied-up in trade debtors, it requires a careful analysis and proper management.

RECEIVABLES—MEANING AND PURPOSE

Receivables are the result of extension of credit facility to the customers. Thus they represent the claims of a firm against its customers. They are known under various titles such as accounts receivable, trade receivables, customer receivables or book debt. Receivables are carried on the assets side of the balance sheet. According to Hampton, John J.,

> receivables are asset accounts representing amounts owed to the firm as a result of
> sale of goods/services in the ordinary course of business.

The purpose of receivables is directly connected with the goals of conducting credit sales. The following are the aims or objectives of credit sales:

(i) **Attaining Growth in Sales:** When a firm conducts credit sales, it can sell more goods than sales on immediate payment. This is because many customers are unable to pay cash immediately on purchase. But such customers can buy goods if payments are postponed.

(ii) **Enhancing Profits:** Usually, a firm can earn higher profit through increase in sales. This is because of increase in the volume of sales and a higher margin of profit on credit sales than cash sales.

(iii) **Facing Competition:** Sometimes a firm resorts to granting credit facilities to its customers as similar facilities are being granted by the competing firms. This helps to avoid the loss of sales from customers who would buy elsewhere unless they receive the expected credit.

RECEIVABLES MANAGEMENT—MEANING

A firm resorts to credit sales to push up sales which ultimately results in enhancing its profit. But credit sales results in blocking of funds in accounts receivable. Consequently, a firm requires additional funds for meeting its operational needs which involve extra costs by way of interest. Further, when receivables increase, the chance of bad debts also goes up. That is why the creation of receivables is both beneficial and dangerous to a firm. However, the basic objective of receivables management is to maximise return on investment. Thus the financial manager of a firm is responsible for the management of receivables. The head of the credit department may report directly to him. All the works of granting credit and supervising the collection of receivables should be carried out by the credit department. Management of accounts receivable, may, therefore, be defined as "the process of making decisions relating to the investment of funds in this asset which will result in maximising the overall return on the investment of the firm."

According to Bolten, S.E.,

> The objective of receivables management is to promote sales and profits until that
> point is reached where the return on investment in further funding of receivables
> is less than the cost of funds raised to finance that additional credit (i.e., cost of
> capital).

Cost of Maintaining Receivables

The costs involved in maintaining accounts receivable are as under.

(i) **Costs of capital:** Maintenance of receivables results in blocking of financial resources in them as there is a time lag between the sale of goods and its payment. Consequently, a firm should make some alternative arrangements for additional funds to meet its own obligations while awaiting payments from its customers. But a firm can raise additional funds either from outside or out of retained earnings. However, a firm incurs a cost in both these cases, i.e., it has to pay interest to the outsider in the former case and there is an opportunity cost to the firm in the latter case.

(ii) **Costs of administration:** When a firm maintains accounts receivables, it has to incur additional administrative costs by way of salaries to the staff kept for this purpose.

(iii) **Cost of collection:** Usually, the collection of payments from credit customers incurs additional cost to a firm. Sometimes, the firm resorts to take additional steps for recovering money from defaulting customers.

(iv) **Defaulting costs:** If a firm cannot recover overdues from the defaulting customers in spite of its serious efforts, such debts are treated as bad debts and have to be written off.

Factors Affecting the Size of Receivables

The size of accounts receivable depends on so many factors. The following are some of the important factors:

(i) **Sales Level:** The size of accounts receivable relates to the level of sales. Usually even in the same industry, a firm which has a large volume of sales should have a higher level of receivables than a firm having a small volume of sales.

Changes in accounts receivable can also be predicted with the help of sales level. For instance, in case a firm predicts that there will be an enhance of 30% in its credit sales for the coming year, it can be expected that there will also be a 30% increase in the level of receivables.

(ii) **Credit Policies:** Credit is one of the many factors that influence the demand for a firm's product. Thus credit policy of a firm can have a significant influence on sales. The term credit policy refers to those decision variables that influence the investment in receivables. (i.e., the amount of trade credit). These variables consist of (i) the quantity of the account accepted; (ii) the length of the credit period; (iii) the size of the cash discount given; (iv) any special terms, such as seasonal datings; and (v) the level of collection expenditures. In each case, the decision should involve a comparison of possible gains from a change in policy with the cost of the change. However, a firm's credit policy determines the amount of risk the firm is willing to undertake in its sales activities. In case a firm has a liberal or lenient credit policy, it will experience a higher level of receivables than a firm having a stringent credit policy on account of the following reasons:

(a) Liberal credit policy results in enhancing the size of the account receivable since it encourages even the financially strong customers to make delays in payment.

(b) As a result of the liberal credit policy, the financially weak customers make further default in payment. This, in turn, results in enhancing the size of the receivables.

(iii) **Credit Terms:** The size of receivables also depends on the terms of credit. Credit terms specify the length of time over which credit is extended to a customer and the discount, if any, given for early payment. Thus the two important components of the credit terms are: (a) Credit period, and (b) Cash discount.

(a) *Credit Period:* The total length of time over which credit is extended to a customer to pay a bill is called the credit period. Usually, it is expressed in terms of a 'net date'. For instance, in case a firm's credit terms are "net 10", it means that the customers are expected to pay within 10 days from the date of credit sale.

(b) *Cash Discount:* A per cent (%) reduction in sales or purchase price allowed for early payment of invoices is called the cash discount. The terms of cash discount contain both the rate of discount and the period for which the discount is allowed. For instance, in case the terms of cash discount are changed from "net 20" to "2/10 net 20", it implies that the credit period is of 20 days but if a customer pays within 10 days, he would get 2% discount on the amount due from him. Although, allowing cash discount results in a loss to the firm, it reduces the volume of receivables and puts extra funds at the disposal of the firm for alternative profitable investment. Thus the amount of loss suffered due to cash discount is compensated by the income otherwise earned by the firm.

Optimum Size of Receivables

Optimum investment in receivables is the level where there is a trade-off between costs and profitability. A liberal credit policy enhances the profitability of the firm on account of higher sales. But such a policy results in increased investment in receivables, more risk of bad debts and higher cost of administration of receivables. In short, a liberal credit policy leads to an increase in the total investment in receivables and, thereby, the problem of liquidity is created. On the contrary, a stringent credit policy declines the profitability, but enhances the liquidity of the firm. Thus optimum credit policy arises at a point where there is a "tradeoff" between liquidity and profitability. This is shown in Figure 11.1

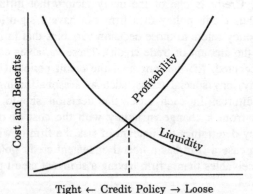

Tight ← Credit Policy → Loose

FIGURE 11.1 Optimum Credit Policy.

Techniques of Determining Credit Policy

A firm's credit policy should be an optimum one, i.e., neither too liberal nor too stringent. A firm can determine its nature of credit policy with the help of the following techniques.

(i) Computation of average age of receivables.

(ii) Aging schedule of receivables.

(i) Computation of Average Age of Receivables

The average age of receivables is a quick and effective method of comparing the liquidity of receivables with the liquidity of receivables of the past and also comparing liquidity of one firm with that of the other competitive firms. It also provides a basis for projecting receivables balance into the future.

The computation of average age of receivables involves the computation of average collection period. This may be computed by any of the following methods:

(i) $$\frac{\text{Months or Days in the Period}}{\text{Accounts Receivable Turnover*}}$$

$$\text{*Accounts Receivable Turnover} = \frac{\text{Credit Sales in the Period}}{\text{Average Accounts Receivable}}$$

(ii) $$\frac{\text{Average Accounts Receivable}}{\text{Average Monthly (or daily) Credit Sales}}$$

(iii) $$\frac{\text{Average Accounts Receivable} \times \text{Months (or days) in the period}}{\text{Sales during the period}}$$

The above methods can be explained with the help of the following illustration.

ILLUSTRATION 11.1

	Rs.
Credit sales for the year, 2000	1,00,000
Accounts receivable as on 1-1-2002	12,000
Accounts receivable as on 31-12-2000	8,000

Compute the average age of receivables.

Solution

Average age of receivables may be computed by any of the following methods.

(i) $$\frac{\text{Months or Days in the Period}}{\text{Accounts Receivable Turnover}}$$

$$\text{Accounts Receivable Turnover} = \frac{\text{Credit sales in the period}}{\text{Average Accounts Receivable}}$$

Thus

$$\text{Account Receivable Turnover} = \frac{1,00,000}{10,000} = 10$$

$$\text{Average Age Receivables (or Debt collection period)} = \frac{12 \text{ months}}{10} = 1.2 \text{ months}$$

(ii) $$\frac{\text{Average Accounts Receivable}}{\text{Average Monthly (or daily) Credit Sales}} = \frac{10,000}{8,000} = 1.2 \text{ months}$$

(iii) $$\frac{\text{Average Accounts Receivable} \times \text{Months (or days) in the Period}}{\text{Sales during the Period}} = \frac{10,000 \times 12}{1,00,000}$$

$$= 1.2 \text{ months}$$

Increase in the average age of receivables or debt collection period is a sign of liberal credit policy or inefficiency in collection. On the other hand, a decrease in the average age of receivables implies a stringent credit policy or efficiency in collection. For instance, in the above illustration in the year 2001, debt collection period goes up to 1.5 months. It indicates that the firm has liberalised its credit policy. On the contrary, in case the collection period decreases to one month, it implies that the firm has moved towards a more stringent credit policy.

Limitation of average age calculation: The technique of average age of receivables should be used with caution. If there are fluctuations in sales pattern then this may give misleading indication. This point can be understood with the help of the following illustration:

ILLUSTRATION 11.2

The collection pattern of a company is as follows:
10% of the sales in the same month.
20% of the sales in the 2nd month.
40% of the sales in the 3rd month, and
30% of the sales in the 4th month.

The sales of the company for the first three quarters of the year are as follows:

Month	Quarter 1	Quarter 2	Quarter 3
First	20,000	10,000	30,000
Second	20,000	20,000	20,000
Third	20,000	30,000	10,000
	Rs. 60,000	Rs. 60,000	Rs. 60,000
Working days	90	90	90

Compute the average age of receivables and comment upon the results.

Solution

The collection pattern of the company shows that outstanding receivables at the end of the each month comprise 90% of the month's sales, 70% of the previous month's sales and 30% of the sales made two months ago.

Thus the amount of accounts receivable and the average age of receivables at the end of each quarter are as follows:

Statement of Accounts Receivable and their Average Age

Sales	1st Quarter	2nd Quarter	3rd Quarter
30% of the 1st Month	6,000	3,000	9,000
70% of the 2nd Month	14,000	14,000	14,000
90% of the 3rd Month	18,000	27,000	9,000
Total Accounts Receivable	**Rs. 38,000**	**Rs. 44,000**	**Rs. 32,000**
Average age of Receivables	$\dfrac{38,000 \times 90}{60,000}$	$\dfrac{44,000 \times 90}{60,000}$	$\dfrac{32,000 \times 90}{60,000}$
	= 57 days	= 66 days	= 48 days

In the light of the above statement, it is clear that the collection process has declined in the 2nd quarter. But it has improved during the 3rd quarter. However, there has been neither any deterioration nor any improvement in the collection machinery. The average age of receivables is different merely on account of fluctuations in the pattern of sales.

(ii) Aging Schedule of Receivables: Aging schedule breaks down receivables in accordance with the length of time for which they have been outstanding. It is prepared to have a closer look over the quality of individual accounts. It can be prepared by checking the receivables ledger for ascertaining the sales made to and payments received from each customer. However, aging schedule may be prepared in the following form:

*Aging Schedule of Receivables

Age Classes days	Month of Sale	As on December 31, 2000		As on December 31, 2001	
		Balance of Receivables	Percentage to Total	Balance of Receivables	Percentage to Total
1–30	December	30,000	23.44	12,000	12.63
31–60	November	70,000	54.69	20,000	21.05
61–90	October	15,000	11.72	50,000	52.63
91–120	September	12,000	9.38	10,000	10.53
121 and more	Earlier	1,000	0.77	3,000	3.16
	Total	**Rs. 1,28,000**	**100**	**Rs. 95,000**	**100**

*All figures are imaginary

In the light of the above schedule, it is clear that there is slackness in the debt collection machinery in 2001 as compared to the year 2000. In 2000, 54.69% of the total account receivables was in the age group of 31 to 60 days. In 2001, this percentage has declined to 21.05. Similarly, in 2000 only 11.72% of the total receivables was in the age group of 61 to 90 days. In 2001, this percentage has increased to 52.63 indicating that more than 50% of the accounts receivable are in this age group.

The finance manager may get such schedule prepared at shorter intervals in lieu of a year. In case the data relating to the competitive firms are available, an inter-firm comparison of the aging schedule of debtors should also be made.

Policies of Managing Receivables

A firm is required to establish the policies of managing receivables after considering both benefits and costs of different policies. These policies relate to (i) Credit Standards, (ii) Credit Terms, and (iii) Collection Procedures.

(i) Credit Standards

The basic criteria for extension for credit to the customers are called the credit standards. In other words, it is the minimum quality of credit worthiness of a credit applicant that is acceptable to the firm. In case a firm's credit standards are relatively loose, its levels of sales and receivables are likely to be high. Usually, the decision concerning the degree of credit standard is largely a matter of judgement. In reaching the credit decision, the credit manager should keep in mind the basic criteria, i.e., five "C's" of credit-capital, capacity, character, collateral and condition. Capital refers to the financial soundness of the firm as indicated primarily by its financial statements. Capacity denotes the ability of the customer to operate successfully as indicated by its profit record. Character relates to the reputation of management for honest and fair dealings. Collateral refers to the security available with the customer in paying the debt. Condition denotes the economic position of the customer.

A firm can collect information about five C's both from internal and external sources. While the internal sources consist of a firm's previous experience with the customer supplemented by its own well developed information system, the external sources comprise a customer's references, trade associations and credit rating organisations such as Don & Brad. Street Inc. of USA.

Having collected all the information about the credit standards of customers, an individual firm can translate its credit information into risk classes or groups in accordance with the probability of loss associated with each class. Hereafter, the firm can determine whether it will be advisable for it to extend credit to a particular class of customers.

ILLUSTRATION 11.3

AB Ltd. is considering pushing up its sales by extending credit facilities to the following categories of customers:

(a) Customers with a 15% risk of non-payment, and

(b) Customers with a 25% risk of non-payment.

The incremental sales expected in the case of category (a) are Rs. 50,000 while in the case of category (b) they are Rs. 60,000.

The cost of production and selling are 50% of sales while the collection costs amount to 7% of sales in the case of category (a) and 12% of sales in the case of category (b).

You are required to advise the firm about extending credit facilities to each of the above categories of customers.

Solution

(a) Extending Credit Facilities with 15% Risk of Non-payment

		Rs.
Incremental Sales		50,000
Less: Loss in Collection (15%)		7,500
Net sales realised		42,500
Less: Production and Selling Costs		
(50% of sales)	25,000	
Collection cost (7% of Sales)	3,500	28,500
Incremental Income		14,000

Thus, the company can have an extra income of Rs. 14,000 by accepting 15% risk group. It may, therefore, lower its credit standard in favour of this category of customers.

(b) Extending Credit Facilities with 25% Risk of Non-payment

		Rs.
Sales by accepting 25% risk group		60,000
Less: Loss on collection (25%)		15,000
Net Sales realised		45,000
Less: Production and Selling Costs		
(50% of sales)	30,000	
Collection Costs (12% of sales)	7,200	37,200
Incremental Income		7,800

Thus the company can have an extra income of Rs. 7,800 by accepting 25% risk class. The company can, therefore, extend credit to such customers as well.

(ii) Credit Terms

The terms under which a firm sells goods on credit to its customers are called the credit terms. They specify the length of time over which credit is extended to a customer and the discount, if any, given for early payment. Thus the two components of the credit terms are: (a) Credit Period and (b) Cash Discount. The approach which can be adopted by a firm in respect of each of these components is as follows:

(a) **Credit Period:** The total length of time over which credit is extended to a customer to pay a bill is called the credit period. Although extending the credit period stimulates sales, it enhances the cost on account of more funds held up in receivables. At the same time, shortening the credit period declines sales, but reduces the cost of held up funds in receivables. By virtue of these situations, there arises the problem of determining the optimum credit period where the marginal profits on increased sales are exactly offset by the cost of carrying the higher amount of accounts receivable.

ILLUSTRATION 11.4

The details regarding the operations of the Z Ltd. during a period of 12 months are as follows:

	Rs.
Sales	15,00,000
Selling Price per unit	12
Variable Cost per unit	8
Total Cost per unit	10
Credit Period allowed to customers	2 months

The company is considering a proposal for a more liberal extension of credit which will result in increasing the average collection period from '2' months to 4 months. This relaxation is expected to push up the sales by 30% from its existing level.

Advise the company regarding the adoption of the new credit policy, assuming that in case company's required return on investment is 30%.

Solution

Computation of New Sales

			Rs.
Present Sales	$1,25,000 \times 12$	=	15,00,000
Additional Sales	$37,500 \times 12$	=	4,50,000
		Total = Rs.	19,50,000

Computation of New Total Cost

			Rs.
Present Sales	$1,25,000 \times 10$	=	12,50,000
Cost of additional Sales	$37,500 \times 8^*$	=	3,00,000
			15,50,000

*Only Variable Costs to be considered

$$\text{New Average Cost per unit} = \frac{\text{New Total Costs}}{\text{New Total Output}} = \frac{15,50,000}{1,62,500}$$

$$= \text{Rs. } 9.54 \text{ per unit}$$

Average Investment in Receivables under New Sales Pattern

Total Annual Sales in units	1,62,500 units
Cost of Sales $(1,62,500 \times 9.54)$	Rs. 15,50,250
Average Collection period	4 months

$$\text{Amount Invested in Receivable} \quad \frac{15,50,250 \times 4}{12} = \text{Rs. } 5,16,750$$

Additional Investment in Receivables = New Investment − Existing Investment

$$= 5,16,750 - {}^*2,08,333 = \text{Rs. } 3,08,417$$

$$= \frac{{}^*12,50,000 \times 2}{12}$$

Profitability of additional sales = Additional units sold × Contribution per unit
$$= 37,500 \times 4 = \text{Rs. } 1,50,000$$

Return on additional investment in receivables $= \dfrac{1,50,000}{3,08,417} = 49\%$

As the actual return on additional investment in receivables comes to 49% in the place of required return of 30%, the proposal should be accepted.

ILLUSTRATION 11.5

Z Ltd. is considering the relaxation of their present credit policy and is in the process of evaluating two proposed policies. At present, the company has annual sales of Rs. 60 lakhs and accounts receivable turnover ratio of 4 times a year. The current level of loss due to bad debts is Rs. 1,00,000. The company is required to give a return of 30% on the investment in new account receivable. The company's variable costs are 60% of the selling price. From the following information given, which is the better option?

	Present policy	Policy Option I	Policy Option II
Annual Credit Sales	Rs. 60,00,000	Rs. 72,00,000	Rs. 78,00,000
Account Receivable Turnover Ratio	4 times	3 times	2.4 times
Bad Debts Losses	Rs. 1,00,000	Rs. 2,00,000	Rs. 3,50,000

Solution

Z Ltd.
Evaluation of Credit Policies

	Present policy	Policy Option I	Policy Option II
Annual Credit Sales	Rs. 60,00,000	Rs. 72,00,000	Rs. 78,00,000
Account Receivable Turnover	4 times	3 times	2.4 times
Average Level of Accounts Receivable	Rs. 15,00,000	Rs. 24,00,000	Rs. 32,50,000
Average Collection Period	3 months	4 months	5 months
Marginal increase in Investment in Receivables less Profit Margin	—	5,40,000	10,50,000
Marginal increase in Sales	—	12,00,000	18,00,000
Profit on Marginal Increase in Sales (40%)	—	4,80,000	7,20,000
Marginal increase in Bad Debts Losses	—	1,00,000	2,50,000
Profit on Marginal increase in sales less Marginal Bad Debts	—	3,80,000	4,70,000
Required Return on Marginal Investment @30%	—	1,62,000	3,15,000
Surplus (loss) after Required Rate of Return	—	2,18,000	1,55,000

In the light of the above analysis, it is clear that both the policy options I and II provide a surplus of Rs. 2,18,000 and Rs. 1,55,000 respectively on the basis of 30% return. Hence, policy option I is better.

(b) **Cash discount:** Cash discount is a per cent (%) reduction in sales or purchase price allowed for early payment of invoices. It is an incentive for credit customers to pay invoices in a timely fashion.

Varying the cash discount involves an attempt to speed up the payment of receivables. Here, the firm should determine whether a speed up in collection would more than offset the cost of an increase in the discount. If it would, the present discount policy should be altered.

Suppose that the company has annual credit sales of Rs. 3 lakhs and an average collection period of two months. Also assume that the sales terms are "net 45", with no cash discount given. As a result, the average receivable balance is Rs. 3,00,000/6 = Rs. 50,000. By initiating terms of "2/10, net 45", the average collection period can be reduced to one month, as 50 per cent of the customers (in sales value) take the benefit of 2 per cent discount. The opportunity cost of the discount to the company is (0.2 × 0.5 × Rs. 3,00,000) Rs. 3,000 annually. The turnover of receivables has gone up to 12 times a year, so that average receivables are declined from Rs. 50,000 to Rs. 25,000 (i.e., Rs. 3,00,000/12 = Rs. 25,000). Thus the company realises Rs. 25,000 from accelerated collections. The value of the funds released is their opportunity cost. In case the company assumes a 20 per cent before-tax rate of return, the opportunity saving is Rs. 5,000. In this case, the opportunity saving arising from a speed up in collection is more than the cost of discount. The company must adopt a 2 per cent discount. In case the speed up in collection had not resulted in sufficient opportunity savings to offset the cost of cash discount, the company should not alter the discount policy. However, it is possible that discounts other than 2 per cent may result in an even greater difference between the opportunity saving and the cost of the discount.

ILLUSTRATION 11.6

XYZ Ltd. has annual credit sales of Rs. 20,00,000. The company grants two months credit to its customers with no cash discount facility. It intends to offer a discount of "2/10, net 60". It is expected that this will decrease the average collection period to one month and 60% of the customers (in value) will take this benefit. The selling price is Rs. 10 per unit and the average cost per unit comes to Rs. 8.50.

Advise the company regarding this new scheme presuming that the required return on investment is 30%.

Solution

	Rs.
Annual Credit Sales	20,00,000.00
Cash Discount Allowed (20,00,000 × 60/100 × 2/100)	24,000.00
Present Investment in Receivables (20,00,000 × 2/12 × 8.5/10)	2,83,333.00
Expected Investment in Receivables (20,00,000 × 1/12 × 8.5/10)	1,41,666.50
Decrease in Investment in Receivables	1,41,666.50
Savings in Capital Costs (1,41,666.50 × 30/100)	42,500.00
Net Savings (Rs. 42,500 – Rs. 24,000)	18,500.00

As the new credit terms will result in a net saving of Rs. 18,500, the company may adopt them.

(iii) Collection Procedures

A firm determines its overall collection policy by the combination of collection procedures it undertakes. These procedures include such things as letters, phone calls, personal visits, and legal action. A stringent collection procedure is expensive for the firm on account of high out-of-pocket costs and loss of goodwill of the firm among its customers. But it minimises the loss due to bad debts. It also enhances savings in terms of lower capital costs because of reduction in the size of receivables. However, the firm's collection policy should be such that it should strike a balance between the costs and benefits of different collection procedures.

― REVIEW QUESTIONS ―

1. What factors determine the size of the investment a company makes in Accounts Receivables? Which of these factors are under the control of the Finance Manager?

2. "The average age of receivables is an important yardstick for testing the efficiency of receivables management of a firm." Discuss.

3. Define credit policy. What is an optimum credit policy?

4. Discuss the important role which receivables play in the total financial picture and how you would control them?

5. Write notes on:
   (a) Credit Policy
   (b) Aging Schedule of Receivables
   (c) Cash Discount
   (d) Credit Period
   (e) Costs of Maintaining Receivables

6. What is receivables management? What are the objectives of receivables management?

7. XYZ Corporation is considering relaxing its present credit policy and is in the process of evaluating two proposed policies. Currently, the firm has annual credit sales of Rs. 50 lakhs and accounts receivable turnover ratio of 4 times a year. The current level of loss due to bad debts is Rs. 1,50,000. The firm is required to give a return of 25% on the investment in new accounts receivable. The company's variable costs are 70% of the selling price. Given the following information, which is the better position?

	Present Policy	Policy Option I	Policy Option II
Annual Credit Sales	Rs. 50,00,000	Rs. 60,00,000	Rs. 67,50,000
Accounts Receivable Turnover Ratio	4 times	3 times	2.4 times
Bad debts losses	Rs. 1,50,000	Rs. 3,00,000	Rs. 4,50,000

(M.Com, Kerala, May 1982)

(**Ans.:** Policy option I gives a surplus of Rs. 18,750 whereas policy option II shows a deficit of Rs. 48,438. Thus policy Option I is better)

8. The details regarding the operations of a firm during a period of 12 months are as follows:

Sales	Rs. 12,00,000
Selling Price per unit	Rs. 10
Variable Cost per unit	Rs. 7
Total Cost per unit	Rs. 9

Credit period allowed to customers one month.

The firm is considering a proposal for a more liberal extension of credit which will result in increasing the average collection period from one month to two months. This relaxation is expected to increase the sales by 25% from its existing level.

You are required to advise the firm regarding adoption of the new credit policy, presuming that if the firm's required return on investment is 25%.

(**Ans.:** The required return on investment is only 25% while the actual return on additional investment in receivables comes to 72%. Thus the proposal should be accepted)

9. The current credit terms of Mayur Ltd. are "net 30". It is considering to change them to "3/15, net 45" credit terms in order to increase its sales. The proposed change is expected to have the following implications:

Current Sales	Rs. 50,00,000
Estimated increase in Sales	10%
Estimated total sales that will avail Discount offer	Rs. 15,00,000
Estimated increased Investment in Receivables	Rs. 4,00,000
Estimated increased costs: Bad Debt Losses	1% of increased sales
Production, Administration and Selling Costs	74% of increased sales
Cash Discount	3% of sales
Required Return on Investment	10%

You are required to state whether it is desirable to introduce the changes in credit terms.

(**Ans.:** Increase in profit on account of increase in sales Rs. 50,400. Opportunity cost of increased investment in receivables Rs. 29,600. Credit standards may be relaxed)

10. The collection pattern of the Z Ltd. is as follows:

10% of the sales in the same month

20% of the sales in the 2nd month

40% of the sales in the 3rd month

30% of the sales in the 4th month

The sales of the company for the first three quarters of the year are as follows:

Month	Quarter I	Quarter II	Quarter III
First	15,000	7,500	22,500
Second	15,000	15,000	15,000
Third	15,000	22,500	7,500
	45,000	45,000	45,000
Working days	90	90	90

Compute the average age of receivables and comment upon the results.

(**Ans.:** Average age of receivables

Quarter I   = 57 days
Quarter II = 66 days
Quarter III = 48 days

The collection process has suffered a serious setback in Quarter II. But it has improved in Quarter III.

The average age of receivables has been different merely because of fluctuations in the sales pattern).

12

Cash Management

*Optimum cash level is that level of cash where the carrying costs
and transactions costs are the minimum.*

— WILLIAM J. BAUMOL

*Cash management implies making sure that all the business generated revenues
are effectively managed and utilised in the best possible manner.*

INTRODUCTION

Since cash is the medium of exchange, it is the most important component of working capital. It is both the basic input required to keep the firm running on a continuous basis and the ultimate output expected to be realised by selling goods and services. Thus cash management is rapidly emerging as a unique area in any organisation. It implies making sure that all the business generated revenues are effectively managed and utilised in the best possible manner. In other words, cash management involves the efficient collection, disbursement, and temporary investment of cash. Although most firms establish a target level of cash balances to maintain, they do not like to keep excess cash balance as interest can be earned if these funds are invested in marketable securities. Thus the main objective of cash management is the optimisation of liquidity through an improved flow of funds.

MEANING OF CASH

In cash management, the term cash is used in both narrow and broad senses. In narrow sense, it includes coins, currency, cheques held by the firm and the balances in its bank accounts. In a broad sense, it also consists of near-cash assets like marketable securities and time deposits with banks. However, the term cash management is generally applied for management of both cash and near-cash assets. The treasurer's department of a company is usually responsible for the firm's cash management system.

MOTIVES OF HOLDING CASH

Although cash does not earn any substantial return for the business, a firm holds cash by virtue of the following motives:

(i) Transaction Motive

This motive refers to the holding of cash for meeting the day-to-day transactions of business. Firms hold cash to make the necessary payments for the goods and services they require. Even if firms hold a major part of transactions balances in cash, they may also hold a part in the form of marketable securities whose maturity conforms to the timing of the anticipated payments, such as, payment of taxes, dividends, etc.

(ii) Precautionary Motive

Precautionary motive refers to the holding of cash to meet unexpected contigencies. It provides a cushion or buffer to withstand unexpected emergencies. Firms hold cash to meet uncertainties, emergencies, running out of cash and fluctuations in cash balances. Thus unexpected cash needs at short notices may arise as a result of:

(a) uncontrollable situations like floods, strikes, droughts, etc;

(b) presentation of bill for settlement earlier than expected;

(c) unexpected delay in collecting trade dues;

(d) hike in material and labour cost; and

(e) cancellation of some orders for goods on account of poor quality.

The more the possibility of such contigencies, the more is the amount that a firm is required to keep in facing them. Sometimes, a portion of such cash balances may also be held in marketable securities.

(iii) Speculative Motive

Speculative motive refers to the holding of cash to take advantage of unexpected opportunities as and when they arise. Sometimes firms hold cash balances above the precautionary level of cash balance to: (a) take advantage of speculative investment opportunities (b) exploit discounts for prompt payment, (c) improve credit rating, etc. Thus speculative motive is positive and aggressive in nature as against the defensive nature of precautionary motive.

(iv) Compensation Motive

Usually, banks provide some services to their customers free of charge. Thus they require clients to keep a minimum cash balance with them. This helps them to earn interest and thus compensate them for the free services so provided.

Normally, business firms do not enter into speculative activities. Thus the primary motives behind holding cash/marketable securities are: the transactions and the precautionary motives.

Objectives of Cash Management

The basic objectives of cash management are as follows: (i) Meeting cash disbursement, and (ii) Minimising funds locked up as cash balances.

(i) Meeting Cash Disbursement

The first and foremost objective of cash management is to meet the payment schedule. In other words, a firm should have enough cash to meet its various requirements such as payment for purchase of raw materials, wages, taxes, purchase of plant, etc. Thus it is needless to say that all the business activities should remain standstill unless proper payment schedule is maintained. Thus cash is aptly described as the "oil to lubricate the everturning wheels of the business, and without it, the process grinds to a halt".

(ii) Minimising Funds Locked Up as Cash Balances

Another objective of cash management is to minimise the amount locked up as cash balances. Usually, the financial manager is confronted with two conflicting views while attempting to do so. On one hand, although the higher cash balance ensures proper payment, this will result in a large balance of cash remaining idle. On the other, hand if a firm keeps its cash balance at low level, it cannot meet its payment schedule. Thus the financial manager should try to have an optimum cash balance by taking into account the above facts.

PROBLEMS OF CASH MANAGEMENT

The problem of cash management can be examined under four heads. They are:

1. Controlling level of cash
2. Controlling inflow of cash
3. Controlling outflow of cash
4. Optimum investment of surplus cash

1. Controlling Level of Cash

One of the fundamental objectives of cash management is the minimisation of the level of cash balance with the firm. This goal can be accomplished in the following ways:

(i) Preparing cash budget (ii) Providing for unpredictable discrepancies (iii) Availability of other sources of funds (iv) consideration of short costs.

(i) Preparing Cash Budget

Cash Budget is an important device to forecast the predictable discrepancies between cash inflows and outflows. It reveals the timing and size of net cash flows and the periods during which excess cash may be available for temporary investment. In large firms, the preparation of cash budget is almost a full-time exercise and it is a common practice to delegate this responsibility to the controller or the treasurer. But in the case of small firms its preparation is relatively a minor job as it does not involve much of complications.

To know the techniques of preparing cash budget refer Chapter 3, Financial Forecasting.

(ii) Providing for Unpredictable Discrepancies

Although cash budget predicts discrepancies between cash inflows and outflows on the basis of normal business activities, it does not consider discrepancies between cash inflows and outflows through unforeseen situations such as strikes, short-term recession, floods, etc. These unforeseen events can either interrupt cash or cause a sudden outflow. Thus a certain portion of cash balance is to be kept for meeting such contingencies and this amount is fixed on the basis of past experience and some intuition regarding the future.

(iii) Availability of Other Sources of Funds

A firm may have external sources to obtain funds on short notice. If a firm has to pay a slightly higher rate of interest than that on a long-term debt, it can avoid holding unnecessary large balance of cash.

(iv) Consideration of Short Costs

The cost which incurs as a result of shortage of cash is called the short cost. Such costs may arise in any of the following forms:

(a) If a firm fails to meet its obligation in time, the creditors may file suit against it. In such a situation, the cost is incurred in terms of fall in the firm's reputation apart from financial costs to be incurred in defending the suit.

(b) Sometimes, a firm may resort to borrowings at high rates of interest. In such a situation, if the firm fails to meet its obligation to bank in time, it is required to pay penalties.

2. Controlling Inflows of Cash

In order to manage cash efficiently, the process of cash inflow can be accelerated by way of systematic planning and refined techniques. Thus an important problem for the financial manager is to control cash inflows. He has to devise action not only to prevent fraudulent diversion of cash receipts but also to speed up collection of cash. However, the proper installation of internal check can minimise the possibility of misuse of cash. Moreover, collection of cash can be expedited through the adoption of various techniques such as (a) concentration banking and (b) lock-box system. These techniques have been found to be very useful and effective in the United States of America.

(a) Concentration Banking

It is a system of decentralising collection of accounts receivables in the case of big firms having business spread over a large area. Under this system, the firm establishes a large number of collection centres in different areas selected on geographical basis and opens its Bank accounts in local banks of different areas. These collection centers are required to collect and deposit remittances in local banks and from the local banks they are transferred to the firm's head office bank. However, fast movement of funds is effected by means of wire transfer or telex.

The system of concentration banking has the following advantages:

(i) Reduction of Mailing Time: Under the system of concentration banking, as the collection centres themselves collect cheques from the customers and immediately deposit them in local bank account, the mailing time is reduced. Further, the mailing time in sending bills to the customers can also be declined if the local collection centres are also used to prepare and send bills to customers in their areas.

(ii) Reduction of Time Required to Collect Cheques: As the cheques deposited in the local bank accounts are usually drawn on banks in that area, the time required to collect cheques also comes down.

(iii) Expediting Collection of Cash: The system of concentration banking also helps in quicker collection of cash.

(b) Lock-Box System

Lock-box is a post office box maintained by a firm's bank that is used as a receiving point for customer remittance. Lock-box system is another step in expediting collection of cash. This system is developed to eliminate the time gap between actual receipt of cheques by a collection centre and its actual depositing in the local bank account under concentration banking. Under lock-box system, the firm hires a post-office box and instructs its customers to mail their remittances to the box. The firm's local bank is given the authority to pick up the remittances directly from the local box. The bank collects from the box several times a day. It deposits the cheques, clears them locally and credits the cash in the firm's account. Local banks are given standing instructions to transfer funds to the Head Office when they exceed a particular limit.

The following are the advantages of lock-box system.

(i) It helps to eliminate the time lag between the receipt of cheques by a firm and their deposit into the bank.

(ii) This system helps to reduce the overhead expenses.

(iii) It facilitates control by separating remittance from the accounts section.

(iv) It also helps to reduce the credit losses by speeding up the time at which data are posted to the ledger.

Apart from the above systems, the firms adopt other systems also for prompt collection.

3. Control Over Cash Outflows

In order to conserve cash and reduce financial requirements, the firm should have strong control over its cash outflows or disbursements. It aims at slowing down disbursements as much as possible as against the maximum acceleration of collection in the case of control over inflows. However, the combination of fast collections and slow disbursements will result in the maximum availability of funds.

A firm can beneficially control outflows if the following points are considered:

(i) The firm should follow the centralised system for disbursements as against decentralised system for collections. Under centralised system, as all payments are made from a single control account, there will be delay in presentation of cheques for payment by parties who are away from the place of control account.

(ii) The financial manager should generally stress on the value of maintaining careful controls over the timing of payments so as to ensure that bills are paid only as they become due. When a firm makes payment on due dates, it should neither lose cash discount nor its prestige on account of delay in payments. Thus all payments should be made on due dates, neither before nor after.

(iii) The firm should adopt the technique of 'playing float' for maximising the availability of funds. The term "float" refers to the amount tied up in cheques that have been drawn but have not been presented for payment. Usually, there is a time gap between the issue of cheque by the firm and its actual presentation for payment. Consequently, the firm's actual balance at bank is greater than the balance as shown by its books. The longer the "float period", the higher the benefit to the firm.

If the financial manager can accurately estimate the dates on which the cheques will be actually presented for payment, the remittance shall be made by issue of cheques even if there is no balance in the firm's bank account in accordance with the books. In the course of time, he has to arrange funds so as to meet the payment of cheques the dates on which they are presented. For instance, a company issues cheques for Rs. 5 lakhs to various creditors on a certain day after banking hours. On the next day itself, all these cheques will not be presented for payment. Some of them may be presented the next day while others may be presented in the next four-five days. But in the case of outstation cheques, even longer time may be taken. Thus a prudent finance manager should keep in his bank account only the amount required to clear the cheques likely to be presented for payment on that day. If he expects that only cheques for Rs. 2 lakhs will be presented by the creditors for payment the next day, only Rs. 2 lakhs and no excess will be arranged in the firm's bank account. Moreover, playing float is all the more essential when a firm does not get any return on idle cash lying in its current account with the Bank.

'Playing float' is a risky game and the firm should play it very cautiously. However, the finance manager should have a close contact with the bank to ensure that no cheques issued by the firm are dishonoured due to insufficiency of funds as it may adversely affect the firm's goodwill.

4. Investing Surplus Cash

Cash in excess of the firm's normal cash requirement is surplus cash. It may be temporary or it may exist more or less on permanent basis. Temporary cash surplus is composed of funds that are available for investment on a short-term basis as they are required to meet regular obligations such as dividend and tax liabilities. Cash surplus may also be maintained more or less permanently as a hedge against unforeseen heavy expenses. Cash may also be accumulated over several years as a measure of a long-term plan.

The basic problems regarding the investment of surplus cash are as follows:

    (i) Determining the amount of surplus cash

    (ii) Determining the channels of investment.

(i) Determining the Amount of Surplus Cash

Cash kept by the firm in excess of its normal needs is called the surplus cash. Thus the finance manager is required to consider the minimum cash balance that the firm should keep to avoid the cost of running out of funds, while determining the amount of surplus cash. Such minimum level may be termed as the "Safety level for cash".

Determination of Safety Level of Cash: While determining the safety level of cash, the finance manager should consider both normal periods and peak periods. In these cases, he should decide the 'desired days of cash', i.e., the number of days for which cash balance should be sufficient to cover payments and the 'average daily cash outflows', i.e., the average amount of disbursements which will have to be made daily. Having determined both the desired days of cash and the average daily cash outflows, the finance manager can compute the safety level of costs as under:

During Normal Periods:

> Safety level of Cash = Desired days of Cash × Average daily Cash Outflows

For instance, in case it is felt that a safety level should provide sufficient cash to cover cash payments for ten days and the firm's average daily cash outflows are Rs. 10,000, the safety level of cash is Rs. 1,00,000. (i.e., 10 × 10,000).

During Peak Periods:

> Safety level of cash = Desired days of cash at the peak period ×
> Average of highest daily cash outflows.

For instance, during the four peak days in the month of January, the firm's cash outflows were Rs. 7,000, Rs. 8,000, Rs. 10,000 and Rs. 11,000. The average cash outflows come to Rs. 9,000. In case the finance manager likes to have enough cash for covering cash payments for six days during the peak periods, the safety level should be Rs. 54,000 (i.e., Rs. 9,000 × 6).

These ratios are highly useful in monitoring the level of cash balances. The finance manager of a firm should compare the actual cash balance with the daily cash outflows to find out the number of days for which cash is available. He should then compare such number of days with the desired days of cash to determine whether the firm is below or above the safety level.

ILLUSTRATION 12.1

From the following information, determines whether the firm has surplus or deficiency of cash.

	Normal periods	Peak periods
Desired days of Cash	7	6
Average daily Outflows	25,000	40,000
Actual Cash Balance	1,25,000	1,60,000

Solution

During Normal Periods

The firm has a cash balance of Rs. 1,25,000. The average daily cash outflows are Rs. 25,000. It implies that the firm has cash available only for 5 days (i.e., 1,25,000/25,000) as compared to that required for 7 days. Thus the firm has deficiency of cash.

During Peak Periods

The firm has a cash balance of Rs. 1,60,000. The average daily outflows are estimated at Rs. 40,000. It implies that the firm has cash available only for '4' days (i.e., 1,60,000/40,000) as compared to that required for '6' days. Thus the firm has deficiency of cash.

(ii) Determining the Channels of Investment

Having determined both the temporary and permanent cash surplus, the finance manager should decide the channels of investment. In most of the firms, there are no formal written instructions for investing the surplus. However, it is left to the discretion of the finance manager. Usually the finance manager considers the following factors or criteria while exercising such discretion.

- **(a) Security:** To ensure security, the finance manager may restrict himself to that type of investment which remains relatively stable in price.
- **(b) Liquidity:** To ensure liquidity, the money should be invested in short-term securities including short-term fixed deposits with banks.
- **(c) Yield:** Smaller companies with relatively limited amounts of surplus to invest are not much concerned with maximising yield. Such companies stick close to short-term Government securities. But some corporate managers feel that they should attempt to maximise yield through more aggressive investment practices. In short, however, most corporate managers provide less emphasis to yield in comparison with security and liquidity of investment.
- **(d) Maturity:** The finance manager should select securities in accordance with their maturities keeping in view the period for which surplus cash is available. He can maximise the yield and maintain the liquidity of investment in case such securities are selected carefully.

For instance, a firm may break its surplus cash available into the following three major groups.

- (i) Surplus funds, i.e., the primary reserve which is made available for meeting unforeseen disbursements. In the case of such cash, as security is more important than yield, it should be invested in assets which can be immediately sold without much loss. Thus assets in primary reserve are regarded as equivalent of cash.

(ii) Surplus cash which is made available on certain definite dates for some specific requirements like tax payments, dividends, capital expenditures, etc. Thus such cash should be invested in securities whose maturities coincide with the dates of payment.

(iii) Surplus cash, i.e., general reserve which is not required to meet any specific payment. Thus such cash can be invested in securities with longer maturities and more favourable yields.

Cash Management Models

To help in determining optimum cash balance, several types of cash management models have been designed. Out of such models, two of them are: (1) Baumol's Model, i.e., optimum cash balance under certainty, and (2) The Miller-Orr Model i.e., Optimum cash balance under uncertainty.

1. Baumol's Model

Baumol's model, suggested by William J. Baumol, considers cash management similar to an inventory management problem. It is a formal approach in determining a firm's optimum cash balance under certainty. According to this model, optimum cash level is that level of cash where the carrying costs and transactions costs are the minimum. As such, the firm attempts to minimise the cost of holding cash and the cost of converting marketable securities into cash.

The Baumol's model is subject to the following assumption.

(i) The firm can forecast its cash requirement with certainty.

(ii) The firm's cash payments are uniform over a period of time.

(iii) The firm's opportunity cost of holding cash is known and it is the same over time.

(iv) Whenever the firm converts securities into cash, its transaction cost will be the same.

It is assumed that the firm sells securities and starts with a cash balance of 'C' rupees. Since cash is spent, the firm's cash balance declines steadily and reaches zero. By selling marketable securities, the firm replenishes its cash to 'C' rupees. This process continues over a period of time. As the cash balance declines steadily, the average cash balance is $C/2$. This process is shown in Figure 12.1.

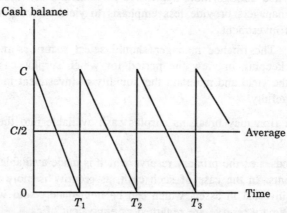

FIGURE 12.1 Baumol's model for cash balance.

Carrying Cost

It is the cost of holding cash i.e., the interest foregone on marketable securities. It is also termed as opportunity cost of keeping cash balance. In case the opportunity cost is K, then the firm's carrying cost for maintaining an average cash balance is :

$$\text{Carrying cost} = K(C/2)$$

Transaction Cost

It is the cost involved in getting the marketable securities converted into cash. If per transaction cost is 'C', then the total transaction cost is:

$$\text{Transaction cost} = C(T/C)$$
$$C = \text{Cash Balance}$$
$$T = \text{Total funds requirements, i.e., total number of transactions during the year.}$$

Thus the total cost of the demand for cash is:

$$\text{Total Cost} = K(C/2) + c(T/C)$$

There is an inverse relationship between the carrying costs and transaction costs. When one goes up, the other comes down. Thus there is a trade-off between the carrying cost and the transaction cost. Figure 12.2 shows this trade-off. The optimum cash level will, therefore, be at that point where these two costs are equal. The formula for optimum cash balance is:

$$C^* = \sqrt{\frac{2cT}{K}}$$

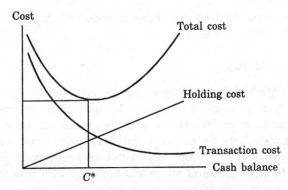

FIGURE 12.2 Cost trade-off: Baumol's Model.

where C^* is the optimum cash balance, 'c' is the cost per transaction. 'T' is the total cash needed during the year and 'K' is the opportunity cost of holding cash balance. The optimum cash balance will increase with increase in the per transaction cost and total funds required and decrease with the opportunity cost.

Optimum cash model has the following drawbacks:

(i) It is assumed that cash payments are to be steady during a specified period. When the cash payment becomes lumpy, it may be appropriate to decrease the period for which calculations are made so that expenditures during the period are relatively steady.

(ii) Cash payments are seldom predictable. Thus the model may not provide a cent per cent correct result.

ILLUSTRATION 12.2

PQR Ltd. estimates its total cash requirement as Rs. 90,00,000 next year. The firm's opportunity cost of fund is 10% per annum. The firm will have to incur Rs. 100 per transaction when it converts its short-term securities to cash. Compute the optimum cash balance. How much is the total annual cost of the demand for the optimum cash balance? How many deposits will have to be made during the year?

Solution

Optimum Cash Balance, i.e., $C^* = \sqrt{\dfrac{2cT}{K}}$

$$C^* = \sqrt{\dfrac{2(100)(90,00,000)}{0.10}} = \text{Rs. } 1,34,164$$

The annual cost will be

Total Cost = 100(90,00,000/1,34,164) + 0.10(1,34,164/2)
= 100(67) + 0.10(67,082)
= 6,700 + 6,708 = Rs. 13,408

During the year, the firm will have to make 67 deposits, i.e., converting marketable securities to cash.

2. Miller-Orr Model

Miller-Orr (MO) Model helps in determining the optimum level of cash when the demand for cash is not steady and cannot be known in advance. Thus this model helps to overcome the limitation of Baumol model where the cash flows are not allowed to fluctuate. MO model assumes that net cash flows are normally distributed with a zero value of mean and a standard deviation. In other words, MO model deals with each management problem under the assumption of random cash flows by laying down control limits for cash balances. These limits comprise of upper limit (h), lower limit (O) and return point (Z). When the firm's cash flows fluctuate randomly and hit the upper limit, it buys sufficient marketable securities to come back to a normal level of cash balance (the return point). Similarly, in case the firm's cash flows wander and hit the lower limit, it sells sufficient marketable securities to bring the cash balance back to the normal level (the return point). However, no transaction between cash and marketable securities is made during the period when the cash balance stays between these upper and lower limits. This model is illustrated in Figure 12.3

The upper and lower limits are set on the basis of opportunity cost of holding cash, degree of likely fluctuation in cash balance and the fixed cost associated with a securities transaction. Thus the difference between the upper limit and the lower limit depends on:

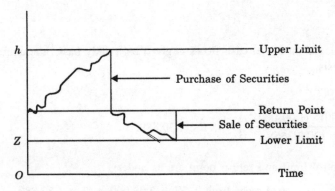

FIGURE 12.3 Miller-Orr Model.

(a) the Transaction Cost (C)

(b) the Interest Rate (i), and

(c) the Standard Deviation (σ) of net cash flows.

The formula for determining the distance between upper and lower control limits (called Z) is:

(Upper Limit – Lower Limit) = (3/4 × Transaction cost × Cash Flow Variance/Interest Rate)$^{1/3}$

$$Z = (3/4 \times c\sigma^2/i)^{1/3}$$

When transaction cost is higher or cash flows show greater fluctuations, the upper and lower limits will be far off from each other (i.e., Z will be larger). However, the limits come closer as the interest goes up. Thus 'Z' is inversely related to the interest rate.

Figure 12.3 shows that the upper control limit is three times above the lower control limit. But the return point lies between the upper and the lower limits. Thus,

Upper Limit = Lower Limit + 3Z

Return Point = Lower Limit + Z

Thus the firm holds the average cash balance equal to:

Average Cash Balance = Lower Limit + (4/3)Z

Since MO model allows variation in cash balance within lower and upper limits, it is more realistic. Thus the lower limit of cash balance of the firm can be set by taking into account its liquidity requirement. Once both these limits are set, attention is needed only when the deviation is made.

ILLUSTRATION 12.3

AB Ltd. has a policy of maintaining a minimum cash balance of Rs. 3,00,000. The standard deviation of the firm's daily cash flows is Rs. 1,00,000. The annual interest rate is 10 per cent. The transaction cost of buying and selling securities is Rs. 100 per transaction. Compute the upper control limit and return point of AB Ltd. under Miller-Orr model.

Solution

Since the standard deviation of net cash flows is given on a daily basis, the annual interest rate is changed to daily basis.

$$Z = (3/4 \times c\sigma^2/i)^{1/3}$$

$$Z = \left(\frac{3}{4} \times \frac{(100) \times (1,00,000)^2}{(0.10/365)} \right)^{1/3} = \text{Rs. } 1,39,889$$

The upper control limit and return point are as under:

Upper Limit = Lower limit + 3Z = 3,00,000 + (3 × 1,39,889)
= Rs. 7,19,667

Return Point = Lower limit + Z = 3,00,000 + 1,39,889
= Rs. 4,39,889

Average cash balance = Lower Limit + (4/3) Z

$$= 3,00,000 + \frac{4}{3} \times 1,39,889$$

= Rs. 4,86,518

AB Ltd. will not allow the lower limit of cash balance of Rs. 3,00,000. If the company's cash balance touches this limit, it will sell marketable securities with (Z) Rs. 1,39,889 and restore return point to Rs. 4,39,889 cash balance level. On the contrary, when the cash balance of AB Ltd. touches the upper limit of Rs. 7,19,667 it will buy marketable securities worth (2Z) Rs. 2,79,778 and bring cash balance to the return point.

— REVIEW QUESTIONS —

1. What is cash in cash management? What are the motives of holding cash?
2. What is cash management? What are the objectives of cash management?
3. "Efficient cash management will aim at maximising the availability of cash inflows by decentralising collections and decelerating cash outflows by centralising disbursements". Discuss.
4. Write notes on:
   (a) Concentration Banking
   (b) Cash Management Model
   (c) Lock-Box System
   (d) Playing Float
5. Discuss the Miller-Orr Model used for determining the cash balance of a firm.
6. Explain Baumol's Model used for determining the cash balance of a firm.
7. From the following information, you are required to compute optimum cash balance of a firm as per Baumol's Model.

Monthly cash requirements	Rs. 60,000
Fixed cost per transaction	Rs. 10
Interest rate on marketable securities	6%

(**Ans.:** Rs. 15,422 or say Rs. 15,000)

13

Sources of Finance

The term source implies the agencies from which funds are procured.

CONTENTS

- Introduction
- Shares
- Debentures
- Public deposits
- Specialised financial institutions
- Case study
- Review questions

INTRODUCTION

The term "source" implies the agencies from which funds are procured. The sources of raising finance can be brought into the following categories on the basis of the period for which funds are required:

(i) **Long-term Finance:** Funds needed for acquiring fixed assets like land and building, plant and machinery, etc., are known as long-term finance. The long-term sources of finance such as shares, debentures and retained earnings are raised mainly for a period of not less than 10 years.

(ii) **Medium-term Finance:** Funds required for meeting long-term needs of working capital are known as medium-term finance. The medium-term sources of finance such as debentureholders, financial institutions, public deposits and commercial banks are raised for a period between 1 year and 10 years.

(iii) **Short-term Finance:** Funds required for meeting the short-term needs of working capital are known as short-term finance. The short-term sources of finance such as public deposits, trade credits and commercial banks are raised for a period of 1 year and less than one year.

Types of Securities

A business concern can raise funds by issuing two types of securities. They are as follows:

(i) Ownership securities or owned capital.

(ii) Creditorship securities or borrowed capital.

Figure 13.1 shows the types of securities.

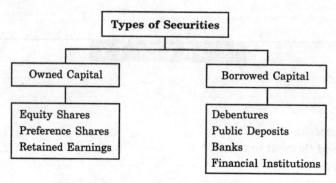

FIGURE 13.1 Types of Securities.

Owned Capital

The capital contributed by the owners (sole proprietor, partners or shareholders) is known as "*owned capital*". This consists of initial capital contribution and the profits re-invested in the business. Owned capital as a source of finance has the following features:

1. **Source of Permanent Capital:** Since owned capital remains in the concern so long as the concern is alive, it is a source of permanent capital. Although a part of the owned capital may be used as working capital, it is generally used to acquire fixed assets. Unlike the borrowed capital, owned capital is not refundable.

2. **Risk Capital to the Business:** The owner gets all the benefits if the concern earns large profits. On the other hand, the owners bear the whole risk of loss if the concern incurs loss. Thus ownership security provides risk capital to the business.

3. **Management and Control:** As the owners have control over the management of the business, the managers should follow the policies laid down by the owners.

4. **Residual Profit in the Form of Dividend:** Dividends to the ownership securities are to be distributed only if there are profits.

Advantages

1. It provides risk capital.
2. It is permanently available in the business.
3. The owners get high returns, if the business is good.
4. It acts as a basis for the control and management of the concern.

Disadvantages

1. The sum invested in a concern is not withdrawable especially if the concern is a joint-stock company.
2. A company may find it difficult to raise additional ownership capital unless it has high profit earning capacity, or growth prospects.
3. The amount of capital which may be raised as owners fund depends on the number of persons prepared to bear the risk involved, and their personal savings.

Borrowed Capital

Finance raised by way of loans and credit from the public, banks and financial institutions is known as "borrowed capital". The sources of borrowed funds like debentures, public deposits, banks, etc., may serve the purposes of long-term, medium-term and short-term finance. Borrowed capital as a source of finance has the following features:

Available for a fixed period

1. Usually, borrowed capital is raised for a fixed period such as long-term, medium-term and short-term. When this fixed period is over, it has to be paid back.
2. It involves the payment of fixed rate of interest at regular intervals.
3. It is backed by the security of tangible assets of the company.
4. The lenders do not have any control over the company.
5. The lenders are not treated as owners of the company.

Advantages

1. It does not effect the owners control over management.
2. It can be used for expansion or modernisation when additional share capital is not readily available.
3. Since interest on loan is fixed, the charge on profits remains the same.
4. Since interest on loan can be written off as expense, borrowed capital has a tax advantage.
5. It is a flexible source of finance as the amount of loan can be so adjusted as to suit the exigencies of the situation.
6. Loans can be repaid in instalments as and when sufficient funds are available. This will reduce interest burden.
7. The lenders are treated as creditors only.

Disadvantages

1. It involves fixed payment of interest.
2. It is not available for permanent use.
3. Any default in payment of loan should adversely affect the business.
4. Funds can be borrowed only if a concern can offer suitable assets as security.

Distinction between Ownership Capital and Creditorship Capital

Ownership Capital	*Creditorship Capital*
1. It comprises the amounts contributed by the owners and their profits reinvested in the business.	1. It consists of funds available in the form of loan or credit.
2. It is permanently invested in the business.	2. It is not a permanent source of finance.
3. It is the risk capital of the business.	3. It is generally safe.

SHARES

The capital of a company is usually divided into certain indivisible units of a definite sum. These units are called "*Shares*". Shares represent the interest of shareholders in a company measured in terms of money. They carry with them certain rights and liabilities. Shares are also called ownership securities and can be transferred from one person to another person. Those who subscribe shares are called shareholders. They are the owners of the company. In India, a public limited company may issue two kinds of shares. They are: (1) Preference Shares and (2) Equity Shares.

Preference Shares

Preference shares are those shares which carry preferential rights in respect of dividend and repayment of capital in the event of winding up of the company. Companies may resort to this technique as long-term capital on account of the above advantages. Since preference shareholders have no voting rights, they do not have to take any risk and hence ownership is not affected.

Holders of preference shares enjoy certain privileges which cannot be claimed by the equity shareholders. These privileges are:

(i) the cumulative dividend if in any year dividend is not paid,

(ii) the right to convert their shares into equity shares,

(iii) the right to participate in profits left after payment of dividend to the preference and equity shareholders.

By virtue of these special privileges enjoyed by preference shareholders, they are denied the right to take part in the matters which may be discussed at the general body meeting. They cannot also take part in the election of directors. In effect, the management and control of the company vests with the equity shareholders.

Kinds of Preference Shares

(i) **Cumulative Preference Shares:** Preference shares which guarantee a fixed rate of dividend is known as "Cumulative Preference Shares". If the dividend at a fixed rate cannot be paid in any year on account of inadequate profits, arrears of dividend will accumulate and will have to be paid out of the profit of future years. All preference shares are considered cumulative unless otherwise mentioned.

(ii) **Non-cumulative Preference Shares:** *"Non-cumulative Preference Shares"* are those shares on which the dividend does not go on accumulating. In the case of such shares, a fixed rate of dividend is paid out of the profits of the company. If no profits are available in any year, the shareholders get nothing, nor can they claim unpaid fixed dividend in subsequent years.

(iii) **Participating Preference Shares:** *"Participating Preference Shares"* are shares which are not only entitled to a fixed preferential dividend but also to participate in the surplus profits along with the equity shareholders.

(iv) **Non-participating Preference Shares:** *"Non-participating Preference Shares"* are shares which entitle the shareholders, only the fixed preferential dividend.

(v) **Convertible Preference Shares:** The holders of convertible preferential shares have the option to convert them into equity shares within a certain period.

(vi) **Non-convertible Preference Shares:** These are the shares which are to be redeemed or refunded at the expiry of a fixed period.

(vii) **Irredeemable Preference Shares:** *"Irredeemable preference Shares"* are those shares which are repayable on the winding up of the company only.

Advantages of Preference Shares

The company has the following benefits through the issue of preference shares:

(a) The preference shares attract funds from those investors who prefer safety and a fixed rate of return on their investment.

(b) Since the preference shareholders have only restricted voting rights, the management can retain control over the company by issuing preference shares to outsiders.

(c) Preference shareholders are entitled to a fixed rate of dividend.

(d) As preference shares carry fixed rate of dividend, they do not impose heavy burden on the company.

(e) A company can raise finance for a long-term without creating any charge over its assets.

Disadvantages of Preference Shares

In spite of the above advantages, preference shares are subject to the following limitations:

(a) Preference shares are costlier.

(b) Investors do not prefer these shares.

(c) Preference shares adversely affect the credit worthiness of the company.

(d) Redeemable preference shares are to be repaid after a fixed time. This becomes a burden to the company.

Equity Shares

Shares which do not enjoy any of the preference attached to the preference shares are known as "*equity shares*" or "*ordinary shares*". Equity shares are the most important sources of finance for fixed capital and they represent the ownership capital of a company. Equity shareholders are the real owners of the company and bear the risk of business. Hence they are known as risk bearers and the capital they contribute is called venture capital. Dividend on equity shares is paid after the dividend on preference shares has been paid. In the case of winding up, equity capital can be paid back only after every claim including those of preference shareholders has been settled.

Advantages

Equity share offers the following benefits as it is regarded as the corner-stone of the capital structure of a company:

(i) It is the permanent resource of the company.

(ii) It does not impose any obligation on the company.

(iii) It does not create any charge over the assets of the company.

(iv) It provides risk capital which serves as a base for outside borrowings.

(v) As it enjoys free transferability, it provides liquidity to the investors funds.

Disadvantages

Equity shares of finance are subject to the following limitations:

(i) The affairs of the company may be manipulated as the control rests with the equity shareholders.

(ii) Excessive issue of equity shares sometimes leads to over-capitalisation.

(iii) If the company issues only equity shares, it will lose the opportunity of trading by issuing other securities.

(iv) Equity shares are not attractive to cautious investors as they are risky.

(v) Higher dividends on equity shares during prosperous periods push up their market values. This will give an opportunity for speculative trading.

Distinction between Preference Shares and Equity Shares

Equity Share	Preference Share
1. Its nominal value is generally lower.	1. Its nominal value is generally higher.
2. Its rate of dividend varies in accordance with the profits of the company.	2. Its rate of dividend is fixed.
3. It has no right to get the arrears of dividend.	3. Holders of cumulative preference shares have a right to get the arrears of dividend.

Continued

Distinction between Preference Shares and Equity Shares (*Continued*)

Equity Share	*Preference Share*
4. It cannot be redeemed.	4. It is redeemable.
5. It has voting rights on all matters.	5. It has no voting right except on matters affecting it.
6. It has comparatively more risk.	6. It has comparatively less risk.
7. There is no priority for the equity shareholders in the matter of dividend and repayment of capital.	7. There is priority regarding payment of dividend and repayment of capital.
8. It is highly speculative as the rate of dividend varies.	8. It is less speculative as the rate of dividend is fixed.

Retained Profits or Ploughing-back of Profits

When a company retains a part of undistributed profits in the form of free resources and the same is utilised for further expansion, it is known as "*Ploughing-back of profits*" or "*retained earnings*". Profits which are undistributed among the shareholders are re-invested into the business year after year for further expansion and modernisation. The amount so retained should have otherwise gone to shareholders as dividend. It is, therefore, treated as "ownership fund".

Ploughing-back of profit is also known as "*self-financing*" because it is an internal source of finance. It is just like individuals saving a part of their current earnings to meet future requirements. Thus it is strictly not a method of raising finance. The sum raised through internal savings is to be shown as a reserve in the financial statement.

Although ploughing-back of profit is essentially a means of financing for extension and development of a company, its availability depends upon the following factors:

(a) The rate of taxation.

(b) The dividend policy of the firm.

(c) Government policy on the payment of dividends by the corporate sector.

(d) Extent of available surplus and upon the company's appropriation policy.

Need for Retained Earnings

The need for retained earnings arises on account of the following reasons:

(i) To expand both fixed capital as well as working capital for further expansion and development.

(ii) To improve the efficiency of the plant and equipment.

(iii) Unreliability on the statement of accounts compels management to retain a part of the substantial profit.

Advantages

1. It makes the company financially strong.

2. As it is an internal source of financing, no obligation is created.

3. It does not involve any cost for raising finance.

4. It has been broadly found to be useful for financing expansion and modernisation.

5. It enhances business reputation.

6. It increases capital formation which is very significant for the development of the economy.

Disadvantages

1. It results in reduction of the current rate of dividend to shareholders.

2. Continuous ploughing-back of profits for a long period may result in converting the company into a monopolistic organisation.

3. The management may misuse the funds to manipulate the value of the company's shares in the stock exchange.

4. It may result in over-capitalisation.

5. It reduces the regular income of the shareholders.

6. It affects the balanced industrial growth of the economy.

DEBENTURES

Debenture is one of the important sources of raising finance for a company. Under Section 2(12) of the Companies Act, 1956, "debentures include debenture stocks, bonds and other securities of a company whether or not constituting a charge on the assets of the company". In other words, debenture is a certificate issued by a company under its seal acknowledging a debt due by it to its holders. It is a creditorship security. Debentureholders are, therefore, known as the creditors of the company. They are entitled to periodical payment of interest at a fixed rate.

Characteristics

1. Debenture is a creditorship security of the company.

2. It carries fixed rate of interest.

3. Debentureholders are the creditors of the company.

4. They do not carry voting rights.

5. Debentures are repayable after a fixed period which is specified at the time of issue.

Types of Debentures

Debentures are classified into the following categories:

1. **Registered Debentures:** The names of such debentureholders are found in the register of debentureholders of the company. In other words, interest is payable or the repayment of debenture is made to that person whose name is registered in the books of the company. These debentures are not negotiable instruments.

2. **Bearer or Unregistered Debentures:** *"Bearer debentures"* are those debentures which are payable to the bearer. Such debentures are just like negotiable instruments. Interest is paid at the end of the stipulated period to the person who will possess them.

3. **Secured Debentures:** When debentures are secured by a charge on the assets of the company, they are known as *"secured or mortgage debentures"*. The charge may be fixed or floating.

4. **Unsecured Debentures:** When debentures are issued without any security in respect of interest or the repayment of the principal they are known as *"unsecured or naked debentures"*. They are like unsecured creditors and hence the solvency of the company is the only security.

5. **Redeemable Debentures:** *"Redeemable Debentures"* are those which are redeemed either at par or at a discount after the expiration of the specified period. The same can be re-issued even after redemption if not cancelled.

6. **Irredeemable Debentures:** *"Irredeemable or Perpetual debenture"* is one which contains no clause as to the payment or which contains a clause that it shall not be paid back.

7. **Convertible Debentures:** These are debentures which give an option to the debenture-holders to convert them into preference or equity shares at a stated rate of exchange.

Advantages

1. Since debentureholders have no voting rights, the issue of debentures does not weaken the control of existing shareholders.

2. Debentures help to provide flexible capital structure.

3. The company can enjoy tax benefit by issuing debentures as the interest paid can be deducted from the profits of the company.

4. It is desirable to raise a part of long-term finance by issuing debentures as they can help trading on equity.

5. Debentures bear less cost as compared to public deposits and bank loan.

6. Debentureholders have a safe investment as they have a fixed and regular income.

Disadvantages

1. The company should bear a fixed burden of interest every year irrespective of profits earned.

2. Creditors like debentures as they prefer safety for their investment.

3. The issue of debentures may not be possible on account of the inadequacy of assets to be offered as security.

4. Debentureholders do not have any voting rights in the company.

Distinction between Shares and Debentures

Shares	Debentures
1. It is a part of the ownership capital of the company.	1. It is a part of the creditorship capital of the company.
2. A shareholder is an owner.	2. A debentureholder is a creditor.
3. A shareholder has a right to vote.	3. A debentureholder has no right to vote.
4. A shareholder gets dividend.	4. A debentureholder gets interest.
5. No dividend unless the company has earned profit.	5. Interest is always payable whether there is profit or not.
6. Shareholders have no charge on the assets of the company.	6. Debentureholders have charge on the assets of the company.
7. Subject to certain legal restrictions, shares can be issued at a discount.	7. Debentures can be issued at a discount without any legal restrictions.
8. In the case of winding up, shareholders have no prior claim over the debenture-holders.	8. In the case of winding-up debentureholders have prior claim over the shareholders.

PUBLIC DEPOSITS

The deposits made by the public with the joint-stock companies are known as *"public deposits"*. These deposits are taken from the members or directors of the company or from the general public at a specified rate of interest for a specified period. They are not secured loans. Thus the depositors are ordinary creditors. Industrial and commercial enterprises resort to this mode of financing for meeting their medium-term financial requirements.

In India, this method of financing is becoming popular at present as the bank credit is becoming costlier. Moreover, a company can accept deposits from the public only in accordance with the rules framed by the Central Government under the Companies Act. As per the existing provisions, a company can accept public deposits for different periods ranging from six months to thirty six months. But deposits can be renewed. However, a company can receive public deposits up to ten per cent of the paid-up capital and free reserves for a minimum period of three months for meeting working capital requirements. But overall a company can collect or renew public deposits only to the extent of thirty five per cent of its paid-up capital and free reserves.

There are two methods of raising fund under this scheme. They are:

(a) cumulative deposits, and

(b) fixed deposits.

(a) Cumulative Deposits

Under this method, there is a specified period of time (generally three years) at the end of which the depositors should be paid their maturity values which include an interest up to 55 per cent of initial deposits, i.e., 18.5 per cent per annum simple interest or 15 per cent per annum compound interest.

(b) Fixed Deposits

Under this method, payment of interest at different rates (generally from 12 to 16 per cent per annum in India) is made for the period ranging from one to three years. An extra amount of interest at 5 per cent per annum is offered to the shareholders or employees.

However, under both these methods, a minimum amount is laid down. If there is any deposit which is above that minimum level, the same is accepted in multiples of certain amount which are specified.

Advantages

Public deposit, as a source of finance has the following advantages:

1. It is less expensive.
2. It is simple to operate as it involves few legal formalities.
3. It does not create any charge on the company's assets as it is an unsecured loan.
4. It serves as a valuable source of medium-term finance.
5. There is no restriction on the use of funds collected in this way.
6. It facilitates payment of higher dividends to the shareholders.
7. It enjoys tax exemption, i.e., loan finance enables the company to save the company from taxation.
8. It has no effect on management as depositors are mere creditors.

Disadvantages

In spite of the aforesaid advantages, public deposit is subject to the following limitations:

1. It is uncertain and unreliable: when the company is prospering, the public is quite willing to give deposits; when the company shows a sign of weakening, the deposits are withdrawn. Thus public deposits are called "fair weather friends".
2. It is available for a short period. Thus it is not advisable for long-term financing.
3. It is generally not available to new companies and those with uncertain earnings.
4. It is an inelastic source of finance, i.e., it cannot be regulated according to the needs of company finance.
5. It is undesirable for the development of sound capital market as investors are deprived of the benefits accruing from good securities.

Commercial Banks

Commercial banks play a very significant role in financing the short-term requirements of companies. They provide finance by way of loans, overdrafts, cash credit and discounting bills.

"*Loan*" is granted for a specific project or purpose such as purchase of plant and machinery. Under "*overdraft*" arrangement, a customer having a current account with the bank is allowed to overdraw his account. Under the "*cash credit*" scheme, the bank fixes a cash credit limit for the customer. The customer can withdraw up to this limit any number of times. But interest is charged only on the amount actually utilised. Commercial banks extend credit to industries by discounting their bills and promissory notes. They discount these documents at the price less than their face value. The difference is the amount of interest charged by the bank.

Advantages

The advantages of bank finance are as follows:

1. It is cheaper compared to any other source of short-term finance.
2. It is readily available.
3. Banks do not interfere with the ownership and management of the borrowing concern.
4. Banks grant credit to small units at concessional rates under their special schemes.

Disadvantages

The disadvantages of bank finance are as follows:

1. A number of legal formalities have to be complied with.
2. Banks rarely provide unsecured credit to companies.
3. Although the business is running at a loss, the interest is to be paid at a fixed rate.

SPECIALISED FINANCIAL INSTITUTIONS

A number of financial institutions have been set up by the Central and State Governments to provide long- and medium-term financial assistance to industrial concerns. These specialised institutions help in the promotion of new concerns apart from providing financial assistance to the existing concerns. Thus they are known as *"Development Banks"*.

Since independence, a number of specialised institutions have been started at the national and state level. They are Industrial Finance Corporation of India (IFCI), Industrial Development Bank of India (IDBI), Industrial Credit and Investment Corporation of India (ICICI), State Financial Corporation (SFC's), State Industrial Development Corporation (SIDC's), etc.

Industrial Finance Corporation of India (IFCI)

Industrial Finance Corporation was set up on 1st July 1948 under the Industrial Finance Corporation Act, 1948. Later it was converted into a company under the Companies Act, 1956 for making the functioning of the corporation more effective. The objective behind its establishment is to make medium- and long-term loans more readily available to industrial enterprises. It will offer assistance to those concerns that are engaged in the manufacturing, processing or preservation of goods or in mining, shipping and hotel keeping or in generation and distribution of electricity or other forms of powers, transport services and certain other specified activities. Usually, loans of over rupees 10 lakhs are granted for a period ranging from 12 to 15 years. However, the maximum amount of loan to an industrial concern cannot go beyond rupees one crore or 10 per cent of the paid-up capital of the corporation.

The IFCI's authorised capital was initially rupees 10 crores. It was raised to rupees 20 crores in December 1972. Its paid-up capital was rupees 5 crores but it was raised to rupees 15 crores in September 1979. The value of each share is rupees five thousands. The share capital of the corporation has been subscribed by the Central Government, the Reserve Bank of India, the Life Insurance Corporation of India, the scheduled banks, insurance companies and co-operative Banks.

Functions

The important functions of the corporation are as follows:

1. Granting loans and advances to industrial concerns.
2. Subscribing to the debentures floated by them.
3. Subscribing directly to the shares of industrial concerns.
4. Underwriting the issues of shares and bonds by industrial concerns.
5. Guaranteeing loans raised by industrial concerns.
6. Guaranteeing the payment for the purchase of capital goods from abroad or within India.
7. Providing assistance, under the self-loan scheme, to the selected industries.
8. Undertaking promotional activities of new industrial concerns.

IFCI now charges interest at 14 per cent per annum on rupee loans as well as foreign currency loans subject to the rebate of ½ per cent per annum for rupee loans in backward areas.

Industrial Development Bank of India (IDBI)

Industrial Development Bank of India was established in July 1964 by a Special Act of Parliament. It was originally a subsidiary of the Reserve Bank of India. But it was later delinked from the RBI and made an independent corporation.

The IDBI's authorised and paid-up capital are rupees 500 crores and 300 and 85 crores respectively. The whole of paid-up capital is held by the Central Government.

The IDBI has a board of directors consisting of:

(i) A chairman, and a managing director appointed by Central Government.

(ii) A deputy governor of the RBI nominated by it.

(iii) Not more than twenty directors nominated by the Central Government as follows:

   (a) Two directors who are the officials of the Central Government.

   (b) Five directors from the financial institutions, viz, ICICI, IFC, LIC and UTI.

   (c) Two directors amongst the employees of IDBI and the aforesaid financial institutions—one from the officer employees and the other from workmen employees.

   (d) Six directors from the State Bank of India, Nationalised Banks and SFC.

   (e) Five directors having special knowledge and professional experience in science, technology, economics, industrial co-operatives, law, industrial finance, investment, accountancy, marketing or any other matter useful to IDBI.

Objectives

The main objectives of IDBI are:

1. to serve as the apex institution for term-finance for industry in India,
2. to serve as a reservoir from which the existing financial institutions can draw,
3. to plan, promote and develop new industries in the key and basic sector,
4. to locate and fill up the gaps in the industrial structure, and
5. to undertake market research and surveys.

Functions

The various functions of IDBI are:

1. to grant direct loans and advances to industrial enterprises,
2. to provide technical and administrative assistance to industrial concerns,
3. to provide re-finance to scheduled banks or co-operative banks.
4. to provide re-finance for export credit granted by banks and other financial institutions,
5. to co-ordinate, regulate and supervise the activities of the other financial institutions, and
6. to accept, discount and re-discount bills and promissory notes of industrial concerns.

Industrial Credit and Investment Corporation of India (ICICI)

The Industrial Credit and Investment Corporation of India was set up on 5th January, 1955 as a public limited company. It came into existence as a privately owned institution. But later on, LIC became its major shareholder. Its authorised and paid-up capital were rupees 25 crores and 5 crores respectively. But in May 1978, its paid-up capital was raised to rupees 22 crores. ICICI sanctions its loans to industries related to chemicals and petro-chemicals, machine manufacturing, metal products, automobiles and cotton-textiles, electric equipment, shipping, etc. Now its rate of interest on rupee and foreign currencies is 11 per cent per annum.

Objectives

Its main objectives are:

1. to assist in the promotion, expansion and modernisation of industrial concerns in the private sector,
2. to encourage and promote participation of private capital in such concerns, and
3. to encourage and promote private ownership of industrial activities.

Functions

The major functions of ICICI are:

1. to grant medium- and long-term loans in home and foreign currencies,
2. to participate in the equity share capital of industrial concerns,

3. to secure and furnish technical and managerial services for the industrial concerns,
4. to underwrite public issues of shares and debentures, and
5. to guarantee loans raised by industrial concerns from other institutions.

State Financial Corporations (SFCs)

The State Financial Corporation Act was passed by the Government of India in 1951 to meet the requirements of small concerns. As per this Act, a state government is empowered to establish a financial corporation to operate within its area. State Financial Corporation is complimentary to the IFCI and is expected to concentrate on small, medium and cottage industries. Its minimum and maximum share capital are rupees 50 lakhs and 5 crores respectively. Its share capital is subscribed by the respective state governments, the Reserve Bank of India, Insurance Companies, Commercial Banks, etc.

Functions

The major functions of State Financial Corporations are:

1. to grant loans and advances to the industrial concerns,
2. to guarantee loans raised by industrial concerns,
3. to subscribe to the debentures of industrial concerns,
4. to underwrite the issue of shares, debentures by industrial concerns, and
5. to guarantee deferred payments for the purchase of capital goods within India.

Unit Trust of India (UTI)

The Unit Trust of India was set up on 1st February 1964 under the Unit Trust of India Act, 1963. Its primary objective is to encourage and mobilise savings of the community and channelise them into productive ventures. UTI was started with an initial capital of rupees five crores. This sum was contributed by the Reserve Bank of India, the State Bank of India, Life Insurance Corporation of India and other specified financial institutions. A Board of Trustees is entrusted with the management and business of the trust.

Objectives

The main objectives of the UTI are:

1. to stimulate the propensity of the middle- and low-income groups to save, and
2. to enable them to share the benefits and prosperity of industrialisation.

The above goals can by accomplished by (a) selling units among many investors; (b) investing the sale proceeds of the units together with its capital in corporate securities, and (c) paying dividends to those who have purchased units.

The scope of the operations of the UTI has been enlarged in recent years to mobilise the savings of the community. It has introduced various schemes such as Unit Scheme 1964, Re-investment Plan 1961, Voluntary Saving Plan 1969, Unit Linked Insurance Plan 1971, etc. UTI has a network of approved agents and registered brokers for the sale of units throughout the nation. It has also issued mutual fund shares under various schemes such as Master Shares, MEPs and Master Gains to mobilise the savings of small investors.

CASE STUDY

Some Other Innovative Sources of Finance

Venture Capital. It is a high risk capital normally provided by venture capital companies (VCCS) at the early stage of a company's life.

Venture capital financing involves a high degree of risk. Usually, venture capital companies provide the necessary risk capital to the entrepreneurs so as to meet the promoters' contribution as required by the financial institutions. Apart from providing capital, these VCCS take an active interest in guiding the assisted firms.

Bridge Loan. A temporary loan given to cover the gap between the purchase of an asset and the sale of another asset, the proceeds of which are required to finance the purchase.

The term 'Bridge Finance' refers to the loans taken by firms, generally from commercial banks. Such a finance is generally secured against mortgage of fixed properties and/or hypothecation of movable properties of the borrowing firm. The rate of interest on such a finance is usually higher than that on term loans.

Consortium Lending and Loan Syndication by Banks

When the large financial requirements of a borrower cannot be met by the individual bank, the need of multiple banking arises. It may be in the forms of (i) consortium lending, and (ii) loan syndication.

(i) **Consortium Lending:** If the financial needs of a single unit cannot be met by a single bank, two or more banks come together to finance the unit by jointly spreading the risk and sharing the responsibilities of monitoring and finance. This arrangement is called consortium lending. This is generally formalized by a consortium agreement. There is no limit to the number of banks in consortium. However, the share of each bank should be 5 per cent of the amount sanctioned or Rs. 1 crore, whichever is greater. In the case of consortium arrangement, any bank outside the consortium will not be permitted to extend any additional credit facility or open current account for the borrowers without the knowledge or concurrence of the consortium members. Usually, consortium lending helps the industrial units to mobilise huge funds for their operations.

As per the RBIs recent guidelines, banks which are financing to units requiring huge outlay of funds form a consortium arrangement among banks. Borrowers requiring funds of Rs. 50 crore or more from two or more banks should be brought under consortium arrangement.

(ii) **Loan Syndication:** Like consortium, the concept of loan syndication has been formulated as per the RBI's recent guidelines to meet the borrowers huge financial requirements, which an individual bank finds it difficult to fulfil. There are two methods of syndication. They are (i) direct lending, and (ii), through participation.

Direct lending: Under direct lending, all the lenders sign the loan agreement independently with the borrower and agree to lend up to their respective share. However, the obligations of the syndicate members are several and they do not underwrite one another.

Through participation: Under this method, the lead bank is the only lending bank as far as the borrower is concerned. Here, the lead bank approaches the other lenders without the knowledge of the borrower to participate in the loan. Moreover, as per the agreement between the lead bank and other lenders, the lead bank grants a certain portion of the loan to each participant and pays him a pro rata share of receipts from the borrower.

Participation is generally brought into four types. They are: (i) substitution, (ii) undisclosed agency, (iii) sub-loan, and (iv) assignment.

Substitution: The first step in substitution is an agreement. The borrower, the lead bank and other participants are parties of the agreement. This agreement grants permission to the lead bank to disburse the loan on behalf of the participants.

Undisclosed agency: Under this type of participation, the lead bank is appointed as agent by the syndicate without the knowledge of the borrower before the loan agreement is made. The lead bank is, therefore, the principal as far as the borrower is concerned.

Sub-loan: In this type, each participant of the syndicate grants a conditional loan to the lead bank. On the basis of the condition, the lead bank repays the loan only to the extent of receipts from the borrower.

Assignment: Under this scheme, the lead bank assigns a proportion of the loan and of the benefit of the loan agreement to the participants. This assignment is made in consideration of the purchase price or pro rata share of the loan to be contributed by the participants.

― REVIEW QUESTIONS ―

1. Critically examine the various sources available to Indian businessmen for raising capital.

2. Write notes on:
   (a) Public deposits
   (b) Ploughing back of profits
   (c) Debentures

3. What is ownership capital? How does it differ from creditorship capital?

4. Examine the relative merits of the following forms of financing:
   (a) Preference shares
   (b) Equity shares
   (c) Debentures

5. Distinguish between:
   (a) Shares and Debentures
   (b) Preference Shares and Equity Shares

6. Write notes on:
   (a) Commercial Banks
   (b) Industrial Finance Corporation of India
   (c) Industrial Development Bank of India
   (d) State Financial Corporations
   (e) Unit Trust of India

14
Financial Analysis

Financial statements, essentially, are interim reports presented annually and reflect a division of the life of an enterprise into more or less arbitrary accounting period—more frequently a year.

— ANTONY, ROBERT N.

Financial Analysis refers to the process of evaluating the financial position and the results of operation of a business.

CONTENTS

- Meaning of financial statements
- Types of financial statements
- Financial analysis
- Common-size statements
- Trend analysis
- Case study
- Review questions

MEANING OF FINANCIAL STATEMENTS

A financial statement is a collection of data organised in accordance with logical and consistent accounting procedures. In other words, it is the outcome of summarising process of accounting. According to John N. Myer

> the financial statements provide a summary of the accounts of a business enterprise, the balance sheet reflecting the assets, liabilities and capital as on a certain date and the income statement showing the results of operations during a certain period.

Thus financial statements are periodic financial reports of a company. They reflect the company's overall performance over a period of time and the financial position at a point of time.

The term financial statement generally refers to two basic statements. They are: (i) the Income Statement, and (ii) the Balance Sheet. Now-a-days, business concerns also prepare two more statements. They are: (a) Statement of Retained Earnings or Surplus Statement and (b) Statement of Changes in Financial Position.

TYPES OF FINANCIAL STATEMENTS

A complete set of financial statements consists of:

    (i)   Income Statement or Profit and Loss Account,

    (ii)   Balance Sheet or Position Statement,

    (iii)   Statement of Changes in Owner's Accounts or Surplus Statement, and

    (iv)   Statement of Changes in Financial Position.

1. Income Statement (Profit and Loss Account)

Income statement is a statement of revenues earned and the expenses incurred for earning that revenue. Revenue or income is the golden egg, the centre of attraction of all those interested in the concern. Thus revenue or income statement is a performance report recording the changes in income, expenses, profits and losses as a result of business operations. When the revenues are more than expenditures, there will be a profit. On the other hand, if the expenditures are in excess of revenues, there will be a loss. The income statement is prepared for a particular period, generally a year for determining the operational position of the concern. Thus all incomes and expenditures falling due in that year should be taken into account irrespective of their receipt or payment.

The income statement is prepared in the form of Manufacturing Account to know the cost of production, in the form of Trading Account to find out gross profit or gross loss. It is prepared in the form of a Profit and Loss Account to determine net profit or net loss.

2. Balance Sheet (Position Statement)

The balance sheet is one of the important statements depicting the financial position of the concern. It lists the sources of funds as well as their uses. In fact, it is a classified summary of assets and the sources of financing the assets. *The American Institute of Certified Public Accountants*, defines Balance Sheet as "A tabular statement of summary of balances (debits and credits) carried forward after an actual and constructive closing of books of account and kept according to principles of accounting."

The balance sheet is the backbone of Double Entry System, the master account of General Ledger. It helps the owners and creditors to estimate the financial stability of the related enterprise.

The balance sheet is prepared on a particular date. It is a static statement as it shows the position of the business at a certain moment of time. Generally, there is no strict sequence for showing various assets and liabilities. But the companies registered under the Companies Act, 1956 have to show their assets and liabilities in the balance sheet in accordance with the form prescribed under this Act. These companies are also required to give figures for the previous year along with the current year's figures.

3. Statement of Changes in Owner's Equity (Retained Earnings)

The term owner's equity refers to the claim of the shareholders against the assets of the firm. It comprises: (a) paid-up share capital representing the initial amount of funds invested by the shareholders, and (b) retained earning representing undisturbed profits.

The statement of changes in owner's equity shows the beginning balance of each owner's equity account, the reasons for increases and decreases in each, and its ending balance. However, in most cases, the only owner's equity account that changes significantly is retained earnings and hence the statement of changes in owner's equity becomes merely a *statement of retained earnings*.

The statement of Retained Earnings or Profit and Loss Appropriation Account explains the utilisation of profits of a concern and states the extent of unutilised amount of profits retained as such. The amount of retained earnings as shown by this statement is transferred to the Balance Sheet.

4. Statement of Changes in Financial Position

The statement of changes in financial position shows the changes in assets and liabilities from the end of one period to the end of another point of time. This statement explains the movement of funds (working capital or cash) during a particular period.

The statement of changes in financial position may take place in the following two forms:

(a) **Funds Flow Statement:** The word 'fund' is used to denote working capital. A statement which is prepared to explain the movement of working capital is known as *"Funds Flow Statement"*. This statement shows the sources from which the funds are received and the uses (or applications) to which these have been put. Thus funds flow statement enables one to have a better understanding of the affairs of the business.

(b) **Cash Flow Statement:** A statement which is prepared to explain the movement of cash is termed "Cash Flow Statement". This statement focuses attention on cash changes only and describes the sources of cash and its uses.

Nature of Financial Statement

A financial statement is prepared on the basis of recorded facts. Thus it is the end-product of financial accounting. *The American Institute of Certified Public Accountants* states the nature of financial statement as "Financial Statements are prepared for the purpose of presenting a periodical review of report on progress by the management and deal with the status of investment in the business and the results achieved during the period under review." They reflect a combination of recorded facts, accounting principles and personal judgements.

In the words of John N. Myer "the financial statements are composed of data which are the result of a combination of: (1) recorded facts concerning the business transactions, (2) conventions adopted to facilitate the accounting technique, (3) postulates, or assumptions made to and (4) personal judgements used in the application of the conventions and postulates.

On the analysis of the above statements, it can be seen that the data exhibited in the financial statements are affected by recorded facts, accounting conventions and postulates, and personal judgements.

1. Recorded Facts

The term recorded facts refers to the data taken out from the accounting records. Business transactions are recorded in the books of accounts of a concern at the same date and at the same value at which they take place. But with the passage of time, these records become historical in nature. The financial statements are prepared on the basis of data taken out from these very accounts and books. Thus the basis of preparing financial statements is said to be recorded facts. Since the recorded facts are not based on replacement costs, the financial statements do not show the current financial condition of the concern.

2. Accounting Conventions

Accounting conventions imply certain accounting principles developed over time by custom or tradition. Certain accounting conventions such as disclosure, materiality, consistency and conservatism are followed while preparing financial statements. For example, the convention of valuing inventory at cost or market price whichever is less is followed at the time of preparing financial statements. The use of accounting conventions makes the financial statements comparable, simple and realistic.

3. Postulates

The postulates or concepts are assumptions upon which the accounting records are made. The accountant makes certain assumptions while making accounting records. One of these assumptions is that the enterprise is treated as a going concern. The other alternative to this postulate is that the concern is to be liquidated. Thus the "rupee value" shown in the Balance Sheet is *"going concern value"* whereas the realisable value at the time of liquidation may be more or less than the rupee value. Another important assumption is that the value of rupee is constant at all times though there is drastic change in the purchasing power of money. Thus the data disclosed by the financial statements are useful and meaningful only till the concern survives.

4. Personal Judgements

The personal judgement of the accountant plays an important role in preparing financial statements although certain standard accounting conventions are followed. It may sometimes be found that the financial statements prepared by two different persons in the same organisation provide different results mainly on account of the difference in their personal judgements in applying postulates and conventions. For example, in applying the cost or market value whichever is less to inventory valuation, the accountant will have to use his judgement in computing the cost in a particular case. He may follow one of the various methods such as last in first out, first in first out, average cost method, standard cost, base stock method, etc., for valuing materials. Thus it is found that the financial statements are greatly affected by the personal judgements of the accountants.

Objectives of Financial Statements

The primary objective of a financial statement is to provide information to decision-makers. *The Accounting Principles Board of America* (APB) mentions the following objectives of a financial statement:

1. It provides reliable financial information about economic resources and obligations of a business concern.

2. It provides other needed information about changes in such economic resources and obligations.

3. It provides reliable information about changes in net resources (resources less obligations) arising out of business activities.

4. It provides financial information that helps in estimating the earning potential of a business.

5. It discloses, to the extent possible, other information related to the financial statements that is relevant to the needs of the users of these statements.

Characteristics of Ideal Financial Statements

The financial statements reflect the financial position and operating strengths or weaknesses of the concern. Thus the financial statement should be prepared in such a way that it can give a clear and orderly picture of the concern.

A financial statement is said to be ideal when it possesses the following characteristics:

1. **Relevance:** The financial statements should be relevant to the objectives of the organisation. The information which is not relevant to the statements should be avoided by applying the skill and efficiency of the person preparing these statements.

2. **Exhibit True Financial Position:** The facts and figures incorporated in the financial statement should be such that a true and correct view of the state of affairs of the concern is taken. While preparing these statements care should be taken to ensure that no material information is withheld.

3. **Intelligible to Common Man:** The financial statements should be presented in a simple and lucid form so that they are easily understandable even to a person who is not well-versed with accounting terminology.

4. **Easiness:** The financial statements can be prepared easily as the facts which are to be incorporated in them are readily available from the books of accounts of the concern. Moreover, the size of the statement should not be very large and the columns to be used for giving information should be less. All these enable to save time in preparing the statements.

5. **Attractive:** The financial statements should be prepared in such a way that they should attract the eye of the reader.

6. **Facilitates Comparison:** The financial statements should facilitate all sorts of comparison. They should be prepared in a way that can be compared with the previous years statements and the figures of other concerns of the same nature. All these help for the proper assessment for the working of the concern.

7. **Brief:** The financial statement should be presented briefly so that the reader can form an idea about the various figures easily. In other words, the financial statements should not be stuffed with unnecessary details.

8. **Promptness:** The financial statements should be prepared and presented immediately at the close of the financial year.

9. **Analytical Representation:** Another feature of an ideal financial statement is that the data of similar nature are presented at the same place. This will help the analysts in establishing relationships between figures of similar nature with less effort.

Use and Importance of Financial Statements

Financial statements are largely useful to management, investors, creditors, bankers, workers, government and public in general. George O. May* states the following major uses of financial statements:

1. As a report of stewardship.
2. As a basis for fiscal policy.
3. To determine the legality of dividends.
4. As a guide to wise dividend action.
5. As a basis for granting credit.
6. As informative for prospective investors in an enterprise.
7. As a guide to the value of investment already made.
8. As an aid to government supervision.
9. As a basis for price or rate regulation.
10. As a basis for taxation.

The uses of financial statement to various parties are as follows:

1. **For Management:** The management usually requires correct and reliable information for proper execution of its function. The financial statements provide such information. On the basis of these informations the management can spot out the efficiency and inefficiency of various departments. Thus the financial statements are highly useful to the management for exercising cost control.

2. **For Creditors:** The creditors are usually interested in the current solvency of an organisation as their claims are to be paid within a short span out of current assets. The calculation of current ratio and liquid ratio with the help of data obtained from financial statements will enable the creditors to assess the current financial position of the organisation in relation to their debts.

3. **For Bankers:** The bankers are usually in need of the detailed information regarding their customers' financial position as they are interested to see that loan amount is secure and the customer can pay the interest regularly. It is through the financial statements that a banker can get all the information useful in taking decisions regarding

---

*May, George O., *Financial Accounting—Distillation of Experience*, p. 3.

the extension of loans to their customers and the amount of securities it will ask from the customers as a cover for the loans.

4. **For Investors:** The financial statements are useful for both short-term and long-term investors. They are much concerned with the security of their investment and the capability of the concern in making regular interest payments. Thus the investors will have to analyse both the present financial position and the future prospects and expansion plans of the concern. The investors should get all the required information for making the various analyses from the financial statements.

5. **For Government:** The financial statements are highly useful to the government in the following respects:

   (a) To assess the tax liability of the concern.

   (b) To study the economic situations of the country.

   (c) To ascertain whether the business is following various rules and regulations or not.

   (d) To frame and amend various laws for the regulation of the business.

6. **For Trade Association:** Trade Associations may analyse the financial statements with a view to providing various information to their members. They may develop standard ratios and design uniform system of accounts.

7. **For Stock Exchange:** The stock exchanges deal with the purchase and sale of securities of various concerns. Thus the financial statements are highly useful to stock brokers in judging the financial position of various concerns. Moreover, the determination of prices of stocks and shares, to a great extent, is based on financial statements.

Limitations of Financial Statements

Although financial statements convey relevant and useful information to the interested parties, they do not present a final picture of the concern. Thus the financial statements are subject to the following limitations:

1. Only Interim Report

The financial statements do not present a final picture of the concern. The actual position of the concern can be known only when the business is closed down as the data given in the statements are approximate. However, the financial statements are required to be prepared for different accounting periods. But they serve as interim reports only.

2. Do not Disclose Correct Financial Position

The financial statements do not disclose the exact financial position of the concern. Usually, the financial position of a concern depends on several factors like economic, social and financial. But the data incorporated in the financial statements reflect only financial factors.

3. On the Basis of Historical Cost

The financial statements are prepared on the basis of historical cost or original cost. In other words, the statements are not prepared keeping in view the current price changes although the value of assets decreases with the passage of time. Thus the values of assets shown in the balance sheet are neither the values at which they can be sold nor the values at which they can be replaced. That is why the exact financial position of the concern cannot be assessed from the balance sheet.

Similarly, the profit disclosed by the profit and loss account may not represent the earning capacity of the concern. The increase in profits need not be due to an increase in efficiency and may be due to an increase in prices or due to some abnormal causes.

4. Failure to State the Impact of Non-monetary Factors

The success of a business largely depends on certain non-monetary factors such as the energy, ability and efficiency of the men who are concerned with the operation of the business. But these factors are not stated in the financial statements as they could not be measured in the monetary terms.

5. Lack of Precision

The information given by the financial statements are not precise. The data used for preparing financial statements are developed by conventional procedures followed over the years. Moreover, they are largely affected by the personal judgements of the parties concerned.

FINANCIAL ANALYSIS

The importance of financial statements lies not in their preparation but in their analysis. 'Analysis' is the mathematical classification of the data. Thus "Financial Analysis" refers to the process of evaluating the financial position and the results of operation of a business. It is the last step of accounting and results in the presentation of information useful to the business managers, investors and creditors.

The various steps involved in financial analysis are:

1. to select the information from the total information in the financial statements which is relevant for a decision.

2. to highlight important relationships by arranging the information contained in the financial statements, and

3. to interpret important relationships and give explanations of the importance.

The term financial statement analysis consists of both analysis and interpretation. However, distinction can be drawn between the two terms 'analysis' and 'interpretation'. While analysis is the methodological classification of the data, interpretation involves explaining the meaning and significance of the data so classified. In fact both analysis and interpretation are complementary to each other. Analysis is useless without interpretation and interpretation without analysis is difficult or even impossible. However, most of the authors have used the term analysis only to cover the meanings of both analysis and interpretation.

Types of Financial Analysis

The various types of financial analysis can be brought into different categories depending upon

(i) the material used and (ii) the method of operation followed in the analysis or modus operandi of analysis. According to material used, the financial analysis may be either external analysis or internal analysis. But on the basis of the modus operandi, it can be classified into horizontal analysis and vertical analysis.

External Analysis

This analysis is done on the basis of information available from published records. Thus an analysis which is done by outsiders who do not have access to the detailed records of the company is known as external analysis. Outsiders include investors, credit agencies, government agencies and other creditors. External analysis serves only a very limited purpose.

Internal Analysis

This analysis is done on the basis of information obtained from internal records. Thus an analysis which is conducted by persons who have access to the detailed records of the concern is known as internal analysis. Such an analysis is usually performed by executives and employees of the organisation and government officials. Analysis for managerial purpose is one of the examples of internal analysis.

Horizontal Analysis

Horizontal analysis is also known as dynamic analysis or trend analysis. Analysis which is done by analysing the financial data of a company for several years is called horizontal analysis. Under this analysis, the analysts compare the figures of the various years with that of the standard or base year to know the periodical trend of various items shown in the statements with the passage of time. Horizontal analysis helps the management to focus attention on items that have significantly changed during the period under review.

Vertical Analysis

Vertical Analysis is also known as static analysis or structural analysis. Analysis which is done by analysing a single set of financial statement is known as vertical analysis. Under this analysis, the figures from financial statement of a year are compared with a base selected from the same year's statement.

Vertical analysis is not very conducive to a proper analysis of financial statements as it considers data for one period only. However, it may be used along with horizontal analysis to make it more meaningful.

Tools and Techniques of Financial Analysis

A host of methods or techniques is used to study the relationship between different statements. However, the following methods of analysis are generally used:

1. Comparative Financial Statements
2. Common-size Statement
3. Trend Analysis

4. Ratio Analysis
5. Funds Flow Analysis
6. Cash Flow Analysis

Comparative Financial Statements

Comparative Financial Statements are statements of financial position at different periods of time. Usually, two financial statements (Balance Sheet and Income Statement) are prepared in a comparative form placing figures for two or more periods side by side. These statements facilitate comparison of absolute figures (rupee amounts) pertaining to two or more periods in order to find out their increase or decrease over the period/periods under consideration.

The financial data are said to be comparative only if the same accounting principles are used in preparing these statements. If there is any variation in the use of accounting principles that should be stated at the foot of financial statements. The analyst must be conscious in using these statements.

The two comparative statements used in the process of analysis are:

(i) Balance Sheet and
(ii) Income Statement

Comparative Balance Sheet

This analysis is the study of the trend of the same items in two or more balance sheets of the same concern on different dates. The changes can be determined by comparing the balance sheet at the beginning and at the end of a period. With the help of these changes, the analyst can form an opinion about the progress of the concern.

The comparative balance sheet should have altogether four columns. The first two columns are for the data of the original balance sheets and fourth and fifth columns are used to show increases/decreases in figures and percentage of increases/decreases respectively.

Guidelines for Analysing Comparative Balance Sheet

While analysing the Comparative Balance Sheet, the analyst should observe:

(i) the current financial position and liquidity position
(ii) the long-term financial position and
(iii) the profitability of the concern.

The current financial position of a concern can be known by studying the working capital of both the years. Working capital is the excess of current assets over current liabilities. The current financial position is said to be good or improved when the working capital shows an increase. But an increase in current assets accompanied by the increase in current liabilities of the same amount should not show any change in the current financial position.

The long-term financial position of a concern can be known by analysing the changes in fixed assets, long-term liabilities and capital. A change in fixed assets should be compared to the change in long-term loans and capital. When the change in fixed assets is greater than the change in long-term securities, it is said that the part of fixed assets has been financed from the working capital. On the contrary, when the change in long-term securities is higher than the change in fixed assets, it is said that fixed assets have not only been financed from long-term sources but part of working capital has also been financed from long-term sources. However, a firm's policy is said to be wise when fixed assets are financed by raising long-term funds.

The profitability of a concern can be known by analysing the changes in retained earnings, various resources and surpluses etc. The profitability of a concern is said to be increased when there is an increase in the balance of Profit and Loss Account and other resources created from profits. On the other hand, decrease in such accounts may mean payment of dividend, issue of bonus shares or deterioration in profitability of the concern.

ILLUSTRATION 14.1

Prepare a Comparative Balance Sheet and study the financial position from the following Balance Sheets of a concern for the years 1996 and 1997.

Balance Sheet
as on 31st December

Liabilities	1996 Rs.	1997 Rs.	Assets	1996 Rs.	1997 Rs.
Equity Share Capital	8,00,000	10,00,000	Land & Building	5,70,000	4,70,000
Reserve & Surplus	4,00,000	3,00,000	Furniture & Fixtures	15,000	20,000
Debentures	3,00,000	4,00,000	Plant & Machinery	4,75,000	6,83,000
Long-term Loans on			Other Fixed Assets	1,25,000	1,30,000
Mortgage	1,50,000	2,00,000	Cash in Hand	15,000	70,000
Sundry Creditors	80,000	1,00,000	Bills Receivable	1,55,000	1,00,000
Bills Payable	70,000	65,000	Sundry Debtors	2,50,000	3,00,000
Other Current Liabilities	5,000	10,000	Stock	2,00,000	3,00,000
			Prepaid Expenses	2,000	
	18,05,000	20,75,000		18,05,000	20,75,000

Solution

Comparative Balance Sheet of a Company
For the year ending December 31, 1996 and 1997

Assets	Year ending 31 December 1996 Rs.	1997 Rs.	Increase/ Decrease Amounts Rs.	Increase/ Decrease (%)
Current Assets:				
Cash in Hand	15,000	70,000	+55,000	+366.6
Bills Receivable	1,55,000	1,00,000	–55,000	–35.4

Continued

| | Year ending 31 December | | Increase/ Decrease Amounts | Increase/ Decrease (%) |
| | 1996 | 1997 | 1997 | |
Assets	Rs.	Rs.	Rs.	
Sundry Debtors	2,50,000	3,00,000	+50,000	+20.00
Stock	2,00,000	3,00,000	+1,00,000	+50.00
Prepaid Expenses	—	2,000	+2,000	
Total Current Assets	6,20,000	7,72,000	+1,52,000	+24.52
Fixed Assets:				
Land & Buildings	5,70,000	4,70,000	–1,00,000	–14.03
Furniture & Fixtures	15,000	20,000	+5,000	+33.33
Plant & Machinery	4,75,000	6,83,000	+2,08,000	+43.78
Other Fixed Assets	1,25,000	1,30,000	+5,000	+4.00
Total Fixed Assets	11,85,000	13,03,000	+1,18,000	+9.95
Total Assets	**18,05,000**	**20,75,000**	**+2,70,000**	**+14.95**
Liabilities & Capital:				
Current Liabilities	Rs.	Rs.	Rs.	
Sundry Creditors	80,000	1,00,000	+20,000	+25
Bills Payable	70,000	65,000	–5,000	–7.1
Other Current Liabilities	5,000	10,000	+5,000	+100
Total Current Liabilities	1,55,000	1,75,000	+20,000	+12.9
Debentures	3,00,000	4,00,000	+1,00,000	+33.33
Long-term Loans on Mortgage	1,50,000	2,00,000	+50,000	+33.33
Total Liabilities	6,05,000	7,75,000	+1,70,000	+28.09
Equity Share Capital	8,00,000	10,00,000	+2,00,000	+25
Reserve & Surplus	4,00,000	3,00,000	–1,00,000	–25
Total	18,05,000	20,75,000	+2,70,000	+14.9

Interpretation:

1. The comparative balance sheet of the company shows that during 1997, there has been an increase in fixed assets of Rs. 1,18,000 i.e., 9.95% while long-term liabilities to outsiders have relatively increased by Rs. 1,50,000 and equity share capital has increased by Rs. 2,00,000. This reveals that the policy of the company is to buy fixed assets from the long-term sources of finance. Thus it should not affect the working capital.

2. The current assets have increased by Rs. 1,52,000 i.e., 24.52% and cash has increased by Rs. 55,000. On the contrary, there has been an increase in inventories amounting to Rs. 1,00,000. The current liabilities have increased only by Rs. 20,000 i.e., 12.9%. This further reveals that the company has raised long-term finances even for the current assets resulting in an improvement in the liquidity position of the company.

3. Reserves and surpluses have decreased from Rs. 4,00,000 to Rs. 3,00,000 i.e., 25% which reveals that the company has utilised reserves and surpluses for the payment of dividends to shareholders either in cash or by the issue of bonus shares.

4. The overall financial position of the company is satisfactory.

Comparative Income Statement

The results of the operation of a concern can be known from the income statement. Thus an idea of the progress of a concern over a period of time should be obtained from the comparative income statement. Moreover, the profitability of a concern can be analysed with the help of changes in absolute data in money values and its percentages.

The income statement also has four columns. When the first two columns give figures of various items for two years, the third and fourth columns are used to show changes in figures in absolute amounts and percentages respectively.

Guidelines for Analysing Income Statements

The analysis of income statement involves the following steps:

1. First of all, the amount of gross profit should be analysed. For this purpose, the change in sales should be compared with the change in cost of goods sold. When the change in sales is higher than the change in cost of goods sold, the profitability of the concern will be high.

2. Next, the operational profits of the concern should be analysed. Operating profit is gross profit minus operating expenses such as office and administrative expenses, selling and distribution expenses. An increase in operating profit is a sign of increase in sales and efficiency in controlling operating expenses. On the other hand, a decrease in operating profits will result from inefficiency in controlling operating expenses or decrease in sales.

3. The last step of analysis should be the study of net profit. Net profit is operating profit minus non-operating expenses such as interest paid, losses from sale of assets, writing of deferred expenses, payment of taxes, etc. An increase in the net profit is a sign of the overall profitability or progress of the concern.

ILLUSTRATION 14.2

The income statements of XY Ltd., are given for the year ending on 31st Dec. 1996 and 1997. Rearrange the figures in a comparative form and study the profitability position of the company.

	1996 Rs. (000)	1997 Rs. (000)
Net Sales	800 ·	950
Cost of Goods Sold	500	600
Operating Expenses:		
General & Administrative Expenses	80	82
Selling Expenses	90	100
Non-operating Expenses:		
Interest Paid	30	35
Income Tax	50	60

Solution

Comparative Statement for the year ended
31st December, 1996 and 1997

Assets	31 December 1996 Rs. (000)	1997 Rs. (000)	Increase (+) Decrease (–) Rs. (000)	Increase (+) Decrease (–) (%)
Net Sales	800	950	+150	+18.75
Less: Cost of Goods Sold	500	600	+100	+20.00
Gross Profit	300	350	+50	+16.66
Operating Expenses:				
General Administrative Expenses	80	82	+2	+2.5
Selling Expenses	90	100	+10	+11.1
Total Operating Expenses	170	182	+12	+7.05
Operating Profit	130	168	+38	+29.2
Less: Other Deductions:				
Interest Paid	30	35	+5	+16.6
Net Profit before Tax	100	133	+33	+33.0
Less: Income Tax	50	60	+10	+20.0
Net Profit after Tax	50	73	+23	+46.0

Interpretation:

The above comparative income statement shows that there has been an increase in net sales of 18.75% while the increase of cost of goods sold is 20%. Thus the resulting increase of gross profit is 16.66%. Even though the operating expenses have increased by 7.05% the increase in gross profit is enough to compensate for the increase in operating expenses. Thus there has been an overall increase in operational profits amounting to Rs. 38,000, i.e., 29.2% despite an increase in financial expenses of Rs. 5,000 for interest and Rs. 10,000 for income-tax. There is an increase in net profits after tax amounting to Rs. 23,000, i.e., 46%. Thus it is concluded that the company's progress and overall profitability is attractive.

COMMON-SIZE STATEMENTS

The common-size statements (balance sheet and income statement) are generally shown in analytical percentages. Common-size statements are those in which figures are stated after converting them into percentage to some common base. These statements are often called component percentages or 100 per cent statements because each statement is reduced to the total of 100 and each individual item is stated as a percentage of the total of 100. Thus the common-size statements can be prepared in the following manner:

1. The total of assets or liabilities are taken as 100.
2. The individual assets are expressed as a percentage of total assets, i.e., 100 and different liabilities are calculated in relation to total liabilities. For instance, if total assets are Rs. 10 lakhs and the value of sundry debtors is Rs. 2 lakhs, then it will be 20 per cent of total assets, i.e.,

$$= \frac{2,00,000 \times 100}{10,00,000}$$

The common-size statements may be: (i) common-size balance sheet and (ii) common-size income statement.

Common-size Balance Sheet

Common-size Balance Sheet is one in which the total of assets or liabilities will be taken as 100 and all the figures in it will be stated as a percentage of this total. For instance, the following assets are shown in a common-size balance sheet:

	Rs.	*Percentage*
Cash in Hand	10,000	2.50
B/R	90,000	22.50
Land and Building	50,000	12.50
Furniture and Fixtures	50,000	12.50
Plant and Machinery	2,00,000	50.00
Total Assets	4,00,000	100.00

The total figure of assets Rs. 4,00,000 is taken as 100 and all other assets are expressed as percentage of total assets. The relation of each asset to total asset is expressed in the statement.

In the same manner, the relation of each liability to total liabilities can also be expressed.

ILLUSTRATION 14.3

Compare the financial position of AB Co. and XY Co. with the help of common-size Balance Sheet from the information given below:

Balance Sheets
as on December 31, 1997

Liabilities	*AB Co.*	*XY Co.*
Preference Share Capital	1,40,000	1,80,000
Equity Share Capital	1,70,000	4,20,000
Reserve and Surpluses	15,000	20,000
Long-term Loans	1,20,000	1,40,000
Sundry Creditors	15,000	5,000
Bills Payable	2,000	–
Outstanding Expenses	11,000	7,000
Proposed Dividend	12,000	92,000
	4,85,000	8,64,000

Liabilities	AB Co.	XY Co.
Assets		
Land and Building	90,000	1,43,000
Plant and Machinery	3,54,000	6,20,000
Temporary Investments	3,000	45,000
Inventories	15,000	31,000
Book-debts	10,000	9,000
Cash and Bank Balance	12,000	13,000
Prepaid Expenses	1,000	3,000
	4,85,000	8,64,000

Solution

Common-size Balance Sheet
As on December 31st 1997

	AB Co.		XY Co.	
	Amount (Rs.)	%	Amount (Rs.)	%
Assets				
Fixed Assets:				
Land & Building	90,000	18.56	1,43,000	16.55
Plant and Machinery	3,54,000	72.99	6,20,000	71.76
Total Fixed Assets	4,44,000	91.55	7,63,000	88.31
Current Assets:				
Temporary Investments	3,000	0.62	45,000	5.21
Inventories	15,000	3.09	31,000	3.59
Book-debts	10,000	2.06	9,000	1.04
Cash and Bank Balance	12,000	2.47	13,000	1.50
Prepaid Expenses	1,000	0.21	3,000	0.35
Total Current Assets	41,000	8.45	1,01,000	11.69
Share Capital and Reserves				
Preference Share Capital	1,40,000	28.87	1,80,000	20.83
Equity Share Capital	1,70,000	35.05	4,20,000	48.61
Reserves and Surpluses	15,000	3.09	20,000	2.31
Total Capital and Reserves	3,25,000	67.01	6,20,000	71.75
Long-term Loans	1,20,000	24.74	1,40,000	16.21
Current Liabilities				
Sundry Creditors	15,000	3.09	5,000	0.58
Bills payable	2,000	0.41	–	–
Outstanding Expenses	11,000	2.27	7,000	0.81
Proposed Dividend	12,000	2.48	92,000	10.65
	40,000	8.25	1,04,000	12.04
Total Liability Side	4,85,000	100.00	8,64,000	100.00

Comments:

1. The pattern of financing of both the companies reveals that XY Co. is more traditionally financed as compared to AB Co. As shown by the balance sheet, the XY Co. has depended more on its own funds. Out of total investments of this company, the outsiders funds are only 28.25% and the remaining 71.75% accounts for proprietors funds. But AB Co. has depended more on outsiders funds as the outsiders funds account for 32.99% and proprietors funds are only the remaining 67.01%. Thus it is concluded that although XY Co. is more financed on traditional lines, both the companies have good financial planning.

2. The working capital position of AB Co., is not inadequate as current assets are more than current liabilities by 0.2%. But XY Co. is suffering from an inadequacy of working capital as the percentage of current assets in this company is less than the percentage of current liabilities by 0.35%.

3. The analysis also shows that in both the companies investments in fixed assets have been financed from working capital. In AB Co. fixed assets account for 91.55% of total assets while long-term funds account for 91.75% of total funds. In XY Co. fixed assets account for 88.31% whereas long-term funds account for 87.96% of total funds.

4. XY Co. is required to raise working capital either by issuing more capital or by raising long-term loans.

Common-size Income Statement

The various items in P/L A/c or income statement are to be shown as percentage of sales with a view to establishing the relation of each item to sales. The change in volume of sales should also change the selling expenses and not administrative or financial expenses. But if there is significant or considerable increase the volume of sales, the administrative and financial expenses may also increase. Thus a relationship is established between sales and other items in income statement. This relationship is highly useful for the appraisal of operational activities of the concern.

ILLUSTRATION 14.4

Prepare a common-size income statement from the following statements of a company for the years ending December 1996 and 1997:

	1996 (Rs. In '000)	1997 (Rs. In '000)
Sales	600	700
Miscellaneous Income	25	20
	625	720
Expenses:		
Cost of Sales	350	535
Office Expenses	30	35
Selling Expenses	35	50
Interest	30	35
	445	655
Net Profit	180	65
	625	720

Solution

Common-size Income Statement
For the years ending December 1996 and 1997

	1996		1997	
	('000) (Rs.)	%	('000) (Rs.)	%
Sales	600	100	700	100
Less: Cost of Sales	350	58.33	535	76.42
Gross Profit	250	41.67	165	23.58
Operating Expenses:				
Office Expenses	30	5.00	35	5.00
Selling Expenses	35	5.83	50	7.14
Total Operating Expenses	55	10.83	85	12.14
Operating Profit	195	32.50	80	11.42
Miscellaneous Income	25	4.16	20	2.85
Total Income	220	36.66	100	14.27
Less : Non-operating expenses				
Interest	30	5.00	35	5.00
Net Profit	190	31.66	65	9.27

Interpretation:

1. In 1997 (as compared to 1996) the sales and gross profit have gone up in absolute figures but the percentage of gross profit to sales has decreased in 1997.

2. The hike in cost of sales as a percentage of sales has brought down the profitability from 41.67% to 23.58%.

3. The operating expenses have increased in 1997 but the non-operating expenses have remained the same in both the years. An increase in operating expenses in the latter year will reduce the profits.

4. Net profits have decreased both in absolute figures and as a percentage in 1997 as compared to 1996.

5. On account of the increase in cost of sales, the overall profitability has come down in 1997. Thus the company should take immediate steps to control its cost of sales.

TREND ANALYSIS

The financial statement may be analysed by calculating the trends of a series of information. Trend analysis involves the computation of percentage relationship that each statement item bears to the same item in the base year. The base year may be the earliest year involved in comparison or the latest year or any intervening year. The trend percentages disclose changes in the financial and operating data between specific periods. Thus the analyst can form an opinion as to whether favourable or adverse tendencies are reflected by the data.

For instance, in case sales figures for the years 1992 to 1997 are to be studied, the sales of 1992 will be taken as 100 and the percentage of sales for all other years shall be computed in relation to the base year, i.e., 1992. Suppose the following trends are found out:

1992	–	100
1993	–	115
1994	–	105
1995	–	125
1996	–	140
1997	–	150

In the above trends of sales, it is clear that since 1995 sales are more in all the years. The sales are shown an upward trend except in 1994. However, a detailed study of trends shows that the rate of increase in sales is less in the years 1996 and 1997. The increase in sales is 20 per cent in 1995 as compared to 1994 and increase is 15 per cent in 1996 as compared to 1995 and 10 per cent in 1997 as compared to 1996.

Although sales are more compared to the base year, the rate of increase has not been constant and requires a study by comparing these trends to other items like cost of productions, etc.

Procedure for Calculating Trends

1. One year is to be taken as a base year. Usually, the first or last year is taken as base year.
2. The figure of base year is to be taken as 100.
3. The trend percentage is to be computed in relation to base year by dividing each year's figure with the base year's figure.

In case a figure in the other year is more than the figure in the base year, the trend percentage will be more than 100. On the other hand, the trend percentage will be less than 100 if a figure in the other year is less than that of the base year.

The trend analysis of financial data should be done cautiously as the mere increase or decrease in trend percentages may give misleading results, if studied in isolation. Thus it is essential that the trend ratio of one item should be compared with that of another item which has a logical relationship with each other. For instance, an increase in sales may not result in an increase of profits in case such an increase is coupled with an increase in the cost of production. Again the figures will not be comparable unless the accounting procedures and conventions used for collecting data and preparation of financial statements are similar.

ILLUSTRATION 14.5

From the following figures of ABC Ltd., calculate the trend percentages and interpret them. The year 1993 is taken as the base.

(Rs. In lakhs)

Year	Sales	Stock	Profit before tax
1993	2,000	800	350
1994	2,500	900	480
1995	3,000	950	500
1996	3,300	1,000	570
1997	4,000	1,200	680

Solution

Trend Percentages
(Base Year 1993 = 100)

Year	Sales		Stock		Profit before tax	
	Amount (Rs. Lakhs)	Trend Percentage	Amount (Rs. Lakhs)	Trend Percentage	Amount (Rs. Lakhs)	Trend Percentage
1993	2,000	100	800	100.0	350	100.0
1994	2,500	125	900	112.5	480	137.1
1995	3,000	150	950	118.7	500	142.8
1996	3,300	165	1,000	125.0	570	162.8
1997	4,000	200	1,200	150.0	680	194.2

Interpretation:

1. The sales figures have shown a continuous increase. Its percentage in 1997 is 200 as compared to 100 in 1993. Thus the increase in sales is quite attractive.

2. The stock figures have also shown an increase from 1993 to 1997. The increase in stock is more in 1997 as compared to earlier years.

3. Profit before tax has also shown a substantial increase. In five years time it has nearly doubled. The comparative increase in profits is much higher in 1996 and 1997 as compared to 1995.

The increase of profit more than sales, shows that there is a proper control over cost of goods sold. The overall performance of the company is quite satisfactory.

CASE STUDY

Comparative Financial Statement Analysis of United Electrical Industries Limited (UEI) and Transformers and Electricals Kerala Limited (TELK)

United Electrical Industries Limited (UEI) was incorporated in 1950 with an authorized capital of Rs. 400.00 lakh. It is the first factory set up in India for producing electricity meters. At present, the main products of the company consist of electricity meters, motor starters, plastic film capacitors and street light contractors.

Transformers and Electricals Kerala Limited (TELK), a government undertaking, started the production of transformers in the year 1963. The authorized and paid-up capital of the company as on 31st March 2004 is Rs. 1500.00 lakh and Rs. 1357.54 lakh respectively. At present, the products of the TELK comprise transformers, gas circuit breakers and oil integrated paper condenser bushings.

Table 14.1 shows the common size balance sheet of UEI and TELK as on 31st March 2004.

Table 14.1 Balance Sheet of UEI and TELK As on 31st March 2004

Assets	UEI Amount (Rs. in lakh)	%	TELK Amount (Rs. in lakh)	%
Fixed Assets	55.35	3.98	236.34	1.87
Current Assets:				
Cash & Bank Balance	167.37	11.99	1049.41	8.34
Bills Receivables	—	—	12.43	0.09
Sundry Debtors	517.47	37.09	3543.52	28.15
Stock	264.38	18.96	1504.74	11.95
Other Currents Assets	123.01	8.82	483.17	3.84
Total Current Assets	1072.23	76.86	6593.27	52.37
Miscellaneous Expenditure not Written off/adjusted	267.32	19.16	5758.19	45.76
Total Assets	1394.90	100.00	12587.80	100
Share Capital and Reserves:				
Paid-up Capital	399.03	28.61	1357.54	10.78
Reserve & Surplus	166.66	11.94	2939.42	23.35
Total Capital & Reserves	565.69	40.55	4296.96	34.13
Long-term Loans	331.28	23.75	2398.69	19.05
Current Liabilities	497.93	35.70	5892.15	46.82
Total of Liability Side	1394.90	100.00	12587.80	100.00

Source: Review of Public Enterprises in Kerala.

In the light of the above statement it is clear that UEI is more traditionally financed as compared to TELK. Share capital and reserves consists of 40.55% of total investments while the percentage is 34.13 in TELK. The UEI has relied more on shareholders funds. But the financial planning of both these companies cannot be considered as safe since the shareholders investments are less than 50% of total investments, TELK has 34.13% investments from shareholders and has relied on outsiders for other funds. So financial structure of UEI is more safe as compared to TELK.

Both the companies have followed the policy of financing fixed assets from long-term funds. In UEI, investments in fixed assets are 3.98% while long-term funds are 64.30%, whereas in TELK, these figures are 1.87% and 53.18%. This shows that both the companies have financed working capital from long-term funds also.

The working capital position of both the companies is good. UEI has 76.86% of current assets while current liabilities are 35.70% of total investments. In TELK, current assets are 52.37% while current liabilities are 46.82%. Looking at the difference of percentage of current assets and current liabilities, the position of UEI looks better. The current ratio of UEI is 2.15:1, whereas in TELK this is 1.12:1.

The analysis of various figures shows that both the companies have satisfactory long-term and short-term financial position. In comparison, UEI has better financial position than that of TELK.

— REVIEW QUESTIONS —

1. What is meant by financial statement? Discuss briefly the various types of financial statements.

2. Explain the nature of financial statements.

3. Discuss the features of ideal financial statements.

4. Explain briefly the significance and limitations of financial statements.

5. What is financial analysis? Discuss the various types of financial analysis.

6. Write notes on:
   (a) Trend Analysis
   (b) Common-size Income Statements
   (c) Comparative Balance Sheet
   (d) Horizontal and Vertical Analysis

7. Prepare a Comparative Balance Sheet of XY Ltd. and study the financial position from its following Balance Sheet for the years ending 31st December 1996 and 1997.

Liabilities	1996 Rs.	1997 Rs.	Assets	1996 Rs.	1997 Rs.
Equity Shared Capital	3,00,000	4,30,000	Fixed Assets		
Preference Share Capital	1,00,000	1,50,000	Less Depreciation	3,40,000	4,50,000
Reserves	20,000	30,000	Stock	40,000	50,000
Profit and Loss A/c	15,000	20,000	Debtors	1,00,000	1,25,000
Bank Overdraft	50,000	50,000	Bills Receivables	20,000	60,000
Creditors	40,000	50,000	Prepaid Expenses	10,000	12,000
Provision for taxation	20,000	25,000	Cash in hand	40,000	53,000
Proposed Dividend	15,000	25,000	Cash at bank	10,000	30,000
	5,60,000	7,80,000		5,60,000	7,80,000

(**Ans.:** Current financial position of the company is satisfactory. It should issue more long-term funds)

8. The comparative income statements of Gopal Industries Limited are given for the years 1995 and 1996. Analyse and interpret the significance of changes in these statements.

	31st December 1995 Rs.	31st December 1996 Rs.
Sales	10,00,000	8,00,000
Less: Discounts, Returns, etc.	15,000	10,000
Net Sales	9,85,000	7,90,000
Less: Cost of Goods Sold	6,20,000	4,50,000
Gross Profit	3,65,000	3,40,000
Less: Administrative and General Expenses	60,000	40,000
Less: Selling Expenses	1,80,000	1,60,000

Continued

	31st December 1995 Rs.	31st December 1996 Rs.
Net Operating Profit	1,25,000	1,00,000
Less: Interest on Loans	15,000	20,000
Net Profit Before Taxes	1,10,000	80,000
Corporation Tax	40,000	20,000
Net Profit for the year	70,000	60,000

(**Ans.:** There is a fair rate of increase in profitability)

9. Convert the following Balance Sheet into common-size balance sheet and interpret the results.

Balance Sheets
As on 31st December 1996 and 1997

Liabilities	1996 Rs.	1997 Rs.	Assets	1996 Rs.	1997 Rs.
			Current Assets:		
Equity Share Capital	1,200	1,500	Debtors	550	490
Capital Reserves	90	185	Cash	200	15
General Reserves	500	450	Stock	320	250
Sinking Fund	90	100	Investments	300	250
Debentures	450	650	Fixed Assets:		
Sundry Creditors	300	250	Building Less		
Others	15	20	Depreciation	1,000	1,700
			Land	198	345
			Furniture and Fixture	77	105
	2,645	3,155		2,645	3,155

(**Ans.:** The overall financial position of the company is good except current assets).

10. You should study Income Statement of AB Ltd with the help of Common-size Statement from the following figures relating to the activities of AB Ltd. for the year ending 31st December 1996.

	Rs.
Sales	8,00,000
Purchase	4,00,000
Opening Stock	80,000
Closing Stock	90,000
Administrative Expenses:	
Salaries	40,000
Rent	15,000
Postage and Stationery	6,000
Provision for Taxation	60,000

Continued

Selling and Distribution Expenses:

Salaries	20,000
Advertising	7,000
Commission on Sales	8,000
Discount	2,500
Non-operating Expenses:	
Interest	5,000
Loss on sale of Assets	10,000
Non-operating Income:	
Profit on sale of Investments	12,000

(**Ans.:** The profitability of the company is satisfactory)

11. From the following information, interpret the result of operations of Rama Krishna Engineering Company Ltd., using trend ratios:

(Rs. Lakhs)

	1994	1995	1996	1997
Sales (Net)	120	110	140	170
Less: Cost of Goods Sold	70	70	80	90
Gross Profit	50	40	60	80
Less: Operating Expenses	15	15	20	25
Net Operating Profit	35	25	40	55
Less Taxes	20	15	20	30
Profit After Tax	15	10	20	25

(**Ans.:** The overall growth is satisfactory. The profitability has sufficiently increased. The operating expenses should be kept under control.)

15

Ratio Analysis

The term "Accounting Ratios" is used to describe significant relationships which exist between figures on a Balance Sheet, in a Profit and Loss Account, in a Budget Control System or in any other part of the accounting organisation.

— J. BATTY, *Management Accountancy* (Orient Longmans, 1966), p. 374

CONTENTS

- Introduction
- Types of ratios
- Summary of ratios
- Case study
- Review questions

INTRODUCTION

Ratio analysis is the most popular technique of financial analysis. It is "the technique of analysing and interpreting financial statements with the help of accounting ratios." A ratio is a mathematical relationship between two items expressed in quantitative forms. It may be defined as the indicated quotient of two mathematical expressions. But a financial ratio is the relationship between two accounting figures expressed mathematically.

A ratio may be expressed in three methods. They are: (i) simple or pure ratio (ii) percentage and (iii) rate

Simple or pure ratios are expressed by the simple division of one number by another. Current ratio is the most commonly used pure ratio.

$$\text{Current Ratio} = \frac{\text{Current Assets}}{\text{Current Liabilities}}$$

$$\text{Say, Current Ratio} = \frac{\text{Rs. 6,00,000}}{\text{Rs. 3,00,000}}$$

The current ratio expressed as pure ratio in the above case is 2:1, i.e., current assets are twice as those of current liabilities.

When the relation between two items is expressed in hundreds, it is known as *Percentages*. Gross profit and net profit are commonly expressed in percentages.

$$\text{Net Profits Ratio} = \frac{\text{Net profit}}{\text{Net Sales}} \times 100 \ \text{say} \ \frac{\text{Rs. 40,000}}{\text{Rs. 2,00,000}} \times 100$$

The net profit ratio expressed as percentage in the above case is 20 per cent, i.e., out of every Rs. 100 sales, the net profit is Rs. 20.

When the relation between two items is expressed in number of times, it is known as *rate*. Turnover ratios such as debtors turnover, creditors turnover and stock turnover are commonly expressed in number of times.

$$\text{Stock Turnover Ratio} = \frac{\text{Cost of Sales}}{\text{Average Stock}} \ \text{say} \ \frac{\text{Rs. 2,00,000}}{\text{Rs. 40,000}}$$

The stock turnover ratio expressed as rate, in the above case is '5' times a year.

Significance of Ratio Analysis

The inter-relationship that exists among the different items appeared in the Financial Statement, are revealed by accounting ratios. Hence, ratio analysis is highly useful to the internal management, prospective investors, creditors and outsiders. It is used as a device to analyse and interpret the financial health of a concern. The significance of ratio analysis as a technique of financial management arises because of the following facts:

1. **Simplifying Financial Information:** Ratio analysis helps to simplify and summarise various complex data contained in the financial statements. Ratios such as return on investment and debt equity ratio are very useful to lenders and financial institutions for determining the financial health of a concern.

2. **Converting Absolute Figures:** Ratio analysis helps to convert absolute figures of financial statements into relative ones. Absolute figures standing alone often convey no meaning. They become significant only when considered along with other figures. For instance, a firm earns a profit of Rs. 2 lakhs. This information is meaningless unless either the figure of capital employed to earn it or of sales affected is available.

3. **Helps in Control:** Ratio analysis also helps in bringing about effective control of the concern. The top management may lay down the standards of various ratios. These standards are used to make a comparison with actual ratios at the end of the year. Thus the top management can initiate corrective actions, in case of wide variations.

4. **Trend Analysis:** Accounting ratios tabulated for a number of years indicate the trend of the change. This helps in the preparation of estimates for the future.

5. **Helps in Decision-making:** Ratio analysis helps in making decision from the information given in the financial statements. Thus it is useful to the management and outsiders. For instance, a bank or investor would like to know the liquidity, profitability and long-term solvency of the concern before advancing money.

Liquidity ratios help to know the liquidity of the concern, i.e., whether the concern is able to meet its current obligations when they become due. These ratios are used by banks, and financial institutions in credit analysis.

Profitability ratios help to know the growth and profitability of the concern in the present as well as the future. An investor may purchase shares or debentures of a concern whose profitability is attractive.

Long-term solvency ratios help to know the strength of a concern. This information is highly essential to the long-term creditors.

6. **Help in Inter-firm Comparison:** Ratio analysis helps to make an inter-firm comparison either between the different departments of a firm or between two firms employed in the identical types of business or between the same firm of two different dates. For instance, the stock turnover ratio of one steel plant can be compared with the other steel plant. This shows the relative position of a company in comparison with the competitors.

Limitations of Ratio Analysis

In spite of the above advantages, ratio analysis is subject to the following limitations:

1. Ratio analysis is only a beginning as it gives only a little information for the purpose of decision-making.

2. Ratios alone are inadequate.

3. Ratios are computed from past accounting records which have their own limitations.

4. Past is not an exact indicator of the future. A particular ratio is not a sure indicator of bad or good management.

5. Price changes are not taken into account in the ratios.

6. Ratios are tools of quantitative analysis only. Normally, qualitative factors are needed to draw conclusions.

7. Lack of standard formulae for working out ratios makes it difficult to compare them.

TYPES OF RATIOS

On the basis of the objectives of analysis, ratios are broadly classified into the following categories:

1. Profitability Ratios
2. Liquidity Ratios
3. Activity Ratios
4. Solvency Ratios
5. Leverage/Capital Structure Ratios

1. Profitability Ratios

Profitability is an indication of the efficiency with which the operations of the concern are carried on. If profit is what is left for shareholders after all the charges have been paid, profitability is a ratio. Being a ratio profitability is a meaningful measure and reveals the relation of different individual items with sales of the concern. Profitability of a concern can be known through the analysis of general and overall profitability. Thus profitability ratios are brought into two groups. They are:

(a) General Profitability Ratios and

(b) Overall Profitability Ratios

(a) General Profitability Ratios

The important general profitability ratios are:

(i) Gross Profit Ratio

(ii) Net Profit Ratio

(iii) Operating Ratio

(iv) Operating Profit Ratio

(v) Expense Ratio

(i) Gross Profit Ratio

Gross profit ratio measures the relationship of gross profit to net sales. It is usually represented as percentage and hence it is calculated by dividing the gross profit by sales.

$$\text{G.P. Ratio} = \frac{\text{Gross Profit}}{\text{Net Sales}} \times 100$$

or

$$\text{G.P. Ratio} = \frac{\text{Net Sales} - \text{Cost of Goods Sold}}{\text{Net Sales}} \times 100$$

ILLUSTRATION 15.1

Calculate Gross Profit Ratio:

Total Sales = Rs. 30,00,000
Sales Return = Rs. 5,00,000
Cost of Goods Sold = Rs. 20,00,000

Solution

$$\text{Gross Profit Ratio} = \frac{\text{Gross Profit}}{\text{Net Sales}} \times 100$$

Net Sales	= Total Sales − Sales Returns
	= Rs. 30,00,000 − 5,00,000
	= Rs. 25,00,000
Gross Profit	= Net Sales − Cost of Goods Sold
	= Rs. 25,00,000 − 20,00,000
	= Rs. 5,00,000

$$\text{Gross Profit Ratio} = \frac{5,00,000}{25,00,000} \times 100$$

$$= 20\%$$

If gross profit ratio is deducted from 100 the ratio of cost of goods sold will get.

Ratio of cost of goods sold to sales in the above example

$$= 100 - \text{Gross Profit Ratio}$$
$$= 100 - 20\% = 80\%$$

Significance: The gross profit ratio indicates the degree to which the selling price of goods per unit may decline without resulting in losses on operations of a firm. It reflects the efficiency with which a firm produces its products.

There is no standard norm for gross profit ratio. It may vary from concern to concern. But the gross profit should be adequate to cover operating expenses and to provide for fixed charges, dividends and accumulation of reserves. A low gross profit ratio is an indication of the high cost of goods sold due to unfavourable purchasing policies, lesser sales, etc.

A comparison of gross profit ratio over time or for different firms in the same industry is a good measure of profitability.

(ii) Net Profit Ratio

Net profit ratio establishes the relationship between net profit and sales. It indicates the efficiency of the management in manufacturing, selling, administrative and other activities of the concern. It is calculated as:

$$\text{Net Profit Ratio} = \frac{\text{Net Operating Profit}}{\text{Net Sales}} \times 100$$

ILLUSTRATION 15.2

Net Sales	= Rs. 2,00,000
Net Operating Profit	= Rs. 40,000

Calculate Net Profit Ratio.

Solution

$$\text{Net Profit Ratio} = \frac{\text{Net Operating Profit}}{\text{Net Sales}} \times 100$$

$$= \frac{40,000}{2,00,000} \times 100 = 20\%$$

Significance: The two elements of this ratio are net profits and sales. Thus this ratio shows the number of rupees that remains out of every 100 rupees of sales. An increase in the ratio over the previous period is an indication of improvement in the operational efficiency of the concern, provided the gross profit is constant. Hence net profit ratio is described as an index of operational efficiency. The higher the ratio, the more successful the business is. But a lower ratio indicates that the concern has a large amount of manufacturing expenses.

(iii) Operating Ratio

Operating ratio measures the cost of operation per rupee of sales. It is generally represented as a percentage. Thus two elements of this ratio are operating cost and net sales. Operating cost is the sum of operating expenses (Administrative and office expenses and selling and distribution expenses) and the cost of goods.

$$\text{Its formula is: } \frac{\text{Operating Cost}}{\text{Net Sales}} \times 100$$

or

$$\frac{\text{Cost of Goods Sold + Operating Expenses}}{\text{Net Sales}} \times 100$$

ILLUSTRATION 15.3

Calculate Operating Ratio: *Rs.*

Cost of Goods Sold	=	7,00,000
Office and Administrative Expenses	=	60,000
Selling and Distribution Expenses	=	40,000
Net Sales	=	10,00,000

Solution

$$\text{Operating Ratio} = \frac{\text{Operating Cost}}{\text{Net Sales}} \times 100$$

$$= \frac{8,00,000}{10,00,000} \times 100 = 80\%$$

Significance: This ratio is a yardstick of operating efficiency. The higher the ratio, the less favourable it is, as it should have a small operating profit to cover interest, income-tax, dividend and reserves.

(iv) Operating Profit Ratio

Operating profit is net sales minus operating cost. In other words, operating profit is net sales − (cost of goods sold + administrative and office expenses + selling and distribution expenses).

Thus operating profit ratio is calculated by dividing operating profit by sales. This ratio is also calculated as: 100 − operating ratio.

ILLUSTRATION 15.4

Calculate operating profit ratio:

Net Sales	=	Rs. 12,00,000
Cost of Goods Sold	=	Rs. 8,00,000
Administrative Expenses	=	Rs. 70,000
Selling Expenses	=	Rs. 90,000

Solution

$$\text{Operating Profit Ratio} = \frac{\text{Operating Cost}}{\text{Net Sales}} \times 100$$

$$
\begin{aligned}
\text{Operating Profit} &= \text{Sales} - (\text{Cost of goods sold} + \text{Administrative expenses} \\
&\quad + \text{Selling expenses}) \\
&= 12,00,000 - (8,00,000 + 70,000 + 90,000) \\
&= 12,00,000 - 9,60,000 \\
&= \text{Rs. } 2,40,000
\end{aligned}
$$

$$\therefore \text{Operating Profit Ratio} = \frac{2,40,000}{12,00,000} \times 100 = 20\%$$

(v) Expense Ratio

It is the relationship of various expenses to net sales. It is calculated by dividing each item of expenses or groups of expenses with the net sales to analyse the cause of variation of the operating ratio. The smaller the ratio, the higher is the profitability; and the greater the ratio, the lower is the profitability.

$$\text{Particular Expense Ratio} = \frac{\text{Particular Expense}}{\text{Net Sales}} \times 100$$

Individual or specific expense ratio is calculated as:

(a) $\text{Cost of Goods Sold Ratio} = \dfrac{\text{Cost of Goods Sold}}{\text{Sales}} \times 100$

(b) $\text{Administrative and Office Expenses Ratio} = \dfrac{\text{Administrative and Office Expenses}}{\text{Sales}} \times 100$

(c) $\text{Selling and Distribution Expenses Ratio} = \dfrac{\text{Selling and Distribution Expenses}}{\text{Sales}} \times 100$

(d) $\text{Non-operating Expenses Ratio} = \dfrac{\text{Non-Operating Expenses}}{\text{Sales}} \times 100$

ILLUSTRATION **15.5**

The following is the P/L A/c of the Gopal Engineering Co. Ltd for the year ended 31st December 1997:

Dr.				Cr.
	Rs.			*Rs.*
To Opening Stock	2,00,000	By Sales		5,60,000
To Purchases	2,54,000	By Closing Stock		1,00,000
To Wages	5,000			
To Gross Profit c/d	2,01,000			
	6,60,000			6,60,000
To Administrative Expenses	30,000	By Gross Profit		2,01,000
To Selling and Distribution Expenses	69,000	By Interest on Investment (Outside business)		13,000
To Non-Operating Expenses	30,000			
To Net Profit	85,000			
	2,14,000			2,14,000

You are required to calculate:

1. Gross Profit Ratio
2. Net Profit Ratio
3. Operating Ratio
4. Operating Profit Ratio
5. Administrative Expenses Ratio

Solution

1. Gross Profit Ratio $= \dfrac{\text{Gross Profit}}{\text{Net Sales}} \times 100$

$= \dfrac{2,01,000}{5,60,000} \times 100 = 35.9\%$

2. Net Profit Ratio $= \dfrac{\text{Net Profit (after tax)}}{\text{Net Sales}} \times 100$

$= \dfrac{85,000}{5,60,000} \times 100$

$= 15.1\%$

3. Operating Ratio $= \dfrac{\text{Cost of Goods Sold} + \text{Operating Expenses}}{\text{Net Sales}}$

Cost of Goods Sold	= Opening Stock + Purchases + Wages − Closing Stock
	= 2,00,000 + 2,54,000 + 5,000 − 1,00,000
	= Rs. 3,59,000
Operating Expenses	= Administrative + Selling and Distribution Expenses
	= 30,000 + 69,000
	= Rs. 99,000

$$\text{Operating Ratio} = \frac{\text{Cost of Goods Sold} + \text{Operating Expenses}}{\text{Net Sales}}$$

$$= \frac{4,58,000}{5,60,000} \times 100$$

$$= 81.7\%$$

4. Operating Profit Ratio = 100 − Operating Ratio
   = 100 − 81.7% = 18.3%

5. Administrative Expenses Ratio = $\dfrac{\text{Administrative Expenses}}{\text{Net Sales}} \times 100$

$$= \frac{30,000}{5,60,000} \times 100$$

$$= 5.3\%$$

(b) Overall Profitability Ratios

The following are the important overall profitability ratios:

(i) Return on Shareholders' Investment or Net Worth Ratios

(ii) Return on Equity Capital

(iii) Earning Per Share

(iv) Return on Capital Employed

(v) Capital Turnover Ratio

(vi) Dividend Yield Ratio

(vii) Dividend Pay-out Ratio

(viii) Price Earning (Earning Yield) Ratio

(i) Return on Shareholders Investment or Net Worth Ratio

Return on shareholders investment is also known as ROI or return on shareholders'/Proprietors' funds. This ratio establishes the relationship between net profits (after tax and interest) and proprietors' funds and is calculated as:

$$\frac{\text{Net Profit (after interest \& tax)}}{\text{Shareholders Funds}}$$

The two basic components of this ratio are net profits and shareholders' funds. The shareholders' funds consist of equity share capital, preference share capital, free reserves such as share premium, revenue reserve, capital reserve, retained earning and surplus, less accumulated losses, if any. But net profits here mean those profits which are arrived at after deducting interest on long-term borrowings and income-tax.

ILLUSTRATION 15.6

Issued and Subscribed Capital   *Rs.*

3,000 Equity Shares of Rs. 100 each	3,00,000
2,000 7% Preference Shares of Rs. 100 each	2,00,000
	5,00,000

Reserve and Surplus   *Rs.*

Revenue Reserve	50,000	
Reserve for Contingencies	30,000	
Capital Reserve	20,000	1,00,000
Net Profit Before Interest and Tax		2,00,000
Interest Charges		20,000
Tax Rate 50%		

Calculate return on shareholders' investment.

Solution

Shareholders' Investment	=	Equity share capital + Preference share capital + Reserve and Surplus
	=	Rs. 3,00,000 + 2,00,000 + 1,00,000
	=	Rs. 6,00,000
Net Profit Before Interest and Tax	=	Rs. 2,00,000
Less Interest	=	20,000
		1,80,000
Less Income Tax @ 50%	=	90,000
Net Profit After Interest and Tax	=	90,000

$$\text{Return on Shareholders' Investment} = \frac{\text{Net Profit After Interest \& Tax}}{\text{Shareholders' Investment}}$$

$$= \frac{90,000}{6,00,000} \times 100$$

$$= 15\%$$

Significance: This ratio is used to measure the overall efficiency of a concern. The higher the ratio the better the results will be as this ratio reveals how well the resources of a concern are being used.

(ii) Return on Equity Capital

The performance of a concern is usually judged on the basis of return on equity capital. It is the relationship between the profits of a concern and its equity capital and is calculated as:

$$\frac{\text{Net Profit After Tax} - \text{Preference Dividend}}{\text{Equity Share Capital (Paid-up)}}$$

ILLUSTRATION 15.7

Calculate return on equity capital from the following information:

12,000 Equity Shares of Rs. 10 each Rs. 8 paid	96,000
10% 4,000 Preference Shares of Rs. 20 each	80,000
Profit Before Tax	90,000
Rate of Tax	50%

Solution

$$\text{Return on Equity Capital} = \frac{\text{Net Proft After Tax} - \text{Preference Dividend}}{\text{Equity Share Capital (Paid-up)}} \times 100$$

Profits available for equity shareholders:

	Rs.
Profits	90,000
Less Tax @50%	45,000
Profits After Tax	45,000
Less Preference Dividend	8,000
	37,000

$$\text{Return on Equity Capital} = \frac{37,000}{96,000} \times 100$$

$$= 38.5\%$$

Significance: This ratio is highly meaningful to the equity shareholders who are interested in knowing the profits earned by the concern. The higher the ratio, the better the results will be.

(iii) Earning Per Share (E.P.S.)

E.P.S. is measured by dividing the net profits after taxes and preference dividend by the total number of equity shares.

$$\text{E.P.S.} = \frac{\text{Net Profit after tax} - \text{Preference Dividend}}{\text{No. of Equity Shares}}$$

Earning per share is a small variation of return on equity capital. It provides a view of the comparative earnings when it compares with that of similar other companies. Thus the earnings per share is a good measure of profitability.

In the above Illustration

$$\text{E.P.S.} = \frac{45,000 - 8,000}{12,000}$$

$$= \frac{37,000}{12,000} = \text{Rs. 3.08}$$

(iv) Return on Capital Employed

It measures the relationship between profits and the capital employed.

The total investment made in a concern is known as capital employed. It may be: (a) Gross capital employed (b) Net capital employed and (c) Proprietors net capital employed.

If gross capital employed is fixed assets plus current assets, the net capital employed is the excess of total assets over current liabilities i.e., Total Assets – Current Liabilities.

Proprietors net capital employed is the shareholders' funds or investments in the business. In other words, it is the excess of total assets (both fixed and current) over outside liabilities, i.e., Fixed Assets + Current Assets – Outside Liabilities.

Apart from the above concepts of capital employed, sometimes a firm prefers the concept of average capital employed as the earnings are on an average for a particular period. It is calculated in any one of the following methods:

$$\frac{\text{Opening Capital Employed} + \text{Closing Capital Employed}}{2}$$

(b) Closing capital employed – ½ of profit earned during the year

(c) Opening capital employed + ½ of profit earned during the year

Calculation of Capital Employed: There are two approaches for computing capital employed in a concern. They are as follows:

(A) Assets Approach and

(B) Liabilities Approach

(A) *Assets Approach:* Under this approach, gross capital employed can be computed by adding the following:

  (a) All fixed assets at their net values (i.e., after deducting depreciation)

  (b) Investment inside the business

  (c) All current assets.

To obtain net capital employed, current liabilities are to be deducted from the total of the assets as computed above.

However, the following items should be excluded from capital employed:

  (a) Idle assets—assets which cannot be used in the concern.

  (b) Intangible assets such as goodwill, patents, trademarks, etc. But if they have sale value or they have been purchased, they may be included.

  (c) Any excess balance of cash or bank over the required sum for the smooth running of the concern.

  (d) Obsolete assets—assets which cannot be used or sold.

(B) *Liabilities Approach:* Under this approach, the gross capital employed can be computed as follows:

	Rs.
Total of All Liabilities	....
Add:	
Increase in the Value of Assets on Replacement Cost	....
Less:	
Accumulated Losses	....
Fictitious Assets	....
Intangible Assets	....
Idle and Obsolete Assets	....
Investment Outside the Business	....

To obtain net capital employed, current liabilities are to be deducted from the total of liabilities as computed above.

ILLUSTRATION 15.8

The following is the Balance Sheet of M/s Krishna Ltd. for the year ended 31st December 1997:

Liabilities	Rs.	Assets	Rs.
60,000 Equity Shares of		Goodwill	60,000
Rs. 10 each fully paid	6,00,000	Plant and Machinery	3,00,000
15,000 Preference Shares		Land and Building	6,00,000
of Rs. 20 each fully paid	3,00,000	Furniture	35,000
P&L A/c (including Rs. 50,000	1,10,000	Stock	2,00,000
current year's profits)		Debtors	30,000
6% Debentures	1,90,000	Cash at Bank	1,60,000
Bills Payable	1,50,000	Preliminary Expenses	15,000
Sundry Creditors	50,000		
	14,00,000		14,00,000

The value of the Plant and Machinery will be Rs. 2,50,000

Find out:

(i) Gross Capital Employed

(ii) Net Capital Employed

(iii) Average Capital Employed.

Solution

For ascertaining capital employed, the revised values of assets should be taken.

Capital Employed:		*Rs.*
Plant and Machinery		2,50,000
Land and Building		6,00,000
Furniture		35,000
Stock		2,00,000
Debtors		30,000
Cash at Bank		1,60,000
(i) Gross Capital Employed		12,75,000

(ii) Net Capital Employed = All Tangible Assets − Current Liabilities

Total Tangible Assets		12,75,000
Less: Sundry Creditors	50,000	
Less: Bills Payable	1,50,000	2,00,000
Net Capital Employed		10,75,000

(iii) Average Capital Employed = Capital Employed − One half of the current year's profits

Average Capital Employed:

(a) Gross = Gross Capital Employed − ½ of current year's profits
$$= Rs. \ 12,75,000 − ½ \ (50,000)$$
$$= Rs. \ 12,50,000$$

(b) Net = Net Capital Employed − ½ of current year's profits
$$= Rs. \ 10,75,000 − ½ \ (50,000) = Rs. \ 10,50,000$$

Calculation of Profits for Return on Capital Employed: The net profit for ascertaining the return on capital employed is to be adjusted in the following manner:

(a) Net profit should be taken before the payment of tax or provision for taxation.

(b) Net Profit should be considered before payment of interest on long-term as well as short-term borrowings in case the gross capital employed is taken.

(c) Only interest on long-term borrowings should be added back to the net profit in case the net capital employed is used.

(d) While calculating net profits, income from excluded assets (for computing capital employed) should not be considered.

(e) Net profit should be adjusted for profit/loss on sale of fixed assets.

(f) Net profit should be adjusted for depreciation based on replacement cost in case assets have been added at replacement cost.

Thus Return on capital employed is calculated as:

$$\text{Return on Gross Capital Employed} = \frac{\text{Adjusted Net Profits}}{\text{Gross Capital Employed}} \times 100$$

$$\text{Return on Net Capital Employed} = \frac{\text{Adjusted Net Profits}}{\text{Net Capital Employed}} \times 100$$

Significance: The return on capital employed reveals the rate of the earning capacity of the concern. It also indicates whether the proprietors funds have been used properly or not. The higher the ratio, the greater will be the return for the owners and the better the profitability.

ILLUSTRATION 15.9

The following are the Profit and Loss A/c and Balance Sheet of X & Y Ltd. for the year ended 31st December 1997.

Profit and Loss Account

	Rs.		Rs.
To Opening Stock	2,00,000	By Sales	14,20,000
To Purchases	9,00,000	By Closing Stock	2,10,000
To Wages	80,000		
To Gross Profit	4,50,000		
	16,30,000		16,30,000
To Officer and Administrative			
Expenses	2,05,000	By Gross Profit	4,50,000
To Selling and Distribution		By Interest on Government	
Expenses	5,000	Securities	11,000
To Interest on Debentures	8,000	By Profit on Sale of Plant	9,000
To Interest on Bank Overdraft	7,000		
To Depreciation	14,000		
To Loss on Sale of Machine	11,000		
To Provision for Tax	1,00,000		
To Net Profit	1,20,000		
	4,70,000		4,70,000

Balance Sheet

Liabilities	Rs.	Assets	Rs.
Equity Share Capital	5,00,000	Land & Building (Net)	2,75,000
10% Preference Share Capital	3,00,000	Plant & Machinery (Net)	4,75,000
Reserve	55,000	Investment in Government	
Profit & Loss A/c	45,000	Securities	1,00,000
11% Debentures	1,00,000	Stocks	2,50,000
Bank Overdraft	75,000	Sundry Debtors	60,000
Other Current Liabilities	1,25,000	Cash	30,000
		Discount on Issue of Shares	10,000
	12,00,000		12,00,000

Calculate:

(i) Return on Gross Capital Employed

(ii) Return on Net Capital Employed

Solution

Gross Capital Employed	*Rs.*
Land and Building	2,75,000
Plant and Machinery	4,75,000
Stocks	2,50,000
Sundry Debtors	60,000
Cash	30,000
	10,90,000

Net Capital Employed = Gross Capital Employed – Current Liabilities
$$= 10,90,000 - (75,000 + 1,25,000)$$
$$= \text{Rs. } 8,90,000$$

Calculation of Adjusted Profits:		*Rs.*
Net Profits as per P/L A/C		1,20,000
Add: Loss on Sale of Machinery		11,000
Interest on Debentures		8,000
Provision for Tax		1,00,000
		2,39,000
Less: Interest on Govt. Securities	11,000	
Profit on sale of Plant	9,000	20,000
Adjusted Profit for Return on Net Capital Employed		2,19,000

To calculate adjusted profits for return on gross capital employed, further Rs. 7,000 should be added back to Rs. 2,19,000 for interest on Bank Overdraft.

Return on Gross Capital Employed:

$$= \frac{\text{Adjusted Net Profits}}{\text{Gross Capital Employed}} \times 100$$

$$= \frac{2,26,000}{10,90,000} \times 100 = 20.73\%$$

Return on Net Capital Employed

$$= \frac{\text{Adjusted Net Profits}}{\text{Gross Capital Employed}} \times 100$$

$$= \frac{2,19,000}{8,90,000} \times 100 = 24.6\%$$

(v) Capital Turnover Ratio

It is the relationship between cost of goods sold and the capital employed. In other words, capital turnover ratio is the relationship between sales (when information about cost of goods sold is not available) and the capital employed.

Capital turnover ratio can be measured as:

$$\frac{\text{Cost of Goods Sold or Sales}}{\text{Capital Employed}}$$

Capital turnover ratio can be classified into: (a) Fixed Assets Turnover and (b) Working Capital Turnover as capital employed in a business comprises investment in fixed assets and working capital.

Fixed assets turnover is the relationship between cost of goods sold or sales and fixed assets employed in a business. It is calculated as:

$$\frac{\text{Cost of Goods Sold or Sales}}{\text{Fixed Assets Employed}}$$

Working capital turnover measures the velocity of the utilisation of net working capital. It is calculated as:

$$\frac{\text{Cost of Goods Sold or Sales}}{\text{(Average) Working Capital}}$$

Working capital turnover ratio can further be separated into: (a) inventory turnover ratio (b) debtors turnover ratio and (c) creditors turnover ratio. These ratios can be discussed under the head activity ratios.

Significance: Capital turnover ratio measures the efficiency or effectiveness with which a concern utilises its resources. This ratio is also a good indicator of overall profitability of a concern.

(vi) Dividend Yield Ratio

Dividend yield ratio is measured to evaluate the relationship between dividend per share paid and the market value of the share. Thus it is calculated as:

$$\frac{\text{Dividend Per Share (DPS)}}{\text{Market Value Per Share (MVPS)}}$$

$$\text{Dividend per share} = \frac{\text{Dividend paid to Shareholders}}{\text{Number of Shares}}$$

(vii) Dividend Payout Ratio or Payout Ratio

It is the relationship between the returns belonging to the equity shareholders and the dividend paid to them. Thus it is calculated as:

$$\frac{\text{Dividend Per Share (DPS)}}{\text{Earning Per Share}}$$

or

$$\frac{\text{Total Dividend to Equity Sharehoders (Cash Dividend)}}{\text{Total Net Profit available to Equity Shareholders}}$$

This ratio is measured mainly to know the extent to which earnings per share have been retained in the business.

(viii) Price-Earning Ratio/Earning Yield Ratio

It is the ratio between market price per equity share and earnings per share. Thus it is calculated as:

$$\frac{\text{Earning Per Share}}{\text{Market Price Per Share}}$$

This ratio is widely used by the prospective investors to determine whether or not to buy shares in a particular company.

ILLUSTRATION 15.10

The capital of XY Ltd. is as follows:

	Rs.
1,00,000 Equity Shares of Rs. 10 each	10,00,000
10% 50,000 Preference Shares of Rs. 10 each	5,00,000

The following information is obtained from the books of the company:

Profit after tax at 50%	Rs. 3,00,000
Depreciation	Rs. 70,000
Equity Dividend paid	20%
Market Price of Equity Share	Rs. 50

You are required to calculate:

(i) Dividend yield on equity share

(ii) Cover for the preference dividend

(iii) Cover for the equity dividend

(iv) Earnings per share

(v) The price-earning ratio

(vi) Net cash flow

Solution

(i) Dividend yield on Equity Share $= \dfrac{\text{Dividend Per Share}}{\text{Market Price Per Share}} \times 100$

$= \dfrac{2 (\text{i.e., } 20\% \text{ of Rs. } 10)}{50}$

$= .04 \text{ or say } 4\%$

(ii) Cover for the Preference Dividend $= \dfrac{\text{Profit After Tax}}{\text{Preference Dividend}}$

$= \dfrac{3,00,000}{50,000 \ (\text{i.e., } 10\% \text{ of } 5,00,00)} = 6 \text{ times}$

(iii) Cover for the Equity Dividend $= \dfrac{\text{Profits After Tax and Preference Dividend}}{\text{Equity Dividend}}$

$$= \dfrac{3,00,000 - 50,000}{2,00,000 \text{ (i.e., 20\% of 10,00,000)}}$$

$$= \dfrac{2,50,000}{2,00,000} = 1.45 \text{ times}$$

(iv) Earnings per Share $\quad = \dfrac{\text{Profits After Tax and Preference Dividend}}{\text{Number of Equity Shares}}$

$$= \dfrac{2,50,000 \text{ (i.e., 3,00,000 - 50,000)}}{1,00,000}$$

$$= \text{Rs. } 2.5$$

(v) Price-Earning Ratio $\quad = \dfrac{\text{Market Price per Share}}{\text{Earnings per Share}}$

$$= \dfrac{50}{2.5} = 20\text{:}1$$

(vi) Net Cash Flow
$$= \text{Total Cash Flow} - \text{Dividend}$$
$$= (\text{Net Profit} + \text{Depreciation} - \text{Dividend})$$
$$= (3,00,000 + 70,000) - (50,000 + 2,00,000)$$
$$= 3,70,000 - 2,50,000$$
$$= \text{Rs. } 1,20,000$$

2. Liquidity Ratios

Liquidity means the ability of a concern to meet its current obligations as and when these become due. Thus the liquidity ratios indicate the ability of a concern to meet its short-term obligations. Ratios measuring the liquidity of a concern are:

(i) Current Ratio

(ii) Quick or Acid Test or Liquid Ratio

(iii) Absolute Liquid or Cash Position Ratio

(i) Current Ratio or Working Capital Ratio

Current Ratio is defined as the relationship between current assets and current liabilities. Thus the two basic components of current ratio are: Current assets and current liabilities. "Current assets" consist of debtors, bills receivable, inventory, cash in hand, cash at bank, pre-paid expenses and short-term investments. The term inventory comprises raw materials, work-in-progress, finished goods and stores and spares.

'Current liabilities' include creditors, bills payable, advance received, bank overdraft, outstanding liabilities for expenses and interest accrued but not due. Some authors are of the view that bank overdraft should not be taken as a current liability as it is a continuing arrangement with the bank. Thus unless otherwise it is specifically mentioned that bank overdraft is a long-term arrangement, it should be considered as a current liability.

$$\text{Current Ratio is calculated as: } \frac{\text{Current Assets}}{\text{Current Liabilities}}$$

ILLUSTRATION 15.11

Current Assets   = Rs. 8,00,000
Current Liabilities = Rs. 4,00,000

Calculate Current Ratio:

Solution

$$\text{Current Ratio} = \frac{\text{Current Assets}}{\text{Current Liabilities}}$$
$$= \frac{8,00,000}{4,00,000} = 2:1$$

Significance: An ideal current ratio is 2:1. Thus this ratio is also known as 2:1 ratio. Current ratio is an index of the concern's financial stability. If a higher current ratio is an indication of inadequate employment of funds, a poor current ratio is a danger signal to the management.

(ii) Quick or Acid Test or Liquid Ratio

Quick ratio is a more rigorous test of liquidity than the current ratio. It can be ascertained by comparing the liquid assets to current liabilities. Liquid assets consist of cash in hand and at bank, debtors less provision for bad and doubtful debts, realisable investments and other current assets which can be realised immediately.

$$\text{Quick Ratio is calculated as: } \frac{\text{Liquid Assets}}{\text{Current Liabilities}}$$

ILLUSTRATION 15.12

Calculate Quick Ratio:

Quick Assets   = Rs. 2,00,000
Current Liabilities = Rs. 1,50,000

Solution

$$\text{Quick Ratio} = \frac{\text{Liquid Assets}}{\text{Current Liabilities}}$$
$$= \frac{2,00,000}{1,50,000} = 1.33$$

Some accountants prefer the term *"Liquid Liabilities"* for current liabilities for ascertaining liquid ratio. Liquid liabilities mean current liabilities minus the bank overdraft and cash credit facilities. Then the formula is:

$$\frac{\text{Liquid Assets}}{\text{Liquid Liabilities}}$$

Significance: Quick ratio measures the firm's capacity to pay off claims of current creditors immediately. The ideal quick ratio is '1'. Usually, a high quick ratio is an indication that the firm is liquid and has the ability to meet its current or liquid liabilities in time. On the other hand, a low quick ratio represents that the firm's liquidity position is not good.

Quick ratio is used as a complementary ratio to the current ratio. But quick ratio provides a more stringent test of solvency than current ratio and hence it is also known as acid test ratio.

(iii) Absolute Liquidity Ratio

It is the relationship between absolute liquid assets and current liabilities. Absolute liquid assets consist of cash in hand and at bank and marketable securities or temporary investments. In other words, absolute liquid assets mean current assets minus Debtors and Bills receivables.

Absolute Liquid Ratio is calculated as:

$$\frac{\text{Absolute Liquid Assets}}{\text{Current Liabilities}}$$

ILLUSTRATION 15.13

Calculate Absolute Liquid Ratio:

	Rs.
Cash in Hand	25,000
Cash at Bank	50,000
Marketable Securities	1,50,000
Current Liabilities	2,50,000

Solution

Absolute Liquid Ratio:

$$= \frac{\text{Absolute Liquid Assets}}{\text{Current Liabilities}}$$

$$= \frac{25,000 + 50,000 + 1,50,000}{2,50,000}$$

$$= \frac{2,25,000}{2,50,000} = 0.9$$

Significance: The absolute liquidity of the concern can be ascertained by calculating absolute liquid ratio along with current ratio and acid test ratio. The acceptable norm for this ratio is 50% or 0.5:1 or 1:2 i.e., Re. 1 worth absolute liquid assets are considered adequate to pay

Rs. 2 worth current liabilities in time as all the creditors are not expected to demand each at the same time. Moreover, cash may also be realised from debtors and inventories.

ILLUSTRATION 15.14

The following is the Balance Sheet of ABC Ltd., for the year ending 31st December 1997.

Liabilities	Rs.	Assets	Rs.
10% Preference share capital	3,00,000	Goodwill	1,00,000
Equity share capital	12,00,000	Land & Building	5,00,000
8% Debentures	1,50,000	Plant & Machinery	9,50,000
Long-term Loans	1,50,000	Furniture & Fixtures	1,50,000
Sundry Creditors	50,000	Bills Receivable	90,000
Bills Payable	80,000	Sundry Debtors	80,000
Bank Overdraft	50,000	Bank Balance	55,000
Outstanding Expenses	5,000	Short-term Investment	25,000
		Pre-paid Expenses	10,000
		Stock	25,000
	19,85,000		19,85,000

Calculate:

(i)   Current Ratio

(ii) Acid-test Ratio

(iii) Absolute Liquid Ratio

Solution

(i) Current Ratio $= \dfrac{\text{Current Assets}}{\text{Current Liabilities}}$

Current Assets $= 90,000 + 80,000 + 55,000 + 25,000 + 10,000 + 25,000$

$= \text{Rs. } 2,85,000$

Current Liabilities $= 50,000 + 80,000 + 50,000 + 5,000$

$= \text{Rs. } 1,85,000$

Current Ratio $= \dfrac{2,85,000}{1,85,000}$

$= 1.54$

(ii) Acid-test Ratio $= \dfrac{\text{Liquid Assets}}{\text{Current Liabilities}}$

Liquid Assets $= 90,000 + 80,000 + 55,000 + 25,000$

$= \text{Rs. } 2,50,000$

Stock and pre-paid expenses have been excluded from current assets with a view to arriving at liquid assets:

$$\text{Current Liabilities} = \text{Rs. } 1,85,000$$

$$\text{Acid-test Ratio} = \frac{2,50,000}{1,85,000}$$

$$= 1.35$$

(iii) $\text{Absolute Liquid Ratio} = \dfrac{\text{Absolute Liquid Assets}}{\text{Current Liabilities}}$

$$\text{Absolute Liquid Assets} = 55,000 + 25,000 = \text{Rs. } 80,000$$

$$\text{Absolute Liquid Ratio} = \frac{80,000}{1,85,000} = 0.43$$

3. Activity Ratios

Activity ratios measure the efficiency or effectiveness with which a concern manages its resources or assets. Activity ratios are also known as turnover ratios as they indicate the speed with which assets are converted or turned over into sales. The important activity or current assets movement ratios are:

(i)   Inventory/Stock Turnover Ratio
(ii) Debtors Turnover Ratio
(iii) Creditors/Payable Turnover Ratio
(iv) Working Capital Turnover Ratio

(i) Inventory Turnover/Stock Turnover Ratio

Inventory turnover ratio measures whether investment in inventory is efficiently used or not. It is the relationship between cost of goods sold and the average inventory. It is also known as stock velocity and is normally calculated as sales/average inventory or cost of goods sold/average inventory.

Its formula is:

$$\text{I.T. Ratio} = \frac{\text{Cost of Goods Sold}}{\text{Average Inventory}}$$

$$\text{Average Inventory} = \frac{\text{Opening Inventory} + \text{Closing Inventory}}{2}$$

When cost of goods sold is not known, the I.T. ratio may be calculated by dividing net sales by average inventory at cost. When average inventory at cost is not known, then the inventory at selling price is taken as the denominator. If opening inventory is not known, then the closing inventory figure may be taken as the average inventory.

ILLUSTRATION 15.15

Rs.

Cost of Goods Sold = 8,00,000
Opening Inventory   = 1,00,000
Closing Inventory   = 3,00,000

Calculate I.T. ratio.

Solution

$$\text{Inventory Turnover Ratio} = \frac{\text{Cost of Goods Sold}}{\text{Average Inventory}}$$

$$\text{Average Inventory} = \frac{\text{Opening Inventory} + \text{Closing Inventory}}{2}$$

$$= \frac{1,00,000 + 3,00,000}{2}$$

$$= \text{Rs. } 2,00,000$$

$$\therefore \text{ I.T. Ratio} = \frac{8,00,000}{2,00,000} = 4 \text{ times}$$

Here inventory turnover ratio is 4. It means that inventory is replaced 4 times in a year.

Significance: I.T. ratio signifies the liquidity of the inventory. It indicates the number of times the stock has been turned over during the period and evaluate the efficiency with which a firm is able to manage its inventory. If higher I.T. ratio indicates brisk sales, a low I.T. ratio results in blocking of funds in inventory.

It is difficult to establish a standard ratio of inventory. However, the following general guidelines can be used:

(a) The raw material should not exceed 2–4 months consumption in the year.

(b) The finished goods should not exceed 2–3 months sales.

(c) Work-in-progress should not exceed 15–30 days cost of completed work.

Inventory Conversion Period

It is the average time taken for clearing the stocks. It can be calculated as:

$$\frac{\text{Days in a year}}{\text{Inventory Turnover Ratio}}$$

(ii) Debtors Turnover Ratio

Two types of ratios may be calculated to evaluate the quality of debtors. They are:

(a) Debtors/Receivables Turnover/Debtors Velocity and

(b) Average Collection Period Ratio

(a) Debtors / Receivables Turnover Ratio

It measures the number of times average debtors (Receivables) are turned over during a year. It is calculated as:

$$\frac{\text{Net Credit Annual Sales}}{\text{Average Trade Debtors}}$$

Trade debtors comprise sundry debtors, bills receivables and accounts receivables:

$$\text{Average trade debtors} = \frac{\text{Opening Trade Debtors} + \text{Closing Trade Debtors}}{2}$$

No provision for bad and doubtful debts should be deducted from debtors. They should be taken at gross value.

If the information about opening and closing balances of the trade debtors and credit sales is not available, then debtors turnover ratio is ascertained as:

$$\frac{\text{Total Sales}}{\text{Debtors}}$$

Significance: There is no norm for interpreting this ratio. However, the higher the values of debtors turnover, the more efficient will be the management of debtors/sales. On the other hand, low debtors turnover implies inefficient management of debtors/sales.

(b) Average Collection Period Ratio

The average collection period indicates the average number of days for which a concern has to wait before its receivables are converted into cash. It is calculated as:

$$\frac{\text{Average Trade Debtors (Drs + B/R)}}{\text{Sales Per Day}}$$

$$\text{Sales per day} = \frac{\text{Net Sales}}{\text{No. of Working Days}}$$

Thus the two basic components of the ratio are debtors and sales per day. Trade debtors are inclusive of bills receivables.

$$\text{Average trade debtors} = \frac{\text{Opening Debtors} + \text{Closing}}{2}$$

When information about opening and closing debtors is not available, the balance of debtors given can be taken.

Net sales means sales after deducting return inwards, if any. When credit sales information is not available then the total sales may be taken to calculate the ratio.

Significance: Average collection period ratio indicates the quality of debtors. Generally, the shorter the average collection period, the better is the quality of debtors. On the other hand, a higher collection period is a sign of inefficient collection performance.

There is no norm for interpreting this ratio. However, the average collection period should be compared with the concern's credit terms and policy to evaluate its collection efficiency.

ILLUSTRATION 15.16

Calculate (i) Debtors Turnover, and (ii) Average Collection Period from the following information:

	31st March, 1997	31st March, 1998
	Rs.	Rs.
Debtors in the beginning	70,000	80,000
Debtors at the end	90,000	1,00,000
Annual credit sales	6,00,000	7,00,000

Days to be taken for the year: 360

Solution

$$\text{Average Debtors} = \frac{\text{Opening Debtors} + \text{Closing Debtors}}{2}$$

$$\text{Debtors Turnover} = \frac{\text{Net Credit Annual Sales}}{\text{Average Debtors}}$$

	Year 1997	Year 1998
Average Debtors	$= \dfrac{70,000 + 90,000}{2}$	$\dfrac{80,000 + 1,00,000}{2}$
	= Rs. 80,000	= Rs. 90,000
(i) Debtors Turnover	$= \dfrac{6,00,000}{80,000}$	$\dfrac{7,00,000}{90,000}$
	= 7.5 times	= 7.77 times

$$\text{(ii) Average Collection Period} = \frac{\text{No. of Working Days}}{\text{Debtors Turnover}}$$

	Year 1997	Year 1998
Average Collection Period	$= \dfrac{360}{7.5}$	$\dfrac{360}{7.77}$
	= 48 days	= 46.3 days or 46 days (approximately)

(iii) Creditors/Payables Turnover Ratio

Creditors turnover ratio is the relationship between trade creditors and average daily purchases. Like debtors turnover ratio, creditors turnover ratio can be ascertained in two forms:

(a) Creditors/Payable Turnover Ratio

$$= \frac{\text{Net Credit Annual Purchases}}{\text{Average Trade Creditors}}$$

When information about credit purchases is not available, the figure of total purchases may be taken as the numerator. The trade creditors consist of sundry creditors and bills payable. When opening and closing balance of creditors are not available, the balance of creditors given may be taken to calculate the ratio.

Significance: This ratio measures the velocity with which the creditors are turned over in relation to purchases. The larger the creditors velocity, the better the result is. On the other hand, the lower the creditors velocity, less favourable is the result.

(b) Average Payment Period Ratio

The average payment period ratio represents the average number of days taken by the firm to pay its creditors. It is calculated as:

$$\frac{\text{Average Trade Creditors (Creditors + Bills Payable)}}{\text{Average Daily Purchases}}$$

$$\text{Average Daily Purchases} = \frac{\text{Annual Purchases}}{\text{No. of Working days in a Year}}$$

or

$$\text{Average Payment Period} = \frac{\text{No. of Working Days}}{\text{Creditors Turnover Ratio}}$$

When information about credit purchases is not given, total purchases may be taken as the credit purchases.

Significance: The higher the ratio, the less liquid the position of the concern is. It also implies lesser discount facilities availed or higher prices paid for the goods purchased on credit. On the other hand, the lower the ratio, the better is the liquidity position of the concern.

ILLUSTRATION 15.17

Calculate creditors turnover ratio and average payment period from the following information:

	Rs.
Total Purchases	5,00,000
Cash Purchases (included in the above)	1,00,000
Purchases Returns	30,000
Creditors at the end	80,000
Bills Payable at the end	20,000
Reserve for Discount on Creditors	10,000

Take 365 days in a year.

Solution

$$\text{Creditors Turnover Ratio} = \frac{\text{Annual Net Purchases}}{\text{Average Trade Creditors}}$$

Net Credit Purchases: *Rs.*

Total Purchases   = 5,00,000
Less Cash Purchases   = 1,00,000
    ――――――――
    4,00,000
Less Returns   =   30,000
    ――――――――
    3,70,000
    ――――――――
Creditors Turnover Ratio = 3,70,000
    ――――――――――
    80,000 + 20,000

(Trade Creditors consist of Creditors and Bills Payable)

$$= \frac{3,70,000}{1,00,000}$$

$$= 3.7 \text{ times}$$

$$\text{Average payment Period} = \frac{\text{No. of Days}}{\text{Creditors Turnover Ratio}}$$

$$= \frac{365}{3.7}$$

$$= 98 \text{ days (approximately)}$$

Reserve for discount on creditors is not taken into account while calculating average collection period as total creditors before deducting such reserves are to be taken.

(iv) Working Capital Turnover Ratio

Working Capital = Current Assets – Current Liabilities. The working capital turnover ratio indicates the number of times the working capital is turned over in the course of a year. It is calculated as:

$$\frac{\text{Cost of Sales}}{\text{Average Working Capital}}$$

$$\text{Average Working Capital} = \frac{\text{Opening Working Capital} + \text{Closing Working Capital}}{2}$$

When the figure of cost of sales is not available, the figure of sales is considered instead.

If opening working capital is not disclosed, then closing working capital will be used. In such a case, the ratio is:

$$\text{Working Capital Turnover Ratio} = \frac{\text{Cost of Sales}}{\text{Net Working Capital}}$$

Significance: The working capital turnover ratio measures the efficiency with which the working capital is being used by a firm. A higher ratio represents efficient utilisation of working capital, and a low ratio represents otherwise.

ILLUSTRATION 15.18

From the following information calculate working capital turnover ratio:

	Rs.
Cash	10,000
Bills Receivable	4,000
Sundry Debtors	20,000
Stocks	14,000
Sundry Creditors	25,000
Cost of Sales	1,40,000

Solution

Working Capital Turnover Ratio	$= \dfrac{\text{Cost of Sales}}{\text{Net Working Capital}}$
Current Assets	$= 10,000 + 4,000 + 20,000 + 14,000$
	$= \text{Rs. } 48,000$
Current Liabilities	$= 25,000$
Net Working Capital	$= \text{CA} - \text{CL}$
	$= \text{Rs. } 48,000 - \text{Rs. } 25,000$
	$= \text{Rs. } 23,000$
So, Working Capital Turnover Ratio	$= \dfrac{1,40,000}{23,000}$
	$= 6.04 \text{ times}$

4. Solvency Ratios

The *solvency or leverage* ratios measure the financial position of a concern. Such ratios reflect the ability of the concern to assure the payment of long-term creditors in time.

The important ratios which determine the solvency of the concern are:

(i)   Debt-Equity Ratio

(ii)   Funded-Debt to Total Capitalisation Ratio

(iii) Proprietary Ratio or Equity Ratio

(iv)   Solvency Ratio or Ratio of Total Liabilities to Total Assets

(v)   Fixed Assets to Net Worth or Proprietor's Funds Ratio

(vi)   Fixed Assets to long-term Funds or Fixed Assets Ratio

(vii) Ratio of Current Assets to Proprietor's Funds

(viii) Debt Service Ratio or Interest-Coverage Ratio

(ix)   Cash to Debt-Service Ratio

(i) Debt-Equity Ratio

Debt-Equity ratio is determined to measure the soundness of the long-term financial policies of the concern. It is also known as External-Internal Equity Ratio and indicates the relationship between the external equities or the outsiders funds and the internal equities or the shareholders' funds. It is calculated as:

$$\frac{\text{Long-Term Debts}}{\text{Shareholders' Funds}}$$

or

$$\frac{\text{Long-Term Debts}}{\text{Internal Equities}}$$

Shareholders funds or internal equities (net worth) consist of equity capital and reserves and surplus of the concern.

Significance: Debt-Equity ratio measures ultimate solvency of a concern. It provides a margin of safety to the creditors. Thus the smaller this ratio, the more secured are the creditors. An appropriate debt-equity ratio is 0.33. A ratio higher than this is an indication of risky financial policies.

ILLUSTRATION 15.19

Calculate Debt-Equity Ratio from the following information:

	Rs.
Equity Capital of a company	40,00,000
Reserves and Surplus	20,00,000
Long-term Debts	30,00,000

Solution

$$
\begin{aligned}
\text{Debt-Equity Ratio} &= \frac{\text{Long-Term Debts}}{\text{Shareholders' Funds}} \\
&= \frac{30,00,000}{40,00,000 + 20,00,000} \\
&= \frac{30,00,000}{60,00,00} \\
&= 1:2
\end{aligned}
$$

(ii) Funded Debt to Total Capitalisation Ratio

The two term used in this ratio are: (a) Funded debt and (b) Total capitalisation:

Funded debt consists of debentures, mortgage loans, bonds and other long-term loans.

Total capitalisation comprises equity share capital, preference share capital, reserves and surpluses, other undistributed reserves, debentures, mortgage loans, bonds and other long-term loans.

Thus this ratio establishes a relationship between the long-term funds raised from outsiders and total long-term funds available in the business. Funded Debt to total Capitalisation Ratio is calculated as:

$$\frac{\text{Funded Debt}}{\text{Total Capitalisation}} \times 100$$

Significance: There is no norm for this ratio. However, up to 50% or 55%, this ratio is considered as good. The smaller the ratio, the better the position will be.

ILLUSTRATION 15.20

Calculate Funded Debt to Total Capitalisation Ratio from the following information relating to the liabilities side of a concern:

	Rs.
60,000 Equity Shares of Rs. 10 each fully paid	6,00,000
30,000 10% Preference Shares of Rs. 10 each fully paid	3,00,000
General Reserve	60,000
Profit and Loss Account	1,50,000
8% Debentures	1,60,000
Mortgage Loans	70,000
Sundry Creditors	1,30,000
Bills Payable	75,000
	15,45,000

Solution

Funded Debt to Total Capitalisation Ratio = $\dfrac{\text{Funded Debt}}{\text{Total Capitalisation}} \times 100$

Funded Debt = 8% Debentures + Mortgage Loan
= 1,60,000 + 70,000
= Rs. 2,30,000

Total Capitalisation = Proprietors' Funds + Funded Debt
                                  or
Equity Share Capital + Preference Share Capital + General Reserve + P/L A/C + 8% Debentures + Mortgage Loans
= 6,00,000 + 3,00,000 + 60,000 + 1,50,000 + 1,60,000 + 70,000
= Rs.13,40,000

Funded Debt to Total Capitalisation = $\dfrac{\text{Rs. }2,30,000}{\text{Rs. }13,40,000} \times 100$

= 17.16%

Here the ratio is very low. Thus there is enough scope for the concern to raise long-term loans from outsiders.

(iii) Proprietary Ratio or Equity Ratio

Proprietory ratio shows the relationship between shareholders' funds to total assets of the concern. The shareholders' funds are equity share capital, preference share capital, undistributed profits, reserves and surpluses. Accumulated losses should be deducted out of this sum. The total assets denote the total resources of the concern. This ratio is calculated as:

$$\frac{\text{Shareholders' Funds}}{\text{Total Assets}}$$

ILLUSTRATION 15.21

Calculate proprietary ratio from the following information:

	Rs.
Shareholders' Funds	5,00,000
Total Assets	8,00,000

Solution

$$\text{Proprietary Ratio} = \frac{\text{Shareholders' Funds}}{\text{Total Assets}}$$

$$= \frac{5,00,000}{8,00,000} = 5:8$$

In percentage this ratio represents the percentage of owner's capital to total capital of the concern. Thus

$$\text{Proprietary Ratio} = \frac{5,00,000}{8,00,000} \times 100$$

$$= 62.5\%$$

Significance: The higher the ratio the better the long-term solvency of the company will be.

(iv) Solvency Ratio or Ratio of Total Liabilities to Total Assets

Solvency ratio is a small variant of equity ratio. It is calculated as:

$$100 - \text{Equity ratio}$$

In the above illustration Solvency Ratio:

$$= 100 - 62.5 \quad \text{or}$$
$$= 37.5\%$$

Solvency ratio shows the relationship between total outsiders liability to total assets of a concern. It is calculated as:

$$\frac{\text{Total Outsiders Liabilities}}{\text{Total Assets}}$$

ILLUSTRATION 15.22

Calculate solvency ratio:

	Rs.
Total Outsiders Liabilities	2,50,000
Total Assets	8,00,000

Solution

$$\text{Solvency Ratio} = \frac{\text{Total Outsiders Liabilities}}{\text{Total Assets}}$$

$$= \frac{2,50,000}{8,00,000} \times 100 = 31.2\%$$

Significance: The smaller the ratio, the more satisfactory will be the long-term solvency position of a concern.

(v) Fixed Assets to Net Worth Ratio or Ratio of Fixed Assets to Proprietor's Funds

Fixed assets to net worth ratio measures the relationship between fixed assets and shareholders' funds. It is calculated as:

$$\frac{\text{Fixed Assets (After Depreciation)}}{\text{Shareholders' Funds}}$$

ILLUSTRATION 15.23

Calculate Fixed assets to Net Worth Ratio:

	Rs.
Depreciated value of Fixed Assets	10,00,000
Equity Capital	8,00,000
Reserves	1,00,000
Surpluses	1,00,000

Solution

Fixed Assets to Net Worth Ratio:

$$\frac{\text{Fixed Assets (After Depreciation)}}{\text{Shareholders' Funds}}$$

$$= \frac{10,00,000}{8,00,000 + 1,00,000 + 1,00,000} \times 100$$

$$= \frac{10,00,000}{10,00,000} \times 100 = 100\%$$

Significance: There is no norm for this ratio. But 60 to 65 per cent is considered to be satisfactory in the case of industrial concerns. If the ratio is more than 100 per cent, it shows that owners' funds are not sufficient to finance the fixed assets. Thus the concern has to depend on outsiders to finance the fixed assets.

(vi) Fixed Assets Ratio or Fixed Assets to Total Long-term Funds

Fixed assets ratio is the relationship between fixed assets and total long-term funds. The long-term funds include shareholders' funds plus long-term borrowings. This ratio is calculated as:

$$\frac{\text{Fixed Assets (After Depreciation)}}{\text{Total Long-term Funds}}$$

ILLUSTRATION 15.24

Calculate Fixed Assets Ratio:

	Rs.
Fixed Assets after Depreciation	5,00,000
Total Long-term Funds	6,00,000

Solution

Fixed Assets Ratio: $\dfrac{\text{Fixed Assets (After Depreciation)}}{\text{Total Long-term Funds}}$

$$= \frac{5,00,000}{6,00,000} \times 100 = 83.3\%$$

Significance: This ratio shows the extent to which the total of fixed assets are financed by long-term funds of the concern. When the total long-term funds are more than total fixed assets, it means that a part of the working capital requirements is met out of the long-term funds of the concern.

(vii) Ratio of Current Assets to Proprietors' Funds

The ratio of current assets to proprietors' funds establishes the relationship between the current assets and shareholders' funds. It is calculated as:

$$\frac{\text{Current Assets}}{\text{Shareholders' Funds}} \times 100$$

Significance: There is no norm for this ratio. On the basis of the nature of business, there may be different ratios for different concerns. However, this ratio indicates the extent to which proprietors' funds are invested in current assets:

ILLUSTRATION 15.25

Calculate the ratio of Current Assets to Proprietors' Funds.

	Rs.
Current Assets	3,00,000
Shareholders' Funds	5,00,000

Solution

Ratio of Current Assets to Proprietors' Funds

$$= \frac{\text{Current Assets}}{\text{Shareholders' Funds}} \times 100$$

$$= \frac{3,00,000}{5,00,000} \times 100 = 60\%$$

(viii) Interest Coverage Ratio or Debt Service Ratio

Interest coverage ratio or Fixed charges cover or Time interest earned establishes the relationship between net profit before interest and taxes and fixed interest charges. It is calculated as:

$$\frac{\text{Net Profit (Before Interest and Taxes)}}{\text{Fixed Interest Charges}}$$

Significance: Interest coverage ratio measures the number of times interest is covered by the profits available to pay the charges. This ratio is used to test the debt-servicing capacity of a concern. Generally, higher the ratio, the more safe are the long-term creditors.

ILLUSTRATION 15.26

Calculate Interest Coverage Ratio:	Rs.
Net Profit (after Taxes)	1,00,000
Fixed Interest charges on Long-term Borrowings	20,000
Rate of Tax	50%

Solution

Interest Coverage Ratio:

$$= \frac{\text{Net Profit (Before Interest and Taxes)}}{\text{Fixed Interest Charges}}$$

$$= \frac{1,00,000 + 1,00,000 + 20,000}{20,000}$$

$$= \frac{2,20,000}{20,000} = 11 \text{ times}$$

The interest coverage ratio does not take into account other fixed obligations such as payment of preference dividend and repayment of loan instalments. Thus total coverage ratio can be found out. It is as follows:

$$\text{Total Coverage or Fixed Charge Coverage} = \frac{\text{Net Profit (Before Interest and Taxes)}}{\text{Total Fixed Charges}}$$

Similarly, Preference Dividend Coverage Ratio can be measured. It is:

$$= \frac{\text{Net Profit (After Interest and Taxes)}}{\text{Preference Dividend}}$$

(ix) Cash to Debt Service Ratio

It is an improvement over the interest coverage ratio and is also called debt cash flow coverage ratio. It is calculated as:

$$\frac{\text{Annual Cash Flow (Before Interest \& Taxes)}}{\text{Interest} + \dfrac{\text{Sinking Fund Appropriation on Debt}}{1 - \text{Tax Rate}}}$$

or

$$\text{CFCD} = \frac{\text{CF}}{I + \dfrac{\text{SFD}}{1 - T}}$$

Here,

CF = Annual Cash Flow Before Interest & Tax

I = Interest Charges

SFD = Sinking Fund Appropriation on Debt

T = Rate of Tax

Significance: This ratio is used to measure the long-term solvency of a concern. The more the coverage, the better will be the long-term solvency of the concern.

ILLUSTRATION 15.27

From the following information, calculate cash to debt service ratio:

	Rs.
Net Profit after tax	25,000
Fixed Interest Charges	3,000
Depreciation Charged	4,000
Tax Rate	50%

Sinking Fund Appropriation 10% of Outstanding Debentures

10% Debentures   20,000

Solution

Debt Cash Flow Coverage (CFCD)

$$= \frac{CF}{I + \dfrac{SFD}{1-T}}$$

$$= \frac{25,000 + 25,000 \text{ (tax)} + 3,000 \text{ (fixed interest)} + 4,000 \text{ (depreciation)}}{3,000 + \dfrac{2,000 \text{ (Sinking Fund Appropriation)}}{1 - \dfrac{50}{100}}}$$

$$= \frac{57,000}{3,000 + \left(\dfrac{2,000}{0.5}\right)} = \frac{57,000}{3,000 + \left(\dfrac{2,000 \times 10}{5}\right)}$$

$$= \frac{57,000}{3,000 + 4,000} = \frac{57,000}{7,000}$$

$$= 8.14 \text{ times}$$

5. Leverage or Capital Structure Ratios

Leverage ratios are found out mainly to test the long-term financial position of a concern. The important leverage or capital structure ratios are:

- (i) Capital Gearing Ratio
- (ii) Debt-Equity Ratio
- (iii) Total Investment to Long-term Liabilities
- (iv) Ratio of Fixed Assets to Funded Debt
- (v) Ratio of Current Liabilities to Proprietors' Funds
- (vi) Ratio of Reserves to Equity Capital

(i) Capital Gearing Ratio

Capital gearing is the relationship between ownership capital (equity share capital including reserves and surpluses) and creditorship capital (preference share capital and other fixed interest bearing loans). It may be either 'low gear' (ownership capital is more) or 'high gear' (creditorship capital is more).

Capital gearing is calculated as:

$$\frac{\text{Equity Share Capital} + \text{Reserves \& Surpluses}}{\text{Preference Capital} + \text{Long-term debt bearing Fixed Interest}}$$

ILLUSTRATION 15.28

Calculate Capital Gearing Ratio from the following information.

	1996 Rs.	1997 Rs.
Equity Share Capital	6,00,000	5,00,000
Reserves & Surplus	4,00,000	3,00,000
10% Preference Share Capital	3,00,000	3,50,000
8% Debentures	3,00,000	5,50,000

Solution

$$\text{Capital Gearing Ratio} = \frac{\text{Equity Share Capital} + \text{Reserves \& Surpluses}}{\text{Preference Capital} + \text{Long-term debt bearing Fixed Interest}}$$

$$\text{In 1996} = \frac{6,00,000 + 4,00,000}{3,00,000 + 3,00,000} = \text{5:3 (Low Gear)}$$

$$\text{In 1997} = \frac{5,00,000 + 3,00,000}{3,50,000 + 5,50,000} = \text{8:9 (High Gear)}$$

Significance: The company should keep gearing in such a way that it can maintain a steady rate of dividend. Low gearing is good for a new company.

Classification of Leverages

Leverage can be brought into:

   (a) Financial leverage

   (b) Operating leverage

   (c) Combined leverage

   (a) **Financial Leverage:** A concern is said to be in financial leverage or trading on equity when it uses long-term interest bearing debt and preference share capital along with the equity share capital. Financial leverage is calculated as:

$$\frac{\text{Earnings Before Interest \& Tax (EBIT)}}{\text{Earnings Before Interest \& Tax} - \text{Interest \& Preference Dividend}}$$

   (b) **Operating Leverage:** It establishes the relationship between contribution (Sales – Variable Cost) and EBIT (Earnings before interest and tax). It is calculated as:

$$\frac{\text{Contribution}}{\text{Earnings Before Interest \& Tax}}$$

   (c) **Combined Leverage:** It is the combination of both financial leverage and operating leverage.

ILLUSTRATION 15.29

From the following information calculate (i) Financial Leverage (ii) Operating Leverage and (iii) Combined Leverage:

Sales (30,000 units @Rs. 10)	3,00,000
Variable Cost (Rs. 5 per unit)	1,50,000
Fixed Cost	70,000
Earnings Before Interest and Tax (EBIT)	80,000
Less Interest	10,000
Profit Before Tax (EBT)	70,000
Tax @50%	35,000
Profit after tax	35,000

Solution

Contribution = Sales – Variable Cost
= 3,00,000 – 1,50,000
= Rs. 1,50,000

(i) Financial Leverage = $\dfrac{\text{EBIT}}{\text{EBIT} - \text{Interest}}$

= $\dfrac{80,000}{70,000}$ = 1.14

(ii) Operating Leverage = $\dfrac{\text{Contribution}}{\text{EBIT}}$

= $\dfrac{1,50,000}{80,000}$ = 1.87

(iii) Combined Leverage = Financial Leverage × Operating Leverage
= 1.14 × 1.87 = 2.13

(ii) Debt-Equity Ratio

This ratio has already been discussed under the head solvency ratios.

(iii) Total Investment to Long-term Liabilities

This ratio establishes the relationship between total of long-term funds and long-term liabilities. It is calculated as:

$$\frac{\text{Shareholders Fund} + \text{Long-term Liabilities}}{\text{Long-term Liabilities}}$$

(iv) Ratio of Fixed Assets to Funded Debt

It is the relationship between the fixed assets and the funded debts. It is highly useful to the long-term creditors. It is calculated as:

$$\frac{\text{Fixed Assets}}{\text{Funded Debt}}$$

(v) *Ratio of Current Liabilities to Proprietors' Funds*

It establishes the relationship between current liabilities and the proprietors funds. It is calculated as:

$$\frac{\text{Current Liabilities}}{\text{Shareholders Funds}}$$

(vi) *Ratio of Reserve to Equity Capital*

This ratio establishes the relationship between Reserves and Equity Share Capital. This is calculated as:

$$\frac{\text{Reserves}}{\text{Equity Share Capital}} \times 100$$

Significance: This ratio shows how much profits are retained by the concern for future growth. The higher the ratio the better will be the position.

SUMMARY OF RATIOS

Objective of Analysis	Relations to be Computed	Formula	Unit of Expression	Reference Levels
A. Analysis of Profitability				
(i) General Profitability	1. Gross Profit Ratio	$\dfrac{\text{Gross Profit}}{\text{Net Sales}} \times 100$	%	......
	2. Operating Ratio	$\dfrac{\text{Operating Cost}}{\text{Net Sales}} \times 100$	%	......
	3. Expense Ratio	$\dfrac{\text{Particular Expense}}{\text{Net Sales}} \times 100$	%	......
	4. Net Profit Ratio	$\dfrac{\text{Net Profit (After Tax)}}{\text{Net Sales}} \times 100$	%	......
	5. Operating Profit Ratio	$\dfrac{\text{Operating Profit}}{\text{Net Sales}} \times 100$	%	......
(ii) Overall Profitability	1. Return on shareholders Investment or Net Worth (R.O.I.)	$\dfrac{\text{Net Profit (After Tax \& Interest)}}{\text{Shareholders Fund}} \times 100$	%	......
	2. Return on Equity Capital	$\dfrac{\text{Net Profit (After Tax)} - \text{Preference Dividend}}{\text{Paid-up Equity Capital}} \times 100$	%	......
	3. Earnings Per Share (E.P.S.)	$\dfrac{\text{Net Profit After Tax \& Preference Dividend}}{\text{No. of Equity Capital}} \times 100$	Per share	......
	4. Return on Gross Capital Employed	$\dfrac{\text{Adjusted Net Profit}}{\text{Gross Capital Employed}} \times 100$	%	......
	5. Return on Net Capital Employed	$\dfrac{\text{Adjusted Net Profit}}{\text{Net Capital Employed}} \times 100$	%	......

Objective of Analysis	Relations to be Computed	Formula	Unit of Expression	Reference Levels
B. Test of Liquidity or Short-term Financial Position	1. Current Ratio	$\dfrac{\text{Current Assets}}{\text{Current Liabilities}}$	Times	2:1
	2. Quick or Acid Test or Liquid Ratio	$\dfrac{\text{Liquid/Quick Assets}}{\text{Current Liabilites}}$	Times	1:1
	3. Absolute Liquid Ratio	$\dfrac{\text{Absolute Liquid Assets}}{\text{Current Liabilites}}$	Times	1:2
C. Activity Ratios or Current Assets Movement	1. Inventory/Stock Turnover Ratio	$\dfrac{\text{Cost of Goods Sold}}{\text{Average Inventory at Cost}}$	Times	9:1
	2. Debtors or Receivables Turnover Ratio/Velocity	$\dfrac{\text{Net Credit Annual Sales}}{\text{Average Trade Debtors}}$	Times	......
	3. Average Collection Period	$\dfrac{\text{Total Trade Debtors}}{\text{Sales Per Day}}$	Times	......
	4. Creditors/Payable Turnover Ratio/Velocity	$\dfrac{\text{Net Credit Annual Purchases}}{\text{Average Trade Creditors}}$	Times	......
	5. Average Payment Period	$\dfrac{\text{Total Trade Creditors}}{\text{Average Daily Purchases}}$	Days	......
	6. Working Capital Turnover Ratio	$\dfrac{\text{Cost of Sales}}{\text{Net Working Capital}}$	Times	......
D. Test of Solvency or Analysis of Long-term Financial Position	1. Debt-Equity Ratio	$\dfrac{\text{Outsiders' Funds}}{\text{Shareholders' Funds}}$ or $\dfrac{\text{External Equities}}{\text{Internal Equities}}$	%	0.33
	2. Funded Debt to Total Capitalisation Ratio	$\dfrac{\text{Funded Debt}}{\text{Total Capitalisation}} \times 100$	%	50% or 55%
	3. Ratio of Long-term Debt to shareholders Fund (Debt-Equity)	$\dfrac{\text{Long-term Debt}}{\text{Shareholders' Fund}}$	%	......
	4. Proprietory or Equity Ratio	$\dfrac{\text{Shareholders' Fund}}{\text{Total Assets}}$	% or Times	......

Objective of Analysis	Relations to be Computed	Formula	Unit of Expression	Reference Levels
	5. Solvency Ratio	$\dfrac{\text{Total Liabilities to Outsiders}}{\text{Total Assets}}$	%	......
	6. Fixed Asset Net Worth Ratio	$\dfrac{\text{Fixed Assets (After Depreciation)}}{\text{Shareholders' Funds}}$	%	60 to 65%
	7. Fixed Assets Ratio or Fixed Assets to long-term funds	$\dfrac{\text{Fixed Assets (After Depreciation)}}{\text{Total Long-term Funds}}$	%	......
	8. Ratio of Current Assets to proprietors Funds	$\dfrac{\text{Current Assets}}{\text{Shareholders' Funds}}$	%	......
	9. Debt-Service, or Interest Coverage Ratio	$\dfrac{\text{Net Profit (Before Interest and Taxes)}}{\text{Fixed Interest Charges}}$	Times	......
	10. Total Coverage or Fixed-charge coverage	$\dfrac{\text{Net Profit (Before Interest and Taxes)}}{\text{Total Fixed Charges}}$	Times	......
	11. Preference Dividend Coverage Ratio	$\dfrac{\text{Net Profit (Before Interest and Taxes)}}{\text{Preference Dividend}}$	Times	......
	12. Cash to Debt Service Ratio or Debt Cash Flow Coverage	$\dfrac{\text{Annual Cash (Before Interest and Taxes)}}{\text{Interest} + \dfrac{\text{Sinking Fund Appropriation on Debt}}{1 - \text{Tax Rate}}}$	Times	......
E. Test of Leverage or Analysis of Capital Structure	1. Capital Gearing Ratio	$\dfrac{\text{Equity Share Capital} + \text{Reserve and Surplus}}{\text{Preference Capital} + \text{Long-term Debt Bearing Fixed Interest}}$	Times	......
	2. Total Investment to Long-term Liabilities	$\dfrac{\text{Shareholders' Funds} + \text{Long-term Liabilities}}{\text{Long-term Liabilities}}$	Times	......
	3. Debt-Equity Ratio	$\dfrac{\text{Outsiders' Funds}}{\text{Shareholders' Funds}}$	Times	......
	4. Ratio of Fixed Assets to Funded Debt	$\dfrac{\text{Fixed Assets}}{\text{Funded Debt}}$	Times	......
	5. Ratio of Current Liabilities to Proprietors Funds	$\dfrac{\text{Current Liabilities}}{\text{Shareholders' Funds}}$	Times	....

Objective of Analysis	Relations to be Computed	Formula	Unit of Expression	Reference Levels
	6. Ratio of Reserves to Equity Capital	$\dfrac{\text{Reserves}}{\text{Equity Share Capital}} \times 100$	Times	......
	7. Financial Leverage	$\dfrac{\text{Earnings Before Interest and Tax (EBIT)}}{\text{EBIT-Interest and Preference Dividend}}$	Times	......
	8. Operating Leverage	$\dfrac{\text{Contribution}}{\text{EBIT}}$	Times	......

CASE STUDY

Ratio Analysis of Traco Cable Company Limited

Traco Cable Company Limited was incorporated on 5th February 1960. It is a public sector undertaking on a profit basis and provides employment to 235 persons. PUC cable made out of copper and aluminium wires and metal cables without covering are its main products. The company's authorized and paid-up capital as on 31st March 2004 is Rs. 1500.00 lakh and Rs. 1301.80 lakh respectively. Table 15.1 shows various Financial/Operating ratio of Traco Cable Company Limited from 2001–02 to 2003–04.

Table 15.1 Financial/Operating Ratios of Traco Cable Company

	Financing/Operating Ratio	2001–02	2002–03	2003–04
(i)	Debt-equity ratio	1.08:1	1.20:1	1.34:1
(ii)	Current ratio	1.58:1	1.37:1	1.10:1
(iii)	Receivables turnover (in times)	1.88	2.05	1.88
(iv)	Stock turnover (in times)	2.34	3.63	3.92
(v)	Net profit to sales (%)	–26.40	–30.32	–32.96
(vi)	Return on investment (%)	–40.69	–58.99	–93.24

Source: Review of Public Enterprises in Kerala.

The debt-equity ratio helps to measure the extent to which debt financing has been used in business. The debt-equity ratio of the Traco Cable Company shows an upward trend from 2001–02 to 2003–04. It indicates that the claims of outsiders (creditors) are increasing year after year and are greater than those of owners. Such a situation may not be considered by the creditors because it gives a lesser margin of safety for them at the time of liquidation of the company.

The current ratio of the Traco Cable Company showed a downward trend year after year, i.e., from 2001–02 to 2003–04. It indicates that there has been a deterioration in the liquidity position of the company. A current ratio equal or near to the rule of thumb of 2:1 is considered to be satisfactory. The idea of having double the current assets as compared to current liabilities is to provide for delays and losses in the realization of current assets. The current ratio of Traco Company during 2001–02 was 1.58:1, but during the following two years, this ratio came down to 1.37:1 and 1.10:1 respectively. This may be due to the insufficiency of funds to pay off liabilities and/or overtrading without considering the company's capacity.

Receivables turnover indicates the number of times the receivables of the company are turned over during a year. Generally, the higher the value of receivables turnover, the more efficient is the management of receivables/sales or more liquid are the receivables. The receivables turnover of Traco Cable Company shows a wide fluctuation during the periods under review. This was 1.88, 2.05 and 1.88 respectively, during 2001–02, 2002–03 and 2003–04. There is no "rule of thumb" which may be used as a norm to interpret the ratio as it may be different from company to company, depending upon the nature of business. However, this ratio should be compared with the ratios of other companies doing similar business to find the trend. This helps to make a better interpretation of the ratio.

Stock turnover of Traco Cable Company measures the speed of conversion of stock into sales. This ratio of the company showed an increasing trend year after year. This was 2.34, 3.63 and 3.92 respectively during 2001–02, 2002–03 and 2003–04. A high stock turnover (i.e., 3.63 and 3.92) during 2002–03 and 2003–04 indicates efficient management of stock because the more frequently the stocks are sold, the lesser amount of money is required to finance the inventory. On the other hand, a low stock turnover (i.e., 2.34) during 2001–02 implies over investment in stock, dull business, poor quality of business, stock accumulation, accumulation of obsolete and slow moving goods and low profits as compared to total investments. It is also pointed out here that there are no "rules of thumb" or generally accepted norms for interpreting this ratio. The norms may be different for different firms depending upon the nature of industry and business conditions. However, a too high stock turnover may not necessarily always imply a favourable situation.

Net profit to sales ratio of a firm indicates its capacity to face adverse economic conditions such as price competition, low demand, etc. Obviously, higher the ratio, the better the profit-ability. Net profit to sales of the Traco Cable Company is –26.40%, –30.32% and –32.96% respectively during the period under review. This is an indication that the loss of the company goes upwards year after year on account of price competition or low demand. However, it is noted that the performance of profits of Traco Cable must also be seen in relation to its investments or capital.

The return on investment reveals how well the resources of a company are being used. Generally, higher the ratio, the better the result. The return on investment of Traco Cable during the initial period under review shows a loss of 40.69%. But this loss is going upwards year after year. This is an indication of deterioration in the company's profitability and efficiency.

— REVIEW QUESTIONS —

1. What is ratio analysis? Discuss its significance?
2. Explain the merits and demerits of ratio analysis?
3. Write short notes on:
   (a) Current Ratio
   (b) Debt to Equity Ratio
   (c) Inventory Turnover Ratio
   (d) Operating Ratio
4. "Return on Investment is considered to be the master ratio which reflects the overall performance of the company". Elucidate.

5. What are the profitability ratios? Explain and illustrate.

6. Explain and illustrate the following terms:
   (a) Gearing on Capital
   (b) Operating Leverage
   (c) Price Earning Ratio
   (d) Return on Investment

7. From the following balance sheet of AB Ltd. as on 31st December 1997 calculate:
   (a) Solvency Ratio and
   (b) Liquidity Ratio

AB Ltd.
As on 31st December 1997

Liabilities	Rs.	Assets	Rs.
Share Capital	2,50,000	Fixed Assets	3,00,000
Fixed Liabilities	1,25,000	Current Assets	2,00,000
Current Liabilities	1,25,000		
	5,00,000		5,00,000

(**Ans.:** Solvency Ratio = 50%
Liquidity Ratio = 160%)

8. Calculate:
   (i) Current Assets
   (ii) Liquid Assets
   (iii) Inventory

   Current Ratio = 2.6:1
   Liquid Ratio = 1.5:1
   Current Liabilities = Rs. 40,000

   (**Ans.:** (i) Rs. 1,04,000; (ii) Rs. 60,000; (iii) Rs. 44,000)

9. The following are the Trading Account, Profit and Loss Account of XYZ Ltd. for the year ending 31st December 1997, and the Balance Sheet as on that date:

Trading and P/L A/C for the year ending December 31st 1997

	Rs.		Rs.
To Opening Stock	1,45,000	By Sales	7,50,000
To Purchases	6,10,000	By Closing Stock	1,55,000
To Gross Profit	1,50,000		
	9,05,000		9,05,000
To Sundry Expenses	80,000	By Gross Profit	1,50,000
To Net Profit	70,000		
	1,50,000		1,50,000

Balance Sheet as on 31st December 1997

		Rs.		Rs.
Share Capital		7,00,000	Net Stock	5,50,000
Reserve and Surplus			Current Assets:	
Balance	50,000		Stock	1,55,000
Profit for the year	70,000	1,20,000	Debtors	80,000
Bank Overdraft		35,000	Cash	2,20,000
Creditors		1,50,000		
		10,05,000		10,05,000

Calculate the following ratios:

(a) Current Ratio
(b) Quick Ratio
(c) Gross Profit to Sales
(d) Stock Turnover
(e) Debtors turnover, and
(f) Net Profit to paid-up capital

(**Ans.:** (a) 2.5:1; (b) 1.6:1; (c) 20%; (d) 20%; (e) 10.67%; (f) 10%)

10. The capital of Krishnan & Co. is as follows:

9% 30,000 Preference Shares of Rs. 10 each	3,00,000
80,000 Equity Shares of Rs. 10 each	8,00,000
	11,00,000

The Accountant has ascertained the following information:

Profit after tax @10%	Rs. 2,70,000
Depreciation	Rs. 60,000
Equity Dividend Paid	20%
Market Price of Equity	Rs. 40

Calculate:

(i) The dividend yield on the Equity Shares
(ii) The cover for the Preference and Equity dividends
(iii) The earnings per share
(iv) The price earning ratio
(v) The net cash flow

(**Ans.:** (i) 5%; (ii) For Preference Shares = 10 times, i.e., 9% of Rs. 3,00,000
For Equity Shares = 1.52 times, i.e., 20% of Rs. 8,00,000; (iii) Rs. 3.03;
(iv) Rs. 13.17; (v) Rs. 1,43,000)

11. Calculate (a) Current Liabilities (b) Current Assets (c) Liquid Assets (d) Stock from the following information given:

Current Ratio	2.5
Liquid Ratio	1.5
Working Capital	Rs. 60,000

(**Ans.:** (a) Rs. 40,000; (b) Rs. 1,00,000; (c) Rs. 60,000; (d) Rs. 40,000)

12. From the following information of Gopal & Co. for the year ending December 31, 1997, calculate Inventory Turnover:

Cash Sales	Rs. 80,000
Credit Sales	Rs. 2,00,000
Return Inwards	Rs. 10,000
Opening Stock	Rs. 25,000
Closing Stock	Rs. 30,000
Gross Profit Ratio	25%

(**Ans.:** 7.36 times)

16

Funds Flow Analysis

The funds flow statement is an important device for bringing to light the underlying financial movements the ebb and flow of funds.

— PATON & PATON

INTRODUCTION

The operation of a business concern involves the conversion of cash into non-cash assets. These non-cash assets when used are recovered back in cash form. The funds used in this circuit flow can be raised through various means. But the soundness of financial programme of a business concern depends on the selection of means to raise funds along with its associated uses. Hence, there is a need of preparing a statement which gives information about the various sources of funds and their respective uses. Such a statement is known as *"Funds Flow Statement"*.

MEANING OF FUNDS FLOW STATEMENT

Funds flow statement is also known as (i) statement of sources and applications of funds (ii) where got where gone statement (iii) analysis of working capital changes, (iv) funds statements, etc. It is a condensed report of how the activities of the business have been financed and how the financial resources have been used during a particular period. It shows the flow of funds into and out of a business. In the words of R.N. Anthony,

> funds flow statement summarises the events of the period (account period) ... it describes the sources from which additional funds were derived and the uses to which these funds were put.

Thus funds flow statement is not a statement of financial position but it is a report of the financial operations of a business concern. It discloses the results or the policies followed by the financial management.

Objectives of Preparing a Funds Flow Statement

Funds flow statement usually discloses the analytical information about the different sources of funds and the applications of the same in an accounting cycle. Thus the major objectives of preparing this statement are:

1. to know the important items relating to sources and applications of funds of fixed assets, long-term loans including capital;

2. to know how far the assets derived from normal activities of the concern are being utilised properly with adequate consideration;

3. to reveal how much out of the total funds is being collected by disposing of fixed assets, how much from issuing shares or debentures, how much from long-term or short-term loans and how much from normal operational activities of the concern;

4. to provide the information about the specific utilisation of such funds, i.e., how much has been applied for acquiring fixed assets, how much for repayment of long-term or short-term loans as well as for payment of tax and dividend, etc., and

5. to help the management in preparing budgets and formulating the policies that will be adopted for future operational activities.

Uses of Funds Flow Statement

Funds flow statement is a supplementary to financial statements. It is a useful tool in the financial manager's analytical kit. It helps in determining how resources are to be obtained and how they are to be used in future. Moreover, funds flow statement is an important indicator of financial analysis and control. It is a valuable aid to the financial manager to evaluate the future flows of a concern on the basis of past data and to assess the (a) growth of the concern, (b) its resulting financial needs and (c) to determine the best way to finance those needs.

Funds flow statement is used widely by the shareholders, prospective investors, bankers and creditors. The shareholders and prospective investors can assess the skill and effectiveness of the management in using the funds of the business. Thus the funds flow statement helps them to know the amount of funds available for payment of dividend and interest. Funds flow statements are used by the bankers and creditors to get an idea about the size of risk which they have to undertake while sanctioning credit to a business concern.

Various useful information of the company such as financial methods used in the past, dividend policies followed and the contribution of funds derived from the operations to the growth of the concern can be derived from the comparative funds flow statements covering several years of a company's operations. Moreover, they also provide reliable clues as to the future financial requirements.

Limitations of Funds Flow Statement

In spite of the above uses, funds flow statement is subject to the following limitations:

1. It is only a re-arrangement of data given in the financial statements and not an original statement.

2. It does not disclose continuous changes.

3. It provides only some additional information regarding changes in working capital. Hence it cannot be considered as a substitute of an income statement or a balance sheet.

4. As it is historic in nature, the projected funds flow statement cannot be prepared with much accuracy.

5. As far as financial management is concerned, the changes in cash are more relevant than the working capital.

FUNDS FLOW STATEMENT, INCOME STATEMENT AND BALANCE SHEET

Funds flow statement is not a substitute of an income statement and a balance sheet. It is a tool of management for financial analysis and helps in making decisions. The *income statement or profit and loss account* is an explanation of the impact of profit—seeking operations on shareholders' equity. It reports the operating results of the business during a definite accounting period. Although it reflects the operating results of the business, it does not reveal the inflows and outflows of funds of business during a particular period.

Balance Sheet is a statement showing the financial position of a business on a particular date. It reports various resources of a concern and the deployment of these resources in various assets on a particular date. However, balance sheet is distinct from funds flow statement. While funds flow statement is dynamic in nature, balance sheet is a static one as it is prepared at the end of the accounting period showing the financial position on a particular date. Usually, the funds flow statement tells many facts which the balance sheet cannot disclose. Moreover, if balance sheet is the end result of all accounting operations on a given date, funds flow statement is essentially a post balance sheet exercise.

Meaning of the Term Funds

The word 'Funds' has been defined in different senses. However, the term 'Funds' has a special meaning with reference to 'Funds Flow Statement'.

Funds Flow Statement Vs Income Statement

Funds Flow Statement	*Income Statement*
1. It is prepared with the help of income statement and hence it is complementary to income statement.	1. It is not prepared from funds flow statement.
2. It highlights the changes in the financial position of a concern by indicating the sources and applications of funds.	2. It depicts the items of income and expenses and does not reveal the inflows and outflows of funds.
3. It considers both capital and revenue items.	3. It considers only revenue items.
4. It has no prescribed format.	4. It is prepared in a prescribed format.

Funds Flow Statement Vs Balance Sheet

Funds Flow Statement	*Balance Sheet*
1. It is a tool of management in financial analysis and helps in making decisions.	1. It is not much help to management in making decisions.
2. It is dynamic in nature as it is a statement of changes in financial position.	2. It is static in nature as it is a statement of financial position on a given date.
3. It reflects the sources and applications of funds in a particular period of time.	3. It depicts the assets and liabilities at a particular point of time.
4. It is usually prepared after preparing the schedule of working capital.	4. It is prepared after preparing the profit and loss account.

In a *narrow sense*, the term 'Funds' means cash only. A funds flow statement prepared on this basis is known as a cash flow statement as it enumerates the net effect of the various business transactions on cash.

In a *broader sense*, the term 'Funds' refers to money values in whatever form it may exist. Here 'Funds' means all financial resources such as men, material, money, machinery and others used in business.

In *popular sense*, the term 'Funds' means working capital which is also called 'Free' or 'Net Current Assets', i.e., the excess of current assets over current liabilities. Thus 'Funds' in the Funds Flow Statement is what might be termed Working Capital Funds as distinguished from Actual Cash Funds. So *Bierman* rightly holds that Working Capital and Funds will be used interchangeably.

Usually, the analysis based on cash or working capital concept of funds (narrower concept) does not reveal some significant items like purchase of building in exchange of shares or payment of bonus in the form of shares which do not affect cash or working capital. Although this concept fails to reveal the changes in the total financial resources of a business, the concept of funds as working capital is the most popular one. Thus in this chapter the term 'funds' is referred to as working capital and a funds flow statement as sources and applications of funds.

Meaning of Flow of Funds

The term '*Flow*' refers to movement and includes both 'inflow' and 'outflow'. Thus the term 'flow of funds' means the transfer of economic values from one asset of equity to another. Under the working capital concept of funds, the term 'flow of funds' refers to the changes in the funds or working capital by a business transaction. The flow of funds takes place by those transactions which;

(i) Increase the current assets but do not bring any increase in current liabilities and vice-versa.

(ii) Decrease the current assets but do not bring any decrease in current liabilities and vice-versa.

When the effect of a transaction results in the increase of funds, it is known as a source of funds and when it results in the decrease of funds, it is called an application of funds.

When the current assets and current liabilities change in the same direction and by the same quantum, there would be no flow of funds as the working capital remains unchanged. For instance, if creditors are being paid in cash, the total of current assets and that of current liabilities is decreased but the difference between the two is not affected. Similarly, there would be no flow of funds or change of working capital if the transactions do not affect current assets and current liabilities. For instance, the redemption of preference shares through the issue of equity shares will not affect current assets and current liabilities and hence working capital will also remain unchanged implying no flow of funds.

Transactions that do not cause the Flow of Funds

The following transactions do not cause any flow of funds or change in the working capital:

(a) Transactions which represent conversion of one current asset into another current asset.

(b) Transactions which amount to one current liability with another current liability.

(c) Transactions which increase (or decrease) current assets causing a corresponding increase (or decrease) in current liabilities by the same amount.

(d) Transactions which relate to non-current items only, i.e., which neither affect current assets nor current liabilities.

Transactions that cause the Flow of Funds

The following transactions may cause the flow of funds:

(a) Transactions between current assets and fixed assets.

(b) Transactions between current assets and capital and long-term liabilities.

(c) Transactions between current liabilities and fixed assets.

(d) Transactions between current liabilities and capital and long-term liabilities.

Figure 16.1 shows the flow of funds.

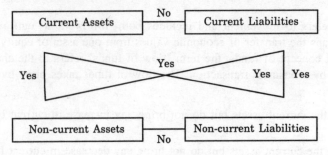

FIGURE 16.1 Flow of Funds.

Procedure for Preparing Funds Flow Statement

The preparation of funds flow statement comprises two parts. They are:

.1. Schedule of Changes in Working Capital, and

2. Statement of Sources and Applications of Funds.

1. Schedule of Changes in Working Capital

The working capital is said to be the excess of current assets over current liabilities. The schedule of changes in working capital is the statement showing the changes of working capital between the two balance sheet dates. It can be prepared with the help of current assets and current liabilities derived from two balance sheets. The changes in current assets and current liabilities and its impact on working capital can be ascertained with the help of the following rules:

   (i) An increase in current assets will increase the working capital.

  (ii) A decrease in current assets will decrease the working capital.

 (iii) An increase in current liabilities will decrease the working capital.

 (iv) A decrease in current liabilities will increase the working capital.

Thus it is clear that the changes in current assets are positively correlated to the changes in the working capital and the changes in current liabilities are inversely related to the changes in the working capital.

A Pro forma of Schedule of Working Capital Changes is shown below:

When the Schedule of Working Capital Changes is prepared only current assets and current liabilities from the Balance Sheet should be taken into account. But additional information relating to these items should be ignored if these are not incorporated into books of accounts.

Moreover, at the time of preparing the schedule, one of the main problems is the recognition of a particular item of asset or liability, i.e., whether a particular asset is an item of current asset and a particular item of liability is an item of current liability. However, the correctness of the schedule depends on the correct diagnosis of a particular asset or liability. Although in most cases, such diagnosis can clearly be made, doubts may arise in respect of certain items which are:

Schedule of Working Capital Changes

	End of the Year		Working Capital Changes	
	Current Year (Rs.)	Previous Year (Rs.)	Increase (Rs.)	Decrease (Rs.)
Current Assets:				
Cash in Hand				
Cash at Bank				
Bill Receivable				
Sundry Debtors				
Temporary Investments				
Stocks/Inventories				
Pre-paid Expenses				
Accrued Incomes				
Total Current Assets				
Current Liabilities:				
Bills Payable				
Sundry Creditors				
Outstanding Expenses				
Bank Overdraft				
Short-term Advances				
Dividends Payable				
Proposed Dividends*				
Provision for Taxation*				
Total Current Liabilities				
Working Capital (CA – CL)				
Net Increase or Decrease in Working Capital				

*May or may not be a current liability.

1. Provision for tax
2. Provision for bad debts
3. Proposed dividend
4. Investments

The above items are discussed in the following pages as these require particular care at the time of preparing a funds flow statement.

ILLUSTRATION 16.1

From the following balance sheets of Bharat Company, prepare a schedule of working capital changes.

	Ending on 31st December	
	1996	*1997*
	Rs.	*Rs.*
Sundry Creditors	70,000	80,000
Sundry Debtors	1,30,000	1,50,000
Bills Receivable	10,000	8,000
Bills Payable	7,000	5,000
Prepaid Expenses	1,000	1,500
Outstanding Expenses	5,000	6,500
Stock	1,80,000	1,70,000
Investment in Govt: Securities	—	30,000

Solution

Schedule of Working Capital Changes

	31st December		Working Capital Changes	
Particulars	1997	1996	Increase	Decrease
Current Assets:				
Sundry Debtors	1,50,000	1,30,000	20,000	—
Bills Receivable	8,000	10,000	—	2,000
Prepaid Expenses	1,500	1,000	500	—
Stock	1,70,000	1,80,000	—	10,000
Investments	30,000	—	30,000	—
Total	3,59,500	3,21,000		
Current Liabilities:				
Sundry Creditors	80,000	70,000	—	10,000
Bills Payable	5,000	7,000	2,000	—
Outstanding Expenses	6,500	5,000	—	1,500
Total	91,500	82,000		
Working Capital (CA – CL)	2,68,000	2,39,000		
Increase in Working Capital			—	29,000
Total			52,500	52,500

ILLUSTRATION 16.2

Prepare a Schedule of Working Capital Changes from the following Balance Sheets of Z Ltd.

	31st Dec. 1997 Rs.	31st Dec. 1996 Rs.
Assets:		
Goodwill	10,000	15,000
Cash	80,000	35,000
Debtors	1,15,000	1,20,000
Closing Stock	1,25,000	92,000
Long-term Investments	30,000	26,000
Preliminary Expenses	6,000	8,000
	3,66,000	2,96,000
Liabilities:		
Bills Payable	10,000	5,000
Sundry Creditors	90,000	80,000
Loans (Payable during 1998)	30,000	—
Share Capital	1,60,000	1,40,000
Profit & Loss Account	76,000	71,000
	3,66,000	2,96,000

Solution

Schedule of Working Capital Changes

Particulars	31st December 1997	31st December 1996	Working Capital Changes Increase	Working Capital Changes Decrease
Current Assets:				
Cash	80,000	35,000	45,000	—
Debtors	1,15,000	1,20,000	—	5,000
Closing Stock	1,25,000	92,000	33,000	—
Total	3,20,000	2,47,000		
Current Liabilities:				
Bills Payable	10,000	5,000	—	5,000
Sundry Creditors	90,000	80,000	—	10,000
Loans (payable during 1998)	30,000	—	—	30,000
Total	1,30,000	85,000		
Working Capital (CA – CL)	1,90,000	1,62,000		
Increase in working Capital				28,000
Total			78,000	78,000

2. *Statement of Sources and Applications of Funds*

Funds flow statement is a statement which represents various sources from which funds are obtained during a particular period and the uses (applications) to which these funds are being put during that period. The different sources and applications of funds are:

Sources (Inflows)	Rs.	Applications (Outflows)	Rs.
Issue of Shares (after adjusting share Premium or Discount on Issue of Shares)	....	Purchase of Fixed Assets/ Investments	....
		Redemption of Preference Shares (after adjusting Premium or Discount)	....
Issue of Debentures (after adjusting Premium or Discount)	....	Redemption of Debentures (after adjusting Premium or Discount)	....
Sale of Fixed Assets/ Investments	....		
Long-term Loans	....	Repayment of any Loan	....
		Payment of Dividend*	....
Trading Profit or Funds from Operation (adjusted)	....	Payment of Tax*	....
Non-Trading Income, etc.	....	Trading loss (adjusted)	....
Decrease in Working Capital (derived from the schedule of Working Capital changes)	....	Increase in Working Capital (derived from the schedule of Working Capital changes)	....
Total		Total	

*Payment of dividend and tax will appear as an application of funds only when these items are appropriations of profits and not current liabilities.

SOURCES OF FUNDS

1. **Issue of Shares:** If there is any increase in the share capital during the year it is an indication of raising of capital during the year. Thus the issue of shares and the calls received from partly paid shares during the year constitute an inflow of funds. In this connection, it should be borne in mind that only the net proceeds (i.e., including the amount of premium or excluding discount, if any) from the issue of share capital shall become the source of funds.

When shares are issued otherwise than in cash, the following rules should be followed:

(a) Issue of shares or making of partly paid shares as fully paid out of the accumulated profits in the form of bonus shares does not amount to inflow of funds.

(b) Issue of shares for consideration such as against purchase of land, machines, etc. (other than current assets) is not a source of funds.

(c) Conversion of debentures into shares is not a source of funds.

In the above three cases, both the amounts do not involve in current assets but involve in non-current assets.

2. **Issue of Debentures and Raising of Loans, etc.:** Issue of debentures or raising of loans, whether secured or not, amounts to source of funds. Here the inflow of funds is the actual proceeds (i.e., including the amount of premium or excluding discount, if any) from the issue of such debentures or raising of loans. However, loans raised for consideration other than a current asset (i.e., for purchase of building) will not constitute a source of funds.

3. **Sale of Fixed Assets/Investments:** When any fixed or non-current asset (i.e., plant and machinery, land and building, furniture and fittings, long-term investments, etc.) is sold, it is an item of source of funds. However, if one fixed asset is exchanged for another fixed asset, it does not amount to an inflow of funds as no current assets are involved.

4. **Trading Profit (i.e., Funds from Operation):** Trading profit or funds from operations is the most regular and significant source of fund. A concern's purchase of fixed asset, payment of dividend, repayment of loans, etc., should depend on this source. In a business, sales lead on inflow of funds as they increase current assets (cash, debtors or bills receivable) but at the same time funds flow out of the business for cost of goods sold along with the other operating expenses. Thus the net effect of the operation will be a source of funds (or inflow of funds) when sales revenue exceeds the cost of goods sold and operating expenses (output flow of funds) during the period and vice versa.

In this connection, it should be borne in mind that funds from operations do not necessarily mean the profits as shown by the profit and loss account of a concern as there are many non-fund items (i.e., depreciation charged to profit and loss account, funds really do not move out of business) and non-operating items (i.e., loss on sale of machinery or payment of dividends) which may have been either debited or credited to profit and loss account.

The example of such items on the debit side of a profit and loss account are: Amortisation of fictitious and intangible assets such as Goodwill, Preliminary expenses and Discount on issue of shares and debentures written off; Appropriation of retained earnings such as Transfers to reserves, etc., Depreciation and depletion; Loss on sale of fixed assets; Payment of dividend, etc.

Trading Profit can be ascertained under the following two methods:

(i) the first method is to prepare the profit and loss account afresh. In this case, only the fund and operational items which involve funds and are related to the normal operations of the business are taken into consideration. Then the balancing figure will be either funds generated from operations or funds lost in operations.

(ii) the second method is to proceed from the figure of net profit or net loss as arrived at from the profit and loss account already prepared.

This method is generally followed in companies. The funds from operation under this method can be calculated as under:

(A) Calculation of Funds from Operations

Closing Balance of P/L A/C or Retained Earning   Rs.
(as given in the balance sheet)

Add: Non-fund and Non-operating items which have been already debited
to P/L A/C:

(i) Depreciation and Depletion

(ii) Amortisation of Ficticious and Intangible Assets such as

    (a) Goodwill

    (b) Patents

    (c) Trade marks

    (d) Preliminary expenses

    (e) Discount on issue of shares, etc.

(iii) Appropriation of Retained Earnings such as

    (a) Transfer to General Reserve

    (b) Dividend Equilisation Fund

    (c) Transfer to Sinking Fund

    (d) Contingency Reserve, etc.

(iv) Loss on Sale of any Non-current (fixed) Assets

(v) Dividends including:

    (a) Interim Dividend

    (b) Proposed Dividend (if it is an appropriation of profit and not taken
    as current liability)

(vi) Provision for Taxation (if it is not taken as current liability)

**(vii) Any other non-fund/non-operating items which have been debited
to P/L A/C.**

Total (A)

Less: Non-fund or Non-operating items which have already been credited
to P/L A/C.

    (i) Profit or Gain from the Sale of Non-current (fixed) Assets.

    (ii) Appropriation in the value of Fixed Assets, such as increase in the
    value of land if it has been credited to P/L A/C.

    (iii) Dividends Received

    (iv) Excess Provision retransferred to P/L A/C or written off.

    (v) Any other Non-operating item which has been credited to P/L A/C.

    (vi) Operating Balance of P/L A/C or Retained Earnings
    (as given in the balance sheet).

Total (B)

Total (A) – Total (B) = Funds generated by operations.

(B) Calculation of Funds from Operation through Adjusted Profit and Loss Account

Adjusted Profit and Loss Account

	Rs.		Rs.
To Write Offs:		By Opening Balance	
Goodwill	....	(of P/L A/C)	....
Preliminary Expenses	....	By Dividend Received	....
Discount on issue of		By Profit on sale of	
Shares/Debentures	....	Fixed Assets	....
Interim Dividend	....	By Funds from Operation	....
Depreciation on Asset	....	(balancing figure in case debit	
Provision for Tax	....	side exceeds credit side)	
Proposed Dividend	....		
Reserve Fund (transfer)			
Loss on sale of Fixed			
Assets, etc.	....		
To Closing balance			
(of P/L A/C)	....		
To Funds lost in Operations			
(balancing figure,	....		
in case credit side			
exceeds the debit side)			

ILLUSTRATION 16.3

From the following information of the AB Company Ltd., calculate funds from operations:

Profit and Loss Account

	Rs.		Rs.
To Expenses:		By Gross Profit	2,30,000
Operation	1,20,000	By Gain on sale of Plant	22,000
Depreciation	50,000		
To Loss on sale of Building	12,000		
To Advertisement Suspense A/C	6,000		
To Discount			
(allowed to customers)	1,000		
To Discount on issue of			
Shares written off	1,000		
To Goodwill	15,000		
To Net Profit	47,000		
	2,52,000		2,52,000

Solution

Calculation of Funds from Operations

		Rs.
Net Profit (as given)		47,000
Add: Non-fund or Non-operating items which have been debited to P/L A/C:		
	Rs.	
Depreciation	50,000	
Loss on sale of Building	12,000	
Advertisement written off	6,000	
Discount on issue of Shares written off	1,000	
Goodwill written off	15,000	84,000
		1,31,000
Less: Non-fund or Non-operating Items which have been credited to P/L A/C:		
Gain on sale of Plant	22,000	22,000
Funds from Operations		1,09,000

Alternatively:

Adjusted Profit and Loss Account

	Rs.		Rs.
To Depreciation	50,000	By Opening balance	....
To Loss on sale of Building	12,000	By Gain on sale of Plant	22,000
To Advertisement Suspense A/C	6,000	By Funds from Operations	
To Discount on issue of Shares	1,000	(balancing figure)	1,09,000
To Goodwill	15,000		
To Closing Balance	47,000		
	1,31,000		1,31,000

ILLUSTRATION 16.4

From the following information of 'Z' Company Ltd. on 31st March, 2000, calculate "Funds From Operations":

(i) Net profit for the year ended 31st March, 2000 Rs. 7,00,000.

(ii) Gain on the sale of building Rs. 40,000.

(iii) Goodwill appears in the books Rs. 2,00,000 out of that 10 per cent has been written off during the year.

(iv) Old machinery worth Rs. 10,000 has been sold for Rs. 8,000 during the year.

(v) Rs. 1,40,000 have been transferred to the General Reserve Fund.

(vi) Depreciation at 10% has been provided during the year on machinery cost Rs. 4,00,000.

Solution

Calculation of Funds from Operations

	Rs.	Rs.
Net Profit for the year (as given)		7,00,000
Add: Non-fund and Non-operating items		
which have been debited to P/L A/C:		
Goodwill written off	20,000	
Loss on sale of Machinery	2,000	
(Rs. 10,000 – 8,000)		
Transfer to General Reserve Fund	1,40,000	
Depreciation at 10% on 4,00,000	40,000	2,02,000
		9,02,000
Less: Non-fund and Non-operating items		
which have been credited to P/L A/C:		
Gain on sale of Building	40,000	40,000
Funds from Operations		8,62,000

Alternatively:

Adjusted Profit and Loss Account

	Rs.		Rs.
To Goodwill	20,000	By Opening Balance	....
To Loss on sale of Machinery	2,000	By Gain on sale of Building	40,000
To Transfer to General		By Funds from Operation	8,62,000
Reserve Fund	1,40,000	(balancing figure)	
To Depreciation	40,000		
To Closing Balance	7,00,000		
	9,02,000		9,02,000

5. **Non-Trading Receipts:** Since the non-trading receipts such as dividend received, refund of tax, rent received are inflow of funds, they should be treated as source of funds. Such incomes need not be included in the funds from operation.

6. **Decrease in Working Capital:** Any decrease of working capital during the current year compared to the previous year constitutes a source of funds.

Applications or Uses of Funds

1. **Purchase of any Non-current or Fixed Asset:** When any fixed asset (i.e., plant and machinery, land and building, furniture and fittings etc.) is acquired or purchased, the same is treated as an *"Application of Funds"*. However, the purchase of fixed asset for a consideration of issue of shares or debentures, or exchange of one fixed asset for another is not an application of funds as it does not involve the outflow of funds.

2. **Redemption of Preference Share Capital:** Any redemption of preference shares during the year is an application of funds as it amounts to an outflow of funds. When the shares are redeemed at premium or discount, the net amount paid (i.e., including premium or excluding discount) should be taken into account. But if shares are redeemed in exchange of some other type of shares or debentures, it is not an outflow of funds as no current asset is involved in this process.

3. **Redemption of Debentures or Repayment of Loans, etc.:** Like the redemption of preference shares, the redemption of debentures or repayment of loans also constitutes an application of funds.

4. **Payment of Dividends and Tax:** The actual payment of dividend (including interim dividend) and tax constitutes an application of funds as it involves outflow of funds. However, the mere declaration of dividend or creating of a provision for taxation does not involve an outflow of funds.

5. **Funds Lost in Operation:** If the result of trading in an accounting year is a loss, it is an application of funds as it amounts to an outflow of funds.

6. **Increase in Working Capital:** The increase of working capital during the current period compared to the previous period is an application of funds as it involves outflow of funds.

Some Important Items

1. Digging out Hidden Information

While preparing a funds flow statement, the non-current assets and non-current liabilities have to be further analysed to find out the hidden information relating to the sale or purchase of non-current assets, issue or redemption of share capital, raising or repayment of long-term loans, transfers to reserves and provisions, etc. By preparing concerned accounts of non-current assets and non-current liabilities, the hidden information can be dug out.

ILLUSTRATION 16.5

Prepare necessary accounts to find out sources/applications of funds from the following extracts of Balance Sheets of AB Company Ltd.

	As on 31st March 1996 Rs.	As on 31st March 1997 Rs.
Equity Share Capital	6,00,000	7,00,000
10% Preference Share Capital	3,00,000	2,50,000

Additional Information

(i) Equity shares were issued during the year against purchase of machinery for Rs. 75,000.

(ii) 10% preference shares worth Rs. 1,50,000 were redeemed during the year.

Solution

Equity Share Capital A/C

	Rs.		Rs.
To Balance c/d	7,00,000	By Balance b/d	6,00,000
		By Machinery A/C	75,000
		By Cash-issue	25,000
		(balancing figure source)	
	7,00,000		7,00,000

10% Preference Share Capital A/C

	Rs.		Rs.
To Cash (application)	1,50,000	By Balance b/d	3,00,000
To Balance c/d	2,50,000	By Cash-issue	1,00,000
		(balancing figure, source)	
	4,00,000		4,00,000

Working Notes:

1. Issue of equity shares against purchase of machinery is neither a source nor an application of funds.

2. Issue of equity shares worth Rs. 25,000 for cash is a source of funds.

3. Redemption of preference shares worth Rs. 1,50,000 is an application of funds.

4. Issue of preference shares of Rs. 1,00,000 is a source of funds.

2. Investments

Investment may be either temporary (short-term) or permanent (long-term). Thus the treatment of investments in funds flow statement depends on their nature. If the investments are temporary in nature, they should be treated as current assets and hence shown in the schedule of changes in Working Capital. On the contrary, if the investments are permanent in nature, they should be treated as fixed assets and hence not shown in the schedule of changes in working capital. In such a case an investment account should be prepared to ascertain the cost of investments purchased or sold during the year and the profit or loss on sale of such investments, if any. Sometimes, the investments are purchased cum-dividend and the pre-acquisition dividend received is credited to profit and loss account.

If there is a profit on sale of such investments and it has been credited to profit and loss account, it should be deducted while ascertaining funds from operation as such a profit is not an operating profit. On the other hand, if there is a loss on sale of such investments and it has been debited to profit and loss account, it should be added back while ascertaining funds from operation as such a loss is not an operating loss. The proceeds realised from the sale of non-current investments is a source of funds and the amount utilised for the purchase of such investments is an application of funds.

ILLUSTRATION 16.6

The extract of a balance sheet of 'XY' company Ltd. reveals that there is an opening balance of trade investments amounting to Rs. 30,000 and a closing balance of Rs. 40,000, Rs. 4,000 by way of dividends have been received during the year including Rs. 1,500 from pre-acquisition profits which have been credited to investments account.

Ascertain the Cost of Investments purchased during the year to be shown as application of funds.

Solution

Investment Account

	Rs.		Rs.
To Balance b/d (Opening balance)	30,000	By Dividend A/C (Pre-acquisition)	1,500
To Cash (Purchase during the year-balancing figure)	11,500	By Balance c/d (Closing Balance)	40,000
	41,500		41,500

Alternatively:

Calculation of Purchase of Investments

	Rs.
Opening Balance	30,000
Less: Dividend being pre-acquisition credited to Investment A/C	1,500
	28,500
Closing Balance	40,000
Purchase of Investments during the year (balancing figure)	11,500

3. Provision for Taxation

The provision for taxation may be treated either as a charge against profit or as an appropriation of profit. If it is treated as a charge against profit, it should be taken simply as a current liability. Hence no adjustment is necessary either in 'profit and loss account' or in the 'statement of sources and applications of funds'. On the other hand, if provision for taxation is treated as an appropriation of profit, the amount of tax which should be provided out of profit is to be debited to 'profit and loss account' and the actual amount of tax which is to be paid is to be shown as an application in the 'Statement of Sources and Applications of Funds'.

However, it is preferable to assume provision for taxation as a current liability as generally it is an immediate obligation of the company to pay it.

In short, the provision for taxation should be treated in the following manner:

1. When the amount of Provision for Taxation is given only in the liabilities side of the Balance sheet.

EXAMPLE 1

Balance Sheet

Liabilities	1996 (Rs.)	1997 (Rs.)
Provision for Taxation	15,000	20,000

Solution

Here, the provision for taxation can be treated in any one of the following two methods:

(a) It is treated as a current liability. Hence, it will be deducted from the total current assets when preparing the schedule of working capital changes.

(b) The amount of provision for the year 1996 (i.e., 1st year) is to be shown as an 'Application of Funds' and the amount of provision for the year 1997 (i.e., 2nd year) is to be recorded in the debit side of the 'Profit and Loss Account'.

2. When the amount of Provision for Taxation is given both in the liabilities side of the Balance Sheet and also in the adjustment by way of additional information.

EXAMPLE 2

Liabilities	1996 (Rs.)	1997 (Rs.)
Provision for Taxation	10,000	15,000

Additional Information

Tax paid during the year Rs. 12,000

Solution

Here, the provision for taxation may be treated as under:

Dr.	Provision for Taxation A/C		Cr.
	Rs.		*Rs.*
To Bank A/C	12,000	By Balance b/d	10,000
To Balance c/d	15,000	By Profit and Loss A/C (Balancing figure)	17,000
	27,000		27,000

Here Rs. 12,000 is to be shown as on 'Application of fund' and Rs. 17,000 is to be recorded in the debit side of 'Profit and Loss Account'.

If provision of tax is given in the problem, in such a case, the amount to be paid is the balancing figure.

Same principle is to be applied for 'Proposed Dividend'.

In the case of 'Interim Dividend', it should appear in the debit side of 'Profit and Loss (Adjusted) Account' and the same will be shown as 'Application of Funds' as it is an item of appropriation of profit.

4. Write offs

The items like goodwill, preliminary expense, discount on issue of shares and debentures, advertisement expense A/C should be written off against profit and loss account (adjusted).

5. Provision for Depreciation

The provision for depreciation may be treated in any one of the following two methods:

(a) It can be considered as a source of funds.

(b) It can be adjusted against Profit and Loss (adjusted) Account for ascertaining the adjusted trading profit.

The second method can be explained here through an illustration.

ILLUSTRATION 16.7

Balance Sheet of AB Company Ltd. (Extracts) as.......

Liabilities	1996 (Rs.)	1997 (Rs.)	Assets (Rs.)	1996 (Rs.)	1997
Provision for Depreciation	70,000	80,000	Fixed Assets	6,00,000	7,00,000

Additional information:

1. A fixed asset costing Rs. 1,20,000 (written down value Rs. 80,000) was sold for Rs. 25,000, the loss being transferred to P/L A/C.

Solution

Dr.		Provision for Depreciation of Fixed Assets A/C		Cr.
	Rs.			Rs.
To Fixed Asset a/c (Dep.)	40,000	By Balance b/d		70,000
To Balance c/d	80,000	By Profit and Loss A/C (Balancing figure)		50,000
	1,20,000			1,20,000

Fixed Assets A/C

	Rs.			Rs.
To Balance b/d	6,00,000	By Provision for Dep. on F.A. A/C		40,000
To Bank A/C – Purchase (Balancing Figure)	2,20,000	By Bank—Sale		25,000
		By P/L A/C—Loss on Sale		55,000
		By Balance c/d		7,00,000
	8,20,000			8,20,000

Where the provision for depreciation is given in the adjustment (i.e., not given in the liabilities side of the B/S or not deducted from the fixed asset from the asset side of the B/S) the treatment will, however, be changed as the fixed assets are given at written down value.

Consider the following illustration:

ILLUSTRATION **16.8**

Balance Sheet of AB Company Ltd. (Extracts) as @.......

Liabilities	1996 (Rs.)	1997 (Rs.)	Assets (Rs.)	1996 (Rs.)	1997
			Land and Building	1,00,000	2,20,000

Additional information:

(i) Accumulated Depreciation

	1996 (Rs.)	1997 (Rs.)
Land and Building	50,000	60,000

(ii) Depreciation charged during the year

Land and Building   Rs. 10,000

Solution

Dr.	Provision for Depreciation on Land and Building A/C		Cr.
	Rs.		*Rs.*
To Balance c/d	60,000	By Balance b/d	50,000
		By Profit and Loss A/C	
		(Dep: for the year)	10,000
	60,000		60,000

Dr.		Land and Building A/C			Cr.
		Rs.			*Rs.*
To Balance b/d			By Balance c/d		
Opening:	1,00,000		Closing:	2,20,000	
Add:			Add:		
Accumulated			Accumulated		
Dep:	50,000	1,50,000	Dep:	60,000	2,80,000
To Bank—Purchase,		1,30,000			
(Balancing Figure)					
		2,80,000			2,80,000

Since the written down value of Land and Building Account is given, in order to ascertain the book value, the accumulated depreciation of the opening and closing balances is to be added with the respective opening and closing balances of the Land and Building Account. And the actual amount of depreciation for the year is adjusted against Provision for Depreciation on Land and Building Account.

6. Profit or Loss on Sale of Fixed Assets

The profit or loss on sale of fixed asset is to be adjusted against Profit and Loss (Adjusted) Account for ascertaining the trading profit. The amount of depreciation should also be considered for this purpose. When there is no provision for depreciation, the amount of depreciation will be adjusted through an entry i.e.,

Profit and Loss A/C Dr.
To Particular Asset A/C

All these cases can be explained through the following illustrations:

ILLUSTRATION 16.9

Where there is no Provision for Depreciation:

Balance Sheet of XY Company Ltd (Extracts) as @ ....

Assets	1996 (Rs.)	1997 (Rs.)
Plant and Machinery A/C	50,000	60,000

Additional Information:

A plant and machinery costing Rs. 30,000
(W.D.V. Rs. 18,000) was sold for Rs. 9,000

Solution

Dr.		Plant and Machinery A/C	Cr.
	Rs.		*Rs.*
To Balance b/d	50,000	By Bank A/C – Sale	9,000
To Bank—Purchase	30,000	By Profit and Loss A/C loss on sale	9,000
		By Profit and Loss A/C Depreciation	12,000
		By Balance c/d	60,000
	80,000		80,000

Loss on Sale = W.D.V. – Selling Price
= 18,000 – 9,000
= Rs. 9,000

The amounts of depreciation on plant and machinery and the loss on sale of plant and machinery should be shown in the debit side of the Profit and Loss (adjusted) Account.

ILLUSTRATION 16.10

Where Provision for Depreciation on Asset Account is maintained:

Balance Sheet of Z Ltd. (Extracts) as @......

Liabilities	1996 (Rs.)	1997 (Rs.)	Assets (Rs.)	1996 (Rs.)	1997 (Rs.)
Provision for Depreciation on Plant and Machinery A/C	1,50,000	2,10,000	Plant and Machinery A/C	5,00,000	7,00,000

Additional Information:

A plant costing Rs. 40,000 (W.D.V. Rs. 24,000) was sold for Rs. 20,000.

Solution

Dr.		Plant and Machinery A/C		Cr.
	Rs.			*Rs.*
To Balance b/d	5,00,000	By Plant and Machinery Disposal A/C		40,000
To Bank – Purchase (Balancing Figure)	2,40,000	By Balance c/d		7,00,000
	7,40,000			7,40,000

Provision for Depreciation Plant and Machinery A/C

	Rs.		*Rs.*
To Disposal of Machinery A/C	16,000	By Balance b/d	1,50,000
To Balance c/d	2,10,000	By Profit and Loss A/C (Balancing Figure)	76,000
	2,26,000		2,26,000

Dr.		Plant and Machinery Disposal A/C		Cr.
	Rs.			*Rs.*
To Plant and Machinery A/C (Balancing Figure)	40,000	By Bank A/C – Sale		20,000
		By Provision for Dep. on Plant and Machinery A/C		16,000
		By Profit and Loss A/C – Loss on Sale		4,000
	40,000			40,000

7. Provision Against Current Asset

Sometimes provisions are to be made against the anticipated losses on current assets. They are provision for bad and doubtful debts, provision for loss on stock etc. These provisions can be treated in any one of the following three methods:

(1) The amount of such provision may directly be deducted from the asset concerned while preparing the schedule of working capital changes (i.e., only net amount is to be shown in the schedule).

(2) The current asset should be shown as its gross amount and the amount of such provision may be added with the current liabilities. Afterwards the same should be deducted from the total current assets while preparing the schedule of working capital changes.

(3) Where excess provision has been created, it may be treated as an appropriation of profits. Thus the same should be added while calculating funds from operation.

However, the amount of excess provision should not be shown in the schedule of working capital changes.

SPECIMEN FUNDS FLOW STATEMENT

The funds flow statement can be prepared in two formats. They are as follows:

(a) Report Form

(b) Account Form or T Form

Specimen Report Form of Funds Flow Statement

Sources of Funds	
Funds from Operations	....
Issue of Share Capital	....
Raising of Long-term loans	....
Receipts from partly Paid Shares, called-up	....
Sales of Non-current (fixed) Assets	....
Non-trading receipts, such as Dividends received	....
Sales of Investments (Long-term)	....
Decrease in Working Capital (as per schedule of Working Capital changes)	....
Total	....
Applications or Uses of Funds	
Funds lost in Operations	....
Redemption of Preference Share Capital	....
Redemption of Debentures	....
Repayment of Long-term Loans	....
Purchase of Non-current (Fixed) Assets	....
Purchase of Long-term Investments	....
Non-trading Payments	....
Payment of Dividends	....
Payment of Tax	....
Increase in Working Capital (as per Schedule of Working Capital Changes)	....
Total	....

Account Form or Self Balancing Type Funds Flow Statement
(For the year ended ....)

Sources	Rs.	Applications	Rs.
Funds from Operations	......	Funds lost in Operations	......
Issue of Share Capital	......	Redemption of Preference Share Capital	......
Issue of Debentures	......	Redemption of Debentures	....
Raising of Long-term Loans	......	Repayment of Long-term Loans	....
Receipts from partly Paid Shares called-up	......	Purchase of Non-current (Fixed) Assets	......
Sales of Non-current (fixed assets)	......	Purchase of Long-term Investments	....
Non-trading receipts such as Dividends	......	Non-trading Payments	....
Sale of Long-term Investments	......	Payment of Dividends	....
Net Decrease in Working Capital	......	Payment of Tax	....
		Net Increase in Working Capital	......
	......		......

Comprehensive Illustrations

ILLUSTRATION **16.11**

Prepare schedule of working capital changes and a statement showing sources and applications of funds from the following Balance Sheets of the 'Z' Company Ltd. for the year ending 31st December 1996 and 31st December 1997.

Liabilities	31st Dec. 1996 (Rs.)	31st Dec. 1997 (Rs.)	Assets	31st Dec. 1996 (Rs.)	31st Dec. 1997 (Rs.)
Share Capital	4,00,000	5,00,000	Plant & Machinery	70,000	80,000
Sundry Creditors	1,50,000	1,20,000	Furniture and Fixtures	90,000	95,000
P/L A/C	20,000	35,000	Stock-in-trade	1,00,000	1,20,000
			Debtors	1,80,000	1,70,000
			Cash	1,30,000	1,90,000
	5,70,000	6,55,000		5,70,000	6,55,000

Solution

Schedule of Working Capital Changes

	31st December 1996 (Rs.)	31st December 1997 (Rs.)	Changes in Working Capital Increase (Rs.)	Changes in Working Capital Decrease (Rs.)
Current Assets:				
Cash	1,30,000	1,90,000	60,000	....
Debtors	1,80,000	1,70,000	....	10,000
Stock-in-trade	1,00,000	1,20,000	20,000	....
	4,10,000	4,80,000		*Continued*

Schedule of Working Capital Changes

	31st December 1996 (Rs.)	31st December 1997 (Rs.)	Changes in Working Capital Increase (Rs.)	Changes in Working Capital Decrease (Rs.)
Current Liabilities:				
Sundry Creditors	1,50,000	1,20,000	30,000	
	1,50,000	1,20,000		
Working Capital	2,60,000	3,60,000		
Increase in Working Capital				1,00,000
			1,10,000	1,10,000

Statement of Sources and Applications of Funds

	Rs.
Source of Funds:	
Issue of Share Capital	1,00,000
Funds from Operations	15,000
	1,15,000
Application of Funds:	
Purchase of Plant & Machinery (80,000 – 70,000)	10,000
Purchase of Furniture and Fixtures (95,000 – 90,000)	5,000
Increase in Working Capital	1,00,000
	1,15,000
Working Notes:	
Funds from Operations: Balance of P/L A/C 1997	35,000
Less Balance of P/L A/C in the beginning of the year	20,000
Funds from Operations	15,000

ILLUSTRATION 16.12

From the following comparative Balance Sheets of 'AB' Ltd. prepare (i) Statement showing the Changes in Working Capital and (ii) Statement of Sources and Applications of Funds.

	31st December 1997 (Rs.)	31st December 1996 (Rs.)
Assets:		
Cash	5,000	3,300
Accounts Receivable	11,000	12,000
Plant & Machinery	7,000	4,500
Stock	9,000	8,000
	32,000	27,800
Liabilities:		
Sundry Creditors	4,000	6,500
Capital	25,000	20,000
Retained Earning	3,000	1,300
	32,000	27,800

Solution

(i) State of Working Capital Changes

Particulars	31st December		Working Capital Changes	
	1997	1996	Increase	Decrease
Current Assets:				
Cash	5,000	3,300	1,700	......
Account Receivable	11,000	12,000	......	1,000
Stock	9,000	8,000	1,000	......
	25,000	23,300		
Current Liabilities:				
Sundry Creditors	4,000	6,500	2,500	......
	4,000	6,500		
Working Capital	21,000	16,800		
Increase in Working Capital				4,200
			5,200	5,200

(ii) Statement of Sources and Applications of Funds

	Rs.	Rs.
Source of Funds:		
Net Profit for the year	1,700	
Issue of further Shares	5,000	
		6,700
Applications of Funds:		
Purchase of Plant & Machinery	2,500	
Increase in Working Capital	4,200	
		6,700

ILLUSTRATION 16.13

The Balance Sheet of 'Z' Ltd., shows the following position:

(Figure in lakhs)

Liabilities	1996 (Rs.)	1997 (Rs.)	Assets	1996 (Rs.)	1997 (Rs.)
Share Capital	100	150	Fixed Assets (Net)	43	45
Reserve and Surplus	25	25	Investments	10	20
Debentures	8	......	Current Assets and		
			Loans, etc.	130	135
Current Liabilities and					
Provisions	50	25			
	183	200		183	200

For the year 1997 the amount of depreciation provided was Rs. 8 lakhs. From the above particulars prepare a Statement of Sources and Applications.

Solution

Schedule of Working Capital Changes (Rs. in lakhs)

Particulars	31st December 1997	31st December 1996	Working Capital Changes Increase	Working Capital Changes Decrease
Current Assets:				
Current Assets, etc.	130	135	5	......
	130	135		
Current Liabilities:	50	25	25	......
	50	25		
Working Capital	80	110		
Increase in Working Capital				30
			30	30

Statement of Sources and Applications of Funds

(Rs. Lakhs)

	Rs.	Rs.
Sources of Funds:		
Issue of Further Shares	50	
Profit from Operations	8	58
Applications of Funds:		
Purchase of Fixed Assets	10	
Purchase of Investments	10	
Redemption of Debentures	8	
Increase in Working Capital	30	58

Working Notes:

(i) Funds from Operations:	*Rs.*	
Profit for the year	Nil	
Add: Depreciation	8	
Funds from Operation	8	

Fixed Asset A/C

	Rs.		Rs.
To Balance b/d	43	By Depreciation	8
To Cash-purchase		By Balance c/d	45
(Balancing figure)	10		
	53		53

ILLUSTRATION 16.14

Prepare a Funds Flow Statement from the following information:

Assets:		1997 (Rs.)		1996 (Rs.)
Cash		10,000		15,000
Debtors		27,000		26,000
Stock		45,000		40,000
Investments		....		6,000
Fixed Assets:				
Cost	90,000		80,000	
Less: Dep:	8,000	82,000	26,250	53,750
Goodwill		....		5,000
		1,64,000		1,45,750
Liabilities:				
Sundry Creditors		34,000		36,000
Short-term Liabilities		16,000		17,500
Accrued Expenses		8,000		7,500
Mortgage		24,000		20,000
Share Capital		65,000		50,000
Retained Earnings		17,000		14,750
		1,64,000		1,45,750

Depreciation provided during the year 1997 amounted to Rs. 2,000 and Goodwill was written off out of retained profits. Dividend paid during the year 1997 amounted to Rs. 4,000.

Solution

Schedule of Working Capital Changes

	31st December		Working Capital Changes	
Particulars	1997 (Rs.)	1996 (Rs.)	Increase (Rs.)	Decrease (Rs.)
Current Assets:				
Cash	10,000	15,000	......	5,000
Debtors	27,000	26,000	1,000	......
Stock	45,000	40,000	5,000	......
	82,000	81,000		
Current Liabilities:				
Sundry Creditors	34,000	36,000	2,000	......
Short-term Liabilities	16,000	17,500	1,500	......
Accrued Expenses	8,000	7,500	......	500
	58,000	61,000		
Working Capital	24,000	20,000		
Increase in Working Capital				4,000
			9,500	9,500

Statement of Sources and Applications of Funds

	Rs.	Rs.
Sources of Funds:		
Profit from Operation	13,250	
Issue of Further Shares	15,000	
Sale of Investments	6,000	
Loan on Mortgage	4,000	
		38,250
Applications of Funds:		
Purchase of Fixed Assets	30,250	
Payment of dividends	4,000	
Increase in Working Capital	4,000	38,250

Working Notes:

Adjusted Profit and Loss Account

	Rs.		Rs.
To Dividend paid	4,000	By Balance b/d	14,750
To Goodwill written off	5,000	By Funds from Operation	
To Depreciation	2,000	(balancing figure)	13,250
To Balance c/d	17,000		
	28,000		28,000

Fixed Asset A/C

	Rs.		Rs.
To Balance b/d	53,750	By Depreciation	2,000
To Cash-Purchase	30,250	By Balance c/d	82,000
(Balancing figure)			
	84,000		84,000

ILLUSTRATION 16.15

From the following summaries of the Balance Sheet of XY Ltd. as at 31st December 1996 and 1997 and additional information, prepare a statement showing sources and applications of funds and a schedule of changes in working capital:

Liabilities	1996 (Rs.)	1997 (Rs.)	Assets	1996 (Rs.)	1997 (Rs.)
Share Capital	2,50,000	3,00,000	Land & Building	2,25,000	2,15,000
General Reserve	55,000	65,000	Plant	1,75,000	1,99,000
Profit and Loss Account	31,000	31,500	Stock	1,10,000	79,000
Bank Loan (Short-term)	80,000	....	Debtors	90,000	69,900
Sundry Creditors	1,60,000	1,40,200	Cash	6,000	8,00
Provision for Taxation	30,000	35,000	Bank	....	8,000
	6,06,000	5,71,700		6,06,000	5,71,700

Additional Information:

(i) Depreciation was written off plant Rs. 15,000 in 1997.

(ii) Dividend of Rs. 22,000 was paid during 1997.

(iii) Income Tax provision made during the year was Rs. 30,000.

(iv) A piece of land has been sold during the year at cost.

Solution

Schedule of Working Capital Changes

Particulars	31st December		Working Capital Changes	
	1997 (Rs.)	1996 (Rs.)	Increase (Rs.)	Decrease (Rs.)
Current Assets:				
Stock	1,10,000	79,000	....	31,000
Debtors	90,000	69,900	....	20,100
Cash	6,000	800	....	5,200
Bank	....	8,000	8,000	....
Total	2,06,000	1,57,700		
Current Liabilities:				
Bank Loan	80,000	....	80,000	....
Sundry Creditors	1,60,000	1,40,200	19,800	....
Total	2,40,000	1,40,200		
Working Capital	(–) 34,000	17,500		
Increase in Working Capital				51,500
			1,07,800	1,07,800

Statement of Sources and Applications of Funds

	Rs.	Rs.
Source of Funds:		
Funds from Operation	77,500	
Issue of Capital	50,000	
Sales of Land & Building	10,000	
		1,37,500
Application of Funds:		
Purchase of Plant	39,000	
Dividend Paid	22,000	
Income-tax paid during 1997	25,000	
Increase in Working Capital	51,500	
		1,37,500

Plant A/C

	Rs.		Rs.
To Balance b/d	1,75,000	By Depreciation	15,000
To Cash-Purchase	39,000	By Balance c/d	1,99,000
(Balancing figure)			
	2,14,000		2,14,000

Provision for Taxation A/C

	Rs.		Rs.
To Cash – Tax paid	25,000	By Balance b/d	30,000
(Balancing figure)		By Adjusted P/L A/C	30,000
To Balance c/d	35,000		
	60,000		60,000

Adjusted Profit and Loss A/C

	Rs.		Rs.
To Transfer to General Reserve	10,000	By Balance b/d	31,000
To Depreciation	15,000	By Funds from Operation	77,500
To Provision for Taxation	30,000		
To Dividend	22,000		
To Balance c/d	31,500		
	1,08,500		1,08,500

ILLUSTRATION 16.16

The following are the summaries of the balance sheets of 'XYZ' Ltd., as at 31st December 1996 and 1997.

	1996 (Rs.)	1997 (Rs.)
Sundry Creditors	40,000	42,000
Bills Payable	34,000	12,000
Bank Overdraft	60,000	....
Provision for Taxation	50,000	60,000
Reserves	50,000	50,000
Profit and Loss Account	40,000	42,000
Share Capital	3,00,000	3,60,000
	5,74,000	5,66,000
Cash	3,000	3,200
Sundry Debtors	85,500	73,000
Sundry Advances	2,350	1,000
Stock	1,21,500	1,07,500
Land and Buildings	1,98,700	1,95,100
Plant & Machinery	1,62,950	1,66,200
Goodwill	....	20,000
	5,74,000	5,66,000

The following additional information is obtained from the general ledger:

1. During the year ended 31st December 1997, an interim dividend of Rs. 30,000 was paid.
2. The assets of another company were purchased for Rs. 60,000 payable in fully paid shares of the company. The assets consisted of stock Rs. 20,000, machinery Rs. 20,000 and goodwill Rs. 20,000 in addition, sundry purchases of plant were made for Rs. 6,000.
3. Income-Tax paid during the year amounted to Rs. 30,000.
4. The net profit for the year before tax was Rs. 72,000.

Prepare a statement showing the sources and applications of funds for the year 1997 and a schedule of working capital changes.

Solution

Schedule of Working Capital Changes

| | 31st December | | Working Capital Changes | |
Particulars	1997 (Rs.)	1996 (Rs.)	Increase (Rs.)	Decrease (Rs.)
Current Assets:				
Cash	3,000	3,200	200	....
Sundry Debtors	85,500	73,000	....	12,500
Sundry Advances	2,350	1,000	....	1,350
Stock	1,21,500	1,07,500	....	14,000
Total	2,12,350	1,84,700		
Current Liabilities:				
Sundry Creditors	40,000	42,000	....	2,000
Bills Payable	34,000	12,000	22,000	....
Bank Overdraft	60,000	....	60,000	....
Total	1,34,000	54,000		
Working Capital (CA – CL)	78,350	1,30,700		
Increase in Working Capital				52,350
			82,200	82,200

Statement of Sources and Applications of Funds

	Amount (Rs.)	Amount (Rs.)
Sources of Funds:		
Issue of Share Capital (Stock)	20,000	
Funds from Operations	98,350	
		1,18,350
Applications of Funds:		
Purchase of Machinery	6,000	
Payment of Dividend	30,000	
Payment of Income Tax	30,000	
Increase in Working Capital	52,350	
		1,18,350

Notes and Assumptions:

(a) Although there is an increase in share capital amounting to Rs. 60,000 only, Rs. 20,000 has been issued against stock (i.e., current asset has been taken as a source). The balance of capital has been issued against purchase of fixed assets, machinery and goodwill. It has neither been taken as a source nor an application.

(b) As Bank Overdraft has not been paid in 1997, it has been assumed as a current liability.

(c) Provision for taxation has not been treated as a current liability.

Share Capital A/C

	Amount (Rs.)		Amount (Rs.)
To Balance c/d	3,60,000	By Balance b/d	3,00,000
		By Stock (Source of Funds)	20,000
		By Machinery	20,000
		By Goodwill	20,000
	3,60,000		3,60,000

Plant & Machinery A/C

	Amount (Rs.)		Amount (Rs.)
To Balance b/d	1,62,950	By Adjusted P/L A/C	22,750
To Share Capital-Purchase	20,000	(Depreciation-Balancing figure)	
To Cash-Purchases	6,000	By Balance c/d	1,66,200
	1,88,950		1,88,950

Land & Building A/C

	Amount (Rs.)		Amount (Rs.)
To Balance b/d	1,98,700	By Adjusted P/L A/C (Depreciation-Balancing figure)	3,600
		By Balance c/d	1,95,100
	1,98,700		1,98,700

Provision for Taxation A/C

	Amount (Rs.)		Amount (Rs.)
To Cash (paid)	30,000	By Balance b/d	50,000
To Balance c/d	60,000	By Adjusted P/L A/C	40,000
	90,000		90,000

Adjusted Profit and Loss A/C

	Amount (Rs.)		Amount (Rs.)
To Depreciation:		By Balance b/d	40,000
Plant & machinery	22,750	By Funds from Operation	
Land & Building	3,600	(Balancing Figure)	98,350
To Provision for Taxation	40,000		
To Dividend	30,000		
To Balance c/d	42,000		
	1,38,350		1,38,350

ILLUSTRATION 16.17

The following was the Balance Sheet of XY Ltd. as on 31st December 1997 and 1996. Prepare a source and application of funds statement with a supporting schedule of working capital changes:

Balance Sheet of XY Ltd.

Liabilities	31st Dec. 1997 (Rs.)	31st Dec. 1996 (Rs.)	Assets	31st Dec. 1997 (Rs.)	31st Dec. 1996 (Rs.)
Bills Payable	15,000	20,000	Cash	56,000	35,000
Bonds Payable	70,000	25,000	Bills Receivable	42,000	50,000
Reserve for Depreciation	19,000	10,000	Inventory	35,000	25,000
on Plant			Plant	1,50,000	1,00,000
Common Stock	1,20,000	1,00,000			
Surplus	59,000	55,000			
	2,83,000	2,10,000		2,83,000	2,10,000

The Surplus Account on 31st December, 1997 was as follows:

Surplus Account

Date	Particulars	Amount (Rs.)	Date	Particulars	Amount (Rs.)
1997 June 20	To Cash dividend	12,000	1997 Jan. 1	By Balance b/d	55,000
December 31	To Balance c/d	59,000		By Net Profit	16,000
				for the year	
		71,000			71,000

A plant expansion of Rs. 50,000 was complete during the year. Depreciation is computed at 6% a year.

Solution

Schedule of Working Capital Changes

Particulars	31st December 1997 (Rs.)	1996 (Rs.)	Working Capital Changes Increase (Rs.)	Decrease (Rs.)
Current Assets:				
Cash	35,000	56,000	21,000	....
Bills Receivable	50,000	42,000	....	8,000
Inventory	25,000	35,000	10,000	....
Total	1,10,000	1,33,000		
Current Liabilities:				
Bills Payable	20,000	15,000	5,000	....
Total	20,000	15,000		
Working Capital (CA – CL)	90,000	1,18,000		
Increase in Working Capital				28,000
			36,000	36,000

Statement of Sources and Applications of Funds

	Rs.	Rs.
Sources of Funds:		
Issue of Bonds Payable	45,000	
Issue of Common Stock (capital)	20,000	
Funds from Operations	25,000	
		90,000
Application of Funds:		
Purchase of Plant	50,000	
Payment of Dividend	12,000	
Increase in Working Capital	28,000	
		90,000

Working Notes:

Bonds Payable A/C

	Rs.		Rs.
To Balance c/d	70,000	By Balance b/d	25,000
		By Cash-Issue (Balancing figure)	45,000
	70,000		70,000

Common Stock A/C

	Rs.		Rs.
To Balance c/d	1,20,000	By Balance b/d	1,00,000
		By Cash-Issue	
		(Balancing figure)	20,000
	1,20,000		1,20,000

Adjusted Profit and Loss A/C

	Rs.		Rs.
To Depreciation on Plant	9,000	By Balance b/d	55,000
To Dividend	12,000	By Funds from Operations	25,000
To Balance c/d	59,000	(Balancing figure)	
	80,000		80,000

— REVIEW QUESTIONS —

1. What is meant by Funds Flow Statement? Explain its uses and objectives.
2. "A Funds Flow Statement is a better substitute for an Income Statement". Discuss.
3. Distinguish between:
   (a) Funds Flow Statement and Income Statement
   (b) Balance Sheet and Funds Flow Statement
4. Explain in detail the procedure of making a Funds Flow Statement.
5. Write Notes on:
   (a) Flow of Funds
   (b) Applications of Funds
   (c) Sources of Funds
6. You are given the following comparative Balance Sheets of XY Ltd:

		31st December	
		1996	1995
Assets:			
Cash		4,700	3,000
Bills Receivable		11,500	12,000
Land		6,600	5,000
Stock		9,000	8,000
		31,800	28,000
Liabilities:		Rs.	Rs.
Bills Payable		4,500	7,000
Capital		25,000	20,000
Retained Earnings		2,300	1,000
		31,800	28,000

You are required to prepare the Schedule of Working Capital Changes.

(**Ans.:** Increase in Working Capital Rs. 4,700)

7. From the following two balance sheets as on 31st December 1995 and 1996, you are required to prepare statement showing flow of funds.

	31st December 1995	1996
Assets:		
Cash	30,000	47,000
Debtors	1,20,000	1,15,000
Stock-in-trade	80,000	90,000
Land	50,000	66,000
	2,80,000	3,18,000
Capital and Liabilities:		
Share Capital	2,00,000	2,50,000
Trade Creditors	70,000	45,000
Retained Earnings	10,000	23,000
	2,80,000	3,18,000

(**Ans.:** Increase in Working Capital Rs. 47,000, Funds from operations Rs. 13,000, Total of Sources and Application of Funds Rs. 63,000 respectively.)

8. The following are the summarised balance sheets of XY Ltd. on 31st December 1995 and 31st December 1996:

Liabilities	1995 Rs.	1996 Rs.	Assets	1995 Rs.	1996 Rs.
Share Capital	6,00,000	8,00,000	Plant &	4,00,000	6,45,000
Debentures	2,00,000	3,00,000	Machinery		
Profit and Loss A/C	1,25,000	2,50,000	(at cost)		
Creditors	1,15,000	90,000	Land & Building	3,00,000	4,00,000
Provision for Bad	6,000	3,000	(at cost)		
and Doubtful Debts			Stock	3,00,000	3,50,000
Provision for Dep:	20,000	24,000	Bank	20,000	40,000
On Land & Building			Preliminary	7,000	6,000
On Plant & Machinery	30,000	35,000	Expenses		
			Debtors	69,000	61,000
	10,96,000	15,02,000		10,96,000	15,02,000

Additional Information:

(a) During the year a part of machinery costing Rs. 70,000 accumulated depreciation thereon Rs. 2,000 was sold for Rs. 6,000.

(b) Dividends of Rs. 50,000 were paid during the year.

You are required to ascertain:

(i) Changes in Working Capital for 1996

(ii) Funds Flow Statement

(**Ans.:** Increase in Working Capital Rs. 90,000, Funds From Operation Rs. 2,49,000; Total of Sources and Applications of Funds Rs. 5,55,000 respectively)

9. From the following extracts of balance sheets of AB Company Ltd., calculate funds from operation:

	31st Dec. 1996	31st Dec. 1997
	Rs.	*Rs.*
Balance of Profit and Loss A/C	1,00,000	1,50,000

Additional Information: *Rs.*

(a) Depreciation charged on assets	10,000
(b) Preliminary expenses written off	5,000
(c) Amount transferred to Dividend Equalisation Fund	15,000
(d) A plant having a book value of Rs. 60,000 was sold for	65,000
(e) Interim dividend paid	10,000

(**Ans.:** Funds from Operations Rs. 85,000)

10. Prepare a Funds Flow Statement from the following particulars:

	1997		1996	
	Rs.		*Rs.*	
Assets:				
Cash	9,000	15,000		
Debtors	27,000	25,000		
Stock	40,000	35,000		
Investments	....	5,000		
Fixed Assets:				
Cost	80,000		70,000	
Less Dep.	7,000	73,000	25,250	44,750
Goodwill		—		5,000
		1,49,000		1,29,000

Liabilities:		
	Rs.	*Rs.*
Trade Creditors	29,000	31,000
Short-term Liabilities	15,000	16,500
Accrued Expenses	8,000	7,500
Mortgage	15,000	10,000
Share Capital	65,000	50,000
Retained Earnings	17,000	14,700
	1,49,000	1,29,750

Depreciation provided during the year 1997 amounted to Rs. 1,750 and Goodwill was written off out of retained profits. Dividend paid during the year 1997 amounted to Rs. 3,500.

(**Ans.:** Increase in Working Capital Rs. 4,000; Profits from operations Rs. 12,500; Purchase of Fixed Assets Rs. 30,000; Total of Sources and Applications of Funds Rs. 37,500 respectively)

11. You have been given the following financial statement of XYZ Ltd. as at 31st December 1996 and 1997.

	31-12-1997 Rs.	31-12-1996 Rs.
Assets:		
Fixed Assets less Depreciation	6,00,000	3,00,000
Investments	10,000	11,250
Stock	1,96,000	1,42,500
Sundry Debtors	1,40,000	90,700
Cash at Bank	45,000	1,30,000
Prepaid Expenses	21,000	14,000
	10,12,000	7,48,450
Liabilities:	Rs.	Rs.
Share Capital (Rs. 100 per share)	2,30,000	1,97,000
Reserves and Surpluses	3,12,000	1,48,000
Bank Loan (Secured)	—	87,000
Sundry Creditors	2,98,000	2,51,450
Provision for Taxation	1,72,000	65,000
	10,12,000	7,48,450

The following further information is available from the records:

(a) The provision in respect of Reserve and Surplus is as under:

	Rs.
Balance on 1-1-1997	1,48,000
Net Profit for the year	1,98,500
	3,46,500
Less Dividend	34,500
	3,12,000

(b) On 31-12-1997 the accumulated depreciation on fixed assets was Rs. 1,80,000 and on 31-12-1996 Rs. 1,60,000. Machinery costing Rs. 20,000 which was half depreciated was discarded and written off in 1997. Depreciation for the year 1997 amounted to Rs. 30,000.

(c) Investment costing Rs. 5,000 was sold during the year 1997 for Rs. 4,800 and Government Securities of the face value of Rs. 4,000 was purchased during the year for Rs. 3,750.

You are required to prepare:

(i) Statement of Sources and Applications of Funds, and
(ii) Statement showing in detail the increase in Net Working Capital.

(**Ans.:** Decrease in Working Capital: Rs. 43,000; Addition of Fixed Assets – Rs. 2,80,000; Total of Sources and Applications of Funds – Rs. 3,14,500 respectively. It has been assumed that the machine has been written off from P/L A/C)

12. From the following balance sheets supplied by Premier Engineering company for the year ended 31-12-1996 and 31-12-1997, prepare a Funds Flow Statement and Schedule of Working Capital Changes.

	1996 Rs.	1997 Rs.		1996 Rs.	1997 Rs.
Equity Share Capital	4,00,000	5,00,000	Fixed Assets	5,00,000	6,00,000
8% Redeemable Pref. Shares	1,00,000	....	Investments	1,30,000	70,000
			Current Assets	3,00,000	4,20,000
General Reserve	....	20,000	Discount on	20,000	10,000
Share Premium	50,000	60,000	issue of Shares		
General Reserve	1,00,000	1,50,000			
Taxation Reserve	70,000	80,000			
Profit and Loss Account	80,000	1,00,000			
Provision for Depreciation	50,000	60,000			
Creditors	80,000	90,000			
Proposed Dividend	20,000	40,000			
	9,50,000	11,00,000		9,50,000	11,00,000

Additional Information:

(a) Investment was sold at a profit of Rs. 20,000, the profit being transferred to capital reserve.

(b) A fixed asset costing Rs. 1,00,000 (written down value Rs. 60,000) was sold for Rs. 20,000, the loss being transferred to Profit and Loss Account.

(c) Preference dividend was paid during the year.

(d) Discount on issue of shares was charged against Share Premium Account.

(e) Proposed Dividend of 1996, together with an Interim Dividend of Rs. 40,000 were paid during the year.

(f) Taxation liability for 1997 comes to Rs. 40,000, the balance being transferred to Share Premium Account.

(g) 8% Preference Shares are redeemed at a premium of 15%, the premium being charged against Share Premium Account, the balance, if any, being charged against General Reserve.

(**Ans.:** Increase in Working Capital Rs. 1,10,000
Income from Operations Rs. 3,33,000; Total of Sources and
Applications of Funds Rs. 5,33,000 respectively.)

17

Cash Flow Analysis

*A cash flow state is a statement of changes in the
financial position of firm on cash basis.*

C O N T E N T S

- Meaning
- Distinction between cash flow statement and funds flow statement
- Procedure for preparing cash flow statement
- Case study
- Review questions

The working capital concept of fund comprises not only cash/bank but also other current assets and current liabilities. Thus a change in working capital (Funds) does not necessarily mean a change in cash/bank. Such a change may be because of change in non-cash current assets and/or in current liabilities. Sometimes, the management of a concern may face the situation of huge profit, sound working capital and inadequate cash/bank position. This leads to the inability of the concern in paying tax and dividends in time. Such a situation may arise due to the fact that cash is not received despite huge profits or cash so received is drained out (used) for some other purposes. As far as management is concerned, this movement of cash has unique significance. Thus the statement prepared with this end in view is known as "Cash Flow Statement" or "Statement of Accounting for Variation in Cash".

MEANING

Cash flow signifies the movements of cash in and out of a business concern. While the inflow of cash is a source of cash, the outflow, of cash is a use of cash. Thus a cash flow statement is a statement of changes in the financial position of firm on cash basis. It summarises the causes of changes in cash position of a business concern between two balance sheet dates and enumerates the net effects of various business transactions on cash.

DISTINCTION BETWEEN CASH FLOW STATEMENT AND FUNDS FLOW STATEMENT

The difference between cash flow statement and funds flow statement are as follows:

1. Cash flow statement is based on a narrower concept of funds, i.e., cash which is only one of the components of working capital. But funds flow statement is based on a wider concept of funds, i.e., working capital.

2. Cash flow statement is based on cash basis of accounting, while funds flow statement is based on accrual basis of accounting.

3. No schedule of working capital changes is prepared in cash flow statement. But in the case of funds flow statement, a schedule of changes in working capital is prepared to show the changes in current assets and current liabilities.

4. Cash flow statement is concerned with changes in cash position only. But funds flow statement is concerned with the changes in working capital between two balance sheet dates.

5. Cash flow statement is prepared with opening balance as starting point and ends with closing balance. But no such opening or closing balance appears in funds flow statement.

6. Cash flow statement is useful for short-term analysis and cash planning. But funds flow statement is useful in planning intermediate and long-term financing.

Utility and Significance of Cash Flow Statement

Being a tool of financial analysis for short-term planning, the cash flow statement possesses the following advantages and utilities:

1. Cash flow statement is highly useful for the evaluation of the cash position of the concern as it is based on the cash basis of accounting.

2. It is highly useful and appropriate for short-term financial planning.

3. It helps the management to evaluate the ability of the concern to meet its obligations such as payment of creditors, repayment of bank loan, payment of interest, taxes and dividends, etc.

4. The trend of a firm's liquidity can be determined with the help of a series of intra-firm and inter-firm cash flow statements.

5. It helps for making appraisal of various capital investment projects just to determine their viability and profitability.

6. It is highly useful to external analysts like bankers for reviewing the financial position of the borrowers.

7. It is used to explain the anomaly of substantial profits and poor cash position.

Limitations of Cash Flow Statement

In spite of a number of uses, cash flow statement suffers from the following drawbacks:

1. Although cash flow statement reveals the inflow and outflow of cash, it excludes the near cash items from cash. This obscures the true reporting of the firm's liquidity position.

2. The term 'cash' cannot be precisely defined. There are controversies over a number of items such as cheques, stamps, postal orders etc., to be included in cash.

3. Cash flow statement is not a substitute for income statement as both of them have separate functions to perform.

4. As working capital is a wider concept of funds, a funds flow statement presents a more complete picture than cash flow statement.

PROCEDURE FOR PREPARING CASH FLOW STATEMENT

Cash flow statement is prepared with the help of financial statement such as balance sheet and profit and loss account and some additional information. It starts with the opening balance of cash and balance at bank. All the inflows of cash are added to the opening balance and the outflows of cash are deducted from the total. Thus the preparation of cash flow statement involves the determination of inflows of cash and outflows of cash.

Sources of Cash Inflows

The following are the main sources of cash inflows:

1. Cash from operation
2. Increase in existing liabilities or creation of new liabilities
3. Reduction in or sale of assets
4. Non-trading receipts.

1. Cash from Operations

Cash from operations is an important source of cash inflow. It is equal to cash sales during a particular period minus cash purchase and cash operating expenses. But its calculation is not so simple as it appears to be. This is so because of certain non-operating expenses or incomes charged to the income statement. However, cash from operations can be ascertained by following any one of the three methods such as:

(a) From Cash Sales

(b) From net Profit/Net Loss and

(c) Cash Operating Profit

(a) From Cash Sales

Cash from operations can be ascertained by deducting cash purchases and cash operating expenses from cash sales. In other words:

Cash from Operations = Cash Sales – (Cash Purchases + Cash Operating Expenses)

Calculation of Cash Sales: The amount of cash sales is ascertained by deducting the amount of credit sales from the amount of total sales. The amount of credit sales during a particular period is equal to the amount of increase in debtors/bills receivable during that period.

Similarly, the decrease in debtors/bills receivables is to be added to total sales. But decrease in debtors/bills receivables may be shown separately as a source of cash inflow.

Calculation of Cash Purchases: The amount of cash purchases is found out by deducting the amount of credit purchases from the amount of total purchases. The amount of credit purchases, which remains unpaid, is known as creditors/bills payables. Thus the amount of credit purchases during a particular period is equal to the amount of increase in creditors/bills payables during the period.

Similarly, the decrease in creditors/bills payables is added to total purchases. But the decrease in creditors/bills payables may be shown separately as use of cash.

Calculation of Cash Operating Expenses: The cash operating expenses can be ascertained by deducting non-cash expenses such as depreciation, writing off goodwill, trademarks and preliminary expenses, and deferred expenditures from total operating expenses. In the absence of any information, all expenses may be assumed to be cash expenses. In case outstanding expenses and pre-paid expenses are shown in the Balance Sheets of two dates, the decrease in outstanding expenses and increase in pre-paid expenses are added to the concerned item of expenditure and the increase in outstanding expenses and the decrease in pre-paid expenses are deducted from the concerned item of expenditure.

Thus cash from operations under this method is:

	Amount
Sales	......
Less: Credit Sales or Increase in accounts receivables	......
Cash Sales	......
Less: Cash Purchases (Purchases – Credit purchases or increase in payables)	......
Less: Cash Operating expenses (after adjusting pre-paid and outstanding expenses)	......
Cash from trading Operations	......

ILLUSTRATION 17.1

From the data given below, calculate cash from operations:

	Rs.
Total Sales	90,000
Debtors at the beginning	7,000
Debtors at the end	11,500
Total Purchases	65,000
Creditors at the beginning	11,000
Creditors at the end	14,500
Total operating expenses	7,000
Pre-paid expenses at the beginning	2,000
Pre-paid expenses at the end	1,200
Outstanding expenses at the end	2,300

Solution

(i)	Cash Sales:			
	Total Sales			90,000
	Less: Increase in Debtors			4,500
				85,500
(ii)	Cash Purchases:			
	Total Purchases			65,000
	Less: Increase in Creditors			3,500
				61,500
(iii)	Cash Operating Expenses:			
	Total Operating Expenses			7,000
	Less: Decrease in Pre-paid Expenses:	800		
	Less: Increase in Outstanding Expenses:	2,300		3,100
				3,900

∴ Cash from Operations = Cash Sales − (Cash Purchases + Cash Operating Expenses)
= 85,500 − (61,500 + 3,900)
= Rs. 20,100

(b) From Net Profit/Net Loss

If the information regarding sales is not available, cash from operations can be ascertained on the basis of net profit. Under this method, all non-cash items of expenses, are added to the net profit and all non-operating incomes shown in the income statement are deducted from net profit.

Moreover, the increase in current assets such as debtors/bills receivables are to be deducted from net profit and the increase in current liabilities such as creditors/bills payables are to be added to net profit. But, the decrease in current assets may not be added to net profit and may be shown separately as source. Similarly, decrease in current liabilities may not be deducted from net profit and may be shown separately as use. Thus cash from operations under this method can be tabulated as follows:

Calculation of Cash from Trading Operations

	Amount
Net Profit as given	
Add: Non-cash and Non-operating items	
Which have already been debited to P/L A/C:	
Depreciation	
Transfer to Reserves	
Transfer to Provisions	
Goodwill written off	
Preliminary Expenses written off	
Other Intangible Assets written off	
Loss on Sale or Disposal of Fixed Assets	
Increase in Account Payable	
Increase in Outstanding Expenses	
Decrease in Pre-paid Expenses·	
Less: Non-cash and Non-operating Items which have already been credited to P/L A/C:	
Increase in Accounts Receivables	
Decrease in Outstanding Expenses	
Increase in Pre-paid Expenses	
Cash from Operations	

ILLUSTRATION 17.2

The net profit of A Ltd for the year 1997 is Rs. 6,000 after debiting inter alia depreciation of Rs. 1,200, loss on sale of furniture Rs. 600 and goodwill Rs. 1,100. The following data are also available:

	1996 Rs.	1997 Rs.
Stock	10,000	11,000
Debtors	14,000	18,000
Creditors	6,000	8,000
Bills Receivables	6,000	9,000
Outstanding Expenses	4,000	6,000
Bills Payable	5,000	3,000
Pre-paid Expenses	1,500	1,000

Calculate Cash from Operations.

Solution

	Rs.
Net Profit for the year	6,000
Add: Non-cash expenses:	
Depreciation	1,200
Loss on sale of furniture	600
Goodwill written off	1,100
	9,900
Add: Decrease in Pre-paid Expenses	500
Increase in Creditors	2,000
Increase in Outstanding Expenses	2,000	4,500
	14,400
Less: Increase in Stock	1,000
Increase in Debtors	4,000
Increase in B/R	3,000
Decrease in B/P	2,000
	10,000
Cash from Operations	4,400

ILLUSTRATION 17.3

From the following information calculate net profit and cash from operations:

	Rs.
Opening Stock	12,000
Purchases	35,000
Sales	60,000
Closing Stock	20,000
Expenses	12,000

Solution

Profit and Loss A/C

	Amount (Rs.)		Amount (Rs.)
To Opening Stock	12,000	By Sales	60,000
To Purchases	35,000	By Closing Stock	20,000
To Gross Profit	33,000		
	80,000		80,000
To Expenses	12,000	By Gross Profit	33,000
To Net Profit	21,000		
	33,000		33,000

Calculation of Cash from Operations

	Rs.
Net profit for the year	21,000
Add: Opening Stock	12,000
	33,000
Less: Closing Stock	20,000
Cash from Operations	13,000

(c) Cash Operating Profit

Under this method of ascertaining cash from operations, the increase or decrease in accounts payable and accounts receivable is not adjusted with net profit or net loss. But it is directly shown in the cash flow statement as an inflow or outflow of cash as the case may be. The cash from operations so ascertained is generally called operating profit.

Calculation of Cash Operating Profit

	Amount
Net Profit (as given) or Closing Balance of Profit and Loss A/C	
Add: Non-cash and Non-operating items which have already been deducted to P/L A/C:	
Depreciation	
Transfer to Reserves and Provisions	
Writing off Intangible Assets	
Outstanding Expenses (Current year)	
Pre-paid Expenses (Previous year)	
Loss on Sale of Fixed Assets	
Dividend paid, etc.	
Less: Non-cash and Non-operating Items which have already been credited to P/L A/C:	
Profit on Sale or Disposal of Fixed Assets	
Non-trading receipts such as dividend received, rent received, etc.	
Re-transfers from Provisions (excess Provisions charged back)	
Outstanding income (current year)	
Pre-received Income (in previous year)	
Opening Balance of P/L A/C	
Cash Operating Profit	

When this method is followed, special care should be given in respect of outstanding and pre-paid expenses.

Outstanding/accrued expenses of the current year are added back while ascertaining cash operating profit as no cash is paid during the year although these expenses are charged to profit and loss account. In case some outstanding expenses of the previous year are also given, these may be assumed to have been paid during the year. Thus these may be shown as an outflow of cash in the cash flow statement.

Pre-paid expenses of the current year should be taken as an outflow of cash in the cash flow statement because these are paid in advance and are not charged to P/L A/C. But pre-paid expenses of the previous year (related to the current year) should be added back while ascertaining cash operating profit as these do not involve outflow of cash in current year but are charged to P/L A/C.

ILLUSTRATION 17.4

From the following information, calculate cash operating profit for the year ended 31st December 1996.

Comparative Balance Sheets

Liabilities	31-12-1995 Rs.	31-12-1996 Rs.	Assets	31-12-1995 Rs.	31-12-1996 Rs.
Equity Capital	1,40,000	1,40,000	Fixed Assets (Net)	90,000	87,000
Reserves	74,000	1,05,000	Cash	75,000	97,000
Sundry Creditors	32,000	35,000	Sundry Debtors	43,000	40,000
Wages Outstanding	3,000	4,000	Inventory	49,000	58,000
Misc. Expenses Outstanding	11,000	3,000	Pre-paid Rent	3,000	5,000
	2,60,000	2,87,000		2,60,000	2,87,000

Accumulated Depreciation was Rs. 16,000 at the end of 1995 and Rs. 19,000 at the end of 1996.

Other Information	Rs.
Sales	3,00,000
Wages	23,000
Misc. Operating Exp.	47,000
Cost of Goods Sold	1,90,000
Rent	6,000
Depreciation	3,000

Solution

Cash Operating Profit:	Rs.
Closing Balance of Reserve (31-12-1996)	1,05,000
Add: Non-cash/Non-operating items:	
Depreciation	3,000
Wages Outstanding (1996)	4,000
Misc. Expenses Outstanding (1996)	3,000
Pre-paid Expenses (1995)	3,000
	1,18,000
Less: Opening Balance of Reserve (31-12-1995)	74,000
	44,000

ILLUSTRATION **17.5**

From the following Balance Sheet and Profit and Loss Account, calculate Cash from operations and Cash Operating Profit by all the three methods.

Balance Sheets

Rs. in lakhs

Liabilities	1996	1997	Assets	1996	1997
Share Capital	140	140	Fixed Assets (net)	100	182
6% Debentures	—	80	Inventories	30	80
Retained Earnings	14	20	Receivables	10	40
Payables	28	78	Pre-paid Expenses	4	8
Outstanding Expenses	2	6	Cash	40	14
	184	324		184	324

Profit and Loss Account (for 1997)

(Rs. In lakhs)

Sales		200
Cost of Goods Sold:		
Purchases	30	
Inventory (Opening)	196	
	226	
Less: Closing Inventory	80	146
Gross Profit		54
Less: Other Expenses:		
General Expenses	30	
Depreciation	16	46
Net Profit		8
Less: Dividend		2
		6
Add: Retained Earnings (1-1-1997)		14
Retained Earnings (31-12-1997)		20

Solution

1. From Sales	(Rs. In lakhs)
Sales	200
Less: Increase in Receivables	30
Cash Sales	170
Less: Operating Expenses:	
Cost of goods sold	146
Add: Increase in Inventories	50

Purchases		196
Less: Increase in Payables		50
		146
General Expenses	30	
Add: Increase in Pre-payments	4	
	34	
Less: Increase in outstanding expenses	4	30
		176
Cash Lost in Operation		6

2. From Net Profit

Net Profit as given		8
Add:		
Depreciation		16
Increase in Payables		50
Increase in Outstanding Expenses		4
		78
Less:		
Increase in Inventories	50	
Increase in Pre-paid Expenses	4	
Increase in Receivables	30	
		84
Cash Lost in operations		6

3. Cash Operating Profit:

Closing Balance of Retained Earnings	20
Add:	
Depreciation	16
Dividend Paid	2
Outstanding Expenses (1997)	6
Pre-paid Expenses (1996)	4
	48
Less:	
Opening Balance of Retained Earnings	14
Cash Operating Profit	34

2. Increase in the Existing Liabilities or Creation of New Liabilities

In case there is an increase in existing liabilities or new liabilities are created, it results in an incoming of cash into the business. The liability may be either long-term liabilities such as equity share capital, preference share capital, debentures, long-term loans, etc., or short-term liabilities such as sundry creditors, bills payables, etc. Incoming of cash may be either actual or notional. While the long-term liabilities result in actual incoming of cash, the short-term liabilities result in inflow of notional cash.

3. Reduction in or Sale of Assets

Whenever a reduction in or sale of any assets (fixed or current) occurs (other than depreciation), there is an incoming of cash into the business. Such incoming may be actual or notional cash. When assets are sold for cash there is an actual incoming of cash. On the other hand, when assets are sold or disposed off on credit, there is notional incoming of cash.

4. Non-Trading Receipts

When non-trading receipts such as dividend received, rent received, refund of tax, etc. are made, there is an incoming of cash into the business. Hence, they should be taken in the cash flow statement.

Applications of Cash or Cash Outflows

1. Cash Lost in Operations
2. Decrease in or Discharge of Liabilities
3. Increase in Purchase of Assets
4. Non-trading payments

1. **Cash Lost in Operations:** When cash sales are less than cash purchases plus cash operating expenses, it is known as cash lost in operations. Such a loss is shown as an outflow of cash in cash flow statement.

2. **Decrease in or Discharge of Liabilities:** When any liability (long-term or short-term) is discharged or decreased, there is an outflow of cash from the business. Such an outflow of cash may be either actual or notional. There is an outflow of actual cash when redeemable preference shares are redeemed and loans are repaid. On the other hand, there is a notional outflow of cash when debentures are redeemed by the issue of shares.

3. **Increase in or Purchase of Assets:** The increase in fixed assets shown in the Balance Sheets of two dates indicates the purchase of fixed assets. Thus the increase or purchase of any asset is an outflow of cash.

4. **Non-Trading Payments:** Since profit from operation is treated as an incoming of cash, the payment of dividend and income-tax should be treated as an item of cash outflow.

Specimen of Cash Flow Statement

Cash flow statement can be prepared either in report form or in 'T' form.

Report Form (Specimen)

	Rs.
Cash Balance in the Beginning	
Add: Cash Inflows:	
Cash Flow from Operations	
Sales of Assets	
Issue of Shares	
Issue of Debentures	
Raising of Loans	
Collection from Debtors	
Non-trading Receipts such as:	
Dividend Received	
Income-tax Refund	
Less: Applications or Outflows of Cash:	
Redemption of Preference Shares	
Redemption of Debentures	
Repayment of Loans	
Purchase of Assets	
Payment of Dividend	
Payment of Taxes	
Cash lost in Operations	
Cash Balance at the end	

T Form (Specimen)

	Rs.		Rs.
Cash balance in the beginning		Outflow of Cash	
Add: Cash Inflows:		Redemption of Preference Shares	
Cash flow from Operation		Redemption of Debentures	
Sales of Assets		Repayment of Loans	
Issue of Shares		Purchase of Assets	
Issue of Debentures		Payment of Dividends	
Raising of Loans		Payment of Tax	
Collection from Debtors		Cash lost in Operations	
Dividends Received		Cash Balance at the end	
Refund of tax			

Some Practical Hints for Preparing Cash Flow Statement:

1. An increase in a liability as a source of cash or cash inflow.

2. A decrease in a liability is an application or outflow of cash.

3. An increase in an asset is an application or outflow of cash.

4. A decrease in an asset is a source or inflow of cash.

Comprehensive Illustrations

ILLUSTRATION 17.6

From the following information of Ramakrishna & Co. Ltd. for the year ended December 31, 1998, prepare a Cash Flow Statement:

Balance Sheet

Liabilities	1997 (Rs.)	1998 (Rs.)	Assets	1997 (Rs.)	1998 (Rs.)
Share Capital	80,000	80,000	Plant and Machinery	60,000	1,01,000
Secured Loans	....	50,000	Stock	15,000	50,000
(Repayable 1999)			Debtors	6,000	21,000
Creditors	15,000	30,000	Cash	20,000	7,000
Tax Payable	1,000	3,000	Pre-paid Expenses	2,000	4,000
P/L A/C	7,000	20,000			
	1,03,000	1,83,000		1,03,000	1,83,000

Profit and Loss Account for the Year ended December 31, 1998

	Rs.		Rs.
To Opening Stock	15,000	By Closing Stock	50,000
To Purchases	1,00,000	By Sales	1,10,000
To Gross Profit	45,000		
	1,60,000		1,60,000
To General Expenses	12,000	By Gross Profit b/d	45,000
To Depreciation	10,000		
To Taxes	5,000		
To Net Profit c/d	18,000		
	45,000		45,000
To Dividend	5,000	By Balance b/d	18,000
To Balance c/d	20,000	By Net Profit b/d	7,000
	25,000		25,000

Solution

Cash Flow Statement
For the year ended 31st, Dec., 1998

Cash Inflows:	Rs.
1. Opening Balance of Cash on 1-1-1998	20,000
2. Loan Raised	50,000
	70,000

Cash Outflows:

1. Purchase of Plant & Machinery		51,000
2. Dividend Paid		5,000
3. Net Cash Lost in operations		7,000
4. Closing Balance of Cash on 31-12-1998		7,000
		70,000

Working Notes:

		Rs.	Rs.
1. Cash from operations:			
Sales		1,10,000	
Less: Increase in Debtors		15,000	
Collection from Sales		95,000	95,000
Less Expenses (operating) :			
Purchases	1,00,000		
Less: Increase in creditors	15,000		
		85,000	
General Expenses		12,000	
Increase in Pre-paid Expenses		2,000	
Taxes	5,000		
Less: Increase in Taxes payable	2,000	3,000	1,02,000
Net Cash lost in Operations			7,000

Taxes of Rs. 5,000 have been assumed to be operating expenses, alternatively if taxes are not an operating expense, it will be added while finding cash from operations and then to be shown as an application.

2. Purchase of Plant and Machinery:		
Opening Balance of Plant and Machinery		60,000
Less: Depreciation		10,000
		50,000
Closing Balance		1,01,000
Purchased during the year		51,000

ILLUSTRATION 17.7

From the following details of AB company Ltd., prepare a Cash Flow Statement.

Liabilities	31-12-96 Rs.	31-12-97 Rs.	Assets	31-12-96 Rs.	31-12-97 Rs.
Share Capital	80,000	85,000	Cash	12,000	10,800
Debentures	15,000	9,000	Debtors	19,900	23,700
Trade Creditors	11,000	12,600	Stock	55,000	48,500
P/L A/C	10,200	10,900	Land	20,300	30,600
Reserve for doubtful debts	1,000	1,100	Goodwill	10,000	5,000
	1,17,200	1,18,600		1,17,200	1,18,600

1. Dividend paid total Rs. 4,000
2. Land was purchased for Rs. 10,300. Amount provided for amortization of goodwill Rs. 5,000.
3. Debenture paid off Rs. 6,000

Solution

Cash Flow Statement

Cash Inflows:	Rs.
1. Cash Balance 1-1-1996	12,000
2. Issue of Share Capital	5,000
3. Increase in Trade Creditors	1,600
4. Cash Inflow from Operations	9,800
5. Decrease in Stock	6,500
	34,900

Cash Outflows:	
1. Purchase of Land	10,300
2. Increase in Debtors	3,800
3. Redemption of Debentures	6,000
4. Dividends paid	4,000
5. Closing Balance of Cash on 31-12-1997	10,800
	34,900

Working Notes:

1. Cash Inflow from operations:

		Rs.
Balance of P/L A/C on 31-12-1997		10,900
Add: Non-fund/Cash and Non-operating Items which have already been debited to P/L A/C:		
Dividend paid		4,000
Goodwill written off		5,000
Reserve for Doubtful Debts		100
		20,000
Less: Opening Balance of P/L A/C and Non-operating Incomes:		
Opening Balance of P/L A/C: (On 31-12-1996)	10,200	10,200
Cash inflow from Operations		9,800

2. Increase in trade creditors should be treated as cash inflows in lieu of purchases and increase in debtors should be treated as cash outflows instead of credit sales.

ILLUSTRATION **17.8**

Balance Sheets of M/s X and Y as on 1st January and 31st December 1998 were as follows:

Liabilities	1-1-1998 Rs.	31-12-1998 Rs.	Assets	1-1-1998 Rs.	31-12-1998 Rs.
Capital	1,25,000	1,53,000	Cash	10,000	7,000
Mrs. Y's Loan	25,000	....	Debtors	30,000	50,000
Loan from Bank	40,000	50,000	Stock	35,000	25,000
Creditors	40,000	44,000	Machinery	80,000	55,000
			Land	40,000	50,000
			Buildings	35,000	60,000
	2,30,000	2,47,000		2,30,000	2,47,000

During the years, a machine costing Rs. 10,000 (total depreciation written off Rs. 3,000) was sold for Rs. 5,000. The provision for depreciation against machinery as on 1-1-1998 was Rs. 25,000 and on 31-12-1998 Rs. 40,000. Net profit for the year 1998 amounted to Rs. 45,000. Prepare a Cash Flow Statement.

Solution

Cash Flow Statement

	Rs.
Cash Inflows:	
1. Opening Balance of cash on 1st January 1998	10,000
2. Loan from Bank	10,000
3. Increase in Sundry Creditors	4,000
4. Decrease in Stock	10,000
5. Sale of Machine	5,000
6. Operating Profit	65,000
	1,04,000
Cash Outflows:	
1. Purchase of Land	10,000
2. Purchase of Building	25,000
3. Increase in Debtors	20,000
4. Mrs. Y's Loan repaid	25,000
5. Drawings	17,000
6. Cash Balance on 31-12-1998	7,000
	1,04,000

Working Notes:

		Rs.
(i)	Operating Profit: (including Non-funds/Cash Items)	
	Net profit for the year as given	45,000
	Add: Non-fund/Cash and Non-operating items:	
	Depreciation on Machinery	18,000
	Loss on sale of Machinery	2,000
		65,000

(ii) Depreciation on Machinery:

Total Depreciation 31-12-1998		40,000
Total Depreciation up to 1-1-1998	25,000	
Less: Depreciation on Machine sold	3,000	22,000
Depreciation for 1998		18,000

(iii) Loss on Sale of Machine

Cost of Machine		10,000
Less Total Depreciation		3,000
		7,000
Less Sale Proceeds		5,000
Loss on Sale		2,000

(iv) Drawings:

Capital on 1-1-1998		1,25,000
Add: Profit for the year		45,000
		1,70,000
Less: Capital at the end of the year		
On 31-12-1998		1,53,000
Drawings		17,000

ILLUSTRATION 17.9

The comparative Balance Sheets of Lalji & Company are as follows:

Liabilities	1997 Rs.	1998 Rs.	Assets	1997 Rs.	1998 Rs.
Share Capital	40,000	50,000	Cash	5,150	4,600
Debentures	10,000	5,000	Book Debts	8,450	9,850
Creditors	5,200	6,000	Stocks	27,600	22,350
Provision for Doubtful Debts	500	600	Land	15,000	28,000
Profit and Loss	5,500	5,700	Goodwill	5,000	2,500
	61,200	67,300		61,200	67,300

Additional information available:

(i) Dividend paid amounted to Rs. 2,000

(ii) Land was purchased for Rs. 13,000 and amount provided for the amortization of goodwill amounted to Rs. 2,500.

(iii) Debentures were paid to the extent of Rs. 5,000.

You are required to prepare a Cash Flow Statement.

Solution

Cash Flow Statement

Cash Inflows:

	Rs.
1. Cash Balance 1-1-1998	5,150
2. Issue of Shares	10,000
3. Cash from Operations	9,450
	24,600

Cash Outflows:

1. Purchase of Land	13,000
2. Payment of Dividend	2,000
3. Repayment of Debentures	5,000
4. Cash Balance 31-12-1998	4,600
	24,600

Working Notes:

Increase in debtors (Rs. 1,400) should be treated as credit sales and similarly increase in creditors (Rs. 800) should be treated as credit purchases. These will be adjusted to profit figure as such:

Cash from operations:	Rs.
P/L A/C 1998	5,700
Less: P/L A/C 1997	5,500
	200
Add: Dividend	2,000
Add: Goodwill written off	2,500
Add: Decrease in Stocks	5,250
Add: Increase in Provision for Doubtful debts	100
Add: Increase in Creditors	800
	10,850
Less: Increase in Debtors	1,400
Cash from operations	9,450

ILLUSTRATION 17.10

The following is the summary of annual accounts of Dures Ltd. for the two years 1997 and 1998:

Comparative Balance Sheets

Liabilities and Capital	1997 Rs.	1998 Rs.	Assets	1997 Rs.	1998 Rs.
Notes Payable	20,000	......	Cash	5,000	3,000
Accounts payable	5,000	8,000	Marketable securities	5,000	7,000
Accrued Taxes	3,000	5,000	A/Cs Receivable	10,000	15,000
Accrued Wages	2,000	2,000	Inventory	12,000	15,000
Long-term Loan	......	15,000	Fixed Asset (Net)	50,000	55,000
Shareholders Fund	60,000	70,000	Other Assets	8,000	5,000
	90,000	1,00,000		90,000	1,00,000

Profit & Loss Account
(for the year ending December 31, 1998)

	Rs.	Rs.
Net Sales		50,000
Expenses:		
Cost of Goods Sold	25,000	
Selling & Administrative Expenses	5,000	
Depreciation	5,000	
Interest	1,000	36,000
Net Profit Before Tax		14,000
Less: Income-tax (50%)		7,000
Net Profit after Tax		7,000
Add: P/L A/C Balance (1-1-1998)		40,000
		47,000
Less: Dividends		3,000
P/L A/C Balance 31-12-1998		44,000

Prepare a Cash Flow Statement.

Solution

DURES Ltd.
Cash Flow Statement

Cash Inflows:	Rs.
1. Cash Balance 1-1-1998	5,000
2. Long-term Loan	15,000
3. Issue of Shares	6,000
4. Sale of Assets (Other)	3,000
5. Cash from operations	14,000
	43,000

Cash Outflows:	
1. Purchase of Fixed Assets	10,000
2. Payment of Dividends	3,000
3. Taxes Paid	5,000
4. Decrease in Notes Payable	20,000
5. Purchase of Securities	2,000
6. Cash Balance on 31-12-1998	3,000
	43,000

Working Notes:

1. Cash from operations:
(a) Cash Sales:

Total Sales	50,000
Less: Increase in Accounts Receivables	5,000
	45,000

(b) Cash Purchases:

Cost of Sales	25,000
Add: Increase in Inventory	3,000
	28,000
Less: Increase in Accounts Payable	3,000
	25,000

(c) Cash Operating Expenses:

Selling & Administration	5,000
Interest	1,000
	6,000

Cash from Operations
= 45,000 − (25,000 + 6,000)
= Rs. 14,000

2. Issue of Shares:

	Rs.	Rs.
Shareholders Fund 31-12-1998	70,000	
Less: P/L A/C Balance 31-12-1998	44,000	
Equity Share Capital 31-12-1998		26,000
Shareholders Funds 31-12-1997	60,000	
Less: P/L A/C Balance 31-12-1997	40,000	
Equity Share Capital 31-12-1997		20,000
		6,000
Further Issue of Shares		55,000

3. Purchase of Fixed Assets:

Fixed Assets (Net) 31-12-1998		
Fixed Assets (Net) 31-12-1997	50,000	
Less: Depreciation for 1998	5,000	
		45,000
Purchases		10,000

4. Taxes Paid:

Amount Paid	7,000
Less: Increase in Accrued Taxes	2,000
Tax Paid	5,000

ILLUSTRATION 17.11

The Balance Sheets of XY Ltd. as at 31st December 1997 and 1998 were as under:

Liabilities and Capital	1997 Rs.	1998 Rs.	Assets	1997 Rs.	1998 Rs.
Share Capital	40,000	40,000	Freehold Property at cost	32,500	34,000
Reserves	22,500	24,000	Plant & Machinery (at cost: less dep:)	14,500	17,500

Continued

Liabilities and Capital	1997 Rs.	1998 Rs.	Assets	1997 Rs.	1998 Rs.
6% Debentures (unsecured)	8,500	8,500	Investment in Shares of companies under the same	16,000	16,000
Mortgage on Freehold Property	3,000	2,000	management (Unquoted) Investment in Shares of	11,250	11,250
Creditors	5,000	5,000	other Companies (quoted)		
Proposed Dividend	2,250	2,325	Stock	5,750	8,000
Provision for tax	2,300	4,000	Debtors	4,500	8,075
Secured Overdraft	2,000	9,000	Bank	1,050	......
	85,550	94,825		85,550	94,825

The following information for the year 1998 is relevant:

		Rs.
(i)	Credit Sales	67,500
(ii)	Credit Purchases	52,000
(iii)	Overheads	8,375
(iv)	Depreciation on Plant & Machinery	1,750
(v)	Dividend for 1997 was paid in full	
(vi)	Amount paid towards Tax for 1997	2,100

You are required to prepare a Cash Flow Statement.

Solution

XY Ltd.
Cash Flow Statement

Cash Inflows:	Rs.
1. Bank Balance 1-1-1998	1,050
2. Cash from Operations	3,550
3. Further Overdraft	7,000
	11,600

Cash Outflows:	Rs.
1. Purchase of Freehold Property	1,500
2. Purchase of Plant etc.	4,750
3. Repayment of Mortgage	1,000
4. Payment of Dividend	2,250
5. Payment of Tax	2,100
6. Cash Balance on 31-12-1998	Nil
	11,600

Working Notes:

1. Cash from operations   *Rs.*

(a) Cash Sales:

Credit Sales	67,500
Less: Increase in Debtors	3,575
Cash Sales	63,925

(b) Cash purchases:

There is no increase in creditors. Thus total purchases (52,000) will be treated as cash purchases.

Cash from Operations = Cash Sales – (Cash Purchases + Overheads)
= 63,925 – (52,000 + 8,375)
= Rs. 3,550

2. Purchase of Plant, etc.

	Rs.	*Rs.*
Book Value 31-12-1998		17,500
Book Value 31-12-1997	14,500	
Less: Depreciation for 1998	1,750	12,750
Purchases		4,750

ILLUSTRATION 17.12

From the following particulars prepare a Cash Flow Statement of Mr. Rama Krishnan.

	1st Jan. 1997 Rs.	31st Dec. 1997 Rs.
Cash	10,000	8,000
Debtors	80,000	90,000
Stock	60,000	50,000
Machinery	1,40,000	1,60,000
Land	60,000	80,000
Building	1,00,000	1,10,000
	4,50,000	4,98,000
Current Liabilities	70,000	80,000
Loan form Mrs. Lekshmi	......	50,000
Bank Loan	80,000	60,000
Capital	3,00,000	3,08,000
	4,50,000	4,98,000

During the year Mr. Rama Krishnan brought an additional capital of Rs. 20,000 and his drawings during the year were Rs. 62,000.

Provision for depreciation on machinery—opening balance Rs. 60,000. Closing balance Rs. 80,000.

No depreciation need be provided for other assets.

Solution

Cash Flow Statement

Cash Inflows:		Rs.
1. Opening Balance of Cash on Jan. 1, 1997		10,000
2. Additional Capital introduced		20,000
3. Decrease in Stock		10,000
4. Increase in Current Liabilities		10,000
5. Loan raised from Mrs. Lekshmi		50,000
6. Cash Operating Profit		70,000
		1,70,000

Cash Outflows:		
1. Purchase of Land		20,000
2. Purchase of Building		10,000
3. Purchase of Machinery		40,000
4. Increase in Debtors		10,000
5. Repayment of Bank Loan		20,000
6. Drawings		62,000
7. Closing Balance of Cash on Dec. 31st 1997		8,000
		1,70,000

Working Notes:

1. Calculation of Profit:		
Capital on 31st Dec. 1997		3,08,000
Add: Drawings		62,000
		3,70,000
Less: Capital on 1st Jan. 1997	3,00,000	
Less: Additional Capital introduced	20,000	3,20,000
Profit		50,000

2. Cash Operating Profit:		
Profit made during the year		50,000
Add: Dep: Charged during the year being Non-cash Item		20,000
Cash Operating Profit		70,000

3. Purchase of Machinery:		
Machinery – 31st Dec. 1997		1,60,000
Machinery – 1st Jan. 1997	1,40,000	
Less: Depreciation (80,000 – 60,000)	20,000	1,20,000
Cash – Purchases		40,000

4. Purchase of Land		
Land – 31st Dec. 1997		80,000
Land – 1st Jan. 1997		60,000
Cash – Purchases		20,000

5. Purchase of Building:		
Building – 31st Dec. 1997		1,10,000
Building – 1st Jan. 1997		1,00,000
Cash – Purchases		10,000

CASE STUDY

Cash Flow Statement of Larsen and Toubro Limited (L&T)

The capital structure and cost of capital of L&T have been analysed in Chapters 5 and 7 respectively. In this section, cash flow statement of L&T is analysed.

A comprehensive cash flow statement is now prepared by most of the listed public limited companies in India. It shows changes in cash flows from operating activities, investment activities and financing activities.

Table 17.1 provides cash flow statement of Larsen and Toubro (L&T) during 2003–04 and 2004–05. The following points may be observed in the light of the analysis of the cash flow statement of L&T.

- L&T utilised Rs. 84.96 crore in 2004–05 in its investment activities. About 45 per cent of these funds were invested in fixed assets (real assets) and 55 per cent in acquiring securities (financial assets) of subsidiary and other companies.

- L&T generated Rs. 353.24 crore cash flow from its operating activities that contributed cent per cent of the company's investment needs.

- L&T raised a net amount of Rs. 188.17 crore from financing activities. In fact, the company issued share capital of Rs. 14.93 crore.

- L&T's net cash flow from its operating, investment and financing activities during 2004–05 was Rs. 456.45 crore. The increase in net cash flow during 2003–04 was Rs. 81.99 crore.

- Overall, L&T's cash flow statement indicates a sound liquidity position.

TABLE 17.1   Cash flow statement of L&T for the year ended March 31, 2005

	2004–05 Rs. crore	2003–04 Rs. crore
A. Cash flow from Operating Activities:		
Net Profit before tax	1405.23	1068.07
Adjustments for:		
Dividend received	(3.69)	(63.75)
Depreciation (including obsolescence), impairment and amortisation	212.20	206.54
Lease Equalisation	38.53	32.22
Unrealised foreign exchange difference net (gain)/loss	(13.11)	(19.62)
Interest (net)	102.10	86.57
(Profit)/Loss on sale of fixed assets (net)	(23.69)	(30 57)
(Profit)/Loss on sale of investments (net)	(385.45)	(12.50)
Employee Stock Option Compensation debited to Profit and Loss Account	16.30	—
Provision/(reversal) for diminution in value of investments	(0.65)	5.32
Gain on disposal of subsidiaries pursuant to Scheme of Arrangement	—	(146.66)
Operating profit before working capital changes	**1347.77**	**1125.62**
Adjustments for:		
(increase)/Decrease in trade and other receivables	(1211 57)	(630.92)
(Increase)/Decrease in inventories	(461.84)	(514.45)

Continued

	2004–05 Rs. crore	2003–04 Rs. crore
(increase)/Decrease in miscellaneous expenditure	7.20	10.76
Increase/(Decrease) in trade payables	981.76	859.06
Cash generated from operations	**663.32**	**850.07**
Direct taxes refund/(Paid) (net)	(310.08)	(165.91)
Net Cash from Operating Activities	**353.24**	**684.16**
B. Cash flow from Investing Activities:		
Purchase of fixed assets (including interest capitalised Rs. 0.28 crore, previous year Rs. 0.80 crore)	(416.98)	(193.48)
Sale of fixed assets (including monies received as advance)	72.89	135.69
Purchase of investments	(5426.97)	(6304.06)
Sale of investments	5768.57	6238.03
Loans/Deposits made with associates and third parties (net)	(150.03)	(8.95)
Advances towards equity commitment	(12.26)	(10.63)
Interest received	41.26	50.87
Distribution received from Associates in the form of dividends/under buyback of equity	11.13	14.94
Dividend received from other investments	3.69	63.75
Cash and cash equivalents acquired pursuant to acquisition of subsidiary	3.68	0.26
Consideration paid on acquisition of a subsidiary company	(2.97)	–
Consideration received on disposal of a subsidiary company	23.03	–
Net Cash (used in)/from Investing Activities	**84.96**	**13.58**
C. Cash flow from Financing Activities:		
Proceeds from issue of share capital	14.93	1.35
Proceeds from long-term borrowings	1636.51	742.43
Repayment of long-term borrowings	(1294.82)	(795.51)
(Repayments)/Proceeds from other borrowings (net)	359.32	(151.46)
Dividends paid	(328.88)	(186.801)
Additional tax on dividend	(55.95)	(23.93)
Interest paid	(142.94)	(174.67)
Net Cash (used in)/from Financing Activities	**188.17**	**588.59**
Net (decrease)/increase in cash and cash equivalents (A + B + C)	**456.45**	**81.99**
Cash and cash equivalents at the beginning of the year	**537.20**	
Less: Transferred pursuant to disposal of subsidiary/demerger of Cement business	3.29	
	533 91	455.21
Cash and cash equivalents at the end of the year	**990.36**	**537.20**

Source: Annual Return

— REVIEW QUESTIONS —

1. What do you mean by Cash Flow Statement? Distinguish between funds flow statement and a cash flow statement?

2. Discuss the uses of preparing cash flow statement. What are its limitations?

3. Discuss the procedure of preparing cash flow statement.

4. Write notes on:
   (a) Cash Flow
   (b) Sources of Cash Inflow
   (c) Cash from Operations

5. From the following information, calculate cash from operations.

	Rs.
Net Profit for the year 1996	80,000
Interest received in advance on 1-1-'96	5,000
Interest received in advance on 31-12-'96	10,000
Expenses outstanding on 1-1-'96	10,000
Expenses outstanding on 31-12-'96	15,000

(Ans.: Cash from operations – Rs. 90,000)

6. From the data given below, calculate cash from operations:

	Rs.
Total Sales	80,000
Debtors at the beginning	6,000
Debtors at the end	11,000
Total Purchases	60,000
Creditors at the beginning	10,000
Creditors at the end	15,000
Total Operating Expenses	6,000
Pre-paid Expenses at the beginning	2,000
Pre-paid Expenses at the end	1,000
Outstanding Expenses at the end	2,000

(Ans.: Cash from operations Rs. 17,000)

7. The net profit of A Ltd for the year 1996 is Rs. 5,500 after debiting interalia depreciation of Rs. 1,000 loss on sale of furniture Rs. 500 and goodwill Rs. 1,000. The following data are also available.

	1995	1996
	Rs.	Rs.
Stock	10,000	12,000
Debtors	15,000	20,000
Creditors	5,000	7,500
Bills Receivables	5,000	8,000
Outstanding Expenses	3,000	5,000
Bills Payable	4,000	2,000
Pre-paid Expenses	1,000	500

Calculate Cash from Operations

(Ans.: Cash from operations Rs. 1,000)

8. Gopal Ltd. has presented the following Balance Sheets as at 31st December, 1995 and 1996.

Liabilities	1995 Rs.	1996 Rs.	Assets	1995 Rs.	1996 Rs.
Share Capital	3,00,000	3,00,000	Building less Dep.	2,50,000	2,40,000
General Reserve	13,250	6,000	Plant less Dep.	45,000	42,500
Sundry Creditors	4,250	2,000	Stock	2,500	500
			Debtors	7,500	5,000
			Cash	12,500	20,000
	3,17,500	3,08,000		3,17,500	3,08,000

Sales made by the company amounted to Rs. 10,92,000 during the year 1996. No dividend has been paid by the company. The changes in Building and Plant value are fully due to depreciation charges for 1996.

Prepare a Cash Flow Statement.·

(**Ans.:** Cash From operations Rs. 5,250; Total of Statement Rs. 22,000)

9. Following are the comparative Balance sheets of Mr. Ramakrishnan

Liabilities	1995 Rs.	1996 Rs.	Assets	1995 Rs.	1996 Rs.
Capital	5,00,000	4,00,000	Building	3,00,000	2,80,000
Creditors	50,000	45,000	Plant & Machinery	1,00,000	70,000
			Stock	80,000	30,000
			Debtors	50,000	55,000
			Cash	20,000	10,000
	5,50,000	4,45,000		5,50,000	4,45,000

Additional information:

(a) There was no purchase or sale of any fixed assets.

(b) There were no drawings

Prepare a Cash Flow Statement.

(**Ans.:** Cash Lost in Operation: Rs. 50,000; Total of Statement Rs. 70,000)

10. The following are the comparative Balance Sheets of ABC Ltd., as on 31st December 1997 and 1998:

Liabilities	1995 Rs.	1996 Rs.	Assets	1995 Rs.	1996 Rs.
Share Capital	3,50,000	3,70,000	Land	1,00,000	1,50,000
(Shares of			Stocks	2,46,000	2,13,500
Rs. 10 each)			Goodwill	50,000	25,000
Profit & Loss A/C	50,400	52,800	Cash and Bank Balance	45,000	39,000
8% Debentures	60,000	30,000	Debtors	71,000	84,500
Creditors	51,600	59,200			
	5,12,000	5,12,000		5,12,000	5,12,000

Other particulars provided to you are: (a) Dividends declared and paid during the year Rs. 17,500 (b) Land was revalued during the year at Rs. 1,50,000 and the profit on revaluation transferred to Profit and Loss account. You are required to prepare a Cash Flow Statement for the year ended 31-12-1998.

(**Ans.:** Cash Lost in operations Rs. 5,100 Cash Flow Statement Total Rs. 1,05,100)

11. Following are the details relating to the business run by Mr. Gopal Sharma.

Balance Sheets (as at 31st December)

Liabilities	1997 Rs.	1998 Rs.	Assets	1997 Rs.	1998 Rs.
Share Capital	70,000	74,000	Cash	9,000	7,800
Debentures	12,000	6,000	Investments	14,900	17,700
Reserve for B/D	700	800	Stock	49,200	42,700
Trade Creditors	10,360	11,840	Land	20,000	30,000
P/L Account	10,040	10,560	Goodwill	10,000	5,000
	1,03,100	1,03,200		1,03,100	1,03,200

In addition you are informed:

 (i) Dividend paid total Rs. 3,500
 (ii) Land was purchased for Rs. 10,000
 (iii) Amount provided for amortization of goodwill Rs. 5,000
 (iv) Debentures paid off Rs. 6,000

Prepare a Cash Flow Statement.

(**Ans.:** Cash from operations Rs. 17,100 (From Net Profit): Total of Statement Rs. 30,100)

12. From the following particulars prepare a Cash Flow Statement of Mr. Ganesh.

	1st Jan. 1998 Rs.	31st Dec. 1998 Rs.
Cash	5,000	4,000
Debtors	40,000	45,000
Stock	30,000	25,000
Land	30,000	40,000
Building	50,000	55,000
Machinery	70,000	80,000
	2,25,000	2,49,000
Current Liabilities	35,000	40,000
Loan from Mrs. Subha	—	25,000
Bank Loan	40,000	30,000
Capital	1,50,000	1,54,000
	2,25,000	2,49,000

During the year Mr. Ganesh brought an additional capital Rs. 10,000 and his drawings during the year were Rs. 31,000.

Provision for depreciation on machinery—opening balance Rs. 30,000, closing balance Rs. 40,000.

No depreciation need be provided for other assets.

(**Ans.:** Cash operating profit Rs. 35,000; Total of Statement Rs. 85,000)

13. From the following information prepare a Cash Flow Statement and Comparative Balance Sheets.

Liabilities	1997 Rs.	1998 Rs.	Assets	1997 Rs.	1998 Rs.
Equity Capital	1,40,000	1,40,000	Fixed Assets (Net)	90,000	87,000
Reserves	74,000	1,05,000	Sundry Debtors	43,000	40,000
Creditors	32,000	35,000	Inventory	49,000	58,000
Wages Outstanding	3,000	4,000	Prepaid Rent	3,000	5,000
Misc. Expenses:			Cash	75,000	97,000
Outstanding	11,000	3,000			
	2,60,000	2,87,000		2,60,000	2,87,000

Accumulated depreciation was Rs. 16,000 at the end of 1997 and Rs. 19,000 at the end of 1998.

Other Information:	Rs.
Sales	3,00,000
Wages	23,000
Misc. Operating Expenses	47,000
Cost of Goods Sold	1,19,000
Rent	6,000
Depreciation	3,000

(**Ans.:** Cash from Operations Rs. 97,000)

14. Following are the summarised Balance Sheets of SreeKrishna Ltd. as on 31-12-1997 and 31-12-1998.

Liabilities	1997 Rs.	1998 Rs.	Assets	1997 Rs.	1998 Rs.
Share Capital	2,00,000	3,00,000	Plant & Machinery	2,00,000	3,00,000
Share Premium	.....	10,000	Land & Building	50,000	1,10,000
8% Debentures	1,00,000	50,000	Investments	10,000	50,000
General Reserve	50,000	80,000	Stock	80,000	60,000
Profit and Loss A/c	50,000	70,000	Debtors	90,000	80,000
Provision for Taxation	30,000	40,000	Cash at Bank	70,000	50,000
Proposed Dividend	20,000	30,000			
Sundry Creditors	50,000	70,000			
	5,00,000	6,50,000		5,00,000	6,50,000

Additional information:

1. Investment costing Rs. 8,000 was sold for Rs. 15,000, the profit being credited to Profit and Loss Account.
2. An interim dividend of Rs. 20,000 was paid during the year.
3. Accumulated Depreciation on:

	1997 Rs.	1998 Rs.
Land and Building	30,000	40,000
Plant & Machinery	40,000	60,000

4. Depreciation charged during the year:

Land and Building	10,000
Plant and Machinery	20,000

5. Debentures were redeemed at par
6. Profit and Loss A/C (balance) 1997

Profit and Loss A/C (balance) 1997	50,000
Add: Profit for the year	40,000
	90,000
Less: Interim Dividend	20,000
	70,000

Prepare a Cash Flow Statement for the year ended 31-12-1998.

(**Ans.:** Total Statement Rs. 3,58,000
Funds from operations Rs. 33,000
Cash Purchase of Machinery Rs. 1,20,000
Cash Purchase of Land and Building Rs. 70,000
Cash purchase of Investment Rs. 48,000)

18

Dividend Policy

*Dividend is a distribution to shareholder out of
profits or reserves available for this purpose.*

— INSTITUTE OF CHARTERED ACCOUNTANTS OF INDIA

*Dividend policy refers to the policy concerning quantum
of profits to be distributed as dividend.*

CONTENTS

- Introduction
- Form of dividend
- Dividend policy
- Dividend theories
- Case study
- Review questions

INTRODUCTION

Dividend policy of the firm is one of the crucial areas of financial management. Its objective should be to maximise shareholders return which consists of two components: dividends and capital gains. Dividend is the share of profits of a company divided amongst its shareholders. It may be defined as divisible profit which is distributed amongst the members of a company in proportion to their shares in such a manner as is prescribed by the Memorandum and Articles of Association of a company.

FORMS OF DIVIDEND

Dividends may be brought into different categories in accordance with the forms in which they are paid. The following are the various forms of dividends.

1. Cash Dividend

Dividend is usually paid in cash. When dividend is paid in cash, it is known as cash dividend. But the payment of dividends in cash involves outflow of funds from the firm. Thus a firm should have enough cash in its bank account when cash dividends are declared. When a firm follows a stable dividend policy, it should prepare a cash budget for the coming period to indicate the necessary funds which would be needed to meet its regular dividend payments. However, the preparation of cash planning in anticipation of dividend needs is relatively difficult if a firm follows an unstable dividend policy.

When cash dividend is paid, both the cash account and the reserves account of the firm will be curtailed. Hence, both the net worth and the total assets of the firm are reduced when the cash dividend is distributed. Moreover, the market price of the share comes down in most cases by the amount of the cash dividend distributed.

2. Stock Dividend (Bonus Shares)

When a firm issues its own shares to the existing shareholders in lieu of or in addition to cash dividend, it is called stock dividend or scrip dividend, in the U.S.A. In India, the payment of stock dividend is popularly termed as "issue of bonus shares". The issue of bonus shares has the effect of increasing the number of outstanding shares of the firm. The shares are distributed proportionately. Hence, a shareholder retains his proportionate ownership of the firm.

For instance, in case a shareholder owns 200 shares at the time when a 10 per cent (i.e., 1:10) bonus issue is made, he will receive 20 additional shares.

The declaration of the bonus shares will enhance the paid-up share capital and curtail the reserve and surplus (retained earnings) of the firm. However, the total networth is not affected by the bonus issue. In fact, a bonus issue represents a recapitalisation of the owner's equity portion, i.e., reserves and surplus. In short, bonus issue is merely an accounting transfer from reserves and surplus to paid-up capital. However, bonus shares cannot be issued in lieu of dividend.

Advantages

The important advantages derived from the issue of bonus shares are as follows:

1. It conserves the company's liquidity as no cash leaves the company.
2. The shareholder who receives a dividend can be converted into cash as and when he wants through selling the additional shares.
3. It broadens the capital base and enhances image of the company.
4. It helps to decline the market price of the shares, rendering the shares more marketable.
5. It is an indication to the prospective investors about the financial soundness of the company.
6. It is one of the best ways of bringing the paid up capital of the company in line with actual capital employed in the business.

7. It is an inexpensive method of raising capital by which the cash resources of the company are preserved.

8. It absolves the liability of the shareholders when bonus is applied for converting partly paid-up shares into fully paid-up.

Disadvantages

1. After bonus issue, there is a sharp fall in the future market price of the share.

2. The rate of dividend in future will come down.

3. Lengthy legal procedures and approvals are involved in the issue of bonus shares.

4. When the conversion of partly paid-up shares into fully paid-up shares is made, the company foregoes cash equivalent to the amount of bonus applied for this purpose.

Guidelines on Bonus Issues

The company shall, while issuing bonus shares, ensure the following guidelines issued by the Securities Exchange Board of India (SEBI) on 11th June, 1992.

1. The bonus issue is made out of free reserves built out of the genuine profits or share premium collected in cash only.

2. Reserves created by revaluation of fixed assets are not capitalised.

3. The development rebate reserve or the investment allowance reserve is considered as free reserve in order to calculate residual reserve test.

4. The residual reserves after the proposed capitalisation shall not be less than 40 per cent of the increased paid-up capital.

5. All contingent liabilities disclosed in the audited accounts which have the bearing on the net profits shall be considered for computing residual reserves.

6. The declaration of bonus issue, in lieu of dividend, is not made.

7. The bonus issue is not made unless the partly-paid shares, if any existing, are made fully paid-up.

8. No bonus issue shall be made within 12 months of any public/right issue.

9. No bonus issue shall be made which will dilute the value or rights of the holders of debentures, convertible fully or partly.

10. Consequent to the issue of bonus shares if the subscribed and paid-up capital exceed the authorised share capital, a resolution shall be passed by the company at its general body meeting for enhancing the authorised capital.

11. There should be a provision in the Articles of Association of the company for capitalisation of reserves, etc., And if not, the company shall pass a resolution at its general body meeting making provisions in the Articles for capitalisation.

12. A company which announces its issue after the approval of the Board of directors should implement the proposals within a period of six months from the date of such approval and shall not have option of changing the decision.

Impact on Balance Sheet, Share Price and EPS

When company issues bonus shares to the shareholders, it receives no money from them. Thus it does not affect the asset side of the Balance Sheet. But on the liability side of the Balance Sheet the reserve is reduced by the amount of the increase in the equity share capital. The enhancement of the number of shares traded will come down the market price of shares and earnings per share (EPS). This can be amplified in the light of the following illustration.

ILLUSTRATION 18.1

The Balance Sheet of XYZ Ltd. as on 31st March, 2001 is given below:

Liabilities	Rs.	Assets	Rs.
Equity Share Capital 2,00,000		Fixed Assets	32,00,000
Shares of 10 each fully paid	20,00,000	Current Assets	18,00,000
General Reserve	30,00,000		
	50,00,000		50,00,000

Net profit after tax is Rs. 18,00,000 during 2000–2001. On 10th April 2001 the company has issued one Bonus share for every two shares held. Draw a revised Balance Sheet after the Bonus issue and also show its impact on EPS.

Solution

XYZ Ltd.
Balance Sheet as at 10th April 2001 (After Bonus Issue)

Liabilities	Rs.	Assets	Rs.
Equity Share Capital 3,00,000		Fixed Assets	32,00,000
Shares of Rs. 10 each fully paid-up	30,00,000	Current Assets	18,00,000
General Reserve	20,00,000		
	50,00,000		50,00,000

$$\text{Calculation of EPS} = \frac{\text{Net Profit After Tax}}{\text{No. of Equity Shares}}$$

$$\text{EPS prior to Bonus Issue} = \frac{\text{Rs. } 18,00,000}{2,00,000 \text{ Shares}}$$

$$= \text{Rs. 9 per share}$$

$$\text{EPS after Bonus Issue} = \frac{\text{Rs. } 18,00,000}{3,00,000 \text{ Equity Shares}}$$

$$= \text{Rs. 6 per Share}$$

The EPS has reduced from Rs. 9 to Rs. 6 per share after the bonus issue.

3. Bond Dividend

In India, bond dividend is not popular. A firm may issue bonds for the amounts due to shareholders by way of dividends if it does not have enough funds to pay dividend in cash. The purpose behind such an issue is the postponement of payment of immediate dividend in cash. Here the bondholders get regular interest on their bonds in addition to the bond money on the due date.

4. Property Dividend

Property dividend is also not popular in India. When a firm pays dividend in the form of assets other than cash, it is called property dividend. The payment of such a dividend may be in the form of a firm's product or in the form of certain assets which are not required by the firm.

5. Interim Dividend

A dividend which is declared before the declaration of the final dividend is called the interim dividend. In other words, interim dividend is a dividend which is declared between two annual general meetings. If the profits of the company appears to be justified for the payment of interim dividend, the Board of directors may from time to time pay to the members such dividends. While deciding to declare an interim dividend, the directors should take into consideration the future prospects of the profits, cash resources etc., of the company.

DIVIDEND POLICY

Dividend policy is the policy concerning the quantum of profits to be distributed as dividend. Usually companies through their Board of Directors evolve a pattern of dividend payment which has a bearing on future action. But most of the companies do not follow this procedure. They simply consider each dividend decision independent of every other decision. This is mainly on account of the fact that the financial manager cannot do anything about it as he works only in an advisory capacity. However, the power to recommend/declare dividends vests completely in the board of directors of the company.

Factors Affecting Dividend Policy

The factors affecting dividend policy are divided into: (i) External factors and (ii) Internal factors.

External Factors

The following are the various external factors affecting dividend policy of the company:

1. **General State of Economy:** The management's decision to retain or distribute earnings of the firm mainly relates to the general state of economy. However, the management may prefer to retain the whole or part of the earnings with a view to building up reserves during:

    (i) uncertain economic and business conditions;

    (ii)   depression (withholding the payment of dividends for maintaining the liquidity position of the firm);

    (iii) prosperity (as there are large investment opportunities); and

    (iv) inflation (to replace worn-out parts).

2. **State of Capital Market:** The extent to which the firm has access to the capital market also affects its dividend policy. A firm can follow a liberal dividend policy if it has an easy access to the capital market on account of its financial strength or favourable conditions prevailing in the capital market. However, a firm is likely to adopt a more conservative dividend policy if it has no easy access to capital market because of its weak financial position or unfavourable conditions in the capital market.

3. **Legal Restrictions:** A firm may also be legally restricted from declaring and paying of dividends. For instance, the Companies Act of 1956 contains several restrictions relating to the declaration and payments of dividends. The following are some of these restrictions.

    (i)   A company is entitled to pay dividend only out of its: (a) current profits, (b) past accumulated profits or (c) money provided by the Central or State Governments for the dividend payments in pursuance of the guarantee given by the Government. However, the dividend payment out of capital is illegal.

    (ii) A company is not entitled to pay dividend unless (a) it has provided for current and all arrears of depreciation, (b) a certain percentage of net profits of that year (as prescribed by the Central Government not exceeding ten per cent) has been transferred to the reserves of the company.

    (iii) A company can use the past accumulated profits for the declaration of dividends only in accordance with the rules framed by the Central Government in this behalf.

Moreover, the Income-tax Act also prescribes certain restrictions about the payment of dividend. The management should consider all the legal restrictions before taking the dividend decision.

4. **Contractual Restrictions:** Restrictions which are imposed by the lenders of the firm are called contractual restrictions. Usually, the lenders of the firm lay down restrictions on dividend payment to protect their interest particularly during the period when the firm is experiencing liquidity or profitability crisis. For instance, it may be provided in the loan agreement that the firm shall not pay dividend to its shareholders more than eight per cent until the loan is repaid or dividend shall not be declared unless the liquidity ratio is found to be more than 1:1.

5. **Tax Policy:** The tax policy followed by the Central Government also affects the dividend policy of the firm. For instance, sometimes the government provides tax incentives to those companies which retain most of their earnings. In such a situation, the management is inclined to retain a larger amount of the firm's earnings.

Internal Factors

Various internal factors which affect the dividend policies of the firm are as follows:

(i) **Desire of the Shareholders:** As the shareholders are technically the owners of the company, their desire cannot be overlooked in spite of the directors liberty of the disposal of firm's earnings.

Usually, shareholders expect returns from their investment in a firm in the form of both capital gains and dividends. Capital gain relates to the profit as a result of the sale of capital investment, i.e., equity shares in the case of shareholders. Dividends are the regular return expected by the shareholders on their investment in a firm. Generally, the desire of the shareholders to get dividends takes priority over the desire to earn capital gains on account of the following reasons.

(a) *Reduce Uncertainty:* Future distribution of earnings is more uncertain than a distribution of current earnings.

(b) *Indicate Strength:* The declaration and payment of cash dividend is a sign of a firm's reasonable strength and health.

(c) *Need for Current Income:* As most of the shareholders are in need of income from the investment to meet their current living expenses, they are generally reluctant to dispose their shares for the purpose of capital gain.

(ii) **Dividend Payout Ratio:** Dividend payout ratio is the percentage share of the net earnings/profits distributed to the shareholders by way of dividends. It involves the decisions either to pay out the earnings or to retain the same for re-investment within the firm. However, the prudent management should give more weightage to the financial needs of the company than the desire of the shareholders. While retained earnings help for the further growth of the firm, the payment of dividend will adversely affect both the owner's wealth and long-term growth of the firm. Thus a firm requires an optimum dividend policy which should maximise the firm's wealth and provide enough funds for the growth in future.

(iii) **Nature of Earnings:** A firm whose income is stable can afford to have a higher dividend pay out ratio than a firm which does not have such stability in its earnings. For instance, public utility concerns which have some monopoly rights, can have a higher dividend pay out ratio than a firm which works under highly competitive conditions.

(iv) **Liquidity Position:** The payment of dividends usually involves cash outflow. Thus sometimes, a firm which has adequate earnings may not have sufficient cash to pay dividends. It is, therefore, the duty of the management to see the liquidity aspect of the firm before and after payment of dividends while taking the dividend decision. In case there is a shortage of cash, the question of payment of dividend does not arise despite the firm's large profit. In this connection, the management should note that in no case can the liquidity ratio be less than 1:1 after the payment of dividends.

(v) **Desire of Control:** The desires of the shareholders or management should also influence the dividend policy of the firm. If a firm issues additional equity shares for raising funds, it will dilute control which is detrimental to the existing equity shareholders. On the other hand, if a firm raises additional funds through long-term loan, it may prove disastrous to the interest of the shareholders in times of financial crisis. Thus in the case of strong desire for control, the management prefers a smaller dividend payout ratio and hence the rate of dividend will be low. However, if the management is strongly in control of the firm (on account of substantial shareholdings or the shares being widely held) it can afford to have a high dividend pay out ratio.

Stability of Dividend

As the equity shareholders prefer stable dividend to fluctuating ones, the dividend policy of the firm should have a degree of stability, i.e., earnings/profits may fluctuate from year to year but not the dividend. Stable dividends relate to the consistency or lack of variability in the streams of dividends payments. In short, it means a regular payment of a certain minimum amount as dividend.

The stability of dividends can be in any of the following three forms:

(i) Constant Dividend per Share

Under this policy, the firm pays a certain fixed amount per share by way of dividends. For instance, a firm may pay a fixed amount of, say, Rs. 10 as dividend per share having a face value of Rs. 30. This fixed sum per share is paid year after year irrespective of the level of earnings of the firm. However, it does not necessarily mean that the amount of dividend will remain fixed for all times in future. When the earning increases, the amount of dividend also increases if the firm can maintain the new level in future. Moreover, there will not be any change in the payment of dividend in the case of temporary increase in earnings. The relationship between earning per share and (EPS) and dividend per share (DPS) can well be understood from Figure 18.1.

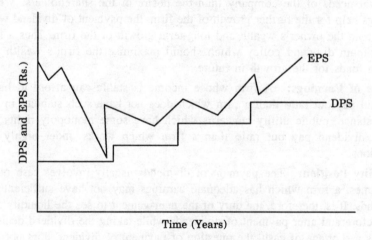

FIGURE 18.1 Stable Dividend Policy per Share.

Figure 18.1 shows that although earnings (EPS) fluctuate from year to year, the dividend per share (DPS) remains constant.

(ii) Constant Percentage

Under this policy, a certain percentage of net earnings/profits is paid year after year as dividend to the shareholders. In the case of constant pay out ratio policy (i.e., constant percentage of net earnings), the amount of dividend fluctuates in direct proportion to the earnings of the firm. As per this policy when the earnings of a firm decrease, the dividend will naturally be low. For instance, if a firm adopts a 50 per cent dividend payout ratio, it indicates that for every one rupee earned by the firm, it will distribute 50 paise among its shareholders.

The relationship between the EPS and DPS under this policy can be understood well from Figure 18.2.

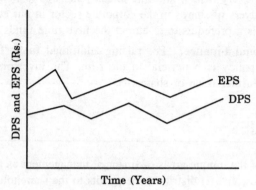

FIGURE 18.2 **Stable Dividend policy under Constant Payout Ratio.**

(iii) Constant Dividend per Share Plus Extra Dividend

Under this policy, fixed dividend per share is paid to the shareholders. But during market prosperity, additional or extra dividend is paid over and above the regular dividend. This extra dividend is waived immediately on the return of normal conditions.

Of the above three dividend policies, the most appropriate policy is the constant dividend per share. This is due to the fact that most investors expect a fixed rate of return from their investment which should gradually go up over a period of time. But in the case of the constant percentage of net earnings policy, the return to the shareholders varies in accordance with the earnings. The management may be in favour of constant percentage policy as it correlates the amount of dividend to the firm's ability to pay dividend. However, the shareholders are against it as it involves uncertainties. But the constant dividend per share plus extra dividend policy is not preferred by the shareholders because of its general uncertainty about the extra dividend.

Significance of Stability of Dividend

A stable dividend policy is advantageous from the point of view of shareholders and the firm on account of the following reasons.

(i) **Expectation of Current Income:** Many investors such as retired persons, widows, etc., consider dividend as a source of income to meet their current living expenses. Such expenses are almost fixed in nature and hence a stable dividend policy should have least inconvenience to these investors.

(ii) **Perception of Stability:** When a firm declares regular dividend, the shareholders usually accept it as a sign of normal operation. However, a decline in the rate of dividend will be considered (by most of the shareholders) as a token of expected trouble in the future. Thus most of the shareholders would like to dispose their shares without further checking. As a result, the market value of the firm's shares will come down. However, such uncertainties can be avoided if the firm follows a stable dividend policy.

(iii) **Requirements of Institutional Investors:** Usually, the shares of the companies are acquired both by individuals and institutions (i.e., financial, educational and social institutions). But every firm would like to sell its shares to financial institutions as they are the largest buyers of shares in the corporate sector in our country. As such, a stable dividend policy is a prerequisite to attract the investible funds of these institutions.

(iv) **Raising Additional Finance:** For raising additional funds from external sources, a stable dividend policy is beneficial to the firm. The investors develop confidence in such a firm for further issue of shares.

DIVIDEND THEORIES

Dividend decision is one of the unique areas of financial management as the firm is to choose one between the two alternatives, viz, (i) distribute the profits to the shareholders as dividend, and (ii) retain profits in the business (i.e., ploughing back of profit). However, if a firm pays dividend in cash, the same will bring down the amount of retention which is also equally essential for the growth and development of a firm. Thus it is required to consider which alternative use is consistent with the object of wealth maximisation. In other words, the net profit of the firm may be used for the payment of dividend if it helps to maximise the owner's wealth. In the opposite case, the firm is advised to retain the said profits for financing various investment opportunities. That is why it is said that there is relationship between dividends and value of the firm which should be carefully considered before any dividend decision. But there are conflicting theories regarding impact of dividend decision on the valuation of a firm. According to one school of thought dividend decision materially affects the shareholders' wealth and the valuation of the firm. On the other hand, according to another school of thought dividend decision does not affect the shareholders' wealth and so also the valuation of the firm.

However, the view-points of the these two schools of thought may be brought under the following two groups:

1. Relevance Concept of Dividend
2. Irrelevance Concept of Dividend

1. Relevance Concept of Dividend

Myron Gordon, James Walter, John Linter and Richardson, among others are associated with the relevance concepts of dividend. According to them, dividend policy of a firm has a direct effect on the position of a firm in a stock market. While the higher dividends enhance the value of stock, the lower dividends reduce its value. This is mainly due to the fact that dividends actually communicate information relating to the profit earning capacity of a firm to the investors. Thus two notable theories, viz, (a) Gordon's Model, and (b) Walter's Model are examined below.

(a) Gordon's Model (Dividend Growth Valuation Model)

Myron Gordon assumes a constant level of growth in dividends in perpetuity. According to him, the dividends of most companies are expected to grow and evaluation of value of shares based on dividend growth is often used in valuation. Gordon's model is based on the following assumptions:

Assumptions

(i) Retained earnings represent the only source of financing.

(ii) Rate of return is constant.

(iii) The firm has perpetual or long life.

(iv) Cost of capital remains constant and is greater than growth rate.

(v) Growth rate of the firm is the product of retention ratio and its rate of return.

(vi) Tax does not exist.

This model implies that when the rate of return is more than the discount rate, the price per share goes up as the dividend ratio comes down and in case the return is less than discount rate it is vice versa. However, the price per share remains constant in case the rate of return and discount rate are equal.

According to Gordon's model, the market value of a share is equal to the present value of an infinite future stream of dividends. The formula is:

$$P_E = \left[\frac{do(1 + g)}{K_E - g)} \right]$$

where

P_E = Market price per share (ex-dividend)

do = Current year dividend

g = Constant annual growth rate of dividends

K_E = Cost of Equity Capital (expected rate of return)

ILLUSTRATION 18.2

XY Ltd. is an established company having its shares quoted in the major stock exchanges. Its share current market price after dividend distributed at the rate of 20% per annum having a paid-up share capital of Rs. 40 lakhs is Rs. 10 each. Annual growth rate in dividend expected is 4%. The expected rate of return on its equity capital is 15%.

Compute the value of XY Ltd's share based on Dividend growth model.

Solution

Dividend distributed during the year = $40,00,000 \times \dfrac{20}{100}$

= Rs. 8,00,000

$$P_E = \left[\frac{do(1+g)}{K_E - g} \right] = \left[\frac{8,00,000(1+0.04)}{0.15-0.04} \right]$$

$$= \left[\frac{8,00,000(1.04)}{0.11} \right] = \frac{8,32,000}{0.11} = Rs.\,75,63,636$$

Say Rs. 75,64,000

$$\text{Value per share} = \frac{75,64,000}{4,00,000} = Rs.\,18.91$$

(b) Walter's Valuation Model

Prof. James E. Walter suggests that dividend policy and investment policy of a firm are interlinked and hence the dividend decision always affects the value of a firm. His proposition clearly states the relationship between the firm's internal rate of return (i.e., Ra) and its cost of capital (i.e., Rc). In short, in case the firm's return on investment is more than the cost of capital, it must retain its earnings and otherwise it should distribute its earnings to the shareholders. Thus Walter's model implies that:

(a) The optimal payout ratio (i.e. *D/P*) for a growth firm (i.e., Ra > Rc) is nil. A firm is said to be a growth firm when it has adequate profitable investment opportunities.

(b) The optimal payout ratio (i.e., *D/P*) for a normal firm (i.e., Ra = Rc) is irrelevant. A firm is said to be normal when its dividend policy does not affect the market price of a share.

(c) The optimal payout ratio (i.e. *D/P*) for a declining firm (i.e., Ra < Rc) is 100%. A firm is said to be a declining firm when it does not have profitable investment opportunities to invest its earnings.

Assumptions

Walter's model is based on the following assumptions:

(i) All financing is done through retained earnings and external sources of funds like debt or new equity capital are not used.

(ii) The firm has an infinite life and is a going concern.

(iii) It assumes that the internal rate of return (Ra) and cost of capital (Rc) are constant.

(iv) All earnings are either distributed as dividend or invested internally at once.

(v) There is no change in the key variables such as EPS and DPS.

Prof. Walter has evolved a mathematical formula with a view to arriving at the appropriate dividend decision, to find out the expected market price of a share which is given below:

$$P = \frac{\left[D + \dfrac{Ra}{Rc}(E - D) \right]}{Rc}$$

where

P = Market price of equity share
D = Dividend per share
E = Earnings per share
$(E - D)$ = Retained earnings per share
Ra = Internal rate of return on investment
Rc = Cost of capital

In case Ra is more than 1, lower dividend should maximise the value per share and vice versa.

Criticisms

Since some of the assumptions made in Walter's model are unrealistic in real world situations, it is subject to the following criticisms:

(i) Walter assumes that the financial needs of a firm are met only by retained earnings and not by external financing. However, it is seldom true in real world situations. Whenever, a firm is in need of additional funds, it usually raises funds by new equity shares or debentures.

(ii) Walter also assumes that the firm's internal rate of return remains constant. This assumption does not hold good. Because, when more investment proposals are taken, Ra also generally comes down.

(iii) The model also assumes that the cost of capital, i.e., Rc remains constant. This assumption does not hold good in the real world situation. Because, if the risk pattern of a firm changes, there is a corresponding change in the cost of capital.

ILLUSTRATION 18.3

Compute the market price of XY Ltd's share under Walter's Model.

Earnings per Share	Rs. 5
Dividend per Share	Rs. 3
Cost of Capital	15%
Internal Rate of Return	16%

Solution

Walter's formula:

$$P = \frac{D + \dfrac{Ra}{Rc}(E - D)}{Rc}$$

$$= \frac{3 + \dfrac{0.16}{0.15}(5 - 3)}{0.15} = Rs.\ 34.22$$

ILLUSTRATION **18.4**

The earnings per share of AB company Ltd. is Rs. 10 and the rate of capitalisation applicable is 12%. The company has before it an option of adopting (i) 50% , (ii) 75% and (iii) 100% dividend payout ratio. Calculate the market price of the company's quoted shares as per Walter's Model if it can earn a return of (i) 20%, (ii) 16%, and (iii) 12% on its retained earnings.

Solution

Walter's formula:

$$P = \frac{D + \dfrac{Ra}{Rc}(E - D)}{Rc}$$

where

P = Market price per Share
D = Dividend per Share
Ra = Internal Rate of Return on Investment
Rc = Cost of Capital, i.e., 12% or 0.12
E = Earnings per Share i.e., Rs. 10

Now, Market price per share based on various IRRs and dividend payout ratios can be computed.

(i) Market price per share when Ra = 20%

   (a) When dividend payout ratio is 50%
       Dividend paid = 10 × 50/100 = Rs. 5

       $$P = \frac{5 + \dfrac{0.20}{0.12}(10 - 5)}{0.12} = \text{Rs. } 111$$

   (b) When dividend payout is 75%
       Dividend paid = 10 × (75/100) = Rs. 7.5

       $$P = \frac{7.5 + \dfrac{0.20}{0.12}(10 - 7.5)}{0.12} = \text{Rs. } 97$$

   (c) When dividend payout is 100%
       Dividend paid = Rs. 10

       $$P = \frac{10 + \dfrac{0.20}{0.12}(10 - 10)}{0.12} = \text{Rs. } 97$$

(ii) Market price per share when Ra = 16%

   (a) When dividend payout ratio is 50%
       Dividend paid = 10 × (50/100) = Rs. 5

       $$P = \frac{5 + \dfrac{0.16}{0.12}(10 - 5)}{0.12} = \text{Rs. } 97$$

(b) When dividend payout ratio is 75%

Dividend paid = 10 × (75/100) = Rs. 7.5

$$P = \frac{7.5 + \frac{0.16}{0.12}(10 - 7.5)}{0.12} = \text{Rs. } 90$$

(c) When dividend payout ratio is 100%

Dividend paid = 10

$$P = \frac{10 + \frac{0.16}{0.12}(10 - 10)}{0.12} = \text{Rs. } 94$$

(iii) Market price per share when Ra = 12%

(a) When dividend payout ratio is 50%

Dividend paid = 10 × (50/100) = Rs. 5

$$P = \frac{5 + \frac{0.16}{0.12}(10 - 5)}{0.12} = \text{Rs. } 83$$

(b) When dividend payout ratio is 75%

Dividend paid = 10 × (75/100) = Rs. 7.5

$$P = \frac{7.5 + \frac{0.12}{0.12}(10 - 7.5)}{0.12} = \text{Rs. } 83$$

(c) When dividend payout ratio is 100%

Dividend paid = Rs. 10

$$P = \frac{10 + \frac{0.12}{0.12}(10 - 10)}{0.12} = \text{Rs. } 91.66$$

Rs. 92 (approx.)

2. Irrelevance Concept of Dividend

This concept is associated with Franco Modigliani and Morton H. Miller and E. Solomon. According to them, dividend policy has no effect on the share prices of a company and, as such, it has no significance. In their opinion, investors do not differentiate between dividends and capital gains. Their ultimate desire is to earn higher return on their investment. Usually, the investors would be content with the company returning the earnings if it has adequate investment opportunities which yields a higher rate of return than the cost of retained earnings. However, in the opposite case, the investors would prefer to receive the earnings (i.e., dividends). Hence, the dividend decision is nothing but a financing decision, i.e., whether to finance the company's financial needs by retained earnings or not. If the company has profitable investment opportunities, it will retain the earnings for investment purposes, otherwise, distribute them. However, the shareholders are only interested in income whether it is in the form of dividend or in capital gains.

Modigliani-Miller (M-M) Hypothesis

The irrelevance concept of dividend is provided by Modigliani and Miller in a comprehensive manner. They argue that a firm's dividend policy has no effect on its value of assets. For instance, in case the rate of dividend declared by a company is less, its retained earnings will increase and also its net worth and vice versa. They have also argued that the value of shares of a firm is determined by its earning potentiality and investment policy and never by the pattern of income distribution. Thus the value of the firm is unaffected by dividend policy, i.e., dividends are irrelevant to shareholders wealth. They build their arguments on the basis of the following assumptions:

1. Capital markets are perfect.
2. There are no personal or corporate income taxes.
3. The firm's capital investment policy is independent of its dividend policy.
4. Investors behave rationally. They freely get information and there are no floatation and transaction costs.
5. Dividend policy has no effect on the firm's cost of equity.
6. Risk or uncertainty does not exist.

The crux of M-M hypothesis is that the value of the firm is determined by its basic earnings and its risk class. Thus the firm's value depends on its asset investment policy rather than on how earnings are split between dividends and retained earnings.

Proof for M-M Hypothesis

In accordance with the M-M hypothesis, the market value of a share in the beginning of the period is equal to the present value of dividends paid at the end of the period plus the market price of the share at the end of the period. Thus the market price of a share after dividend declared is computed by applying the following formula.

$$P_0 = \frac{P_1 + D_1}{1 + K_e}$$

where

P_0 = Prevailing Market Price of a Share
K_e = Cost of Equity Capital
D_1 = Dividend to be received at the end of period one
P_1 = Market Price of a Share at the end of period one

From the above equation, the following equation can be derived for ascertaining the value of P_1.

$$P_1 = P_0(1 + K_e) - D_1$$

The number of new shares to be issued to implement the new project is determined with the help of the following formula.

$$\Delta N = \frac{I - (E - nD_1)}{P_1}$$

n = Number of Shares outstanding at the beginning of the period

ΔN = Change in the number of Shares outstanding during the period (i.e., No. of new shares to be issued)

I = Total Investment amount required for Capital Budget

E = Earnings of Net Income of the firm during the period.

ILLUSTRATION 18.5

Z Ltd. belongs to a risk class of which the appropriate capitalisation rate is 12%. It currently has 90,000 shares selling at Rs. 100 each. The company is contemplating declaration of a dividend of Rs.5 per share at the end of the current fiscal year which has just begun. Answer the following questions based on Modigliani and Miller Model and assumption of no taxes.

(i)   What will be the price of the shares at the end of the year if a dividend is not declared?

(ii) What will be the price if dividend is declared?

(iii) Assuming that the company pays dividend, has net income of Rs. 12 lakhs and makes a new investment of Rs. 25 lakhs during the period, how many new shares should be issued?

Solution

$$P_0 = \frac{P_1 + D_1}{1 + K_e}$$

where

P_1 = Market price of a Share at the year end (to be determined)

D_1 = Contemplated Dividend per Share, i.e., Rs. 5

P_0 = Existing Market Price of Share, i.e., Rs. 100

K_e = Cost of Equity Capital or Rate of Capitalisation, i.e., 12% or 0.12

(i)   If dividend is not declared

$$P_0 = \frac{P_1 + D_1}{1 + K_e}$$

$$100 = \frac{P_1 + 0}{1 + 0.12}$$

$$100 = \frac{P_1}{1.12}$$

$$100 \times 1.12 = P_1$$

$$P_1 = \text{Rs. } 112$$

(ii) If dividend is declared

$$P_0 = \frac{P_1 + D_1}{1 + K_e}$$

$$100 = \frac{P_1 + 5}{1 + 0.12}$$

$$100 = \frac{P_1 + 5}{1.12}$$

$$100 \times 1.12 = P_1 + 5$$

$$112 = P_1 + 5$$

$$P_1 = 112 - 5$$

$$P_1 = \text{Rs. } 107$$

(iii) Calculation of No. of shares to be issued

Particulars	Dividend Declared	Dividend not Declared
Net Income	12,00,000	12,00,000
Less: Dividends paid	4,50,000	
Retained earnings	7,50,000	12,00,000
New investments	25,00,000	25,00,000
Amounts to be raised by Issue of new Shares (A)	17,50,000	13,00,000
Market price per Share (B)	Rs. 107	Rs. 112
New Shares to be issued (C) (A)/(B)	16,355	11,607

Alternatively, the number of new shares to be issued is calculated as follows:

$$\Delta N = \frac{I - (E - nD_1)}{P_1}$$

where,

n = No. of shares outstanding at the beginning of the period, i.e., 90,000 shares

ΔN = Change in the number of shares outstanding during the period (to be computed)

I = Total investment required for capital budget, i.e., Rs. 25,00,000

E = Earnings of the firm during the period after payment of dividend

If Dividend is declared   = Rs. 12,00,000 − 4,50,000

                          = Rs. 7,50,000

If no Dividend is declared = Rs. 12,00,000

Now, the number of new shares to be issued can be computed:

(i) If dividend is declared

$$\Delta N = \frac{25,00,000 - 7,50,000}{107} = 16,355 \text{ shares}$$

(ii) If no dividend is declared

$$\Delta N = \frac{25,00,000 - 12,00,000}{112} = 11,607 \text{ shares}$$

Verification of M-M Dividend Irrelevancy Theory

Particulars		If dividend is declared	If dividend is not declared
Existing Shares		90,000	90,000
New Shares issued		16,355	11,607
Total no. of Shares at the year end	(i)	1,06,355	1,01,607
Market price per Share	(ii)	Rs. 107	Rs. 112
Total Market Value of Shares at the year end	(i) × (ii)	Rs. 1,13,79,985	Rs. 1,13,79,984, i.e., Rs. 1,13,79,985

Thus, whether dividends are paid or not, value of the company remains the same as per M-M approach.

Criticism of M-M Hypothesis

M-M hypothesis is subject to severe criticism by virtue of unrealistic nature of assumptions. They are as follows:

(i) **Tax Differential:** M-M hypothesis assumes that taxes do not exist. This assumption is far from reality. In real life, the shareholders will have to pay tax. But there are different rates of tax for capital gains and dividends. Thus the cost of internal financing is cheaper than that of external financing. In fact, the shareholders are in favour of a dividend policy with retention of earnings as against the payment of dividends by virtue of tax differential.

(ii) **Existence of Floatation Costs:** M-M also assumes that both the internal as well as the external financing are equivalent and same. But in true sense, the external financing is costlier than internal financing since the companies are required to pay floatation costs by way of underwriting fees and brokers' commission as and when the funds are raised externally.

(iii) **Transaction Costs:** M-M also assumes that whether dividends are paid or not, the shareholders wealth will be the same. This assumption is also far from facts. The shareholders are required to pay brokerage fee, etc., whenever they want to dispose the shares. Thus they prefer dividends to retain their earnings.

(iv) **Discount Rate:** M-M hypothesis assumes that the discount rate is the same whether a company chooses internal or external financing. This is not correct. In case the shareholders want to diversify their portfolios, they would like to distribute earnings which they may be able to invest in such dividends in other companies. In such a case, the shareholders will have a higher value of discount rate if internal financing is being used and vice-versa.

CASE STUDY

Dividend Policy Analysis of Larsen and Toubro Limited (L&T)

The capital structure, cost of capital and cash flow statement of L&T have been analysed in Chapters 5, 7 and 17 respectively. In this section, the dividend policy of L&T is to be analysed. Table 18.1 provides financial data of L&T from 1995–96 to 2004–05.

Behaviour of EPS, DPS and Payout

Both EPS and DPS of L&T from 1995-96 to 2004–05 shown an upward trend. However, EPS has shown wide fluctuations, but DPS has been steadily growing (Figure 18.3). Consequently, dividend payout ratio shows wide variations ranging between 24.4% to 47.3% (Figure 18.4). The average payout ratio during the past 10 years (1995–96 to 2004–05) is 34%.

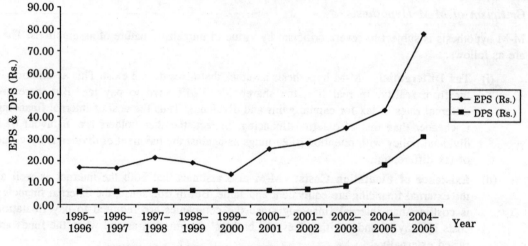

FIGURE 18.3   L&T's EPS and DPS from 1995-96 to 2004-05.

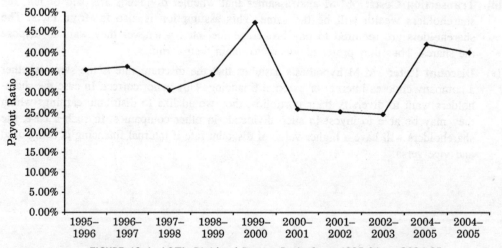

FIGURE 18.4   L&T's Dividend Payout Ratio from 1995-96 to 2004-05.

Behaviour of Share Price

The share price of L&T has been steadily increasing since 1995–96 (Figure 18.5). This may be on account of the good earnings performance of the company and the steadily growing dividend per share. The average market price (AMP) of the share seems to have a strong relationship with DPS. The maximum average share price of Rs. 900 was reached in 2004–05. The share price after declining to Rs. 260 in 1996–97, increased to Rs. 280 in 1997–98 and was at Rs. 900 in 2004–05.

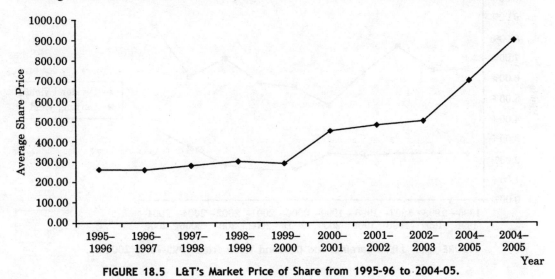

FIGURE 18.5   L&T's Market Price of Share from 1995-96 to 2004-05.

TABLE 18.1   L&T's EPS, DPS and Other Financial Data

Year	EPS (Rs)	DPS (Rs.)	Average Share Price (Rs.)	Book Value Per Share (Rs.)	Dividend Payout Ratio	Dividend Yield	Earning Yield	ROE
1995–1996	16.88	6.00	262.00	112.67	35.50%	2.30%	6.50%	15.00%
1996–1997	16.55	6.00	260.00	122.04	36.30%	2.30%	6.40%	13.60%
1997–1998	21.39	6.50	280.00	134.99	30.40%	2.30%	7.60%	15.80%
1998–1999	18.94	6.50	300.50	146.48	34.30%	2.20%	6.30%	12.90%
1999–2000	13.74	6.50	290.00	152.13	47.30%	2.30%	4.70%	9.00%
2000–2001	25.34	6.50	450.00	157.31	25.70%	1.50%	5.60%	16.10%
2001–2002	27.90	7.00	480.00	130.25	25.10%	1.50%	5.80%	21.40%
2002–2003	34.83	8.50	500.00	139.15	24.40%	1.70%	7.00%	25.00%
2003–2004	42.82	18.00	700.50	216.74	42.00%	2.60%	6.10%	19.80%
2004–2005	77.62	31.00	900.00	253.91	39.90%	3.50%	8.60%	30.60%
Average	29.60	10.25	442.30	156.57	34.10%	2.20%	6.50%	17.90%

Source: Annual Report of L&T

Earnings and Dividend Yields

The dividend yield of L&T was steady up to 1999–2000 and then started declining except during 2003–04 and 2005–05. However, it has remained below 3 per cent except during 2004–05. The average dividend yield for the past ten years is 2.2 per cent which is below the all India average dividend yield. This indicates that the L& T's share price has been growing faster than the growth in DPS.

The earnings yield of L & T showed a high degree of flexibility (Figure 18.6). It peaked to 8.6 per cent in 2004–05. The average earnings yield during 1995–96 to 2004–05 was 6.5 per cent.

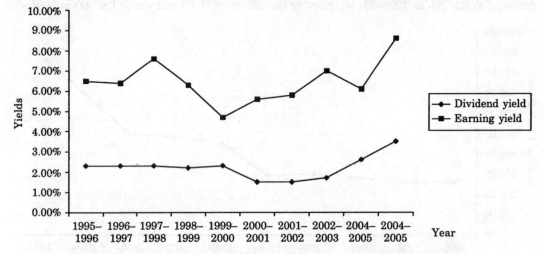

FIGURE 18.6 L&T's Earnings and Dividend Yields from 1995-96 to 2004-05.

– REVIEW QUESTIONS –

1. To what extent are firms able to establish a definite long-run dividend policy. What factors would affect these policies?

2. Write a short note on stable dividend policy?

   (M.Com, Kerala, April 1982)

3. Critically examine the assumptions underlining the irrelevance hypothesis of Modigliani and Miller regarding dividend distribution.

   (C.A. Final, November 1990)

4. What do you understand by Dividend Policy? What are the main determinants of dividend policy in a corporate enterprise?

   (C.A. Final, December 1988)

5. What is the Modigliani-Miller's approach of irrelevance concept of dividends? Under what assumptions do the conclusions hold good?

   (M.Com, Delhi, 1993)

6. Write notes on:
   (a) Cash dividend
   (b) Stock dividend
   (c) Walter's approach to dividend policy

7. Explain fully Walter's formulation on dividend policy. How far does it explain the dividend practices of companies?

   (C.A. Final, May 1985)

8. Explain Gordon's Growth Model on dividend policy. Under what assumptions do the conclusions hold good?

9. The earnings per share of XY company is Rs. 8 and the rate of capitalisation applicable is 10%. The company has before it an option of adopting (i) 50% (ii) 75% and (iii) 100% dividend payout ratio. Compute the market price of the company's quoted shares as per Walter's model if it can earn a return of (i) 15%, (ii) 10% and (iii) 5% on retained earnings.

Ans.:

    (i) When Dividend payout ratio is 50% = Rs. 100
        When Dividend payout ratio is 75% = Rs. 90
        When Dividend payout ratio is 100% = Rs. 80

    (ii) When Dividend payout ratio is 50% = Rs. 80
        When Dividend payout ratio is 75% = Rs. 80
        When Dividend payout ratio is 100% = Rs. 80

    (iii) When Dividend payout ratio is 50% = Rs. 60
        When Dividend payout ratio is 75% = Rs. 70
        When Dividend payout ratio is 100% = Rs. 80

10. Gopal Ltd. is an established company having its shares quoted in the major stock exchanges. Its share current market price after dividend distributed at the rate of 21% p.a. having a paid up share capital of Rs. 50 lakhs of Rs. 10 each. Annual growth rate in dividend expected is 3%. The expected rate of return on its equity capital is 16%. Calculate the value of Gopal Ltd's share based on dividend growth model.

(Ans.: Rs. 16.64)

11. 'Z' Ltd belongs ot a risk class of which the appropriate capitalisation is 10%. It currently has 1,00,000 shares selling at Rs. 100 each. The firm is contemplating declaration of a dividend of Rs. 6 per share at the end of the current fiscal year which has just begun. Answer the following questions based on Modigliani and Miller Model and assumption of no taxes.

    (i) What will be the price of the shares at the end of the year if a dividend is not declared?

    (ii) What will be the price if dividend is declared?

    (iii) Assuming that the firm pays dividend, has net income of Rs. 10 lakhs and makes new investments of Rs. 20 lakhs during the period, how many new shares must be issued?

(Ans.: (i) Rs. 110; (ii) Rs. 104; (iii) If dividend is declared 15,385 shares
If Dividend is not declared 9.091 shares)

12. X company earns Rs. 5 per share, is capitalised at a rate of 10% and has a rate of return on investment at 18%.

According to Walter's formula what should be the price per share at 25% dividend payout ratio? Is this the optimum payout ratio according to Walter?

(M.Com, Delhi, 1974)

(Ans.: Rs. 80. This is not the optimum Dividend Payout Ratio since Walter suggests a zero per cent Dividend Payout Ratio in situation where Ra > K)

13. The Agro-Chemical Company belongs to a risk class for which the appropriate capitalisation is 10%. It currently has 1,00,000 shares selling at Rs. 100 each. The firm is contemplating the declaration of Rs. 5 as dividend at the end of the current financial year, which has just begun. What will be the price of the share at the end of the year, if a dividend is not declared? What will it be if one is declared? Answer these on the basis of Modigliani and Miller model and assume no taxes.

(M.Com, Delhi, 1977)

(**Ans.:** (i) Rs. 135, (ii) Rs. 110)

19

Budgeting

Budget is a predetermined detailed plan of action developed and distributed as a guide to current operations and as a partial basis for the subsequent evaluation of performance.

— GORDON AND SHILLINGLAW

CONTENTS

- Introduction
- Meaning of budget
- Budgetary control
- Budget preparation
- Classification and types of budget
- Review questions

INTRODUCTION

Every business, no matter how small, needs the use of control techniques for surviving in the modern world economy. There are several control techniques adapted to manage the business operations and budget is one such control technique. It is the most significant tool of profit planning and control and also acts as an instrument of coordination.

This chapter contains a general view of budgeting, its meaning, essential features and classification of budgets.

MEANING OF BUDGET

Budget is a statement of management policy expressed in physical and monetary terms. There is no planning without policy. Thus policy is pre-requisite to planning and budget is the detailed and coordinated plan-statement. In short, budget is an estimate facilitating planning and control of business. The term budgeting is used for preparing budget and other procedures for planning, co-ordination and control of business undertakings.

In the words of J. Fred Meston,

> a budget is the expression of firm's plan in financial form for a period of time in future.

According to I.C.W.A., London, A budget is a financial and/or quantitative statement prepared prior to a defined period of time, of the policy to be pursued during that period for the purpose of attaining a given objective. Thus the essentials of a budget are as follows.

(i) It is a statement expressed in monetary and/or physical units. For instance a budget may provide for a sale of Rs. 2,00,000 (i.e., monetary units) or for a sale of 20,000 units (i.e., physical units), (ii) It contains "specific period" of operation. Emphasis is given to the time element, (iii) It is prepared in advance, and (iv) It relates to future and is based on objectives to be attained.

Estimate and Forecast: Estimate is the expectation based on some principle (i.e., average of past records). It may be for present or future. But forecast is an estimate based on some basis for the future only.

Standard and Budget: Standard is a target to be attained having regard to technical and financial circumstances. It is fixed for operational activity like production, sales, etc., and expressed per unit.

Budget sets the ceiling of expenses and targets of incomes in total. It is made for all activities like purchase, production, sales, selling expenses, capital expenditures, cash, etc., and prepared for a specific period.

Budget and Budgeting: A budget is a blue print of a plan expressed in quantitative terms. It is the individual objective of a department, etc.

Budgeting is a technique for formulating budgets. Thus budgeting may be said to be the act of building budgets.

Budgeting and Forecasting: Forecast is a statement comprising the facts which are likely to happen at a future date. These facts may not occur in accordance with the estimate. There will be an element of variation. It is a statement of probable events. However, the degree of accuracy of forecasts is judged only after making comparison with the actual performance.

Forecast acts as a basis for the formulation of budgets. In other words, budgeting begins where forecasting ends. The actual performance of the past, the present situation and likely trends in the future are taken into account while preparing budgets. Thus a budget relates to planned events and is a quantitative expression of business plans and policies to be pursued in the future.

BUDGETARY CONTROL

Budgetary control refers to the principles, procedures and practices of accomplishing given objectives through budgets. It is an overall management tool for the business planning and control. In the words of Brown and Howard, budgetary control is a system of controlling costs which includes the preparation of budgets, co-ordinating the departments and establishing responsibilities, comparing actual performance with the budgeted and acting upon results to achieve maximum profitability.

The above definition points out that budgetary control is a control system adopted in an organisation through which every business operation has to be carried out as per the plan. The performance appraisal is made at the end and the whole control activity takes place with the objective of maximizing profit. Thus budgetive is only an estimated plan of action to be carried out in the coming period whereas budgetary control is concerned with the successful implementation of the budget.

Essentials of Budgetary Control

The following steps are involved for the successful implementation of budgetary control system.

1. Organisation of budgetary control, 2. Budget centres, 3. Budget officer, 4. Budget manual, 5. Budget committee, 6. Budget period, and 7. Determination of key factor.

1. Organisation for Budgetary Control: Proper organisation is required for the successful preparation and maintenance of budgets. It defines levels in the management hierarchy, shows authority and power enjoyed by each level and the responsibility to be discharged. The volume and nature of business determines the structure of the organisation. This structure helps in preparing the master budget, functional and sub-functional budget. An organisation chart for budgetary control is given in Figure 19.1.

As shown in Figure 19.1, the chief executive is the overall in-charge of budgetary system. He constitutes a budget committee for the preparation of budgets. There is a budget officer who

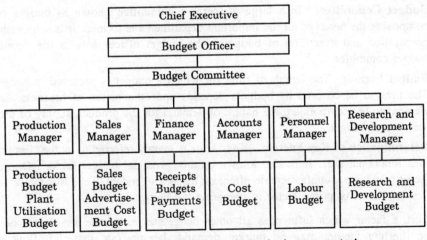

FIGURE 19.1 Organisation chart for budgetary control.

is the convenor of the budget committee. He has to coordinate the budgets of various departments. However, the managers of various departments are responsible for their departmental budgets.

2. **Budget Centre:** A budget centre is that part of the organisation for which the budget is formed. It is a point selected for controlling cost. So it is also known as cost centre. Costs are to be controlled at the points at which they are incurred. The selected point must be suitable for cost control.

3. **Budget Manual:** Budget manual is a written document for facilitating the formulation of budget. It spells out the duties and responsibilities of the various executives concerned with the budgets. Thus the budget manual covers the following matters:

   - It clearly defines the objectives of budgetary control system and gives the benefits and principles of this system.
   - It provides the duties and responsibilities of various persons involved in the preparation and execution of budgets.
   - It provides information about the sanctioning authorities of various budgets.
   - It contains cost classification and procedure for the estimation of each category of cost.
   - It suggests the procedure to be followed for the operation of budgetary control system.
   - It defines the responsibilities of functional and departmental budget centres.
   - It clearly gives the length of various budget periods and control points.
   - It states a method of accounting to be used for various expenditures.

4. **Budget Officer:** The budget officer is empowered to scrutinise the budgets prepared by various departmental heads and to bring changes if the need arises. He will see to the regular periodical budget reports from every department. He determines the deviations in the budget and takes necessary steps to rectify the deficiencies, if any. He also apprises the top management about the performance of various departments.

5. **Budget Committee:** In a large concern, a committee known as budget committee comprising the heads of all the important departments is formed. It is responsible for the preparation and execution of budgets. The budget officer acts as the coordinator of budget committee.

6. **Budget Period:** The length of time for which a budget is prepared is budget period. The time to be covered by budgets depends upon the nature of business, the control element to be incorporated, the nature of demand for the product, supply of product and the type of budget.

7. **Determination of Key Factor:** Key factor is mainly referred to as the 'limiting factor' in a functional area. It is also known as the 'principal budget factor'. One particular factor may have an unfavourable effect on the whole budget. Thus this factor becomes a limiting factor or prime factor in preparing the budget.

In short, a factor which influences all other budgets is called the key factor or principal factor. The limiting factors may be market demand, labour, raw material, flow of funds, government policy, demography, market structure, etc. There may be a limitation on the quantity of goods a firm may sell. In such a situation, sales will be a key factor. Hence, all other budgets should be prepared by keeping in view the quantity of goods the firm is able to sell. However, the key factor may not necessarily remain the same. For instance, the raw material supply may be limited at one time but it may be easily available at another time.

BUDGET PREPARATION

The preparation of budget involves several steps or stages. They are as follows:

(i) Collection of relevant data, (ii) Forecasting the activities, (iii) Establishing organisation chart, budget committee, etc., (iv) Preparing accounting records, (v) Framing guidelines, (vi) Awareness of task, (vii) Preparation of budget manual, (viii) Submission of budgets prepared for discussion, and (ix) Implementation of budgets.

Collection of Relevant Data: Budget formulation commences with the collection of relevant data (i.e., immediate past data) and analysis. This analysis sheds light on the trend of capital movement, profit growth, etc., which provide a strong base for the preparation of budget.

Forecasting the Activities: Each functional department should be asked to forecast its activities and assess its resources. This helps in preparing functional budgets. The goal of the concern, the key factor of the function, and the way of overcoming the key factor, should also be considered while framing the functional budget.

Establishing Organisation Chart, Budget Committee, etc.: An organisation chart should be established to define the functional responsibilities of each member of the management team associated with the preparation of budget. Fixing the budget period and the establishment of budget committee and budget centre should also be taken care of at this stage.

Preparing Accounting Records: Budget formulation requires several accounting records. A chart showing the requirement of accounting records of each functional area should be prepared. This helps in facilitating the analysis and interpretation of the accounting information required for the preparation of budget.

Framing Guidelines: The guidelines required for the preparation of budget should be framed. Such guidelines are related to production, stock levels, channel choice, product promotion and general investment policies.

Awareness of Task: For the smooth preparation of budget, everyone concerned with its preparation should be made known his task.

Preparation of Budget Manual: The budget manual assigning the responsibility to each person engaged in the preparation of budget is to be prepared at this stage.

Submission of Budget Prepared for Discussion: Every functional department is required to place the budget prepared as per the set guidelines before the budget committee for discussion and reformation. The budget approved by the budget committee in turn should be sent to the top management for approval.

Implementation of Budget: The budget committee should send the approved budgets to the concerned departments for implementation. It should have the responsibility to conduct periodic reviews for assessing the performance of each functional area. It should also ascertain whether actuals conform with the budget.

CLASSIFICATION AND TYPES OF BUDGETS

Budgets are usually classified according to various activities. They are: (i) Functions, (ii) Nature of expenditure, (iii) Time, and (iv) Activity level. Table 19.1 shows the various categories of budgets prepared in accordance with this classification.

TABLE 19.1 Classification of budget.

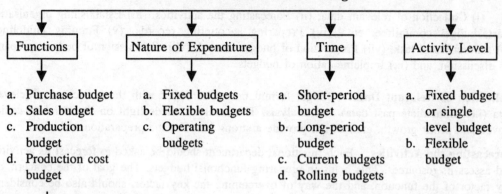

Functions	Nature of Expenditure	Time	Activity Level
a. Purchase budget	a. Fixed budgets	a. Short-period budget	a. Fixed budget or single level budget
b. Sales budget	b. Flexible budgets	b. Long-period budget	
c. Production budget	c. Operating budgets	c. Current budgets	b. Flexible budget
d. Production cost budget		d. Rolling budgets	

1. Materials budget
2. Labour budget
3. Factory overhead budget

e. Administrative overhead budget
f. Selling and distribution overheads budget
g. Plant utilization budget
h. Research and development budget
i. Capital budgeting
j. Cash budget

1. Receipt payment method
2. Adjusted profit & loss method
3. Balance sheet method

Classification According to Function

Budgets can be classified according to the functions they are meant to perform. Thus these budgets are termed as functional budgets. The various functional budgets are as follows.

(a) Purchase Budget

The budget which guides the management in making necessary purchases to be made during the budget period is known as purchase budget. This budget is based on other budgets such as sales budget, production budget, cost budget, stock levels, economic order quantity (EOQ), etc. Purchase budget is mainly concerned with the raw materials in the case of a manufacturing concern. The budget shows the actual raw material required in terms of physical or monetary units.

ILLUSTRATION 19.1

Prepare a purchase budget from the particulars given below:

Materials used	X	Y	Z
Price per ton (in Rs.)	10,000	50,000	1,00,000
Opening Stock (in tons)	200	300	400
Closing Stock (in tons)	100	150	1500
Estimated Consumption (in tons)	1500	2500	3000

Budget period 1-1-2004 to 31-12-2004
Purchase Budget (Period 1-1-2004 to 31-12-2004)

Particulars	Material X (Tons)	Material Y (Tons)	Material Z (Tons)
Expected use of Materials	1500	2500	3000
Add: Closing Stock to be held	100	150	500
Total required	1600	2650	3500
Less: Stock held	200	300	400
Quantity to be Purchased	1400	2350	3100
Price per ton (in Rs.)	10,000	50,000	1,00,000
Estimated Cost of Material to be purchased (in Rs.)	1,40,00,000	11,75,00,000	31,00,00,000

(b) Sales Budget

Sales budget is the nerve centre or backbone of an organisation and is the basis of budgetary control. It is an estimate of expected sales during a budgeted period. The budget can be expressed either in monetary terms or in physical units.

A sales budget is the starting point on which other budgets are based. The degree of accuracy with which sales are estimated should decide the practicability of operating budgets. As the people involved in the preparation of sales budget have to take into account uncontrollable factors, forecasting of sales needs some amount of creativity. But the possible factors to be considered while preparing a sales budget are (i) past sales figures, (ii) assessment and reports by salesmen, (iii) availability of raw materials, (iv) seasonal fluctuations, (v) availability of finance, and (vi) plant capacity.

The sales budget can be prepared on the basis of:

(i) region or territories in which the sales are made,

(ii) the consumer behaviour (i.e., in accordance with the class or type of consumers)

(iii) budget period (ie. yearly, half-yearly, quarterly, monthly and weekly).

(iv) product (i.e., separate sales budgets for each product in the case of multi-product).

(v) according to salesmen (separate sales budget for each salesman).

Steps in Preparing Sales Budget

The sales director in consultation with the top management and field force of sales should prepare the sales budget. However, he should follow certain steps which are given below.

(i) Analysis of past sales data, (ii) Collective opinion from sales force, (iii) Study of environmental factors, (iv) Study of market conditions, (v) Cost-benefit analysis.

ILLUSTRATION 19.2

Ramaraj & Co. Kerala, estimate their annual sales as 5,00,000 units at Rs. 10 per unit. The monthly sales on the basis of an index is given below:

Month	Units
January	20,000
February	20,000
March	42,000
April	40,000
May	50,000
June	60,000
July	60,000
August	50,000
September	60,000
October	28,000
November	30,000
December	40,000
	5,00,000

The district-wise sales in each of the five districts shows the following results.

Month	Trivandrum	Kollam	Alappuzha	Kottayam	Ernakulam
January	15%	10%	15%	25%	25%
February	20%	15%	10%	20%	15%
March	20%	25%	30%	15%	10%
April	30%	20%	10%	20%	10%
May	20%	30%	10%	20%	10%
June	30%	15%	20%	15%	10%

Prepare the sales budget for the first six months in terms of quantity and value.

Solution

Sales Forecast (Period from January to June)

Month	Trivandrum Qty.	Trivandrum Value Rs.	Kollam Qty.	Kollam Value Rs.	Alappuzha Qty.	Alappuzha Value Rs.	Kottayam Qty.	Kottayam Value Rs.	Ernakulam Qty.	Ernakulam Value Rs.
January	3,000	30,000	2,000	20,000	3,000	30,000	5,000	50,000	5,000	50,000
February	4,000	40,000	3,000	30,000	2,000	20,000	4,000	40,000	3,000	30,000
March	8,400	84,000	10,500	1,05,000	12,600	1,26,000	6,300	63,000	4,200	42,000
April	12,000	1,20,000	8,000	80,000	4,000	40,000	8,000	80,000	4,000	40,000
May	10,000	1,00,000	15,000	1,50,000	5,000	50,000	10,000	1,00,000	5,000	50,000
June	18,000	1,80,000	9,000	90,000	12,000	1,20,000	9,000	90,000	6,000	60,000
Total	55,400	5,54,000	47,500	4,75,000	38,600	3,86,000	42,300	4,23,000	27,200	2,72,000

ILLUSTRATION 19.3

From the following data for the year 2004, prepare a sales budget.

(i) Estimated sales for 2003

Product	Trivandrum	Kollam	Kottayam
A	15000 @ Rs. 10	12000 @ Rs. 10	10000 @ Rs. 10
B	5000 @ Rs. 15	10000 @ Rs. 15	6000 @ Rs. 15
C	4000 @ Rs. 20	20000 @ Rs. 20	5000 @ Rs. 20

(ii) Actual sales for the year 2003

Product			
A	18000 @ Rs. 10	15000 @ Rs. 10	12000 @ Rs. 10
B	7000 @ Rs. 15	12000 @ Rs. 15	8000 @ Rs. 15
C	3000 @ Rs. 20	15000 @ Rs. 20	4000 @ Rs. 20

After the market study, the following decisions are taken.

(a) To increase the sales:

	A	B	C
Trivandrum	50%	40%	20%
Kollam	70%	50%	–
Kottayam	50%	50%	–

(b) Reduce sales by 15% of product C in Kollam and Kottayam.

The prices are refixed by the budget committee and are as follows:

A – Rs. 15
B – Rs. 20
C – Rs. 25

Solution

Sales Budget for 2004

Places	Product	Budgeted Sales – 2003 Units	Price Rs.	Value Rs.	Actual Sales – 2003 Units	Price Rs.	Value Rs.	Budgeted Sales – 2004 Units	Price Rs.	Value Rs.
Trivandrum	A	15,000	10	1,50,000	18,000	10	1,80,000	22,500	15	3,37,500
	B	5,000	15	75,000	7,000	15	1,05,000	7,000	20	1,40,000
	C	4,000	20	80,000	3,000	20	60,000	4,800	25	1,20,000
		24,000		**3,05,000**	**28,000**		**3,45,000**	**34,300**		**5,97,500**
Kollam	A	12,000	10	1,20,000	15,000	10	1,50,000	20,400	15	3,06,000
	B	10,000	15	1,50,000	12,000	15	1,80,000	15,000	20	3.00,000
	C	20,000	20	4,00,000	15,000	20	3,00,000	17,000	25	4,25,000
		42,000		**6,70,000**	**42,000**		**6,30,000**	**52,400**		**10,31,000**

Continued

Sales Budget for 2004

Places	Product	Budgeted Sales – 2003			Actual Sales – 2003			Budgeted Sales – 2004		
		Units	Price Rs.	Value Rs.	Units	Price Rs.	Value Rs.	Units	Price Rs.	Value Rs.
Kottayam	A	10,000	10	1,00,000	12,000	10	1,20,000	15,000	15	2,25,000
	B	6,000	15	90,000	8,000	15	1,20,000	9,000	20	1,80,000
	C	5,000	20	1,00,000	4,000	20	80,000	4,250	25	1,06,250
		21,000		2,90,000	24,000		3,20,000	28,250		5,11,250
Total	A	37,000	10	3,70,000	45,000	10	4,50,000	57,900	15	8,68,500
	B	21,000	15	3,15,000	27,000	15	4,05,000	31,000	20	6,20,000
	C	29,000	20	5,80,000	22,000	20	4,40,000	26,050	25	6,51,250
		87,000		12,65,000	94,000		12,95,000	1,14,950		21,39,750

(c) Production Budget

Production budget is a forecast of the production for the budget period. It is prepared only after the sales budget is prepared. Sales budget determines the quantity of the products to be produced. The production department arranges the production programme on the basis of this sales quantity. Production budget is usually prepared for the number of units to be produced. It is also called an output budget as it forecasts the quantity of products to be produced in the budget period or control period.

The preparation of production budget involves the following:

Production Planning: Production budget can be prepared only with the help of a suitable production planning schedule. While preparing a production plan, the utilization of optimum plant capacity and avoidance of bottlenecks on account of shortage of materials and labour should be considered.

Consideration of Plant Capacity: The capacity which the plant can work throughout the budget period should be determined. However, the capacity should not be fixed either too high or too low. The quantity of various products to be manufactured should be determined on the basis of plant capacity.

Stock Quantity to be Held: The quantity of finished goods to be carried forward should be determined. This quantity depends on factors such as sales potential, storage facilities available and cost of the stock. The requisite closing stock figures should be added to the estimated sales figures and opening stock figures should be deducted from it while fixing the production target. The work-in-progress should also be considered at the time of fixing a production target.

Consideration of Sales Budget: The production budget is prepared with reference to sales budget. The sales budget should provide guidelines for production planning. Unless both the budgets are coordinated, there may arise problems of shortages and surpluses.

The following is the format of production budget:

(d) Production Cost Budget

The production cost budget shows the cost involved in the production of various products estimated to be manufactured. The production budget determines the number of units to be produced. When these units are converted into monetary terms, it becomes a production cost budget. Thus production cost budget is a consolidated cost budget containing the expenditure to be incurred on elements like raw material, labour and overheads.

Production Budget
for the year ended 31st Dec., 2004

Month	Units Required for Sale	Add Closing Stock of Finished Goods	Total Units Required	Less Opening Stock of Finished Goods	Units to be Produced
January					
February					
March					
April					
May					
June					
July					
August					
September					
October					
November					
December					
Total					

ILLUSTRATION 19.4

Prepare a production budget for each month and a summarized production cost budget, for the six months period ending 31st December, 2004, from the following data of product 'A'.

   (i)   The units to be sold for different months are as follows:

July 2004	1200
August 2004	1200
September 2004	1800
October 2004	2000
November 2004	3000
December 2004	2800
January 2005	2400

  (ii) There will be no work-in-progress at the end of any month.

 (iii) Finished units equal to half the sales for the next month will be in stock at the end of each month (including June, 2004).

 (iv) Budgeted production and production cost for the year ending 31st December, 2004 are as follows:

Production (units)	25,000
Direct materials (per unit)	Rs. 10
Direct wages (per unit)	Rs. 5
Total factory overheads apportioned to products	Rs. 90,000

Solution

(i) Production Budget
for each month from July to Dec., 2004

Month 2004	Sales (Units)	Add Closing Stock (Units)	Less Opening Stock (Units)	Production Units
July	1200	600	600	1200
August	1200	900	600	1500
September	1800	1000	900	1900
October	2000	1500	1000	2500
November	3000	1400	1500	2900
December	2800	1200	1400	2600
			Total	12,600

Production = Sales + Closing stock − Opening stock

(ii) Production Cost Budget
for six month ending 31st Dec., 2004

	Rate per unit (Rs.)	(Production Units 12,600) Amount Rs.
Direct Materials	10.00	1,26,000
Direct Wages	5.00	63,000
Factory Overheads $\left(\dfrac{90,000}{25,000}\right)$	3.60	45,360
	Total	2,34,360

ILLUSTRATION 19.5

Ratan Enterprises Ltd. manufactures two products X and Y and the budgeted data for the year are as follows:

	Product X (Rs.)	Product Y (Rs.)
Sales price per unit	90	80
Direct materials per unit	30	20
Direct wages per unit	7	6
Total works overhead	10,000	9,000
Total marketing overhead	1,500	1,400

The sales manager forecasts the sales in units as follows:

	Product X (Units)	Product Y (Units)
January	30	12
February	30	14
March	28	18
April	22	22
May	18	26
June	18	26
July to December, each month	20	24

It is assumed that (i) there will be no work-in-progress at the end of any month, and (ii) finished units equal to half the sales for the following month will be kept in stock.

Prepare a production budget for each month and production cost budget.

Solution

Production Budget Units

Month	Product X				Product Y			
	Sales	Add Closing Stock	Less Opening Stock	Production	Sales	Add Closing Stock	Less Opening Stock	Production
January	30	15	15	30	12	7	6	13
February	30	14	15	29	14	9	7	16
March	28	11	14	25	18	11	9	20
April	22	9	11	20	22	13	11	24
May	18	9	9	18	26	13	13	26
June	18	10	9	19	26	12	13	25
July	20	10	10	20	24	12	12	24
August	20	10	10	20	24	12	12	24
September	20	10	10	20	24	12	12	24
October	20	10	10	20	24	12	12	24
November	20	10	10	20	24	12	12	24
December	20	10	10	20	24	12	12	24
Total	266			261	262			268

Note: Opening stock is half of the budgeted sales for the same month because closing stock of finished goods is equal to half the sales in the next month.

Summarised Production Cost Budget

	Product X261 Units	Product Y268 Units	Total
Direct material			
X : @ Rs. 30	7,830	5,360	13,190
Y : @ Rs. 20			
Direct labour			
X : @ Rs. 7	1,827	1,608	3,435
Y : @ Rs. 6			
Works Overheads	10,000	9,000	19,000
Total Production Cost	19,657	15,968	35,625
Cost per unit	75	60	

1. **Raw Material Budget:** The budget which is concerned with determining the quantity of raw materials required for production is called raw material budget. This budget considers the expenditure to be incurred on the estimated raw material, time involved in procuring it, the terms of purchase etc. Usually the raw materials budget will serve the following purposes.

   (i)   It enables to know the total quantity of raw material required for the production of estimated units of product.

   (ii) It helps to draw a purchase programme.

   (iii) It assists to estimate the cost of raw material required for each product.

   (iv) It enables to know the stock of raw materials.

The format of raw material budget is as follows:

Format of Raw Material Budget

	Material – P			Material – Q		
	Qty	Rate	Amount (Rs.)	Qty	Rate	Amount (Rs.)
Required material	......			......		
Material P ... Units for ... units of finished goods	......	......	......			
Material Q ... Units for ... units of finished goods				......	......	......
Estimated closing balance	......	......	......	......	......	......
Materials on order (closing)	......	......	......	......	......	......
	......	......	......	......	......	......
Less: Opening balance of materials (Budgeted)	......	......	......	......	......	......
	......	......	......	......	......	......
Less: Materials on order (opening)	......	......	......	......	......	......
Required materials	......	......	......	......	......	......

ILLUSTRATION 19.6

From the following data, prepare raw material purchase budget.

	X	Y
Material used		
Opening Stock of Materials (in units)	12,000	8,000
Materials to be held in units at close	20,000	10,000
Expected consumption of materials (in units)	1,00,000	80,000
Standard price (per unit)	Rs. 1	Rs. 2

Solution

Purchase Budget – Raw materials

Particulars	Material X in units	Material Y in units
Expected Consumption	1,00,000	80,000
Add Closing Stock	20,000	10,000
	1,20,000	90,000
Less Opening Stock	12,000	8,000
Quantity to be purchased	1,08,000	82,000

Estimated cost of purchase.

X = 1,08,000 × Rs. 1 = Rs. 1,08,000
Y = 82,000 × Rs. 2 = Rs. 1,64,000

2. **Labour Budget:** Several categories of labourers are involved in the production process. Thus the labour required for production may be classified into direct and indirect labour. The labour required for manufacturing the product is called the direct labour. This is one of the major elements in the production cost. Since indirect labour cannot be specified with production, it is made a part of manufacturing overhead. Hence, only direct labour budget is prepared from the costing point of view.

3. **Factory Overheads Budget:** Under this budget, the cost of indirect materials, indirect labour and indirect factory expenses are estimated. This sum should be allocated between fixed and variable costs. However, the allocation should be exercised with great skill and diligence. The fixed costs are determined on the basis of past data. But the variable and semi-variable costs are projected on the basis of expected production.

(e) Administrative Overheads Budget

The budget which covers the expenses of all administrative offices and of management salaries is called the administrative overhead budget. This budget can easily be prepared as most of the expenses are fixed in nature. The previous years budget can be used to know the type of expenditure and the expenditure level.

(f) Selling and Distribution Overhead Budget

The budget which estimates the expenses involved in selling and distributing the product is known as selling and distribution overhead budget. The responsibility for the preparation of this budget rests with the executives of the sales division. They should analyse the market situation, advertising policies, research programmes and the fixed and variable elements before commencing the preparation of this budget.

(g) Plant Utilisation Budget

The budget which estimates the extent of plant and machinery to be used in the production process is called the plant utilization budget. The plant utilization is expressed in terms of machine hours (i.e., the hours the plant is to be worked). This enables to know the machine load for the target production. In the case of overload, it has to be corrected by adopting some alternative actions. If there is underload, it indicates the need for some aggressive sales promotion activity.

(h) Research and Development Budget

The budget which is prepared to know the estimated cost on research and development comes under the category of research and development budget. First of all, costs on research (fundamental or applied research) for new product or improved methods should be estimated. Afterwards, the cost involved on product design and development should be assessed. A budget is then prepared for research and development.

(i) Capital Budgeting

Capital project planning or capital budgeting is the process by which funds are allocated to various investment projects designed to ensure profitability and growth. It involves (i) the search for new and more profitable investment proposals, and (ii) the making of an economic analysis to determine the profit potential of each investment proposal.

Refer Chapter 21 capital budgeting for more details.

(j) Cash Budget

The budget which shows the cash requirements for a future period is called the cash budget. It is the summary of the firm's expected cash inflows and outflows over a projected time period.

The cash budget helps the management in (i) determining the future cash requirements (ii) planning for financing those requirements, and (iii) exercising control over cash and liquidity.

A cash budget can be prepared by any of the following methods:

(i) Receipts and payments method

(ii) The adjusted profit and loss account method and

(iii) The balance sheet method

Refer Chapter 3, financial forecasting for more details.

Master Budget

Master budget is the final product in the budget process. It is a comprehensive budget package prepared for a company. In the words of Rowland and William H. Harr,

> The master budget is a summary of the budget schedule in capsule form made for the purpose of presenting in a single report with the highlights of the budget forecast.

Hence, master budget is a summary budget which incorporates all other budgets. It contains the detailed plan of operations for all departments for the budget period.

The master budget is prepared by the budget officer. It needs the approval of the budget committee before it is put into operation. Usually, this budget is used to coordinate the activities of various functional departments and also to serve as a control device.

The various steps involved in the construction of master budget comprise the preparation of (i) sales budget, as the basic starting point; (ii) production budget; (iii) cost of production budget; (iv) cash budget; and (v) the projected income statement and the balance sheet.

ILLUSTRATION 19.7

A Thermos Flask manufacturing company asks you to prepare a master budget from the following data for the year 2004.

Sales:

Size – I	Rs. 3,00,000
Size – II	Rs. 5,00,000

Direct Material cost is 60% of sales
Direct Wages 20 workers @ Rs. 150 per month
Factory Overheads:
Indirect Labour

(i) Works supervisor Rs. 500 per month

(ii) Foreman Rs. 400 per month

Stores and Spares 2½% on Sales

	Rs.
Depreciation on Machinery	12,600
Light and Power	5,000
Repairs and Maintenance	8,000

Other Sundries 10% on Direct Wages

Administration, Selling and Distribution Expenses Rs. 20,000 per year.

Solution

Master Budget for the Year 2004

			Rs.
I.	Sales Budget		
	Size – I		3,00,000
	Size – II		5,00,000
			8,00,000
II.	Production Cost Budget		
	Direct Materials, 60% of Sales		4,80,000
	Direct Wages		36,000
	Prime Cost		5,16,000
	Factory Overheads:		
		Rs.	
	Variable: Stores and Spares	20,000	
	(2½% on Sales)		
	Light and Power	5,000	
	Repairs and Maintenance	8,000	33,000
			5,49,000
	Fixed: Indirect Labour:		
	Works Supervisor	6,000	
	Foreman	4,800	
	Depreciation	12,600	
	Sundries	3,600	27,000
	Works Cost		5,76,000
III.	Gross Profit (I – II)		2,24,000
IV.	Administration, Selling and Distribution cost		20,000
V.	Expected Net Profit (III – IV)		2,04,000

Classification According to the Nature of Expenditure

On the basis of nature of expenditure, budgets are classified as (i) fixed budgets, (ii) flexible budgets, and (iii) operating budgets.

Fixed Budgets

A budget prepared on the basis of standard or fixed level of activity is called the fixed budget or single level budget. Usually, this budget is prepared when activities can be fairly forecast with reasonable certainty. According to I.C.W.A., London, "a fixed budget is a budget which is designed to remain unchanged irrespective of the level of activity actually attained". Thus a fixed budget does not change with the change in the level of activity.

Flexible Budgets

A budget which is designed to change in accordance with the level of activity actually attained is called the flexible budget or dynamic budget. This budget is usually prepared after taking into account the fixed and variable elements of cost and the expected changes for each item at various levels of operation.

Flexible budget helps in studying cost behaviour pattern and preparing budgets for different levels, rather than single level. It provides information useful in modifying plans. Thus flexible budget has the following unique features.

(i) It is directed to all levels of activity within a range, (ii) It is flexible in character, and (iii) It provides scope for performance appraisal.

Methods of Preparing a Flexible Budget

A flexible budget can be prepared in any one of the three methods such as (i) multi-activity method, (ii) formula method, and (iii) graphic method.

Multi-activity Method: Multi-activity method involves the computation of budget figures for various levels of activity within a range. The budget preparation under this method involves the following steps.

(i) Determining the unit in which the different levels of activity are to be expressed.

(ii) Fixing the budget cost allowance for the budget centres.

(iii) Determining the various levels of activity for which the flexible budget is to be prepared.

ILLUSTRATION 19.8

A manufacturing company produces 2000 units at 100% capacity, and the costs at this level are given below:

Variable	Rs. 4 per unit
Semi-variable	Rs. 6 per unit (50% variable)
Fixed	Rs. 6000

Prepare a flexible budget for 80%, 90% and 100% levels of activity.

Solution

Flexible Budget

	Levels of activity		
	80%	*90%*	*100%*
Units	1600	1800	2000
Variable costs	6,400	7,200	8,000
Semi-variable costs:			
Fixed	6,000	6,000	6,000
Variable	4,800	5,400	6,000
Fixed Costs	6,000	6,000	6,000
Total Costs	23,200	24,600	26,000

In the above illustration, budgeted figures for various levels of activity within the range of 80% to 100% have been ascertained for any level of activity. For instance, in case the actual level of activity is only 85%, the figures for this level of activity are given below:

	Rs.
Variable Costs (@ Rs. 4 for 1700 units)	6,800
Semivariable Costs:	
Fixed	6,000
Variable (@ Rs. 3 for 1700 units)	5,100
Fixed Costs	6,000
	23,900

ILLUSTRATION 19.9

The expenses for the production of 6,000 units in a company are as follows:

	Per unit Rs.
Materials	50
Labour	15
Variable Overheads	20
Fixed Overheads (Rs. 60,000)	10
Administrative expenses (10% variable)	10
Selling expenses (20% fixed)	10
Distribution expenses (10% fixed)	8
Total Cost of Sales per unit	Rs. 123

Prepare a budget for the production of 8,000 units

Solution

Flexible Budget

Particulars	Output 6,000 Units Per Unit Rs.	Output 6,000 Units Amount Rs.	Output 8,000 Units Per Unit Rs.	Output 8,000 Units Amount Rs.
Materials	50.00	3,00,000	50.00	4,00,000
Labour	15.00	90,000	15.00	1,20,000
Prime Cost	65.00	3,90,000	65.00	5,20,000
Factory Overheads:				
Variable Overheads	20.00	1,20,000	20.00	1,60,000
Fixed Overheads:	10.00	60,000	7.50	60,000
Works Cost	95.00	5,70,000	92.50	7,40,000
Administrative Expenses	10.00	60,000	7.75	62,000
Cost of Production	105.00	6,30,000	100.25	8,02,000
Selling & Distribution Expenses:				
Selling Expenses	10.00	60,000	9.50	76,000
Distribution Expenses	8.00	48,000	7.80	62,400
Total Cost of Sales	123.00	7,38,000	117.55	9,40,400

ILLUSTRATION 19.10

The following information relates to a flexible budget at 60% capacity. Compute the overhead costs at 50% and 70% capacity and also determine the overhead rates:

Variable Overheads:	Expenses at 60% capacity
	Rs.
Indirect Labour	10,500
Indirect Materials	8,000
Semi-variable Overheads:	
Repairs and Maintenance	6,000
(60% Fixed, 40% Variable)	
Electricity (40% fixed, 60% variable)	24,000
Fixed Overheads:	
Office Expenses including Salaries	60,000
Insurance	5,000
Depreciation	20,000
Estimated Direct Labour Hours	90,000

Flexible Budget and Overhead Rates

Particulars	50% Capacity	60% Capacity	70% Capacity
	Rs.	Rs.	Rs.
Variable Overheads:			
Indirect Labour	8,750.00	10,500.00	12,250.00
Indirect Materials	6,666.67	8,000.00	9,333.34
Semi-variable Overheads:			
Repairs and Maintenance (1)	5,600.00	6,000.00	6,400.00
Electricity (2)	21,600.00	24,000.00	26,400.00
Fixed Overheads:			
Office Expenses including Salaries	6,000.00	6,000.00	6,000.00
Insurance	5,000.00	5,000.00	5,000.00
Depreciation	20,000.00	20,000.00	20,000.00
Total Overheads	73,616.67	79,500.00	85,383.34
Estimated Direct Labour hours	75,000	90,000	1,05,000
Overhead Rate	0.99	0.89	0.82

Working notes:

1. Repairs and maintenance amount to Rs. 6,000 at 60% capacity. Out of this 60% (i.e, Rs. 3,600) is fixed and 40% (i.e., Rs. 2,400) is variable. Rs. 3,600 will remain the same at all capacities while variable part will vary. Variable cost at 50% capacity will be $\left(\dfrac{2,400}{60} \times 50\right)$ Rs. 2,000 and 70% capacity $\left(\dfrac{2,400}{60} \times 70\right)$ Rs. 2800. So, the total expenditure will be (3,600 + 2,000) Rs. 5,600 and (3,600 + 2,800) Rs. 6,400 at 50% and 70% capacities respectively.

2. Electricity at 60% capacity is Rs. 24,000 of which 40% part (i.e., Rs. 9,600) is fixed and 60% is variable. Rs. 9,600 will be the same at all capacities but variable will be at 50% capacity $\left(\dfrac{14,400}{60}\times 50\right)$ Rs. 12,000 and at 70% capacity $\left(\dfrac{14,400}{60}\times 70\right)$ Rs. 16,800. Total electricity cost will be (9,600 + 12,000) Rs. 21,600 and (9,600 + 16,800) Rs. 26,400 at 50% and 70% capacities respectively.

Formula Method: Formula method is otherwise known as the budget cost allowance method. The preparation of budget under this method involves the following steps:

(i) A budget should be formed for the expected normal level of activity.

(ii) Ratios should be computed showing the relationship of each expense or group of expenses per unit level of activity.

ILLUSTRATION 19.11

Normal level of Activity	90%
Output at this level	900 units
Variable Costs	Rs. 9,000
Fixed Costs	Rs. 6,000

Compute the total cost in case the actual level of activity is 100%.

Solution

From the above question, it is clear that variable cost per 1% level of activity is Rs. 100.

Variable costs @100% level	Rs. 10,000
(Rs. 9,000 + 10 × Rs. 100)	
Fixed costs	6,000
Total costs	16,000

Thus, the total costs for any level of activity can be ascertained on the basis of the formula given below:

Total costs = Fixed costs + (Actual units of activity × Variable Costs per unit of activity)

Graphic Method: Under this method, the costs are classified is accordance with their variability-fixed, variable and semi-variable. Afterwards, the estimates should be made for various costs for various levels of activity. The data should then be plotted on a graph paper showing the costs at various levels of activity. The amounts of budgeted costs and the budgeted levels of activity should be on the vertical and horizontal scales respectively.

ILLUSTRATION 19.12

From the following information for 60% activity, compute the costs at 90% activity by the Graphic Method

Output	600 units
Variable Costs per unit	Rs. 6
Fixed Costs (Total)	Rs. 6,000
Semi-variable Costs (50% fixed)	Rs. 12,000

Solution

For determining the costs by the graphic method, the costs at various levels of activity should be computed and then plotted on the graph.

Costs at various levels of activity

Level of activity	Variable Costs (Rs. 6 + Rs. 10)	Fixed Costs (Rs. 6,000 + Rs. 6,000)	Total Costs
20% (200 units)	3,200	12,000	15,200
40% (400 units)	6,400	12,000	18,400
60% (600 units)	9,600	12,000	21,600
80% (800 units)	12,800	12,000	24,800
100% (1000 units)	16,000	12,000	28,000

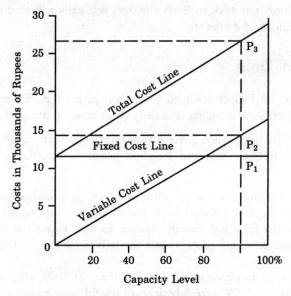

FIGURE 19.2 Flexible budget.

At 90% capacity: Fixed Costs   Rs. 12,000 (P₁)

Variable Costs   Rs. 14,400 (P₂)

Total Cost   Rs. 26,400 (P₃)

Operating Budget

A firm may prepare operating budget on the basis of programmes or responsibility areas. Thus it may comprise (i) programme budget, and (ii) responsibility budget.

Programme Budget: A budget comprising expected revenues and costs of various products or projects (that are termed as the major programmes of the concern) is termed programme budget. It may be constructed for each product line or project showing revenues, costs and the relative profitability of the different programmes.

Programme budget is useful in locating areas where efforts are required to bring down costs and enhance revenues.

Responsibility Budget: An operating budget prepared in terms of responsibility areas (i.e., cost centre, profit centre, investment centre, etc.) is called the responsibility budget. This budget shows the plans in terms of persons responsible for accomplishing them. The management can adopt this budget as a control device to appraise the performance of executives who are in-charge of various cost centres.

Refer Chapter 20, new horizons in budgeting for more details.

Classification According to Time

In terms of time, budget is classified into (a) long-term budget, (b) short-term budget, (c) current budget, and (d) rolling budget.

Long-term Budget: A budget which is designed for a long period (i.e., a period of 5 to 10 years) is termed as a long-term budget. Such a budget is usually prepared in physical units for the planning of the operations of a concern.

Budgets Based on Time

Short-term Budget: A budget designed for a short period (i.e., not exceeding 5 years) is termed as short-term budget. Such a budget is usually constructed in physical and monetary units.

Current Budgets: Budgets which cover a very short period (i.e., a month or a quarter) are current budgets. These budgets are prepared for short period in accordance with the prevailing conditions.

Rolling Budgets: Rolling budgets are also known as progressive budgets. Firms which follow such budgets will always be planned for a year ahead. A fresh budget is constructed after the end of each month/quarter for a full year in advance. In such a case, the figures for the month or quarter which has rolled down are dropped and the figures for the next month or quarter are added.

For instance, if a budget has been constructed for the year 2003, after the expiration of the first quarter ending 31st March 2003, a fresh budget for the full year ending 31st March 2004 will be constructed by dropping the figures of the quarter which has rolled down (i.e., quarter ending 31st March 2003) and adding figures for the new quarter ending 31st March 2004. If required, the figures for the remaining period (i.e., three quarters ending 31st December 2003) may also be revised. Whenever a quarter ends and a new quarter begins, this procedure will continue.

Financial Engineering

Increased competition as a result of rapid reforms and globalisation of markets has prompted the innovation of many financial products for prosperity in the long run. As such the concept of financial engineering emerged within given physical and budgetary constraints. The term 'engineering' refers to the practical application of mathematical or scientific principles to solve problems and design products. Hence financial engineering is the process of designing developing and implementing innovative financial instruments and formulating creative solutions to problems in finance. It lies in innovation and creativity to promote market efficiency and involves the construction of innovative asset liability structures (using combination of basic instruments) to obtain hybrid instruments. Thus financial engineering is very unique and of great help in corporate finance, investment management, money management, trading activities and risk management.

Financial engineering should be based on the period of financial requirements (i.e., short- or long-term) of a firm. A debt based instrument would be strategically attractive in the case of short-term requirement. Usually a firm requires engineering instruments on account of its (i) difficulty to meet repayment obligations, (ii) need to replace high rate servicing funds with lower rate funds, and (iii) requirement of modernization, expansion and financing of a project. Hence financial engineering is applied specifically on a firm to firm basis where (i) the straight route to equity is not difficult to obtain, and (ii) the interest rates of the term lending route through financial institutions may vary between 15 to 24 per cent, which prove to be torturous.

Notwithstanding constraints, financial engineering is intended to ensure the following:

(i) Raising of maximum funds which does not require servicing.

(ii) Servicing of funds raised to be deferred as long as possible.

(iii) Raising of funds from the cheapest source and at minimum cost.

(iv) Cost of capital is minimum.

Features of Instruments Devised by Financial Engineering

- It is a document in the nature of bond or debenture with warrants entitling shares after a certain period issued at par or at discount.
- It may be partly convertible or non-convertible.
- Its conversion is to be made at a pre-determined price or at a price to be determined by the company and at a certain ratio.
- Its interest rate is within the band of administered rates for long-term deposits and/or slightly higher than the minimum cap on working capital loan.
- Its lock-in period may be stipulated.
- It creates complexity for the investor in understanding his rate of return on investment and the cash-inflows, the present value thereof.

However, the success of the engineering instruments depends on the following presumptions.

(i) Increase of share price so as to make conversion at a premium.

(ii) Decrease in earnings per share on account of enhanced number of shares arising on conversion will be off-set by the reduced incidence of interest and increased profit after tax.

(iii) The instruments should be actively traded at the exchanges.

− REVIEW QUESTIONS −

1. What do you understand by budgetary control? Describe the essential steps of a budgetary control system.

2. What is budget? Bring out clearly the role of key factor in budgeting.

3. What is meant by the term budgeting? Describe the organisation for the preparation of budgets.

4. "Budgetary control improves planning, aids in coordination and helps in having comprehensive control". Elucidate.

5. Write notes on:

    (a) Programme budgeting·
    (b) Budgeting vs forecasting
    (c) Standard and estimate
    (d) Master budget

6. Explain in detail the principal factors that should be considered in developing sales budget.

7. Discuss the procedure for preparing the following budgets.

    (a) Production budget
    (b) Purchase budget
    (c) Sales budget

8. What is flexible budget? Explain the procedure for preparing flexible budget.

9. Write notes on:

    (a) Fixed budget
    (b) Operating budget
    (c) Rolling budgets
    (d) Cash budget
    (e) Financial engineering

10. From the following particulars, prepare a Purchase Budget

		P	Q	R
1.	Materials used			
2.	Price per ton Rs.	20,000	30,000	1,50,000
3.	Opening Stock in tons	300	400	500
4.	Closing Stock in tons	150	200	600
5.	Estimated Consumption in tons	1000	2000	2500
6.	Budget period 1-1-2000 to 31-12-2000			

(**Ans.:** Estimated cost of material to be purchased: P = 1,70,00,000; Q = 5,40,00,000; and R = 39,00,00,000)

11. Gopal Enterprises Ltd. manufactures two products A and B. A sales forecast for the first seven months of 2002 is given below:

Product	Jan.	Feb.	Mar.	April	May	June	July
A	2000	2400	3200	4000	4800	4800	4000
B	5600	5600	4800	4000	5200	3200	3600

It is expected that (i) finished goods equal to half the sales for the next month will be in stock at the end of each month, and (ii) the work-in-progress will be nil at the end of each month.

(Ans.:

Production required	Jan.	Feb.	Mar.	April	May	June
A	2200	2800	2600	4400	4800	4400
B	5600	5200	4400	4600	4200	3400)

12. Prepare a Production Budget for three months ending March 31, 2001 for a factory producing four products, on the basis of the following information.

Type of Product	Estimated Stock on Jan. 1, 2001	Estimated Sales during Jan. – March 2001	Desired Closing Stock on March 31 2001
	(units)	(units)	(units)
A	2000	10,000	3000
B	3000	15,000	5000
C	4000	13,000	3000
D	3000	12,000	2000

(Ans.: Units to be produced

Product: A – 11,000

B – 17,000

C – 12,000

D – 11,000

13. A Glass Manufacturing Company requires you to calculate and present the budget for the next year from the following information.

Sales:

Toughened glass	Rs. 3,00,000
Bent toughened glass	5,00,000
Direct Material Cost	60% of sales
Direct Wages	20 workers @ Rs. 150 per month

Factory overheads:

Indirect Labour:

Works manager Rs. 500 per month	
Foreman Rs. 400 per month	
Stores and Spares	2½ % on sales
Depreciation on Machinery	Rs. 12,000
Light and Power	5,000
Repairs and Maintenance	10% on Direct Wages

Administration, Selling and Distribution Expenses Rs. 14,000 per year

(Ans.: Net Profit: Rs. 2,10,000)

14. From the following details against production of 8000 units in 2002 prepare a flexible budget for 10,000 and 12,000 units for 2003.

	Rs.
Materials	40,000
Direct Expenses	16,000
Wages	30,000
Factory Expenses	20,000
Administrative Expenses	40,000
Selling Expenses	30,000
	1,76,000
Sales value	2,40,000
Profit	64,000

Material cost is likely to go up by 2% per unit. Wages are paid at a piece rate of Rs. 3 per unit. The fixed benefits paid to labour are likely to go up by 10% in the next year. Administrative expenses may go up by 5% due to normal increment, etc. Selling expenses rise by 5% against increase of 20% or any part thereof above 8,000 units. All selling prices are to be reduced by 10%, if production above 10,000 units is to be sold.

(**Ans.:** Level of activity 10,000 units; Profit – Rs. 97,400;
Level of activity 12,000 units; Profit – Rs. 99,700)

20

New Horizons in Budgeting

Budget is a pre-determined detailed plan of action developed and distributed as a guide to current operations and as a partial basis for the subsequent evaluation of performance.

— GORDON AND SHILLINGLAW

INTRODUCTION

Budget is a plan in respect of future financial requirements presented in written form. According to Harry L. Wylie,

> Budgets are finished products—they are formal programmes of future operations and expected results. Budgets result from forward thinking and planning.

The definition reveals that budget is a tool which may be used by the management in planning the future course of actions and in controlling the actual performance. Its basic purpose,

449

therefore, is to assist management in its main functions—Planning, Co-ordination and Control. Budget is the end result of budgeting. If budget is a future financial plan presented in written form, budgeting is the procedure for preparing plan in respect of future financial requirements. The procedure to be followed in preparing budget varies from business to business. However, in normal case, the following steps are involved in preparing the budgets.

STEPS IN BUDGET PREPARATION

    (i) Formulation of Policy: Business policies are the base for budget construction. The management should, therefore, formulate policies in regard to various plans such as sales, production, inventory, capital expenditure, cash etc., before the construction of budgets.

    (ii) Preparation of Forecasts: After formulating business policies, forecasts are made by considering past, present and future expectations in respect of various business activities. While making forecasts proper weightage should be given to key factor, if any.

    (iii) Comparison of Alternative Combination of Forecast: Having made the forecasts, the alternative combinations of forecasts are to be compared with a view to selecting the maximum profit-yielding combination of forecasts. When such forecasts are selected, they should be treated as final.

    (iv) Preparation of Budgets: After selecting the best combination of forecasts, it should be presented in written form. The forecasts presented in such a form are known as budgets. On the basis of forecasts for various functions, different functional budgets should be prepared. When all these functional budgets are co-ordinated and combined into one, it is known as Master Budget.

In the light of the above discussion, it is clear that the budgeting process followed in formulating budget is based on the current level of operations. A budget which is based on current level of operations is popularly known as traditional budgeting or line-item budgeting. The top management will have to face a number of problems on account of such type of budgeting. A few of them are as follows:

    (a) No proper identification of activities and programmes involving wasteful expenditures.

    (b) No encouragement on the part of managers for defining, identifying and evaluating alternative means of accomplishing the same objectives.

    (c) Lack of rigorous analysis of all proposed benefits and costs. This leads to irrational decision-making.

    (d) Inherent tendency of managers to inflate their budget requests. This causes more demand for funds than are available.

    (e) No search for key areas. As a result, priorities cannot be fixed.

The above problems of traditional budgeting can be overcome with the help of the following new techniques:

    1. Zero-base Budgeting

    2. Programme Budgeting

3. Performance Budgeting
4. Responsibility Accounting.

1. ZERO-BASE BUDGETING

Zero-base budgeting is the act of starting budgets from 'SCRATCH' or requiring each programme to be justified from the bottom up. It provides the ability to reduce budgets on a rational basis and reallocate resources without a decrease in the overall budget. It also provides a complete re-examination of all programmes, instead of incremental analysis and incremental budgeting. For example, suppose that the 2004 budget for programmes was 5 million rupees, and we would expect a 10 per cent increase in programme activity for 2005. In the incremental approach, the budget would be proposed for 5.5 million rupees. Emphasis would be placed on justifying the increase of Rs. 5,00,000. In the ZBB approaches, the budgeting activity would concern with justifying the entire budget request of 5.5 million rupees and not simply the incremental difference from 2004. But in the process of utilizing Zero-base budgeting, the complete budget is examined and a tendency to increase the budget by a flat amount of 10 per cent is rejected.

Zero-base budgeting was developed originally by *Peter A. Pyhrr* at Texas Instruments. He has defined ZBB as "an operating, planning and budgeting process which requires each manager to justify his entire budget request in detail from scratch (hence Zero Base) and shifts the burden of proof to each manager to justify why he should spend any money at all".

Following the article by Mr. Pyhrr on ZBB, Jimmy Carter implemented ZBB in the state of Georgia, USA. In Georgia, the use of ZBB is credited with the reduction of the administrative costs of government by more than one half and opportunity to provide substantially improved services without any tax increases. In addition, a number of companies and research organisations began experimenting with and using ZBB.

Process of ZBB

The Zero-base budgeting involves the following process:

(i) Identification of decision units.
(ii) Preparation and development of decision packages.
(iii) Ranking of decision packages.
(iv) Approval and funding.

(i) Identification of Decision Units

A decision unit should be identified in terms of either functional responsibility centre or cost centre. It may be a programme, an organisational unit, an activity or an appropriation item. Such decision units can be defined as major projects or capital projects. In each case, the decision units should have identifiable managers. While spelling out decision units, it is necessary to consider the size of them. If the decision unit selected is too small, considerable detail is required with little payoff in the budget process. On the other hand, if the decision unit derived is too large, the alternatives may not be properly evaluated.

Decision Unit = Project manager + Project team or Activity manager and his team

(ii) Preparation and Development of Decision Packages

The concept of decision package is at the very heart of ZBB. It has in a way revolutionised the whole process of budgeting. Decision package is a document that identifies and describes each decision unit so that management can evaluate and rank it. There may be several decision packages for one decision unit.

While formulating decision packages, it is necessary to assume that in each decision unit, budget request is made up of a sum of a series of decision packages. Moreover, each decision package specifies a discreet set of services, activities and resources. The first package, the one that is given the higher priority, represents a minimum level of fund (i.e., substantially less than the current level say 10 to 20 per cent less). The number of decision package is a summary of all aspects of an activity that helps management to take decision. The aspects included in are: purpose of activity, various proposed methods of its performance, alternative levels of performance, costs of its performance, benefits that would accrue to the organisation by its performance and the consequences of its non-performance.

(iii) Ranking of Priorities

Having completed the compilation process of decision packages, the next step is to rank all decision packages for a decision unit in descending priority. There are three different questions for ranking: (1) What goals/objectives, (2) How many resources, and (3) How many major goals. Thus it is required to rank all decision packages for a decision unit in descending priority. The ranking may be performed by an individual manager or a committee. Firms have developed extensive techniques for conducting the ranking procedures. But at successively higher organisational levels, a series of rankings may be required.

The ranking process establishes priorities among the functions as described in the decision packages. The ranking would be made by top-management to analyse the trade-off among profit centres and specifically to compare the marginal benefits of funding additional decision-packages against the organisation's profit needs. With the decision packages ranked in order of priority, management can continually revise budgets by revising the cut-off level on any or all ranking.

(iv) Funding

After ranking, the next process in ZBB is funding. It means the allocation of available resources of the organisation to various decision units in accordance with the ranking process. In case the available resources are not adequate to meet the requirements of the selected alternatives, the alternatives with the second highest rank is selected for funding and inclusion in the budget for the organisation.

Benefits of ZBB

The main benefits of ZBB are as follows:

1. It ensures optimum use of financial resources as allocation is made on the basis of cost-benefit analysis.
2. It identifies the alternative ways to meet objectives.
3. It identifies the tradeoffs between and within programmes.

4. It provides the managers at all levels with better information on the relative priority associated with budget request and decision.

5. It eliminates duplicate and overlapping programmes.

6. It results in undertaking only essential and high priority scheme in the organisation.

7. It forces the management to look ahead and becomes more effective and efficient in administering the business operations.

8. It helps to co-ordinate, integrate, and balance the efforts of various departments in the light of the overall objectives.

9. It improves the quality of communication which results in better understanding and harmonious relations among managers and subordinates.

10. It develops an atmosphere of profit mindedness and cost consciousness as projects/ programmes have to pass the acid test of objectivity before these are funded.

11. It makes the budgeting exercise itself more rational and systematic and less political and arbitrary.

Limitations of ZBB

Although ZBB is a systematic approach to the solution of problems, it is not foolproof. Thus it is subject to the following limitations:

1. It requires more time and effort than traditional budgeting.

2. It expects high degree of managerial skill because its success depends upon the precision of estimates.

3. It cannot directly be applied to direct materials, direct labour and overheads associated with production function. Thus its application is limited.

Criticism of ZBB

1. An organisation which introduces ZBB should face the difficulty of defining the decision units and decision packages.

2. Every manager is not expected to do the scientific technique of ranking the decision packages.

3. The ranking of inter-related decision packages is a too tough task.

4. It requires high cost of administration because of too much paper work.

5. It is not elastic as there is no system of revision for contingencies.

6. It challenges the fundamental accounting postulate of continuity as it regards irrelevancy of the past. Moreover, budget is a continuous process.

Distinction between Traditional Budgeting and ZBB

Traditional Budgeting	ZBB
1. It is accounting-oriented as it lays main stress on previous level of expenditure.	1. It is decision-oriented as all programmes (existing and new) are to compete for scarce resources afresh.

Continued

Distinction between Traditional Budgeting and ZBB

Traditional Budgeting	ZBB
2. It makes first reference to previous year's level of expenditure and then budget demand for hike is made.	2. It develops and ranks both old and new programmes so as to enable the top management to focus attention only on decision package having top priority.
3. It tempts managers to inflate budget request in such a way that even after the cuts, they would still get what they desire.	3. It exposes such managers because top management accords approval to only those decision packages which are carefully devised and result-oriented.
4. It is the responsibility of the top management to justify why a particular amount be spent on a programme.	4. It is the responsibility of the decision unit manager to justify why a particular amount be spent on a programme.

2. PROGRAMME BUDGETING

A budgeting which focuses on the achievement of specific goals and missions and on the output (results) is known as programme budgeting. The term is used in conjunction with planning, programming and budgetary system. Programme budgeting was introduced originally by the *Second Hoover Commission* in 1961 in the U.S. Department of Defence where budgeting was mainly an allocation process and it was to be linked to long-range planning and overall national goals. Later in 1968, its use was extended to all federal and local government departments. In Britain, it is known as *"Output Budgeting"*.

The basic theme of programme budgeting is to build budgeting around each result-oriented plan for the future and make a rational attempt for relating available resources to such plans. Programme budgeting integrates all planning activities of the organisation into a total system. For this purpose, the programmes for the mission of the organisation are identified and each programme is broken down into elements. For each element, resources are identified and allocation of resources to various programmes over the period is considered. Thus programme budgeting involves the following steps:

(a) Identification the programmes to achieve the mission.

(b) Identification of various elements of programme.

(c) Allocation of resources to programme.

(d) Forecast and analysis of alternatives.

Objectives

Programme budgeting has the following three partially separable objectives:

(i) Classification of government goals and objectives.

(ii) Comparison of costs and outcomes and the exploration of alternative means of achieving outcomes.

(iii) Long-range planning of governmental programmes.

Merits of Programme Budgeting

The benefits of programme budgeting are as follows:

(i) It emphasises the purposes and objectives of the programme.

(ii) It helps for allocating resources through strategic decision-making.

(iii) It helps the decision-makers by providing relevant and future data in appropriate format.

(iv) It facilitates the analysis of alternatives in the light of benefits and costs.

3. PERFORMANCE BUDGETING

The concept of performance budgeting was originally used in the USA by the *First Hoover Commission* in 1949 when it recommended the adoption of a budget based on functions, programmes and activities. In India, Administrative Reforms Commission suggested the use of performance budgeting by the Government. Performance budgeting implies the technique of presenting the budget in terms of functions, programmes, activities, projects and objects, costs involved, along with evaluative aspects. It correlates the physical and financial aspects of various activities and establishes a meaningful relationship between inputs and outputs. In other words, performance budgeting shows costs matching with operations and helps in knowing whether the concern is getting adequate results for the money spent. Thus performance budget is a work plan which expresses target for accomplishment based on accepted norms. Moreover, one of the pertinent aspects of performance budget is the measurement of actual performance both in physical and financial terms in relation to the expressed targets.

Features of Performance Budget

The following are the basic features of performance budget:

1. It integrates the accounting systems with the plan objectives.

2. It correlates the physical and financial aspects of planning.

3. It clearly defines the precise details of job or services to be performed.

4. It brings into account the functional classification of budget (i.e., presenting budget expenditure in terms of functions, programmes, activities, and projects).

5. It helps in resource allocation.

6. It involves the techniques for the measurement of output in relation to input.

7. It facilitates performance audit.

8. It reshapes the entire finance function as per the needs of the development as envisaged in national development plans.

Ingredients of Performance Budgeting

1. **Objective Formulation:** Before preparing performance budget, the objectives of the concern should be formulated in concrete terms as the performance budgeting indicates the appraisal of the performance of the concern in the light of its objectives.

2. **Programme/Activity Classification:** A meaningful activity classification in tune with the objectives of the concern should be incorporated in the performance budget. However, such classification of activities is to be tailored to the needs of both the organisation and the various levels of management.

3. **Accounting Structure:** The concept of performance budgeting should also be built into the structure of accounts of the concern in order to operationalise the scheme of performance budgeting.

4. **Norms and Standards:** The functioning of the system of performance budgeting largely depends on the techniques evolved for the measurement of output in relation to input. Thus it is highly necessary to set physical targets in a scheme of performance budgeting for attainment in respect of each programme and activity.

5. **Decentralised Responsibility Structure and Delegation:** A style of management based on decentralised responsibility structure is required in performance budgeting technique. Such responsibility structure necessitates the delegation of financial power commensurate with the responsibilities to be discharged at various levels.

6. **Reporting and Review of Performance:** A continuous and regular flow of information relating to financial and physical aspects of a programme or activity to each responsibility level assume vital significance in performance budgeting. The information so collected should be compared with the budgeted plan to find out variances, if any. Then report is to be made for its submission to various levels of management. Such a report should also contain the information relating to variance analysis, directing the causes, isolating the key factors and so on.

Objectives of Performance Budgeting

The various objectives of performance budgeting are:

1. to integrate the physical and financial aspects of each activity and programme,
2. to improve budget formulation,
3. to facilitate better appreciation and review of organisational activities by the top management,
4. to measure progress towards long-term goals,
5. to help for effective performance audit,
6. to help in better appreciation and review by controlling authorities like legislature, PAC, Board of Trustee, etc.

Distinction between Performance Budgeting and Programme Budgeting

Performance Budgeting	Programme Budgeting
1. It focuses on activity analysis.	1. It focuses on output analysis.
2. It treats work and activities as ends in themselves.	2. It regards work and services as intermediate aspects, i.e., the process of converting resources into output.
3. It lays greater emphasis on cost accounting and scientific management.	3. It derives its core ideas from economics and systems analysis.
4. It is based on the past performance.	4. It is essentially based on the future programmes.
5. It defines budgeting as a tool for management and the budget as a work programme.	5. It treats budgeting as an allocative process among competitive claims and budget as a statement of policy.

Distinction between Performance Budgeting and Traditional Budgeting

Performance Budgeting	*Traditional Budgeting*
1. It is based on prospective approach, i.e., it focuses on future impact of current decisions.	1. It is based on retrospective approach, i.e., it measures what was done with current means in estimating for the next budget.
2. It makes budgeting decisions by emphasising output categories such as goals, objectives, products, etc.	2. It makes budgeting decisions by emphasising input categories like materials, salaries, facilities, etc.
3. Its decisions flow downwards.	3. Its decisions flow upwards.

4. RESPONSIBILITY ACCOUNTING

The basic objectives of a concern is to run in an effective manner by reducing its cost and maximising its profit as much as possible. The personnel at different levels in the concern are the best centres for achieving the cost control and cost reduction. The centres may be the divisions or departments of the sections and regions of the activities of the concern. In a responsibility accounting system, the responsibility centres form the decentralised units of a concern. Moreover, responsibility centres are divisionalisation or creating subdivisions of a concern to guage executive performance. Each responsibility centre has a defined executive head to control operations.

Responsibility accounting is also known as activity accounting, profitability accounting and management by objectives through the accounting control system. It is a system of control wherein costs are identified with the person responsible for them. In other words, responsibility accounting is a system of accounting that identifies responsibility centres as units of divisibility in a concern, the performance of which is measured in terms of its goals through accounting criteria. It lays emphasis upon the decision of a concern among different levels in such a way that each level becomes the responsibility of an individual manager. Each manager is held responsible for these activities which are under his direct control. Thus responsibility accounting is an accounting control system that reflects the performance of a decentralised concern. In the words of Charles T. Hongren,

> responsibility accounting is a system of accounting that recognises various responsibility centres throughout the organisation and that reflects the plan of action of each of these centres by allocating particular revenues and costs to the one having the pertinent responsibility.

Essentials of Responsibility Accounting

The essentials of responsibility accounting are:

1. to create suitable responsibility centres in the organisation,
2. to fix the area of authority and responsibility for each centre,
3. to have a clear-cut idea, on the part of each manager as to what is expected of him,
4. to mention only the revenues, expenses, profits and investments controllable by the manager in the performance report of each centre.

5. to highlight variances and items requiring management's attention in the performance report of each centre.

Steps in Responsibility Accounting

One of the essential elements of responsibility accounting is the effective communication of accurate information to the right person at the right time. For this purpose, the responsibility accounting should have the following steps:

1. Setting targets and communicating them to each manager/executive.
2. Putting into operation the continuous appraisal of actual performance and conveying the result to each manager of concerned responsibility centre.
3. Reporting of variances to the higher management along with the names of managers of concerned responsibility centres.
4. Suggesting corrective measures and communicating them to the concerned manager of the centre.

Major Considerations in Responsibility Accounting

Major considerations required in responsibility accounting are:

1. to express, as far as possible and feasible, all inputs and outputs in monetary terms.
2. to measure output in terms of total cost of services offered if monetary measurement of output is impossible.
3. to measure the financial performance of a manager by controllable factors manageable by him.

Responsibility Centres

Responsibility Accounting focuses attention on the responsibility centres. Responsibility centre is any point in an organisation where control is exercised over the costs or generating of revenue is found. Such a point may be an individual, an operation, a department, a company, a division, or the centre or organisation itself. The various responsibility centres are:

(i) The cost centre
(ii) The profit centre
(iii) The investment centre

The Cost/Expense Centre

A cost centre is the smallest area of responsibility where costs are accumulated. A manager of a cost centre is responsible for costs incurred in that centre. The cost centre records only the cost incurred and not the revenue earned. Hence cost centres are service departments providing services to other departments such as public relations, R&D, personnel, etc.

A cost centre is to be taken as an index of performance for departments whose product/output cannot be measured and expressed in financial figures, like consultancy, personal and administrative. It, therefore, reflects productivity of inputs, i.e., cost per unit of service.

The Profit Centre

A Profit centre is a big area of activity that is responsible for both inputs (costs) and outputs (revenues). The prime responsibility of a profit centre is to generate earnings. Hence it has full control over both costs and revenues and is expected to contribute a fair rate of return on the assets it deploys. Managers of profit centres are assessed on their ability to generate earnings. In a profit centre approach, the profit may be targeted and the manager has full authority:

(i) to control costs,

(ii) to earn revenue,

(iii) to effect cost-revenues,

(iv) to decide internal competition (i.e., transfer pricing policies),

(v) to decide external competition.

The Investment Centre

It is the area of managerial responsibility in which an individual is held responsible to report profit as well as profit in relation to investment, i.e., the investment required to generate the profit. The manager of an investment centre has full control over costs, revenues and investment funds. The performance of this centre is measured in terms of ROI.

Limitations of Responsibility Centre

The implementation of responsibility accounting in an organisation is really a tough task because of its limitations as listed below:

1. Difficulty in designing an organisation chart with clearly delineating lines of authority and responsibility.

2. Difficulty in implementation on account of conflict between individual interest and organisation interest.

3. Ignoring the personal reactions of the personnel involved in the implementations.

4. Requiring a good reporting system to make the system useful and meaningful.

Clubbing of Responsibility Accounting with Zero-Base Budgeting

Zero-base budgeting would give out the solution to the problem of lack of base for cost control and reduction. But it requires a check on each individual concerned with the incurring of the expenditure. For each individual, some expenditures are controllable and others non-controllable. A detailed budget should, therefore, be prepared mentioning the quantum of controllable and non-controllable expenditures. This enables to hold the concerned person responsible for the control of his controllable cost and thus leads to better cost control and cost reduction. Moreover, when each individual becomes aware of the outlay he is going to control and the output he is going to give out, he will become a true asset for the concern.

The concept of responsibility accounting may be explained in a proper way with the help of the following data based case.

ABC Company Ltd.

(a) Budget for the Process Division   *Rs.*

Budgeted Total Expenditure   1,20,000
Breaking Activities:

1. Training   60,000
2. Welfare Programme   14,000
3. Facilities & Fringe Benefits   40,000
4. Other Expenses   6,000

(b) The above Budget expressed under Responsibility Accounting Concept.

Process Division:

Activity/Executive	Mr. X Rs.	Mr. Y Rs.	Mr. Z Rs.
1. Training	20,000	20,000	20,000
2. Welfare Programme	5,000	5,000	4,000
3. Facilities & Fringe Benefits	13,000	13,000	14,000
4. Other Expenses	2,000	2,000	2,000
Total Budget (Rs. 1,20,000)	40,000	40,000	40,000

Each executive of the concerned activity should be considered as a centre of responsibility and the expenditure should be allotted to this centre. As each expenditure is now controllable for each centre, the control over such expenditure becomes the sole responsibility of the individual who is treated as the centre of responsibility. However, the responsibility should not be more or less than the authority and both these would be properly defined as to their quantum, nature and relations to the output expected. Once the quantum of responsibility is properly defined, the evaluation criteria in respect of various centres such as cost centre, profit centre and investment centre become easy to be formulated. They are as follows:

(a) **For Cost Centre:** (i) Operating ratios (ii) Output-input ratio (iii) Waste & Scrap data (iv) Quality variance (v) Cost variance.

(b) **For Profit Centre:** (i) Profitability (ii) Capital turnover (iii) Inventory turnover (iv) Profit trend (v) Return on investment.

(c) **For Investment Centre:** a & b above (i) Capital expenditure variance (ii) Assets turnover (iii) Cost of capital (iv) Comparative study of the incremental cost of funds and incremental revenue from these funds (v) Debt-Equity ratio (vi) Solvency liquidity ratio.

The concept of responsibility accounting is very much essential in public sector enterprises although the same is difficult to introduce in such enterprises. The performance of such enterprises can be evaluated with the help of profitability criterion. But some academicians and professionals criticise the idea of responsibility accounting as an idea based on 'free trade and free competition' which is not suitable to the public enterprises in Indian economy. However, they forget that these public enterprises use public money and the public has every right to expect an increasing ROI from their money invested.

In brief, if Zero-base budgeting is properly clubbed with the idea of responsibility accounting then it can give out the cost control and cost reduction on both the macro and micro levels. Zero-base budgeting is the proforma idea of performance budgeting whereas responsibility accounting is the tool to use this pro forma successfully.

— REVIEW QUESTIONS —

1. Discuss the problems of traditional budgeting. How can these problems be overcome?
2. What is Zero-base budgeting? Distinguish between Zero-base budgeting and traditional budgeting.
3. Discuss the process of Zero-base budgeting. Explain its merits and demerits.
4. Distinguish between:
   (a) Performance budgeting and Programme budgeting.
   (b) Performance budgeting and Traditional budgeting.
   (c) Budget and Budgeting.
5. What is performance budgeting? Discuss its ingredients and objectives.
6. What is responsibility accounting? Discuss its steps and limitations.

21

Capital Budgeting

Capital Budgeting is a long-term planning for making
and financing proposed capital outlays.

— CHARLES T. HORNGREN

CONTENTS

- Meaning and definition
- Process of capital budgeting
- Capital Budgeting—methods of appraisal (investment criteria)
- Review questions

The allocation of funds of a concern mainly depends on its investment decision. It is a choice of assets such as short-term or current assets and long-term or fixed assets where funds will be invested. The investment decision which relates to the short-term or current assets is known as working capital management or current assets investment decision whereas the investment decision relating to the long-term or fixed assets is known as capital budgeting or capital expenditure decision or long-term investment decision.

MEANING AND DEFINITION

Capital budgeting is the planning of capital expenditure which provide yields over a number of years. In other words, it is the firm's decision to invest its funds most efficiently in long-term activities against an anticipated flow of future benefits over a number of years. Thus under capital budgeting, proposed capital expenditure and their financing are considered and projects assuring the most profitable use of given resources are undertaken. In the words of Charles T. Horngren,

> Capital Budgeting is a long-term planning for making and financing proposed capital outlays.

A similar view has been expressed by Max. D. Richards and Paul S. Greenlaw,

> when they hold Capital Budgeting generally refers to acquiring inputs with long-term returns.

Capital budgeting is a decision-making process through which a business concern evaluates the purchase of various fixed assets for expansion, replacement, etc. In this sense Hampton John. J. has put,

> Capital Budgeting refers to firm's formal process for the acquisition and investment of capital.

A similar view has been expressed by Gitman L.J. when he holds,

> Capital Budgeting refers to the total process of generating, evaluating, selecting and following up on capital expenditure alternatives.

PROCESS OF CAPITAL BUDGETING

The various steps involved in capital budgeting process depend upon large number of factors such as size of the concern, nature of projects, their numbers, complexities and diversities and so on. According to Quinin G. David, the following five steps are involved in the process of capital budgeting:

(i) Project Generation

(ii) Project Evaluation

(iii) Project Selection

(iv) Project Execution

(v) Follow-up

(i) Project Generation: A continuous generation of capital expenditure proposals like proposals expanding the revenues and proposals reducing the cost is highly essential to make efficient and full use of funds of the concern. If the proposals expanding the revenues relate to the proposals to add new products and to expand the capacity in existing lines, the proposals reducing the costs are designed to bring savings in cost in existing lines without changing the scale of operations.

(ii) Project Evaluation: This process deals with judging the suitability and desirability of a project by applying various criteria. Thus the process of project evaluation involves estimating the costs and benefits in terms of cash flows, and selecting an appropriate criterion for judging the desirability of the projects.

(iii) Project Selection: This step deals with screening and selecting the projects. Usually, projects under consideration can be screened at various levels of management. But the final approval of them should be given by the top management.

(iv) Project Execution: After the projects are selected, the funds are to be allocated for them. Such a formal plan for the allocation of fund is known as capital budget. The top management or executive committee should ensure that funds are spent as per the allocation made in the capital budgets.

(v) **Follow-up:** Follow-up deals with comparison of actual performance with the budgeted data. This will ensure better forecasting and also help in sharpening the technique of forecasting.

Features of Capital Budgeting

Capital budgeting is a multi-facet activity involving the search for new and more profitable investment proposals, investigating and predicting the effects of accepting the proposal and making profitability—analysis of each and every project. Thus the salient features of capital budgeting are:

(i) Potentially large anticipated benefits;

(ii) A relatively high degree of risk; and

(iii) A relatively long period between the initial outlay and the anticipated return.

Significance of Capital Budgeting

In financial decision-making, capital budgeting decisions have primary significance as they have a vital impact on the profitability aspect of the firm. Moreover, capital budgeting is significant due to the following:

1. **It has Long-term Implications:** The most significant reason for capital budgeting decisions is that they have long-term implications for a firm. Usually, the effects of a capital budgeting decision extend into the future and have to be put up with for a longer period than the consequences of current operating expenditures.

2. **It requires a Large Amount of Funds:** The capital investment decisions must be thoughtful, wise and correct as they require large amounts of funds. But a wrong/ incorrect decision would result in losses which prevent the firm earning profits from other investments as well as due to scarcity of resources.

3. **It is the Most Critical and Difficult Decision:** The decision relating to capital investment is the most critical and difficult in the sense that such a decision will have a far-reaching influence on a firm's profitability in future.

4. **It is not Reversible:** Once the decisions relating to capital investment are taken, they are not easily reversible. This is because of the fact that the second-hand capital assets may have neither any market nor any possibility of conversion into other usable assets. Then the only solution is to dispose the same sustaining a heavy loss to the firm.

CAPITAL BUDGETING—METHODS OF APPRAISAL (Investment Criteria)

Capital expenditure decision involves a long-term commitment in the sense that current investment yields benefit in future. Such a decision assumes great significance because the future development and the competitive power of the concern depends on it. A concern should, therefore, adopt a sound appraisal method to measure the economic worth of each investment project. However, an appraisal method or investment criterion is said to be sound if it possesses the following features or conditions:

(i) It should provide a basis for distinguishing acceptable and rejectable proposals.

(ii) It should provide a basis for ranking of projects in accordance with desirability.

(iii) It should help in choosing the right one among alternative projects if any.

(iv) It should be a criterion applicable to any investment project.

(v) It should recognise that early benefits are preferable to later benefits.

The various investment criteria or appraisal methods which are widely used for evaluating the capital expenditure proposals are broadly classified into the following two groups:

1. Traditional or unsophisticated Method and
2. Time-Adjusted or sophisticated Method

The traditional method consists of (a) pay-back period method and (b) average rate of return method. The time adjusted rate of return method is also known as discounted cash flow technique which comprises: (a) present value method, (b) net present value method, (c) internal rate of return method, (d) benefit-cost ratio or profitability index method, and (e) terminal value method.

1. Traditional or Unsophisticated Method

(a) Pay-Back Period

The pay-back period method or pay-out method is the unsophisticated method of capital budgeting. It describes the relationship between annual savings (cash inflows) and total amount of capital expenditure (investment) in terms of time. In other words, the pay-back method reveals the period which is required to get back the original cost of investments by annual savings. To be more precise, pay-back period is the investment divided by annual savings. The operating savings here mean cash inflows before interest and depreciation but after taxes, if any.

However, the computation of pay-back period depends on whether the cash flow accrues at even rate or at uneven rate.

(i) When cash flow accrues at even rate, i.e., where there is equal cash inflow:

$$\text{Pay-Back Period (P.B.P.)} = \frac{\text{NI}}{\text{OS}}$$

$$\text{Here NI} = \text{Net Investment}$$
$$\text{OS} = \text{Operating Savings}$$

ILLUSTRATION 21.1

A project requires an investment of Rs. 2,00,000 with a life of 10 years which yields an expected annual net cash flow of Rs. 50,000. Compute the pay-back period.

Solution

$$\text{Pay-Back Period (PBP)} = \frac{NI}{OS} = \frac{Rs.\,2,00,000}{Rs.\,50,000}$$

$$= 4 \text{ years}$$

ILLUSTRATION 21.2

Gopal Industries Ltd., is considering the purchase of a new machine which would carry out some operations at present being performed by hands. The two alternative models under consideration are "DUPLEX" and "GAMELEX".

The following information is available in respect of the two models:

	DUPLEX Rs.	GAMELEX Rs.
Cost of Machines	10,00,000	15,00,000
Estimated Life (in years)	10	15
Estimated Savings in Scrap (p.a.)	60,000	80,000
Additional Cost of Supervision (p.a.)	65,000	85,000
Additional Cost of Maintenance (p.a.)	35,000	50,000
Cost of Indirect Material (p.a.)	30,000	40,000
Estimated savings in wages:		
(i) Wages per worker p.a.	3,000	3,000
(ii) No. of workers not required	200	250

Using the method of Pay-back Period, suggest as which model should be bought. Ignore tax.

Solution

Statement of Annual Savings or OS (Operating Savings)

	Model DUPLEX Rs.	Model GAMELEX Rs.
Estimated Saving p.a.		
(i) Scrap	60,000	80,000
(ii) Wages	6,00,000	7,50,000
	6,60,000	8,30,000

Estimated Additional Cost:

(i)	Cost of Supervision	65,000	85,000
(ii)	Cost of Maintenance	35,000	50,000
(iii)	Indirect Material	30,000	40,000
		1,30,000	1,75,000
	Operating Saving p.a. (OS)	5,30,000	6,55,000
	Pay-back period:		
(a)	Net Investment	10,00,000	15,00,000
(b)	Operating Savings	5,30,000	6,55,000
(c)	(a) divided by (b)	1.8 years	2.2 years
		(Approximately)	(Approximately)

Thus it may be recommended that Model, DUPLEX be bought because it has comparatively lower pay-back period.

(ii) When Cash Flow accrues at uneven rate, i.e., where there is unequal cash inflow

The pay-back period may be calculated by adding up the cash inflows until the total is equal to the initial cash investment.

In the formula form:

$$\text{Pay-back period} = E + \frac{B}{C}$$

E = No. of years immediately preceding the year of recovery.
B = Balance amount of investments to be recovered.
C = Savings (Cash Inflow) during the year of final recovery.

ILLUSTRATION 21.3

Calculate the pay-back period for a project which requires a cash outlay of Rs. 50,000 but the same generates a cash inflow of Rs. 20,000; Rs. 15,000; Rs. 10,000; Rs. 8,000.

Solution

Year	Savings	Cumulative Savings
1	20,000	20,000
2	15,000	35,000
3	10,000	45,000
4	8,000	53,000

Note: Cumulative total is to be done up to the point where such total equals or just exceeds the total cost.

$$\text{P.B.P.} = E + \frac{B}{C} = 3 \text{ years} + \frac{50,000 - 45,000}{8,000} \text{ years}$$

$$= 3 + \frac{5}{8} = 3\frac{5}{8} \text{ years}$$

ILLUSTRATION 21.4

The following are the details relating to Project A and Project B.

	Project A Rs.	Project B Rs.
Cost of Project	2,00,000	2,50,000
Estimated Scrap	20,000	30,000
Estimated Savings:		
Year 1	30,000	50,000
Year 2	40,000	70,000
Year 3	60,000	70,000
Year 4	60,000	70,000
Year 5	50,000	40,000
Year 6	40,000	30,000
Year 7	10,000	—

Calculate Pay-back periods and consider which project is better.

Solution

Year	Project A		Project B	
	Savings Rs.	Cum. Sav. Rs.	Savings Rs.	Cum. Sav. Rs.
1	30,000	30,000	50,000	50,000
2	40,000	70,000	70,000	1,20,000
3	60,000	1,30,000	70,000	1,90,000
4	60,000	1,90,000	70,000	2,60,000
5	50,000	2,40,000	—	—

Note: Cumulative total is to be calculated up to the point where such total equals or just exceeds the total cost.

Pay-Back Period:

$$\text{Projct A — P.B.P.} = 4 \text{ years} + \frac{2,00,000 - 1,90,000}{50,000} \text{ years}$$

$$= 4 + \frac{1}{5} = 4\frac{1}{5} \text{ years}$$

$$\text{Projct B — P.B.P.} = 3 \text{ years} + \frac{2,50,000 - 1,90,000}{70,000} \text{ years}$$

$$= 3 + \frac{6}{7} \text{ years} = 3\frac{6}{7} \text{ years}$$

Project B is better because it has comparatively lower pay-back period.

Advantages

1. It is an important guide to investment policy.
2. It lays a great emphasis on liquidity.
3. It is simple to operate and easy to understand.
4. It acts as a yardstick in comparing the profitability of two projects.
5. It weighs early returns heavily and ignores distant returns.
6. It enables a firm to determine the period required to recover the original investment with some percentage return. This helps the firm to know the degree of risk associated with the investment.

Disadvantages

1. It fails to consider the period over which an investment is likely to fetch incomes.
2. It ignores the time value of money.
3. It recognises only the recovery of purchase costs, not the profits earned during the working life of the asset.
4. It fails to consider that profits from different projects may arrive at an uneven rate.
5. It over-emphasises liquidity and ignores capital wastage and the economic life of an asset.
6. It does not consider the cost of capital which is a base for sound investment decisions.

Improvements in Traditional Approach to Pay-back Period

Pay-back method is very popular in Western countries in spite of its many weaknesses. Some authorities in the field of Management Accounting have, therefore, ventured to bring some modifications in traditional approach. These modifications are as follows:

(i) Pay-Back Profitability
(ii) Discounted Pay-Back Period
(iii) Pay-Back Reciprocal

Pay-back Profitability

Pay-back profitability is the modified version of pay-back method. This method recognises that the total cash flow remains after recovering the cost of investment. Hence, a project is to be selected on the basis of post pay-back profitability which is calculated as:

Net cash flow of savings × (Expected life of the project – Pay-back Period)

ILLUSTRATION 21.5

The following are the particulars relating to two alternative machines:

	Machine A	*Machine B*
Purchase Price	Rs. 50,000	Rs. 84,000
Estimated Life (years)	8	10
Net Earnings after Tax but Before Depreciation (p.a.)	Rs. 10,000	Rs. 12,000

Calculate the profitability of the investment on the basis of pay-back profitability.

Solution

Profitability Statement

	Machine A	Machine B
Cost of Investment	Rs. 50,000	Rs. 84,000
Estimated Life	8	10
Net earnings (after Tax but Before Depreciation)	Rs. 10,000	Rs. 12,000
Pay-Back Period	50,000	84,000
	$\frac{50,000}{10,000}$ = 5 years	$\frac{84,000}{12,000}$ = 7 years
Profitability:		
Net Savings ×	$10,000 \times (8-5)$	$12,000 \times (10-7)$
(Expected Life – Pay-Back Period)	= Rs. 30,000	= Rs. 36,000

From the above statement, it is clear that Machine-B is a profitable investment. But if the pay-back period is considered Machine-A appears to be more profitable as its pay-back period is shorter i.e., 5 years in comparison with Machine-B which has a pay-back period of 7 years. Since, the Machine-B contributes Rs. 6,000 more (36,000 – 30,000) after recovering its capital cost, it is more profitable to invest in Machine-B than in Machine-A.

(ii) Discounted Pay-Back Period

When pay-back period is calculated by taking into account the discounting or interest factors, it is known as Discounted Pay-back Period. This method actually recognises the time value of money by combining pay-back with Net Present Value (Discount Cash Flow).

Under this method, after ascertaining the present value of each year's savings, cumulative totals of all discounted values should be made. The procedure for computing the Discounted Pay-back Period on the basis of cumulative totals will be the same as mentioned in the traditional approach.

ILLUSTRATION 21.6

Calculate the pay-back period from the following particulars using (i) the traditional method and (ii) the discounted pay-back method:

Cost of the Project Rs. 50,000
Life   5 years
Cost of Capital   10%

Year	Operating Savings Rs.	P.V. of Rs. 1 at 10%
1	5,000	0.909
2	20,000	0.826
3	30,000	0.751
4	30,000	0.683
5	10,000	0.621

Solution

(i) Pay-back Period under Traditional Method

Year	Annual Savings Rs.	Cum. Savings Rs.
1	5,000	5,000
2	20,000	25,000
3	30,000	55,000

$$\text{P.B.P.} = E + \frac{B}{C} = 2 \text{ years} + \frac{5,0000 - 25,000}{30,000} \text{ years}$$

$$= 2 + \frac{5}{6} \text{ years} = 2 \text{ years and 10 months}$$

(ii) Discounted Pay-back Period

Years	Savings Rs.	P.V. Factor	Discounted Savings Rs.	Cum. Dis. Savings Rs.
1	5,000	0.909	4,546	4,546
2	20,000	0.826	16,530	21,076
3	30,000	0.751	22,539	43,615
4	30,000	0.683	20,490	64,105

$$\text{D.P.B.P.} = E + \frac{B}{C} = 3 \text{ years} + \frac{50,000 - 43,615}{20,490} \text{ years}$$

$$= 3 + \frac{1}{3} \text{ approximately} = 3 \text{ years 4 months}$$

(iii) Pay-Back Reciprocal

As explained, the traditional pay-back period expresses the profitability in terms of years. But it neglects time factor and does not highlight upon the rate of return. Hence pay-back reciprocal is utilised to rectify these situations. However, pay-back reciprocal is useful where the cash flow/earning is relatively consistent and the life of the asset is at least double the pay-back period. The formula for computing Pay-back Reciprocal is:

$$\text{Pay-back Reciprocal} = \frac{1}{\text{Pay-back Period}}$$

ILLUSTRATION 21.7

From the following particulars relating to two machines, compute Pay-back Reciprocal.

	Machine X	Machine Y
Purchase Price	Rs. 25,000	Rs. 42,000
Estimated Life (years)	8	10
Net Earnings (after Tax but before Depreciation) p.a.	Rs. 5,000	Rs. 6,000

	Machine X	*Machine Y*
Pay-Back Period	$\dfrac{25,000}{5,000} = 5$ years	$\dfrac{42,000}{6,000} = 7$ years
Pay-Back Reciprocal		
$\dfrac{1}{\text{Pay-Back Period}} \times 100$	$\dfrac{1}{5} \times 100 = 20\%$	$\dfrac{1}{7} \times 100 = 14.3\%$

(b) Average Rate of Return (A.R.R.)

This method, also known as Accounting Rate of Return, is used to measure the rate of return on an investment in a project. Under this method average annual profit (after tax) is expressed as percentage of investment. Thus A.R.R. is found out by dividing the average annual profit after tax by the average investment. Here, average investment should be equal to the original investment divided by two. If there is scrap value, then cost minus scrap value will be divided by two and to this, Scrap Value should be added. If there is additional working capital required by the project, it should also be added.

Average Rate of Return expressed as a percentage can be determined with the help of the following:

$$\text{A.R.R.} = \frac{\text{Average Annual Profit after Tax}}{\text{Average Investment}} \times 100$$

Average annual profit after tax is determined by adding the after tax expected profits for each year of the life of the project and dividing the same by the number of years.

ILLUSTRATION 21.8

Gopal Ltd. wants to purchase a machine. Two machines, viz., A and B, are available in the market. The cost of each machine is Rs. 2,00,000. The expected life of these machines are 5 years. Net profits before tax during the expected life of the machines are given below:

	Machine	
Year	*A*	*B*
	Rs.	*Rs.*
1	20,000	14,000
2	30,000	26,000
3	26,000	30,000
4	40,000	50,000
5	34,000	40,000
Total	1,50,000	1,60,000

The average rate of tax is 50%. Calculate which machine is more profitable.

Solution

Comparative Profitability Statement

	Machine A	Machine B
Cost Price	Rs. 2,00,000	Rs. 2,00,000
Estimated Life (years)	5	5
Total Net Profit	Rs. 1,50,000	Rs. 1,60,000
Average Annual Profit (before tax)	$\dfrac{1,50,000}{5}$ = Rs. 30,000	$\dfrac{1,60,000}{5}$ Rs. 32,000
Average Annual Profit (after tax) Tax Rate 50%	Rs. 15,000	Rs. 16,000
Average Investment	$\dfrac{2,00,000}{2}$ = Rs. 1,00,000	$\dfrac{2,00,000}{2}$ = Rs. 1,00,000
A.R.R. = $\dfrac{\text{Average Annual Profit after tax}}{\text{Average Investment}}$	$\dfrac{15,000}{1,00,000} \times 100$ = 15%	$\dfrac{16,000}{1,00,000} \times 100$ = 16%

Hence, Machine B is more profitable as it gives the higher return.

ILLUSTRATION 21.9

Determine the average rate of return from the following data of two Machines A and B:

	Machine A	Machine B
Cost	Rs. 56,125	Rs. 56,125
Estimated Life in years	5	5
Estimated Salvage Value	Rs. 3,000	Rs. 3,000
Average Income-tax Rate	55%	55%
Additional Working Capital	Rs. 5,000	Rs. 6,000

Annual estimated income after depreciation and income-tax:

	Machine A	Machine B
1st year	Rs. 3,375	Rs. 11,375
2nd year	Rs. 5,375	Rs. 9,375
3rd year	Rs. 7,375	Rs. 7,375
4th year	Rs. 9,375	Rs. 5,375
5th year	Rs. 11,375	Rs. 3,375
	Rs. 36,875	Rs. 36,875

Depreciation has been charged on straight line basis.

(Delhi, M.Com)

Solution

	Machine A	Machine B

Average Earnings after Dep. and Tax $= \dfrac{36,875}{5} =$ Rs. 7,375 $\quad \dfrac{36,875}{5} =$ Rs. 7,375

Average Investment $= \dfrac{Cost - Scrap}{2} + W.C. + Scrap$

Machine-A $= \dfrac{56,125 - 3,000}{2} + 5,000 + 3,000$

$= 26,562.50 + 8,000$

$=$ Rs. 34,562.50

Machine-B $= \dfrac{56,125 - 3,000}{2} + 6,000 + 3,000$

$= 26,562.50 + 9,000$

$=$ Rs. 35,562.50

A.R.R. Machine-A $= \dfrac{7,375 \times 100}{34,562.50} = 21.34\%$

A.R.R. Machine-B $= \dfrac{7,375 \times 100}{35,562.50} = 20.74\%$

ILLUSTRATION 21.10

Cash flows of Projects X and Y requiring an investment of Rs. 3,000 each are given below:

Year	Cash Flow After Taxes		Depreciation	
	X	Y	X	Y
1	1,300	900	600	600
2	1,100	900	600	600
3	900	900	600	600
4	640	900	600	600
5	640	900	600	600
Total	4,580	4,500	3,000	3,000

The Cash Flow includes Rs. 40 as interest payment for each year. Find out the Average Rate of Return.

Solution

	Project X	Project Y

Average earnings after tax – Dep. – Interest

$\dfrac{4,580 - 3,000 - 200}{5} = \dfrac{1,380}{5}$ $\quad$ $\dfrac{4,500 - 3,000 - 200}{5} = \dfrac{1,300}{5}$

$= Rs.\ 276$ $\qquad\qquad\qquad$ $= Rs.\ 260$

Average Investment $\qquad \dfrac{3,000}{2}$ = Rs. 1,500 $\qquad \dfrac{3,000}{2}$ = Rs. 1,500

A.R.R. $\qquad = \dfrac{276}{1,500} \times 100 = 18.4\%$ $\qquad = \dfrac{260}{1,500} \times 100 = 17.3\%$

Advantages of A.R.R.

1. It is simple to calculate and easy to understand and hence it is widely used.
2. It considers savings over the entire life of the project.
3. It recognises the concept of the net earnings, i.e., earnings after providing for depreciation on capital assets.
4. It facilitates the comparison of new product project with that of cost-reducing project or other projects of competitive nature.

Disadvantages of A.R.R.

1. It does not recognise the timings of cash inflows and outflows as it is based on accounting income in lieu of cash flows.
2. It does not take into account life period of the various investments. While average earning is calculated by taking life period into account, investment (whether initial or average) is ascertained without reference to the life period.
3. In the case of long-term investments, it may not reveal true and fair view. There is always the fear of over-valuation of the position.

2. Discounted Cash Flow Techniques/Sophisticated Techniques

In order to overcome the limitations of Pay-back Period and A.R.R., Discounted Cash Flow (DCF) methods are recognised. These methods recognise the time value of money and provide a more objective basis. They also consider all benefits and costs occurred during the life of the project. The various D.C.F. evaluation methods are discussed here.

(a) Present Value Method

Present Value Method recognises that cash inflows and outflows at different periods differ in value. Thus comparison can be made only when they are expressed in terms of common denominator. The various steps involved in this method are:

(i) To determine cash outflows (initial investments and subsequent outlay) and cash outflows for different periods.
(ii) To determine discounting rate, i.e., cut-off rate which is generally taken to be equal to the cost of capital.
(iii) To calculate present value of cash inflows at different periods with the help of discounting rate. For this purpose, present value factor (P.V.F.) is taken from the annuity tables or is calculated by $\dfrac{1}{(1+i)^n}$.
(iv) To add together the present value of all cash inflows for different periods.

Here, the scarp value and working capital released at the end of project's life should also be considered as cash inflows are duly discounted to present values.

(v) To discount cash outflows at the subsequent periods by the same P.V.F. However, cash outflows at the initial period (zero period of time) need not be discounted.

Then the present values of cash inflows should be compared with present values of cash outflows. In case, the present value of cash inflows are greater than (or equal to) the present value of cash outflows (or initial investment), the project would be accepted and vice-versa.

ILLUSTRATION 21.11

From the following details relating to two machines X and Y, suggest which machine should be accepted:

	Machine-X Rs.	Machine-Y Rs.
Cost	56,125	56,125
Estimated Life	5 years	5 years
Estimated Salvage Value	3,000	3,000

Annual income after tax and depreciation:

	Rs.	Rs.
Year I	3,375	11,375
Year II	5,375	9,375
Year III	7,375	7,375
Year IV	9,375	5,375
Year V	11,375	3,375

Overhauling charges at the end of 3rd year: Rs. 25,000
Depreciation has been charged at Straight Line Method. Discounting rate is 10%. P.V.F. at 10% for five years are: 0.909, 0.829, 0.751, 0.683, 0.621.

Solution

(i) Present Value of Cash Outflows

	Machine-X Rs.	Machine-Y Rs.
Initial Investment	56,125	56,125
Overhauling Charges		
25,000 × 0.751	18,775	......
	Rs. 74,900	Rs. 56,125

(ii) Present Value of Cash Inflows
(Machine-X)

Year	Income after Tax and Dep. Rs.	Dep. Rs.	CFAT (2 + 3) Rs.	P.V.F. Rs.	P.V. Rs.
I	3,375	10,625	14,000	0.909	12,726
II	5,375	10,625	16,000	0.826	13,216
III	7,375	10,625	18,000	0.751	13,518
IV	9,375	10,625	20,000	0.683	13,660
V	11,375	10,625	22,000	0.621	13,662
					66,782
			Value of Scrap 3,000 × 0.621		1,863
				Total	68,645

(iii) Present Value of Cash Inflows
(Machine-Y)

Year	Income after Tax and Dep. Rs.	Dep. Rs.	CFAT (2 + 3) Rs.	P.V.F. Rs.	P.V. Rs.
I	11,375	10,625	22,000	0.909	19,998
II	9,375	10,625	20,000	0.826	16,520
III	7,375	10,625	18,000	0.751	13,518
IV	5,375	10,625	16,000	0.683	10,928
V	3,375	10,625	14,000	0.621	8,694
					69,658
			Value of Scrap 3,000 × 0.621		1,863
					71,521

Now for:

Machine-X 68,645 < 74,900
Machine-Y 71,521 > 56,125
Hence Machine-Y should be accepted.

(b) Net Present Value Method (N.P.V.)

N.P.V. is the time value of money approach for evaluating the investment proposals. This is also known as Excess Present Value (E.P.V.) or Investor's Method and is just a variation of Present Value Method. Under this method, all cash flows (cash outflows and cash inflows) are discounted at a given rate and their present values are computed. The present value of the cash outflows is subtracted from the sum of present values of various cash inflows. The surplus is the net present value. If the N.P.V. is positive (the forecast return is more than the required return), the proposal is acceptable. On the other hand, if the N.P.V. is negative, (the forecast return is less than the required return) the proposal is not acceptable. Thus under N.P.V., the decision rule is to accept the proposal if the N.P.V. is positive and reject if it is negative or:

(a) N.P.V. > Zero = Accept

(b) N.P.V. < Zero = Reject

The P.V.F. for given rate of discounting may be obtained from Annuity Table (Table I). It may also be derived by solving the following formula for v with the help of Log and Antilog.

$$V = \frac{a}{i}\left(1 - \frac{1}{(1+i)^n}\right)$$

ILLUSTRATION 21.12

You are required to find out the net present worth of the following projects, assuming that the cost of capital is 10% and the initial investment is Rs. 1,600 each:

Year	Project A Net Cash Flows Rs.	Project B Net Cash Flows Rs.
1	800	200
2	800	400
3	400	400
4	200	400
5	...	600
6	...	800

Solution

Calculation of N.P.V.

Year	P.V.F. at 10% Rs.	Project A		Project B	
		Cash Inflows Rs.	P.V. Rs.	Cash Inflows Rs.	P.V. Rs.
1	0.909	800	727.28	200	181.82
2	0.826	800	661.16	400	330.58
3	0.751	400	300.52	400	300.52
4	0.683	200	136.60	400	273.20
5	0.621	....	....	600	372.56
6	0.564	....	....	800	451.58
		Total	1,825.56		1,910.26
	Less Initial Investment		1,600.00		1,600.00
	N.P.V.		+225.56		+310.26

Thus, N.P.V. is positive in both the cases. Since cost is the same, Project-B is to be preferred because it provides higher N.P.V. as compared to Project-A.

ILLUSTRATION 21.13

Your company can make either of the following two investments at the beginning of 2000. The following particulars are available in this respect:

	Project-I	Project-II
Estimated Cost (to be incurred initially)	Rs. 20,000	Rs. 28,000
Estimated Life (Years)	4	5
Scrap Value at the end of estimated life	Nil	Nil
Estimated Net Cash Flow (Rs.)		
End of 2000	5,500	5,600
End of 2001	7,000	9,000
End of 2002	8,500	9,000
End of 2003	7,500	9,000
End of 2004	...	9,000

It is estimated that each of the alternative projects will require an additional working capital of Rs. 2,000 which will be received back in full after the expiry of each project life. In estimating net cash flow, depreciation has been provided under straight line method.

Cost of finance to your company may be taken at 10% p.a. The present value of Rs. 1 to be received at the end of each year, at 10% is given below:

Year	1	2	3	4	5
P.V.	0.91	0.83	0.75	0.68	0.62

Evaluate the investment proposals using Net Present Value.

(I.C.W.A. – Final)

Solution

Calculation of N.P.V.

End of the Year	P.V.F. at 10% Rs.	Project-I		Project-II	
		Cash Inflows Rs.	P.V. Rs.	Cash Inflows Rs.	P.V. Rs.
2000	0.91	5,500	5,005	5,600	5,096
2001	0.83	7,000	5,810	9,000	7,470
2002	0.75	8,500	6,375	9,000	6,750
2003	0.68	7,500	5,100	9,000	6,120
2004	0.62	...	...	9,000	5,580
Working Capital to be received back at the end of life					

Continued

End of the Year	P.V.F. at 10% Rs.	Project-I Cash Inflows Rs.	Project-I P.V. Rs.	Project-II Cash Inflows Rs.	Project-II P.V. Rs.
2003	0.68	2,000	1,360	...	...
at the end of life 2004	0.62	...	...	2,000	1,240
		Total	23,650		32,256
Less: Initial Investment:					
Estimated Cost	20,000				
Working Capital	2,000		22,000		
Estimated Cost	28,000				
Working Capital	2,000				30,000
			+1,650		+2,256

Hence, Project II is more profitable because its N.P.V. is higher.

ILLUSTRATION 21.14

SP & Co. have been using a machine costing Rs. 15,000 for the past 5 years. The machine has 15 years of life and it has been depreciated @ 10% p.a. The current salvage value would be Rs. 2,000 and the company has been paying 50% of its profits as taxes (i.e., it is subjected to 50% flat tax rate.)

Now the management desires to replace it by new machine costing Rs.10,000 with salvage value of Rs. 2,000. The new machine has a life of 10 years and will be depreciated @ 10% p.a. The cost of capital is 10% and the expected savings is likely to be Rs. 3,000 p.a.

Should the company go for a new machine?

(A.C.S. Final – adapted)

Solution

	Rs.
Cash Outflow:	
Investment in New Machine	10,000
Less: Salvage Value of existing machine	2,000
	8,000
Tax Savings on loss of sale of machine to be calculated as under:	
Cost of the Existing Machine	15,000
Less: Dep. @ 10% for 5 years on Straight Line basis (1,500 × 5)	7,500
Written Down Value (WDV)	7,500
Less: Salvage Value	2,000
Loss on Sale	5,500
Less: Tax @ 50%	2,750
Net Cash Outflow	2,750

Continued

Cash Inflow:	
Annual Savings	3,000
Less: Dep. $\dfrac{10,000 - 2,000}{10 \text{ years}}$	800
	.....
Profit before tax	2,200
Less: Tax @ 50%	1,100
Profit after tax	1,100
Add: Dep. (non-cash item)	800
Annual Cash inflow for 10 years	1,900

Present Values of Cash Inflow

	Discounting Factor @ 10%	Present Value Rs.
Annual Cash Inflow for 10 years 1,900	6.1446 (as per Table given in Appendix)	11,675
Salvage Value of new machine 2,000	0.38554 (as per Table given in Appendix)	771
	Total	12,446
	Less: Total Cash Outflow (Calculated above)	5,250
	Net Present Value	7,195

The company should go for the new machine.

Advantages of N.P.V.

1. It is superior to other methods of evaluating the economic worth of investments.
2. It recognises all cash flows throughout the life of the project.
3. It helps to satisfy the objectives for maximising firm's values.
4. It recognises the time value of money.
5. It is generally accepted by economist.

Disadvantages of N.P.V.

1. It fails to give satisfactory answer when projects under consideration involve different amounts of investments and with different economic life periods.
2. It gives the same decision for mutually exclusive projects as in the case of discounted benefit-cost ratio.
3. It fails to indicate the rate of return which is expected to be earned.

However, the desired rate of return cannot be determined easily as many line managements frequently fail understand this concept.

(c) *Internal Rate of Return or Yield Method*

Internal rate of return was first introduced by Joel Dean. This method is also known as yield on investment, marginal efficiency of capital, rate of return over cost, time adjusted rate of return and so on. But it is appropriately called as internal rate of return as it exclusively depends on the initial outlay and cash proceeds of the projects, and not by any rate determined outside the investment.

Internal rate of return is a rate which actually equates the present value of cash inflows with the present value of cash outflows. It is actually the rate of return which is earned by a project, i.e., it is a rate at which the N.P.V. of investment is zero. Under this method, a project is accepted when I.R.R. is greater or equal to the cut-off rate (generally, cost of capital). In the opposite case, a project is rejected. But if there are a number of alternative projects, the acceptance criterion can be considered only after analysing the following:

(a) Determine the I.R.R. in each alternative case.

(b) Compare the I.R.R. with cut-off rate and reject those projects whose I.R.R. is less than the cut-off rate.

(c) Compare the I.R.R. of each alternative and select that one which gives the highest rate.

The I.R.R., which coincides with discounting rate, can be computed in the following manner:

(a) *When Savings are Even for all the Years*

The present values of future savings can be ascertained from the Annuity Table by Trial and Error Method, if savings are even. Then the following procedures are to be adopted:

(i) Divide the investment by annual savings.

(ii) Look at the Annuity Table and find the line for the number of years savings will generate.

(iii) Move across this line until a figure is found nearly equal to the amount calculated in (i) above. The rate mentioned by this column is I.R.R.

The above procedures can be amplified with the help of an example. Suppose the cost of investment is Rs. 6,000 and annual savings are Rs. 2,000 p.a. for five years, i.e., economic life. Now the present value factor is 6,000/2,000 = 3.00. Looking at Cumulative Present Value Table and moving across five year line we get 2.991 which is close to 3.00. This is 20% column of Cumulative Present Value. Thus I.R.R. is 20% in this case.

However, the present values of future can also be computed with the help of the following formula:

$$V = \frac{a}{i}\left(1 - \frac{1}{(1+i)^n}\right)$$

Here, V = Cost of Investment
$\quad\quad a$ = Annual Savings
$\quad\quad n$ = Number of Years
$\quad\quad i$ = IRR

The formula can be solved for (i) with the help of Log and Anti-Log Tables. Moreover, the exact rate may be interpolated as under:

$$I.R.R. = L.R. + \frac{H.P.V. - P.V.F}{\text{Difference in Calculated Present Value}} \times \text{Difference in Rate}$$

(b) When Savings are not Even

If savings are uneven, the I.R.R. can be found only through Trial and Error Method. Here, the main problem is to compute a rate on which the present value of uneven savings are just equal to the cost of investment. Thus I.R.R. in this case is: Cash Outflows – Cash Inflows = 0. For this purpose, the present values of cash inflows are ascertained at varying rates. In that process, the rate on which present values of cash inflows are closest to the cost of investment is taken to be I.R.R.

The following procedures are involved in this process.

1. Find out the average of the cash inflows at different years.
2. Divide the net investment by average cash inflows. The resultant figure is the present value factor.
3. Ascertain the rate from the Present Value Table for the present value factor.
4. Calculate the present values of cash inflows of several years with the above rate.
5. Compare the total of such present values with the cost of investment. If the total of present values is more than the cost of investment, then further interpolation be done at a higher rate. On the contrary, in case the total of present values is less than the cost of investment the further interpolation be carried on at lower rate. The actual I.R.R. can be ascertained by following such trial and error.

$$I.R.R. = L.R. + \frac{\text{Calculated P.V.} - \text{P.V. of Cash Outflow}}{\text{Difference in Calculated Present Value}} \times (\text{Difference in Rate})$$

ILLUSTRATION 21.15

From the following particulars relating to two projects X and Y, compute I.R.R. and state which of the two projects is better.

	Project X	Project Y
Economic Life	10 Years	8 Years
Cost	Rs. 1,80,000	Rs. 2,00,000
Estimated Savings	Rs. 30,000	Rs. 40,000

Solution

	Project X	Project Y
Present Value Factor (NI/OS)	6.00	5.00

Closest present values to 6.00 from Cumulative P.V. Table (Table II) for 10 years in the case of Project X are:

P.V.	Rate	
6.145	10%	Thus, I.R.R. will be between
5.650	12%	10% and 12%

$$\text{I.R.R.} = \text{LR} + \frac{\text{H.P.V.} - \text{P.V.F.}}{\text{Difference in Calculated P.V.}} \times \text{Difference in Rate}$$

$$= 10\% + \frac{0.145}{0.495} \ (12\% - 10\%) = 10\% + 0.6\%$$

$$= 10.6\%$$

Closest Present Values to 5.00 from Cumulative P.V. Table for 8 years in the case of Project Y are:

P.V.	Rate	
5.335	10%	Thus, I.R.R. will be between
4.968	12%	10% and 12%

$$\text{I.R.R.} = \text{LR} + \frac{\text{H.P.V.} - \text{P.V.F.}}{\text{Difference in Calculated P.V.}} \times \text{Difference in Rate}$$

$$= 10\% + \frac{0.335}{0.367} \ (12\% - 10\%) = 10\% + 1.8\%$$

$$= 11.8\%$$

On the basis of I.R.R. Project Y is ranked I and it is better.

ILLUSTRATION 21.16

From the following information of two Projects X and Y, calculate I.R.R. and suggest which project is preferable.

	Project X Rs.	Project Y Rs.
Cost	22,000	20,000
Cash Inflows:		
Year 1	12,000	2,000
Year 2	4,000	2,000
Year 3	2,000	4,000
Year 4	10,000	20,000

Solution

	Project X	Project Y
P.V.F. (NI/Average OS)	$\dfrac{22,000}{7,000} = 3.14$	$\dfrac{20,000}{7,000} = 2.86$

Closest Present Values to 3.14 from Annuity Table II for 4 years in the case of Project-X are 3.170 at 10% and 3.07 at 12%. Hence, I.R.R. can be interpolated by trial and error procedure using discounting rates of 10% and 12%.

I.R.R. of Project – X

Year	Cash Inflows Rs.	P.V.F. 10%	P.V. Rs.	P.V.F. 12%	P.V. Rs.
1	12,000	0.909	10,908	0.893	10,716
2	4,000	0.826	3,304	0.797	3,188
3	2,000	0.751	1,502	0.712	1,424
4	10,000	0.683	6,830	0.636	6,360
	Total		22,544		21,688

Excess (+) or Deficient (–)

	Over NI	+544	–312

Thus,

$$\text{I.R.R.} = \text{L.R.} + \frac{\text{Calculated P.V.} - \text{P.V. of Cash Outlay}}{\text{Difference in Calculated Present Values}} \times \text{(Difference in Rate)}$$

$$= 10 + \frac{544}{544 + 312} \times (12 - 10) = 10 + \frac{544}{856} \times 2$$

$$= 10 + 1.27 = 11.27\%$$

In the case of Project-Y, the closest Present Values to 2.86 from Annuity Table II for four years are 2.914 at 14% and 2.855 at 15%. Thus I.R.R. in this case should be tried using 14% and 15% discounting factors.

I.R.R. of Project – Y

Year	Cash Inflows Rs.	P.V.F. 15%	P.V. Rs.	P.V.F. 14%	P.V. Rs.
1	2,000	0.870	1,740	0.877	1,754
2	2,000	0.756	1,512	0.769	1,538
3	4,000	0.658	2,632	0.675	2,700
4	20,000	0.572	11,440	0.592	11,840
	Total		17,324		17,832
Excess (+) or Deficiency (–) over NI			–2,676		–2168

As the Present Values at 15% and 14% are less than investment of Rs. 20,000 a much lesser rate is to be used. Let us use 10% rate.

Year	Cash Inflows Rs.	P.V. at 10%	P.V. Rs.
1	2,000	0.909	1,818
2	2,000	0.826	1,652
3	4,000	0.751	3,004
4	20,000	0.683	13,660
			20,134
Excess (+) or Deficiency (–) Over NI			+134

Thus,

$$\text{I.R.R.} = \text{L.R.} + \frac{\text{Calculated P.V.} - \text{P.V. of Cash Outlay}}{\text{Difference in Calculated Present Values}} \times (\text{Difference in Rate})$$

$$= 10 + \frac{134}{134 + 2,168}(14 - 10) = 10 + \frac{134 \times 4}{2,302}$$

$$= 10 + 0.23$$

$$= 10.23\%$$

It appears that I.R.R. of Project-X is more than that of Project-Y. Thus Project-X is preferable.

Advantages of I.R.R.

The advantages of Internal Rate of Return Method are as follows:

1. It provides more precise information regarding profitability.
2. It helps the firm to choose from among different alternatives.
3. It recognises the time value of money like N.P.V. Method.
4. It takes into account the cash flows throughout the life of the project.
5. It restricts investment expenditure to the amount of funds internally generated by a firm.

Disadvantages of I.R.R.

In spite of its theoretical soundness, the I.R.R. is not free from snags. Some of them are given below:

1. Its computation is quite tedious and complicated.
2. It uses accounting information and does not explain the cash flow position.
3. It may present inconsistent result with the N.P.V. method when the projects actually differ from their expected life or cash outflows or timing of cash flows.
4. It does not provide significant answers under all situations.

(d) Profitability Index (P.I.) or Benefit-Cost Ratio (B/C Ratio)

Profitability index is one of the time-adjusted techniques for evaluating investment proposals. It is also known as Benefit Cost Ratio (B/C Ratio) because the numerator measures benefits and the denominator measures costs. Profitability index is the relation between present value of future net cash flows and the initial cash outlay and is expressed either in per rupee or in percentage. It is computed as under:

$$\text{P.I. (per rupee)} = \frac{\text{P.V. of Cash Inflows}}{\text{P.V. of Cash Outflows (cost)}}$$

$$\text{P.I. (\%)} = \frac{\text{P.V. of Cash Inflows} \times 100}{\text{P.V. of Cash Outflows (cost)}}$$

Under this method, an investment proposal may be accepted when the Profitability Index (PI) exceeds one (or hundred if it is expressed in percentage).

However, in the case of mutually exclusive proposals, the acceptance criterion is: the higher the index, the more profitable are the proposals and vice-versa.

Profitability index is similar to the N.P.V. approach. The only one difference is that if P.I. is relative measure (as it measures the present value of return per rupee invested), N.P.V. is an absolute measure (as it depends on the difference between P.V. of N.C.F. and P.V. of cash outflow).

ILLUSTRATION 21.17

Initial Cash Outflows		Rs. 25,000

Cash Inflow:

End of the year	*Rs.*
1	10,000
2	7,500
3	12,500
4	5,000

Calculate the N.P.V. and P.I. of the project assuming that the discount factor is 10%.

Solution

Calculation of Profitability Index

Year	Cash Inflow Rs.	Discount Factors @ 10%	P.V. of N.C.F. Rs.
1	10,000	0.909	9,090
2	7,500	0.826	6,195
3	12,500	0.751	9,388
4	5,000	0.683	3,415
		Total	28,088
		Less Initial Outlay	25,000
		N.P.V.	3,088

$$\therefore \text{ Profitability Index (P.I.)} = \frac{\text{P.V. of Cash Inflows}}{\text{Initial Cash Outlay}}$$

$$= \frac{\text{Rs. 28,088}}{\text{Rs. 25,000}}$$

$$= 1.12$$

Here the project is acceptable because the profitability index (P.I.) is greater than one.

Advantages of P.I.

The advantages of P.I. Method of evaluating investment proposals are as follows:

1. It is a conceptually sound technique of evaluating investment project because it satisfies the requirements of time value of money, totality of benefit, etc.

2. It evaluates the worth of projects in terms of their relative magnitude. Hence, it is superior to N.P.V. method.

3. It can be used to choose between mutually exclusive projects by computing incremental benefit-cost ratio.

Disadvantages of P.I.

Despite the superiority of P.I. of N.P.V. method, P.I. is not free from limitations. They are as follows:

1. It involves more calculations than the traditional methods (i.e., Payback and A.R.R.) and hence it is very difficult to understand.

2. In some cases of mutually exclusive nature, P.I. is inferior to N.P.V. method.

(e) Terminal Value Method (T.V.)

This method is based on the assumption that the cash flow of each year is re-invested in another asset at a certain rate of return from the moment of its receipt till the end of the economic life of the project. But the cash flows of the last year of the project will not be re-invested. In short, the N.C.F. and the outlay are compounded forward on the basis of compounding factor obtained from compound interest table (Table III).

This method is also based on the assumption that the total sum of the compounded cash inflows is received at the end of the life of the project and hence should be discounted at present values on the basis of discounting rate. Then the present values of compounded cash inflows should be compared with present values of cash outflows. If the present values of compounded cash inflows are greater than the present value of outflow, the project should be accepted and vice-versa. In other words, if NCF has a higher terminal value in comparison with the outlay, the project is accepted and vice-versa. In case both the terminal value and the outlay are equal, the management will be indifferent. If there are mutually exclusive projects, the project which has the highest positive terminal value should be accepted.

Both T.V. and N.P.V. methods are similar in most cases. The only difference is that in the case of former, the values are compounded and in the case of latter the values are discounted. However, both of them will present the same result provided the rate is same (i.e., discounting and compounding).

ILLUSTRATION 21.18

From the following information, evaluate the proposal using T.V.

Initial Outlay	Rs. 20,000
Project Life	5 years
Net Cash Inflow	Rs. 8,000 each for 5 years
Cost of Capital	@ 10% (K)

Expected interest rates:

End of the year	Percentage
1	6%
2	6%
3	8%
4	8%
5	8%

Solution

It should be remembered that the first year's cash inflows will be re-invested for 4 years, second year's for 3 years and so on. Cash inflows of 5th year will not be re-invested. The compounding factors are taken from Table III. Hence, the compounded cash inflows are:

Year	Cash Inflows	Rates of Return	Period of Re-investment	Compounding Factors	Compounded Cash Inflows
1	8,000	6%	4	1.262	10,096
2	8,000	6%	3	1.191	9,528
3	8,000	8%	2	1.166	9,328
4	8,000	8%	1	1.080	8,640
5	8,000	8%	0	1.000	8,000
	Total				45,592

Here the discount rate represents the cost of capital (K) (10%). We are also to find out the P.V. of Rs. 45,592 which will actually be received at the end of the 5th year.

P.V.F. for 5th year at 10% is 0.621

P.V. of Compounded Cash Inflows = 45,592 × 0.621
                                 = Rs. 28,312.63

Since Rs. 28,312.63 is more than Rs. 20,000 (initial cash outflows), the project is acceptable.

Here T.V. is positive, i.e., Rs. 8,313 (28,312 − 20,000)

Advantages of T.V.

1. It is mathematically easier and makes the evaluation procedure simple.
2. It is simple to understand.
3. It avoids the influence of cost of capital.
4. It is more suitable where cash budget is in operation.

Disadvantages of T.V.

1. It does not consider the comparative evaluation of two or more mutually exclusive proposals.
2. It relates to the projected rates of return at which cash inflows of different years may be re-invested.

— REVIEW QUESTIONS —

1. Define Capital Budgeting. Discuss the importance of capital budgeting.

2. Discuss the salient features of 'Present Value Method' of project evaluation and examine its rationality.

3. Define and explain the following with their respective merits and demerits:
   (a) Pay-back Period
   (b) Discounted Pay-Back method, and
   (c) Average Rate of Return

4. "Despite all limitations of the method of Pay-Back Period, it has still significance in project appraisal". Discuss.

5. What does the profitability index signify? What is the criterion for judging the worth of investment in the capital budgeting technique based on the profitability index?

6. What do you mean by Internal Rate of Return? State its advantages and limitations.

7. Write notes on:
   (a) Profitability Index
   (b) Terminal Value Method
   (c) Net Present Value Method

8. A project requires an investment of Rs. 2,00,000. It yields an annual cash flow of Rs. 40,000 for 9 years. Find out the pay-back period of the project.

   (**Ans.:** 5 years)

9. Calculate the Pay-back period for a project which requires a cash outlay of Rs. 40,000 but the same generates a cash inflow of Rs. 16,000; Rs. 12,000; Rs. 10,000 and Rs. 6,000.

   (**Ans.:** 3 years plus 4 months)

10. There are two alternative machines, you are asked to compute the profitability of the investment on the basis of pay-back profitability.

	Machine X	*Machine Y*
Purchase Price	Rs. 25,000	Rs. 42,000
Estimated Life (years)	8	10
Net Earnings (After Tax but Before Depreciation) p.a.	Rs. 5,000	Rs. 6,000

    (**Ans.:** Profitability: Machine X – Rs. 15,000; Machine Y – Rs. 18,000 p.a.
    Machine Y is profitable)

11. The following are the details of three projects A, B and C

	A	*B*	*C*
Cost (Rs.)	50,000	70,000	70,000
Life (years)	10	12	14
Estimated Surplus (Rs.)	5,000	10,000	7,000
Annual Profit (less tax) (Rs.)	5,000	6,000	5,500

Select the best one using:

(i) Pay-back Period

(ii) Surplus life over pay-back period, and

(iii) Surplus cash flow, as decision criterion

(A.C.S. – Final)

Ans. (i) Pay-Back Period:

Project-A = 5.26 years, Rank-1

Project-B = 6.36 years, Rank-2

Project-C = 7 years, Rank-3

(ii) Surplus life over pay-back period

Project-A = 4.74 years, Rank-3

Project-B = 5.64 years, Rank-2

Project-C = 7 years, Rank-1

(iii) Surplus Cash Flows:

Project-A = 50,000, Rank-3

Project-B = 72,000, Rank-2

Project-C = 77,000, Rank-1

12. X Ltd. is contemplating an investment of Rs. 10,00,000 in a new plant, which will provide a salvage value of Rs. 80,000 at the end of its economic life of 5 years. The profits after depreciation and tax are estimated to be as under:

Year	Rs.
1	50,000
2	75,000
3	1,25,000
4	1,30,000
5	80,000

Calculate the Average Rate of Return.

(**Ans.:** A.R.R. = 20%; Average Savings Rs. 92,000, Average Investments Rs. 4,60,000)

13. The management of Z Ltd. proposes to invest Rs. 8,000 in a project which will give earnings for five years as under:

Year	Rs.
1	3,000
2	4,000
3	3,000
4	2,000
5	2,000
	14,000

Suggest whether this project is worthwhile to be taken up. You may take the rate of 10% as discounted rate of present value.

(**Ans.:** P.V. Rs. 10,892 and N.P.V. Rs. 2,892. Project is worthwhile)

14. A machine purchased six years ago for Rs. 3,00,000 has been depreciated to a book value of Rs. 1,80,000. Its economic life was 15 years with no salvage value. If this machine is replaced by a new machine costing Rs. 4,50,000, the operating costs would be reduced by Rs. 60,000 for the next 10 years. The old machine could also be sold for Rs. 1,00,000. The cost of capital is 10%. The new machine will be depreciated on straight line basis over an eight-year life with Rs. 50,000 as salvage value. The company's tax rate is 55%. Using N.P.V. determine whether old machine should be replaced.

(Ans.: Cash Outflows:

	Rs.
Cost of new Machine	4,50,000
Less: Sale Proceeds (Cash 1,00,000 + Tax savings Rs. 44,000)	1,44,000
Net Cash Outflow	3,06,000
Annual Cash Inflows	Rs. 43,500
P.V. of Cash Inflows (including P.V. of Salvage)	Rs. 2,55,379
Less: N.P.V.	Rs. 50,621

15. From the following information calculate I.R.R.:

Initial Outlay	Rs. 40,000
Annual Net Cash Flow (N.C.F.)	Rs. 12,000
Estimated Life	5 years

(Ans.: I.R.R. = 15.24%)

16. From the following information, calculate N.P.V. and P.I. of the project:

Initial Cash Outflow   Rs. 50,000

Cash Inflow:

End of the Year	Rs.
1	20,000
2	15,000
3	25,000
4	10,000

Assume discount factor at 10%

(Ans.: P.V. 56, 175, N.P.V. 6, 175, P.I. = 1.12)

22

Risk Analysis in Capital Budgeting

Risk is the variability that is likely to occur in future
between the estimated and the actual return.

INTRODUCTION

A firm usually makes decisions on the basis of forecasts which themselves depend upon future events. The occurrence of these events cannot be anticipated with absolute certainty on account of factors such as economic, social, fiscal, political, etc. Hence risk is linked with business decisions. It may be defined as the chance that the actual outcome differs from the expected outcome. But in the current context, risk is the chance that the actual return differs from the expected return.

The decision situations as to risk may be classified into: (i) certainty (or no risk), (ii) uncertainty, and (iii) risk. Under risk situations, the probabilities of a specific event happening are known. But in an uncertain situation, the probabilities of such an event are quite unknown. In other words, while in risk situation, the chance of future loss can be predicted with the help of past experience, in an uncertainty the future loss cannot be anticipated. Hence, the management will not be able to deal with the uncertain situation in the planning process.

Business Risk and Financial Risk

Business is exposed to many internal and external dangers or risks. These risks arise from various points such as products, competitors, properties, employees and its customers. While some of these risks are general, others are connected with finances of the firm. Thus the total risk of a firm can be broken down into business risk and financial risk.

Business risk is one which relates to the general business of an environment. It is determined by how a firm invests its funds (i.e., the type of projects). Usually business risk of a firm is influenced by so many factors such as its competitive position, the industries in which it operates, its market share, etc. Risk which relates to finances of the firm is called the financial risk. It is determined by how a firm finances its various investments. Financial risk of a firm is primarily influenced by the level of financial gearing, interest cover, operating leverage, and cash flow adequacy.

RISK ANALYSIS IN PROJECT SELECTION

A firm's acceptance of projects mainly depends upon their cash flows and risk. While cash flow comprises net operational cash receipts (i.e., operational cash receipts less operational cash expenditures) and investment outlay, risk relates to the volatility of the expected outcome and the spread of likely returns around the expected return. A firm should consider risk while estimating the required rate of return on a project.

Every financial decision contains an element of return in addition to an element of risk. The relationship between risk and return, therefore, exists in the form of a risk-return trade-off. It shows that higher return can be earned only by accepting higher risk. In short, risk and return are positively correlated, an increase in one is accompanied by an increase in the other (Figure 22.1).

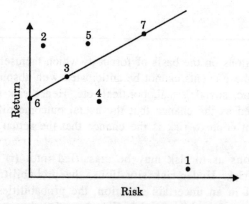

FIGURE 22.1 Risk-return relationship for alternative projects.

Figure 22.1 shows the risk-return relationship of seven projects. Among the different available projects, the best one is number 2 which has high return and low risk. It also presents the most desirable combination of the features of risk-return. The least desirable project is number 1. It is a low return and high risk project. Investment number 3 should be preferred to investment number 4 as it has more return for the same level of risk. The highest return project is number 7, but it has high expectations of return. Project 6 is a zero risk investment with a certain outcome. Such an investment may be a short dated Government security, where the exact interest rate is known ahead.

Since three projects such as 6, 3 and 7 are on the risk-return line, they have zero net present values. Their expected returns are just enough to compensate for their risk. Investors can be logical in their choice patterns and yet select either 6 or 3 or 7.

SENSITIVITY ANALYSIS

Sensitivity analysis is a modelling procedure used in forecasting. It refers to the study of key assumptions or calculations on which a management decision is based with a view to predicting alternative outcomes of that decision if various assumptions are made. Sensitivity analysis is of great help in determining the value of information and the range of variations in the co-efficients over which the solutions will remain optional. The variations can be brought into five heads. They are (i) variations in the objective function coefficients, (ii) variations in the technical coefficients, (iii) variations in the constrain vector coefficients, (iv) the addition or deletion of constraints, and (v) the addition or deletion of variables.

Steps in Sensitivity Analysis

Sensitivity analysis involves the following five steps:

(i) Listing the key factors or parameters. For instance, while estimating the profitability factors of a project to be considered, the analyst should take into account the market growth rate, market share, selling price, and the costs of direct labour and direct material.

(ii) Attaching the most likely values to each of these parameters. This process helps in predicting the most likely level of profit.

(iii) Calculating the effect of variance in values of all or a selected few of these parameters.

(iv) Listing the outcomes of alternative assumptions and making a subjective assessment of their likelihood.

(v) Drawing conclusions on any action required. This would help the earlier accomplishment of better outcomes.

Benefits of Sensitivity Analysis

(a) Sensitivity analysis helps in preventing rash predictions about the outcome of plans by (i) ensuring the examination of assumptions on which the plans are based, and (ii) gauging the effect of variations in these assumptions.

(b) It indicates the areas where improvements are likely to have the greatest impact on results.

(c) It facilitates the development of alternative or contingency plans in case the basic assumptions have to be varied.

ILLUSTRATION 22.1

Kamal Industries Ltd. has prepared the following budgeted profitability statement for the current year operations.

		Rs.
Sales	3000 units × Rs. 5	15,000
Variable Cost:		
Materials	6,000	
Labour	4,000	10,000
Contribution		5,000
Less: Fixed Cost		3,000
Profit		2,000

Make a sensitivity analysis based on the above data.

Solution

The variations in the sales revenues and costs on profit can be evaluated in the light of sensitivity analysis as given below:

(i) If selling price is brought down by more than 13.33 per cent of the budgeted price, the firm would incur a loss.

(ii) If the sales are brought down by more than 13.33 per cent of the budgeted sales, the firm should incur a loss.

(iii) If labour costs enhance by more than 50 per cent of the budgeted costs, the firm would make a loss.

(iv) If material costs increase by more than 33.33 per cent of the budgeted costs, the firm would incur a loss.

(v) If the fixed costs increase by more than 66.66 per cent of the budgeted costs, the firm would incur a loss.

In case the sensitivity of the above data is observed, it is found that the sales units and selling price are more sensitive than other items of cost. So these areas require careful consideration.

INCORPORATION OF RISK FACTOR

The techniques of capital budgeting involves the estimation of future cash inflows and outflows. However, it should be based on the factors such as (i) expected economic life of the project, (ii) salvage value of the asset at the end of the economic life, (iii) capacity of the project, (iv) selling price of the project, (v) production cost, (vi) depreciation, (vii) rate of taxation, and (viii) future demand of the project. But on account of uncertainties about the future, these factors cannot be exactly foreseen. For instance, owing to unexpected technological developments, a product may become obsolete much earlier than anticipated. Hence, while making a decision on investment proposal, all these elements of uncertainty or risk factors should be considered. However, incorporation of risk factor in capital budgeting decisions is a too tough task. But some allowances are to be provided for the element of risk.

Methods for Accounting Risk

The following methods are suggested for accounting of risk in capital budgeting.

(i) Risk adjusted discount rate, (ii) Certainty technique, (iii) Sensitivity technique, (iv) Probability technique, (v) Standard deviation method, (vi) Co-efficient of variation method, and (vii) Decision tree analysis.

Risk Adjusted Discount Rate

The risk adjusted discount rate or method of varying discount rate is a composite discount rate that takes into account both time and discount factors. This method needs the determination of both risk-free rate and risk premium rate. Risk-free rate is the rate at which the future cash inflows should be discounted in case there is no risk. But risk premium rate is the extra return expected by the investor over and above the normal rate (i.e., the risk free rate) because of the risky project. Thus the risk adjusted discount rate is based on the presumption that investors expect a higher rate of return on risky projects than that of less risky projects.

ILLUSTRATION 22.2

Gopal Engineering Company Ltd. is considering a new project. Two alternative projects are available (X and Y) each costing Rs. 2,00,000. Cash inflows are expected to be as under:

	Cash Inflows	
Year	Investment X Rs.	Investment Y Rs.
1	80,000	1,00,000
2	70,000	80,000
3	50,000	60,000
4	40,000	60,000

The company has a target return on capital of 10%. Risk premium rates are 2% and 8% respectively for investments X and Y. State which project is better.

Solution

The profitability of the two projects can be compared on the basis of net present values of cash inflows adjusted for risk premium rates as given below:

Year	Project X			Project Y		
	Discount Factor @ 10% + 2% = 12%	*Cash Inflows Rs.*	*Present Value Rs.*	*Discount Factor @ 10% + 8% = 18%*	*Cash Inflows Rs.*	*Present Value Rs.*
1	0.893	80,000	71,440	0.847	1,00,000	84,700
2	0.797	70,000	55,790	0.718	80,000	57,440
3	0.712	50,000	35,600	0.609	60,000	36,540
4	0.635	40,000	25,400	0.516	60,000	30,960
			1,88,230			2,09,640

Project X   Project Y
Net Present Value = Rs. 1,88,230 – 2,00,000   Rs. 2,09,640 – 2,00,000
                  = Rs. (–) 11,770   = Rs. 9,640

Since even at a higher discount rate, project Y gives a higher net present value, project Y is better.

Certainty Equivalent Method

Certainty equivalent coefficient is the ratio of riskless (i.e., certain) cash flow to risky (i.e., uncertain) cash flow. Riskless cash flow is one which the management is prepared to accept unless there is risk. Usually, the cash flow of riskless project is less than that of the risky project.

Under this method, the estimated cash flows are brought down to a certain level by applying correction factor (i.e., certainty equivalent coefficient). It can be employed by multiplying the expected cash flows by certainty equivalent coefficient as to convert the uncertain cash flows to certain cash flows.

ILLUSTRATION 22.3

There are two projects A and B. Each involves an investment of Rs. 80,000. The expected cash inflows and the certainty coefficients are as follows.

Year	Project A		Project B	
	Cash Inflow Rs.	*Certainty Coefficient*	*Cash Inflow Rs.*	*Certainty Coefficient*
1	50,000	0.8	40,000	0.9
2	40,000	0.7	60,000	0.8
3	40,000	0.9	40,000	0.7

Risk-free cut of rate is 10%. State which project is better.

Solution

Calculation of Cash Inflows with Certainty

	Project A			Project B		
Year	Cash Inflow Rs.	Certainty Coefficient	Certain Cash Inflow Rs.	Cash Inflow Rs.	Certainty Coefficient	Certain Cash Inflow Rs.
1	50,000	0.8	40,000	40,000	0.9	36,000
2	40,000	0.7	28,000	60,000	0.8	48,000
3	40,000	0.9	36,000	40,000	0.7	28,000

Calculation of Present Values of Cash Inflows

		Project A		Project B	
Year	Discount Factor @10%	Cash Inflows Rs.	Present Values Rs.	Cash Inflows Rs.	Present Values Rs.
1	0.909	40,000	36,360	36,000	32,724
2	0.826	28,000	23,128	48,000	39,648
3	0.751	36,000	27,036	28,000	21,028
			86,524		93,400

	Project A	Project B
Net Present Value =	Rs. 86,524 − 80,000	Rs. 93,400 − 80,000
	= Rs. 6,524	= Rs. 13,400

Since the net present value of project B is higher than that of project A, project B is better.

Sensitivity Technique

In case cash inflows are very sensitive in various cases, two and more forecasts of the future cash inflows may be made. These inflows are regarded as 'Optimistic', 'Most Likely', and 'Pessimistic'. Further, cash inflows are discounted to ascertain the net present values in these three situations. The net present value explains how sensitive the cash inflows are in these three cases. If this value differs widely, it implies that there is a great risk in the project. Hence the investor's decision to accept or reject a project depends on his risk bearing capacities.

ILLUSTRATION 22.4

XY Ltd. is considering two mutually exclusive projects P and Q. From the following information, you are required to advise the company.

	Project P (Rs.)	Project Q (Rs.)
Cost of the Investment	1,00,000	1,00,000
Forecast cash inflows per annum for 5 years:		
Optimistic	60,000	80,000
Most likely	40,000	40,000
Pessimistic	30,000	10,000

(The cut-off rate may be assumed to be 15%)

Solution

Calculation of net present value of cash inflows at a discount rate of 15% annuity of Rs. 1 for 5 years

	Project P				Project Q			
	Annual Cash Inflow Rs.	Discount Factor @15%	Present Value Rs.	Net Present Value Rs.	Annual Cash Inflow Rs.	Discount Factor @15%	Present Value Rs.	Net Present Value Rs.
Optimistic	60,000	3.3522	2,01,132	1,01,132	80,000	3.3522	2,68,176	1,68,176
Most likely	40,000	3.3522	1,34,088	34,088	40,000	3.3522	1,34,088	34,088
Pessimistic	30,000	3.3522	1,00,566	566	10,000	3.3522	33,522	66,478

The net present values of the each project show that the project Q is more risky than project P. But in favourable circumstances, it is more profitable as well. However, the acceptance of the project depends on the company's attitude towards risk. In case the company is able to bear more risk, project Q is more profitable.

Probability Technique

Probability means the likelihood of an occurrence of an event in future. In other words, it is the relative frequency with which an event may happen in future. For instance, when an event has 1 probability, it means that it is bound to occur. If it has 0 probability, it means that it is not going to occur.

When the future estimates of cash inflows have various probabilities, the expected money values may be ascertained by multiplying cash inflow, with the probability assigned. Further, the expected monetary values may be discounted to compute the present values. The project which provides more net present value may be accepted.

ILLUSTRATION 22.5

AB Ltd is considering two investment projects P and Q requiring an equal investment of Rs. 12,000.

From the following available information, you are requested to give your opinion regarding the selection of the project.

Cash Inflow Year	Project P Rs.	Probability	Project Q Rs.	Probability
1	8,000	0.2	16,000	0.2
2	16,000	0.6	18,000	0.6
3	24,000	0.2	18,000	0.2

Assume cost of capital at 10%.

Solution

Calculation of net present values of the two projects

Year	P.V. factor @10%	Project P Cash Inflows	Project P Probability	Project P Monetary Value	Project P Present Value	Project Q Cash Inflows	Project Q Probability	Project Q Monetary Value	Project Q Present Value
1	0.909	8,000	0.2	16,000	1,454	16,000	0.2	3,200	2909
2	0.826	16,000	0.6	9,600	7,930	18,000	0.6	10,800	8921
3	0.751	24,000	0.2	4,800	3,605	18,000	0.2	3600	2704

Total present Value	12,989	14,534
Less: Cost of Investment	12,000	12,000
Net present value	989	2,534

Standard Deviation

Standard deviation is a measure of dispersion. It is defined as the square root of squared deviations calculated from the mean. In capital budgeting, this measure is adopted to compare the variability of possible cash flows of different projects from their respective mean or expected values. A project having higher standard deviation is more risky than that of lower standard deviation.

The various steps involved in calculating the standard deviations of the possible cash flows of a project are given below:

(i) Computing mean value of the possible cash flows.

(ii) Ascertaining deviations between the mean value and the possible cash flows.

(iii) Squaring of deviations

(iv) Multiplying squared deviations by the assigned probabilities which give weighted squared deviations.

(v) Totaling of the weighted squared deviations and finding their square root. The resulting figure is the standard deviation.

ILLUSTRATION 22.6

On the basis of information given below, ascertain which project is more risky by adopting standard deviation approach.

Project P Cash Inflow Rs.	Project P Probability	Project Q Cash Inflow Rs.	Project Q Probability
4,000	0.2	4,000	0.1
8,000	0.3	8,000	0.4
12,000	0.3	12,000	0.4
16,000	0.2	16,000	0.1

Solution

Calculation of Standard Deviation

Project X

Cash Inflows Rs.	Deviation from Mean (d) (10,000)	Square of Deviations (d²)	Profitability	Weighted Sq. Deviations (fd²)
1	2	3	4	5
4,000	−6,000	3,60,00,000	0.2	72,00,000
8,000	−2,000	40,00,000	0.3	12,00,000
12,000	+2000	40,00,000	0.3	12,00,000
16,000	+6000	3,60,00,000	0.2	72,00,000
			$n = 1$	$\Sigma(fd^2) = 1,68,00,000$

$$\text{Standard Deivaition } (\sigma) = \sqrt{\frac{\Sigma fd^2}{n}}$$

$$= \sqrt{\frac{1,68,00,000}{1}}$$

$$= 4,099$$

Project Y

1	2	3	4	5
4,000	−6,000	3,60,00,000	0.1	36,00,000
8,000	−2,000	40,00,000	0.4	16,00,000
12,000	+2000	40,00,000	0.4	16,00,000
16,000	+6000	3,60,00,000	0.1	36,00,000
			$n = 1$	$\Sigma(fd^2) = 1,04,00,000$

$$\text{Standard Deivaition } (\sigma) = \sqrt{\frac{\Sigma fd^2}{n}}$$

$$= \sqrt{\frac{1,04,00,000}{1}}$$

$$= 3,225$$

Since the standard deviation of Project X is greater than that of Project Y, X is more risky.

Coefficient of Variation Method

It is the relative measure of variation. Coefficient of variation (i.e., relative measure) should be ascertained to judge the relative position of the risk involved, in case the projects have same cost but different net present values. It can be computed as

$$\text{Coefficient of Variation} = \frac{\text{Standard Deviation}}{\text{Mean}} \times 100$$

ILLUSTRATION 22.7

From the above illustration, calculate coefficient of variation and suggest which proposal can be accepted.

Solution

$$\text{Coefficient of Variation} = \frac{\text{Standard Deviation}}{\text{Mean}} \times 100$$

For project X, $= \dfrac{4,099}{10,000} \times 100 = 40.99\%$

For project Y $= \dfrac{3,225}{10,000} \times 100 = 32.25\%$

Since the coefficient of variation of Project X is greater than that of Y, Project X is more risky. Hence, Project Y can be selected.

Decision Tree Analysis

A decision tree is a branching diagram which represents the relationship between a present decision and future events, future decisions and their consequences. The sequence of events is mapped out over time in a format resembling branches. Hence, the analysis is called the decision tree analysis. This analysis is helpful in tackling risky capital investment proposal.

Decision trees are constructed from left to right. The branches represent the possible alternative decisions that can be made and the various possible outcomes that may arise. It helps to differentiate between the two types of branches.

The decision tree analysis involves various steps. They are (i) identifying the problem, (ii) tracing the alternatives, (iii) exhibiting the decision tree showing the decision points, chance events, etc. (iv) specifying probabilities and monetary values of cash inflows, and (v) analysing alternatives.

ILLUSTRATION 22.8

PQR Ltd is considering the purchase of a new plant requiring a cash outlay of Rs. 40,000. The expected returns during the life of the investment are given below.

Year I

Event	Cash Inflow	Probability
(i)	16,000	0.3
(ii)	24,000	0.5
(iii)	20,000	0.2

Year II

Cash inflows in year I are:

	Rs. 16,000		Rs. 24,000		Rs. 20,000	
	Cash Inflows Rs.	Probability	Cash Inflows Rs.	Probability	Cash Inflows Rs.	Probability
(i)	30,000	0.2	40,000	0.1	50,000	0.2
(ii)	40,000	0.6	60,000	0.8	80,000	0.5
(iii)	50,000	0.2	80,000	0.1	1,20,000	0.3

Assuming that 10% is the cost of capital, plot the above data in the form of decision tree and suggest whether the project should be accepted or not.

Solution

Calculation of net present values of cash inflows

	Alterna-tives	Cash Inflows Year I Rs.	Cash Inflows Year II Rs.	Discount Factor 10% Year I	Discount Factor 10% Year II	Present Values Year I Rs.	Present Values Year II Rs.	Total Rs.	Net Present Value Rs.
(a)	(i)	16,000	30,000	0.909	0.826	14,544	24,780	39,324	−676
	(ii)	16,000	40,000	0.909	0.826	14,544	33,040	47,584	7,584
	(iii)	16,000	50,000	0.909	0.826	14,544	41,300	55,844	15,844
(b)	(i)	24,000	40,000	0.909	0.826	21,816	33,040	54,856	14,856
	(ii)	24,000	60,000	0.909	0.826	21,816	49,560	71,376	31,376
	(iii)	24,000	80,000	0.909	0.826	21,816	66,080	87,896	47,896
(c)	(i)	20,000	50,000	0.909	0.826	18,180	41,300	59,480	19,480
	(ii)	20,000	80,000	0.909	0.826	18,180	66,080	84,260	44,260
	(iii)	20,000	1,20,000	0.909	0.826	18,180	99,120	1,17,300	77,300

Decision Tree Analysis

(1) Year 0	(2) Year I Probability Cash Inflow	(3) Year II Probability Cash Inflow Rs.	(4) Net Present Value of Inflow Rs.	(5) Joint Probability	(6) = (4) × (5) Expected Net Present Value Rs.
	0.3 16,000	0.2 30,000	− 676	0.06	− 40.56
		0.6 40,000	7,584	0.18	1,365.12
		0.2 50,000	15,844	0.06	950.32
Cash Outflow Rs. 40,000	0.5 24,000	0.1 40,000	14,856	0.50	742.80
		0.8 60,000	31,376	0.40	12,550.40
		0.1 80,000	47,896	0.05	2,394.80
	0.2 20,000	0.2 50,000	19,480	0.04	779.20
		0.5 80,000	44,260	0.10	4,426.00
		0.3 1,20,000	77,300	0.06	4,638.00
		Total		1.00	27,806.08

Since the proposal yields a net present value of +27,806.08 at a discount factor of 10%, the proposal may be accepted.

CAPITAL RATIONING

Capital rationing is a situation where a company has more investment proposals than it can finance. Thus capital rationing refers to a situation where a company cannot undertake all profitable projects (i.e., Positive NPV projects) it has identified because of shortage of capital. Usually, a company is forced to reject some of the viable projects having profit on account of paucity of funds. However, in practice, the company fixes the size of the annual capital expenditure budget on the basis of the volume of funds available and other considerations. In such an event, the company has not only to select profitable projects but has also to rank the projects from the highest to lowest priority. A cut-off point is then fixed. Proposals above the cut-off point should be chosen and those below the cut-off point should be rejected or delayed. The company usually fixes the cut-off point keeping in view the number of projects, the objectives of the firm and the availability of capital to finance the capital expenditure.

Factors of Capital Rationing

The situation of capital rationing arises due to both external and internal factors. Factors such as imperfections of capital market or deficiencies in market information are brought under external causes. A company may not get the required amount of funds to carry out all of its profitable projects because of these imperfections. The various internal factors which cause capital rationing are the reluctance of the company: (i) to financing by external equities for avoiding further risk; (ii) to broaden the equity share base for fear of losing control, and (iii) to accept some viable projects because of its inability to manage the concern in the scale of operation.

Steps in Capital Rationing

Selecting projects under the situation of capital rationing involves two steps. They are (i) Ranking projects in accordance with profitability index or internal rate of return, and (ii) Selecting projects in descending order of profitability under the budget figures are exhausted keeping in view the objective of maximizing the value of the concern.

ILLUSTRATION 22.9

A company has the following investment proposals.

Proposals	Initial Outlay	Profitability Index
1	2,00,000	1.46
2	2,50,000	0.98
3	2,50,000	2.31
4	3,50,000	1.32
5	2,00,000	1.25

The available funds are Rs. 8 lakh. Advise the company regarding the acceptance of the proposals.

Solution

In this illustration all proposals except No. 2 give profitability index exceeding one and are profitable investments. The total outlay required to be invested in all other (profitable) projects is Rs. 10,00,000 (1 + 3 + 4 + 5) but total funds available within the concern are Rs. 8,00,000 and hence, the concern has to do capital rationing and select the most profitable combination of projects within the total cash outlay of Rs. 8,00,000. Project No. 5 which has the lowest profitability index among the profitable proposals cannot be taken.

— REVIEW QUESTIONS —

1. "Risk analysis of capital investments is one of the most complex controversial and slippery areas in finance". Comment.

2. Define risk. Explain the various techniques used for incorporating risk factor in capital budgeting decisions.

3. Write notes on:
   (a) Sensitivity analysis
   (b) Capital rationing
   (c) Decision tree analysis
   (d) Certainty equivalent coefficient

4. What is capital rationing? Explain the factors leading to capital rationing.

5. From then following data, state which project is better:

Project Cash flows Year	X	Y
0	−10,000	−10,000
1	4,000	5,000
2	4,000	6,000
3	2,000	3,000

Riskless discount rate is 5%. Project X is less risky as compared to Project Y. The management considers risk premium rates at 5% and 10% respectively appropriate for discounting the cash inflows.

   (**Ans.:** Project Y is superior to Project X. Since NPV is positive it may be accepted)

6. X Ltd is considering a project with the following cash flows:

Year	Purchase of Plant / Rs.	Running Costs / Rs.	Savings Rs.
0	(7,000)		
1		2,000	6,000
2		2,500	7,000

The cost of capital is 8%. Measure the sensitivity of the project to changes in the level of plant value, running costs and savings (considering each factor at a time) such that net present value becomes zero. Which factor is most sensitive to effect the acceptability of the project. The present value factors at 8% are as follows:

Year	Factor
0	1.00
1	0.93
2	0.86

(**Ans.:** Saving is the most sensitive factor to affect the acceptability of the project)

7. Two mutually exclusive investment proposals are being considered. The following information is available.

	Project X		Project Y	
	Rs.		Rs.	
Cost	6,000		6,000	
Cash Inflow				
Year	Rs.	Probability	Rs.	Probability
1	4,000	0.2	8,000	0.2
2	8,000	0.6	9,000	0.6
3	12,000	0.2	9,000	0.2

Assuming cost of capital at 10%, advise the selection of the project.

(**Ans.:** Project Y is more profitable)

8. From the following information ascertain which project is more risky on the basic of standard deviation.

Project A		Project B	
Cash Inflow	Probability	Cash Inflow	Probability
Rs.		Rs.	
2,000	0.2	2,000	0.1
4,000	0.3	4,000	0.4
6,000	0.3	6,000	0.4
8,000	0.2	8,000	0.1

(**Ans.:** Project A is more risky)

9. Mr. M is considering the purchase of a new plant requiring a cash outlay of Rs. 20,000. The plant is expected to have a useful life of 2 years without any salvage value. The cash flows and their associated probabilities for the two years are as under.

Ist year	Cash Flow (Rs.)	Probability
(i)	8,000	0.3
(ii)	11,000	0.4
(iii)	15,000	0.3

2nd year. If cash flows in 1st year are:

	Rs. 8,000		Rs. 11,000		Rs. 15,000	
	Cash Flows	Probability	Cash Flows	Probability	Cash Flows	Probability
(i)	4,000	0.2	13,000	0.3	16,000	0.1
(ii)	10,000	0.6	15,000	0.4	20,000	0.8
(iii)	15,000	0.2	16,000	0.3	24,000	0.1

presuming that 10% is the cost of capital, you plot the above data in the form of a decision tree and suggest whether the project should be taken up or not.

(**Ans.:** Since the project gives a positive net present value of Rs. 2513 at 10% discount factor it may be accepted)

23

Human Resource Accounting

Human resource accounting is the measurement and quantification of human organisational inputs, such as recruiting, experience and commitment.

— Stephen Knauf

CONTENTS

- Introduction
- Methods of human resource accounting
- Human resource accounting in India
- Review questions

INTRODUCTION

The economic development of any nation mainly depends on the exploitation of her human and non-human resources. But in the case of an industrial concern, human resources are virtually mother resources because of the fact that they are not only its inputs but also its final consumer. However, an enterprise with competent people can make the unit successful in a short span of time. Then the question is why are people not treated as assets? The reason is that human assets are not owned and are not transferable on the basis of transactions like other assets. Moreover, there is no assurance of future benefits from human resources. When fixed assets are purchased, the cost incurred is the estimated potential value of the benefits likely to be gained. While assessing the potential benefits and services of fixed assets, the uncertainties of changes in technology and production process and premature obsolescence of these assets is taken into account. But there is no reason why human assets should not be amenable to the same treatment. Another objection is that the human assets may not be recognised by tax-laws.

In actual practice, even now the profit and loss accounts prepared on the basis of existing conventions have to be redrawn for tax purposes. It should, therefore, be possible to overcome the difficulties of tax laws by incorporating the value of human resources in the financial statements.

Definitions

The American Accounting Association's Committee on HRA has defined human resource accounting, "As the process of identifying, measuring and communicating information relating to human resources in order to facilitate effective management within the organisation". It involves measuring the costs incurred by business firms to recruit, select, hire, train and develop human assets and giving this information to those who are interested in it. Human resource accounting is intended basically as an information system which reflects the changes in human resources over a period of time. Such information is vital to management in the planning and control of human resources and budgeting of personnel. According to Eric Flamholtz of University of California, Los Angeles,

> Human resource accounting is an accounting for people as organisational resources. It is the measurement of the cost and value of people for the organisation.

Eric explains that HRA is a tool to measure the cost of human resources in the organisation. R. Likert has defined it as the activity devoted to attaching dollar estimates to the value of a firm's human organisation and its customer goodwill.

Objectives of Human Resources Accounting

The human being constitutes an important asset for organisational success. Without men all money and material resources cannot be effectively geared for achieving the goal of an enterprise. The variables in human behaviour like group loyalty, skill, motivation and capacity for effective interaction, communication and decision-making are the true indicators of organisational health. The study of human resources in an enterprise is, therefore, required with the following objectives in mind:

1. It helps in evaluating the return on investment in human capital.

2. It helps in communicating the worth of human resources to the organisation and the general public.

3. It helps in knowing whether the human resources have been properly utilised or not.

4. It provides quantitative information on human resources which will help managers and investors in making decisions.

Need for Human Resource Accounting

The need for human resources accounting cannot be over emphasised in knowing whether human asset is being built up in the business or not. But in traditional accounting practice, the value of human capital is completely ignored. As such, real assessment of a firm's resources is not possible because manpower forms a vital part of the total assets.

Moreover, in traditional accounting system, the amount spent on selection, recruitment, training, welfare, development and incentive payments for improving the efficiency of employees are treated as current costs and charged against current revenue. Hence, management has absolutely no information regarding investment in human resources even if these costs are investment in human resources. But at the same time information about human assets is highly essential to management for planning and control in the same way as data regarding other resources are needed for presentation in the financial statements. If the value of both human and physical assets is shown together in the balance sheet, a more realistic assessment of the firm can be presented before the investors, financers, creditors, government and the public in general. However, such needs of the management can be fulfilled through a system of human resource accounting.

To sum up, there is a growing need to shift inert priorities from getting the best out of non-human capital to getting the best out of human capital. If the man behind the machine is tended, mended and given proper treatment, he will blossom to health to give encouraging results in the best interest of the enterprise. As such, today there is a greater awareness to focus attention on the scientific study of social behaviour and its effect on cost and quality of the end product.

Advantages of Human Resources Accounting

The advantages of human resources accounting are as follows:

1. Human resources accounting reflects the cost of developing human resources in the business. This will help the management to ascertain the cost of labour turnover.

2. It helps the management to compare the investment in human resources with the benefits derived. This further helps to avoid the wasteful expenditure on human beings.

3. The accurate return on investment can be ascertained only when expenditure on employees is treated as an asset. Thus the real return on investment can be calculated with the help of HRA.

4. It helps the management in planning and executing the personnel policies such as transfers, promotions, training, retirement and retrenchment of human resources.

5. Human resources accounting will motivate employees to improve their worth as they come to know the cost incurred on them and the returns given by them in the form of output.

6. It also helps the management to know whether the firm has made proper investments in human resources or not. If it is found excess, the management can take steps to control it at the right time.

METHODS OF HUMAN RESOURCE ACCOUNTING

A number of approaches has been developed to measure human resources, one approach is based on cost which may be historical cost, replacement cost, standard cost or opportunity cost and the other approach is to measure the economic value of the resources based on capitalisation of earnings, i.e., the present value of future earnings, economic value, return on effort employed and goodwill approach.

1. Historical Cost Approach

This approach was developed by *Brummet, Flamholtz* and *Pyle*. As per this approach, the costs of recruitment, training, hiring and developments, etc., incurred up to the stage of making an employee ready for providing service are capitalised. The sum of historical costs for all employees of the firm is the total value of human resources. The cost so capitalised has to be written off over the expected period for which an employee is likely to remain with the firm. In case he leaves the firm prematurely, the unamortised cost remaining in the books has to be written off against the revenue of that year. On the contrary, if he has a longer life than expected, his cost of amortisation is rescheduled.

Advantages

1. It is easy to calculate and simple to understand.
2. It follows the traditional accounting concept of matching cost with the revenue.
3. It helps the firm to ascertain a return on human asset.

Disadvantages

1. It is a tough task to estimate the number of years an employee will remain in a firm.
2. It is very difficult to determine the number of years over which the effect of investment in human assets will be realised.
3. It is also difficult to fix a rate of return as human assets can generally be written off on a constant basis.
4. In the course of time, the utility of employees increases due to the acquisition of experience and training. Thus it is very difficult to see the contribution of each person although it is easy to measure the total cost of human factor.

2. Replacement Cost Approach

This approach was put forward by *Rensis Likert* and *Eric G. Flamholtz*. According to them, the value of human assets of a firm is to be found out by calculating how much it would cost to replace the existing human assets with other persons of equivalent experience and talent. In other words, under this approach the cost of recruiting, selecting, training, developing, etc., of new employees to reach the level of competence of existing employees are measured to find out the value of human assets of a firm. However, the replacement cost approach differs from historical cost approach in the sense that it allows for changes in the cost of acquiring and developing employees.

Advantages

1. It provides more realistic value in inflationary times as it adjusts the human value of price trends in the economy.
2. It provides estimates of the current cost of employing personnel.

Disadvantages

1. It is not always possible to ascertain the exact replacement of an employee.
2. It is a tough task to ascertain the cost of replacing human resources as different persons may arrive at different estimates.

3. Opportunity Cost Approach

This method was first advocated by *Hekimian* and *Jones* for a company with several divisional heads bidding for the services of various people they need among themselves and then include in the investment base. This approach values human resources on the basis of the economic concept of opportunity cost. The opportunity cost is linked with scarcity. There is no opportunity cost for those employees who are not scarce and also those at the top will not be available for auction. As such, only scarce people should comprise the value of human resources. In other words, employees not considered scarce are not included in the human asset base of a firm.

The opportunity cost approach can work for some of the people at shop-floor and middle order management. But it fails to provide a value for total human resources. Moreover, valuation on the basis of opportunity cost is restricted to alternative uses within the organisation. In real life, such alternative uses may not be identifiable on account of the constraints in an organisational environment.

4. Present Value of Future Earnings Method

Under this method, the value of an employee is the present value of his future earnings from employment.

Suppose Vr is the value of human asset relating to an employee r years old, T is the age of retirement, $E(t)$ is the annual earnings up to the age of retirement and r is the rate of return on investment, i.e., discount rate (cost of capital), then

$$\text{Vr} = \sum_{t=r}^{T} \frac{E(t)}{(1+r)t-r}$$

The asset value would be $\text{Vr} \times e$, where e is the efficiency ratio.

Human asset calculated in this way if compared with non-human assets will give an idea about the degree of labour intensiveness in the enterprise. It is assumed that employees will serve the firm in the same position until death or retirement.

5. Economic Value Method

Another approach to the evaluation of human assets in a firm is to calculate their economic values. The economic value of the firm is determined by obtaining the present value of future earnings. The commonly used method is that group-wise future earnings of employees are estimated, then discounted and resulting figures being aggregated.

A number of valuation models has been developed for determining the present value of future earnings. They are:

(a) The Lev and Schwartz Model (1971)

(b) Flamholtz Model (1971)

(c) Morse Net Benefit Model (1973)

6. Return on Effort Employed Method

This method is similar to that of return on investment measured in financial accounting. Here the quality and quantity of effort employed are rated numerically. The level of work done is determined on the basis of salary grades of jobs. Job grades are assigned numbers in descending order for the purpose of quantitative assessment of performance. Similarly, experience and efficiency that travel together up to a point are also allotted numbers. The product of all the factors provides the measure of effort contributed by individual employee. The sum of products of all employees taken together gives the figure of total effort employed. The rate of return on human efforts for profits earned is then expressed per unit of effort. The rate of return on human efforts forms the basis of comparison from year to year in the firm or among different business centres of the firm in the same year. This information leads management to question why there are such differences and how improvement can be achieved.

7. Goodwill Approach

In valuing human resources under this method, only the permanent factors leading to super profits are considered. As it is risky to proceed the valuation of human resources only on the basis of profit, a careful assessment should also be made of other factors in operation. These factors are as follows:

(i) Return on investment in the light of:
  (a) Shares of the market and the growth rate of sales,
  (b) Value added,
  (c) Replacement programme of assets.

(ii) Research and Development made in the light of:
  (a) Development of new products,
  (b) Development of new markets and uses.

(iii) Management capability measured in the light of:
  (a) Executive development,
  (b) Employee satisfaction and morale,
  (c) Customer satisfaction, and
  (d) Awareness of changes in the social, technological and economic environment and the ability to meet them.

Besides, the general image that the firm enjoys among the government, bankers, financiers and the general public for its products and services should also be considered.

Objections Against Human Resource Accounting

The main objections raised against human resources accounting are as follows:

1. Human resources cannot be valued like other assets as there is a difference between other assets and human assets.

2. Although there are different methods for valuation of human resources, they are different from each other. All of them give results.

3. Human resource asset is only a theoretical concept as it is not recognised by tax laws.

4. The factors to be included for valuing human resources are not precisely measurable in monetary terms as they are abstract.

HUMAN RESOURCE ACCOUNTING IN INDIA

In India, companies prepare financial statements as per the Companies Act of 1956. The Act, however, does not contain any provision for the disclosure of human resources in the financial statements. But the only provision contained in the Act is regarding the disclosure of information about the employees getting remuneration of Rs. 36,000 per annum or more as footnote in the Profit and Loss Account. However, leading public sector companies such as BHEL, SAIL, ONGC, HMT, etc., have already commenced reporting valuation of human resources in their Annual Reports as additional information.

In India, BHEL have adopted Lev and Schwartz model for human resources accounting. This model states that the value of human capital embodied in an individual is the present value of his remaining future earnings from employment in the form of salaries and wages. This model is also based on assumptions that the promotion policy and the pay scales remain constant.

BHEL reported the following figures of human assets from their published accounts for the year ended March 31, 1973:

	Million Rs.
Executives	1,094
Supervisors	655
Skilled Artisans	1,291
Supporting Technical Staff	199
Clerical and Office-Supporting Staff	288
Unskilled employees	500
	4,027

It is the human resources as a whole that has to be valued and the value should be based on the benefits likely to accrue to the concern and not the cost it incurs on human assets. This method is regarded as the most scientific as compared with other methods because it provides a future-oriented economic value of human capital. The practical difficulty is that of quantifying and pricing services of employee-groups in respect of jobs which do not yield any physical output.

— REVIEW QUESTIONS —

1. What is human resource accounting? Explain its objectives and significance in the present context.

2. Explain the various methods of valuing human resource assets.

3. Discuss the Historical Cost Approach of human resource accounting. What are its merits and demerits?

4. Explain the Lev and Schwartz model of human resource accounting in the context of public sector companies in India.

5. Writes notes on:

   (a) Objections against human resources accounting.
   (b) Replacement cost approach of human resource accounting.
   (c) Human resource accounting in India.
   (d) Goodwill approach of human resource accounting.
   (e) Need for human resource accounting.

24

Lease Financing

*Leasing separates ownership and use as two economic activities,
and facilitates asset use without ownership.*

— MILLER M.H. AND C.W. UPTRON

CONTENTS

- Introduction
- Meaning
- Types of leasing
- Review questions

INTRODUCTION

After identifying the attractive projects, the financial manager of a firm has to consider the sources from which the investments for these projects are to be raised. In the recent few decades, apart from debt and equity financing, leasing has emerged as a third important source of medium and long-term financing. It has proved to be an effective system for financing capital equipment in Europe, Japan and U.S.A. Although capital equipment leasing is widely used in Western countries, it is a recent practice in India. Of course, leasing concerned with real estate was prevalent in our country before 1950. As a formal instrument of industrial finance, the country witnessed the emergence of leasing companies in the early 1970. The pioneer in this field was the establishment of the "First Leasing Company of India Ltd" in Madras. The company commenced its business in 1973. At present, we have a number of large-sized companies in this field.

MEANING

A contract of lease may be defined as "a contract whereby the owner of an asset grants to another party the exclusive right to use the asset usually for an agreed period of time in return for the payment of rent". In other words, leasing is an arrangement that provides a firm with the use and control over assets without buying and owning the same. Thus leasing distinguishes the two significant rights to the property i.e., right to own and right to use. Here, the owner of the asset is called lessor and the person who uses the asset is known as lessee.

Steps in Leasing

The following steps are involved in a leasing transaction:

1. The lessee has to decide about the type of asset required and his other requirements such as design, specifications of the price, warranties, terms of delivery, etc.

2. The lessee has to determine the manufacturer or supplier for the supply of the asset required.

3. The lessee has to enter into a lease agreement with the lessor with regard to:

    (a) the irrevocability of the lease during the basic lease period,

    (b) the amount and timing of the periodical rental payments during the basic lease period,

    (c) the option to renew the lease or to purchase the asset at the end of the basic lease period, and

    (d) the responsibility for payment of cost of maintenance and repairs, taxes, insurance and other expenses.

4. After signing the agreement, the lessor has to contact the manufacturer or supplier to supply the asset to the lessee.

5. After the asset is delivered and accepted by the lessee, the lessor has to make the payment to the manufacturer or the supplier.

TYPES OF LEASING

The lease transactions are mainly of two types. They are:

1. Operating or Service Lease
2. Financial Lease

1. Operating or Service Lease

An operating lease is defined as a contract in which the lessee is not committed to paying more than the original cost of equipment during contractual period. In other words, an operating lease is one which does not satisfy any of the following conditions:

    (a) The lessor transfers title to the lessee at the end of the lease period.

    (b) The lease contains an option to purchase the asset at a bargaining price.

(c) The lease period is equal to or greater than seventy five per cent of the estimated economic life of the asset.

(d) At the beginning of the lease the present value of the minimum lease payments equals to or exceeds ninety per cent of the fair value of the leased property to the lessor (less any investments and tax credits realised by the lessor).

The operating lease is also known as "Open-end Lease Arrangement" as the lessee has the option to terminate the agreement by notice. Under an operating lease, the cost of maintenance of the equipment is borne by the lessor. It is used often in leasing of specialized office machinery, computers, etc., which require expert technical staff for maintenance.

2. Financial Lease

Like an instalment loan, financial lease is a legal commitment to pay for the entire cost of the equipment plus interest over a specified period of time. Lessee commits to a series of payments which in total exceed the original cost of the equipment (cost of equipment and interest). Financial lease is usually for a longer period and non-cancellable. In India, most of the leases are financial leases which are commonly used for leasing land, building, machinery and fixed equipment. The main features of financial lease are as follows:

1. It is non-cancellable by the lessee prior to the date of its expiry.
2. It provides the lessee an option of renewing the lease for further period at a nominal cost.
3. Its contract period covers essentially the expected useful life of the asset.
4. It normally excludes provisions for maintenance or taxes which are paid separately by the lessee.
5. Its risk of obsolescence and under-utilisation is borne by the lessee.

Forms of Financial Lease

Various kinds of financial lease arrangements are as follows:

(i) Sale and Lease Back

Under a sale and lease back arrangement, a firm sells an asset to another person who in turn leases it back to the firm. The firm usually sells the asset at its market value and receives the sales price in cash and gets the right to use the asset during the basic lease period. The firm, in turn, contracts to make periodic lease payments and gives up title to the asset. The lessors such as insurance companies, institutional investors, finance companies, etc., generally engage in sale and lease-back arrangement.

(ii) Leveraged Lease

Leveraged lease is a special form of leasing developed in recent years in U.S.A. in conjunction with the financing of assets requiring large capital outlays. It is an arrangement under which the lessor borrows funds, for purchasing the asset, from a third party called lender which is usually a bank or a finance company. The loan is usually secured by a mortgage on the asset besides assignment of the leased assets and rental payments.

Leveraged lease arrangement involves three parties—the lessee, the lessor and the lender. Here, the lessee agrees to make periodic payments over the basic lease period and gets the right to use the asset over the agreed period of time. The lessor acquires the asset in keeping with the lease arrangements but finances only a part of the total investment, says 25 per cent. The remaining 75 per cent is provided by a long-term lender or lenders. The lessor acts both as the owner and the borrower. The lender is usually a bank, insurance company, financial institution or a private financing company.

(iii) Direct Leasing

Under direct leasing, a firm acquires the use of an asset without owning it. There are a wide variety of direct leasing arrangements available to meet the various needs of the firm. The manufacturers, finance companies and independent leasing companies are the major types of lessors.

A direct lease may be arranged either from the manufacturer/supplier directly or through the leasing company. In the first case, the manufacturer/supplier himself acts as the lessor. But in the second case, the lessee firm arranges the purchase of the asset for the lessor (leasing company) from the manufacturer or the supplier and also enters into an agreement with the lessor for the lease of the asset.

(iv) Straight Lease and Modified Lease

A lease is said to be straight when the lease agreement does not provide any modifications to the terms and conditions of the basic lease. Under straight lease, the leasee firm is required to pay the lease rent over the expected life of the asset.

A modified lease, on the other hand, is one which provides several options to the lessee during the lease period. For example, the lease agreement provides an option of terminating lease either by purchasing the asset or by returning the same.

(v) Primary and Secondary Lease

(Front-ended and Back-ended Lease)

A lease is said to be primary when the lessor charges lease rent in such a manner that it covers the cost of the asset and acceptable profit during the initial period of the lease. On the other hand, a lease is said to be secondary when the lessor charges only nominal rent during the secondary period of the lease. However, the rental charged by the lessor during the primary period, is much higher than that of the secondary period. The primary and secondary lease is also called front-ended and back-ended lease.

Financial Evaluation of Leasing

A. Lessee's Point of View (Lease or Buy Decisions)

After evaluating the economic viability of an asset, the intending user has to consider the alternative method of financing the investment, i.e., whether to buy the asset or take it on lease. While comparing buying with leasing, the cost of financing the asset through debt and equity should also be compared with the cost of leasing. Thus lease finance decisions basically involve comparison between the cost of debt-financing and lease financing.

The evaluation of 'buying' and 'leasing' (lease financing decisions) can be made in accordance with the discounted cash flow technique, using net present value (NPV) method. The various steps involved in this process are as follows:

1. Calculate the present value of cash flows under the buying alternatives.

2. Ascertain the present value of cash flows associated with the leasing alternatives.

3. Determine whether to buy or lease or reject the proposal by comparing the N.P.V. under each of the alternative.

The alternative with higher NPV will be preferred. If the NPVs of both the alternatives are negative, the proposal will altogether be rejected.

ILLUSTRATION 24.1

A bulldozer, which has a service life of 10 years, can be purchased for Rs. 1,80,000. It can also be hired at the rate of Rs. 45,000 per annum payable at the beginning of each year. Operating costs are to be borne by the user.

A contractor requiring the use of the bulldozer only for a period of two years seeks your advice. If purchased, he expects to use it for 2 years and then sell it at 80 per cent of the purchase price. He can finance its purchase by his own resources to the extent of Rs. 80,000 and the balance by borrowing at an interest rate of 18 per cent per annum. The interest on the loan is payable annually at the end of each year and the loan can be repaid out of the sale proceeds of the bulldozer.

For income-tax purposes, depreciation is an admissible deduction at 25 per cent on diminishing balance method. Excess realisation, if any, over the written down value is subject to tax. The effective tax rate for the contractor is 50 per cent. Tax liabilities can be assumed to arise at the close of each year.

The contractor expects a minimum internal rate of 10 per cent net of taxes on his own funds. Prepare a suitable statement and advise the contractor, indicating clearly the basis for your recommendation.

(C.A., Final (N.S.), May 1977, AIMA, June 1988)

Solution

The operating costs and gross revenues from the use of the bulldozer will be the same whether it is bought or taken on lease. Thus it will be proper to work out only the cash inflows and outflows that will be different under the two alternatives.

A. Purchase of the Bulldozer

(i) Outflows:

	Amount Rs.	P.V. Factor at 10% p.a.	Discounted Value Rs.
Cash Outflows on Purchase (see note)	80,000	1.000	80,000
*Interest on Borrowing for first year	9,000	0.909	8,181
*Interest on Borrowing for second year	9,000	0.826	7,434
Income-tax Payable on Profit on sale of the bulldozer (see Note 2)	21,375	0.826	17,657
	1,19,375		1,13,272

*The rate of Income-tax being 50% of the real incidence of interest on the firm will be only ½ of Rs. 18,000.

(ii) Outflows:	Amount Rs.	P.V. Factor at 10% p.a.	Discounted Value Rs.
Cash received on sale of the bulldozer after repaying borrowings (see Note 3)	44,000	0.826	36,344
Savings in Tax because of depreciation			
First year	22,500	0.909	20,453
Second Year (See Note 4)	16,875	0.826	13,939
	83,375		70,736

Thus the purchase of the bulldozer will result in a net discounted cash outflow Rs. 42,536 (i.e., Rs. 1,13,272 – 70,736).

B. Hiring (or leasing) of the Bulldozer

(i) Outflows:	Amount Rs.	P.V. Factor at 10% p.a.	Discounted Value Rs.
Hire charges for the first year	45,000	1.000	45,000
Hire charges for the Second year	45,000	0.909	40,905
	90,000		85,905

(ii) Outflows:	Amount Rs.	P.V. Factor at 10% p.a.	Discounted Value Rs.
Tax savings in the first year on Hire charges (see Note 5)	22,500	0.909	20,453
Tax Savings on Hire charges For the Second year	22,500	0.826	18,585
	45,000		39,038

The net outflows if the bulldozer is hired will be Rs. 46,867 (i.e., Rs. 85,905 – Rs. 39,038).

Thus it is clear that the net discounted outflows if the bulldozer is bought are less than the net discounted outflows if it is taken on hire. Hence, the proposal of buying should be accepted, in case there are no uncertainties involved.

If the amount realisable on the sale of the bulldozer at the end of two years (Rs. 1,44,000) is rather uncertain and, on the face of it, 80% of the original cost appears to be high, the conclusion may well be in favour of hiring. Furthermore, the rate of return specified is the minimum of 10%. If it is possible to utilise the sum of Rs. 80,000 in some other profitable venture, it may be better to take the bulldozer on hire.

Working Notes:

1. The net cash outflow on purchase is only Rs. 80,000, as Rs. 1,00,000 is borrowed and repaid at the end of two years. However, the interest on such borrowings is an outflow.

2. The written down value of the bulldozer after two years of use is Rs. 1,01,250 (depreciation is Rs. 45,000 in the first year and Rs. 33,750 in the second). Thus there is

a profit of Rs. 42,750. It is presumed that the tax on this profit is payable immediately at the end of two years.

3. Cash realised on sale is Rs. 1,44,000. However, Rs. 1,00,000 (loan) has to be paid back. The net cash flow, therefore, is Rs. 44,000.

4. Depreciation is Rs. 45,000 and Rs. 33,750 for the first and the second years respectively. Saving in tax would be 50% of these amounts.

5. The hire charges will be paid in the beginning of the year, but the tax savings on the same will accrue only at the end of the year.

B. Lessor's Point of View

From the point of view of lessor, the evaluation of leasing out an asset can be made with the help of the following two time adjusted methods of capital budgeting:

(a) Present Value Method

(b) Internal Rate of Return Method

(a) **Present Value Method:** Under this method, the following steps are involved:

(i) Determining cash outflows by deducting tax advantage of owning an asset such as investment allowance, if any.

(ii) Determining cash inflows after tax.

(iii) Determining the present value of cash outflows and after tax cash inflows by discounting at weighted average cost of capital of the lessor.

(iv) Compare the present value of cash inflows with the present value of cash outflows. If P.V. of cash inflows is more than the P.V. of cash outflows, it is desirable to lease out the asset and vice-versa.

ILLUSTRATION 24.2

From the following information, you are required to advise about leasing out of the asset.

Cost of Equipment	Rs. 5,00,000
Average Cost of Capital to the Lessor	12%
Depreciation (Allowable)	25% on original cost
Expected Life of Asset	5 years
Salvage Value	Nil
Lease Rent payable at the end of each of 5 years	Rs. 1,75,000
Corporate Tax (applicable to lessor)	50%

P.V. of an annuity of Rs. 1 for 5 years at 12% is Rs. 3.605.

Solution

(i) Calculation of Cash Outflows:

	(Rs.)
Cost of Equipment	Rs. 5,00,000
Less: Tax advantage if any	Nil
Cash Outflow	5,00,000

(ii) Calculation of After-Tax Inflows:

Lease Rent	1,75,000
Less: Depreciation	1,25,000
Earnings before Tax (EBT)	50,000
Less: Tax at 50%	25,000
Earnings After Tax (EAT)	25,000
Add: Depreciation	1,25,000
Cash Inflows After Tax (CFAT)	1,50,000

(iii) Calculation of Present Value (P.V.) of Cash Outflows:

Year	Cash Outflow	P.V. Discount Factor @ 12%	P.V. of Cash Outflow (Rs.)
0	5,00,000	1.000	5,00,000

(iv) Calculation of P.V. of Cash Inflows:

Year	Cash Flow After Tax (CFAT)	P.V. Discount Factor @ 12%	P.V. of Cash Inflows (Rs.)
1 – 5	1,50,000	3.605	5,40,750

(v) Calculation of Net Present Value:

Present value of Cash Inflows	5,40,750
Less: P.V. of Cash Outflows	5,00,000
Net Present Value of Cashflows	40,750

Since N.P.V. is positive, it is desirable to lease out the asset.

(b) Internal Rate of Return Method: It is the rate of discount at which the Present Value of cash-inflows is equal to the present value of cash outflows.

Internal Rate of Return (I.R.R.) can be computed with the help of present value tables. The various steps involved in its computation are as follows:

1. Determining the future net cash flows for the period of the lease.
2. Determining the rate of discount at which the present value of cash inflows is equal to the present value of cash outflows. This can be determined as follows:

(c) When the Annual Cash Flows are even over the Life of the Asset: First of all, calculate Present Value Factor by using the following formula:

$$\text{Present Value Factor} = \frac{\text{Initial Outlay}}{\text{Annual Cash Flow}}$$

Afterwards, consult present value annuity tables with the number of years equal to the life of the asset and find out the rate at which the calculated present value factor is equal to the present value given in the table.

Moreover, the exact rate may be interpolated as under:

$$I.R.R. = LR + \frac{H.P.V. - P.V.F}{\text{Difference in Calculated Present Value}} \times \text{Difference in Rate}$$

ILLUSTRATION 24.3

Initial Outlay	–	Rs. 1,00,000
Life of the Asset	–	5 years
Estimated Annual Cash Flow	–	Rs. 25,000

Compute I.R.R.

Solution

$$\text{Present Value Factor} = \frac{\text{Initial Outlay}}{\text{Annual Cash Flow}}$$

$$= \frac{1,00,000}{25,000} = 4$$

Consulting Present Value Annuity tables for 5 year period at Present Value Factor of 4:

$$I.R.R. = 8\% \text{ approx.}$$

(as seen from the table that at 8% for 5 year period, the present value is 3.9927 which is nearly equal to 4)

ILLUSTRATION 24.4

Initial Outlay	Rs. 3,60,000
Economic Life of the Asset	10 years
Estimated Annual Cash Flow	Rs. 60,000

Calculate I.R.R.

Solution

$$\text{Present Value Factor} = \frac{\text{Initial Outlay}}{\text{Annual Cash Flow}}$$

$$= \frac{3,60,000}{60,000} = 6$$

Closest present values to 6.00 from cumulative P.V. Table (Table II) for 10 years are:

P.V.	Rate
6.145	10%
5.650	12%

Thus I.R.R. will be between 10% and 12%

$$\text{I.R.R.} = LR + \frac{H.P.V. - P.V.F.}{\text{Difference in Calculated Present Value}} \times \text{Difference in Rate}$$

$$= 10\% + \frac{0.145}{0.495} \ (12\% - 10\%)$$

$$= 10\% + 0.6\%$$

$$= 10.6\%$$

∴ I.R.R. = 10.6%

(b) When the Annual Cash Flows are Uneven over the Life of the Asset: If savings are unequal, the I.R.R. can be ascertained only through Trial and Error Method. Here, the main problem is to compute a rate on which the present value of unequal savings are just equal to the cost of investment. Thus I.R.R. in this case is: Cash outflows – Cash inflows = 0. For this purpose, the present values of cash inflows are computed at varying rates. In that process, the rate on which present values of cash inflows are closest to the cost of investment is taken to be I.R.R.

The following procedures are involved in this process:

1. Find out the average of the cash inflows at different years.

2. Divide the net investment by average inflows. The resultant figure is the present value factor.

3. Ascertain the rate from the Present Value Table for the present value factor.

4. Calculate the present values of cash inflows of several years with the above rate.

5. Compare the total of such present values with the cost of investment. If the total of present values is more than the cost of investment, then further interpolation be done at a higher rate. On the contrary, in case the total present value is less than the cost of investment, the further interpolation be carried on at lower rate. The actual I.R.R. can be ascertained by following such trial and error.

$$\text{I.R.R.} = LR + \frac{\text{Calculated P.V.} - \text{P.V. of Cash Outflow}}{\text{Difference in Calculated Present Values}} \times (\text{Difference in Rate})$$

6. Accept the proposal in case the I.R.R. is more than or equal to the minimum required rate of return, i.e., the cost of capital or cut off rate.

7. In the case of alternative proposals, select the proposal with the highest rate of return as long as the rates are more than the cost of capital or cut-off rate.

ILLUSTRATION **24.5**

Initial Investment = Rs. 44,000
Life of the Asset = 4 years

Estimated Net Annual Cash Flows:

1st year = Rs. 24,000
2nd year = Rs. 8,000
3rd year = Rs. 4,000
4th year = Rs. 20,000

Calculate the I.R.R. and also advise the lessor about the leasing out decision if the expected minimum rate of return is 12%.

Solution

$$P.V.F. = \frac{Initial\ Investment}{Average\ Cash\ Inflows} = \frac{44,000}{14,000}$$

$$= 3.14$$

Closest Present Values to 3.14 from Annuity Table II for 4 years are 3.170 at 10% and 3.037 at 12%. Hence, I.R.R. can be interpolated by trial and error procedure using discounting rates of 10% and 12%.

I.R.R. at Discount Rates of 10% and 12%

Year	Cash Inflows (Rs.)	P.V.F. 10%	P.V. (Rs.)	P.V.F. 12%	P.V. (Rs.)
1	24,000	0.909	21,816	0.893	21,432
2	8,000	0.826	6,608	0.797	6,376
3	4,000	0.751	3,004	0.712	2,848
4	20,000	0.683	13,660	0.636	12,720
		Total	45,088		43,376
Excess (+) or Deficiency (−) over NI			+1,088		−624

Thus,

$$I.R.R. = LR + \frac{Calculated\ P.V. - P.V.\ of\ Cash\ Outlay}{Difference\ in\ Calculated\ Present\ Values} \times (Difference\ in\ Rate)$$

$$= 10 + \frac{1,088}{1,712} \times (12 - 10)$$

$$= 10 + \frac{1,088}{1,712} \times 2$$

$$= 10 + 1.27 = 11.27\%$$

Method of Computing Lease Rentals

The various steps involved in computing lease rentals are as follows:

1. Determining the cost of the asset. It comprises the actual purchase price and expenses such as freight, insurance, taxes, installation, etc.
2. Determining the cash flows to the lessor by way of ownership of the asset. These consist of tax advantage provided by depreciation and investment allowance.
3. Computing the present value of cash flows.
4. Deducting the present value of cash flows of ownership advantage from the cost of the asset.
5. Computing the post-tax lease rentals. These can be obtained by dividing the minimum required net recovery through lease rentals by present value factor of annuity.
6. Calculating the pre-tax lease rentals. These can be obtained by adjusting the post-tax lease rentals for the tax factor.

ILLUSTRATION 24.6

Gopal Leasing is considering to lease out a machinery costing Rs. 5,00,000 for five years. The machinery has an expected life of five years and has an estimated salvage value of Rs. 50,000. Gopal Leasing can claim a depreciation of 20% on w.d.v. of the asset but is not eligible for investment allowance. The firm falls under a tax rate of 50% and the minimum post-tax required rate of return is 12%. You are required to compute the lease rental which the firm should charge.

Note: (1) Present Value Factor at 12% discount rate is as follows:
Year 1 = 0.893, year 2 = 0.797, year 3 = 0.712
Year 4 = 0.636 and year 5 = 0.567

(2) Annuity Discount Factor at 12% for 5 years = 3.605

Solution

(i) The cost of the equipment = Rs. 5,00,000 (given)
(ii) Calculation of Cash Flows to the Lessor on account of the ownership of the Asset.

Year	Amount of Depreciation (Rs.)	Tax Advantage on Depreciation (Rs.)	Tax Advantage Investment Allowance (Rs.)	Salvage Value (Rs.)	Total C.F. (Rs.)
1	1,00,000	50,000	....	....	50,000
2	80,000	40,000	....	....	40,000
3	64,000	32,000	....	....	32,000
4	51,200	25,600	....	....	25,600
5	40,960	20,480	....	50,000	70,480

(iii) Calculation of Present Value of Cash Flow

Year	Cash Flows (Rs.)	P.V. Factor at 12%	P.V. of Cash Flow Rs.
1	50,000	0.893	44,650
2	40,000	0.797	31,880
3	32,000	0.712	22,784
4	25,600	0.636	16,282
5	70,480	0.567	39,962
		Total	1,55,558

(iv) Minimum Required Net Recovery through Lease Rentals

$$MRLR = 5,00,000 - 1,55,558$$
$$= Rs.\ 3,44,442$$

(v) Post-tax lease Rental

$$PTLR = \frac{3,44,442}{3,605}$$
$$= Rs.\ 95,546$$

(vi) Pre-tax Lease Rental

$$LR = 95,546 \times \frac{100}{50}$$
$$= Rs.\ 1,91,092$$

∴ Lease Rent expressed in terms of lease financing

$$= 1,91,092 \times \frac{1,000}{5,00,000} \times \frac{1}{12}$$
$$= 31.85\ per\ thousand\ per\ month$$
$$I.R.R. = 11.27\%$$

As the I.R.R. is less than the minimum rate of return, the lessor should not lease out the asset.

Pros and Cons of Leasing

The advantages accruing from leasing can be examined from the point of view of the lessee and the lessor.

Advantages of Leasing to the Lessee

1. **No Initial Cash Outlay:** Under leasing, lessee has no initial cash outlay for acquiring the use of an asset by way of margin money. The margin in the case of loan financing varies from 25% to 30%. However, some leasing companies insist that first lease rental be paid in advance.

2. **Minimum Delay:** Usually, processing of leasing proposals involves much lesser time as against the lengthy procedure involved in the term-loan financing. Thus a concern can avoid delay in the use of an asset by taking it on lease.

3. **Shifting the Risk of Obsolescence:** In the case of leased equipment, the risk of obsolescence is transferred to the lessor. This is an advantage to the lessee in case the asset is exposed to the risk of high rate of obsolescence.

4. **Increased Liquidity:** As leasing releases funds for investment in working capital, it enables the lessee to pay for fixed assets out of the earnings of the assets acquired on lease. Thus sale and lease back arrangement helps the lessee to improve the liquidity position by releasing funds invested in fixed assets.

5. **Getting an Opportunity for Tax Planning:** The lessee gets an opportunity for tax planning regarding the fixation of rentals. He can amortise the assets within a short span under leasing as against buying the asset to be depreciated within a specified period.

6. **Easy Source of Finance:** Leasing is one of the easiest sources of medium and long-term financing. Since the ownership of asset remains with the lessor, leasing does not require any mortgage of the assets.

7. **Greater Degree of Flexibility:** Leasing allows the lessee a greater degree of flexibility in additional financing as against debt financing.

8. **No Dilution of Ownership:** In leasing, the dilution of ownership can be avoided as it does not have convertibility clause.

9. **Higher Return on Capital Employed:** The lessee need not show the leased asset on the asset side of the balance sheet as he acquires only the right to use the asset without owning it. This implies greater earnings against capital employed and greater rate of return on capital employed.

10. **Less Costs:** Leasing reduces the cost of raising capital as against raising of debentures from the capital market.

Disadvantages of Leasing for the Lessee

1. **Higher Cost:** Leasing is regarded as a form of financing at higher cost because lease rentals consist of margin for the lessor and also the cost of risk of obsolescence.

2. **Not Suitable for Project Financing:** Project Financing can hardly be arranged under lease because rentals become payable immediately on entering into a lease contract. But in a new project cash generation commences only after a long gestation period.

3. **No Incentives:** In the case of leased equipment, the lessee may not be entitled to certain incentives/tax benefits such as backward area incentives and central subsidy. These incentives are based on the amount of fixed capital employed.

4. **No Alteration in Asset:** The lessee cannot make any substantial change in the asset as he is not the owner of the asset.

5. **Difficulty in Termination:** The lessee may not be in a position to terminate the lease contract except by paying heavy penalties even when he may wish to discontinue a particular line of business.

6. **Risk of Being Deprived of the Use of Asset:** The lessee may be deprived of the use of the asset on account of deterioration in the financial position of the lessor or winding up of the leasing company.

7. **Loss of Salvage Value of the Asset:** Since the lessee is not the owner of the asset, he cannot realise the salvage value which the asset has at the expiration of the useful life. But at the same time, he has to return the asset to the lessor.

Advantages of Leasing to the Lessor

1. **High Profits:** Profits generated by leasing are high both in terms of back profits and cash accruals.

2. **Lower Gestation Period:** Since leasing forms an activity with a lower gestation period as compared to other investment opportunities, the lessor gets quick returns in the form of lease rentals.

3. **Postponement of Tax Liability:** Under leasing, the lessor is entitled to depreciation including additional depreciation and investment allowance on the total cost of the asset. This enables him to write off a large amount in the initial years resulting in the postponement of tax liability.

4. **Enhanced Sales:** Leasing through third parties has helped manufacturers to enhance their sales. Thus lessors are also in a position to demand certain concessions from the manufacturers.

Disadvantages for the Lessor

1. **Competitive Market:** Since a number of leasing companies have emerged in recent years, they have to compete with one another for survival. As a result, the lessor cannot obtain enough lease rent to recover the cost of the asset and expected return on investment.

2. **High Risk of Obsolescence:** Leasing involves a high risk of obsolescence for the lessor on account of technological improvement and competitive situation in the market.

3. **Management of Cash Flows:** Since the success of the leasing business depends on the efficient management of cash flows, the inflows are not allowed to remain idle by revolving them effectively. For this purpose, the lessor is required to be on his toes in search for good investment opportunities.

4. **Unexpected Fluctuations:** Leasing costs are often subject to unexpected fluctuations. This will throw the lessor's entire profit out of focus if an escalation clause is not incorporated into the lease contract.

5. **Locking-up of Funds:** The leasing business may involve locking-up of funds unless due care has been exercised in monitoring of cash flows.

6. **Long-term Investment:** It usually takes considerable time to recover the capital tied up in leases through accumulated profits from the business of leasing. This indicates that the lessor has to adopt a conservative policy for the distribution of dividend and to rely largely on self-financing for the growth of his business.

7. **Liquidity Crisis:** Under leasing, the lessor heavily depends on public deposits. This leads to diversion of short-term funds for long-term use resulting in liquidity crisis.

— REVIEW QUESTIONS —

1. What is meant by leasing? State its merits and demerits?

2. Discuss the methods of evaluating the leasing proposal?

3. Distinguish the following:
   (a) Leveraged Lease and Sale and Lease-back Lease
   (b) Primary and Secondary Lease
   (c) Straight Lease and Modified Lease
   (d) Finance Lease and Operating Lease

4. Define leasing. What are the steps involved in leasing?

5. Leasing Finance has proved its unique adaptability to various financial problems. Discuss its merits as compared to other methods of financing.

6. A concern desires to acquire a machine costing Rs. 20 lakhs which has an economic life of ten years at the end of which the asset is not expected to have any residual value. The concern is considering the alternative choice of:

   (a) Taking the machinery on lease; or
   (b) Purchasing the asset by raising a loan.

   Lease payments are to be made in advance and the lessor requires the asset to be completely amortised over its useful period and that the asset will yield him a return of 10%.

   The cost of debt is worked at 16% per annum. Average rate of income tax is 50%. It is expected that the operative costs would remain the same under either method.

   The following factors may also be taken into account.

   (i) The present value discount factors for even stream of each cash flows over the number of years are:

Year	8%	Rate of Interest 10%	16%
1	0.93	0.91	0.86
2	1.78	1.75	1.60
3	2.58	2.49	2.25
4	3.31	3.17	2.80
5	3.99	3.79	3.27
6	4.62	4.35	3.68
7	5.20	4.87	4.04
8	5.75	5.33	4.34
9	6.25	5.76	4.61
10	6.71	6.14	4.83

   (ii) Straight line method of depreciation may be adopted.
   (iii) Investment allowance at 25% is available on original cost.

   As a financial consultant, indicate what your advice will be?

   (**Ans.:** N.P.V. of cash outflows under lease alternative Rs. 11,52,367. N.P.V. of cash outflows under purchasing alternative Rs. 10,97,651. Hence purchasing of the machine is preferable to taking it on lease)

7. A concern has the choice of buying an asset for Rs. 1,00,000 or leasing it for 20 years at an annual rent of Rs. 15,000. If the concern obtains it on leasing, it will have to bear the cost of repairs, maintenance and change in the rates. For tax purposes, lease rent is a permissible deduction. The effective rate of tax applicable to it is 50%. Tax is to be paid annually without delay or postponement. No change in the rate of tax is expected during the period of lease. Advise whether the firm should lease the asset or buy it outright? Assume that if the asset is purchased outright, its resale value after the expiry of the lease period, i.e., 20 years is estimated at Rs. 80,000. Assume further that the sum required for purchasing the asset is obtained through equity shares. The cost of such equity funds is 7% per annum. Finally, also assume that the asset purchased outright attracts no capital allowance.

(**Ans.:** The present value of the whole expression is Rs. 1,04,800.
The net present value is Rs. 4800 (i.e., 1,04,800 − 1,00,000)

Purchasing, therefore, is marginally preferable to leasing it as is apparent by the net present value).

Appendix

Table A.1   Present Value of Re. 1

Years	5%	6%	8%	10%	12%	14%	15%	16%	18%	20%	22%	24%	25%	28%	30%
1	0.952	0.943	0.926	0.909	0.893	0.877	0.870	0.862	0.847	0.833	0.820	0.806	0.800	0.781	0.769
2	0.907	0.890	0.857	0.826	0.797	0.769	0.756	0.743	0.718	0.694	0.672	0.650	0.640	0.610	0.592
3	0.864	0.840	0.794	0.751	0.712	0.675	0.658	0.641	0.609	0.579	0.551	0.524	0.512	0.477	0.450
4	0.823	0.792	0.735	0.683	0.636	0.592	0.572	0.552	0.516	0.482	0.451	0.423	0.410	0.373	0.350
5	0:784	0.747	0.681	0.621	0.567	0.519	0.497	0.476	0.437	0.402	0.370	0.341	0.328	0.291	0.269
6	0.746	0.705	0.630	0.564	0.507	0.456	0.432	0.410	0.370	0.335	0.303	0.275	0.262	0.227	0.207
7	0.711	0.665	0.583	0.513	0.452	0.400	0.376	0.354	0.314	0.279	0.249	0.222	0.210	0.170	0.159
8	0.677	0.627	0.540	0.467	0.404	0.351	0.327	0.305	0.266	0.233	0.204	0.179	0.118	0.139	0.123
9	0.645	0.592	0.500	0.424	0.361	0.308	0.284	0.263	0.225	0.193	0.167	0.144	0.134	0.108	0.094
10	0.614	0.558	0.463	0.386	0.322	0.270	0.247	0.227	0.191	0.162	0.137	0.116	0.107	0.085	0.073
11	0.585	0.527	0.429	0.350	0.287	0.237	0.215	0.195	0.162	0.135	0.112	0.094	0.087	0.066	0.056
12	0.557	0.497	0.397	0.319	0.257	0.208	0.187	0.168	0.137	0.112	0.092	0.076	0.069	0.032	0.043
13	0.530	0.469	0.368	0.290	0.229	0.182	0.163	0.145	0.116	0.093	0.075	0.061	0.055	0.040	0.033
14	0.505	0.442	0.340	0.263	0.205	0.160	0.141	0.125	0.099	0.078	0.062	0.049	0.044	0.032	0.025
15	0.481	0.417	0.315	0.239	0.183	0.140	0.123	0.108	0.084	0.065	0.051	0.040	0.035	0.025	0.200
16	0.458	0.394	0.292	0.218	0.163	0.123	0.107	0.093	0.071	0.054	0.042	0.032	0.028	0.019	0.015
17	0.436	0.371	0.270	0.198	0.146	0.108	0.093	0.080	0.060	0.045	0.034	0.026	0.023	0.015	0.012
18	0.416	0.350	0.250	0.180	0.130	0.095	0.081	0.069	0.051	0.038	0.028	0.021	0.018	0.012	0.009
19	0.396	0.331	0.232	0.164	0.116	0.083	0.070	0.060	0.043	0.031	0.023	0.017	0.014	0.009	0.007
20	0.377	0.312	0.215	0.149	0.104	0.073	0.061	0.051	0.037	0.026	0.019	0.014	0.012	0.007	0.005

Table A.2 Present Value of Re. 1 Received Annually for N Years

Years	5%	6%	8%	10%	12%	14%	15%	16%	18%	20%	22%	24%	25%	28%	30%
1	0.952	0.943	0.926	0.909	0.893	0.877	0.870	0.862	0.847	0.833	0.820	0.806	0.800	0.781	0.769
2	1.859	1.833	1.783	1.736	1.690	1.647	1.646	1.605	1.566	1.528	1.492	1.457	1.440	1.392	1.361
3	2.723	2.676	2.577	2.487	2.402	2.322	2.283	2.246	2.174	2.016	2.042	1.981	1.952	1.868	1.816
4	3.546	3.465	3.312	3.170	3.037	2.914	2.855	2.798	2.690	2.589	2.494	2.404	2.362	2.241	2.166
5	4.330	4.212	3.993	3.791	3.605	3.433	3.352	3.274	3.127	2.991	2.864	2.745	2.689	2.532	2.346
6	5.076	4.917	4.623	4.335	4.111	3.889	3.784	3.685	3.498	3.326	3.167	3.020	2.951	2.759	2.643
7	5.786	5.582	5.206	4.868	4.564	4.288	4.160	4.039	3.812	3.605	3.416	3.242	3.161	2.937	2.802
8	6.463	6.210	5.747	5.335	4.968	4.639	4.487	4.344	4.078	3.837	3.619	3.421	3.329	3.076	2.925
9	7.109	6.802	6.247	5.759	5.328	4.946	4.772	4.607	4.303	4.031	3.786	3.566	3.463	3.184	3.019
10	7.722	7.360	6.710	6.145	5.650	4.216	5.019	4.833	5.494	4.192	3.923	3.682	3.571	5.269	3.092
11	8.306	7.887	7.139	6.495	5.937	5.453	5.234	5.029	4.656	4.327	4.035	3.776	3.656	3.335	3.147
12	8.863	8.384	7.536	6.814	6.194	5.660	5.421	5.197	4.793	4.439	4.127	3.851	3.725	3.387	3.190
13	9.394	8.853	7.904	7.103	6.424	5.842	5.583	5.342	4.910	4.533	4.023	3.912	3.780	3.427	3.223
14	9.899	9.295	8.244	7.367	6.628	6.002	5.724	5.468	5.008	4.611	4.265	3.962	3.824	3.459	3.249
15	10.380	9.712	8.559	7.606	6.811	6.142	5.847	5.575	5.092	4.675	4.315	4.001	3.859	3.483	3.268
16	10.838	10.106	8.851	7.824	6.974	6.265	5.954	5.669	5.162	4.730	4.357	4.033	3.887	3.503	3.283
17	11.274	10.477	9.122	8.022	7.120	6.373	6.047	5.749	5.222	4.775	4.391	4.059	3.910	3.518	3.295
18	11.690	10.828	9.372	8.201	7.250	6.467	5.128	5.818	4.273	4.812	4.419	4.080	3.928	3.529	3.304
19	12.085	11.158	9.614	8.365	7.366	6.550	6.198	5.877	5.316	4.844	4.442	4.097	3.942	3.539	3.311
20	12.462	11.470	9.818	8.514	7.469	6.623	6.259	5.929	5.353	4.870	4.660	4.110	3.954	3.546	3.316

Table A.3 Compound Value of Re. 1

Period	1%	2%	3%	4%	5%	6%	7%	8%	9%	10%	12%	14%	15%
1	1.010	1.020	1.030	1.040	1.050	1.060	1.070	1.080	1.090	1.100	1.120	1.140	1.150
2	1.020	1.040	1.061	1.082	1.102	1.124	1.145	1.166	1.186	1.210	1.254	1.300	1.322
3	1.030	1.061	1.093	1.125	1.158	1.191	1.225	1.260	1.295	1.331	1.405	1.482	1.521
4	1.041	1.082	1.126	1.170	1.216	1.262	1.311	1.360	1.412	1.464	1.574	1.689	1.749
5	1.051	1.104	1.159	1.217	1.276	1.338	1.403	1.469	1.539	1.611	1.762	1.925	2.011
6	1.062	1.126	1.194	1.265	1.340	1.419	1.501	1.587	1.677	1.772	1.974	2.195	2.313
7	1.072	1.149	1.230	1.316	1.407	1.504	1.606	1.714	1.828	1.949	2.211	2.502	2.660
8	1.083	1.172	1.267	1.369	1.477	1.594	1.718	1.851	1.993	2.144	2.476	2.853	3.059
9	1.094	1.195	1.305	1.423	1.551	1.689	1.838	1.999	2.172	2.358	2.773	3.252	3.518
10	1.105	1.219	1.344	1.480	1.629	1.791	1.967	2.159	2.367	2.594	3.106	3.707	4.046
11	1.116	1.243	1.384	1.539	1.710	1.898	2.105	2.332	2.580	2.853	3.479	4.226	4.652
12	1.127	1.268	1.426	1.601	1.796	2.012	2.252	2.518	2.813	3.138	3.896	4.818	5.350
13	1.138	1.294	1.469	1.665	1.886	2.133	2.410	2.720	3.066	3.452	4.363	5.492	6.153
14	1.149	1.319	1.513	1.732	1.980	2.261	2.579	2.937	3.342	3.797	4.887	6.261	7.076
15	1.161	1.346	1.558	1.801	2.079	2.397	2.759	3.172	3.642	4.177	5.474	7.138	8.137
16	1.173	1.373	1.605	1.873	2.183	2.540	2.952	3.426	3.970	4.595	6.130	8.137	9.358
17	1.184	1.400	1.653	1.948	2.292	2.693	3.159	3.700	4.328	5.054	6.866	9.276	10.761
18	1.196	1.428	1.702	2.026	2.407	2.854	3.380	3.996	4.717	5.560	7.690	10.575	12.375
19	1.208	1.457	1.754	2.107	2.527	3.026	3.617	4.316	5.142	6.116	8.613	12.056	14.232
20	1.220	1.486	1.806	2.191	2.653	3.207	3.870	4.661	5.604	6.728	9.646	13.743	16.367
25	1.282	1.641	2.094	2.666	3.386	4.292	5.427	6.848	8.623	10.835	17.000	26.462	32.919
30	1.348	1.811	2.427	3.243	4.322	5.743	7.612	10.063	13.268	17.449	29.960	50.950	66.212

Glossary

ABC Analysis: Analysis of a range of items, e.g., stock levels, customers, sales territories, etc., into three groups A = very important, B = important, C = marginal significance.

Accountable Management: Marking individuals or units responsible for performance measured as objectively as practicable and, as far as possible, with cooperation of those individuals or units. It has much in common with management by objectives and likely to involve the establishment of cost and profit centers.

Accounting Rate of Return (ARR): The return on investment as measured by relating a capital projects average accounting profits to its average (or initial) investment.

Accounts Receivable or Debtors: Accounts on which monies are due from customers.

Accretion: An increase in value which takes place over a period of time.

Accruals Basis: It is the basis of preparing profit and loss which takes into account not merely amounts paid and received but also expenses accrued but not paid and for income accrued but not received. It is the normal basis of the preparations of accounts for commercial undertakings.

Acid Ratio Test: The determination of ratio of total cash, accounts receivable (debtors) and the market value of marketable investments of a business to its current liabilities. The ratio is used by financial and credit analysts as a guide to credit rating. This ratio is also known as quick ratio or liquid ratio.

Active Income: Income which results from production or services provided by an individual or corporation.

Activity Ratio: Comparison showing actual against budgeted output during the given hours of work.

Added Value: The value added to materials by the process of production. It is calculated by deduction from the sales value (gross output), the cost of materials, fuel, etc. used in the production process.

Adjusted Present Value (APV): A present value technique which discounts a firm's cash flows at different rates depending on the risk of the cash flows.

Ageing Schedule: An analysis of the debtors of a business which shows how old each separate element of debt is. It is useful in assessing the success of credit control and, since bad debts first show up as late debts, in determining the correct amount for the charge for bad debts in the profit and loss account.

Agency Costs: The costs that arise as a result of conflicts of interest between a firm's owners and its agents (i.e., its directors and managers). Agency costs decrease the value of the firm.

All-Equity Cost of Capital: The required return on a company's stock in the absence of debts.

American Depository Receipt (ADR): A certificate of ownership issued by a U.S. bank representing a multiple of foreign shares that are deposited in a U.S. bank. ADRs can be traded on the organised exchanges in the U.S. or in the OTC market.

Amortisation: The process of gradually extinguishing a liability, debt or capital expenditure over a period of time.

Annuity: A cash flow pattern in which a constant annual amount is to be paid or received over a defined number of years.

Arm's Length: A term description of negotiation where each party is concerned only to advance his or her own interests and not those of the other party. It may be important to determine whether a transaction was at arm's length in order to ascertain whether a fair value was established by the transaction.

Asset Cover: The extent to which a share is represented by valuable assets.

Asset Stripping: A process whereby a company acquires a controlling interest in another company for the purpose of disposing of its assets.

Auto-financing: The use of part of sales proceeds to provide the means of payment for capital expenditure, i.e., that part which is left over when all cash expenses, taxes and dividends have been paid.

Automatic Data Processing (ADP): The execution of recording operations of an accounting or statistical nature by electronic equipment based on a computer, whereby all stages from original record to ultimate report are carried out without human intervention.

Average Rate of Return: An alternative term for accounting rate of return.

Axe: To cut actual or planned expenditure abruptly. It is usually in response to a situation of emergency.

B

Back-to-Back Loans: A loan involving two parties – two companies located in different countries. Each company borrows funds in its capital market and re-lends to the other company.

Backwardation: The amount by which the price of a commodity for immediate delivery differs from its price for delivery at some specified future date.

Balance of Payments: A country's record of international transactions presented in a double-entry bookkeeping form.

Balance Sheet Hedge: Intended to decrease transaction exposure of an MNC by eliminating the mismatch of exposed net assets and exposed net liabilities denominated in the same currency.

Balloon Note: Repayment of the major or a large part of a loan in a single payment, usually by promissory note, following smaller instalments.

Bankable: Of great value. A person's agreement may be described as bankable if the person is regarded as very reliable.

Barometer Stock: Shares of a company which has such wide-ranging interests that that company's performance can be taken as indicative of the performance of the economy as a whole. The movements of its share price tend to reflect general market trends.

Base Stock: A level of stock regarded as the irreducible minimum with which business can operate.

Basket: A collection of items (for instance, shares, goods or securities) used for the purpose of calculating an index.

Bearer Bond: A bond in which ownership is demonstrated through possession of the bond.

Bed and Breakfast: A stock market term applied to a transaction whereby the holder of a security sells it on one day and buys it back on the next.

Benchmark: A level, point or standard in a scale or range against performance can be evaluated.

Black Check: Accounting/audit term for a detailed examination of a key part of the accounts of a company or organisation.

Black Economy: Economic activities not recorded by officially. These include transactions, such as wage payments on which payment of tax is evaded illegally. This may happen, for example, in some cases of moonlighting.

Blue Chip: A share in an of established company of high reputation and, therefore a sound investment.

Bona Vacantia: Property which has no owners. It could arise when a person dies without leaving a will and where there are no relatives.

Bond Washing: The practice of selling fixed interest securities just before an interest payment is due and then re-buying immediately afterwards.

Bonus Shares: Shares issued by a company free of charge to its existing shareholders on a pro rata basis.

Book Inventory: Theoretical level of stocks or inventory based on records of existing stocks plus incoming goods less outgoing goods. As it is not based on a physical count of the stock items, the book inventory figures will not reveal errors, pilferage, etc.

Book Rate of Return: Alternative term for return on capital or accountant's return.

Book Value: The value at which an asset is shown in the accounting records as distinguished from its intrinsic or market value. Thus book value is the original cost less the accumulated depreciation.

Brainstorming: A type of group discussion process in which members of the group are encouraged to generate as many imaginative and creative ideas and suggestions as possible within a relatively short period of time, under a chairman.

Breakeven Analysis: A method for examining the relationship between sales revenue, fixed costs and variable costs to determine the minimum value of production necessary to break even (i.e., make neither profit nor loss).

Breakeven Chart: A graphic representation normally used to show profitability or otherwise of an undertaking at various levels of activity.

Breakeven Point: The point at which neither profit nor loss is made as shown by a breakdown chart.

Bridging Loan: A temporary loan given to cover the gap between the purchase of an asset and the sale of another asset, the proceeds of which are required to finance the purchase.

Budgeting: A procedure for formalising in quantitative and/or financial terms, the objectives to be achieved for a given period in the future (normally one year) and the policies, methods and resources to be employed to attain these objectives.

Bursar: The person in charge of the finance of an organisation. The term is most commonly used in connection with such institutions as schools, colleges and hospitals rather than with manufacturing or commercial organizations where such an officer is more likely to be called a comptroller or chief accountant.

C

Capacity Usage Ratio: The relationship between the budgeted number of working hours and the maximum number of working hours in a budget period.

Capital Allowance: A scheme of taxation allowances which a company is entitled to claim, in lieu of depreciation, when it invests in certain types of fixed assets.

Capital Asset Pricing Model (CAPM): An asset pricing model which states, in equation form, that the required return on an asset (r), is equal to the risk-free rate (R_f), plus a risk premium, $B(ER_m - R_f)$ expressed as: $r = R_f + B(ER_m - R_f)$. The CAPM is the equation of the security market line (SML).

Capital Budget: A budget concerned with the proposed capital expenditure on fixed assets and their financing.

Capital Budgeting: The process of preparing a plan for the raising of capital funds and for their deployment.

Capital Commitment: An obligation to undertake capital expenditure which has not yet become an actual liability.

Capital Cost: The non-recurrent set-up cost of a project. After capital cost has been incurred there will subsequently be recurring running costs.

Capital Employed: Gross capital employed, i.e., summation of fixed and current assets. Net capital employed, i.e., summation of fixed and current assets minus current liabilities. Proprietor's or shareholder's net capital employed, i.e., paid up share capital plus reserves.

Capital Expenditure: Expenditure on additional fixed assets which increases the capacity and efficiency of existing fixed assets.

Capital Flight: The mass withdrawal by international investors of funds from a country where doubts have arisen about the future course of its economy.

Capital Loss: A loss occasioned by the sale of an asset at an amount below its cost.

Capital Rationing: A restriction on the investment of capital funds other than that arising from their cost or the availability of investment opportunities. Capital rationing is an artificial constraint on the capital budgeting process which can consequently lead to a sub-optimal position.

Capital Reserve: Retained earnings and amounts received from other sources (e.g., share premiums) which are not available for distribution to the shareholders through the profit and loss account.

Capital Structure: The relative proportions of different types of financing used to make up the total long-term financing of a business.

Capital Turnover: The notional rate at which the capital employed by a business flows through the profit earning cycle. It is calculated as

$$\frac{\text{Turnover}}{\text{Capital Employed}}$$

Capitalisation Rate: A rate applied to the annual income produced by an asset in order to determine its capital value.

Cash Budget: A plan which details the time and size of expected receipts and disbursements.

Cash Conversion Cycle: Defined as the firm's operating cycle (average inventory days plus average debtor days) minus average creditor payment days. It represents the amount of time, usually days, that cash is tied up from when the company pays for its inputs from its suppliers and in turn receives payment from its customers for the sale of the same inputs converted into finished product.

Cash Discount: A deduction from a debt which may be made at the stated rate if it is paid within a given period or not later than the specified date.

Cash Flow: It describes the flow of cash required to finance the daily or weekly operating expenses and meet the daily or weekly financial obligations.

Cash Flow Statement: It is a statement which explains how the cash and cash equivalents held by the business have changed between one balance sheet date and the next.

Cash Forecast: It is a flow of cash accruing or expected to accrue from the pursuit of trading operations in terms of predetermined plan or budget.

Cash in Transit: Cash in the process of being transferred from one business to another and not, therefore, appearing in the records of either of them.

Cash Management: It is the management of: handling of cash which a firm has in transaction balances, funds tied up in precautionary cash balances, investment of excess funds at the most favourable rate, and borrowing at the lowest rate when there is temporary cash shortage.

Cash Sale: A sale made against the immediate payment of cash.

Cessation: The discontinuance of business.

Close Company: It is a company controlled by fewer participators or by participators who are directors.

Cluster Analysis: Mathematical technique for analysing the complex information on people, products, etc. and dividing the population into groups or clusters having broadly similar characteristics. This is used particularly in market research.

Collateral: Secondary or supporting security for a loan. A bank might, for example, make a loan against the main security of a mortgage on property. As collateral they might take a policy of life assurance on the life of the borrower.

Collection Period: The time taken from the granting of credit to a customer until payment has been received.

Compensating Balance: Non-interest–bearing demand deposits maintained by a firm to compensate a bank for services provided, credit lines, or loans.

Compliance Cost: The costs imposed on a business by the need to comply with some legislative obligation.

Concentration Analysis: Concentration of those areas which are of major significance, e.g., major customers, key products, stock levels of expensive items, etc. A development of Pareto concept.

Concentration of Investment: The excessive investment, within a portfolio of funds in one company or in one industry.

Consistency: The principle that similar matters should be treated in a similar way whenever they arise.

Consols: An abbreviation of consolidated stock, an irredeemable government security on which a fixed coupon rate of interest is paid.

Consortium: An association between two or more organizations to carry on a joint activity which may or may not provide for the creation of a separate joint organisation.

Contingent Liabilities: Liabilities indefinite either as to amount or occurrence, e.g., legal action for contract, patent infringement.

Convertible debt: Offers the holder the option to convert the debt into equity at some time in the future, under specified terms and conditions.

Cooling off Period: A period of time allowed after an agreement has been reached but before it becomes totally binding.

Corner: To obtain control over the supply and thus the price of some commodity or security by acquiring all, or nearly all, of the available supply.

Cost Discount: A deduction from a debt which may be made at the stated rate if it is paid within a given period or not later than a specified date.

Cost Effectiveness Analysis (CEA): A limited form of cost benefit analysis which is concerned with evaluating and comparing only the costs of alternative ways of producing the same or a similar result or of achieving the same objective. The aim is to find the least cost solution to attain a given objective.

Cost of Capital: The rate of return that must be earned on investments, in order to satisfy the rate of return required by investors. It is the discount rate used to evaluate the firm's capital projects.

Cost of Sales: The total amount expended in producing or acquiring the goods sold during a period of time.

Cost Push Inflation: Inflation (rise in prices) which seems to be primarily related to increases in the cost of business inputs.

Cost Reduction: A procedure involving, among other matters, the careful examination of accounting records, having the objective of reducing the costs of operating an organisation so as to improve its efficiency.

Cost-benefit Analysis (CBA): A comprehensive form of investment appraisal which defines costs and benefits in very broad terms and adapts traditional investment appraisal techniques to its needs.

Cost-Plus Contract: A contract under which the customer agrees to pay the cost of producing the supply with the addition of an agreed percentage as profit.

Cost-price Squeeze: Pressure of increasing costs at a time when competition or other pressures make it difficult to put up prices.

Coupon Rate: The stated rate of interest on a bond; the annual interest payment divided by the bond's face value.

Coverage Analysis: It is a technique of operational research for optimising ordering policy for stock.

Coverage Ratio: Ratios that relate the financial charges of a firm to its ability to service, or cover them.

Credit Rating: Appraisal of creditworthiness of the existing and potential customers/clients.

Credit Standard: The minimum quality of credit worthiness of a credit applicant that is acceptable to the firm.

Critical Path Analysis (CPA): It is a form of network analysis used to determine the continuous chain of operations critical to completion of a project by its scheduled completion date.

Current Cost Reserve: A reserve set up to contain the revaluation arising under current cost accounting. It may also be called revaluation reserve.

Current Liabilities: Liabilities which fall due for payment within a relatively short period, normally less than twelve months, e.g., creditors, bank overdrafts and provision for dividend payments.

Current Ratio: An accounting ratio; total current assets/total current liabilities.

D

Debenture: Any document containing an acknowledgement of indebtedness.

Debenture Redemption Reserve: A reserve representing retentions out of profit made for the purpose of redeeming debentures. The reserve is legally a revenue reserve but, because funds will be used to redeem the debentures, the company may choose to regard it as a capital reserve.

Debit Card: A card similar in appearance to a credit card and which is offered in a similar way in payment for goods and services.

Debt Capacity: The maximum amount of debt that a firm can adequately service.

Debt Factoring: It involves no financing. The service provided is purely administrative. The factor will administer the sales ledger and forward the invoice to the Buyer and collect debt on the due date.

Debt Ratio: Total liabilities divided by total capital to show the weight of credit in a business.

Debt Retirement: The process of removing debt by repaying it.

Debt-service Burden: Cash required during a specific period, usually a year, to meet interest expenses and principal payments. Also called simply debt service.

Decentralisation: A method of business organisation whereby units of the business representing separate products, common functions, etc., are given a large measure of autonomy.

Decision Theory: The study and application of mathematical techniques which provide a rational basis for choosing between alternative courses of action in situation of varying degrees.

Deep Discounted Bonds: Bonds which do pay an annual coupon rate to investors but the rate is at a substantial discount to prevailing market rates of return. However, the bonds will be redeemable at or above par on maturity.

Defalcation: The stealing of money which has been entrusted to the individual concerned.

Defeasance: The termination of an interest in property according to the terms of some deed.

Deflation: The opposite condition to inflation, i.e., there is general fall in the price level.

Degree of Financial Leverage (DFL): The percentage change in a firm's earnings per share (EPS) resulting from one per cent change in operating profit (EBIT).

Degree of Operating Leverage (DOL): The percentage change in a firm's operating profit (EBIT) resulting from a one per cent change in output (sales).

Degree of Total Leverage (DTL): The percentage change in a firm's earnings per share (EPS) resulting from a one per cent change in output (sales). This is also equal to a firm's degree of operating leverage (DOL) times its degree of financial leverage (DFL) at a particular level of output (sales).

Depletion: That process whereby a wasting asset becomes progressively consumed. A quarry, for instance, becomes depleted as the material is removed.

Depository Transfer Cheque (DTC): A non-negotiable cheque payable to a single company account at a concentration bank.

Deprival Value: The maximum amount which a business would be prepared to pay rather than lose a specified asset.

Derivative Security: A financial contract whose value derives in part from the value and characteristics of one or more underlying assets, interest rates, exchange rates, or indices.

Dilution: A decrease in the proportional claim on earnings and assets of a share of common stock because of the issuance of additional shares.

Disbursement Float: Total time between mailing of a cheque by a firm and encashing the cheque or getting it credited into the account of the receiving firm.

Discount Rate: Interest rate used to convert future values to present values.

Discounted Cash Flow (DCF): Any method of investment project evaluation and selection that adjusts cash flows over time for the time value of money.

Disintermediation: The dispensing with financial intermediaries and having a direct relationship between borrower and lender.

Disinvestment: The opposite of investment. It is thus the realisation of investments.

Distress: The action of seizing goods under an order of court.

Distress Value: The value attached to the assets of a business on the basis that they have to be sold quickly in order to meet very pressing commitments or to save of financial collapse.

Dividend Cover: A financial ratio which assesses the firm's ability to pay dividends to shareholders from its after-tax profits. It indicates the vulnerability of dividend payments to a drop in profits. The ratio is calculated as profit after interest and tax (PAIT) divided by dividends payable.

Dividend Reinvestment Plan (DRIP): An optional plan allowing shareholders to automatically reinvest dividend payments in additional shares of the company's stock.

Dividend Valuation Model (DVM): A method of share valuation which determines the value of a share as the present value of all the share's future dividend cash flows discounted at the investors required rate of return.

Dividend Yield: Anticipated annual dividend divided by the market price of the stock.

Dividend-payout Ratio: Annual cash dividends divided by annual earnings; or alternatively, dividends per share divided by earnings per share. The ratio indicates the percentage of a company's earnings that are paid out to shareholders in cash.

Du Pont System: A method of analysing financial accounts so as to assess the underlying health of the business.

E

Earned Income: Income which arises from some personal remunerative effort.

Earnings: The after tax profits of a company attributable to its ordinary shareholders.

Earnings Per Share (EPS): Earnings after taxes (EAT) divided by the number of common shares outstanding.

Earnings Yield: The earnings per share of a company expressed as percentage of its current share price.

EBIT-EPS breakover Analysis: Analysis of the effect of financing alternatives on earnings per share. The break-even point is the EBIT level where EPS is the same for two (or more) alternatives.

Economic Order Quantity (EOQ): The quantity of an inventory item to order so that total inventory costs are minimised over the firm's planning period.

Economic Value: The value of an asset computed by discounting its prospective future generation of cash.

Economic Value Added (EVA): A measure of business performance. It is a type of economic profit that is equal to a company's after-tax net operating profit minus a dollar cost of capital charge.

Economics of Scale: The benefit where the average unit cost falls as volume increases.

Eighty-Twenty Rule: This is an empirical rule which describes a common tendency particularly in inventory control. It suggests that 20 per cent of the stores account for about 80 per cent of the total stores value. Applied to customers, it suggests that 20 per cent of the customers account for 80 per cent of the sales turnover. It can also be applied to suppliers: 20 per cent of the suppliers supply 80 per cent of the goods purchased. The purpose behind the 80–20 rule is to emphasise the need to concentrate management control on the important 20 per cent which account for the bulk of activity or values. This idea is also closely allied to management by exception, ABC method and Pareto's Law.

Electronic Commerce (EC):   The exchange of business information in an electronic (nonpaper) format, including via the Internet.

Electronic Funds Transfer (EFT):   The electronic movements of information between two depository institutions resulting in a value (money) transfer.

Electronic Transfer of Funds: The movement of money effected not by physical means but by means of information sent electronically.

Entity Concept: The concept of accounting which sees a business as an entity in its own right separate from its managers or its properties.

Equipment Leasing: A method of purchasing the use of machinery or equipment, without resorting to existing capital or raising new capital over a definite and relatively long period of time, i.e., normally the asset's useful life.

Ethical Investment: Investment which has regard to the morality of the activity carried out by the companies which are the subject of the investment.

EVOP: Abbr. Evaluating and Optimisation. A systematic procedure for improving quality, waste reduction and improved productivity.

Extrinsic: Determined by outside factors. Assets have an extrinsic (as opposed to intrinsic) value in that it is determined by the state of a market which lies outside any inherent characteristics the asset might itself possess.

F

Face Value: The stated value of an asset. In the case of a bond, the face value is usually $ 100.

Factor: Agent to whom goods are entrusted for the purpose of being resold for the owner.

Factor Analysis: Mathematical technique for clarifying complex data and making meaningful correlations and deductions.

Factoring: The selling of receivables to a financial institution, the factor usually without recourse.

Fair Market Value: The price at which property can be sold in an arm's length transaction.

Feasibility Criterion: A criterion which all accounting techniques must meet if they are to have practical applications.

Feasibility Study: The analysis of accounting or other clerical procedures to assess the suitability of converting to a computer operation.

Feedback: Data extracted from a process or situation and used in controlling, planning or modifying immediate or future inputs into the process or situation.

Fiduciary Loan: One granted without security trusting on the word and honour of the borrower.

Figureless Accounts: The system of management information in which performance, progress or profit are recorded by plus/minus symbols against predetermined norms without recording detailed figures.

Final Accounts: The set of accounting statements produced by a business at the end of its financial year.

Finance: Money which has to be committed to a project or a business enterprise to enable it to operate.

Financial Accounting: Organising and presenting of an organisation's accounts for the internal information of management particularly for reporting to shareholders.

Financial Accounting Standard Board (FASB):   The rule making body of the accounting profession that sets its standards.

Final Dividend: The last dividend to be paid in respect of a given financial periods.

Financial EDI (FEDI):   The movement of financially related electronic information between a company and its bank or between banks.

Financial Intermediaries: Financial institutions that accept money from savers and use those funds to make loans and other financial investments in their own name.

Financial Lease: A long-term lease that is not cancellable.

Financial Leverage: The use of financing costs by the firm. The British expression is gearing.

Financial Management: It is concerned with the acquisition, financing, and management of assets with some overall goal in mind.

Financial Planning: The process of preparing forecasts and budgets so that requirement for finance can be foreseen.

Financial Ratio: An index that relates two accounting numbers and is obtained by dividing one number by the other.

Financial Reporting: The process of reporting the financial position and progress of a business to persons outside that business.

Financial Risk: The added variability in earnings per share (EPS)—plus the risk of possible insolvency—that is induced by the use of financial leverage.

Financial Year: The year during which a business draws up its accounts.

Fiscal Year: The year designated by the government for the tax purposes.

Fixed Cost: Costs which are not affected by variations in the volume of production.

Flexible Budget: Budget which takes account of a range of possible volumes. Sometimes referred to as a multi-volume budget.

Flexing: In budgetary control, the process of adjusting the budget in relation to changes in volumes of production or sales.

Float: Cash kept in a till or petty cash system.

Floating Charge: A floating charge is one which is not attached to a definite property, but covers property of a fluctuating type. The company is left free to deal with the property so charged as it no charge has been created.

Flotation Costs: The costs associated with issuing securities, such as underwriting, legal, listing and printing fees.

Flow of Funds Statement: A summary of a firm's changes in a financial position from one period to another, which is also called a source and use of funds statement or a statement of changes in financial position.

Forecasting: The assessment or calculations of future developments or the anticipated outcomes of planning.

Foreign Direct Investment (FDI):   Investment in a foreign country that gives the MNC a measure of control.

Foreign Exchange Risk: The risk of facing uncertain future exchange rates.

Forfaiting: It is the non-recourse purchase by a bank or other financial institutions (forfaiter) of receivables arising from an export of goods and services.

Format: A style imposed on certain accounting statements.

Franchise: Grant of a licence to a manufacturer or marketer to distribute products or services.

Free on Board (FOB):   When the seller or supplier of goods is responsible for the cost of delivering them to the ship.

Free Reserve: A revenue reserve which has not been allocated to any defined purpose.

G

Galloping Inflation: Rapidly accelerating inflation, possibly leading to economic catastrophe.

Geared Buyout: The purchase of a business, usually by the existing management, financed to a substantial extent by the borrowed money.

Gearing: The ratio of debt finance to equity finance in a company's capital structure.

General Reserve: A revenue reserve created for unspecified purposes. It represents a decision to retain some part of the profit of a company from distribution.

Generally Accepted Accounting Principles: Principles so widely used and accepted that they may be presumed to underlie all accounting statements.

Gilt-edged Security: A security which is guaranteed by the government.

Goan Congruence: The process of seeking harmony between the goals of the organisation as a whole and the goals of the organisation's agent.

Going Concern: A business which has become established and has thus achieved a momentum of activity tending to favour its long-term survival.

Going-concern Value: The amount of a firm could be sold for a continuing operating business.

Golden Handcuff: A term built into a person's contract of service such that there would be substantial financial penalties in leaving that employment.

Golden Handshake: A colloquial expression for compensation for loss of office.

Golden Hello: A colloquial term referring to a situation where a person was induced to leave a previous employment in order to take up the present one by the payment of a large sum of money.

Golden Share: A single share in a company having special voting rights and held by the government following the privatisation of a previously publicly owned business.

Gross Profit Margin: Trading profit before deduction of depreciation as a percentage of turnover.

Gross Working Capital: The firm's investment in the current assets.

Gross Yield: The annual income deriving from a security expressed as a percentage of the capital sum invested and before making any deduction for taxation.

Growth Stock: Shares in a company which are expected to expand over a long period of time.

Guillotine: Method of closing debate or discussions on a subject when the permitted time limit has been reached.

H

Hardware: The machinery and equipment constituting a data-processing system.

Hedging Approach: A method of financing where each asset would be offset with a financing instrument of the same approximate maturity.

Heuristics: An aid to decision-making which eliminates many alternative courses of action at the outset leaving only a few alternatives which need to be examined in order to an optimal solution.

Historical Costing: The ascertainment and/or recording of costs after they have been incurred.

Hot Money: Money which is undesirable to hold for more than a very short period.

Human Resource Accounting: A financial representation of the value of the team of employees which a business possesses.

Hurdle Rate: The minimum required rate of return on an investment in a discounted cash flow analysis; the rate at which a project is acceptable.

Hush Money: Money paid to a person to induce him or her to keep silent about some matter which it is desired should not be made public.

Hybrid Finance: A type of finance which has some of the attributes of equity and some of the attributes of a loan. A convertible debenture is an example of hybrid finance.

Hyperinflation: Inflation so rapid that it completely undermines the value of a currency at a medium of exchange. When hyperinflation occurs price rises amounting to several thousand-fold over a year are experienced.

Hypothecation: The setting aside of a sum of money or identified goods for a specified purpose.

I

Imprest: A method to keep petty cash by means of which a certain sum of money is retained for petty cash expenditure.

Income Tax: A direct tax levied on the active income of an individual or corporation.

Incremental Cost: The increase in total expenditure caused by the addition of one small element to the level of activity.

Index Analysis: An analysis of percentage financial statements where all balance sheet or income statement figures for a base year equal 100 (per cent) and subsequent financial statement items are expressed as percentages of their values in the base year.

Indexation: The process of linking a price or a value to an index.

Indifference Curve: A line representing all combinations of expected return and risk that provide an investor with an equal amount of satisfaction.

Indifference Point (EBIT-EPS indifference point): The level of EBIT that produces the same level of EPS for two (or more) alternative capital structures.

Indirect Tax: A tax levied on a taxpayer's income which was not directly generated by the taxpayer and serves as passive income for the taxpayer.

Induction: Orienting and introducing the new employee to the non-technical aspects of his work, e.g., working conditions and general company policy.

Inflation: A rise in the average level of prices of goods and services.

Initial Margin: An initial collateral deposit needed to establish an asset position.

Integrated Accounting: A form of accounting in which financial accounting and cost accounting records are maintained in the same set of books.

Interest Coverage Ratio: Earnings before interest and taxes divided by interest charges. It shows the firm's ability to cover interest charges.

Internal Rate of Return (IRR): The discount rate that equates the present value of the future net cash flows from an investment project with the project's initial cash outflow.

Intrinsic Value: The price of security "ought to have" based on all factors bearing on valuation.

Investment Appraisal: The process of evaluating an investment opportunity.

Invoice Discounting: An alternative method of financing debtors offered by subsidiaries of the major banks and other specialist finance companies.

J

Joint Venture: A single transaction or group of transactions carried out by more than one person, who however, intend no permanent business association.

Junk Bond: A high-risk, high yield bond rated below investment grade.

Just-in-time (JIT): An approach to inventory management and control in which inventories are acquired at the exact times they are needed.

K

Key Person: A person who is of vital importance to a business. This will usually be because of that person's special knowledge of the business.

Knock-Down: Description of price which has been substantially reduced usually because of adverse trading conditions.

Know-how: Skill and knowledge acquired from research and/or experience.

L

Lead Time: The length of time between the placement of an order for an inventory item and when the item is received in inventory.

Lease: A contract under which one party lessor (owner) of an asset, agrees to grant the use of that asset to another, the lessee, in exchange of periodic rental payments.

Leasehold: A form of tenure of land whereby holder has possession for a defined period of years.

Legacy: An amount of money or other item of value received from a deceased person under the terms of will.

Leverage: The use of fixed costs in an attempt to increase profitability.

Leverage Buyout (LBO): A primarily debt-financed purchase of all the stock or assets of a company, subsidiary, or division by an investor group.

Leveraged Leasing: A lease arrangement in which the lessor provides an equity portion of the leased asset's cost and the third-party lenders provide the balance of the financing.

Lien: A legal claim on certain assets.

Limiting Factor: The factor in a business situation which places a limit on expansion. The limiting factor may be the availability of material, skilled labour or factor capacity.

Liquidity: The ability of an asset to be converted into cash without a significant price concession.

Liquidity Ratio: Ratios that measure a firm's ability to meet short-term obligations.

Lock-box: A post office box maintained by a firm's bank that is used as a receiving point for customer remittances.

Lying Time: The period of time between the end of the working week and actual day that wages are paid.

M

Management Buyout (MBO): A leveraged buyout (LBO) in which prebuyout management ends up with a substantial equity position.

Market Imperfections: Various frictions, such as transaction costs and legal restrictions, that prevent the markets from functioning perfectly.

Market Risk: The part of an asset's risk which cannot be eliminated by diversification.

Market Value: The market price at which an asset trades.

Marketable Securities: Short-term, easily liquidated, low risk, interest earning financial assets.

Master Budget: The overall plan for a business' financial activities to which its sectional plans must relate.

Modigliani and Miller Theory: A theory that capital structure is not a factor in determining the cost of capital. The theory argues that the total value of a business is the same whatever be its method of financing.

Money Markets: Financial markets for trading securities with a short-term to maturity.

N

Net Asset Value: A value attached to a share in a company based on the assets of the business attributable to the shareholders divided by the number of shares issued.

Net Current Assets: Current assets less current liabilities, i.e., working capital.

Net Float: The rupee difference between the balance shown in a firm's cheque book balance and balance on the bank's books.

Net Lease: A lease where the lessee maintains and insures the leased asset.

Net Operating Income (NOI) Approach: A theory of capital structure in which the weighted and the total value of the firm remains constant as financial leverage is changed.

Net Present Value (NPV): The present value of an investment project's net cash flows minus the project's initial cash outflow.

Net Working Capital: Current assets minus current liabilities.

Net Worth: An accounting concept denoting the excess of the book value of all assets over liabilities.

Novation: The substitution in a contract of one debtor for another with the agreement of the creditor.

O

Ombudsman: A person who is appointed to oversee fair play and adjudicate in any dispute.

Operating Activities: Those activities entered into by a business as part of its normal trade. The term is used in a cash flow statement.

Operating Cycle: The length of time from the commitment of cash for purchases until the collection of receivables resulting from the sale of goods or services.

Operating Exposure: The extent to which the firm's operating cash flows will be affected by random changes in the exchange rates.

Operating Lease: A short-term lease that is often cancelable.

Operating Leverage: The use of fixed operating costs by the firm.

Operating Profit: The profit deriving from the operation of the basic business process.

Operating Ratios: Ratios calculated from set of accounts which throw light on the profit making activities for a period of time.

Opportunity Cost: What is lost by not taking the next-best investment alternative.

Optimal Capital Structure: The capital structure that minimises the firm's cost of capital and thereby maximizes the value of the firm.

Order Point: The quantity to which inventory should fall in order to signal that an order should be placed to replenish an item.

Outsourcing: Subcontracting a certain business operation to an outside firm instead of doing in house.

Overcapitalised: Having more funds than can profitably be employed in the business.

Overtrading: Carrying on a level of business activity which cannot be supported financially.

Owner's Equity: The part of the overall value of a business which is attributable to its proprietors. It is thus the total value of the assets less the claims of creditors and lenders to the business.

P

Par Value: The face value of a stock or bond.

Payback Period (PBP): The period of time required for the cumulative expected cash flows from an investment project to equal the initial cash flows.

Perfect Market: The situation where all the potential sellers and buyers are promptly aware of the prices at which transactions take place and of all the offers made by other sellers and buyers and where any buyer can purchase from any seller and vice versa.

Performance Appraised: A systematic appraisal of an individual employee to assess past performance, future potential and salary.

Permanent Working Capital: The total amount in monetary terms, of current assets, required to meet a firm's long-term minimum needs.

Perpetual Inventory: System of continuous stock recording so that the stock of each item is known at all times.

Perpetuity: An ordinary annuity whose payments or receipts continue for ever.

PERT: Programme Evaluation and Review Technique.

Petty Cash: Small amounts of currency maintained to cover trivial day-to-day expenses.

Pin Money: Small amounts of money earned casually by a person to supplement his or her main income.

Piracy: Strictly the term means the seizing of goods from ships on the high sea, i.e., outside any jurisdiction. In business terms, piracy means stealing or copying a company's products (such as software) without obtaining any legal permission or right, and selling the same to the customers illegally.

Pittance: A very small, and thus inadequate, wage.

Plough Back: To allow profits to accumulate in a business rather than to be withdrawn by the proprietors so that extra resources thus made available can be used in financing the expansion of the business.

Pooling of Interests (Method): A method of accounting treatment for a merger based on the net book value of the acquired company's assets. The balance sheets of the two companies are simply combined.

Portfolio: A combination of two or more securities.

Portfolio Planning: Assumes that managing the diversified firm resembles managing a portfolio of investments. Each firm is unique in such things as a growth, cash flow, profits, and tax benefits.

Present Value: The current value of a future amount of money, or a series of payments, evaluated at a given interest rate.

Privatisation: Act of a country divesting itself of ownership and operation of business ventures by turning them over to the free market system.

Profit maximisation: Maximizing a firm's earnings after taxes.

Profitability Ratio: Ratios that relate profits to sales and investment.

Pyramid Selling: A type of selling based on the principle of the chain letter.

Q

Quality Spread Differential (QSD): The difference between the fixed interest rate spread differential and the floating interest rate spread differential of the debt of two counterparties of different creditworthiness.

Quick Assets: Assets which are highly liquid. Cash and bank balances are good examples.

Quoted Company: A company whose shares are quoted on the stock exchange.

Quoted Investments: Investments which are listed on the stock exchange.

R

Ratio: The relationship between one value and another.

Realisable Income: The profit of a business calculated on the basis of valuing all its assets at realisable values.

Realisable Value: The amount which would be received if an asset were sold.

Recapitalisation: An alteration of a firm's capital structure. For instance, a firm may sell bonds to acquire the cash necessary to repurchase some of its outstanding common stock.

Refunding: Replacing an old debt issue with a new one, usually to lower the interest cost.

Regression Analysis: A mathematical method used to establish the relationship, if any, between observed and quantifiable variables.

Regular Dividend: The dividend that is normally expected to be paid by the firm.

Relevant Cost: A cost which would be charged in a proposal under consideration to be implemented but not otherwise. It is relevant costs only which should be considered in decision making.

Relevant Income: The income of a closed company which may be deemed to be distributable for the purpose of making a shortfall assessment to tax.

Replacement Cost: The cost of replacing an asset with another which is identical or equivalent.

Required Rate of Return: The minimum return on investment should provide in order to be of interest to investors.

Reserve Capital: That part of the nominal capital of a business which has not yet been called up.

Residual Value: The value of a leased asset at the end of the lease period.

Responsibility Accounting: Making the executive a cost centre responsible for the financial results of the field for which he is accountable.

Retrospective: Taking effect as though it had occurred at an earlier date.

Return on Capital Employed: Profit related to the investment of capital required to produce it.

Return on Equity (ROE): A measure of the return the firm is earning on the equity funds invested by its shareholders. It is calculated as profit after interest and tax divided by ordinary shareholders' funds.

Revaluation: The process of placing a different valuation on an asset from its current recorded value.

Reversion: The return of property which was the subject of lease to the freeholder at the expiration of the lease.

Revolving Credit Agreement: A formal, legal commitment to extend credit up to some maximum amount over a stated period of time.

Risk Averse: The term applied to an investor who demands a higher expected return, for the higher risk.

Risk Yield: The term used to describe the relationship between yield on investment and the degree of risk.

Risk-adjusted Discount Rate (RADAR): An approach to project risk analysis in which a project's discount rate is modified to incorporate a risk premium.

Risk-return Trade-off: The relationship between risk and return, indicating that additional risk should be rewarded with additional expected returns.

ROAM: Abbr. Return on Assets Managed. An alternative term for return on investment or capital.

ROL: Abbr. Re-ordering Level.

Rolling Budget: A budget which, having been established at the beginning of a period, is then constantly amended to take account of developing circumstances.

S

Safety Stock: Inventory stock held in reverse as a cushion against uncertain demand (or usage) and replenishment lead time.

Sale and Leaseback: A type of agreement whereby a business sells a major asset to a finance company and then continues to use it under a leasing arrangement.

Sales Budget: The quantitative and financial statement prepared prior to a defined period of time of the sales to be achieved during that period.

Scheduling: The determination of times in the future when specified tasks should be completed.

Scrap Value: A realisable value possessed by a fixed asset at the end of its useful life.

Scrip Dividend: A dividend given in the form of extra shares instead of cash.

Shadow Price: The opportunity cost of using an item of stock or other asset.

Shareholders' Equity: Total assets minus total liabilities.

Sinking Fund: The fund established to periodically retire a portion of security issue before maturity.

Slump: A state of an economy of a country in which economic activity is at a very low level.

Soft Currency: A currency, associated with an ailing economy, whose value and convertibility into other currencies is unreliable.

Source and Applications of Funds Statement: A statement showing the main sources of funds arising during a period of time and the application of those funds.

Spontaneous Financing: Trading credit, and other payables and accruals, that arise spontaneously in the firm's day-to-day operations.

Stock Dividend: A payment of additional shares of stock to shareholders.

Stockout: Not having enough items in inventory to fill an order.

Stock Split: An increase in the number of shares outstanding by reducing the par value of the stock.

Stock Turnover: A ratio: cost of sales/over age inventory.

Switching: Moving resources from one investment to another with the object of maximizing long-term gains.

T

Tangible Asset: An asset, either physical or financial in character, e.g., plant, stock, cash, receivables and investments.

Tax Avoidance: The management of a taxpayer's affairs so that his or her liability is legally reduced. Tax avoidance is legal.

Tax Evasion: The escape from the payment of tax which is legally due. Tax evasion usually takes place by a failure to make a full declaration of income. Tax evasion is fraud and if detected, is punishable as such.

Tax Shield: A tax-deductible expense.

Temporary Working Capital: The amount of current assets in monetary terms that varies with seasonal requirements.

Term Loan: Debt originally scheduled for repayment in more than one year, but generally in less than ten years.

Ticket Symbol: A unique, letter-character code name assigned to securities and mutual funds.

Tombstone Advertisement: An announcement placed in newspapers and magazines giving just the most basic details of security offering.

Total Firm Risk: The variability in earnings per share (EPS). It is the sum of business plus financial risk.

Trade Credit: Credit granted from one business to another.

Trade Investments: Investments owned by an organisation which are not held for sale.

Trade Liabilities: Money owed to suppliers.

Trademark: A symbol used by a business to represent itself or its products in a quickly recognisable way.

U

Under-capitalised: The condition of having too little capital invested in the business.

Underwriting: Bearing the risk of not being able to sell a security at the established price by virtue of purchasing security for resale to the public.

Unearned Income: Income acquired other than by the provision of personal effort. Thus it consists of dividends, interest and rental income.

Unsecured Creditor: A creditor whose claim is supported only by the agreement that payment should be made.

Unsecured Loans: A form of debt for money borrowed that is not backed by the pledge of specific asset.

Unsystematic Risk: The variability of return on stocks or portfolios not explained by general market movements. It is avoidable through diversification.

V

Value-Added Tax (VAT): An indirect national tax which is levied on the value added in the production of a good or service as it moves through the various stages of production.

Variable Overhead: Overhead which varies in total amount directly with the volume of the production to which it relates.

Venture Capital: High risk capital normally provided by venture capital companies (VCCs) at the early stage of a company's life.

Virtual Corporation: A business organisational model that involves the largescale outsourcing of business functions.

W

Watered Stock: Shares in a company whose nominal value exceeds the actual market value of the underlying assets.

Weighted Average: A method of calculating an average whereby some constituents are given more influence than others.

Weighted Average Cost of Capital (WACC): The average cost of capital of the firm's existing operations. It is calculated by weighing the cost of each individual source of capital (debt, equity, etc.) in proportion to the total market value of the firm.

White Knight: A company which volunteers to take over another company to rescue the latter from an unwelcome takeover bid from some third party.

Window Dressing: Applied to financial statements (e.g., balance sheets) which give a false impression of the financial position.

Wire Transfer: A generic term for electronic funds transfer using a two-way communications system, like Fedwire.

Working Capital Management: The administration of the firm's current asset and the financing needed to support current assets.

Wrongful Trading: Trading by a limited company which is insolvent.

X

X-axis: The horizontal axis on a graph.

Y

Yield: Return or profit earned on an investment in particular stocks or shares.

Yield Curve: A graph of the relationship between yields and term to maturity for particular securities.

Yield Gap: The gap between the average yield on shares and the average yield on fixed interest securities.

Yield to Maturity (YTM): The expected rate of return on a bond if bought at its current market price and held to maturity.

Z

Zero Balance Account (ZBA): A corporate checking account in which a zero balance is maintained.

Zero Base Budget: A budget constructed on the basis that the inclusion of every item has to be justified and none is taken for granted.

Zero-coupon Bond: A bond that pays no interest but sells at a deep discount from its face value. It provides compensation to investors in the form of price appreciation.

Bibliography

1. Banerjee, B., *Cash Management—A Practical Approach*, The World Press, 1982.

2. Banerjee, B., *Financial Policy and Management Accounting*, The World Press, Calcutta.

3. Basu, C.R., *Organisation and Management*, S. Chand & Company, New Delhi, 1985.

4. Bierman, H. and S. Smidt, *The Capital Budgeting Decisions*, Macmillan Publishing Co., New York, 1978.

5. Bolton, S.E., *Managerial Finance*, Boston, Houghton, Mifftin Co., 1976.

6. Chandra, P., *Capital Budgeting in Indian Industries*, Indian Management, New Delhi, February 1973.

7. Chandra, P., *Financial Management—Theory and Practice*, 3rd ed., Tata McGraw-Hill, New Delhi.

8. Chhabra, T.N., *Principles and Practice of Management*, Dhanpat Rai & Sons, Delhi, 1995.

9. Ciaran, Walsh, *Key Management Ratios*, Macmillan, Delhi 1997.

10. Dean Joel, *Capital Budgeting*, Columbia University Press, 1951.

11. Gupta, S.P., *Management Accounting*, Sahitya Bhavan, Agra, 1993.

12. Guthmann, H.G. and H.E. Dougall, *Corporate Finance Policy*, 3rd ed., Prentice-Hall of India, New Delhi.

13. Hampton. J.J., *Financial Decision Making, Concepts, Problems and Cases*, Prentice-Hall of India, New Delhi, 1983.

14. Homes, Maynard Edwards and Meier, *Intermediate Accounting*, 3rd ed., R.D. Irwin.

15. Jack Clark Francis, *Management of Investments*, McGraw-Hill, Inc., 1993.

16. Joshi, N.B., *Financial Analysis through Current Ratio*, The Management Accountant, ICWAI, Vol. 14, No. 5, p. 462, May 1979.

17. Joy, O.M., *Introduction to Financial Management*, Homewood Illionois, R.D. Irwin, 1979.

18. Keyness, J.M., *The General Theory of Employment, Interest and Money*, Hercourt Brace & Jovanovich, New York, 1936.

19. Khan, M.Y. and P.K. Jain, *Financial Management*, Tata McGraw-Hill, New Delhi, 1982.

20. Kulkarni, P.V., *Financial Management*, Himalaya Publishing House, Bombay, 1996.

21. Kulshrestha, *Management Accounting Concepts and Cases*, Tata McGraw-Hill, New Delhi, 1996.

22. Maheswari, S.N., *Management Accounting and Financial Control*, Sultan Chand & Sons, New Delhi, 1996.

23. Malhotra, Nachhatlar Singh, S.D. Sharma, *Financial Management*, Anmol Publications, New Delhi, 1997.

24. Osteryoung, J.S., *Capital Budgeting, Long-term Assets Selection*, Columbus, Ohio, Grid, 1979.

25. Pandey, I.M., *Financial Management*, Vikas Publishing House, 1996.

26. Pancras, U., *Time Adjusted Current Ratio, The Management Accountant*, Vol. 16, No. 11, November, 1981.

27. Paul, S. Kr., *Advanced Financial Management*, New Central Book Agency, Calcutta, 1997.

28. Pillai, R.S.N. and Bagavathi, *Management Accounting*, S. Chand & Company, New Delhi, 1997.

29. Porwal, L.S., *Capital Budgeting in India*, Sultan Chand & Sons, New Delhi, 1976.

30. Prasad, L.M., *Principles and Practice of Management*, Sultan Chand & Sons, New Delhi, 1998.

31. Quirin, G. David, *The Capital Expenditure Decision*, Richard D. Irwin Inc., Illinois, 1977.

32. Raj, A.B.C., *Public Enterprise Investment Decisions in India*, Macmillan, New Delhi, 1977.

33. Ramamoorthy, V.E., *Working Capital Management*, Madras Institute of Management and Research, 1976.

34. Reddy, P.N. and H.R. Appannaiah, *Management Accounting*, Himalaya Publishing House, Bombay, 1997.

35. Roy, G.D., *Anatomy of Depreciation*, The World Press.

36. Sarkar, J.B., *Depreciation and Working Capital Financing in the Central Government Companies—Lok Udyog*, February 1982.

37. Sharma, R.K. and Shashi K. Gupta, *Management Accounting Principles and Practice*, Kalyani Publishers, Ludhiana, 1996.

38. Srinivasan, N.P., *Management Accounting*, Sterling Publishers, New Delhi, 1992.

39. Upadhyay, K.M., *Financial Management*, Kalyani Publishers, New Delhi.

40. Van Horn, J.C., *Financial Management and Policy*, Prentice-Hall of India, New Delhi, 1979.

Index